Readings from

UNDERSTANDING

AND USING
ENGLISH

Newman P. Birk
and
Genevieve B. Birk

TUFTS UNIVERSITY

THE ODYSSEY PRESS · INC · New York

Copyright 1959
By The Odyssey Press, Inc.
All rights reserved

A 0 9 8 7 6 5 4 3 2

Acknowledgments

The authors are grateful to the following writers, publishers, and literary agents for permission to use the materials listed below.

George Allen & Unwin Ltd.: passage from *The Interpretation of Dreams* by Sigmund Freud (trans. James Strachey).

The American Historical Review: "Everyman His Own Historian" by Carl L. Becker.

Appleton-Century-Crofts: passage from *Science and Christian Tradition* by Thomas Henry Huxley.

Edward Arnold, Ltd.: passage from *The Human Situation* by W. Macneile Dixon.

The Atlantic Monthly: "The Business of a Biographer" by Catherine Drinker Bowen, "A Reasonable Life in a Mad World" by Irwin Edman, and "How Big Is One" by Edward Weeks.

Basic Books, Inc.: passage from *The Interpretation of Dreams* by Sigmund Freud (trans. James Strachey).

Joseph Beaver: "'Technique' in Hemingway" by Joseph Beaver in *College English*, March, 1953.

Brandt & Brandt: passage from *Nineteen Eighty-Four* by George Orwell.

Clarendon Press: passage from *The Manual of Epictetus* translated by P. E. Matheson.

Columbia University Press: entry on George Ryan Brummell in *The Columbia Encyclopedia*, 1942 Edition.

Coward-McCann: "The Life and Death of a Worm" by Alan Devoe.

Farrar, Straus and Cudahy, Inc.: passage from *My Mother's House* by Colette.

Harcourt, Brace and Company: passages from *Orlando* and *The Second Common Reader* by Virginia Woolf, *The Autobiography of Lincoln Steffens*, *Nineteen Eighty-Four* by George Orwell, and *Abraham Lincoln: The War Years* by Carl Sandburg.

Harper & Brothers: passages from *The Mind in the Making* by James Harvey Robinson, "Introduction" to the *Bhagavad-Gita* by Aldous Huxley, *The Second Tree from the Corner* and *One Man's Meat* by E. B. White, and *Roosevelt and Hopkins* by Robert E. Sherwood.

Howard Mumford Jones: "The Attractions of Stupidity."

Alfred A. Knopf, Inc.: passage from *Life with Father* by Clarence Day.

ACKNOWLEDGMENTS

Longmans, Green & Company, Inc.: passage from *The Will to Believe* by William James.

McGraw-Hill Book Company: "Principles of Perception" in *Introduction to Psychology* by Clifford T. Morgan, copyright, 1956, McGraw-Hill Book Co., Inc.

The Macmillan Company: passage from *The Renaissance* by Walter Pater.

Methuen and Co. Ltd., and Les Editions Nagel: passage from *Existentialism and Humanism* by Jean-Paul Sartre (trans. Philip Mairet).

The Nation: "The Riddles of Franklin Roosevelt" by Raymond Swing.

The New Yorker: "Another Go at F.D.R." by Hamilton Basso in *The New Yorker*, June 3, 1950.

New York *Times Book Review:* "Roosevelt's Rendezvous with History" by Adolph Berle, Jr. in the New York *Times Book Review*, June 4, 1950.

New York *Times Magazine:* "Measuring the I.Q. Test" by **David Wechsler**, *Times Magazine*, January 20, 1957.

Oxford University Press: passage from *The Sea Around Us* by Rachel L. Carson.

Philosophical Library, Inc.: "Science and Religion" in *Out of My Later Years* by Albert Einstein.

Random House: "Remarks on Receiving the Nobel Prize" by William Faulkner.

The Reader's Digest: "Slow-Motion Picture of High-Speed Death" by E. A. Walz III and C. B. Wall in *The Reader's Digest*, February, 1957, copyright, 1957, by The Reader's Digest Association, Inc., reprinted with permission.

The Rotarian: "Does Human Nature Change?" by John Dewey.

St. Martin's Press: passage from *The Human Situation* by W. Macneile Dixon.

Charles Scribner's Sons: "The Lantern-Bearers," by Robert Louis Stevenson.

Martin Secker & Warburg Ltd.: "The Principles of Newspeak" from *Nineteen Eighty-Four* by George Orwell, passage from *My Mother's House* by Colette.

Simon and Schuster: passage from *Of Men and Music* by Deems Taylor.

The Technology Review: "The Builders" by Vannevar Bush in *The Technology Review*, January, 1945.

James Thurber: passage from *Ladies' and Gentlemen's Guide to Modern English Usage.*

Time: "Let's Wait" and "An American Storyteller: Ernest Hemingway" by the Editors of *Time.*

The Viking Press: passages from *Candle in the Dark* and *Philosopher's Holiday* by Irwin Edman, and *Viking Portable Library World Bible* by Robert O. Ballou.

Carl B. Wall: "Slow-Motion Picture of High-Speed Death" by E. A. Walz III and C. B. Wall in *The Reader's Digest*, February, 1957.

David Wechsler: "Measuring the I.Q. Test" by David Wechsler in New York *Times Magazine,* January 20, 1957.

Yale University Press: passages from *Modern Democracy* and *New Liberties for Old* by Carl Becker.

Preface to This Edition

This book is section 5 of *Understanding and Using English,* Third Edition with Readings. For the most part, it is unchanged in this edition: the selections, the comment and questions on the selections—even, for the sake of economy, the page numbers—remain the same as before. In the Preface to the Readings, pages 721–724, we tried to explain our objectives in choosing and arranging the readings and in supplying comment and questions on them. These objectives, too, remain the same, and need not be restated here.

The Glossary (pages 1135–1153), however, is new; it represents a kind of experiment which, if successful, could substantially increase the worth of this volume. Because the original book contained a complete rhetoric, it was possible for us to assume that students had some understanding of the vocabulary necessary for intelligent analysis and discussion of their reading. The purpose of the unusually full Glossary is to provide materials for a similar understanding of terms and principles referred to, directly or indirectly, in the comments and questions on the readings.

Of course teachers who choose to do so and students who are given a choice can use this book without reference to the Glossary, but if our own experience as teachers is typical and if the Glossary serves its intended purpose, students will benefit from using it.

The terms included in the Glossary fall into two classes. Those in the first class will sound familiar to college students, but will often turn out to have little precise and practical meaning for them. Examples of such terms are *balance, concreteness, economy, emphasis, organization, rhythm, transitions, style.* Though we have attempted to be brief, we have tried, too, to give enough concrete information about such vaguely familiar terms to make them meaningful and useful. In the second class are semitechnical terms which may be less familiar or totally unfamiliar to most students, but which are useful—perhaps even essential—to those who wish to be fully aware of the art and technique, and the implications, in what they read. Examples of these terms are *charged language, context, dominant impression, irony, pace, slanting, syllogism, tone, value judgment, verifiable fact.*

In selecting and explaining terms in both classes, we have naturally referred, with frequent self-plagiarism, to the fuller treatments in the rhetoric that accompanies these readings in the larger edition. The process of culling out the terms and concepts that seem most important for perceptive reading has caused us to wonder if the selectivity and brevity demanded by a glossary may not have certain advantages. Students sometimes seem to emerge from the study of a complete rhetoric with a blurred knowledge of many things —a knowledge too ill-digested to serve them well in either reading or writing. There may possibly be a gain in knowing a limited number of key terms and principles, using those terms recurrently in close analysis, and understanding how the principles actually operate in effective writing.

With these considerations in mind, we have called our glossary a brief rhetoric. Used with readings that provide a variety of examples and are accompanied by integrated comments and questions, it will, we hope, contribute to the student's growth in the interrelated skills of reading, writing, and thinking, and to his greater awareness of the unity of form and thought.

N. P. B.
G. B. B.

Contents

Preface to the Readings and Organization by Theme ... 721

SECTION 1. Reading Informative Prose ... 725
    Clifford T. Morgan, Principles of Perception ... 725
    Edgar A. Walz III, and Carl B. Wall, Slow-Motion Picture of High-Speed Death ... 729
    Alan Devoe, The Life and Death of a Worm ... 731
    Vannevar Bush, The Builders ... 735
    George Orwell, The Principles of Newspeak ... 737
    Carl L. Becker, The Ideal Democracy ... 747

SECTION 2. Reading Evaluations ... 760
    David Wechsler, Measuring the I.Q. Test ... 760
    John Gunther's *Roosevelt in Retrospect:* Four Reviews ... 765
    Joseph C. Beaver, "Technique" in Hemingway ... 775
    Deems Taylor, The Monster ... 780

SECTION 3. Reading Persuasion ... 784
    William Maxwell Aitken, Lord Beaverbrook, Present and Future ... 784
    Sigmund Freud, Dreams of the Death of Persons of Whom the Dreamer is Fond ... 787
    Winston Churchill, Dunkirk ... 800

SECTION 4. History and Biography: Information and Evaluation ... 809
    Carl L. Becker, Everyman His Own Historian ... 809
    Carl Sandburg, Lincoln Speaks at Gettysburg ... 823
    Rachel L. Carson, The Gray Beginnings ... 837
    Catherine Drinker Bowen, The Business of a Biographer ... 846
    Virginia Woolf, Beau Brummell ... 858
    Editors of *Time,* An American Storyteller: Ernest Hemingway ... 864

CONTENTS

SECTION 5. Reading for Ideas and Values — 875
- James Harvey Robinson, Four Kinds of Thinking — 875
- John Dewey, Does Human Nature Change? — 885
- Plato, *Apology* — 892
- Plato, The Myth of the Cave — 912
- Plato, from the *Symposium* — 919
- Epicurus, Letter to a Friend — 925
- Epictetus, The Quiet Mind — 928
- Jesus, Sermon on the Mount — 935
- John Henry Newman, Enlargement of Mind — 942
- John Stuart Mill, On the Liberty of Thought and Discussion — 950
- Ralph Waldo Emerson, Self-Reliance — 973
- Henry David Thoreau, from *Walden* — 989
- Albert Einstein, Science and Religion — 997
- Thomas Henry Huxley, Agnosticism and Christianity — 1003
- William James, Religious Faith — 1008
- John Henry Newman, Belief in One God — 1015
- Robert O. Ballou, The Jew and the Christian — 1022
- Aldous Huxley, The Bhagavad-Gita and the Perennial Philosophy — 1032
- Jean-Paul Sartre, Existentialism — 1040
- William Faulkner, Remarks on Receiving the Nobel Prize — 1050
- W. Macneile Dixon, The Human Situation — 1052
- Irwin Edman, A Reasonable Life in a Mad World — 1065

SECTION 6. Simple Narrative, Autobiography, and Informal Essays — 1072
- Lincoln Steffens, I Get a Colt to Break In — 1072
- Clarence Day, Father Opens My Mail — 1079
- Colette, My Mother and the Animals — 1084
- James Thurber, Which — 1088
- E. B. White, Calculating Machine — 1090
- E. B. White, Walden, 1939 — 1092
- Irwin Edman, Former Teachers — 1098
- Robert Louis Stevenson, The Lantern-Bearers — 1111
- Howard Mumford Jones, The Attractions of Stupidity — 1120
- Edward Weeks, How Big Is One — 1125

Glossary: A Brief Rhetoric — 1135

Index — 1155

Preface to the Readings

In choosing and editing the readings for this book, we have made certain interlocking assumptions, both positive and negative, about college students, about the nature and aims of liberal education, and about the skills and arts of reading, writing, and thinking.

More than two decades of close association with college students—in class and out of class—have left us with a solid respect for the intelligence and good sense of the young men and women we have taught and known. Our first assumption on the basis of this experience is that when students come to college, their minds are as vital as they will ever be; that freshmen and sophomores *can* think and want to think; that they are ready for, and deserve to have, exciting intellectual experiences. Our purpose in choosing many of these readings is to provide just such experiences.

Although we assume that students are ready to think when they enter college, we do not assume that they have much recondite learning. Matthew Arnold writes of those who have sought to "humanize" knowledge: "those who have a passion for diffusing, for making prevail . . . the best knowledge, the best ideas of their time; who have labored to divest knowledge of all that was harsh, uncouth, difficult, abstract, professional, exclusive; to humanize it, to make it efficient outside the clique of the cultivated and learned, yet still remaining the best knowledge and thought. . . ." In assembling these readings we have tried to make available to young and live minds some of the humanized and humane wisdom contained in the works of good and great minds, past and present; and we have tried to find selections that convey that wisdom without dilution, and without the jargon and the lumber of abstruse terminology.

Another closely related assumption is that the real end of liberal education, one above the mere acquiring of knowledge and refining of skills, is the development of taste and judgment through the search for viable

721

truths—affirmations that one can live by. Most students come to college with sets of accepted and unexamined beliefs. In the process of a liberal education they should be obliged to examine these beliefs: to reject, to modify, to substitute, or to confirm. We think it is important not only to stir the questioning mind but also to provide it with some choice of answers. In the readings as a whole—and particularly in the section entitled "Reading for Ideas and Values"—there is conflict, even outright contradiction, as well as harmony. We hope that these conflicts of opinion will stimulate the student to think for himself, that the diversity of views will enable him to choose meaningful values on which to build his personal philosophy.

Our final assumption is that reading, writing, and thinking are most profitably studied together: that reading and writing are two sides of the same coin, and thought is the metal of which the coin is made. In headnotes and in comments and questions following the selections we have tried to emphasize the unity of these three aspects of the art of communication.

Although we have kept continually in mind this oneness of form and idea, we have shifted our principal emphasis from stress on the study of types and techniques in the early sections to stress on the ideas of the writers in the section "Reading for Ideas and Values" mentioned above. Our plan in this section has been to start with two modern statements on thinking, education, and human nature, to go back then to the ideas of Plato and other early shapers of thought, and to return by way of the nineteenth century to contemporary points of view. We have not hesitated, though, to violate the roughly-chronological order when it seemed desirable to juxtapose pieces on the same general subject. Actually, we are not concerned with the order of readings in this section but with the impact they should have on the student's thinking and his set of values. In the last section of the readings, "Simple Narrative, Autobiography, and Informal Essays," we again, to a degree, emphasize type and technique. This section contains some lighter pieces, and some which may serve as guides to the student in his own writing.

Other kinds of writing assignments—critical and analytical papers on the ideas of one or more writers—will be suggested by the questions following each of the readings, and also by the table below. This table lists the selections according to their subject-matter or theme. The fact that the same selection may appear under different headings indicates the recurrence of major themes; indeed we have by no means exhausted in this listing the interconnections that exist. We strongly recommend that the student use this topically-arranged table as a help in reviewing and in seeing interrelationships. Even though he is not asked to write papers comparing, for example, the views of Einstein, Thomas Huxley, James, and Newman on science and religion, or the views of Plato, Newman, and Dewey on education, he still should find the topical analysis useful as he thinks about his reading, compares and contrasts the ideas and values he has encountered, and attempts to arrive at a synthesis of his own.

Organization of the Readings by Theme

Human Nature and the Human Situation
Orwell, The Principles of Newspeak 737
Becker, The Ideal Democracy 747
Freud, Dreams of the Death of Persons of Whom the Dreamer is Fond 787
Robinson, Four Kinds of Thinking 875
Dewey, Does Human Nature Change? 885
Plato, *Apology* 892
Plato, The Myth of the Cave 912
Epicurus, Letter to a Friend 925
Epictetus, The Quiet Mind 928
Jesus, Sermon on the Mount 935
Emerson, Self-Reliance 973
Thoreau, from *Walden* 989
Einstein, Science and Religion 997
James, Religious Faith 1008
Newman, Belief in One God 1015
Ballou, The Jew and the Christian 1022
Sartre, Existentialism 1040
Faulkner, Remarks on Receiving the Nobel Prize 1050
Dixon, The Human Situation 1052
Edman, A Reasonable Life in a Mad World 1065
Stevenson, The Lantern Bearers 1111
Jones, The Attractions of Stupidity 1120
Weeks, How Big Is One 1125

Freedom of Thought and the Inquiring Mind
Robinson, Four Kinds of Thinking 875
Dewey, Does Human Nature Change? 885
Plato, *Apology* 892
Plato, The Myth of the Cave 912
Newman, Enlargement of Mind 942
Mill, On the Liberty of Thought and Discussion 950
Emerson, Self-Reliance 973
Thoreau, from *Walden* 989
Thomas Huxley, Agnosticism and Christianity 1003
Jones, The Attractions of Stupidity 1120

Education and Mental Enlargement
Bush, The Builders 735
Becker, Everyman His Own Historian 809
Robinson, Four Kinds of Thinking 875
Dewey, Does Human Nature Change? 885
Plato, The Myth of the Cave 912
Plato, from the *Symposium* 919
Newman, Enlargement of Mind 942
Einstein, Science and Religion 997
Edman, Former Teachers 1065
Jones, The Attractions of Stupidity 1120

723

The Individual and Society

Orwell, The Principles of Newspeak   737
Becker, The Ideal Democracy   747
Plato, *Apology*   892
Plato, The Myth of the Cave   912
Epictetus, The Quiet Mind   928
Mill, On the Liberty of Thought and Discussion   950
Emerson, Self-Reliance   973
Thoreau, from *Walden*   989
Sartre, Existentialism   1040
Dixon, The Human Situation   1052
Jones, The Attractions of Stupidity   1120
Weeks, How Big Is One   1125

Language, Literature, and the Arts

Orwell, The Principles of Newspeak   737
Beaver, "Technique" in Hemingway   775
Taylor, The Monster   780
Bowen, The Business of a Biographer   846
Editors of *Time*, An American Storyteller   864
Faulkner, Remarks on Receiving the Nobel Prize   1050
Thurber, Which   1088
White, Calculating Machine   1090
Stevenson, The Lantern Bearers   1111

Science, and Science and Religion

Bush, The Builders   735
Freud, Dreams of the Death of Persons of Whom the Dreamer is Fond   787
Carson, The Gray Beginnings   837
Einstein, Science and Religion   997
Thomas Huxley, Agnosticism and Christianity   1003
James, Religious Faith   1008
Newman, Belief in One God   1015
Dixon, The Human Situation   1052

Religion and Morality

Taylor, The Monster   780
Plato, *Apology*   892
Epicurus, Letter to a Friend   925
Epictetus, The Quiet Mind   928
Jesus, Sermon on the Mount   935
Mill, On the Liberty of Thought and Discussion   950
Emerson, Self-Reliance   973
Einstein, Science and Religion   997
Thomas Huxley, Agnosticism and Christianity   1003
James, Religious Faith   1008
Newman, Belief in One God   1015
Ballou, The Jew and the Christian   1022
Aldous Huxley, The Bhagavad-Gita and the Perennial Philosophy   1032
Sartre, Existentialism   1040
Faulkner, Remarks on Receiving the Nobel Prize   1050
Dixon, The Human Situation   1052

READINGS

SECTION 1

Reading Informative Prose

CLIFFORD T. MORGAN

Principles of Perception*

The following selection from a psychology text illustrates a pattern of analysis, and also the brief definition-and-clarification of semitechnical terms. Mr. Morgan is a well-known psychologist who teaches at Johns Hopkins University.

[1] Perception is so broad a subject that entire books have been written about it. The facts of perception, however, can be summarized in a few general principles. Not only does human perception obey these principles, but the behavior of many animals suggests that their perceptions do too. Many of the principles are obvious—so obvious that we are apt to overlook them—but some are not. These principles are discussed in the following sections.

[2] **Attention.** One of the more obvious characteristics of perception is its selective nature. At any given moment our sense organs are bombarded by a multitude of stimuli. Yet only a few of these stimuli are given a clear channel. We perceive clearly only a very few events at one time. Other events are perceived less clearly, and the rest forms a sort of hazy background of which we are partially or completely unaware. This is another way of saying that, of the various events around us, we *attend* to only a very few. So *attention* is a basic factor in perception.

[3] This factor divides our field of experience, so to speak, into a *focus* and a *margin*. In the focus of experience are the events that we perceive clearly. Because we attend to them, they stand out from the background of our experience. Other items in the margin are less clearly perceived. We are aware

---

* By permission from *Introduction to Psychology*, by Clifford T. Morgan. Copyright, 1956. McGraw-Hill Book Co., Inc.

725

of their presence but less clearly so. Imperceptibly shading off from the margin are other items which are outside our field of attention and of which, for the moment, we are not consciously aware.

[4] Let us illustrate the nature of attention. While watching a football game, our attention is focused on the ball carrier. We are somewhat dimly aware of the tangle of players at the scrimmage line and of the activity of the blockers, but it is the ball carrier and his movements that most clearly stand out. We are at the same time being bombarded by a number of other stimuli. Our feet may be aching with the cold, unpleasant sensations may be coming from our stomach as a result of the last hot dog we ate, and the fellow in back of us may be carrying on a conversation with his girl. While the play is going on we are not aware of any of these things. Only when the play is finished or time out is called do we perceive how cold our feet are or hear the couple behind us.

[5] **Shifting of attention.** The fact that we do at some time hear the conversation behind us and do notice the coldness in our feet illustrates another aspect of our field of attention. Attention is constantly shifting. What is at the focus one minute is marginal the next, and still later may have passed completely from conscious awareness. Even when one activity dominates our attention, its dominance usually is not perfectly continuous. Other perceptions come fleetingly into the focus of our awareness and then are replaced again by the dominant item.

[6] What is it that determines what we will attend to? Although attention does shift, it has a certain orderliness to it. It is not completely chaotic, for if it were we should be unable to carry out any extended activity. Actually, as a good advertising man could explain, there are certain principles that determine the direction of our attention—the principles of attention getting. These tell us what will be most clearly perceived and what may be only dimly perceived or not perceived at all. These principles concern two general classes of factors: *external factors* in the environment, and *internal factors* such as motives, set, and expectancy. We shall first consider the external factors under four headings: (1) intensity and size, (2) contrast, (3) repetition, and (4) movement.

[7] **Intensity and size.** The louder a sound, the more likely a person is to attend to it. The brighter the light, the more likely it is to capture his attention. By the same token he will more likely notice a full-page advertisement than he will a half-column one. This factor of intensity or bigness is most pronounced when he is experiencing something new or unfamiliar; then the items in the environment that are biggest, loudest, or brightest will attract his attention first. In general, if two stimuli are competing for attention, the one that is most intense will be the first to be noticed.

[8] **Contrast.** As human beings, we tend to adapt or become used to the stimulation around us. The ticking of the clock which may be so noticeable when we enter a room is not noticed after a while. A room may seem hot or

cold when we first enter it, but after a few minutes we may hardly be aware of the temperature. On the other hand, if the ticking clock should abruptly stop, we become aware of the sudden silence. As we drive along in a car, we are not aware of the hum of the engine, but let a cylinder misfire and the noise of the engine occupies the center of our attention.

[9] These examples illustrate the role of contrast in determining attention. Any change in the stimulation to which we have become adapted immediately captures our attention. If we are reading in our room and someone turns on the radio in the adjoining room, we are apt to become acutely aware of it. But after a short while it drops from our awareness as we again become absorbed in our reading. Now when the radio is turned off it again receives our ATTENTION for a moment. Both the onset and the termination of a stimulus tend to acquire attention because both contrast with what has preceded them.

[10] The word in capital letters in the above paragraph is another illustration of contrast. Most of you noticed the word as soon as you looked at this part of the page. However, if all the text were in capitals, the word would have gone unnoticed. It attracted attention because it contrasts with the words in lower-case letters.

[11] **Repetition.** There are times when the repetition of a stimulus is attention-getting. A misspelled word is more likely to be noticed if it occurs twice in the same paragraph than if it occurs only once. We are more likely to hear a burst of gunfire than a single shot, or to hear our name if it is called twice. Mother, when she calls Junior in for dinner, shouts his name not once but several times.

[12] The advantage of repetition is twofold. A stimulus repeated twice has a better chance of catching us during one of the periodic wanings of attention to a task in which we may be engaged. In addition, repetition increases our sensitivity or alertness to the stimulus.

[13] **Movement.** Human beings, as well as most animals, are quite sensitive to objects that move in their field of vision. Our eyes are involuntarily attracted to movement in much the same way as the moth is attracted to a flame. Soldiers on a night patrol soon learn this fact and freeze in their tracks when a flare bursts. To fall flat or duck behind shelter is movement that makes their detection more likely than remaining motionless out in the open.

[14] The field of advertising, of course, makes good use of this fact. Some of the most effective advertising signs are those that involve movement, either blinking lights or animated figures.

[15] **Motives.** The factors of intensity, contrast, repetition, and movement that attract attention are external stimulus factors. Of equal importance are human factors of motives, interests, and other internal states. Our needs and interests govern not only what will attract our attention but also what will hold it. Even the sleepiest student in the class can be made to sit on the edge of his chair by the instructor's announcing that he is going to talk

about "Sex Practices of American Females." Appeal to the sex drive is particularly effective in our culture because of the traditional suppression of the drive. Thus advertisements effectively use shapely girls in bathing suits to sell such unrelated items as spark plugs. In a society where food was more scarce than it is in this culture, advertisements showing food objects would probably outnumber those with sex appeal.

[16] Not only are basic motives such as sex and hunger important in directing attention, but any of the great variety of human motives and interests are effective. If a geologist and a bird fancier walk through the same fields, the geologist will notice the detailed features of the terrain, the various kinds of rocks, etc., while the bird lover will notice the number and variety of birds. If you ask the geologist about the birds, he is very apt to say that he did not notice any, much less how many or what kind. And of course the bird lover is not likely to have noted any of the geological features of the terrain.

[17] **Set or expectancy.** Besides our interests and motives, *set* or expectancy plays a major role in selecting what we will perceive. The geologist would have been able to tell you much more about the bird life in the fields he traversed if he had known beforehand that you were going to ask him. A doctor may hear the phone ring in the night, but not hear the baby's crying. His wife, on the other hand, may sleep through the ringing telephone, but the slightest sound from the child probably will bring her wide awake. . . .

[18] Of the various factors that determine attention and thus perception, expectancy is probably the most important, for our sets and expectancies largely direct and order the succession of our perceptual experiences. Without them, our perceiving would be largely at the mercy of random fluctuations in the environmental stimuli.

COMMENT AND QUESTIONS

Like many texts, the one from which this selection is taken indicates important points and divisions in the material by a system of section headings and subheadings. (The title "Principles of Perception" is a section heading within a chapter of the book.) Guided by the subheadings, one should emerge from reading "Principles of Perception" with a clear understanding of the eight terms in boldface type: **Attention, Shifting of attention,** etc. These eight topics are not, however, parallel, or related in precisely the same way to the subject of perception. The good reader will notice how Mr. Morgan relates attention to principles of perception in paragraphs 2–5; how he establishes a further pattern of organization by analysis in paragraph 6, a question-to-answer paragraph; and how he restates that organization in two sentences of summary and transition at the beginning of paragraph 15.

I. Assume that "Principles of Perception" has been assigned as collateral reading in one of your courses, and bring to class reading notes on it.

II. Mr. Morgan skillfully uses brief examples to define or clarify many of his terms. What examples stay in your mind after you have read the selection? What idea does each of these examples clarify?

III. In writing this selection, the author is deliberately making a bid for the attention of his audience of college students. What are some of the devices he uses? Consider the six techniques for interesting the reader listed in question I on "The Life and Death of a Worm," page 734.

IV. If you have read the early chapters of this book before reading this selection, you may find it interesting to consider the following questions: (1) What psychological principles are most likely to influence, or to account for, the unconscious slanting of material? (2) What psychological principles may influence conscious slanting? (3) How might the psychological principles of *intensity, contrast, repetition,* and *movement* be applied to the problem of developing a clear, interesting, and effective style in writing? To what extent and in what ways would the employment of these principles be determined by the audience for whom the communication was intended?

EDGAR A. WALZ, III, AND CARL B. WALL

Slow-Motion Picture of High-Speed Death[*]

The following article from the *Reader's Digest* of February, 1957, is a report illustrating general-to-particular arrangement of material.

"John Collins, 38, of 210 Hill Place, was instantly killed last night when his car struck a tree on Route 35, two miles east. . . ."

Daily newspapers carry thousands of news briefs similar to this every year. It is a tragically common form of death, but one about which very little has been known.

For a number of years researchers like John O. Moore, director of Automotive Crash Injury Research for Cornell University Medical College, and Dr. J. H. Mathewson, of the Institute of Transportation and Traffic Engineering of the University of California, have test-crashed hundreds of cars, studied thousands of accident reports from all over the country, visited the scene and microscopically examined the wreckage of cars in which hundreds have died. Crack safety engineers of the leading automobile-manufacturing companies have cooperated. Distinguished medical experts have written detailed autopsies of crash victims.

[*] Copyright 1957 by The Reader's Digest Association, Inc. Reprinted with permission.

The primary reason for the research has been to reduce fatalities by making cars safer, more crash-proof. Out of it have come recommendations for safety belts, a different type of steering wheel, safety door catches, dashboard padding. But out of the research has also come something else: the terrifying picture of what happens to steel and glass, to flesh and blood, in those last split seconds when a human being is hurled into eternity.

This is the slow-motion, split-second reconstruction of what happens when a car, traveling 55 miles an hour, crashes into a solid, immovable tree:

1/10 of a second—The front bumper and chrome "frosting" of the grillwork collapse. Slivers of steel penetrate the tree to depths of one and a half inches and more.

2/10—The hood crumples as it rises, smashing into the windshield. Spinning rear wheels leave the ground. The grillwork disintegrates. The fenders come into contact with the tree, forcing the rear parts to splay out over the front doors.

In this same second tenth of a second, the heavy structural members of the car begin to act as a brake on the terrific forward momentum of the $2\frac{1}{2}$-ton body. But the driver's body continues to move forward at the vehicle's original speed. This means a force of 20 times gravity; his body weighs 3200 pounds. His legs, ramrod-straight, snap at the knee joints.

3/10—The driver's body is now off the seat, torso upright, broken knees pressing against the dashboard. The plastic-and-steel frame of the steering wheel begins to bend under his terrible death grip. His head is now near the sun visor, his chest above the steering column.

4/10—The car's front 24 inches have been completely demolished, but the rear end is still traveling at an estimated speed of 35 miles an hour. The driver's body is still traveling at 55. The half-ton motorblock crunches into the tree. The rear of the car, like a bucking horse, rises high enough to scrape bark off low branches.

5/10—The driver's fear-frozen hands bend the steering column into an almost vertical position. The force of gravity impales him on the steering-wheel shaft. Jagged steel punctures lung and intercostal arteries. Blood spurts into his lungs.

6/10—So great is the force of the impact that the driver's feet are ripped from his tightly laced shoes. The brake pedal shears off at the floorboards. The chassis bends in the middle, shearing body bolts. The driver's head smashes into the windshield. The rear of the car begins its downward fall, spinning wheels digging into the ground.

7/10—The entire, writhing body of the car is forced out of shape. Hinges tear. Doors spring open. In one last convulsion the seat rams forward, pinning the driver against the cruel steel of the steering shaft. Blood leaps from his mouth. Shock has frozen his heart. He is now dead.

Time elapsed—seven tenths of one second.

COMMENT AND QUESTIONS

We have included this grim article for two reasons. First, though very short, it is a good example of one kind of informative report: the authors state the scope, method, and purpose of the investigation of a common form of death; they give the general conclusions and results of the investigation; and they present the detailed findings of one part of the investigation. Second, the article seems to us to illustrate well the force of concrete words and concrete details. Notice that few attitudinal words are used; the language is largely factual, and from the accumulation of specific facts comes the emotional impact of the article.

Do you think that the primary intention of the authors was to inform or to persuade? Explain.

ALAN DEVOE

The Life and Death of a Worm*

Chronological arrangement and analysis of a mechanism are used together in the following selection to give information about a life process. Particularly worth noting as you read the essay are the techniques used to interest the reader in what could well be a dull subject—a worm. Alan Devoe (1909–1955) was an American author, editor, and naturalist who contributed essays and nature studies to many magazines. "The Life and Death of a Worm" is taken from *Down to Earth*, published in 1940.

[1] In a damp earth tunnel under the subsoil a minute cocoon stirs gently with emergent life. Out of it, presently, there issues a tiny ribbon of pink crawling flesh. An earthworm, commonest of all the annelids, has been born.

[2] The human infant, emerging out of foetal unawareness, comes into a world bright with colors and clamorous with sound. So does a guinea-pig baby or a new-hatched loon. The earthworm's birth is no such transition. Out of the darkness of the egg, this wriggling fragment of flesh and muscle emerges into a world that is hardly more fraught with awareness, hardly more informed by mind, than was the egg mass from which it came. The earthworm is unseeing, for it has no eyes. It is unhearing for it has no ears. The world into which it has been born is only a darkness and a silence.

[3] But this eyeless and earless morsel of blood and skin is sensible of inner

* From *Down to Earth* by Alan Devoe. Copyright, 1940, by Alan Devoe. Reprinted by permission of Coward-McCann, Inc.

urgings, responsive from the moment of its birth to dim behests. It is stirred by vague restlessness, such as never infected a mushroom or a sumac root, and which is token of its membership in animal creation. It is blood brother, this blind, unhearing worm, to the high hawk and the running deer, and it is equipped with compulsions even as these are. It is not exempted from the twin necessities which are visited upon every creature of earth: the necessity to eat and the necessity to beget. These things being so, the earthworm stirs and wriggles in its dark earth-chamber, and sets forth presently on the great adventure of existence.

[4] In obedience to an inner bidding it directs its body upward, toward the topsoil and the outer air. The way of its going is very slow, and it is this: just under the body skin runs a layer of circular muscles, and just under these a layer of muscles that lie longitudinally; alternately the earthworm contracts the circular muscles at its anterior end, rendering the body extended and thin, and contracts the longitudinal muscles, rendering the body short again. It is a slow, laborious way of locomotion, and effects a movement at all only because of a curious device. On each segment of the earthworm's body are arranged four pairs of tiny, spiny hairs, called setae, under the direct control of muscles. They extend obliquely backward from the sides and underparts of the earthworm's body, and the earthworm moves them as though they were little legs. As the worm thrusts upward now, boring blindly toward the outer otherworld which it cannot know exists, the setae press and grip the burrow wall and translate the worm's muscular churnings into a slow but steady movement.

[5] Unhaltingly the earthworm struggles upward through the soil. Its infinitesimal brain, in an anterior segment above the pharynx, is incapable of harboring the thing that men call mind; a subtler and stranger species of impulsion informs the nerve cords and directs the muscles in their work. Mindless, the earthworm is yet gifted with perceptions and recognitions. The pressures and stresses of the soil against its flesh are intelligible to it; the sensations of dryness or of moisture are somehow meaningful. When now, on its upward voyage, the earthworm reaches a stratum of hard dry soil through which it cannot penetrate by muscular effort alone, there comes to it—perhaps out of the misty realm called instinct, perhaps out of an otherwhere never to be plumbed—the knowledge of what must be done. The earthworm begins to eat.

[6] Grain by grain it sucks the hard-packed soil into its muscular pharynx, grain by grain it reduces the barrier impeding its progress. Millimeter by millimeter, as the obstructing earth is nibbled away, the worm ascends toward outer air. It reaches the surface at last, thrusting its wriggling way through grass roots and the final crust, and when ultimately its tunneling is completed it deposits on the surface, in the form of castings, the swallowed earth which has passed through its alimentary canal. No man wholly understands the worm's earth-eating, or comprehends the chemistry whereby its body extracts from the eaten soil the bits of humus and vegetable matter

which will give it nourishment. The feeding process of earthworms is a curious thing, and this much is known of it: from the pharynx the food goes to an oesophagus, and is there mixed with gland secretions which neutralize the acids. Thence it enters a thin-walled crop, and thence a gizzard, where it is ground to bits by spasmodic muscular contractions—and by the sharp grains of sand that have been swallowed—and is rendered ready for entrance into the worm's intestine. The network of tiny veins and arteries by which the earthworm's blood is circulated carries likewise waste products of the digested food, and on every segment of the body is a pair of organs, called nephridia, for the excretion of these wastes. Such is the manner of the earthworm's nourishment, and such the processes which have attended its upward voyage through the earth.

[7] The earthworm has attained the outer world now, although no sight or sound can apprise it of the fact. In the damp darkness (for the ascension has been made at night) the earthworm fastens its tail by the setae to the top of the burrow, and, stretching its soft elastic body to full length, explores the neighborhood in which it finds itself. It is in quest of fallen leaves, of minute fragments of weed stalks and roots and decayed bark. Having no organs of sight, the earthworm is nevertheless able, perhaps by a dim awareness akin to scent, to detect the presence of these morsels and to seize on them; and it is able, further, to single out those foods for which it has a special preference—such foods, for instance, as cabbage leaves and carrots.

[8] Slowly the earthworm investigates the night, thrusting its blind naked head this way and that. Its recognition of the universe is hardly more complete than the recognition possessed by a burdock leaf or a floating water weed. The texture of its awareness is scarcely more complex. From time to time, now, as it forages blindly and deafly in the damp night air, it wriggles suddenly in response to the glinting of light or the vibrance of a tread upon the nearby earth. These are the things to which its delicate flesh responds—these the limits of the universe it can perceive. Presently, when it has taken in a sufficiency of food, it terminates its explorations for the night and withdraws once more to inner earth.

[9] There is small variegation in the pattern of the earthworm's succeeding days. During the sunlit hours the worm stays buried in the cool darkness beneath the surface of the soil, for the thin slime of mucus that covers its skin would be dried up by the sun. But when the nights come—or when the sun is hidden and rain falls—the earthworm grows obscurely aware that it is time for seeking the outer world again, and once more the pink flesh thrusts upward. After this fashion does day follow day, unmarked by any incident but the worm's feeding and breathing. Even the breathing is almost as simple as a plant's. Blind and deaf and unequipped with mind, the earthworm also lacks lungs. It absorbs the oxygen directly through its body walls into the sluggish blood, and similarly, imperceptibly, the carbon dioxide is expelled.

[10] Some time before it dies, the worm must beget young. The individual

earthworm is both male and female, having the reproductive organs of each sex, and when the time for egg-laying comes it secretes from a thickened place in its body—the clitellum—a cocoon in which the eggs are secured. This done, the eggs are then fertilized by the spermatozoa of another worm, and the most vital of all animal rites has been accomplished. A few days or a few weeks longer the earthworm feeds and forages and pursues its eyeless way, and then the life goes out of it as unknowledgeably as it came, and the briefly animated morsel of blood and sinew reverts to parent earth.

[11]   An earthworm, I suppose, will hardly attract the contemplation of the kind of man who can be stirred by no less gaudy natural marvel than a Grand Canyon or a shooting star. Charles Darwin, though, thought earthworms were worth studying for forty years, and Darwin made some curious discoveries. He found, for instance, that in a single acre of ground there may be 50,000 worms, and he found that they carry to the surface, in a single year, some eighteen tons of earth castings. The earthworms in an acre, Darwin learned, would in twenty years carry from the subsoil to the surface a layer of soil three inches thick; and it became evident to him that the honeycombing of the earth by its earthworms was what aerated the soil and made it porous and rendered it fit for man's agriculture.

[12]   It is good sometimes to be reminded that the ephemeral shifts of politics and ideologies are not the things on which our human welfare actually depends. The ultimate welfare of our tribe depends on things like worms.

COMMENT AND QUESTIONS

I. Six closely related techniques for interesting the reader are commonly used in informative writing aimed at a popular audience. These techniques, most of which we have mentioned before, are: (1) beginning with an attention-arousing device (a question, an exclamation, an anecdote); (2) associating the subject with the personal experience and interests of the reader; (3) translating abstract terms into concrete terms which the reader can more easily understand and relate to his own experience; (4) focusing on an individual instead of dealing generally with a large group; (5) using examples or comparisons which appeal to the reader; (6) arousing emotion about the subject in order to keep the reader sufficiently interested to read on and get the information. These devices are, of course, persuasive, although the primary intention of the writing may be informative. How many of these six techniques for interest are used in "The Life and Death of a Worm"? Point out specific examples.

II. In addition to certain other techniques, the writer of this article uses a dramatic, highly colored style. Notice, for example, the sentence structures and choice of words in paragraph 5. One of his stylistic devices is repetition: the fact that the worm is unseeing and unhearing is repeated in such phrases as "this blind unhearing worm," "boring blindly," "having no organs of sight," "its blind naked head," "forages blindly and deafly," "blind and deaf and unequipped with mind," "its eyeless way." Point out other examples in the article of dramatic style and repetition. Are these techniques appropriate to the material? Are they, in your opinion, effectively used, or overused?

III. Paragraphs 4, 6, and 10 contain examples of inconspicuous definition of technical terms (setae, nephridia, clitellum). Also very skillful is the double pattern in the first seven paragraphs, by which the reader, following chronologically the life of the worm, also follows it in its physical progress up through the soil. By what technical means is the reader kept aware of this progress?

IV. What do the last two paragraphs contribute to the article?

VANNEVAR BUSH

The Builders*

In the following selection, a contemporary scientist uses an extended analogy to analyze the process by which the structure of human knowledge is built. Vannevar Bush has had a distinguished career as Professor of Electrical Engineering at the Massachusetts Institute of Technology, inventor of electronic calculating machines, director of the Office of Scientific Research and Development, and President of the Carnegie Institution of Washington. He is also the author of *Modern Arms and Free Men,* published in 1949. "The Builders" appeared in the January, 1945, issue of *The Technology Review.*

[1] The process by which the boundaries of knowledge are advanced, and the structure of organized science is built, is a complex process indeed. It corresponds fairly well with the exploitation of a difficult quarry for its building materials and the fitting of these into an edifice; but there are very significant differences. First, the material itself is exceedingly varied, hidden and overlaid with relatively worthless rubble, and the process of uncovering new facts and relationships has some of the attributes of prospecting and exploration rather than of mining or quarrying. Second, the whole effort is highly unorganized. There are no direct orders from architect or quarry-master. Individuals and small bands proceed about their businesses unimpeded and uncontrolled, digging where they will, working over their material, and tucking it into place in the edifice.

[2] Finally, the edifice itself has a remarkable property, for its form is pre-

* Reprinted from *The Technology Review,* January, 1945, edited at the Massachusetts Institute of Technology.

destined by the laws of logic and the nature of human reasoning. It is almost as though it had once existed, and its building blocks had then been scattered, hidden, and buried, each with its unique form retained so that it would fit only in its own peculiar position, and with the concomitant limitation that the blocks cannot be found or recognized until the building of the structure has progressed to the point where their position and form reveal themselves to the discerning eye of the talented worker in the quarry. Parts of the edifice are being used while construction proceeds, by reason of the applications of science, but other parts are merely admired for their beauty and symmetry, and their possible utility is not in question.

[3] In these circumstances it is not at all strange that the workers sometimes proceed in erratic ways. There are those who are quite content, given a few tools, to dig away unearthing odd blocks, piling them up in the view of fellow workers, and apparently not caring whether they fit anywhere or not. Unfortunately there are also those who watch carefully until some industrious group digs out a particularly ornamental block; whereupon they fit it in place with much gusto, and bow to the crowd. Some groups do not dig at all, but spend all their time arguing as to the exact arrangement of a cornice or an abutment. Some spend all their days trying to pull down a block or two that a rival has put in place. Some, indeed, neither dig nor argue, but go along with the crowd, scratch here and there, and enjoy the scenery. Some sit by and give advice, and some just sit.

[4] On the other hand there are those men of rare vision who can grasp well in advance just the block that is needed for rapid advance on a section of the edifice to be possible, who can tell by some subtle sense where it will be found, and who have an uncanny skill in cleaning away dross and bringing it surely into the light. These are the master workmen. For each of them there can well be many of lesser stature who chip and delve, industriously, but with little grasp of what it is all about, and who nevertheless make the great steps possible.

[5] There are those who can give the structure meaning, who can trace its evolution from early times, and describe the glories that are to be, in ways that inspire those who work and those who enjoy. They bring the inspiration that not all is mere building of monotonous walls, and that there is achitecture even though the architect is not seen to guide and order.

[6] There are those who labor to make the utility of the structure real, to cause it to give shelter to the multitude, that they may be better protected, and that they may derive health and well-being because of its presence.

[7] And the edifice is not built by the quarrymen and the masons alone. There are those who bring them food during their labors, and cooling drink when the days are warm, who sing to them, and place flowers on the little walls that have grown with the years.

[8] There are also the old men, whose days of vigorous building are done, whose eyes are too dim to see the details of the arch or the needed form of its keystone, who have built a wall here and there, and lived long in the

edifice; who have learned to love it and who have even grasped a suggestion of its ultimate meaning; and who sit in the shade and encourage the young men.

COMMENT AND QUESTIONS

Analogy is used in informative writing, as we have said earlier, to make a complex or abstract idea more understandable and concrete. In some analogies, the writer compares abstract idea or situation A with familiar idea or situation F, and then explains, point by point, the likenesses between them. In other analogies the writer, having established his comparison, expands or analyzes situation F, and expects his readers to see its application to A. The reader of such analogy, of which "The Builders" is an example, must make this application. If his reading is successful, he receives simultaneously the literal meaning which the analogy is designed to clarify, and the force of the figurative language in which it is clothed.

I. What, stated in literal terms, are the three ways in which building knowledge differs from building an actual edifice?

II. What actual groups are referred to in the analysis of types of builders in paragraphs 3-8?

III. This analogy is persuasive as well as informative. Which groups of builders is the reader led, by Mr. Bush's treatment, to admire? Which groups is he led to condemn?

GEORGE ORWELL

The Principles of Newspeak[*]

The following essay was written as an appendix to *Nineteen Eighty-Four,* a novel depicting life in a future totalitarian state made up of countries in Europe and America. The essay purports to be a purely informative, objective, semitechnical description and analysis of the official language of the state of Oceania. The reader will soon realize, however, that the writing is ironical: out of the factual language and the apparently impersonal, uncritical tone emerge a number of value judgments. George Orwell (1903-1950), whose real name was Eric Blair, was an English author and critic. *Nineteen Eighty-Four* was published in 1949.

[*] From *Nineteen Eighty-four* by George Orwell. Published by Harcourt, Brace and Company, Inc. Copyright 1949, by Harcourt, Brace and Company, Inc. Permission also from Martin Secker and Warburg, Ltd. (London).

[1] Newspeak was the official language of Oceania and had been devised to meet the ideological needs of Ingsoc, or English Socialism. In the year 1984 there was not as yet anyone who used Newspeak as his sole means of communication, either in speech or writing. The leading articles in the *Times* were written in it, but this was a tour de force which could only be carried out by a specialist. It was expected that Newspeak would have finally superseded Oldspeak (or Standard English, as we should call it) by about the year 2050. Meanwhile it gained ground steadily, all Party members tending to use Newspeak words and grammatical constructions more and more in their everyday speech. The version in use in 1984, and embodied in the Ninth and Tenth Editions of the Newspeak dictionary, was a provisional one, and contained many superfluous words and archaic formations which were due to be suppressed later. It is with the final, perfected version, as embodied in the Eleventh Edition of the dictionary, that we are concerned here.

[2] The purpose of Newspeak was not only to provide a medium of expression for the world-view and mental habits proper to the devotees of Ingsoc, but to make all other modes of thought impossible. It was intended that when Newspeak had been adopted once and for all and Oldspeak forgotten, a heretical thought—that is, a thought diverging from the principles of Ingsoc—should be literally unthinkable, at least so far as thought is dependent on words. Its vocabulary was so constructed as to give exact and often very subtle expression to every meaning that a Party member could properly wish to express, while excluding all other meanings and also the possibility of arriving at them by indirect methods. This was done partly by the invention of new words, but chiefly by eliminating undesirable words and by stripping such words as remained of unorthodox meanings, and so far as possible of all secondary meanings whatever. To give a single example, the word *free* still existed in Newspeak, but it could only be used in such statements as "This dog is free from lice" or "This field is free from weeds." It could not be used in its old sense of "politically free" or "intellectually free," since political and intellectual freedom no longer existed even as concepts, and were therefore of necessity nameless. Quite apart from the suppression of definitely heretical words, reduction of vocabulary was regarded as an end in itself, and no word that could be dispensed with was allowed to survive. Newspeak was designed not to extend but to *diminish* the range of thought, and this purpose was indirectly assisted by cutting the choice of words down to a minimum.

[3] Newspeak was founded on the English language as we now know it, though many Newspeak sentences, even when not containing newly created words, would be barely intelligible to an English-speaker of our own day. Newspeak words were divided into three distinct classes, known as the A vocabulary, the B vocabulary (also called compound words), and the C vocabulary. It will be simpler to discuss each class separately, but the grammatical peculiarities of the language can be dealt with in the section

devoted to the A vocabulary, since the same rules held good for all three categories.

[4] *The A vocabulary.* The A vocabulary consisted of the words needed for the business of everyday life—for such things as eating, drinking, working, putting on one's clothes, going up and down stairs, riding in vehicles, gardening, cooking, and the like. It was composed almost entirely of words that we already possess—words like *hit, run, dog, tree, sugar, house, field*— but in comparison with the present-day English vocabulary, their number was extremely small, while their meanings were far more rigidly defined. All ambiguities and shades of meaning had been purged out of them. So far as it could be achieved, a Newspeak word of this class was simply a staccato sound expressing *one* clearly understood concept. It would have been quite impossible to use the A vocabulary for literary purposes or for political or philosophical discussion. It was intended only to express simple, purposive thoughts, usually involving concrete objects or physical actions.
[5] The grammar of Newspeak had two outstanding peculiarities. The first of these was an almost complete interchangeability between different parts of speech. Any word in the language (in principle this applied even to very abstract words such as *if* or *when*) could be used either as verb, noun, adjective, or adverb. Between the verb and the noun form, when they were of the same root, there was never any variation, this rule of itself involving the destruction of many archaic forms. The word *thought,* for example, did not exist in Newspeak. Its place was taken by *think,* which did duty for both noun and verb. No etymological principle was involved here; in some cases it was the original noun that was chosen for retention, in other cases the verb. Even when a noun and verb of kindred meaning were not etymologically connected, one or other of them was frequently suppressed. There was, for example, no such word as *cut,* its meaning being sufficiently covered by the noun-verb *knife.* Adjectives were formed by adding the suffix *-ful* to the noun-verb, and adverbs by adding *-wise.* Thus, for example, *speedful* meant "rapid" and *speedwise* meant "quickly." Certain of our present-day adjectives, such as *good, strong, big, black, soft,* were retained, but their total number was very small. There was little need for them, since almost any adjectival meaning could be arrived at by adding *-ful* to a noun-verb. None of the now-existing adverbs was retained, except for a very few already ending in *-wise;* the *-wise* termination was invariable. The word *well,* for example, was replaced by *goodwise.*
[6] In addition, any word—this again applied in principle to every word in the language—could be negatived by adding the affix *un-,* or could be strengthened by the affix *plus-,* or, for still greater emphasis, *doubleplus-.* Thus, for example, *uncold* meant "warm," while *pluscold* and *doubleplus- cold* meant, respectively, "very cold" and "superlatively cold." It was also possible, as in present-day English, to modify the meaning of almost any word by prepositional affixes such as *ante-, post-, up-, down-,* etc. By such

methods it was found possible to bring about an enormous diminution of vocabulary. Given, for instance, the word *good,* there was no need for such a word as *bad,* since the required meaning was equally well—indeed, better—expressed by *ungood.* All that was necessary, in any case where two words formed a natural pair of opposites, was to decide which of them to suppress. *Dark,* for example, could be replaced by *unlight,* or *light* by *undark,* according to preference.

[7]   The second distinguishing mark of Newspeak grammar was its regularity. Subject to a few exceptions which are mentioned below, all inflections followed the same rules. Thus, in all verbs the preterite and the past participle were the same and ended in *-ed.* The preterite of *steal* was *stealed,* the preterite of *think* was *thinked,* and so on throughout the language, all such forms as *swam, gave, brought, spoke, taken,* etc., being abolished. All plurals were made by adding *-s* or *-es* as the case might be. The plurals of *man, ox, life* were *mans, oxes, lifes.* Comparison of adjectives was invariably made by adding *-er, -est (good, gooder, goodest),* irregular forms and the *more, most* formation being suppressed.

[8]   The only classes of words that were still allowed to inflect irregularly were the pronouns, the relatives, the demonstrative adjectives, and the auxiliary verbs. All of these followed their ancient usage, except that *whom* had been scrapped as unnecessary, and the *shall, should* tenses had been dropped, all their uses being covered by *will* and *would.* There were also certain irregularities in word-formation arising out of the need for rapid and easy speech. A word which was difficult to utter, or was liable to be incorrectly heard, was held to be ipso facto a bad word; occasionally therefore, for the sake of euphony, extra letters were inserted into a word or an archaic formation was retained. But this need made itself felt chiefly in connection with the B vocabulary. *Why* so great an importance was attached to ease of pronunciation will be made clear later in this essay.

[9]   *The B vocabulary.* The B vocabulary consisted of words which had been deliberately constructed for political purposes: words, that is to say, which not only had in every case a political implication, but were intended to impose a desirable mental attitude upon the person using them. Without a full understanding of the principles of Ingsoc it was difficult to use these words correctly. In some cases they could be translated into Oldspeak, or even into words taken from the A vocabulary, but this usually demanded a long paraphrase and always involved the loss of certain overtones. The B words were a sort of verbal shorthand, often packing whole ranges of ideas into a few syllables, and at the same time more accurate and forcible than ordinary language.

[10]   The B words were in all cases compound words.[1] They consisted of two or more words, or portions of words, welded together in an easily pro-

---

[1] Compound words, such as *speakwrite,* were of course to be found in the A vocabulary, but these were merely convenient abbreviations and had no special ideological color.

nounceable form. The resulting amalgam was always a noun-verb, and inflected according to the ordinary rules. To take a single example: the word *goodthink,* meaning, very roughly, "orthodoxy," or, if one chose to regard it as a verb, "to think in an orthodox manner." This inflected as follows: noun-verb, *goodthink;* past tense and past participle, *goodthinked;* present participle, *goodthinking;* adjective, *goodthinkful;* adverb, *goodthinkwise;* verbal noun, *goodthinker.*

[11] The B words were not constructed on any etymological plan. The words of which they were made up could be any parts of speech, and could be placed in any order and mutilated in any way which made them easy to pronounce while indicating their derivation. In the word *crimethink* (thought-crime), for instance, the *think* came second, whereas in *thinkpol* (Thought Police) it came first, and in the latter word *police* had lost its second syllable. Because of the greater difficulty in securing euphony, irregular formations were commoner in the B vocabulary than in the A vocabulary. For example, the adjectival forms of *Minitrue, Minipax,* and *Miniluv* were, respectively, *Minitruthful, Minipeaceful,* and *Minilovely,* simply because *-trueful, -paxful,* and *-loveful* were slightly awkward to pronounce. In principle, however, all B words could inflect, and all inflected in exactly the same way.

[12] Some of the B words had highly subtilized meanings, barely intelligible to anyone who had not mastered the language as a whole. Consider, for example, such a typical sentence from a *Times* leading article as *Oldthinkers unbellyfeel Ingsoc.* The shortest rendering that one could make of this in Oldspeak would be: "Those whose ideas were formed before the Revolution cannot have a full emotional understanding of the principles of English Socialism." But this is not an adequate translation. To begin with, in order to grasp the full meaning of the Newspeak sentence quoted above, one would have to have a clear idea of what is meant by *Ingsoc.* And, in addition, only a person thoroughly grounded in Ingsoc could appreciate the full force of the word *bellyfeel,* which implied a blind, enthusiastic acceptance difficult to imagine today; or of the word *oldthink,* which was inextricably mixed up with the idea of wickedness and decadence. But the special function of certain Newspeak words, of which *oldthink* was one, was not so much to express meanings as to destroy them. These words, necessarily few in number, had had their meanings extended until they contained within themselves whole batteries of words which, as they were sufficiently covered by a single comprehensive term, could now be scrapped and forgotten. The greatest difficulty facing the compilers of the Newspeak dictionary was not to invent new words, but, having invented them, to make sure what they meant: to make sure, that is to say, what ranges of words they canceled by their existence.

[13] As we have already seen in the case of the word *free,* words which had once borne a heretical meaning were sometimes retained for the sake of convenience, but only with the undesirable meanings purged out of them.

Countless other words such as *honor, justice, morality, internationalism, democracy, science,* and *religion* had simply ceased to exist. A few blanket words covered them, and, in covering them, abolished them. All words grouping themselves round the concepts of liberty and equality, for instance, were contained in the single word *crimethink*, while all words grouping themselves round the concepts of objectivity and rationalism were contained in the single word *oldthink*. Greater precision would have been dangerous. What was required in a Party member was an outlook similar to that of the ancient Hebrew who knew, without knowing much else, that all nations other than his own worshipped "false gods." He did not need to know that these gods were called Baal, Osiris, Moloch, Ashtaroth, and the like; probably the less he knew about them the better for his orthodoxy. He knew Jehovah and the commandments of Jehovah; he knew, therefore, that all gods with other names or other attributes were false gods. In somewhat the same way, the Party member knew what constituted right conduct, and in exceedingly vague, generalized terms he knew what kinds of departure from it were possible. His sexual life, for example, was entirely regulated by the two Newspeak words *sexcrime* (sexual immorality) and *goodsex* (chastity). *Sexcrime* covered all sexual misdeeds whatever. It covered fornication, adultery, homosexuality, and other perversions, and, in addition, normal intercourse practiced for its own sake. There was no need to enumerate them separately, since they were all equally culpable, and, in principle, all punishable by death. In the C vocabulary, which consisted of scientific and technical words, it might be necessary to give specialized names to certain sexual aberrations, but the ordinary citizen had no need of them. He knew what was meant by *goodsex*—that is to say, normal intercourse between man and wife, for the sole purpose of begetting children, and without physical pleasure on the part of the woman; all else was *sexcrime*. In Newspeak it was seldom possible to follow a heretical thought further than the perception that it *was* heretical; beyond that point the necessary words were nonexistent.

[14]   No word in the B vocabulary was ideologically neutral. A great many were euphemisms. Such words, for instance, as *joycamp* (forced-labor camp) or *Minipax* (Ministry of Peace, i.e., Ministry of War) meant almost the exact opposite of what they appeared to mean. Some words, on the other hand, displayed a frank and contemptuous understanding of the real nature of Oceanic society.   An example was *prolefeed,* meaning the rubbishy entertainment and spurious news which the Party handed out to the masses. Other words, again, were ambivalent, having the connotation "good" when applied to the Party and "bad" when applied to its enemies. But in addition there were great numbers of words which at first sight appeared to be mere abbreviations and which derived their ideological color not from their meaning but from their structure.

[15]   So far as it could be contrived, everything that had or might have political significance of any kind was fitted into the B vocabulary. The name

of every organization, or body of people, or doctrine, or country, or institution, or public building, was invariably cut down into the familiar shape; that is, a single easily pronounced word with the smallest number of syllables that would preserve the original derivation. In the Ministry of Truth, for example, the Records Department, in which Winston Smith worked, was called *Recdep,* the Fiction Department was called *Ficdep,* the Teleprograms Department was called *Teledep,* and so on. This was not done solely with the object of saving time. Even in the early decades of the twentieth century, telescoped words and phrases had been one of the characteristic features of political language; and it had been noticed that the tendency to use abbreviations of this kind was most marked in totalitarian countries and totalitarian organizations. Examples were such words as *Nazi, Gestapo, Comintern, Inprecorr, Agitprop.* In the beginning the practice had been adopted as it were instinctively, but in Newspeak it was used with a conscious purpose. It was perceived that in thus abbreviating a name one narrowed and subtly altered its meaning, by cutting out most of the associations that would otherwise cling to it. The words *Communist International,* for instance, call up a composite picture of universal human brotherhood, red flags, barricades, Karl Marx, and the Paris Commune. The word Comintern, on the other hand, suggests merely a tightly knit organization and a well-defined body of doctrine. It refers to something almost as easily recognized, and as limited in purpose, as a chair or a table. *Comintern* is a word that can be uttered almost without taking thought, whereas *Communist International* is a phrase over which one is obliged to linger at least momentarily. In the same way, the associations called up by a word like *Minitrue* are fewer and more controllable than those called up by *Ministry of Truth.* This accounted not only for the habit of abbreviating whenever possible, but also for the almost exaggerated care that was taken to make every word easily pronounceable.

[16] In Newspeak, euphony outweighed every consideration other than exactitude of meaning. Regularity of grammar was always sacrificed to it when it seemed necessary. And rightly so, since what was required, above all for political purposes, were short clipped words of unmistakable meaning which could be uttered rapidly and which roused the minimum of echoes in the speaker's mind. The words of the B vocabulary even gained in force from the fact that nearly all of them were very much alike. Almost invariably these words—*goodthink, Minipax, prolefeed, sexcrime, joycamp, Ingsoc, bellyfeel, thinkpol,* and countless others—were words of two or three syllables, with the stress distributed equally between the first syllable and the last. The use of them encouraged a gabbling style of speech, at once staccato and monotonous. And this was exactly what was aimed at. The intention was to make speech, and especially speech on any subject not ideologically neutral, as nearly as possible independent of consciousness. For the purposes of everyday life it was no doubt necessary, or sometimes necessary, to reflect before speaking, but a Party member called upon to make a political

or ethical judgment should be able to spray forth the correct opinions as automatically as a machine gun spraying forth bullets. His training fitted him to do this, the language gave him an almost foolproof instrument, and the texture of the words, with their harsh sound and a certain willful ugliness which was in accord with the spirit of Ingsoc, assisted the process still further.

[17] So did the fact of having very few words to choose from. Relative to our own, the Newspeak vocabulary was tiny, and new ways of reducing it were constantly being devised. Newspeak, indeed, differed from almost all other languages in that its vocabulary grew smaller instead of larger every year. Each reduction was a gain, since the smaller the area of choice, the smaller the temptation to take thought. Ultimately it was hoped to make articulate speech issue from the larynx without involving the higher brain centers at all. This aim was frankly admitted in the Newspeak word *duckspeak,* meaning "to quack like a duck." Like various other words in the B vocabulary, *duckspeak* was ambivalent in meaning. Provided that the opinions which were quacked out were orthodox ones, it implied nothing but praise, and when the *Times* referred to one of the orators of the Party as a *doubleplusgood duckspeaker* it was paying a warm and valued compliment.

[18] *The C vocabulary.* The C vocabulary was supplementary to the others and consisted entirely of scientific and technical terms. These resembled the scientific terms in use today, and were constructed from the same roots, but the usual care was taken to define them rigidly and strip them of undesirable meanings. They followed the same grammatical rules as the words in the other two vocabularies. Very few of the C words had any currency either in everyday speech or in political speech. Any scientific worker or technician could find all the words he needed in the list devoted to his own specialty, but he seldom had more than a smattering of the words occurring in the other lists. Only a very few words were common to all lists, and there was no vocabulary expressing the function of Science as a habit of mind, or a method of thought, irrespective of its particular branches. There was, indeed, no word for "Science," any meaning that it could possibly bear being already sufficiently covered by the word *Ingsoc.*

[19] From the foregoing account it will be seen that in Newspeak the expression of unorthodox opinions, above a very low level, was well-nigh impossible. It was of course possible to utter heresies of a very crude kind, a species of blasphemy. It would have been possible, for example, to say *Big Brother is ungood.* But this statement, which to an orthodox ear merely conveyed a self-evident absurdity, could not have been sustained by reasoned argument, because the necessary words were not available. Ideas inimical to Ingsoc could only be entertained in a vague wordless form, and could only be named in very broad terms which lumped together and condemned whole groups of heresies without defining them in doing so. One

could, in fact, only use Newspeak for unorthodox purposes by illegitimately translating some of the words back into Oldspeak. For example *All mans are equal* was a possible Newspeak sentence, but only in the same sense in which *All men are redhaired* is a possible Oldspeak sentence. It did not contain a grammatical error, but it expressed a palpable untruth, i.e., that all men are of equal size, weight, or strength. The concept of political equality no longer existed, and this secondary meaning had accordingly been purged out of the word *equal*. In 1984, when Oldspeak was still the normal means of communication, the danger theoretically existed that in using Newspeak words one might remember their original meanings. In practice it was not difficult for any person well grounded in *doublethink* to avoid doing this, but within a couple of generations even the possibility of such a lapse would have vanished. A person growing up with Newspeak as his sole language would no more know that *equal* had once had the secondary meaning of "politically equal," or that *free* had once meant "intellectually free," than, for instance, a person who had never heard of chess would be aware of the secondary meanings attaching to *queen* and *rook*. There would be many crimes and errors which it would be beyond his power to commit, simply because they were nameless and therefore unimaginable. And it was to be foreseen that with the passage of time the distinguishing characteristics of Newspeak would become more and more pronounced—its words growing fewer and fewer, their meanings more and more rigid, and the chance of putting them to improper uses always diminishing.

[20] When Oldspeak had been once and for all superseded, the last link with the past would have been severed. History had already been rewritten, but fragments of the literature of the past survived here and there, imperfectly censored, and so long as one retained one's knowledge of Oldspeak it was possible to read them. In the future such fragments, even if they chanced to survive, would be unintelligible and untranslatable. It was impossible to translate any passage of Oldspeak into Newspeak unless it either referred to some technical process or some very simple everyday action, or was already orthodox (*goodthinkful* would be the Newspeak expression) in tendency. In practice this meant that no book written before approximately 1960 could be translated as a whole. Prerevolutionary literature could only be subjected to ideological translation—that is, alteration in sense as well as language. Take for example the well-known passage from the Declaration of Independence:

[21] *We hold these truths to be self-evident, that all men are created equal, that they are endowed by their Creator with certain inalienable rights, that among these are life, liberty, and the pursuit of happiness. That to secure these rights, Governments are instituted among men, deriving their powers from the consent of the governed. That whenever any form of Government becomes destructive of those ends, it is the right of the People to alter or abolish it, and to institute new Government . . .*

[22] It would have been quite impossible to render this into Newspeak while keeping to the sense of the original. The nearest one could come to doing so would be to swallow the whole passage up in the single word *crimethink*. A full translation could only be an ideological translation, whereby Jefferson's words would be changed into a panegyric on absolute government.

[23] A good deal of the literature of the past was, indeed, already being transformed in this way. Considerations of prestige made it desirable to preserve the memory of certain historical figures, while at the same time bringing their achievements into line with the philosophy of Ingsoc. Various writers, such as Shakespeare, Milton, Swift, Byron, Dickens and some others were therefore in process of translation; when the task had been completed, their original writings, with all else that survived of the literature of the past, would be destroyed. These translations were a slow and difficult business, and it was not expected that they would be finished before the first or second decade of the twenty-first century. There were also large quantities of merely utilitarian literature—indispensable technical manuals and the like—that had to be treated in the same way. It was chiefly in order to allow time for the preliminary work of translation that the final adoption of Newspeak had been fixed for so late a date as 2050.

COMMENT AND QUESTIONS

I. The following questions will serve as a check on your understanding of the factual content and structure of the essay: (1) What are the purposes of Newspeak? (2) What are the chief characteristics of each of the three classes of words? (3) Why does the author choose to discuss the grammar of Newspeak in connection with the A vocabulary instead of discussing it in a section preceding his analysis of the three vocabularies? (4) Why is the B vocabulary discussed more fully than the other two; the C vocabulary less fully? (5) Does there appear to be a plan in the illustrations the author uses; that is, does he seem to be emphasizing any point or points with his examples comparing Newspeak to Oldspeak? (6) Why is easy pronunciation important in Newspeak? (7) What is meant by the ideological translation of older literature? Why is it necessary?

II. We have said earlier that the basis of irony is contrast—contrast, for example, between what is said and what is meant, or between what is expected and what actually occurs, or between what is and what seems to be or should be. What kind or kinds of irony do you find in "The Principles of Newspeak"?

III. Consider the language of the following passages:

Its vocabulary was so constructed as to give *exact and often very subtle expression* to every meaning that a Party member could properly wish to express. . . .

The B words were a sort of verbal shorthand, often packing whole ranges of ideas into a few syllables, and at the same time *more accurate and forcible than ordinary language.*

Each reduction [in vocabulary] was *a gain,* since the smaller the area of choice, the smaller the temptation to take thought.

What sort of attitude toward the subject would normally be communicated by the italicized expressions? In the context of the essay, what do these expressions mean? What does the author gain by stating his meaning thus indirectly instead of directly?

IV. What tendencies toward a simplified language, perfected in Newspeak, can you see in present-day English? Do any of these simplifications seem to you sensible or desirable? Do you think that they would to George Orwell?

V. List as many characteristics as you can of the hypothetical society of 1984 as it appears in this selection. What is the relationship of each of these characteristics to the language of Newspeak? Do the attitudes and the practices of 1984 seem wholly remote from those of our society, or do at least some of them represent extensions of practices now in operation?

VI. Summarize what you take to be Mr. Orwell's ideas about the relationship between language and thought.

CARL L. BECKER

The Ideal Democracy*

Extended definition, analysis of a concept, and cause-and-effect arrangement are illustrated by the following selection. The clear handling of complex material and the lucid, polished style, characteristic of all the writing of Carl L. Becker, are worth careful study. Mr. Becker (1873–1945) was a distinguished American historian. He taught history at Pennsylvania State College, Dartmouth, the Universities of Kansas and Minnesota, and after 1917 at Cornell. Among his books are *The Heavenly City of the Eighteenth Century Philosophers, Every Man His Own Historian, New Liberties for Old, How New Will the Better World Be?* and *Modern Democracy,* from which this selection is taken. "The Ideal Democracy" was originally delivered as a lecture at the University of Virginia in 1940. It therefore combines a generally formal style and tone with a personal speaker-audience relationship.

[1] Democracy, like liberty or science or progress, is a word with which we are all so familiar that we rarely take the trouble to ask what we mean by it. It is a term, as the devotees of semantics say, which has no "referent"—

* From *Modern Democracy* by Carl Becker. Yale University Press.

there is no precise or palpable thing or object which we all think of when the word is pronounced. On the contrary, it is a word which connotes different things to different people, a kind of conceptual Gladstone bag which, with a little manipulation, can be made to accommodate almost any collection of social facts we may wish to carry about in it. In it we can as easily pack a dictatorship as any other form of government. We have only to stretch the concept to include any form of government supported by a majority of the people, for whatever reasons and by whatever means of expressing assent, and before we know it the empire of Napoleon, the Soviet regime of Stalin, and the Fascist systems of Mussolini and Hitler are all safely in the bag. But if this is what we mean by democracy, then virtually all forms of government are democratic, since virtually all governments, except in times of revolution, rest upon the explicit or implicit consent of the people. In order to discuss democracy intelligently it will be necessary, therefore, to define it, to attach to the word a sufficiently precise meaning to avoid the confusion which is not infrequently the chief result of such discussions.

[2] All human institutions, we are told, have their ideal forms laid away in heaven, and we do not need to be told that the actual institutions conform but indifferently to these ideal counterparts. It would be possible then to define democracy either in terms of the ideal or in terms of the real form—to define it as government of the people, by the people, for the people; or to define it as government of the people, by the politicians, for whatever pressure groups can get their interests taken care of. But as a historian, I am naturally disposed to be satisfied with the meaning which, in the history of politics, men have commonly attributed to the word—a meaning, needless to say, which derives partly from the experience and partly from the aspirations of mankind. So regarded, the term democracy refers primarily to a form of government, and it has always meant government by the many as opposed to government by the one—government by the people as opposed to government by a tyrant, a dictator, or an absolute monarch. This is the most general meaning of the word as men have commonly understood it.

[3] In this antithesis there are, however, certain implications, always tacitly understood, which give a more precise meaning to the term. Peisistratus, for example, was supported by a majority of the people, but his government was never regarded as a democracy for all that. Caesar's power derived from a popular mandate, conveyed through established republican forms, but that did not make his government any less a dictatorship. Napoleon called his government a democratic empire, but no one, least of all Napoleon himself, doubted that he had destroyed the last vestiges of the democratic republic. Since the Greeks first used the term, the essential test of democratic government has always been this: the source of political authority must be and remain in the people and not in the ruler. A democratic government has always meant one in which the citizens, or a suf-

ficient number of them to represent more or less effectively the common will, freely act from time to time, and according to established forms, to appoint or recall the magistrates and to enact or revoke the laws by which the community is governed. This I take to be the meaning which history has impressed upon the term democracy as a form of government. It is, therefore, the meaning which I attach to it in these lectures.

[4] The most obvious political fact of our time is that democracy as thus defined has suffered an astounding decline in prestige. Fifty years ago it was not impossible to regard democratic government, and the liberties that went with it, as a permanent conquest of the human spirit. In 1886 Andrew Carnegie published a book entitled *Triumphant Democracy*. Written without fear and without research, the book was not an achievement of the highest intellectual distinction perhaps; but the title at least expressed well enough the prevailing conviction—the conviction that democracy had fought the good fight, had won the decisive battles, and would inevitably, through its inherent merits, presently banish from the world the most flagrant political and social evils which from time immemorial had afflicted mankind. This conviction could no doubt be most easily entertained in the United States, where even the tradition of other forms of government was too remote and alien to color our native optimism. But even in Europe the downright skeptics, such as Lecky, were thought to be perverse, and so hardheaded a historian as J. B. Bury could proclaim with confidence that the long struggle for freedom of thought had finally been won.

[5] I do not need to tell you that within a brief twenty years the prevailing optimism of that time has been quite dispelled. One European country after another has, willingly enough it seems, abandoned whatever democratic institutions it formerly enjoyed for some form of dictatorship. The spokesmen of Fascism and Communism announce with confidence that democracy, a sentimental aberration which the world has outgrown, is done for; and even the friends of democracy support it with declining conviction. They tell us that democracy, so far from being triumphant, is "at the crossroads" or "in retreat," and that its future is by no means assured. What are we to think of this sudden reversal in fortune and prestige? How explain it? What to do about it?

II

[6] One of the presuppositions of modern thought is that institutions, in order to be understood, must be seen in relation to the conditions of time and place in which they appear. It is a little difficult for us to look at democracy in this way. We are so immersed in its present fortunes that we commonly see it only as a "close-up," filling the screen to the exclusion of other things to which it is in fact related. In order to form an objective judgment of its nature and significance, we must therefore first of all get it in proper perspective. Let us then, in imagination, remove from the immediate present scene to some cool high place where we can survey at a glance

five or six thousand years of history, and note the part which democracy has played in human civilization. The view, if we have been accustomed to take democratic institutions for granted, is a bit bleak and disheartening. For we see at once that in all this long time, over the habitable globe, the great majority of the human race has neither known nor apparently much cared for our favorite institutions.

[7] Civilization was already old when democracy made its first notable appearance among the small city states of ancient Greece, where it flourished brilliantly for a brief century or two and then disappeared. At about the same time something that might be called democracy appeared in Rome and other Italian cities, but even in Rome it did not survive the conquest of the world by the Roman Republic, except as a form of local administration in the cities of the empire. In the twelfth and thirteenth centuries certain favorably placed medieval cities enjoyed a measure of self-government, but in most instances it was soon replaced by the dictatorship of military conquerors, the oligarchic control of a few families, or the encroaching power of autocratic kings. The oldest democracy of modern times is the Swiss Confederation, the next oldest is the Dutch Republic. Parliamentary government in England does not antedate the late seventeenth century, the great American experiment is scarcely older. Not until the nineteenth century did democratic government make its way in any considerable part of the world—in the great states of continental Europe, in South America, in Canada and Australia, in South Africa and Japan.

[8] From this brief survey it is obvious that, taking the experience of mankind as a test, democracy has as yet had but a limited and temporary success. There must be a reason for this significant fact. The reason is that democratic government is a species of social luxury, at best a delicate and precarious adventure which depends for success upon the validity of certain assumptions about the capacities and virtues of men, and upon the presence of certain material and intellectual conditions favorable to the exercise of these capacities and virtues. Let us take the material conditions first.

[9] It is a striking fact that until recently democracy never flourished except in very small states—for the most part in cities. It is true that in both the Persian and the Roman empires a measure of self-government was accorded to local communities, but only in respect to purely local affairs; in no large state as a whole was democratic government found to be practicable. One essential reason is that until recently the means of communication were too slow and uncertain to create the necessary solidarity of interest and similarity of information over large areas. The principle of representation was well enough known to the Greeks, but in practice it proved impracticable except in limited areas and for special occasions. As late as the eighteenth century it was still the common opinion that the republican form of government, although the best ideally, was unsuited to large countries, even to a country no larger than France. This was the view of Mon-

tesquieu, and even of Rousseau. The view persisted into the nineteenth century, and English conservatives, who were opposed to the extension of the suffrage in England, consoled themselves with the notion that the American Civil War would confirm it—would demonstrate that government by and for the people would perish, if not from off the earth at least from large countries. If their hopes were confounded the reason is that the means of communication, figuratively speaking, were making large countries small. It is not altogether fanciful to suppose that, but for the railroad and the telegraph, the United States would today be divided into many small republics maneuvering for advantage and employing war and diplomacy for maintaining an unstable balance of power.

[10] If one of the conditions essential to the success of democratic government is mobility, ease of communication, another is a certain measure of economic security. Democracy does not flourish in communities on the verge of destitution. In ancient and medieval times democratic government appeared for the most part in cities, the centers of prosperity. Farmers in the early Roman Republic and in the Swiss Cantons were not wealthy to be sure, but equality of possessions and of opportunity gave them a certain economic security. In medieval cities political privilege was confined to the prosperous merchants and craftsmen, and in Athens and the later Roman Republic democratic government was found to be workable only on condition that the poor citizens were subsidized by the government or paid for attending the assemblies and the law courts.

[11] In modern times democratic institutions have, generally speaking, been most successful in new countries, such as the United States, Canada, and Australia, where the conditions of life have been easy for the people; and in European countries more or less in proportion to their industrial prosperity. In European countries, indeed, there has been a close correlation between the development of the industrial revolution and the emergence of democratic institutions. Holland and England, the first countries to experience the industrial revolution, were the first also (apart from Switzerland, where certain peculiar conditions obtained) to adopt democratic institutions; and as the industrial revolution spread to France, Belgium, Germany, and Italy, these countries in turn adopted at least a measure of democratic government. Democracy is in some sense an economic luxury, and it may be said that in modern times it has been a function of the development of new and potentially rich countries, or of the industrial revolution which suddenly dowered Europe with unaccustomed wealth. Now that prosperity is disappearing round every next corner, democracy works less well than it did.

[12] So much for the material conditions essential for the success of democratic government. Supposing these conditions to exist, democratic government implies in addition the presence of certain capacities and virtues in its citizens. These capacities and virtues are bound up with the assumptions

on which democracy rests, and are available only in so far as the assumptions are valid. The primary assumption of democratic government is that its citizens are capable of managing their own affairs. But life in any community involves a conflict of individual and class interests, and a corresponding divergence of opinion as to the measures to be adopted for the common good. The divergent opinions must be somehow reconciled, the conflict of interests somehow compromised. It must then be an assumption of democratic government that its citizens are rational creatures, sufficiently so at least to understand the interests in conflict; and it must be an assumption that they are men of good will, sufficiently so toward each other at least to make those concessions of individual and class interest required for effecting workable compromises. The citizens of a democracy should be, as Pericles said the citizens of Athens were, if not all originators at least all sound judges of good policy.

[13] These are what may be called the minimum assumptions and the necessary conditions of democratic government anywhere and at any time. They may be noted to best advantage, not in any state, but in small groups within the state—in clubs and similar private associations of congenial and like-minded people united for a specific purpose. In such associations the membership is limited and select. The members are, or may easily become, all acquainted with each other. Everyone knows, or may easily find out, what is being done and who is doing it. There will of course be differences of opinion, and there may be disintegrating squabbles and intrigues. But on the whole, ends and means being specific and well understood, the problems of government are few and superficial; there is plenty of time for discussion; and since intelligence and good will can generally be taken for granted there is the disposition to make reasonable concessions and compromises. The analogy must be taken for what it is worth. States may not be the mystical blind Molochs of German philosophy, but any state is far more complex and intangible than a private association, and there is little resemblance between such associations and the democracies of modern times. Other things equal, the resemblance is closest in very small states, and it is in connection with the small city states of ancient Greece that the resemblance can best be noted.

[14] The Greek states were limited in size, not as is often thought solely or even chiefly by the physiography of the country, but by some instinctive feeling of the Greek mind that a state is necessarily a natural association of people bound together by ties of kinship and a common tradition of rights and obligations. There must then, as Aristotle said, be a limit:

> For if the citizens of a state are to judge and distribute offices according to merit, they must know each other's characters; where they do not possess this knowledge, both the elections to offices and the decisions in the law courts will go wrong. Where the population is very large they are manifestly settled by haphazard, which clearly ought not to be. Besides, in over-populous states foreigners and metics will readily acquire citizenship, for who will find them out?

It obviously did not occur to Aristotle that metics and foreigners should be free to acquire citizenship. It did not occur to him, or to any Greek of his time, or to the merchants of the self-governing medieval city, that a state should be composed of all the people inhabiting a given territory. A state was rather an incorporated body of people within, but distinct from, the population of the community.

[15] Ancient and medieval democracies had thus something of the character of a private association. They were, so to speak, purely pragmatic phenomena, arising under very special conditions, and regarded as the most convenient way of managing the affairs of people bound together by community of interest and for the achievement of specific ends. There is no suggestion in Aristotle that democracy (polity) is intrinsically a superior form of government, no suggestion that it derives from a special ideology of its own. If it rests upon any superiority other than convenience, it is the superiority which it shares with any Greek state, that is to say, the superiority of Greek over barbarian civilization. In Aristotle's philosophy it is indeed difficult to find any clear-cut distinction between the democratic form of government and the state itself; the state, if it be worthy of the name, is always, whatever the form of government, "the government of freemen and equals," and in any state it is always necessary that "the freemen who compose the bulk of the people should have absolute power in some things." In Aristotle's philosophy the distinction between good and bad in politics is not between good and bad types of government, but between the good and the bad form of each type. Any type of government—monarchy, aristocracy, polity—is good provided the rulers aim at the good of all rather than at the good of the class to which they belong. From Aristotle's point of view neither democracy nor dictatorship is good or bad in itself, but only in the measure that it achieves, or fails to achieve, the aim of every good state, which is that "the inhabitants of it should be happy." It did not occur to Aristotle that democracy (polity), being in some special sense in harmony with the nature of man, was everywhere applicable, and therefore destined by fate or the gods to carry throughout the world a superior form of civilization.

[16] It is in this respect chiefly that modern democracy differs from earlier forms. It rests upon something more than the minimum assumptions. It is reinforced by a full-blown ideology which, by endowing the individual with natural and imprescriptible rights, sets the democratic form of government off from all others as the one which alone can achieve the good life. What then are the essential tenets of the modern democratic faith?

III

[17] The liberal democratic faith, as expressed in the works of eighteenth- and early nineteenth-century writers, is one of the formulations of the modern doctrine of progress. It will be well, therefore, to note briefly the historical antecedents of that doctrine.

[18] In the long history of man on earth there comes a time when he remembers something of what has been, anticipates something that will be, knows the country he has traversed, wonders what lies beyond—the moment when he becomes aware of himself as a lonely, differentiated item in the world. Sooner or later there emerges for him the most devastating of all facts, namely, that in an indifferent universe which alone endures, he alone aspires, endeavors to attain, and attains only to be defeated in the end. From that moment his immediate experience ceases to be adequate, and he endeavors to project himself beyond it by creating ideal worlds of semblance, Utopias of other time or place in which all has been, may be, or will be well.

[19] In ancient times Utopia was most easily projected into the unknown past, pushed back to the beginning of things—to the time of P'an Ku and the celestial emperors, to the Garden of Eden, or the reign of King Chronos when men lived like gods free from toil and grief. From this happy state of first created things there had obviously been a decline and fall, occasioned by disobedience and human frailty, and decreed as punishment by fate or the angry gods. The mind of man was therefore afflicted with pessimism, a sense of guilt for having betrayed the divine purpose, a feeling of inadequacy for bringing the world back to its original state of innocence and purity. To men who felt insecure in a changing world, and helpless in a world always changing for the worse, the future had little to offer. It could be regarded for the most part only with resignation, mitigated by individual penance or well-doing, or the hope of some miraculous intervention by the gods, or the return of the god-like kings, to set things right again, yet with little hope that from this setting right there would not be another falling away.

[20] This pervasive pessimism was gradually dispelled in the Western world, partly by the Christian religion, chiefly by the secular intellectual revolution occurring roughly between the fifteenth and the eighteenth centuries. The Christian religion gave assurance that the lost golden age of the past would be restored for the virtuous in the future, and by proclaiming the supreme worth of the individual in the eyes of God enabled men to look forward with hope to the good life after death in the Heavenly City. Meantime, the secular intellectual revolution, centering in the matter-of-fact study of history and science, gradually emancipated the minds of men from resignation to fate and the angry gods. Accumulated knowledge of history, filling in time past with a continuous succession of credible events, banished all lost golden ages to the realm of myth, and enabled men to live without distress in a changing world since it could be regarded as not necessarily changing for the worse. At the same time, a more competent observation and measurement of the action of material things disclosed an outer world of nature, indifferent to man indeed, yet behaving, not as the unpredictable sport of the gods, but in ways understandable to human reason and therefore ultimately subject to man's control.

[21] Thus the conditions were fulfilled which made it possible for men to conceive of Utopia, neither as a lost golden age of the past nor as a Heavenly City after death prepared by the gods for the virtuous, but as a future state on earth of man's own devising. In a world of nature that could be regarded as amenable to man's control, and in a world of changing social relations that need not be regarded as an inevitable decline and fall from original perfection, it was possible to formulate the modern doctrine of progress: the idea that, by deliberate intention and rational direction, men can set the terms and indefinitely improve the conditions of their mundane existence.

[22] The eighteenth century was the moment in history when men first fully realized the engaging implications of this resplendent idea, the moment when, not yet having been brought to the harsh appraisal of experience, it could be accepted with unclouded optimism. Never had the universe seemed less mysterious, more open and visible, more eager to yield its secrets to common-sense questions. Never had the nature of man seemed less perverse, or the mind of man more pliable to the pressure of rational persuasion. The essential reason for this confident optimism is that the marvels of scientific discovery disclosed to the men of that time a God who still functioned but was no longer angry. God the Father could be conceived as a beneficent First Cause who, having performed his essential task of creation, had withdrawn from the affairs of men, leaving them competently prepared and fully instructed for the task of achieving their own salvation. In one tremendous sentence Rousseau expressed the eighteenth-century world view of the universe and man's place in it. "Is it simple," he exclaimed, "is it natural that God should have gone in search of Moses in order to speak to Jean Jacques Rousseau?"

[23] God had indeed spoken to Rousseau, he had spoken to all men, but his revelation was contained, not in Holy Writ interpreted by Holy Church, but in the great Book of Nature which was open for all men to read. To this open book of nature men would go when they wanted to know what God had said to them. Here they would find recorded the laws of nature and of nature's God, disclosing a universe constructed according to a rational plan; and that men might read these laws aright they had been endowed with reason, a bit of the universal intelligence placed within the individual to make manifest to him the universal reason implicit in things and events. "Natural law," as Volney so clearly and confidently put it, "is the regular and constant order of facts by which God rules the universe; the order which his wisdom presents to the sense and reason of men, to serve them as an equal and common rule of conduct, and to guide them, without distinction of race or sect, toward perfection and happiness." Thus God had devised a planned economy, and had endowed men with the capacity for managing it: to bring his ideas, his conduct, and his institutions into harmony with the universal laws of nature was man's simple alloted task.

[24] At all times political theory must accommodate itself in some fashion

to the prevailing world view, and liberal-democratic political theory was no exception to this rule. From time immemorial authority and obedience had been the cardinal concepts both of the prevailing world view and of political and social theory. From time immemorial men had been regarded as subject to overruling authority—the authority of the gods, and the authority of kings who were themselves gods, or descended from gods, or endowed with divine authority to rule in place of gods; and from time immemorial obedience to such divine authority was thought to be the primary obligation of men. Even the Greeks, who were so little afraid of their gods that they could hob-nob with them in the most friendly and engaging way, regarded mortals as subject to them; and when they lost faith in the gods they deified the state as the highest good and subordinated the individual to it. But the eighteenth-century world view, making man the measure of all things, mitigated if it did not destroy this sharp contrast between authority and obedience. God still reigned but he did not govern. He had, so to speak, granted his subjects a constitution and authorized them to interpret it as they would in the supreme court of reason. Men were still subject to an overruling authority, but the subjection could be regarded as voluntary because self-imposed, and self-imposed because obedience was exacted by nothing more oppressive than their own rational intelligence.

[25] Liberal-democratic political theory readily accommodated itself to this change in the world view. The voice of the people was now identified with the voice of God, and all authority was derived from it. The individual instead of the state or the prince was now deified and endowed with imprescriptible rights; and since ignorance or neglect of the rights of man was the chief cause of social evils, the first task of political science was to define these rights, the second to devise a form of government suited to guarantee them. The imprescriptible rights of man were easily defined, since they were self-evident: "All men are created equal, [and] are endowed by their Creator with certain inalienable rights, among which are life, liberty, and the pursuit of happiness." From this it followed that all just governments would remove those artificial restraints which impaired these rights, thereby liberating those natural impulses with which God had endowed the individual as a guide to thought and conduct. In the intellectual realm, freedom of thought and the competition of diverse opinion would disclose the truth, which all men, being rational creatures, would progressively recognize and willingly follow. In the economic realm, freedom of enterprise would disclose the natural aptitudes of each individual, and the ensuing competition of interests would stimulate effort, and thereby result in the maximum of material advantage for all. Liberty of the individual from social constraint thus turned out to be not only an inherent natural right but also a preordained natural mechanism for bringing about the material and moral progress of mankind. Men had only to follow reason and self-interest: something not themselves, God and Nature, would do whatever else was necessary for righteousness.

[26] Thus modern liberal-democracy is associated with an ideology which rests upon something more than the minimum assumptions essential to any democratic government. It rests upon a philosophy of universally valid ends and means. Its fundamental assumption is the worth and dignity and creative capacity of the individual, so that the chief aim of government is the maximum of individual self-direction, the chief means to that end the minimum of compulsion by the state. Ideally considered, means and ends are conjoined in the concept of freedom: freedom of thought, so that the truth may prevail; freedom of occupation, so that careers may be open to talent; freedom of self-government, so that no one may be compelled against his will.

[27] In the possibility of realizing this ideal the prophets and protagonists of democracy exhibited an unquestioned faith. If their faith seems to us somewhat naïve, the reason is that they placed a far greater reliance upon the immediate influence of good will and rational discussion in shaping the conduct of men than it is possible for us to do. This difference can be conveniently noted in a passage from the *Autobiography* of John Stuart Mill, in which he describes his father's extraordinary faith in two things—representative government and complete freedom of discussion:

So complete was my father's reliance on the influence of reason over the minds of mankind, whenever it was allowed to reach them, that he felt as if all would be gained if the whole population were taught to read, if all sorts of opinions were allowed to be addressed to them by word and writing, and if by means of the suffrage they could nominate a legislature to give effect to the opinions they adopted. He thought that when the legislature no longer represented a class interest, it would aim at the general interest, honestly and with adequate wisdom; since the people would be sufficiently under the guidance of educated intelligence to make in general good choice of persons to represent them, and having done so to leave to those whom they had chosen a liberal discretion. Accordingly, aristocratic rule, the government of the few in any of its shapes, being in his eyes the only thing that stood between mankind and the administration of its affairs by the best wisdom to be found amongst them, was the object of his sternest disapprobation, and a democratic suffrage the principal article of his political creed.

[28] The beliefs of James Mill were shared by the little group of Philosophical Radicals who gathered about him. They were, indeed, the beliefs of all those who in the great crusading days placed their hopes in democratic government as a panacea for injustice and oppression. The actual working of democratic government, as these devoted enthusiasts foresaw it, the motives that would inspire men and the objects they would pursue in that ideal democracy which so many honest men have cherished and fought for, have never been better described than by James Bryce in his *Modern Democracies*. In this ideal democracy, says Bryce,

the average citizen will give close and constant attention to public affairs, recognizing that this is his interest as well as his duty. He will try to comprehend the main issues of policy, bringing to them an independent and impartial mind, which thinks first not of its own but of the general interest. If, owing to inevitable differences of opinion as to what are the measures needed for the general welfare, parties become inevitable, he will join one, and attend its meetings, but will repress the impulses of party spirit. Never failing to come to the polls, he will vote for his party candidate only if satisfied by his capacity and honesty. He will be ready to . . . be put forward as a candidate for the legislature (if satisfied of his own competence), because public service is recognized as a duty. With such citizens as electors, the legislature will be composed of upright and capable men, single-minded in their wish to serve the nation. Bribery in constituencies, corruption among public servants, will have disappeared. Leaders may not always be single-minded, nor assemblies always wise, nor administrators efficient, but all will be at any rate honest and zealous, so that an atmosphere of confidence and goodwill will prevail. Most of the causes that make for strife will be absent, for there will be no privileges, no advantages to excite jealousy. Office will be sought only because it gives opportunity for useful public service. Power will be shared by all, and a career open to all alike. Even if the law does not—perhaps it cannot—prevent the accumulation of fortunes, these will be few and not inordinate, for public vigilance will close the illegitimate paths to wealth. All but the most depraved persons will obey and support the law, feeling it to be their own. There will be no excuse for violence, because the constitution will provide a remedy for every grievance. Equality will produce a sense of human solidarity, will refine manners, and increase brotherly kindness.

[29] Such is the ideal form of modern democracy laid away in heaven. I do not need to tell you that its earthly counterpart resembles it but slightly.

COMMENT AND QUESTIONS

One of the best ways to study the very skillful organization of this essay is to examine the first and last sentences of each paragraph, noticing how they state or emphasize topic ideas, and how they establish transitions between paragraphs and sections. The excellent use of examples and concrete statements to clarify abstract material is also worth noting.

I. What phase of the subject is treated in each of the three major divisions of the essay?

II. What methods of definition are used in section I?

III. Upon what material conditions does democracy depend for success? What minimum assumptions does democracy make about the capacities and virtues of its citizens?

IV. How does modern democratic faith differ from early theories about democracy?

V. How did the Christian religion change the idea that Utopia existed only in an unknown past? How did the "secular intellectual revolution" between the fifteenth and eighteenth centuries change still further the concept of Utopia?

VI. What is the "modern doctrine of progress"?

VII. Explain how the world view of the eighteenth century affected political theory and produced the modern democratic ideology.

VIII. Why, according to Becker, were men of the eighteenth and early nineteenth centuries more optimistic than men today about the possibility of achieving ideal democracy?

IX. "The Ideal Democracy" was written some twenty years ago. Does it seem equally true today that democracy "has suffered an astounding decline in prestige," and that "its future is by no means assured"?

X. In what particular ways would you say that democracy-in-practice falls short of the ideal counterpart represented in the last pages of the essay?

XI. A number of Americans at the present time find it difficult to understand why people of other countries—particularly the "undeveloped" areas of the world—have not been and are not enthusiastic about democratic government. In what ways might Mr. Becker's discussion of the history of democracy throw light on the fact that the institutions which seem obviously valuable to us are not equally attractive to all people?

XII. Since "The Ideal Democracy" is the first of three lectures on democracy, it is somewhat inconclusive: the author does not answer all the questions he raises at the end of the first section, and he may leave in doubt his own opinion of democracy as a form of government. That opinion is stated in the following passage from another of Becker's books, *New Liberties for Old:*

To have faith in the dignity and worth of the individual man as an end in himself, to believe that it is better to be governed by persuasion than by coercion, to believe that fraternal good will is more worthy than a selfish and contentious spirit, to believe that in the long run all values are inseparable from the love of truth and the disinterested search for it, to believe that knowledge and the power it confers should be used to promote the welfare and happiness of all men rather than to serve the interests of those individuals and classes whom fortune and intelligence endow with temporary advantage—these are the values which are affirmed by the traditional democratic ideology. . . . The case for democracy is that it accepts the rational and humane values as ends, and proposes as the means of realizing them the minimum of coercion and the maximum of voluntary assent. We may well abandon the cosmological temple in which the democratic ideology originally enshrined these values without renouncing the faith it was designed to celebrate. The essence of that faith is belief in the capacity of man, as a rational and humane creature, to achieve the good life by rational and humane means. The chief virtue of democracy, and the sole reason for cherishing it, is that with all its faults it still provides the most favorable conditions for achieving that end by those means.

READINGS SECTION 2

Reading Evaluations

DAVID WECHSLER

Measuring the I. Q. Test*

A question-to-answer organization of material is used in the following evaluation of intelligence tests. Dr. Wechsler is Chief Psychologist at Bellevue Psychiatric Hospital in New York, and Clinical Professor of Clinical Psychology at New York University College of Medicine. This article was published in the *New York Times Magazine,* January 20, 1957.

[1] In 1957 several million boys and girls in the schools of the United States will be given one or another form of intelligence examination. Added to this number will be several hundred thousand children of pre-school age tested for purposes of adoption, placement and admission to private schools. During the same time almost as many 16- to 18-year-old high school students will be taking college entrance examinations which, though generally referred to as aptitude tests, differ only in part from standard group intelligence tests. This does not exhaust the list. But even if the program is not extended, it is a safe guess that by 1960 at least one of every two persons in the United States between 5 and 50 will have taken an intelligence test at one time or another.

[2] The ever-increasing use of intelligence tests in so many different places and for so many varied purposes has naturally aroused the public's interest and, occasionally, also its concern. One is repeatedly asked, "Do the tests really measure intelligence; are they reliable; are they fair to all who take them; and what about the claim made in recent years that intelligence, after reaching a peak in early adulthood, tends to decline with age?"

---
* Courtesy of Dr. David Wechsler.

[3] The answer to the first of these questions obviously depends on what we mean by intelligence and the extent to which others agree with the definition. Intelligence has been defined in different ways, and no single definition has enjoyed anywhere near universal acceptance. Most psychologists, however, are agreed that intelligence, no matter how defined, involves the following elements: the ability to learn, the ability to think or reason, the ability to deal effectively with one's environment and, finally, the ability to profit from experience.

[4] The typical intelligence test consists of a series of standardized tasks of varying difficulty which the individual is required to perform, usually within certain time limits. His score or rating is based on the number of items correctly answered. Some of these tasks resemble the kind of things one learns in school and to a certain extent are dependent upon school training. Nevertheless, the information which the psychologist tries to obtain from the tests is not a measure of what the subject has learned or even what his special abilities may be, but something more basic. He is looking for an indication of an underlying capacity—namely, the capacity to think and act with insight in situations which are not dependent primarily on knowledge.

[5] An intelligence scale is thus a series of tasks so organized as to enable the individual examined to show to what extent he has this capacity. For this reason, a good intelligence examination generally requires different types of tests so as to enable a subject to communicate and express himself in as many different ways as possible. For most people, language, of course, is the easiest and most direct mode of expression, so intelligence tests will be found to be heavily loaded with various types of verbal items. But provision is also made for individuals who express themselves better spatially or manipulatively by including items involving reproduction of designs, putting objects together, and the like. The latter are usually referred to as performance tests, and may be given separately or together as part of a battery.

[6] On the whole, whether it is a matter of classifying children as to learning ability, of detecting mental defectives, of predicting greater as against lesser success in certain types of occupations, and finally, of appraising over-all adjustment, there is little doubt but that intelligence tests have proved themselves much better predictors than any other *single* measure at present available.

[7] The second question, as to whether intelligence tests are reliable, that is, whether an individual tested on one day will perform at a similar level when retested on a later occasion, may, with some exceptions, also be answered in the affirmative. The consistency of performance will depend, in part, on the age of the individual, the type of test used and the absence of interfering circumstances at the time of examination. In general, test ratings of young children, particularly of infants, are less reliable than those of older children and adults. This is because suitable test items for

young children are difficult to find and because variations in rate of maturation are more of a problem.

[8] This leads us to the important question as to how an intelligence test score can be interpreted. It may be done in a variety of ways, but the two methods most commonly used, and most familiar to the lay person, are the measures defined by the terms Mental Age and I.Q. (Intelligence Quotient). About both there is much misunderstanding. A Mental Age, for example, contrary to what most people think, is just a score. It is a score which the originator of intelligence tests, Alfred Binet, found convenient to express in terms of months and years instead of in so many points.

[9] The second and even more often cited measure of intelligence is the I.Q. An I.Q. is a ratio defining an individual's level of intelligence compared with persons of his own age; it is a measure of relative position. Thus, an I.Q. of 85 represents a low rating (dull normal), an I.Q. of 130 a high rating (superior), irrespective of the subject's age.

[10] The rating assigned to an I.Q. depends upon the test from which it was derived. For most current intelligence scales the I.Q. range 90–110 includes approximately 50 per cent of the population and is accordingly interpreted as representing average intelligence. I.Q.'s of 110–120, which include some 16 per cent, are classified as bright normal; I.Q.'s of 120–130 (about 7 per cent) as superior; and I.Q.'s over 130, the top 2 per cent, as very superior. Comparably, I.Q.'s of 80–90 (approximately 16 per cent) are classified as dull normal; I.Q.'s of 70–80 (6 per cent) as borderline, and I.Q.'s below 70 (2–3 per cent) are usually considered metally retarded or defective. These limits are only approximate; other factors have to be taken into consideration when classifying a person.

[11] Everyone is entitled to know how he rates in intelligence, but it is generally not a good idea for an individual to get tagged with an I.Q. Like any technical number, it can be easily misinterpreted or encourage invidious comparison. An I.Q. does not describe all of an individual's potential and when taken out of context may be incorrectly evaluated. This is particularly true in the case of children's I.Q.'s. For that reason psychologists are loath to release numerical I.Q.'s, especially to parents.

[12] A question that always comes up when one discusses the I.Q. is whether it remains the same over the years. If a person's I.Q. changed significantly with each testing it would have no great value. Many studies have accordingly been made to find out what changes do occur when an individual is retested at different intervals, such as one month, one year, five years or even longer.

[13] These studies, with only few exceptions, show that the changes observed when a subject is retested with the same or similar instrument under comparable conditions are surprisingly small. The average change is approximately five to six points in either direction. About 50 per cent of individuals tested will not vary by more than this amount when re-examined. If a variation of ten points is admitted, some 80 per cent of the subjects will fall within this limit, and so on.

[14] There is always a small percentage of individuals whose performance is unpredictable, and with these individuals it is generally found that some special factors prior to or at the time of one of the examinations can account for the large discrepancy observed. However, it should be emphasized that these represent a relatively small percentage of cases tested and do not justify skepticism regarding the general stability of the I.Q. In particular, it does not justify the hope encouraged by some groups that an I.Q. can be radically changed.

[15] The third question as to the fairness of intelligence tests has two aspects to it. One has to do with the possibility that individuals under emotional or other stress may perform below their actual capacity. There is always such a possibility, but it does not happen very often; when it does, a competent examiner takes the contingency under consideration. When there is reason to believe that a person is so handicapped, the usual procedure is to have the subject retested. The chance of lightning striking the same place twice is small, and good advice to parents would be not to go around shopping for I.Q.'s.

[16] A more serious concern about possible unfairness of intelligence tests is the implication that the content and form of the tests themselves may favor or be prejudicial to certain individuals or groups. For example, one consistent finding is that children of middle and upper socio-economic groups do better, on the average, than those of lower socio-economic level, on all standard intelligence tests. It has also been found that groups of certain national origin or cultural background test higher than others.

[17] The question is whether these differences are due to basic endowment or reflect differences in education, cultural opportunities or even selectiveness in type of item used in the tests. This is a complex question which cannot be answered unqualifiedly either way. There is evidence to show that education and socio-economic factors are related to test performance, and that in general no test can be said to be entirely culture-free. As in the case of physical traits, mental abilities are conditioned and determined by both heredity and environment.

[18] Intelligence tests seek to avert bias, first by avoiding, so far as possible, test items which favor one group as against another, and secondly by taking care that subjects used in the standardization of these tests shall be representative of the populations to whom the tests will be subsequently administered.

[19] Thus, in getting up a vocabulary list, one would avoid words with which individuals of a higher status group would be more familiar than would a lower status group—"peignoir," "chutney" and "litigation," for example. Again, in testing a person for ability to detect missing parts, one would use a picture of a horse rather than a yak, a drum rather than a base viol. Similarly in planning questions of general comprehension one must take into consideration the customs and attitudes of different places. Thus the questions "Why are shoes made of leather?" and "Why does the state require people to get a marriage license?" would be suitable for Europeans

and Americans but might be quite incomprehensible to persons living where shoes are not worn and where the state is not so particular.

[20] However, there is considerable evidence to show that so-called "race" differences have been greatly overestimated. General intelligence seems to be a very general commodity. It is not so much the significance of the differences in ability found between groups as the exploitation of these differences which have sometimes given intelligence tests a bad reputation.

[21] We now come to the last question: Does intelligence really decline with increasing age? Practically all studies employing the cross-sectional method, which is the one usually used, show that mental, like physical, abilities, after reaching a peak somewhere between 20 and 30, begin to decline. This decline is at first relatively small but after 40 is substantial, so that by age 60 or 65 there is a drop of about 25 per cent from the peak. Not all abilities decline at the same rate. Word knowledge (vocabulary) and general information fall off much less, if at all, whereas learning and abstract reasoning may show more than average decline.

[22] Nearly all these findings are based on cross-sectional studies, that is, studies comparing different individuals at different ages. In contrast to these there are some recent longitudinal studies in which the same individuals have been retested at successive age periods, the results of which are more encouraging. They show that intelligence test scores can continue to increase until age 45 or 50. These results are as yet too few to controvert the accumulated earlier findings, but do challenge their interpretation.

[23] Similarly encouraging are the results obtained in the restandardization of this writer's adult intelligence scale. This study showed that from 1939 to 1955 the age at which adults obtained their maximal scores rose from age 23 to age 29 or approximately six years. This rise may have been due in part to better sampling, to increase in educational level of the population and greater layman familiarity with tests. In addition, there is reason to believe that the advance may also be due to the improved general health of the adult population. This inference, if correct, would support the hope that science is not only "adding years to life, but life to years."

[24] The foregoing findings do not alter the fact that older people do less well on intelligence tests than younger ones. Whether the peak age is 25, 30 or 40, there still remain a goodly number of years beyond that point when the older person will consistently show a decline in test performance. This does not necessarily imply a corresponding loss in intelligence. With increasing age there is a change in the nature of intelligence and in the extent to which various factors determine its effectiveness. For example, sheer learning ability counts for less, whereas the ability to integrate what one has already learned counts for considerably more. The older person has the benefit of experience, and the experience can and often does serve as a substitute for ability. Above all, age carries with it an increasing capacity to deal with situations calling for judgment and decision. Psychologists are

aware of this and are now working on tests geared to tap the individual's sagacity as well as his creativity.

[25] The wide interest in intelligence tests is amply justified. The public has correctly sensed that intelligence, to paraphrase a current advertisement, is the country's most important asset.

COMMENT AND QUESTIONS

I. In paragraph 2, the author quotes four questions repeatedly asked about intelligence tests, and, in the remainder of the article, systematically answers them. What, precisely, is his answer to each question? To what extent does he qualify each answer? What evidence does he cite to support his conclusions?

II. Dr. Wechsler supplies his readers with definitions of terms, and description and analysis of tests and scores—information which he might have put into an introductory section. Why, instead, does he weave it into the question-answer organization; for example, why are the working-definition of intelligence and the description of a typical test included in the discussion of question 1, and the data about I.Q. ratings made part of the discussion of question 2?

III. The tone of this article is impersonal and objective, but from time to time Dr. Wechsler seems to be speaking to readers whose ideas about intelligence tests and about the procedure of psychologists need correcting. Who are the readers aimed at, and what are the mistaken attitudes they hold?

IV. Do you feel inclined to question any of Dr. Wechsler's judgments? If so, why?

V. If you find this article convincing and sound, what are your chief reasons for accepting the author's evaluation?

John Gunther's *Roosevelt in Retrospect:* Four Reviews

The four reviews in the following pages are evaluations of the same book. "Roosevelt's Rendezvous With History," by Adolf A. Berle, Jr., appeared in the *New York Times Book Review*, June 4, 1950; "Another Go at F.D.R.," by Hamilton Basso, in *The New Yorker*, June 3, 1950; "Let's Wait," in *Time* magazine, June 5, 1950; and "The Riddles of Franklin Roosevelt," by Raymond Swing, in *The Nation*, June 3, 1950.

1. Roosevelt's Rendezvous with History*
by Adolf A. Berle, Jr.

Men famous enough to be remembered have two careers. One is in life; the second, in history. Struggle begins at death for possession of the name, reputation and memory of a really great man; contesting factors push backward to sanctify, or to blacken, the facts of his actual life. Contest continues through generations, sometimes centuries.

So it is proving in the case of Franklin Roosevelt. He had unquestioned greatness. Undeniably his career in history has begun. Unblushingly, friend and foe seek to establish or diminish his stature.

It is fortunate, then, that John Gunther, perhaps the best-known reporter of our generation, has patiently collected and impartially chronicled a great body of intimate but fugitive fact material of Roosevelt's life which otherwise could easily have been lost. He has done an extensive, rich and authentic job. Of outstanding interest is the careful record of comment, anecdote, conversation and explanation from Roosevelt's own lips borne in the memory of living men; this, save for some such record, would have vanished in a few years.

Yet it is crucial; President Roosevelt's habit was to express his mind freely to his friends, his colleagues, even to casual contacts; the windows of his personality were always open. He kept no diary; and his day-to-day thoughts and impressions survive chiefly through diaries and recollections of his contemporaries. In giving these permanent lodging, Gunther has served history well—and written a thrilling book.

The collection of Lincolniana by Herndon was undertaken because Herndon wanted the fact to prevail over the mounting mythology; Lincoln, the man, he believed, was greater than any legend. Gunther apparently had the same idea about Roosevelt. In any case, as early as 1944 he found a rising tide of myths about Roosevelt, and then planned and now has performed, some part, at least, of the same service for Roosevelt. It was none too soon. Prehensile hands already are clutching at the great name. For a time the Communists strove to annex it; though they rapidly gave up. Conservative extremists seek to make him into the image of a would-be Fuehrer, struggling to become dictator. John T. Flynn contents himself by portraying Roosevelt as an egotist-weakling, justifying the worst suspicions of Roosevelt-haters, while Charles A. Beard saw a Machiavellian steering America into avoidable war under the false banner of peace. Little, if any, of this extremism will survive Gunther's report of fact. But then, Gunther's study will not altogether please those to whom Roosevelt had become as Gunther puts it, "anthropomorphic, a virtual god."

Those who knew and loved the man will welcome the volume. In storm and in sunshine, in weakness, in strength, in laughter and in anger, in times

* From the *New York Times Book Review*, June 4, 1950.

when he was everlastingly right, in times when he was clearly wrong, here is Franklin Roosevelt. As a human being he is incomparably greater than any myth.

And yet, not all the man is here—though this is hardly Gunther's fault. As he said, "the President is inexhaustible," and endless material is not yet in. Published autobiographies and diaries of his intimates (the list is already long and growing) are, as they should be, books primarily about their authors rather than about Roosevelt. He himself, no stranger to historical method, quite realized that he had a rendezvous with history—and enjoyed the idea thoroughly. For that reason he caused to be collected all his papers, running literally into millions, and had them placed in the Hyde Park library for anyone who wished to examine. No living human being has yet put this prodigious record together.

Even when it is distilled into biography, a central mystery will probably remain unsolved; the explanation of one crippled man's power to transmit unlimited hope, confidence and strength to millions upon millions of men and women in all parts of the earth who never saw his face, or to give comfort through a golden, radio-transmitted voice. A poet may solve that problem. A journalist can only record the fact.

In analysis of events, Gunther does as well as perhaps can be done, given the material he was using. Historical research may vary some of his conclusions, though I think the general results will stand up well. Gunther's review of Yalta—the most controversial episode in the Rooseveltian epic—may serve as illustration.

The Yalta Conference, judged in hindsight and by its fruits, was a failure, with tragic consequences. Gunther analyzes it as a Rooseveltian gamble for high stakes: for world peace, based on moral relationships, no less. (He believes that had Roosevelt lived to see the peace through, the gamble might well have been won instead of lost.) His conclusion is that Roosevelt's Yalta policy was largely dictated by the military and that failure was in considerable part attributable to mistaken military intelligence.

This judgment is convincingly supported, and is generally confirmed by serious students. So also is Gunther's demonstration that Roosevelt before his death clearly understood Russian double-dealing, though Gunther thinks Russia shifted to an anti-Western policy immediately after Yalta, which accounts partly for the ensuing misfortunes. This theory is not supported, and is probably not the fact: Russia did undoubtedly conceal her actual objectives which seem to have been determined on some months earlier, and only revealed the change later. Charges of "sell-out" and "betrayal" at Yalta are nevertheless effectively refuted.

The verdict is that Roosevelt, on the advice of his generals, underestimated the strength of the American position and, with Churchill, was out-traded. Gunther states fairly the huge risk run by the President in the light of the knowledge available to him had he alienated Stalin while Japan was still formidable. This is the reasoned analysis of a fair-minded journalist. It should clarify the whole controversy.

Reporting is an art most highly exercised when its skill is most concealed. A brilliant feature of this volume lies in the portraits, sketches on huge canvas, occasionally illuminated by a deft phrase or simile. In reviewing the intimate life of Franklin and Eleanor, the author describes the partnership of the man and his wife in history—noting that the pair are fairly comparable to Ferdinand and Isabella. The story, sometimes humorous, sometimes matter-of-fact, sometimes poignant, is drawn to scale. So also are the more earthy episodes of Roosevelt's strictly political career.

One fact, curiously, fails to find a place in the record. For while he played politics with gusto and skill, the President with one lobe of his brain regarded it as unpleasant, corrosive business. One reason for his constantly calling in new men, not engaged in political life, was a latent desire, occasionally expressed, to liberate his operations, if possible, from the limitations and implications of a game he knew too well. One of his conceptions of himself was as a political engineer, giving reality where possible to the academic thought of his time.

A man of Roosevelt's stature seldom bothers to attempt, and still more rarely succeeds in, conscious explanation of himself or analysis of his "mission." Certainly Roosevelt did not. With sure instinct, Gunther chooses for record the single conscious profession the President ever did make of his own function—that of educator. Evidence exists for this beyond that adduced in this volume. Repeatedly Roosevelt spoke of men who did not understand his social objectives as "illiterate," needing to be taught. The Four Freedoms, thrown out across the world and embodied in the Atlantic Charter, were designed to draw out men's minds in a brilliant combination of instruction and hope.

Again as a result of his teaching, any return to the conception of the Presidency held by, say, Calvin Coolidge, is an intellectual impossibility. His idea that diplomacy is a people's prerogative, not a mysterious rite carried on between sovereigns, has changed the whole conduct of foreign affairs. Roosevelt repeatedly thought of himself as a teacher who, like all great teachers, studied as well as taught.

Because the reporter is recording reality and fighting myth, the book soft-pedals the high emotional content of the material. The passionate love which the President inspired is merely suggested. Only dimly described is the hatred he engendered in certain groups.

Generation of these emotions was a part of the man. It is why some seek to defeat him in history as bitterly as some opposed him in life. It is also the reason why unending thousands file, day by day, in silence through a quiet garden, past a simple stone, on which is inscribed only,

FRANKLIN DELANO
ROOSEVELT
1882–1945

2. Another Go at F.D.R.* by Hamilton Basso

In the foreword to *Roosevelt in Retrospect* (Harper), John Gunther declares that it was not his intention to write a full-dress history of the Roosevelt years or a biography in the orthodox manner. He describes his book as "an attempt at analysis as well as a mere narrative; a gathering of sources and an interpretation rather than a reminiscence or revelation." I am not altogether sure that I know what Mr. Gunther is trying to say (what is a "mere" narrative, how could it have been a reminiscence unless he has something to reminisce about, what does "revelation" mean in the context?), but I deduce that he wishes us to understand that his intention was (1) to accumulate all the material he could about Roosevelt, (2) to tell the story of his life, and (3) to investigate in some detail his character and personality.

Mr. Gunther, in his "Inside" books, has already demonstrated his ability to accumulate masses of material, and he has also shown that he knows how to put a story together, but he is weak in the area of analysis and interpretation. He is the only man alive who can take on a whole continent without losing his breath, yet though I have always admired his journalistic muscularity, I invariably get the impression, after a continent has been made to say uncle, that we are still just where we started. And so it is with this book about Franklin D. Roosevelt. As a fact finder, a gossip gatherer, and an anecdote collector, Mr. Gunther is excellent; as an interpreter, he leaves a great deal to be desired.

Another thing that works against Mr. Gunther is that he is traveling over well-trodden ground. In his bibliography, he lists a hundred and twenty books, the large majority of which are mainly concerned with F.D.R. It is true that Mr. Gunther has gone out and found a considerable amount of material on his own, but it is the same *kind* of material. We have already had enough anecdotes about Roosevelt's humor, his garrulity, his interest in stamps, his fondness for the sea, and his ability to go to sleep as soon as he went to bed. Nor do we need any further information about his reluctance to fire the people he liked, his dependence on Harry Hopkins, the way he and his staff of eminent ghostwriters constructed his speeches, and his opinion of such men as Willkie, Hoover, and Dewey. It has been put into the record over and over again. What is now required is a real attempt at biography. After all this cutting of bait—quite necessary, I might add—the time has come for somebody to start to fish.

Mr. Gunther, in explaining why he wrote the book he did, asserts that a full-length biography must await what he calls "the slow sifting of years of scholarship." The same assertion has been made by others. I doubt, however, whether the difficulties that admittedly exist are so big a hump as

---

* By permission of the author. Copyright, 1950. The New Yorker Magazine, Inc.

he implies. We don't need the complete Roosevelt, in as many volumes as are now being assembled to present the complete Jefferson, to know Roosevelt thoroughly. All of the really essential information is in hand. What we don't know, of course, is the final effect his influence and long administration will have upon the United States and the rest of the world. But that is not a matter of research; it is a matter of waiting for history.

Partisanship is the chief obstacle in the way of a good, judicious biography of Roosevelt. The emotions he stirred up, pro and con, have not yet died down. The Democratic Party is still riding his coat-tails, and the Republicans are still forcefully doing battle with him. Mr. Gunther, it turns out, is one of the more uncritical of Roosevelt's admirers. He is in there all the time getting in his licks for his hero. Here is a sample, and a necessarily long one, of what I mean:

> On another occasion Mr. Steinhardt got a remarkable insight on the way the President's subtle mind worked. Home on leave from Istabul, he asked FDR for a decision on a critical difference then developing between ourselves and the British on Lend Lease in Turkey. . . . Roosevelt hardly appeared to be listening, and brushed him off with a ten-minute monologue on, of all unrelated things, three impending appointments to the Federal judiciary in New York. . . . He had made up his mind on the first two, but not the third. The Democratic National Committee was supporting one . . . candidate, the state chairman another, and a powerful senator still another. FDR himself favored a fourth man, and he asked Steinhardt, with his wide experience of the New York bar, if he knew anything against him. "No," the Ambassador replied. Roosevelt then waved him out cheerfully, adding almost as an after-thought: "Oh—on that Lend Lease matter, see Hopkins." By this technique FDR had killed several birds. He avoided making a decision himself on the Lend Lease dispute, which was already the cause of a serious tussle between Hopkins and Sumner Welles. Moreover, by sending Steinhardt to Hopkins rather than Welles, he implied that he favored the Hopkins view, while not actually taking sides. Finally, he had obtained Steinhardt's opinion on an entirely different matter; the Ambassador had said no more than the single word "No," but Roosevelt was quite capable of using this so that, if anybody did oppose the man he favored, he could claim that Steinhardt had supported him.

Now, this is surely a peculiar performance by Roosevelt. He pays no attention to his Ambassador, he ducks out of making an important decision, he takes sides in a devious manner, and he prepares to hide behind another man's innocent, unsuspecting word. But Mr. Gunther doesn't see it that way; to him, it's a remarkable example of the workings of a subtle mind. And so it goes throughout the book. Item: Although Roosevelt collected everything he could about himself, including a complete newsreel history running to hundreds of thousands of feet of film, he wasn't vainglorious; "perhaps the best analysis would be to say that he had a passionate adhesive interest in history of any kind, and was therefore naturally interested in his own." Item: Although there may be some truth in the charge that Roosevelt got along by sabotaging his friends and placating his enemies, and although some good men "were thrown to the dogs without any thanks at all," there was a sound reason—"A president cannot always give thanks, because the president is an institution, not just a man."

But Mr. Gunther's book fails not only because he writes as a partisan apologist. Much more important is that lack of analytical ability. "I once heard it said that Roosevelt's most effective quality was receptivity," he writes. "But also he transmitted. He was like a kind of universal joint, or rather a switchboard, a transformer. The whole energy of the country, the whole power of one hundred and forty million people, flowed into him and through him; he not only felt this power, but he utilized it, he transmitted it. Why does a country, if lucky, produce a great man when he is most needed? Because it really believes in something and focuses the entire energy of its national desires into a single human being; the supreme forces of the time converge into a single vessel. Roosevelt could manipulate this power, shooting it out at almost any angle, to provoke response, to irradiate ideas and men, to search out enormous issues. He was like a needle, always quivering, oscillating, responding to new impulses, throbbing at the slightest variation in current—a magnetic instrument measuring ceaselessly the tone and intensity of public impact. But no matter how much the needle quivered and oscillated, it seldom varied far from its own true north." This is a fair sample of Mr. Gunther's analytical method. But what does it mean? I don't know. Does Mr. Gunther?

3. Let's Wait* *by the Editors of* Time

Journalist John Gunther has made a career of breezing through countries, even whole continents, and persuading his readers that he is giving them inside stuff. His "Inside" (Europe, Latin America, Asia, U.S.A.) books have considerable popular virtues: they can be read in a hammock, they seldom induce thought, and they almost never leave a deep residue of conviction or concern. Writing with ebullience and wide-eyed surprise, he projects men and events just far enough beyond the daily-news level to satisfy those who dislike being serious but are plagued by the need to seem informed.

In *Roosevelt in Retrospect,* Gunther has brought these talents to bear on the complex personality of Franklin Delano Roosevelt. In spite of his avowed aim of getting at his subject's "root qualities and basic sources of power," Gunther has conspicuously failed to "pin something of his great substance against the wall of time." Getting inside a man is something quite different from getting into a continent or a country; it takes more than visas. What Gunther has achieved is a lively journalistic profile pieced together with materials largely lifted from the mushrooming literature on F.D.R. and loosely held together by Gunther's own surface researches.

* Courtesy of *Time.* Copyright Time, Inc., 1950.

Shudders & Secrets. Writing "as objectively as possible," Gunther is obviously too dazzled by the Roosevelt glitter to do a balanced job. Even when he concedes F.D.R.'s political deviousness and lack of candor, he is much more interested in finding excuses for them than in showing their damaging consequences. They "arose not so much out of duplicity but from . . . agreeableness . . . and his marked distaste for hurting friends."

Gunther's mouth often seems as wide open as his eyes. Noting that F.D.R. and his mother both nearly died at his birth from an overdose of chloroform, he pontificates: "Of such hairbreadths is history made." A shudder passes over him when he recalls that Roosevelt was elected governor of New York in 1928 by only 25,000 votes: "His whole future career was made possible by less than 1 per cent of the electorate. What would have happened to America in the turbulent 1930's—and later—if this minuscule handful of voters had gone the other way?" Admirers of F.D.R. who have as much faith in the U.S. as Roosevelt had will feel that the nation would have survived. At times, Gunther's bald style fails him and his subject entirely: "Young Roosevelt was still at Harvard. Presently he found himself in love with Eleanor. He kept his passion a great secret, however; he did not even tell his roommate. . . . Late in 1903 he asked her to marry him, and she at once accepted." The Roosevelt romance will probably get more imaginative treatment one day.

Poodles & Poker. *Roosevelt in Retrospect* nonetheless has Gunther's reader-tested qualities of liveliness and high quota of anecdote. Example: F.D.R. was economical. As a young man he disliked paying more than $2 for a shirt, and in the White House he charged Mrs. Harry Hopkins 50¢ a day for the keep of her poodle. Gunther names the only man who ever called F.D.R. an s.o.b. to his face: Leon Henderson. Myrna Loy was the President's favorite actress, and he loved poker. He saved and filed Christmas cards and he kept the bullet fired at him by an assassin in Miami. When F.D.R. flew to Casablanca, a strong swimmer was brought along to keep him afloat should the plane crash.

For such tidbits and for its admiring enthusiasm, *Roosevelt in Retrospect* will be attractive reading for a ready-made audience. But it was F.D.R. himself who used to put off would-be biographers with the warning: "Let's wait a hundred years."

4. The Riddles of Franklin Roosevelt[*] *by Raymond Swing*

John Gunther calls his new Roosevelt book both a "profile" and a "summary." It also is a compilation to about a third of its length, composed in the now established Gunther technique, of an impressive assortment of details, some of facts important and trivial, some of ideas deliberately artless and

[*] From *The Nation*, June 3, 1950.

penetrating. Thus the Roosevelt story has been accorded the treatment of the notable "Inside" works that have given Mr. Gunther a unique place in political journalism. It need not be debated whether this treatment assures a satisfactory biography; it does not. Mr. Roosevelt was both too complex and too paradoxical to be illuminated by a catalogue of his contradictions and questions about his qualities. He needs the synthesis of a great interpretative biography, operating like a shaft of light that reveals unity formed out of disunity and harmony underlying discord. Mr. Gunther has not undertaken to write this biography. It is not his method or his art. He is a compiler, as was Mr. Sandburg writing about Lincoln. He does not go in for the portraiture that grows out of selection, that is, the suppression of detail. He must note everything, stop and conjecture about everything, delight in everything, and both marvel and cavil.

All this makes a book that is informative, entertaining, and in this case also important, and because Mr. Gunther is an indefatigable gatherer of detail, a book that is fresh even in the familiar field of Rooseveltiana. But Mr. Gunther has not departed from his established formula. He writes about F.D.R. as he writes about a continent. But since F.D.R. was not a continent, it is clear that Mr. Gunther does not write about him *because* he understands him and feels compelled to share his understanding. He is searching, and we share his search. Mr. Roosevelt will remain one of the most difficult men of destiny to understand. But sooner or later someone will write *as though* he understood him, and a true biography will result.

What Mr. Gunther's book does suggest, though somewhat faintly, is that understanding Mr. Roosevelt is impossible without understanding first the greatness of the era in which he became the most notable world figure. We still are too close to that era to see its dimensions. The depression and America's rescue from it are only a minor part of the drama. The coming war is a larger part; and then the war itself, with its now forgotten dangers and its now unappreciated victory, forms the stupendous climax. What is mysterious about Mr. Roosevelt's career is that he went through each of these phases, not as an intellectual leader who had mastered in advance the requirements of each, but as a political leader who had to come to grips with the problems as they grew acute, and did so groping his way, and only in time became master of events. He conquered the depression not with mind but with spirit. He was slow and tardy in feeling the rising peril of Nazi and Japanese ambition. And once the war was on, he was to lead the country through two years of mortifying defeat and impotence. But in each phase he rallied the forces that came into dominance. Only when a future generation is able to appraise the full nature of the tragic conflict of the era will Mr. Roosevelt's title to historic rank be clear. Mr. Gunther has moments when he is caught up by the forces of the time and feels their overwhelming power both for success or failure. But he does not let himself go in for re-creating this time, and failing to do so he fails to assign Mr. Roosevelt to his final rank. He believes he knows what the rank is, and suggests it persistently by his device of compilation and questioning. But not being ready to write the history of the Roosevelt era in its titanic perspective, he is unable to make Mr. Roosevelt a Titan.

Whatever else can be said about Mr. Roosevelt, he will count in the end for a series of achievements in all of which he began as a novice and then, by his phenomenal political talents, ended as architect and builder—and one who finished what he built. The one exception appears to be in regard to the peace. This he did not complete, and no political heir has had the vision and the power to complete it. Now, because he did not live to build the peace, some of his contemporaries hold it against him, as though it was due to a shortcoming in his nature and genius. And in this view, because men have forgotten the dire perils they were in during World War II, and how near they came to defeat and how dramatic were the developments that staved it off, the victory passes as of minor moment and with it the leadership of Mr. Roosevelt. Mr. Gunther might have expended some of his indubitable gifts in drawing with greater attention the backdrop before which F.D.R. was to act, and thus have established his stature. But though he knows quite well what the stature was, he only affirms it, and does not measure it with the arts of creative writing.

It surely is somewhat unfair to a man who has written a really good book to chide him for not writing a better one. Mr. Gunther may simply have lacked the time—the years—to have tackled the better one. What he has given lies within his quite generous means. He has produced the best new work on Mr. Roosevelt I have seen (excepting Sherwood's, which is also about Hopkins). It is highly readable, arresting, sometimes annoyingly naïve, but always disarmingly honest and scrupulously fair.

A future writer who is to attempt true portraiture will find postulated in this book all the riddles of which Mr. Roosevelt's complicated nature was made. But unless F.D.R. is to remain for all time simply a beloved but bewildering paradox, Mr. Gunther has provided only a sourcebook, albeit one of warmth, candor, and devotion.

COMMENT AND QUESTIONS

I. If you have not read *Roosevelt in Retrospect*, what is your opinion, after reading these four reviews, of John Gunther's book?

II. If you have read the book, which review best accords with your own judgment, and why?

III. Do any of the four reviewers agree on any points about the book? If so, what? On what main points do they disagree?

IV. Do any of the reviewers seem to you to be influenced by their personal feeling about the subject of the book, Franklin D. Roosevelt?

V. What agreement and disagreement do you find in the reviews about the author, John Gunther?

VI. The slanting by means of emphasis in the reviews affords an interesting study. What points are emphasized, to the exclusion of other points, in each review? Does the order in which the reviews appear represent a kind of slanting? If so, is the slanting favorable or unfavorable to Gunther and to Roosevelt? Explain.

VII. Which reviews appeal to emotion? Which make use of irony and ridicule? Comment on the validity and effectiveness of such persuasive techniques in the evaluation of a book.

VIII. Which review seems to you to be the most fair and to give the most convincing evidence to support the reviewer's opinion? Which review seems the least fair and the least convincing?

IX. Read *Roosevelt in Retrospect* and, with the approval of your instructor, write a critical evaluation of the book and of these four reviews.

JOSEPH C. BEAVER

"Technique" in Hemingway*

The following criticism of Ernest Hemingway's work starts with a limited problem: what quality of "good Hemingway" is present in *The Old Man and the Sea* and lacking in *Across the River and into the Trees,* a novel published five years earlier. The author suggests an answer to the problem, and supports his answer with particular references to Hemingway's writing. Mr. Beaver teaches English in Broome Technical Community College. This article was published in *College English,* March, 1953.

[1] With the publication of *The Old Man and the Sea,* a story which has won critical approbation almost to the extent that *Across the River and into the Trees* drew condemnation, we have been afforded an unusual opportunity to re-examine what it is that makes "good Hemingway." For, whatever it is, assuredly it is present in *The Old Man and the Sea,* just as for the most part it was not present in the World War II novel.

[2] Among critics there was some disagreement and haziness as to just what was the matter with *Across the River.* Some who roundly condemned it felt that Hemingway had simply overused elements which have always been his stock and trade; Alfred Kazin called the novel a "travesty" of Hemingway. Others felt (as Maxwell Geismar) that it collected together all that was bad in his previous work. Then there were those who found the novel true and satisfying Hemingway, but a Hemingway on a lesser scale. Among these, for example, was John O'Hara in the *New York Times.*

* By permission from the author.

Making no exorbitant claims for the book itself, O'Hara said in the last paragraph of his review (the only one in that chaotic, irresponsible piece containing anything resembling evaluation) that Hemingway might no longer be able to go the full distance, but he could still hurt you. And to Kate Simon, writing in the *New Republic,* the difference seemed also to be mainly a question of scope and extent: "Although the canvas is now smaller and painted in grayed tones, there is no less art. The mixture is, on a minor scale, as before and still magical."

[3] While doubtless all these positions are tenable, I think no one of them penetrated to the root of the trouble. At first consideration it did appear that the novel had in it nothing that was not in earlier Hemingway and everything that was. But I believe the mixture was really not the same, that there was something lacking, something perhaps a little difficult to isolate. Hemingway himself apparently feared he might be charged with too little action. He said in an interview reported in the *New York Times Book Review* (September 17, 1950): "Sure, they can say anything about nothing happening in *Across the River,* but all that happens is the defense of the lower Piave, the breakthrough in Normandy, the taking of Paris, and the destruction of the 22d Inf. Reg. in Hurtgen forest plus a man who loves a girl and dies."

[4] I submit that the missing element in *Across the River* was not "action" precisely, but rather a treatment of *technique.* I use the word here in the layman's sense—it seems to me that nearly all of Hemingway's work is concerned with the "technique" of performing some job properly, correctly. The common denominator to his best work has been, I think, his delineation of technique in this sense. Back of the correct technique lie the practice and experience in performing the particular job, combined sometimes with inherent artistic talent, which distinguish Hemingway's heroes at their best (and in this sense they *are* heroes, as characters in novels by most other contemporary writers are not). Most of them have no philosophy except the philosophy of performing something correctly and well. They take pride in their mechanical perfection; they are technicians.

[5] Such is the old man in Hemingway's latest novel, and such is almost the entire content of the story. Passages selected almost at random detail the technique of deep-sea fishing:

> Before it was really light he had his baits out and was drifting with the current. One bait was down forty fathoms. The second was at seventy-five and the third and fourth were down in the blue water at one hundred and one hundred and twenty-five fathoms. Each bait hung head down with the shank of the hook inside the bait fish, tied and sewed solid and all the projecting part of the hook, the curve and the point, was covered with fresh sardines. Each sardine was hooked through both eyes so that they made a half-garland on the projecting steel. There was no part of the hook that a great fish could feel which was not sweet smelling and good tasting.

[6] Correct technique is an obsession with Hemingway; he explores the subject tirelessly and has found basic principles which apply in all forms of directed physical activity. In this novel it is clear, both in the old man's conversations with the boy and in his semidelirious reflections, that big-league baseball and deep-sea fishing are kindred occupations.

[7] One basic principle of correct technique, for example, is the performing of an action in measured time, slower than one is capable of performing it. This is true in bull-fighting, hunting, bridge-blowing, and deep-sea fishing. Thus:

> He rowed slowly and steadily toward where the bird was circling. He did not hurry and he kept his lines straight up and down. But he crowded the current a little so that he was still fishing correctly though faster than he would have fished if he was not trying to use the bird.

[8] Technique is something one learns from a teacher. The grounds of the boy's affection for the old man are precisely this: "The old man had taught the boy to fish and the boy loved him." And there always remain further refinements of technique to be acquired:

> He let his hand dry in the air then grasped the line with it and eased himself as much as he could and allowed himself to be pulled forward against the wood so that the boat took the strain as much, or more, than he did.
> I'm learning how to do it, he thought.

[9] There is not enough treatment of technique in *Across the River,* but there was some, and it was because of this that readers found any merit at all in the novel. Colonel Cantwell knows ducks and knows duck-shooting. He is a perfectionist in technique, and he despises those who have not the technique. In the short opening and closing sections of this novel—many reviewers commented that these sections contained the old Hemingway—Hemingway dealt with a thing he had dealt with, in one form or another, in almost every piece he had ever written. In *The Sun Also Rises* it is, in the first part, the technique of getting drunk, and in the last it is the technique of correct, or genuine, bull-fighting. The ability to distinguish the correct from the incorrect, the genuine from the nongenuine, whether in drinking or bull-fighting, is the mark of the "good" character. In *To Have and Have Not* it is the technique of correct deep-sea fishing again, of skilful boat-handling, as well as the technique of love; if this novel is inferior, it is because it lacks a unifying theme, not because it lacks technique and action. In *For Whom the Bell Tolls* Robert Jordan is an expert technician, an artist who blows bridges. He is irritated because the guerrillas are impressed by the blowing of a train, a cheaply sensational job not requiring great skill, or fastidiously correct performance (compare Romero's bull-fighting, in *The Sun Also Rises,* with that of the contemporary crowd-pleasers). It is the technician who works efficiently under the bridge, who

keeps telling himself (like a baseball pitcher counting between pitches) not to work too fast; it is the combat-technician finally who, lying prone, his heart pounding against the pine-needle-covered forest floor, calculates coolly and automatically at what point he will fire. The book is not about a social or political cause, save incidentally. Only the title, with its implication that the Spanish war was the world's concern, has social meaning; in *For Whom the Bell Tolls,* as in his other novels, Hemingway finds expression for his professional interest in the technique of physical action.

[10] If we examine Hemingway's nonfiction writing, we find him still concerned with the same theme. *Death in the Afternoon* is an extensive eulogy of correct technique in bull-fighting and of those who have had the technique. In *The Green Hills of Africa* Hemingway is the hero, and his concern with technique is the subject. Hemingway's characters are always grouped in cliques, whether in his fiction or nonfiction, and the password of the secret order is appreciation of correct technique. Thus M'Cola and P.O.M. are to Hemingway, in *The Green Hills of Africa,* as Bill Gorton and Lady Brett are to Jake Barnes in *The Sun Also Rises.* And Robert Cohen, the outsider who doesn't know the password, has his counterpart in Hemingway's African hunting party in the person of Garrick. *The Green Hills of Africa* is a good book, and it is good, our interest is sustained, because Hemingway concentrates our attention on the proper way of hunting and shooting. He is disgusted with himself when he fires improperly, at the whole body of the animal rather than at a particular point; he is pleased and filled with the joy of living which is the all of life to him when he squeezes the trigger properly, having first "frozen" himself inside. His feelings after gut-shooting a sable are representative:

> But that damned sable bull. I should have killed him; but it was a running shot. To hit him at all I had to use him all as a target. Yes, you bastard, but what about the cow you missed twice, prone, standing broadside? Was that a running shot? No. If I'd gone to bed last night I would not have done that. Or if I'd wiped out the bore to get the oil out she would not have thrown high the first time. Then I would not have pulled down and shot under her the second shot. Every damned thing is your own fault if you're any good. I thought I could shoot a shotgun better than I could and I had lost plenty of money backing my opinion but I knew, coldly and outside myself, that I could shoot a rifle on game as well as any son of a bitch that ever lived.

[11] So through all of Hemingway. There is always the technique of combat, and it is this which has replaced, or which Hemingway implies *is,* the nobility and grandeur of man which art is supposed to reveal. Sometimes it is technique in the more violent sports, frequently it is technique in hunting and killing animals, and frequently it is the technique of war. When this technique is properly handled, the result is characters who are genuine heroes, and novels which are genuinely great. When improperly handled, when the mixture of ingredients is altered, the result is a bad novel, and a character who acts, on occasion, like Walter Mitty in one of his daydreams.

This was true in *Across the River*. Except in the duck-shoot scenes, and except in one or two other short scenes, we did not have technique *in action* in *Across the River*. Hemingway tried to fill this vacuum by having Cantwell *speak* at length of war technique to his lover. But it was not the same thing. It would not take the place of a bull fight, or a Caporetto retreat, or the actual blowing of a bridge. What was lacking in *Across the River* was technique, and in so far as Hemingway's technique has to have its roots in action, Hemingway's fear that his book would be criticized for lack of action was right.

[12] But none of this is true of *The Old Man and the Sea*. Here is technique in action throughout. Indeed, it is Hemingway's most extensive continuous exercise of this theme, and perhaps the most unadulterated. Correct technique can carry one through adversity; it will operate unconsciously when our faculties are bruised and dulled. Returning from his heroic, unbelievable struggle with the marlin, the eighty-year-old man, though sleepless for days, automatically unsteps the sail, furls and ties it, shoulders the mast and bears it in agony up the hill to his room where he stands it against the wall before lying down on the bed to sleep.

[13] A tourist couple at the end of the novel observe the remains of the marlin, and the woman, mistakenly believing it to have been a shark, comments, "I didn't know sharks had such handsome, beautifully formed tails." Her companion replies, "I didn't either."

[14] Here again is the division between the initiate and the uninitiate. The task executed with proper technique, the battle correctly fought—activity which gives an indescribable inward sense of satisfaction—this, to Hemingway, is the glory and dignity of man.

COMMENT AND QUESTIONS

I. Explain the meaning of *technique* as it is used in this article. What is the further meaning of *technique in action?* What is the relationship between technique and character in Hemingway's writing?

II. Mr. Beaver is writing for an audience familiar with Hemingway's work. Do you think that his theory and examples are clear, also, to readers who do not know the books he refers to? What might be the value to such readers in reading a critical article of this kind?

III. If you know Hemingway's writing, can you think of stories or novels in which "technique" is not important?

IV. For further information about Hemingway, and his own comments on technique, see "An American Storyteller: Ernest Hemingway," on page 864.

DEEMS TAYLOR

The Monster*

The following selection by an American composer and critic is an evaluation of a person. Deems Taylor has composed two operas and many symphonic poems and songs, and is a well-known music commentator. "The Monster" is taken from one of his books of criticism, *Of Men and Music,* published in 1937.

[1] He was an undersized little man, with a head too big for his body—a sickly little man. His nerves were bad. He had skin trouble. It was agony for him to wear anything next to his skin coarser than silk. And he had delusions of grandeur.

[2] He was a monster of conceit. Never for one minute did he look at the world or at people, except in relation to himself. He was not only the most important person in the world, to himself; in his own eyes he was the only person who existed. He believed himself to be one of the greatest dramatists in the world, one of the greatest thinkers, and one of the greatest composers. To hear him talk, he was Shakespeare, and Beethoven, and Plato, rolled into one. And you would have had no difficulty in hearing him talk. He was one of the most exhausting conversationalists that ever lived. An evening with him was an evening spent in listening to a monologue. Sometimes he was brilliant; sometimes he was maddeningly tiresome. But whether he was being brilliant or dull, he had one sole topic of conversation: himself. What *he* thought and what *he* did.

[3] He had a mania for being in the right. The slightest hint of disagreement, from anyone, on the most trivial point, was enough to set him off on a harangue that might last for hours, in which he proved himself right in so many ways, and with such exhausting volubility, that in the end his hearer, stunned and deafened, would agree with him, for the sake of peace.

[4] It never occurred to him that he and his doings were not of the most intense and fascinating interest to anyone with whom he came in contact. He had theories about almost any subject under the sun, including vegetarianism, the drama, politics, and music; and in support of these theories he wrote pamphlets, letters, books . . . thousands upon thousands of words, hundreds and hundreds of pages. He not only wrote these things, and published them—usually at somebody else's expense—but he would sit and read them aloud, for hours, to his friends and his family.

---

* From *Of Men and Music,* copyright, 1937, by Deems Taylor. Reprinted by permission of Simon and Schuster, Publishers.

[5] He wrote operas; and no sooner did he have the synopsis of a story, but he would invite—or rather summon—a crowd of his friends to his house and read it aloud to them. Not for criticism. For applause. When the complete poem was written, the friends had to come again, and hear *that* read aloud. Then he would publish the poem, sometime years before the music that went with it was written. He played the piano like a composer, in the worst sense of what that implies, and he would sit down at the piano before parties that included some of the finest pianists of his time, and play for them, by the hour, his own music, needless to say. He had a composer's voice. And he would invite eminent vocalists to his house, and sing them his operas, taking all the parts.

[6] He had the emotional stability of a six-year-old child. When he felt out of sorts, he would rave and stamp, or sink into suicidal gloom and talk darkly of going to the East to end his days as a Buddhist monk. Ten minutes later, when something pleased him, he would rush out of doors and run around the garden, or jump up and down on the sofa, or stand on his head. He could be grief-stricken over the death of a pet dog, and he could be callous and heartless to a degree that would have made a Roman emperor shudder.

[7] He was almost innocent of any sense of responsibility. Not only did he seem incapable of supporting himself, but it never occurred to him that he was under any obligation to do so. He was convinced that the world owed him a living. In support of this belief, he borrowed money from everybody who was good for a loan—men, women, friends, or strangers. He wrote begging letters by the score, sometimes groveling without shame, at others loftily offering his intended benefactor the privilege of contributing to his support, and being mortally offended if the recipient declined the honor. I have found no record of his ever paying or repaying money to anyone who did not have a legal claim upon it.

[8] What money he could lay his hands on he spent like an Indian rajah. The mere prospect of a performance of one of his operas was enough to set him running up bills amounting to ten times the amount of his prospective royalties. On an income that would reduce a more scrupulous man to doing his own laundry, he would keep two servants. Without enough money in his pocket to pay his rent, he would have the walls and ceiling of his study lined with pink silk. No one will ever know—certainly he never knew—how much money he owed. We do know that his greatest benefactor gave him $6,000 to pay the most pressing of his debts in one city, and a year later had to give him $16,000 to enable him to live in another city without being thrown into jail for debt.

[9] He was equally unscrupulous in other ways. An endless procession of women marches through his life. His first wife spent twenty years enduring and forgiving his infidelities. His second wife had been the wife of his most devoted friend and admirer, from whom he stole her. And even while he was trying to persuade her to leave her first husband he was writing to a

friend to inquire whether he could suggest some wealthy woman—*any* wealthy woman—whom he could marry for her money.

[10] He was completely selfish in his other personal relationships. His liking for his friends was measured solely by the completeness of their devotion to him, or by their usefulness to him, whether financial or artistic. The minute they failed him—even by so much as refusing a dinner invitation—or began to lessen in usefulness, he cast them off without a second thought. At the end of his life he had exactly one friend left whom he had known even in middle age.

[11] He had a genius for making enemies. He would insult a man who disagreed with him about the weather. He would pull endless wires in order to meet some man who admired his work, and was able and anxious to be of use to him—and would proceed to make a mortal enemy of him with some idiotic and wholly uncalled-for exhibition of arrogance and bad manners. A character in one of his operas was a caricature of one of the most powerful music critics of his day. Not content with burlesquing him, he invited the critic to his house and read him the libretto aloud in front of his friends.

[12] The name of this monster was Richard Wagner. Everything that I have said about him you can find on record—in newspapers, in police reports, in the testimony of people who knew him, in his own letters, between the lines of his autobiography. And the curious thing about this record is that it doesn't matter in the least.

[13] Because this undersized, sickly, disagreeable, fascinating little man was right all the time. The joke was on us. He *was* one of the world's great dramatists; he *was* a great thinker; he *was* one of the most stupendous musical geniuses that, up to now, the world has ever seen. The world did owe him a living. People couldn't know those things at the time, I suppose; and yet to us, who know his music, it does seem as though they should have known. What if he did talk about himself all the time? If he had talked about himself for twenty-four hours every day for the span of his life he would not have uttered half the number of words that other men have spoken and written about him since his death.

[14] When you consider what he wrote—thirteen operas and music dramas, eleven of them still holding the stage, eight of them unquestionably worth ranking among the world's great musico-dramatic masterpieces—when you listen to what he wrote, the debts and heartaches that people had to endure from him don't seem much of a price. Eduard Hanslick, the critic whom he caricatured in *Die Meistersinger* and who hated him ever after, now lives only because he was caricatured in *Die Meistersinger*. The women whose hearts he broke are long since dead; and the man who could never love anyone but himself has made them deathless atonement, I think, with *Tristan und Isolde*. Think of the luxury with which for a time, at least, fate rewarded Napoleon, the man who ruined France and looted Europe;

and then perhaps you will agree that a few thousand dollars' worth of debts were not too heavy a price to pay for the *Ring* trilogy.

[15] What if he was faithless to his friends and to his wives? He had one mistress to whom he was faithful to the day of his death: Music. Not for a single moment did he ever compromise with what he believed, with what he dreamed. There is not a line of his music that could have been conceived by a little mind. Even when he is dull, or downright bad, he is dull in the grand manner. There is a greatness about his worst mistakes. Listening to his music, one does not forgive him for what he may or may not have been. It is not a matter of forgiveness. It is a matter of being dumb with wonder that his poor brain and body didn't burst under the torment of the demon of creative energy that lived inside him, struggling, clawing, scratching to be released; tearing, shrieking at him to write the music that was in him. The miracle is that what he did in the little space of seventy years could have been done at all, even by a great genius. Is it any wonder that he had no time to be a man?

COMMENT AND QUESTIONS

I. This evaluation is built on a pattern of contrast, with the first eleven paragraphs devoted to Wagner's unpleasant qualities and the last three, introduced by the turn in paragraph 12, to his genius. For an analysis of the essay, list in order the topic ideas in the first eleven paragraphs.

II. What is the reason for the sequence of ideas in these eleven paragraphs? Could the order be changed without loss?

III. How many of the unpleasant qualities discussed in the first section are referred to and justified in the last three paragraphs?

IV. What does Mr. Taylor gain by withholding the "monster's" identity until paragraph 12?

V. How well are the two contrasting judgments of Wagner supported by factual evidence?

VI. If you have read other evaluations in this section of the book, you will notice that "The Monster" is much more personal in tone and emotional in language than, for example, "Measuring the I.Q. Test." Point out some of the techniques Mr. Taylor uses to evoke emotion in his readers. Does the attitudinal language seem to you appropriate and effective in this piece of writing? Explain.

VII. State in the form of a syllogism Mr. Taylor's argument in the last three paragraphs. Do you agree with his major premise?

READINGS

SECTION 3

Reading Persuasion

WILLIAM MAXWELL AITKEN, LORD BEAVERBROOK

Present and Future*

The following World War II document is an example of persuasion by logical argument. The historical context is this: in the summer of 1943, British and American forces had completed a successful campaign against the German forces in North Africa, and the Russian armies had successfully resisted the Germans on the Eastern front; but Allied forces had no foothold in western Europe. In June, 1943, Lord Beaverbrook, Minister of Aircraft Production in England and member of Churchill's war cabinet, presented the following memorandum to Harry Hopkins, the personal representative of President Franklin D. Roosevelt. "Present and Future" analyzes the current (1943) war situation, discusses certain alternative courses of action, and forcefully presents a case for establishing a second front in Europe by an attack through the Dardanelles or a landing in northern France. (The second front was opened a year later, with the Allied landings in Normandy, June 6, 1944.)

[1] It was a year ago that the Prime Minister came to Washington to make the plans which have now culminated in the fall of all North Africa.

[2] The dominant question then was whether to launch a Second Front. The decision, taken against the sombre background of defeat in Libya and impending retreat in Russia, was that the project was too ambitious, and that a lesser objective should be chosen—the clearance of the southern shore of the Mediterranean. Such a plan involved gambling on Russia's ability to stand, *for one more campaign,* on her own. In the event, Russia did hold fast, and North Africa succeeded. These two achievements have meant, for

---

* From *Roosevelt and Hopkins* by Robert E. Sherwood. Copyright, 1948, Robert E. Sherwood. Published by Harper & Brothers.

the British and Americans, that the spectre of defeat has been almost entirely banished.

[3] It is against a new background of established confidence that fresh decisions have now to be taken. The odds have moved heavily in favour of the Allies—the wasting assets of the Luftwaffe, the damage to German industry from the air, the strain on German manpower, the development of American strength, the Russian offensive successes, the opening of the Mediterranean—cumulatively these advantages are impressive.

[4] But for all that, in the West and in the East, the game is still "all to play for." The Russians are only back where they were this time last year. The Anglo-Americans are nowhere on the mainland of Europe.

[5] This year, as last, the dominant question is the Second Front. For this reason: that so long as it is unattempted, there remains for Germany not only the chance, albeit an outside one, to knock out or mortally wound the Russian armies, but also time to prepare the defences of "Festung Europa."

[6] Can *we* afford more time for preparation? The Germans have a most powerful army in the East. The Russians used up men and resources at a heavy rate last winter in an offensive which stopped short of its fullest aims. There is always the risk that Japan will stab in the back. It cannot be said that Moscow, Baku or Leningrad are out of danger. It can still less be said that we and the Americans could in any measurable space of time win without Russian assistance.

[7] Can the Germans ignore the threat of a Second Front? They can and certainly will. To do otherwise would be to allow the initiative to slip finally from their grasp. They are likely to go even further. They will ignore or treat lightly any blow from the West which is not delivered against a vital point. Knowing that the primary object of a Second Front would be to divert troops from the East they will go to almost any lengths to prevent that occurring.

[8] Add to these factors the change in the Anglo-American situation in the last year. Then there were strong grounds for saying that a Second Front would be nothing but a forlorn hope involving the risk of final disaster, and there was much truth in the contention that in a year we should be vastly stronger. Today, of the three major United Nations, we and the Russians are as strong as we shall ever be. Certainly American potential is still developing, and in a year's time the United States will be more powerfully armed. But can we afford the new delay? Even suppose that Germany leaves Russia alone, will she, given a "year of calm" in which to organize for defence, grow much weaker? Can bombing alone make all the difference? We have the weapons now, and the men, and the Germans are uncertain of themselves, their calculations seriously upset. None of these facts can guarantee success for the launching of a major Second Front. They do go far to insuring that its failure will not spell disaster.

[9] Surely the inference is inescapable that the question today must be not whether but where to launch the Second Front. The preliminaries are over,

brilliantly performed. If they do not prove to have been the curtain raiser, the conclusion will be hard to escape, in occupied Europe especially, that the main play is never destined for performance.

[10] But the "where" of the Second Front is all-important. To be more than a diversion the attack must come at a spot where success will bring an immediate *mortal* threat to the enemy. The Second Front can, if it is a real one, apparently fail and yet succeed. It can, if it is only a diversion, apparently succeed and yet in reality fail.

[11] The invasion of Italy? It might prove a major psychological blow at the enemy, but it could not guarantee decisive results. It could be parried by redrawing the southern boundary of the Fortress of Europe at the Alps and Dolomites, fighting a delaying action meanwhile.

[12] The invasion of Northern Norway? It would mean a link-up with the Russians, but again the decisive threat to Europe would be lacking.

[13] A landing in Southern Greece? The passes northwards to the Balkans and the Danube valley could be held by small forces.

[14] When any of these objectives had been achieved, the game, so far as the core of German Europe was the goal (and there can be no other) would be still "all to play for."

[15] But two places of attack promise immediate results. A descent, through the Dardanelles, with Turkish connivance or assistance, on the Eastern Balkans, would lay open the whole Danubian plain and jeopardize all the German forces in southern Russia. A landing in Northern France would point straight at Paris, at the Ruhr and at the Rhine. If either plan succeeded the enemy would be exposed to an intolerable strain before he had time to conserve, perfect and organize his defences.

[16] There are factors, such as the exact shipping position, relative to the Second Front, which may be unknown to the layman. There are two factors which the military will ignore at our peril. One is the danger to Russia, the other the danger of stalemate. There seems a real danger that we shall go on indefinitely sewing the last button on the last gaiter, and the risk is increased by the undoubted fact that a real Second Front will always entail big risks, always remain the most difficult operation in military warfare. But if we are not prepared to accept the risks, face the difficulties, suffer the casualties, then let us concentrate at once exclusively on the production of heavy bombers and think in terms of 1950.

COMMENT AND QUESTIONS

This memorandum is distinctive for its clarity, economy, and force of expression, and for its use of cold analysis in stating a problem, in considering and rejecting alternatives, and in proposing a course of action. Lord Beaverbrook's argument has four parts: (1) reasons for establishing a second front *now;* (2) reasons for rejecting Italy, Norway, and Greece as possible second fronts; (3) reasons for a descent through the Dardanelles or a landing in Northern France; and (4) restatement and emphatic conclusion.

I. Where does each of these parts end, and by what reasoning is each developed?

II. Although broken into a number of short paragraphs, this memorandum has an exceptionally coherent development. What devices of transition are most noticeable? Where is a summary statement used between main points?

III. What in general appears to be Lord Beaverbrook's attitude toward Russia, and what evidences of this attitude can you point to in the actual language of the memorandum?

IV. What is the relevance of paragraph 4 in the development of the whole argument?

V. Explain what Beaverbrook means in paragraph 10 when he makes the statement: "The Second Front can, if it is a real one, apparently fail and yet succeed." What does he mean by a *real* second front, and how do you know?

VI. Comment fully on the meaning and the implication of the last sentence of the memorandum, especially of the last few words: "and think in terms of 1950." (Remember that the memorandum was written in 1943 and that Lord Beaverbrook had been Minister of Aircraft Production. The war with Germany was in fact ended in 1945.)

SIGMUND FREUD

Dreams of the Death of Persons of Whom the Dreamer Is Fond[*]

In the following selection, a pioneer in the study of the unconscious mind presents and argues in favor of a theory which he knows will encounter opposition. Sigmund Freud (1856–1939) was an Austrian physician and the founder of psychoanalysis. Although his theories have been modified, even discarded, by some other psychiatrists, he has had a profound influence on twentieth-century thought. This selection from *The Interpretation of Dreams* (1899) deals with Freud's theory of the embodiment in dreams of repressed wishes, and with what Freud later called the "Oedipus complex." The footnotes are from subsequent editions of *The Interpretation of Dreams;* notes by the translator, James Strachey, are in brackets.

[*] From *The Interpretation of Dreams,* by Sigmund Freud. Translated by James Strachey. Reprinted with permission of Basic Books, Inc., and George Allen & Unwin Ltd.

[1] Another group of dreams which may be described as typical are those containing the death of some loved relative—for instance, of a parent, of a brother or sister, or of a child. Two classes of such dreams must at once be distinguished: those in which the dreamer is unaffected by grief, so that on awakening he is astonished at his lack of feeling, and those in which the dreamer feels deeply pained by the death and may even weep bitterly in his sleep.

[2] We need not consider the dreams of the first of these classes, for they have no claim to be regarded as 'typical.' If we analyse them, we find that they have some meaning other than their apparent one, and that they are intended to conceal some other wish. Such was the dream of the aunt who saw her sister's only son lying in his coffin. It did not mean that she wished her little nephew dead; as we have seen, it merely concealed a wish to see a particular person of whom she was fond and whom she had not met for a long time—a person whom she had once before met after a similarly long interval beside the coffin of another nephew. This wish, which was the true content of the dream, gave no occasion for grief, and no grief, therefore, was felt in the dream. It will be noticed that the affect felt in the dream belongs to its latent and not to its manifest content, and that the dream's *affective* content has remained untouched by the distortion which has overtaken its *ideational* content.

[3] Very different are the dreams of the other class—those in which the dreamer imagines the death of a loved relative and is at the same time painfully affected. The meaning of such dreams, as their content indicates, is a wish that the person in question may die. And since I must expect that the feelings of all of my readers and any others who have experienced similar dreams will rebel against my assertion, I must try to base my evidence for it on the broadest possible foundation.

[4] I have already discussed a dream which taught us that the wishes which are represented in dreams as fulfilled are not always present-day wishes. They may also be wishes of the past which have been abandoned, overlaid and repressed, and to which we have to attribute some sort of continued existence only because of their re-emergence in a dream. They are not dead in our sense of the word but only like the shades in the Odyssey, which awoke to some sort of life as soon as they had tasted blood. In the dream of the dead child in the 'case' what was involved was a wish which had been an immediate one fifteen years earlier and was frankly admitted as having existed at that time. I may add—and this may not be without its bearing upon the theory of dreams—that even behind this wish there lay a memory from the dreamer's earliest childhood. When she was a small child—the exact date could not be fixed with certainty—she had heard that her mother had fallen into a deep depression during the pregnancy of which she had been the fruit and had passionately wished that the child she was bearing might die. When the dreamer herself was grown-up and pregnant, she merely followed her mother's example.

[5] If anyone dreams, with every sign of pain, that his father or mother or

brother or sister has died, I should never use the dream as evidence that he wishes for that person's death *at the present time*. The theory of dreams does not require as much as that; it is satisfied with the inference that this death has been wished for at some time or other during the dreamer's childhood. I fear, however, that this reservation will not appease the objectors; they will deny the possibility of their *ever* having had such a thought with just as much energy as they insist that they harbour no such wishes now. I must therefore reconstruct a portion of the vanished mental life of children on the basis of the evidence of the present.[1]

[6]   Let us first consider the relation of children to their brothers and sisters. I do not know why we presuppose that that relation must be a loving one; for instances of hostility between adult brothers and sisters force themselves upon everyone's experience and we can often establish the fact that the disunity originated in childhood or has always existed. But it is further true that a great many adults, who are on affectionate terms with their brothers and sisters and are ready to stand by them to-day, passed their childhood on almost unbroken terms of enmity with them. The elder child ill-treats the younger, maligns him and robs him of his toys; while the younger is consumed with impotent rage against the elder, envies and fears him, or meets his oppressor with the first stirrings of a love of liberty and a sense of justice. Their parents complain that the children do not get on with one another, but cannot discover why. It is easy to see that the character of even a good child is not what we should wish to find it in an adult. Children are completely egoistic; they feel their needs intensely and strive ruthlessly to satisfy them—especially as against the rivals, other children, and first and foremost as against their brothers and sisters. But we do not on that account call a child 'bad,' we call him 'naughty'; he is no more answerable for his evil deeds in our judgment than in the eyes of the law. And it is right that this should be so; for we may expect that, before the end of the period which we count as childhood, altruistic impulses and morality will awaken in the little egoist and (to use Meynert's terms [e.g. 1892, 169 ff.]) a secondary ego will overlay and inhibit the primary one. It is true, no doubt, that morality does not set in simultaneously all along the line and that the length of non-moral childhood varies in different individuals. If this morality fails to develop, we like to talk of 'degeneracy,' though what in fact faces us is an inhibition in development. After the primary character has already been overlaid by later development, it can still be laid bare again, at all events in part, in cases of hysterical illness. There is a really striking resemblance between what is known as the hysterical character and that of a naughty child. Obsessional neurosis, on the contrary, corresponds to a super-morality imposed as a reinforcing weight upon fresh stirrings of the primary character.

[7]   Many people, therefore, who love their brothers and sisters and would

---

[1] [*Footnote added* 1909:] Cf. my 'Analysis of a Phobia in a Five-Year-Old Boy' (1909*b*) and my paper 'On the Sexual Theories of Children' (1908*c*).

feel bereaved if they were to die, harbour evil wishes against them in their unconscious, dating from earlier times; and these are capable of being realized in dreams.

[8] It is of quite particular interest, however, to observe the behaviour of small children up to the age of two or three or a little older towards their younger brothers and sisters. Here, for instance, was a child who had so far been the only one; and now he was told that the stork had brought a new baby. He looked the new arrival up and down and then declared decisively: 'The stork can take him away again!' [2] I am quite seriously of the opinion that a child can form a just estimate of the set-back he has to expect at the hands of the little stranger. A lady of my acquaintance, who is on very good terms to-day with a sister four years her junior, tells me that she greeted the news of her first arrival with this qualification: 'But all the same I shan't give her my red cap!' Even if a child only comes to realize the situation later on, his hostility will date from that moment. I know of a case in which a little girl of less than three tried to strangle an infant in its cradle because she felt that its continued presence boded her no good. Children at that time of life are capable of jealousy of any degree of intensity and obviousness. Again, if it should happen that the baby sister does in fact disappear after a short while, the elder child will find the whole affection of the household once more concentrated upon himself. If after that the stork should bring yet another baby, it seems only logical that the little favourite should nourish a wish that his new competitor may meet with the same fate as the earlier one, so that he himself may be as happy as he was originally and during the interval.[3] Normally, of course, this attitude of a child towards a younger brother or sister is a simple function of the difference between their ages. Where the gap in time is sufficiently long, an elder girl will already begin to feel the stirring of her maternal instincts towards the helpless newborn baby.

[9] Hostile feelings towards brothers and sisters must be far more frequent in childhood than the unseeing eye of the adult observer can perceive.[4]

---

[2] [*Footnote added* 1909:] The three-and-a-half-year-old Hans (whose phobia was the subject of the analysis mentioned in the preceding footnote) exclaimed shortly after the birth of a sister, while he was suffering from a feverish sore throat: 'I don't *want* a baby sister!' [Freud, 1909*b*, Section I.] During his neurosis eighteen months later he frankly confessed to a wish that his mother might drop the baby into the bath so that she would die. [Ibid., Section II (April 11).] At the same time, Hans was a good-natured and affectionate child, who soon grew fond of this same sister and particularly enjoyed taking her under his wing.

[3] [*Footnote added* 1914:] Deaths that are experienced in this way in childhood may quickly be forgotten in the family; but psycho-analytic research shows that they have a very important influence on subsequent neuroses.

[4] [*Footnote added* 1914:] Since this was written, a large number of observations have been made and recorded in the literature of psycho-analysis upon the originally hostile attitude of children towards their brothers and sisters and one of their parents. The [Swiss] author and poet Spitteler has given us a particularly genuine and naïve account of this childish attitude, derived from his own childhood [1914, 40]: 'Moreover there was a second Adolf there: a little creature who they alleged was my brother, though I could not see what use he was and still less why they made as much fuss of him as of me my-

[10] In the case of my own children, who followed each other in rapid succession, I neglected the opportunity of carrying out observations of this kind; but I am now making up for this neglect by observing a small nephew, whose autocratic rule was upset, after lasting for fifteen months, by the appearance of a female rival. I am told, it is true, that the young man behaves in the most chivalrous manner to his little sister, that he kisses her hand and strokes her; but I have been able to convince myself that even before the end of his second year he made use of his powers of speech for the purpose of criticizing someone whom he could not fail to regard as superfluous. Whenever the conversation touched upon her he used to intervene in it and exclaim petulantly: 'Too 'ickle! too 'ickle!' During the last few months the baby's growth has made enough progress to place her beyond this particular ground for contempt, and the little boy has found a different basis for his assertion that she does not deserve so much attention: at every suitable opportunity he draws attention to the fact that she has no teeth.[5] We all of us recollect how the eldest girl of another of my sisters, who was then a child of six, spent half-an-hour in insisting upon each of her aunts in succession agreeing with her: 'Lucie can't understand that yet, can she?' she kept asking. Lucie was her rival—two and a half years her junior.

[11] In none of my women patients, to take an example, have I failed to come upon this dream of the death of a brother or sister, which tallies with an increase in hostility. I have only found a single exception; and it was easy to interpret this as a confirmation of the rule. On one occasion during an analytic session I was explaining this subject to a lady, since in view of her symptom its discussion seemed to me relevant. To my astonishment she replied that she had never had such a dream. Another dream, however, occurred to her, which ostensibly had no connection with the topic —a dream which she had first dreamt when she was four years old and at that time the youngest of the family, and which she had dreamt repeatedly since: *A whole crowd of children—all her brothers, sisters and cousins of both sexes—were romping in a field. Suddenly they all grew wings, flew away and disappeared.* She had no idea what this dream meant; but it is not hard to recognize that in its original form it had been a dream of the death of all her brothers and sisters, and had been only slightly influenced by the censorship. I may venture to suggest the following analysis. On the occasion of the death of one of this crowd of children (in this instance the children of two brothers had been brought up together as a single family) the dreamer, not yet four years old at the time, must have asked some wise grown-up person what became of children when they were dead. The reply

---

self. I was sufficient so far as I was concerned; why should I want a brother? And he was not merely useless, he was positively in the way. When I pestered my grandmother, he wanted to pester her too. When I was taken out in the perambulator, he sat opposite to me and took up half the space, so that we were bound to kick each other with our feet.'

[5] [*Footnote added* 1909:] Little Hans, when he was three and a half, gave vent to a crushing criticism of his sister in the same words. It was because of her lack of teeth, he supposed, that she was unable to talk. [Freud, 1909b, Section I.]

must have been: 'They grow wings and turn into little angels.' In the dream which followed upon this piece of information all the dreamer's brothers and sisters had wings like angels and—which is the main point—flew away. Our little baby-killer was left alone, strange to say: the only survivor of the whole crowd! We can hardly be wrong in supposing that the fact of the children romping in a *field* before flying away points to butterflies. It is as though the child was led by the same chain of thought as the peoples of antiquity to picture the soul as having a butterfly's wings.

[12]   At this point someone will perhaps interrupt: 'Granted that children have hostile impulses towards their brothers and sisters, how can a child's mind reach such a pitch of depravity as to wish for the *death* of his rivals or of playmates stronger than himself, as though the death penalty were the only punishment for every crime?' Anyone who talks like this has failed to bear in mind that a child's idea of being 'dead' has nothing much in common with ours apart from the word. Children know nothing of the horrors of corruption, of freezing in the ice-cold grave, of the terrors of eternal nothingness—ideas which grown-up people find it so hard to tolerate, as is proved by all the myths of a future life. The fear of death has no meaning to a child; hence it is that he will play with the dreadful word and use it as a threat against a playmate: 'If you do that again, you'll die, like Franz!' Meanwhile the poor mother gives a shudder and remembers, perhaps, that the greater half of the human race fail to survive their childhood years. It was actually possible for a child, who was over eight years old at the time, coming home from a visit to the Natural History Museum, to say to his mother: 'I'm so fond of you, Mummy: when you die I'll have you stuffed and I'll keep you in this room, so that I can see you *all* the time.' So little resemblance is there between a child's idea of being dead and our own![6]

[13]   To children, who, moreover, are spared the sight of the scenes of suffering which precede death, being 'dead' means approximately the same as being 'gone'—not troubling the survivors any longer. A child makes no distinction as to how this absence is brought about: whether it is due to a journey, to a dismissal, to an estrangement, or to death.[7] If, during a

---

[6] [*Footnote added* 1909:] I was astonished to hear a highly intelligent boy of ten remark after the sudden death of his father: 'I know father's dead, but what I can't understand is why he doesn't come home to supper.'—[*Added* 1919:] Further material on this subject will be found in the first [seven] volumes of the periodical *Imago* [1912–21], under the standing rubric of '*Vom wahren Wesen der Kinderseele*' ['The True Nature of the Child Mind'], edited by Frau Dr. H. von Hug-Hellmuth.

[7] [*Footnote added* 1919:] An observation made by a parent who had a knowledge of psycho-analysis caught the actual moment at which his highly intelligent four-year-old daughter perceived the distinction between being 'gone' and being 'dead.' The little girl had been troublesome at meal-time and noticed that one of the maids at the pension where they were staying was looking at her askance. 'I wish Josefine was dead,' was the child's comment to her father. 'Why dead?' enquired her father soothingly; 'wouldn't it do if she went away?' 'No,' replied the child; 'then she'd come back again.' The unbounded self-love (the narcissism) of children regards any interference as an act of *lèse majesté;* and their feelings demand (like the Draconian code) that any such crime shall receive the one form of punishment which admits of no degrees.

child's prehistoric epoch, his nurse has been dismissed, and if soon afterwards his mother has died, the two events are superimposed on each other in a single series in his memory as revealed in analysis. When people are absent, children do not miss them with any great intensity; many mothers have learnt this to their sorrow when, after being away from home for some weeks on a summer holiday, they are met on their return by the news that the children have not once asked after their mummy. If their mother does actually make the journey to that 'undiscover'd country, from whose bourn no traveller returns,' children seem at first to have forgotten her, and it is only later on that they begin to call their dead mother to mind.

[14] Thus if a child has reasons for wishing the absence of another, there is nothing to restrain him from giving his wish the form of the other child being dead. And the psychical reaction to dreams containing death-wishes proves that, in spite of the different content of these wishes in the cases of children, they are nevertheless in some way or other the same as wishes expressed in the same terms by adults.[8]

[15] If, then, a child's death-wishes against his brothers and sisters are explained by the childish egoism which makes him regard them as his rivals, how are we to explain his death-wishes against his parents, who surround him with love and fulfil his needs and whose preservation that same egoism should lead him to desire?

[16] A solution of this difficulty is afforded by the observation that dreams of the death of parents apply with preponderant frequency to the parent who is of the same sex as the dreamer: that men, that is, dream mostly of their father's death and women of their mother's. I cannot pretend that this is universally so, but the preponderance in the direction I have indicated is so evident that it requires to be explained by a factor of general importance.[9] It is as though—to put it bluntly—a sexual preference were making itself felt at an early age: as though boys regarded their fathers and girls their mothers as their rivals in love, whose elimination could not fail to be to their advantage.

[17] Before this idea is rejected as a monstrous one, it is as well in this case, too, to consider the real relations obtaining—this time between parents and children. We must distinguish between what the cultural standards of filial piety demand of this relation and what everyday observation shows it in fact to be. More than one occasion for hostility lies concealed in the relation between parents and children—a relation which affords the most ample opportunities for wishes to arise which cannot pass the censorship.

[18] Let us consider first the relation between father and son. The sanctity

[8] [The adult attitude to death is discussed by Freud more particularly in the second essay of his *Totem and Taboo* (1912-13), Section 3 (*c*), in his paper on 'The Three Caskets' (1913*f*) and in the second part of his 'Thoughts on War and Death' (1915*b*).]

[9] [*Footnote added* 1925:] The situation is often obscured by the emergence of a self-punitive impulse, which threatens the dreamer, by way of a moral reaction, with the loss of the parent whom he loves.

which we attribute to the rules laid down in the Decalogue has, I think, blunted our powers of perceiving the real facts. We seem scarcely to venture to observe that the majority of mankind disobey the Fifth Commandment. Alike in the lowest and in the highest strata of human society filial piety is wont to give way to other interests. The obscure information which is brought to us by mythology and legend from the primaeval ages of human society gives an unpleasing picture of the father's despotic power and of the ruthlessness with which he made use of it. Kronos devoured his children, just as the wild boar devours the sow's litter; while Zeus emasculated his father [10] and made himself ruler in his place. The more unrestricted was the rule of the father in the ancient family, the more must the son, as his destined successor, have found himself in the position of an enemy, and the more impatient must he have been to become ruler himself through his father's death. Even in our middle-class families fathers are as a rule inclined to refuse their sons independence and the means necessary to secure it and thus to foster the growth of the germ of hostility which is inherent in their relation. A physician will often be in a position to notice how a son's grief at the loss of his father cannot suppress his satisfaction at having at length won his freedom. In our society to-day fathers are apt to cling desperately to what is left of a now sadly antiquated *potestas patris familias*; and an author who, like Ibsen, brings the immemorial struggle between fathers and sons into prominence in his writings may be certain of producing his effect.

[19] Occasions for conflict between a daughter and her mother arise when the daughter begins to grow up and long for sexual liberty, but finds herself under her mother's tutelage; while the mother, on the other hand, is warned by her daughter's growth that the time has come when she herself must abandon her claims to sexual satisfaction.

[20] All of this is patent to the eyes of everyone. But it does not help us in our endeavour to explain dreams of a parent's death in people whose piety towards their parents has long been unimpeachably established. Previous discussions, moreover, will have prepared us to learn that the death-wish against parents dates back to earliest childhood.

[21] This supposition is confirmed with a certainty beyond all doubt in the case of psychoneurotics when they are subjected to analysis. We learn from them that a child's sexual wishes—if in their embryonic stage they deserve to be so described—awaken very early, and that a girl's first affection is for her father [11] and a boy's first childish desires are for his mother. Ac-

---

[10] [*Footnote added* 1909:] Or so he is reported to have done according to some myths. According to others, emasculation was only carried out by Kronos on his father Uranus. [This passage is discussed in Chapter X (3) of *The Psychopathology of Everyday Life* (Freud, 1901*b*).] For the mythological significance of this theme, cf. Rank, 1909, [*added* 1914:] and Rank, 1912*c*, Chapter IX, Section 2.—[These sentences in the text are, of course, an early hint at the line of thought developed later by Freud in his *Totem and Taboo* (1912–13).]

[11] [Freud's views on this point were later modified. Cf. Freud, 1925*j* and 1931*b*.]

cordingly, the father becomes a disturbing rival to the boy and the mother to the girl; and I have already shown in the case of brothers and sisters how easily such feelings can lead to a death-wish. The parents too give evidence as a rule of sexual partiality: a natural predilection usually sees to it that a man tends to spoil his little daughters, while his wife takes her sons' part; though both of them, where their judgment is not disturbed by the magic of sex, keep a strict eye upon their children's education. The child is very well aware of this partiality and turns against that one of his parents who is opposed to showing it. Being loved by an adult does not merely bring a child the satisfaction of a special need; it also means that he will get what he wants in every other respect as well. Thus he will be following his own sexual instinct and at the same time giving fresh strength to the inclination shown by his parents if his choice between them falls in with theirs.

[22] The signs of these infantile preferences are for the most part overlooked; yet some of them are to be observed even after the first years of childhood. An eight-year-old girl of my acquaintance, if her mother is called away from the table, makes use of the occasion to proclaim herself her successor: 'I'm going to be Mummy now. Do you want some more greens, Karl? Well, help yourself, then!' and so on. A particularly gifted and lively girl of four, in whom this piece of child psychology is especially transparent, declared quite openly: 'Mummy can go away now. Then Daddy must marry me and I'll be his wife.' Such a wish occurring in a child is not in the least inconsistent with her being tenderly attached to her mother. If a little boy is allowed to sleep beside his mother when his father is away from home, but has to go back to the nursery and to someone of whom he is far less fond as soon as his father returns, he may easily begin to form a wish that his father should *always* be away, so that he himself could keep his place beside his dear, lovely Mummy. One obvious way of attaining this wish would be if his father were dead; for the child has learnt one thing by experience—namely that 'dead' people, such as Granddaddy, are always away and never come back.

[23] Though observations of this kind on small children fit in perfectly with the interpretation I have proposed, they do not carry such complete conviction as is forced upon the physician by psycho-analyses of adult neurotics. In the latter case dreams of the sort we are considering are introduced into the analysis in such a context that it is impossible to avoid interpreting them as *wishful* dreams.

[24] One day one of my women patients was in a distressed and tearful mood. 'I don't want ever to see my relations again,' she said, 'they must think me horrible.' She then went on, with almost no transition, to say that she remembered a dream, though of course she had no idea what it meant. When she was four years old she had a dream that *a lynx or fox* [12] *was walking on the roof; then something had fallen down or she had fallen down;*

[12] [The German names for these animals are very much alike: '*Luchs*' and '*Fuchs*'.]

and then her mother was carried out of the house dead—and she wept bitterly. I told her that this dream must mean that when she was a child she had wished she could see her mother dead, and that it must be on account of the dream that she felt her relations must think her horrible. I had scarcely said this when she produced some material which threw light on the dream. 'Lynx-eye' was a term of abuse that had been thrown at her by a street-urchin when she was a very small child. When she was three years old, a tile off the roof had fallen on her mother's head and made it bleed violently.

[25] I once had an opportunity of making a detailed study of a young woman who passed through a variety of psychical conditions. Her illness began with a state of confusional excitement during which she displayed a quite special aversion to her mother, hitting and abusing her whenever she came near her bed, while at the same period she was docile and affectionate towards a sister who was many years her senior. This was followed by a state in which she was lucid but somewhat apathetic and suffered from badly disturbed sleep. It was during this phase that I began treating her and analysing her dreams. An immense number of these dreams were concerned, with a greater or less degree of disguise, with the death of her mother: at one time she would be attending an old woman's funeral, at another she and her sister would be sitting at table dressed in mourning. There could be no question as to the meaning of these dreams. As her condition improved still further, hysterical phobias developed. The most tormenting of these was a fear that something might have happened to her mother. She was obliged to hurry home, wherever she might be, to convince herself that her mother was still alive. This case, taken in conjunction with what I had learnt from other sources, was highly instructive: it exhibited, translated as it were into different languages, the various ways in which the psychical apparatus reacted to one and the same exciting idea. In the confusional state, in which, as I believe, the second psychical agency was overwhelmed by the normally suppressed first one, her unconscious hostility to her mother found a powerful *motor* expression. When the calmer condition set in, when the rebellion was suppressed and the domination of the censorship re-established, the only region left open in which her hostility could realize the wish for her mother's death was that of dreaming. When a normal state was still more firmly established, it led to the production of her exaggerated worry about her mother as a hysterical counter-reaction and defensive phenomenon. In view of this it is no longer hard to understand why hysterical girls are so often attached to their mothers with such exaggerated affection.

[26] On another occasion I had an opportunity of obtaining a deep insight into the unconscious mind of a young man whose life was made almost impossible by an obsessional neurosis. He was unable to go out into the street because he was tortured by the fear that he would kill everyone he met. He spent his days in preparing his alibi in case he might be charged

with one of the murders committed in the town. It is unnecessary to add that he was a man of equally high morals and education. The analysis (which, incidentally, led to his recovery) showed that the basis of this distressing obsession was an impulse to murder his somewhat over-severe father. This impulse, to his astonishment, had been consciously expressed when he was seven years old, but it had, of course, originated much earlier in his childhood. After his father's painful illness and death, the patient's obsessional self-reproaches appeared—he was in his thirty-first year at the time—taking the shape of a phobia transferred on to strangers. A person, he felt, who was capable of wanting to push his own father over a precipice from the top of a mountain was not to be trusted to respect the lives of those less closely related to him; he was quite right to shut himself up in his room.

[27] In my experience, which is already extensive, the chief part in the mental lives of all children who later become psychoneurotics is played by their parents. Being in love with the one parent and hating the other are among the essential constituents of the stock of psychical impulses which is formed at that time and which is of such importance in determining the symptoms of the later neurosis. It is not my belief, however, that psychoneurotics differ sharply in this respect from other human beings who remain normal—that they are able, that is, to create something absolutely new and peculiar to themselves. It is far more probable—and this is confirmed by occasional observations on normal children—that they are only distinguished by exhibiting on a magnified scale feelings of love and hatred to their parents which occur less obviously and less intensely in the minds of most children.

[28] This discovery is confirmed by a legend that has come down to us from classical antiquity: a legend whose profound and universal power to move can only be understood if the hypothesis I have put forward in regard to the psychology of children has an equally universal validity. What I have in mind is the legend of King Oedipus and Sophocles' drama which bears his name.

[29] Oedipus, son of Laïus, King of Thebes, and of Jocasta, was exposed as an infant because an oracle had warned Laïus that the still unborn child would be his father's murderer. The child was rescued, and grew up as a prince in an alien court, until, in doubts as to his origin, he too questioned the oracle and was warned to avoid his home since he was destined to murder his father and take his mother in marriage. On the road leading away from what he believed was his home, he met King Laïus and slew him in a sudden quarrel. He came next to Thebes and solved the riddle set him by the Sphinx who barred his way. Out of gratitude the Thebans made him their king and gave him Jocasta's hand in marriage. He reigned long in peace and honour, and she who, unknown to him, was his mother bore him two sons and two daughters. Then at last a plague broke out and the Thebans made enquiry once more of the oracle. It is at this point that

Sophocles' tragedy opens. The messengers bring back the reply that the plague will cease when the murderer of Laïus has been driven from the land.

> But he, where is he? Where shall now be read
> The fading record of this ancient guilt? [13]

The action of the play consists in nothing other than the process of revealing, with cunning delays and ever-mounting excitement—a process that can be likened to the work of a psycho-analysis—that Oedipus himself is the murderer of Laïus, but further that he is the son of the murdered man and of Jocasta. Appalled at the abomination which he has unwittingly perpetrated, Oedipus blinds himself and forsakes his home. The oracle has been fulfilled.

[30] *Oedipus Rex* is what is known as a tragedy of destiny. Its tragic effect is said to lie in the contrast between the supreme will of the gods and the vain attempts of mankind to escape the evil that threatens them. The lesson which, it is said, the deeply moved spectator should learn from the tragedy is submission to the divine will and realization of his own impotence. Modern dramatists have accordingly tried to achieve a similar tragic effect by weaving the same contrast into a plot invented by themselves. But the spectators have looked on unmoved while a curse or an oracle was fulfilled in spite of all the efforts of some innocent man: later tragedies of destiny have failed in their effect.

[31] If *Oedipus Rex* moves a modern audience no less than it did the contemporary Greek one, the explanation can only be that its effect does not lie in the contrast between destiny and human will, but is to be looked for in the particular nature of the material on which that contrast is exemplified. There must be something which makes a voice within us ready to recognize the compelling force of destiny in the *Oedipus,* while we can dismiss as merely arbitrary such dispositions as are laid down in [Grillparzer's] *Die Ahnfrau* or other modern tragedies of destiny. And a factor of this kind is in fact involved in the story of King Oedipus. His destiny moves us only because it might have been ours—because the oracle laid the same curse upon us before our birth as upon him. It is the fate of all of us, perhaps, to direct our first sexual impulse towards our mother and our first hatred and our first murderous wish against our father. Our dreams convince us that that is so. King Oedipus, who slew his father Laïus and married his mother Jocasta, merely shows us the fulfilment of our own childhood wishes. But, more fortunate than he, we have meanwhile succeeded, in so far as we have not become psychoneurotics, in detaching our sexual impulses from our mothers and in forgetting our jealousy of our fathers. Here is one in whom these primaeval wishes of our childhood have been fulfilled, and we shrink back from him with the whole force of the repression by which those wishes have since that time been held down within

---

[13] [Lewis Campbell's translation (1883), line 108 f.]

us. While the poet, as he unravels the past, brings to light the guilt of Oedipus, he is at the same time compelling us to recognize our own inner minds, in which those same impulses, though suppressed, are still to be found. The contrast with which the closing Chorus leaves us confronted—

> . . . Fix on Oedipus your eyes,
> Who resolved the dark enigma, noblest champion and most wise.
> Like a star his envied fortune mounted beaming far and wide:
> Now he sinks in seas of anguish, whelmed beneath a raging tide . . .[14]

—strikes as a warning at ourselves and our pride, at us who since our childhood have grown so wise and so mighty in our own eyes. Like Oedipus, we live in ignorance of these wishes, repugnant to morality, which have been forced upon us by Nature, and after their revelation we may all of us well seek to close our eyes to the scenes of our childhood.[15]

[32]   There is an unmistakable indication in the text of Sophocles' tragedy itself that the legend of Oedipus sprang from some primaeval dream-material which had as its content the distressing disturbance of a child's relation to his parents owing to the first stirrings of sexuality. At a point when Oedipus, though he is not yet enlightened, has begun to feel troubled by his recollection of the oracle, Jocasta consoles him by referring to a dream which many people dream, though, as she thinks, it has no meaning:

> Many a man ere now in dreams hath lain
> With her who bare him. He hath least annoy
> Who with such omens troubleth not his mind.[16]

To-day, just as then, many men dream of having sexual relations with their mothers, and speak of the fact with indignation and astonishment. It is clearly the key to the tragedy and the complement to the dream of the dreamer's father being dead. The story of Oedipus is the reaction of the imagination to these two typical dreams. And just as these dreams, when dreamt by adults, are accompanied by feelings of repulsion, so too the

---

[14] [Lewis Campbell's translation, line 1524 ff.]

[15] [*Footnote added* 1914:] None of the findings of psycho-analytic research has provoked such embittered denials, such fierce opposition—or such amusing contortions—on the part of critics as this indication of the childhood impulses towards incest which persist in the unconscious. An attempt has even been made recently to make out, in the face of all experience, that the incest should only be taken as 'symbolic.'—Ferenczi (1912) has proposed an ingenious 'over-interpretation' of the Oedipus myth, based on a passage in one of Schopenhauer's letters.—[*Added* 1919:] Later studies have shown that the 'Oedipus complex' which was touched upon for the first time in the above paragraphs in the *Interpretation of Dreams*, throws a light of undreamt-of importance on the history of the human race and the evolution of religion and morality. (See my *Totem and Taboo*, 1912-13 [Essay IV].)—[Actually the gist of this discussion of the Oedipus complex and of the *Oedipus Rex*, as well as of what follows on the subject of *Hamlet*, had already been put forward by Freud in a letter to Fliess as early as October 15th, 1897. (See Freud, 1950*a*, Letter 71.) A still earlier hint at the discovery of the Oedipus complex was included in a letter of May 31st, 1897. (Ibid., Draft N.)—The actual term 'Oedipus complex' seems to have been first used by Freud in his published writings in the first of his 'Contributions to the Psychology of Love' (1910*h*).]

[16] [Lewis Campbell's translation, line 982 ff.]

legend must include horror and self-punishment. Its further modification originates once again in a misconceived secondary revision of the material, which has sought to exploit it for theological purposes. The attempt to harmonize divine omnipotence with human responsibility must naturally fail in connection with this subject-matter just as with any other.

COMMENT AND QUESTIONS

I. Freud limits his discussion to dreams of the death of relatives in which the dreamer feels grief. Why does he exclude those in which the dreamer is unaffected by grief?

II. On what particular points does Freud anticipate opposition from his readers? How does he try to meet their objections?

III. With what kind of evidence does he support the theory that children wish for the death of brothers and sisters? With what kind of evidence does he support the theory that children entertain death-wishes toward their parents?

IV. How do the legend of Oedipus and the power of Sophocles' play seem to Freud to confirm his hypothesis?

V. Do any parts of Freud's theory and reasoning strike you as being common sense, borne out by your own experience or observation? Do any parts seem far-fetched or unconvincing? Explain.

WINSTON CHURCHILL

Dunkirk

The evacuation of Dunkirk, regarded by military experts as a miracle of World War II, has become a symbol of victory in defeat. Badly defeated in May, 1940, by the Germans in Belgium, the British and French armies fell back to Dunkirk, the only port on the French coast still in Allied hands. A fleet of rescue boats—destroyers, ferries, tugboats, fishing smacks—every boat available—set out from the British coast across the channel and, shuttling back and forth under heavy German attack, rescued 335,000 men from the beaches of Dunkirk. On June 4, 1940, Winston Churchill, Prime Minister of Great Britain, gave the following account of the evacuation to the House of Commons. His address is an informative report, an evaluation, and above all a piece of persuasion designed to inspire courage and strength for the hard days ahead.

[1] From the moment that the French defenses at Sedan and on the Meuse were broken at the end of the second week of May, only a rapid retreat

to Amiens and the south could have saved the British and French Armies who had entered Belgium at the appeal of the Belgian King; but this strategic fact was not immediately realized. The French High Command hoped they would be able to close the gap, and the Armies of the north were under their orders. Moreover, a retirement of this kind would have involved almost certainly the destruction of the fine Belgian Army of over 20 divisions and the abandonment of the whole of Belgium. Therefore, when the force and scope of the German penetration were realized and when a new French Generalissimo, General Weygand, assumed command in place of General Gamelin, an effort was made by the French and British Armies in Belgium to keep on holding the right hand of the Belgians and to give their own right hand to a newly created French Army which was to have advanced across the Somme in great strength to grasp it.

[2] However, the German eruption swept like a sharp scythe around the right and rear of the Armies of the north. Eight or nine armored divisions, each of about four hundred armored vehicles of different kinds, but carefully assorted to be complementary and divisible into small self-contained units, cut off all communications between us and the main French Armies. It severed our own communications for food and ammunition, which ran first to Amiens and afterwards through Abbeville, and it shore its way up the coast to Boulogne and Calais, and almost to Dunkirk. Behind this armored and mechanized onslaught came a number of German divisions in lorries, and behind them again there plodded comparatively slowly the dull brute mass of the ordinary German Army and German people, always so ready to be led to the trampling down in other lands of liberties and comforts which they have never known in their own.

[3] I have said this armored scythe-stroke almost reached Dunkirk—almost but not quite. Boulogne and Calais were the scenes of desperate fighting. The Guards defended Boulogne for a while and were then withdrawn by orders from this country. The Rifle Brigade, the 60th Rifles, and the Queen Victoria's Rifles, with a battalion of British tanks and a thousand Frenchmen, in all about four thousand strong, defended Calais to the last. The British Brigadier was given an hour to surrender. He spurned the offer, and four days of intense street fighting passed before silence reigned over Calais, which marked the end of a memorable resistance. Only thirty unwounded survivors were brought off by the Navy, and we do not know the fate of their comrades. Their sacrifice, however, was not in vain. At least two armored divisions, which otherwise would have been turned against the British Expeditionary Force, had to be sent to overcome them. They have added another page to the glories of the light divisions, and the time gained enabled the Graveline water lines to be flooded and to be held by the French troops.

[4] Thus it was that the port of Dunkirk was kept open. When it was found impossible for the Armies of the north to reopen their communications to Amiens with the main French Armies, only one choice remained.

It seemed, indeed, forlorn. The Belgian, British and French Armies were almost surrounded. Their sole line of retreat was to a single port and to its neighboring beaches. They were pressed on every side by heavy attacks and far outnumbered in the air.

[5] When, a week ago today, I asked the House to fix this afternoon as the occasion for a statement, I feared it would be my hard lot to announce the greatest military disaster in our long history. I thought—and some good judges agreed with me—that perhaps 20,000 or 30,000 men might be re-embarked. But it certainly seemed that the whole of the French First Army and the whole of the British Expeditionary Force north of the Amiens-Abbeville gap would be broken up in the open field or else would have to capitulate for lack of food and ammunition. These were the hard and heavy tidings for which I called upon the House and the nation to prepare themselves a week ago. The whole root and core and brain of the British Army, on which and around which we were later to build, and are to build, the great British Armies in the later years of the war, seemed about to perish upon the field or to be led into an ignominious and starving captivity.

[6] That was the prospect of a week ago. But another blow which might well have proved final was yet to fall upon us. The King of the Belgians had called upon us to come to his aid. Had not this Ruler and his Government severed themselves from the Allies, who rescued their country from extinction in the late war, and had they not sought refuge in what has proved to be a fatal neutrality, the French and British Armies might well at the outset have saved not only Belgium but perhaps even Poland. Yet at the last moment, when Belgium was already invaded, King Leopold called upon us to come to his aid, and even at the last moment we came. He and his brave, efficient Army, nearly half a million strong, guarded our left flank and thus kept open our only line of retreat to the sea. Suddenly, without prior consultation, with the least possible notice, without the advice of his Ministers and upon his own personal act, he sent a plenipotentiary to the German Command, surrendered his Army, and exposed our whole flank and means of retreat.

[7] I asked the House a week ago to suspend its judgment because the facts were not clear, but I do not feel that any reason now exists why we should not form our own opinions upon this pitiful episode. The surrender of the Belgian Army compelled the British at the shortest notice to cover a flank to the sea more than 30 miles in length. Otherwise all would have been cut off, and all would have shared the fate to which King Leopold had condemned the finest Army his country had ever formed. So in doing this and in exposing this flank, as anyone who followed the operations on the map will see, contact was lost between the British and two out of the three corps forming the First French Army, who were still farther from the coast than we were, and it seemed impossible that any large number of Allied troops could reach the coast.

[8] The enemy attacked on all sides with great strength and fierceness,

and their main power, the power of their far more numerous Air Force, was thrown into battle or else concentrated upon Dunkirk and the beaches. Pressing in upon the narrow exit, both from the east and from the west, the enemy began to fire with cannon upon the beaches by which alone the shipping could approach or depart. They sowed magnetic mines in the channels and seas; they sent repeated waves of hostile aircraft, sometimes more than a hundred strong in one formation, to cast their bombs upon the single pier that remained, and upon the sand dunes upon which the troops had their eyes for shelter. Their U-boats, one of which was sunk, and their motor launches took their toll of the vast traffic which now began. For four or five days an intense struggle reigned. All their armored divisions—or what was left of them—together with great masses of infantry and artillery, hurled themselves in vain upon the ever-narrowing, ever-contracting appendix within which the British and French Armies fought.

[9] Meanwhile, the Royal Navy, with the willing help of countless merchant seamen, strained every nerve to embark the British and Allied troops; 220 light warships and 650 other vessels were engaged. They had to operate upon the difficult coast, often in adverse weather, under an almost ceaseless hail of bombs and an increasing concentration of artillery fire. Nor were the seas, as I have said, themselves free from mines and torpedoes. It was in conditions such as these that our men carried on, with little or no rest, for days and nights on end, making trip after trip across the dangerous waters, bringing with them always men whom they had rescued. The numbers they have brought back are the measure of their devotion and their courage. The hospital ships, which brought off many thousands of British and French wounded, being so plainly marked were a special target for Nazi bombs, but the men and women on board never faltered in their duty.

[10] Meanwhile, the Royal Air Force, which had already been intervening in the battle, so far as its range would allow, from home bases, now used part of its main metropolitan fighter strength, and struck at the German bombers and at the fighters which in large numbers protected them. This struggle was protracted and fierce. Suddenly the scene has cleared, the crash and thunder has for the moment—but only for the moment—died away. A miracle of deliverance, achieved by valor, by perseverance, by perfect discipline, by faultless service, by resource, by skill, by unconquerable fidelity, is manifest to us all. The enemy was hurled back by the retreating British and French troops. He was so roughly handled that he did not hurry their departure seriously. The Royal Air Force engaged the main strength of the German Air Force, and inflicted upon them losses of at least four to one; and the Navy, using nearly a thousand ships of all kinds, carried over 335,000 men, French and British, out of the jaws of death and shame, to their native land and to the tasks which lie immediately ahead. We must be very careful not to assign to this deliverance the attributes of a victory. Wars are not won by evacuations. But there was a victory inside this deliverance, which should be noted. It was gained by the Air Force. Many of our

soldiers coming back have not seen the Air Force at work; they saw only the bombers which escaped its protective attack. They underrate its achievements. I have heard much talk of this; that is why I go out of my way to say this. I will tell you about it.

[11] This was a great trial of strength between the British and German Air Forces. Can you conceive a greater objective for the Germans in the air than to make evacuation from these beaches impossible, and to sink all these ships which were displayed, almost to the extent of thousands? Could there have been an objective of greater military importance and significance for the whole purpose of the war than this? They tried hard, and they were beaten back; they were frustrated in their task. We got the Army away; and they have paid four-fold for any losses which they have inflicted. Very large formations of German aeroplanes—and we know that they are a very brave race—have turned on several occasions from the attack of one-quarter of their number of the Royal Air Force, and have dispersed in different directions. Twelve aeroplanes have been hunted by two. One aeroplane was driven into the water and cast away by the mere charge of a British aeroplane, which had no more ammunition. All of our types—the Hurricane, the Spitfire, and the new Defiant—and all our pilots have been vindicated as superior to what they have at present to face.

[12] When we consider how much greater would be our advantage in defending the air above this Island against an overseas attack, I must say that I find in these facts a sure basis upon which practical and reassuring thoughts may rest. I will pay my tribute to these young airmen. The great French Army was very largely, for the time being, cast back and disturbed by the onrush of a few thousands of armored vehicles. May it not also be that the cause of civilization itself will be defended by the skill and devotion of a few thousand airmen? There never has been, I suppose, in all the world, in all the history of war, such an opportunity for youth. The Knights of the Round Table, the Crusaders, all fall back into the past—not only distant but prosaic; these young men, going forth every morn to guard their native land and all that we stand for, holding in their hands these instruments of colossal and shattering power, of whom it may be said that

> "Every morn brought forth a noble chance
> And every chance brought forth a noble knight,"

deserve our gratitude, as do all of the brave men who, in so many ways and on so many occasions, are ready, and continue ready, to give life and all for their native land.

[13] I return to the Army. In the long series of very fierce battles, now on this front, now on that, fighting on three fronts at once, battles fought by two or three divisions against an equal or somewhat larger number of the enemy, and fought fiercely on some of the old grounds that so many of us knew so well—in these battles our losses in men have exceeded 30,000 killed, wounded, and missing. I take occasion to express the sympathy of

the House to all who have suffered bereavement or who are still anxious. The President of the Board of Trade is not here today. His son has been killed, and many in the House have felt the pangs of affliction in the sharpest form. But I will say this about the missing: We have had a large number of wounded come home safely to this country, but I would say about the missing that there may be very many reported missing who will come back home, some day, in one way or another. In the confusion of this fight it is inevitable that many have been left in positions where honor required no further resistance from them.

[14] Against this loss of over 30,000 men, we can set a far heavier loss certainly inflicted upon the enemy. But our losses in material are enormous. We have perhaps lost one-third of the men we lost in the opening days of the battle of 21st March, 1918, but we have lost nearly as many guns—nearly one thousand—and all our transport, all the armored vehicles that were with the Army in the north. This loss will impose a further delay on the expansion of our military strength. That expansion had not been proceeding as fast as we had hoped. The best of all we had to give had gone to the British Expeditionary Force, and although they had not the numbers of tanks and some articles of equipment which were desirable, they were a very well and finely equipped Army. They had the first-fruits of all that our industry had to give, and that is gone. And now here is this further delay. How long it will be, how long it will last, depends upon the exertions which we make in this Island. An effort the like of which has never been seen in our records is now being made. Work is proceeding everywhere, night and day, Sundays and week days. Capital and Labor have cast aside their interests, rights, and customs and put them into the common stock. Already the flow of munitions has leaped forward. There is no reason why we should not in a few months overtake the sudden and serious loss that has come upon us, without retarding the development of our general program.

[15] Nevertheless, our thankfulness at the escape of our Army and so many men, whose loved ones have passed through an agonizing week, must not blind us to the fact that what has happened in France and Belgium is a colossal military disaster. The French Army has been weakened, the Belgian Army has been lost, a large part of those fortified lines upon which so much faith had been reposed is gone, many valuable mining districts and factories have passed into the enemy's possession, the whole of the Channel ports are in his hands, with all the tragic consequences that follow from that, and we must expect another blow to be struck almost immediately at us or at France. We are told that Herr Hitler has a plan for invading the British Isles. This has often been thought of before. When Napoleon lay at Boulogne for a year with his flat-bottomed boats and his Grand Army, he was told by someone, "There are bitter weeds in England." There are certainly a great many more of them since the British Expeditionary Force returned.

[16] The whole question of home defense against invasion is, of course,

powerfully affected by the fact that we have for the time being in this Island incomparably more powerful military forces than we have ever had at any moment in this war or the last. But this will not continue. We shall not be content with a defensive war. We have our duty to our Ally. We have to reconstitute and build up the British Expeditionary Force, once again, under its gallant Commander-in-Chief, Lord Gort. All this is in train; but in the interval we must put our defenses in this Island into such a high state of organization that the fewest possible numbers will be required to give effective security and that the largest possible potential offensive effort may be realized. On this we are now engaged. It will be very convenient, if it be the desire of the House, to enter upon this subject in a secret Session. Not that the Government would necessarily be able to reveal in very great detail military secrets, but we like to have our discussions free, without the restraint imposed by the fact that they will be read the next day by the enemy; and the Government would benefit by views freely expressed in all parts of the House by Members with their knowledge of so many different parts of the country. I understand that some request is to be made upon this subject, which will be readily acceded to by His Majesty's Government.

[17] We have found it necessary to take measures of increasing stringency, not only against enemy aliens and suspicious characters of other nationalities, but also against British subjects who may become a danger or a nuisance should the war be transported to the United Kingdom. I know there are a great many people affected by the orders which we have made who are the passionate enemies of Nazi Germany. I am very sorry for them, but we cannot, at the present time and under the present stress, draw all the distinctions which we should like to do. If parachute landings were attempted and fierce fighting attendant upon them followed, these unfortunate people would be far better out of the way, for their own sakes as well as for ours. There is, however, another class, for which I feel not the slightest sympathy. Parliament has given us the powers to put down Fifth Column activities with a strong hand, and we shall use those powers, subject to the supervision and correction of the House, without the slightest hesitation until we are satisfied, and more than satisfied, that this malignancy in our midst has been effectively stamped out.

[18] Turning once again, and this time more generally, to the question of invasion, I would observe that there has never been a period in all these long centuries of which we boast when an absolute guarantee against invasion, still less against serious raids, could have been given to our people. In the days of Napoleon the same wind which would have carried his transports across the Channel might have driven away the blockading fleet. There was always the chance, and it is that chance which has excited and befooled the imaginations of many Continental tyrants. Many are the tales that are told. We are assured that novel methods will be adopted, and when we see the originality of malice, the ingenuity of aggression, which our enemy displays, we may certainly prepare ourselves for every kind of novel stratagem

and every kind of brutal and treacherous maneuver. I think that no idea is so outlandish that it should not be considered and viewed with a searching, but at the same time, I hope, with a steady eye. We must never forget the solid assurances of sea power and those which belong to air power if it can be locally exercised.

[19] I have, myself, full confidence that if all do their duty, if nothing is neglected, and if the best arrangements are made, as they are being made, we shall prove ourselves once again able to defend our Island home, to ride out the storm of war, and to outlive the menace of tyranny, if necessary for years, if necessary alone. At any rate, that is what we are going to try to do. That is the resolve of His Majesty's Government—every man of them. That is the will of Parliament and the nation. The British Empire and the French Republic, linked together in their cause and in their need, will defend to the death their native soil, aiding each other like good comrades to the utmost of their strength. Even though large tracts of Europe and many old and famous States have fallen or may fall into the grip of the Gestapo and all the odious apparatus of Nazi rule, we shall not flag or fail. We shall go on to the end, we shall fight in France, we shall fight on the seas and oceans, we shall fight with growing confidence and growing strength in the air, we shall defend our Island, whatever the cost may be, we shall fight on the beaches, we shall fight on the landing grounds, we shall fight in the fields and in the streets, we shall fight in the hills; we shall never surrender, and even if, which I do not for a moment believe, this Island or a large part of it were subjugated and starving, then our Empire beyond the seas, armed and guarded by the British Fleet, would carry on the struggle, until, in God's good time, the New World, with all its power and might, steps forth to the rescue and the liberation of the old.

COMMENT AND QUESTIONS

I. The opening paragraphs of "Dunkirk" are chiefly informative, but with elements of evaluation and persuasion. Where, in the first three paragraphs, does Churchill subtly place blame and award praise? Would a French statesman have given exactly the same account? How does Churchill treat the King of the Belgians (in paragraphs 6 and 7), and why? Paragraph 5 is not essential to the report of events; what purpose does this paragraph serve?

II. Paragraphs 8–10 are interesting examples of dramatic narration. What techniques does Churchill use to make the reported action intense and vivid?

III. Summarize Churchill's evaluation of the events which he is reporting to the House of Commons. What is his attitude toward the possible invasion of England?

IV. What passages do you think would have been most effective in arousing zeal and determination for carrying on the war effort? To what emotions do these passages appeal?

V. Churchill's prose, though more formal and rhetorical than most modern expression, is excellent, and worth study for its traits of style. The last paragraph of "Dunkirk" is particularly worth analysis. Notice the length, structure, and rhythm of sentences, and, especially in the famous long last sentence, the variation within the pattern of parallelism and repetition. To what different groups is this paragraph addressed? To what emotions does it appeal?

VI. Earlier in this book we have cited the conclusion of "Dunkirk" as an example of honest, deeply-felt expression of feeling. The story is told that Churchill was forced by the wild cheering in the House of Commons to pause in the delivery of his conclusion, and that, under cover of the uproar, he added, "And beat the **** over the head with bottles. That's all we've got." If this story is true, does it raise a question about the sincerity of the prepared address? Explain.

READINGS   SECTION 4

History and Biography: Information and Evaluation

CARL L. BECKER

Everyman His Own Historian*

In the following essay, published in *The American Historical Review* in 1932, a noted historian addresses other historians on the meaning of history. As the title may indicate, however, Mr. Becker is not concerned with history simply as an academic subject, but with the kind of historical knowledge which man-the-individual and men-in-society need to orient themselves in a today that is necessarily related to yesterday and to tomorrow. If the first duty of the historian is to establish the facts, his main function, Mr. Becker believes, is to evaluate and interpret those facts in terms meaningful to the world in which he lives. For a further note on Carl L. Becker, see page 747.

[1]   Once upon a time, long long ago, I learned how to reduce a fraction to its lowest terms. Whether I could still perform that operation is uncertain; but the discipline involved in early training had its uses, since it taught me that in order to understand the essential nature of anything it is well to strip it of all superficial and irrelevant accretions—in short, to reduce it to its lowest terms. That operation I now venture, with some apprehension and all due apologies, to perform on the subject of history.

[2]   I ought first of all to explain that when I use the term history I mean knowledge of history. No doubt throughout all past time there actually occurred a series of events which, whether we know what it was or not, constitutes history in some ultimate sense. Nevertheless, much the greater part

---
* Reprinted from *The American Historical Review*, 1932, by permission.

of these events we can know nothing about, not even that they occurred; many of them we can know only imperfectly; and even the few events that we think we know for sure we can never be absolutely certain of, since we can never revive them, never observe or test them directly. The event itself once occurred, but as an actual event it has disappeared; so that in dealing with it the only objective reality we can observe or test is some material trace which the event has left—usually a written document. With these traces of vanished events, these documents, we must be content since they are all we have; from them we infer what the event was, we affirm that it is a fact that the event was so and so. We do not say "Lincoln is assassinated"; we say "it is a fact that Lincoln was assassinated." The event *was,* but is no longer; it is only the affirmed fact about the event that *is,* that persists, and will persist until we discover that our affirmation is wrong or inadequate. Let us then admit that there are two histories: the actual series of events that once occurred; and the ideal series that we affirm and hold in memory. The first is absolute and unchanged—it was what it was whatever we do or say about it; the second is relative, always changing in response to the increase or refinement of knowledge. The two series correspond more or less; it is our aim to make the correspondence as exact as possible; but the actual series of events exists for us only in terms of the ideal series which we affirm and hold in memory. This is why I am forced to identify history with knowledge of history. For all practical purposes history is, for us and for the time being, what we know it to be.

[3] It is history in this sense that I wish to reduce to its lowest terms. In order to do that I need a very simple definition. I once read that "History is the knowledge of events that have occurred in the past." That is a simple definition, but not simple enough. It contains three words that require examination. The first is knowledge. Knowledge is a formidable word. I always think of knowledge as something that is stored up in the *Encyclopaedia Britannica* or the *Summa Theologica;* something difficult to acquire, something at all events that I have not. Resenting a definition that denies me the title of historian, I therefore ask what is most essential to knowledge. Well, memory, I should think (and I mean memory in the broad sense, the memory of events inferred as well as the memory of events observed); other things are necessary too, but memory is fundamental: without memory no knowledge. So our definition becomes, "History is the memory of events that have occurred in the past." But events—the word carries an implication of something grand, like the taking of the Bastille or the Spanish-American War. An occurrence need not be spectacular to be an event. If I drive a motor car down the crooked streets of Ithaca, that is an event—something done; if the traffic cop bawls me out, that is an event—something said; if I have evil thoughts of him for so doing, that is an event—something thought. In truth anything done, said, or thought is an event, important or not as may turn out. But since we do not ordinarily speak without thinking, at least in some rudimentary way, and since the psychologists tell

us that we cannot think without speaking, or at least not without having anticipatory vibrations in the larynx, we may well combine thought events and speech events under one term; and so our definition becomes, "History is the memory of things said and done in the past." But the past—the word is both misleading and unnecessary: misleading, because the past, used in connection with history, seems to imply the distant past, as if history ceased before we were born; unnecessary, because after all everything said or done is already in the past as soon as it is said or done. Therefore I will omit that word, and our definition becomes, "History is the memory of things said and done." This is a definition that reduces history to its lowest terms, and yet includes everything that is essential to understanding what it really is.

[4] If the essence of history is the memory of things said and done, then it is obvious that every normal person, Mr. Everyman, knows some history. Of course we do what we can to conceal this invidious truth. Assuming a professional manner, we say that so and so knows no history, when we mean no more than that he failed to pass the examinations set for a higher degree; and simple-minded persons, undergraduates and others, taken in by academic classifications of knowledge, think they know no history because they have never taken a course in history in college, or have never read Gibbon's *Decline and Fall of the Roman Empire*. No doubt the academic convention has its uses, but it is one of the superficial accretions that must be stripped off if we would understand history reduced to its lowest terms. Mr. Everyman, as well as you and I, remembers things said and done, and must do so at every waking moment. Suppose Mr. Everyman to have awakened this morning unable to remember anything said or done. He would be a lost soul indeed. This has happened, this sudden loss of all historical knowledge. But normally it does not happen. Normally the memory of Mr. Everyman, when he awakens in the morning, reaches out into the country of the past and of distant places and instantaneously recreates his little world of endeavor, pulls together as it were things said and done in his yesterdays, and coördinates them with his present perceptions and with things to be said and done in his tomorrows. Without this historical knowledge, this memory of things said and done, his today would be aimless and his tomorrow without significance.

[5] Since we are concerned with history in its lowest terms, we will suppose that Mr. Everyman is not a professor of history, but just an ordinary citizen without excess knowledge. Not having a lecture to prepare, his memory of things said and done, when he awakened this morning, presumably did not drag into consciousness any events connected with the Liman von Sanders mission or the Pseudo-Isidorian Decretals; it presumably dragged into consciousness an image of things said and done yesterday in the office, the highly significant fact that General Motors has dropped three points, a conference arranged for ten o'clock in the morning, a promise to play nine holes at four-thirty in the afternoon, and other historical events of similar import. Mr. Everyman knows more history than this, but at the

moment of awakening this is sufficient: memory of things said and done, history functioning, at seven-thirty in the morning, in its very lowest terms, has effectively oriented Mr. Everyman in his little world of endeavor.

[6] Yet not quite effectively after all perhaps; for unaided memory is notoriously fickle; and it may happen that Mr. Everyman, as he drinks his coffee, is uneasily aware of something said or done that he fails now to recall. A common enough occurrence, as we all know to our sorrow—this remembering, not the historical event, but only that there was an event which we ought to remember but can not. This is Mr. Everyman's difficulty, a bit of history lies dead and inert in the sources, unable to do any work for Mr. Everyman because his memory refuses to bring it alive in consciousness. What then does Mr. Everyman do? He does what any historian would do: he does a bit of historical research in the sources. From his little Private Record Office (I mean his vest pocket) he takes a book in MS., volume XXXV, it may be, and turns to page 23, and there he reads: "December 29, pay Smith's coal bill, 20 tons, $1017.20." Instantaneously a series of historical events comes to life in Mr. Everyman's mind. He has an image of himself ordering twenty tons of coal from Smith last summer, of Smith's wagons driving up to his house, and of the precious coal sliding dustily through the cellar window. Historical events, these are, not so important as the forging of the Isidorian Decretals, but still important to Mr. Everyman: historical events which he was not present to observe, but which, by an artificial extension of memory, he can form a clear picture of, because he has done a little original research in the manuscripts preserved in his Private Record Office.

[7] The picture Mr. Everyman forms of Smith's wagons delivering the coal at his house is a picture of things said and done in the past. But it does not stand alone, it is not a pure antiquarian image to be enjoyed for its own sake; on the contrary, it is associated with a picture of things to be said and done in the future; so that throughout the day Mr. Everyman intermittently holds in mind, together with a picture of Smith's coal wagons, a picture of himself going at four o'clock in the afternoon to Smith's office in order to pay his bill. At four o'clock Mr. Everyman is accordingly at Smith's office. "I wish to pay that coal bill," he says. Smith looks dubious and disappointed, takes down a ledger (or a filing case), does a bit of original research in his Private Record Office, and announces: "You don't owe me any money, Mr. Everyman. You ordered the coal here all right, but I didn't have the kind you wanted, and so turned the order over to Brown. It was Brown delivered your coal: he's the man you owe." Whereupon Mr. Everyman goes to Brown's office; and Brown takes down a ledger, does a bit of original research in his Private Record Office, which happily confirms the researches of Smith; and Mr. Everyman pays his bill, and in the evening, after returning from the Country Club, makes a further search in another collection of documents, where, sure enough, he finds a bill from Brown, properly drawn, for twenty tons of stove coal, $1017.20. The research is

now completed. Since his mind rests satisfied, Mr. Everyman has found the explanation of the series of events that concerned him.

[8] Mr. Everyman would be astonished to learn that he is an historian, yet it is obvious, isn't it, that he has performed all the essential operations involved in historical research. Needing or wanting to do something (which happened to be, not to deliver a lecture or write a book, but to pay a bill; and this is what misleads him and us as to what he is really doing), the first step was to recall things said and done. Unaided memory proving inadequate, a further step was essential—the examination of certain documents in order to discover the necessary but as yet unknown facts. Unhappily the documents were found to give conflicting reports, so that a critical comparison of the texts had to be instituted in order to eliminate error. All this having been satisfactorily accomplished, Mr. Everyman is ready for the final operation—the formation in his mind, by an artificial extension of memory, of a picture, a definitive picture let us hope, of a selected series of historical events—of himself ordering coal from Smith, of Smith turning the order over to Brown, and of Brown delivering the coal at his house. In the light of this picture Mr. Everyman could, and did, pay his bill. If Mr. Everyman had undertaken these researches in order to write a book instead of to pay a bill, no one would think of denying that he was an historian.

[9] I have tried to reduce history to its lowest terms, first by defining it as the memory of things said and done, second by showing concretely how the memory of things said and done is essential to the performance of the simplest acts of daily life. I wish now to note the more general implications of Mr. Everyman's activities. In the realm of affairs Mr. Everyman has been paying his coal bill; in the realm of consciousness he has been doing that fundamental thing which enables man alone to have, properly speaking, a history: he has been reënforcing and enriching his immediate perceptions to the end that he may live in a world of semblance more spacious and satisfying than is to be found within the narrow confines of the fleeting present moment.

[10] We are apt to think of the past as dead, the future as nonexistent, the present alone as real; and prematurely wise or disillusioned counselors have urged us to burn always with "a hard, gemlike flame" in order to give "the highest quality to the moments as they pass, and simply for those moments' sake." This no doubt is what the glow-worm does; but I think that man, who alone is properly aware that the present moment passes, can for that very reason make no good use of the present moment simply for its own sake. Strictly speaking, the present doesn't exist for us, or is at best no more than an infinitesimal point in time, gone before we can note it as present. Nevertheless, we must have a present; and so we create one by robbing the past, by holding on to the most recent events and pretending that they all belong to our immediate perceptions. If, for example, I raise my arm, the total event is a series of occurrences of which the first are past before the last have

taken place; and yet you perceive it as a single movement executed in one present instant. This telescoping of successive events into a single instant philosophers call the "specious present." Doubtless they would assign rather narrow limits to the specious present; but I will willfully make a free use of it, and say that we can extend the specious present as much as we like. In common speech we do so: we speak of the "present hour," the "present year," the "present generation." Perhaps all living creatures have a specious present; but man has this superiority, as Pascal says, that he is aware of himself and the universe, can as it were hold himself at arm's length and with some measure of objectivity watch himself and his fellows functioning in the world during a brief span of allotted years. Of all the creatures, man alone has a specious present that may be deliberately and purposefully enlarged and diversified and enriched.

[11] The extent to which the specious present may thus be enlarged and enriched will depend upon knowledge, the artificial extension of memory, the memory of things said and done in the past and distant places. But not upon knowledge alone; rather upon knowledge directed by purpose. The specious present is an unstable pattern of thought, incessantly changing in response to our immediate perceptions and the purposes that arise therefrom. At any given moment each one of us (professional historian no less than Mr. Everyman) weaves into this unstable pattern such actual or artificial memories as may be necessary to orient us in our little world of endeavor. But to be oriented in our little world of endeavor we must be prepared for what is coming to us (the payment of a coal bill, the delivery of a presidential address, the establishment of a League of Nations, or whatever); and to be prepared for what is coming to us it is necessary, not only to recall certain past events, but to anticipate (note I do not say predict) the future. Thus from the specious present, which always includes more or less of the past, the future refuses to be excluded; and the more of the past we drag into the specious present, the more an hypothetical, patterned future is likely to crowd into it also. Which comes first, which is cause and which effect, whether our memories construct a pattern of past events at the behest of our desires and hopes, or whether our desires and hopes spring from a pattern of past events imposed upon us by experience and knowledge, I shall not attempt to say. What I suspect is that memory of past and anticipation of future events work together, go hand in hand as it were in a friendly way, without disputing over priority and leadership.

[12] At all events they go together, so that in a very real sense it is impossible to divorce history from life: Mr. Everyman cannot do what he needs or desires to do without recalling past events; he cannot recall past events without in some subtle fashion relating them to needs or desires to do. This is the natural function of history, of history reduced to its lowest terms, of history conceived as the memory of things said and done: memory of things said and done (whether in our immediate yesterdays or in the long past of mankind), running hand in hand with the anticipation of things

to be said and done, enables us, each to the extent of his knowledge and imagination, to be intelligent, to push back the narrow confines of the fleeting present moment so that what we are doing may be judged in the light of what we have done and what we hope to do. In this sense all *living* history, as Croce says, is contemporaneous: in so far as we think of the past (and otherwise the past, however fully related in documents, is nothing to us) it becomes an integral and living part of our present world of semblance.

[13] It must then be obvious that living history, the ideal series of events that we affirm and hold in memory, since it is so intimately associated with what we are doing and with what we hope to do, cannot be precisely the same for all at any given time, or the same for one generation as for another. History in this sense cannot be reduced to a verifiable set of statistics or formulated in terms of universally valid mathematical formulas. It is rather an imaginative creation, a personal possession which each one of us, Mr. Everyman, fashions out of his individual experience, adapts to his practical or emotional needs, and adorns as well as may be to suit his esthetic tastes. In thus creating his own history, there are, nevertheless, limits which Mr. Everyman may not overstep without incurring penalties. The limits are set by his fellows. If Mr. Everyman lived quite alone in an unconditioned world, he would be free to affirm and hold in memory any ideal series of events that struck his fancy, and thus create a world of semblance quite in accord with the heart's desire. Unfortunately, Mr. Everyman has to live in a world of Browns and Smiths; a sad experience, which has taught him the expediency of recalling certain events with much exactness. In all the immediately practical affairs of life Mr. Everyman is a good historian, as expert, in conducting the researches necessary for paying his coal bill, as need be. His expertness comes partly from long practice, but chiefly from the circumstance that his researches are prescribed and guided by very definite and practical objects which concern him intimately. The problem of what documents to consult, what facts to select, troubles Mr. Everyman not at all. Since he is not writing a book on "Some Aspects of the Coal Industry Objectively Considered," it does not occur to him to collect all the facts and let them speak for themselves. Wishing merely to pay his coal bill, he selects only such facts as may be relevant; and not wishing to pay it twice, he is sufficiently aware, without ever having read Bernheim's *Lehrbuch,* that the relevant facts must be clearly established by the testimony of independent witnesses not self-deceived. He does not know, or need to know, that his personal interest in the performance is a disturbing bias which will prevent him from learning the whole truth or arriving at ultimate causes. Mr. Everyman does not wish to learn the whole truth or to arrive at ultimate causes. He wishes to pay his coal bill. That is to say, he wishes to adjust himself to a practical situation, and on that low pragmatic level he is a good historian precisely because he is not disinterested: he will solve his problems, if he does solve them, by virtue of his intelligence and not by virtue of his indifference.

[14] Nevertheless, Mr. Everyman does not live by bread alone; and on all proper occasions his memory of things said and done, easily enlarging his specious present beyond the narrow circle of daily affairs, will, must inevitably, in mere compensation for the intolerable dullness and vexation of the fleeting present moment, fashion for him a more spacious world than that of the immediately practical. He can readily recall the days of his youth, the places he has lived in, the ventures he has made, the adventures he has had—all the crowded events of a lifetime; and beyond and around this central pattern of personally experienced events, there will be embroidered a more dimly seen pattern of artificial memories, memories of things reputed to have been said and done in past times which he has not known, in distant places which he has not seen. This outer pattern of remembered events that encloses and completes the central pattern of his personal experience, Mr. Everyman has woven, he could not tell you how, out of the most diverse threads of information, picked up in the most casual way, from the most unrelated sources—from things learned at home and in school, from knowledge gained in business or profession, from newspapers glanced at, from books (yes, even history books) read or heard of, from remembered scraps of newsreels or educational films of *ex cathedra* utterances of presidents and kings, from fifteen-minute discourses on the history of civilization broadcast by the courtesy (it may be) of Pepsodent, the Bulova Watch Company, or the Shepard Stores in Boston. Daily and hourly, from a thousand unnoted sources, there is lodged in Mr. Everyman's mind a mass of unrelated and related information and misinformation, of impressions and images, out of which he somehow manages, undeliberately for the most part, to fashion a history, a patterned picture of remembered things said and done in past times and distant places. It is not possible, it is not essential, that this picture should be complete or completely true: it is essential that it should be useful to Mr. Everyman; and that it may be useful to him he will hold in memory, of all the things he might hold in memory, those things only which can be related with some reasonable degree of relevance and harmony to his idea of himself and of what he is doing in the world and what he hopes to do.

[15] In constructing this more remote and far-flung pattern of remembered things, Mr. Everyman works with something of the freedom of a creative artist; the history which he imaginatively recreates as an artificial extension of his personal experience will inevitably be an engaging blend of fact and fancy, a mythical adaptation of that which actually happened. In part it will be true, in part false; as a whole perhaps neither true nor false, but only the most convenient form of error. Not that Mr. Everyman wishes or intends to deceive himself or others. Mr. Everyman has a wholesome respect for cold, hard facts, never suspecting how malleable they are, how easy it is to coax and cajole them; but he necessarily takes the facts as they come to him, and is enamored of those that seem best suited to his interests or promise most in the way of emotional satisfaction. The exact

truth of remembered events he has in any case no time, and no need, to curiously question or meticulously verify. No doubt he can, if he be an American, call up an image of the signing of the Declaration of Independence in 1776 as readily as he can call up an image of Smith's coal wagons creaking up the hill last summer. He suspects the one image no more than the other; but the signing of the Declaration, touching not his practical interests, calls for no careful historical research on his part. He may perhaps, without knowing why, affirm and hold in memory that the Declaration was signed by the members of the Continental Congress on the fourth of July. It is a vivid and sufficient image which Mr. Everyman may hold to the end of his days without incurring penalties. Neither Brown nor Smith has any interest in setting him right; nor will any court ever send him a summons for failing to recall that the Declaration, "being engrossed and compared at the table, was signed by the members" on the second of August. As an actual event, the signing of the Declaration was what it was; as a remembered event it will be, for Mr. Everyman, what Mr. Everyman contrives to make it: will have for him significance and magic, much or little or none at all, as it fits well or ill into his little world of interests and aspirations and emotional comforts.

[16]   What then of us, historians by profession? What have we to do with Mr. Everyman, or he with us? More, I venture to believe, than we are apt to think. For each of us is Mr. Everyman too. Each of us is subject to the limitations of time and place; and for each of us, no less than for the Browns and Smiths of the world, the pattern of remembered things said and done will be woven, safeguard the process how we may, at the behest of circumstance and purpose.

[17]   True it is that although each of us is Mr. Everyman, each is something more than his own historian. Mr. Everyman, being but an informal historian, is under no bond to remember what is irrelevant to his personal affairs. But we are historians by profession. Our profession, less intimately bound up with the practical activities, is to be directly concerned with the ideal series of events that is only of casual or occasional import to others; it is our business in life to be ever preoccupied with that far-flung pattern of artificial memories that encloses and completes the central pattern of individual experience. We are Mr. Everybody's historian as well as our own, since our histories serve the double purpose, which written histories have always served, of keeping alive the recollection of memorable men and events. We are thus of that ancient and honorable company of wise men of the tribe, of bards and story-tellers and minstrels, of sooth-sayers and priests, to whom in successive ages has been entrusted the keeping of the useful myths. Let not the harmless, necessary word "myth" put us out of countenance. In the history of history a myth is a once valid but now discarded version of the human story, as our now valid versions will in due course be relegated to the category of discarded myths. With our predecessors, the bards and story-tellers and priests, we have therefore this in common: that

it is our function, as it was theirs, not to create, but to preserve and perpetuate the social tradition; to harmonize, as well as ignorance and prejudice permit, the actual and the remembered series of events; to enlarge and enrich the specious present common to us all to the end that "society" (the tribe, the nation, or all mankind) may judge of what it is doing in the light of what it has done and what it hopes to do.

[18] History as the artificial extension of the social memory (and I willingly concede that there are other appropriate ways of apprehending human experience) is an art of long standing, necessarily so since it springs instinctively from the impulse to enlarge the range of immediate experience, and however camouflaged by the disfiguring jargon of science, it is still in essence what it has always been. History in this sense is story, in aim always a true story; a story that employs all the devices of literary art (statement and generalization, narration and description, comparison and comment and analogy) to present the succession of events in the life of man, and from the succession of events thus presented to derive a satisfactory meaning. The history written by historians, like the history informally fashioned by Mr. Everyman, is thus a convenient blend of truth and fancy, of what we commonly distinguish as "fact" and "interpretation." In primitive times, when tradition is orally transmitted, bards and story-tellers frankly embroider or improvise the facts to heighten the dramatic import of the story. With the use of written records, history, gradually differentiated from fiction, is understood as the story of events that actually occurred; and with the increase and refinement of knowledge the historian recognizes that his first duty is to be sure of his facts, let their meaning be what it may. Nevertheless, in every age history is taken to be a story of actual events from which a significant meaning may be derived; and in every age the illusion is that the present version is valid because the related facts are true, whereas former versions are invalid because based upon inaccurate or inadequate facts.

[19] Never was this conviction more impressively displayed than in our own time—that age of erudition in which we live, or from which we are perhaps just emerging. Finding the course of history littered with the *débris* of exploded philosophies, the historians of the last century, unwilling to be forever duped, turned away (as they fondly hoped) from "interpretation" to the rigorous examination of the factual event, just as it occurred. Perfecting the technique of investigation, they laboriously collected and edited the sources of information, and with incredible persistence and ingenuity ran illusive error to earth, letting the significance of the Middle Ages wait until it was certainly known "whether Charles the Fat was at Ingelheim or Lustnau on July 1, 887," shedding their "life-blood," in many a hard fought battle, "for the sublime truths of Sac and Soc." I have no quarrel with this so great concern with Hoti's business. One of the first duties of man is not to be duped, to be aware of his world; and to derive the significance of human experience from events that never occurred is surely an enterprise

of doubtful value. To establish the facts is always in order, and is indeed the first duty of the historian; but to suppose that the facts, once established in all their fullness, will "speak for themselves" is an illusion. It was perhaps peculiarly the illusion of those historians of the last century who found some special magic in the word "scientific." The scientific historian, it seems, was one who set forth the facts without injecting any extraneous meaning into them. He was the objective man whom Nietzsche described— "a mirror: accustomed to prostration before something that wants to be known, . . . he waits until something comes, and then expands himself sensitively, so that even the light footsteps and gliding past of spiritual things may not be lost in his surface and film." "It is not I who speak, but history which speaks through me," was Fustel's reproof to applauding students. "If a certain philosophy emerges from this scientific history, it must be permitted to emerge naturally, of its own accord, all but independently of the will of the historian." Thus the scientific historian deliberately renounced philosophy only to submit to it without being aware. His philosophy was just this, that by not taking thought a cubit would be added to his stature. With no other preconception than the will to know, the historian would reflect in his surface and film the "order of events throughout past times in all places"; so that, in the fullness of time, when innumerable patient expert scholars, by "exhausting the sources," should have reflected without refracting the truth of all the facts, the definitive and impregnable meaning of human experience would emerge of its own accord to enlighten and emancipate mankind. Hoping to find something without looking for it, expecting to obtain final answers to life's riddle by resolutely refusing to ask questions—it was surely the most romantic species of realism yet invented, the oddest attempt ever made to get something for nothing!

[20] That mood is passing. The fullness of time is not yet, overmuch learning proves a weariness to the flesh, and a younger generation that knows not Von Ranke is eager to believe that Fustel's counsel, if one of perfection, is equally one of futility. Even the most disinterested historian has at least one preconception, which is the fixed idea that he has none. The facts of history are already set forth, implicitly, in the sources; and the historian who could restate without reshaping them would, by submerging and suffocating the mind in diffuse existence, accomplish the superfluous task of depriving human experience of all significance. Left to themselves, the facts do not speak; left to themselves they do not exist, not really, since for all practical purposes there is no fact until someone affirms it. The least the historian can do with any historical fact is to select and affirm it. To select and affirm even the simplest complex of facts is to give them a certain place in a certain pattern of ideas, and this alone is sufficient to give them a special meaning. However "hard" or "cold" they may be, historical facts are after all not material substances which, like bricks or scantlings, possess definite shape and clear, persistent outline. To set forth historical facts is not comparable to dumping a barrow of bricks. A brick retains its form and pressure wherever

placed; but the form and substance of historical facts, having a negotiable existence only in literary discourse, vary with the words employed to convey them. Since history is not part of the external material world, but an imaginative reconstruction of vanished events, its form and substance are inseparable: in the realm of literary discourse substance, being an idea, *is* form; and form, conveying the idea, *is* substance. It is thus not the undiscriminated fact, but the perceiving mind of the historian that speaks: the special meaning which the facts are made to convey emerges from the substance-form which the historian employs to re-create imaginatively a series of events not present to perception.

[21] In constructing this substance-form of vanished events, the historian, like Mr. Everyman, like the bards and story-tellers of an earlier time, will be conditioned by the specious present in which alone he can be aware of his world. Being neither omniscient nor omnipresent, the historian is not the same person always and everywhere; and for him, as for Mr. Everyman, the form and significance of remembered events, like the extension and velocity of physical objects, will vary with the time and place of the observer. After fifty years we can clearly see that it was not history which spoke through Fustel, but Fustel who spoke through history. We see less clearly perhaps that the voice of Fustel was the voice, amplified and freed from static as one may say, of Mr. Everyman; what the admiring students applauded on that famous occasion was neither history nor Fustel, but a deftly colored pattern of selected events which Fustel fashioned, all the more skillfully for not being aware of doing so, in the service of Mr. Everyman's emotional needs—the emotional satisfaction, so essential to Frenchmen at that time, of perceiving that French institutions were not of German origin. And so it must always be. Played upon by all the diverse, unnoted influences of his own time, the historian will elicit history out of documents by the same principle, however more consciously and expertly applied, that Mr. Everyman employs to breed legends out of remembered episodes and oral tradition.

[22] Berate him as we will for not reading our books, Mr. Everyman is stronger than we are, and sooner or later we must adapt our knowledge to his necessities. Otherwise he will leave us to our own devices, leave us it may be to cultivate a species of dry professional arrogance growing out of the thin soil of antiquarian research. Such research, valuable not in itself but for some ulterior purpose, will be of little import except in so far as it is transmuted into common knowledge. The history that lies inert in unread books does no work in the world. The history that does work in the world, the history that influences the course of history, is living history, that pattern of remembered events, whether true or false, that enlarges and enriches the collective specious present, the specious present of Mr. Everyman. It is for this reason that the history of history is a record of the "new history" that in every age rises to confound and supplant the old. It should be a relief to us to renounce omniscience, to recognize that every generation, our own

included, will, must inevitably, understand the past and anticipate the future in the light of its own restricted experience, must inevitably play on the dead whatever tricks it finds necessary for its own peace of mind. The appropriate trick for any age is not a malicious invention designed to take anyone in, but an unconscious and necessary effort on the part of "society" to understand what it is doing in the light of what it has done and what it hopes to do. We, historians by profession, share in this necessary effort. But we do not impose our version of the human story on Mr. Everyman; in the end it is rather Mr. Everyman who imposes his version on us—compelling us, in an age of political revolution, to see that history is past politics, in an age of social stress and conflict to search for the economic interpretation. If we remain too long recalcitrant Mr. Everyman will ignore us, shelving our recondite works behind glass doors rarely opened. Our proper function is not to repeat the past but to make use of it, to correct and rationalize for common use Mr. Everyman's mythological adaptation of what actually happened. We are surely under bond to be as honest and as intelligent as human frailty permits; but the secret of our success in the long run is in conforming to the temper of Mr. Everyman, which we seem to guide only because we are so sure, eventually, to follow it.

[23] Neither the value nor the dignity of history need suffer by regarding it as a foreshortened and incomplete representation of the reality that once was, an unstable pattern of remembered things redesigned and newly colored to suit the convenience of those who make use of it. Nor need our labors be the less highly prized because our task is limited, our contributions of incidental and temporary significance. History is an indispensable even though not the highest form of intellectual endeavor, since it makes, as Santayana says, a gift of "great interests . . . to the heart. A barbarian is not less subject to the past than is the civic man who knows what the past is and means to be loyal to it; but the barbarian, for want of a transpersonal memory, crawls among superstitions which he cannot understand or revoke and among people whom he may hate or love, but whom he can never think of raising to a higher plane, to the level of a purer happiness. The whole dignity of human endeavor is thus bound up with historic issues, and as conscience needs to be controlled by experience if it is to become rational, so personal experience itself needs to be enlarged ideally if the failures and successes it reports are to touch impersonal interests."

[24] I do not present this view of history as one that is stable and must prevail. Whatever validity it may claim, it is certain, on its own premises, to be supplanted; for its premises, imposed upon us by the climate of opinion in which we live and think, predispose us to regard all things, and all principles of things, as no more than "inconstant modes or fashions," as but the "concurrence, renewed from moment to moment, of forces parting sooner or later on their way." It is the limitation of the genetic approach to human experience that it must be content to transform problems since it can never solve them. However accurately we may determine the

"facts" of history, the facts themselves and our interpretations of them, and our interpretation of our own interpretations, will be seen in a different perspective or a less vivid light as mankind moves into the unknown future. Regarded historically, as a process of becoming, man and his world can obviously be understood only tentatively, since it is by definition something still in the making, something as yet unfinished. Unfortunately for the "permanent contribution" and the universally valid philosophy, time passes; time, the enemy of man as the Greeks thought; tomorrow and tomorrow and tomorrow creeps in this petty pace, and all our yesterdays diminish and grow dim: so that, in the lengthening perspective of the centuries, even the most striking events (The Declaration of Independence, the French Revolution, the Great War itself; like the Diet of Worms before them, like the signing of the Magna Carta and the coronation of Charlemagne and the crossing of the Rubicon and the battle of Marathon) must inevitably, for posterity, fade away into pale replicas of the original picture, for each succeeding generation losing, as they recede into a more distant past, some significance that once was noted in them, some quality of enchantment that once was theirs.

COMMENT AND QUESTIONS

I. Why does Becker wish to reduce history to its lowest terms? Why does he use the unacademic concrete example of Mr. Everyman and his coal bill? What are the operations of historical research that Mr. Everyman has performed in the process of paying his bill?

II. Notice that paragraph 9 briefly summarizes the preceding material and leads into a major idea in the essay—the enlargement of immediate perception through historical knowledge. What does Becker mean by the "specious present," and what is its importance to man?

III. Paragraph 12 again summarizes the ideas discussed thus far; paragraph 13 introduces the second major idea of the essay—the inevitable variations and changes in "living history." What is the author's reason, in paragraph 13 and the following paragraphs, for returning to Mr. Everyman and his sense of history?

IV. Why, according to Becker, is it impossible for "facts" to speak for themselves, without "interpretation"? Why must history be different for each generation? Does Becker's view seem to accord with, or conflict with, the "principle of selection" discussed early in this book?

V. At the end of his essay, Becker says that with the passage of time "even the most striking events (The Declaration of Independence, the French Revolution, the Great War itself . . .) must inevitably, for posterity, fade away into pale replicas of the original picture . . . losing . . . some significance that once was theirs." This essay was written in 1932; the "Great

War" is, of course, World War I. Do you think that for your generation that "Great War" has already faded into a pale replica?

Suppose you had written a personal, autobiographical history four years ago and were now writing another one. Would events that seemed striking then have lost some of their significance or enchantment now?

What important national and international facts and events of the present time do you think may possibly have faded into pale replicas, or may be seen in a different perspective, when the history of these days is written fifty years from now?

VI. The writing in "Everyman His Own Historian" is of very high quality. Choose several short passages that seem to you particularly good, and analyze the sentence structures, the rhythms, and the choice and arrangement of words.

CARL SANDBURG

Lincoln Speaks at Gettysburg*

The following account of an event in history is part of a long biography of Lincoln. One of the distinctive features of the selection is the skillful weaving of a mass of fact, evidence, and conflicting opinion into a highly readable historical narrative. Carl Sandburg, probably best known as a poet of the Midwest, is the author of *Chicago Poems; Cornhuskers; Smoke and Steel; The American Songbag; The People, Yes;* and *Remembrance Rock,* a novel. His biography of Lincoln, *The Prairie Years* (two volumes) and *The War Years* (four volumes), won the 1940 Pulitzer Prize.

[1] A printed invitation came to Lincoln's hands notifying him that on Thursday, November 19, 1863, exercises would be held for the dedication of a National Soldiers' Cemetery at Gettysburg. The same circular invitation had been mailed to Senators, Congressmen, the governors of Northern States, members of the Cabinet, by the commission of Pennsylvanians who had organized a corporation through which Maine, New Hampshire, Vermont, Massachusetts, Rhode Island, Maryland, Connecticut, New York, New Jersey, Pennsylvania, Delaware, West Virginia, Ohio, Indiana, Illinois, Michigan, Wisconsin, and Minnesota were to share the cost of a decent burying-ground for the dust and bones of the Union and Confederate dead.

[2] In the helpless onrush of the war, it was known, too many of the fallen had lain as neglected cadavers rotting in the open fields or thrust into so

* Condensed from *Abraham Lincoln: The War Years* by Carl Sandburg. Copyright, 1939, by Harcourt, Brace and Company, Inc.

shallow a resting-place that a common farm plow caught in their bones. Now by order of Governor Curtin of Pennsylvania seventeen acres had been purchased on Cemetery Hill, where the Union center stood its colors on the second and third of July, and plots of soil had been alloted each State for its graves.

[3] The sacred and delicate duties of orator of the day had fallen on Edward Everett. An eminent cultural figure, perhaps foremost of all distinguished American classical orators, he was born in 1794, had been United States Senator, Governor of Massachusetts, member of Congress, Secretary of State under Fillmore, Minister to Great Britain, Phi Beta Kappa poet at Harvard, professor of Greek at Harvard, president of Harvard. His reputation as a public speaker began in the Brattle Street Unitarian Church of Boston. Two volumes of his orations published in 1850 held eighty-one addresses, two more volumes issued in 1859 collected one hundred and five speeches. His lecture on Washington, delivered a hundred and twenty-two times in three years, had in 1859 brought a fund of $58,000, which he gave to the purchase and maintenance of Mount Vernon as a permanent shrine. Other Everett lectures had realized more than $90,000 for charity causes. . . . No ordinary trafficker in politics, Everett had in 1860 run for Vice-President on the Bell-Everett ticket of the Constitutional Union party, receiving the electoral votes of Virginia, Kentucky, and Tennessee.

[4] The Union of States was a holy concept to Everett, and the slavery issue secondary, though when president of Harvard from 1846 to 1849 he refused to draw the color line, saying in the case of a Negro applicant, Beverly Williams, that admission to Harvard College depended on examinations. "If this boy passes the examinations, he will be admitted; and if the white students choose to withdraw, all the income of the College will be devoted to his education." Not often was he so provocative.

[5] On the basis of what Everett had heard about Lincoln he wrote in his journal shortly before the inauguration in '61 that the incoming President was "evidently a person of very inferior cast of character, wholly unequal to the crisis." Then on meeting the new President he recorded that he found him of better stuff than he had expected. As a strict worshiper of the Constitution and the Union he was drawn toward Lincoln's moderate slavery policy, writing to critics after the Administration had lost in the '62 fall elections, "It is my purpose to support the President to the best of my ability." Speaking publicly as a man of no party, and as the leading founder of the Mount Vernon memorial to George Washington, he trusted he would offend no candid opponent by saying that the main objection against Mr. Lincoln, "that personally he lacks fixedness of purpose," might on precisely the same grounds be brought against George Washington and his Administration. The President's "intellectual capacity" had been proved in his debates with Douglas. "He is one of the most laborious and indefatigable men in the country," said Everett, "and that he has been able to sustain himself under as great a load of care as was ever laid upon the head

or the heart of a living man is in no small degree owing to the fact that the vindictive and angry passions form no part of his nature and that a kindly and playful spirit mingles its sweetness with the austere cup of public duty." . . .

[6] Serene, suave, handsomely venerable in his sixty-ninth year, a prominent specimen of Northern upper-class distinction, Everett was a natural choice of the Pennsylvania commissioners, who sought an orator for a solemn national occasion. When in September they notified him that the date of the occasion would be October 23, he replied that he would need more time for preparation, and the dedication was postponed till November 19.

[7] Lincoln meanwhile, in reply to the printed circular invitation, sent word to the commissioners that he would be present at the ceremonies. This made it necessary for the commissioners to consider whether the President should be asked to deliver an address when present. Clark E. Carr of Galesburg, Illinois, representing his State on the Board of Commissioners, noted that the decision of the Board to invite Lincoln to speak was an afterthought. "The question was raised as to his ability to speak upon such a grave and solemn occasion. . . . Besides, it was said that, with his important duties and responsibilities, he could not possibly have the leisure to prepare an address. . . . In answer . . . it was urged that he himself, better than any one else, could determine as to these questions, and that, if he were invited to speak, he was sure to do what, under the circumstances, would be right and proper."

[8] And so on November 2 David Wills of Gettysburg, as the special agent of Governor Curtin and also acting for the several States, by letter informed Lincoln that the several States having soldiers in the Army of the Potomac who were killed, or had since died at hospitals in the vicinity, had procured grounds for a cemetery and proper burial of their dead. "These grounds will be consecrated and set apart to this sacred purpose by appropriate ceremonies on Thursday, the 19th instant. I am authorized by the Governors of the various States to invite you to be present and participate in these ceremonies, which will doubtless be very imposing and solemnly impressive. It is the desire that after the oration, you, as Chief Executive of the nation, formally set apart these grounds to their sacred use by a few appropriate remarks."

[9] Mr. Wills proceeded farther as to the solemnity of the occasion, and when Lincoln had finished reading the letter he understood definitely that the event called for no humor and that a long speech was not expected from him. "The invitation," wrote Clark E. Carr, "was not settled upon and sent to Mr. Lincoln until the second of November, more than six weeks after Mr. Everett had been invited to speak, and but little more than two weeks before the exercises were held."

[10] On the second Sunday before the Gettysburg ceremonies were to take place Lincoln went to the studio of the photographer Gardner for a long-

delayed sitting. Noah Brooks walked with him, and he carefully explained to Brooks that he could not go to the photographer on any other day without interfering with the public business and the photographer's business, to say nothing of his liability to be hindered en route by curiosity-seekers "and other seekers." On the White House stairs Lincoln had paused, turned, walked back to his office, and rejoined Brooks with a long envelope in his hand, an advance copy of Edward Everett's address to be delivered at the Gettysburg dedication. It was thoughtful of Everett to take care they should not cover the same ground in their speeches, he remarked to Brooks, who exclaimed over the length of the Everett address, covering nearly two sides of a one-page supplement of a Boston newspaper. Lincoln quoted a line he said he had read somewhere from Daniel Webster: "Solid men of Boston, make no long orations." There was no danger that he should get upon the lines of Mr. Everett's oration, he told Brooks, for what he had ready to say was very short, or as Brooks recalled his emphasis, "Short, short, short." He had hoped to read the Everett address between sittings, but the photographer worked fast, Lincoln got interested in talk, and did not open the advance sheets while at Gardner's. In the photograph which Lincoln later gave to Brooks an envelope lay next to Lincoln's right arm resting on a table. In one other photograph made by Gardner that Sunday the envelope was still on the table. The chief difference between the two pictures was that in one Lincoln had his knees crossed and in the other the ankles.

[11] Lamon noted that Lincoln wrote part of his intended Gettysburg address at Washington, covered a sheet of foolscap paper with a memorandum of it, and before taking it out of his hat and reading it to Lamon he said that it was not at all satisfactory to him, that he was afraid he would not do himself credit nor come up to public expectation. He had been too busy to give it the time he would like to. . . .

[12] Two men, in the weeks just before the Gettysburg ceremonies, had worked on Lincoln, doing their best to make him see himself as a world spokesman of democracy, popular government, the mass of people as opposed to aristocrats, classes, and special interests. John Murray Forbes, having read Lincoln's lively stump-speech letter to the Springfield, Illinois, mass meeting, wrote to Sumner on September 3, "I delight in the President's plain letter to plain people!" Forbes followed this five days later with a letter which Sumner carried to the White House and handed to Lincoln. It began with convincingly phrased praise of the Springfield letter, and proceeded into the unusual question: "Will you permit a suggestion from one who has nothing to ask for himself: one who would accept no office, and who seeks only to do his duty in the most private way possible?" With such an opening it could hardly be doubted that Lincoln read on into the next paragraphs—and read them more than once.

[13] An aristocracy ruled the South and controlled it for war, believed Forbes, pointing to "the aristocratic class who own twenty negroes and up-

wards" as numbering "about 28,000 persons, which is about the 178th part of 5,000,000" whites. So Forbes urged, "Let the people North and South see this line clearly defined between the people and the aristocrats, and the war will be over!" . . .

[14]   Thus while Lincoln shaped his speech to be made at Gettysburg he did not lack specific advice that when the chance came he should stand up and be a world spokesman for those who called themselves democrats and liberals as opposed to what they termed "the aristocratic classes."

[15]   Some newspapers now had it that the President was going to make a stump speech over the graves of the Gettysburg dead as a political play. Talk ran in Washington that by attending Governor Curtin's "show" the President would strengthen himself with the Curtin faction without alienating the opposing Cameron clique.

[16]   Various definite motives besides vague intuitions may have guided Lincoln in his decision to attend and speak even though half his Cabinet had sent formal declinations in response to the printed circular invitations they had all received. Though the Gettysburg dedication was to be under interstate auspices, it had tremendous national significance for Lincoln because on the platform would be the State governors whose cooperation with him was of vast importance. Also a slander and a libel had been widely mouthed and printed that on his visit to the battlefield of Antietam nearly a year before he had laughed obscenely at his own funny stories and called on Lamon to sing a cheap comic song. Perhaps he might go to Gettysburg and let it be seen how he demeaned himself on a somber landscape of sacrifice.

[17]   His personal touch with Gettysburg, by telegraph, mail, courier, and by a throng of associations, made it a place of great realities to him. Just after the battle there, a woman had come to his office, the doorman saying she had been "crying and taking on" for several days trying to see the President. Her husband and her three sons were in the army. On part of her husband's pay she had lived for a time, till money from him stopped coming. She was hard put to scrape a living and needed one of her boys to help.

[18]   The President listened to her, standing at a fireplace, hands behind him, head bowed, motionless. The woman finished her plea for one of her three sons in the army. He spoke. Slowly and almost as if talking to himself alone the words came and only those words:

[19]   "I have two, and you have none."

[20]   He crossed the room, wrote an order for the military discharge of one of her sons. On a special sheet of paper he wrote full and detailed instructions where to go and what to say in order to get her boy back.

[21]   In a few days the doorman told the President that the same woman was again on hand crying and taking on. "Let her in," was the word. She had found doors opening to her and officials ready to help on seeing the President's written words she carried. She had located her boy, camp, regi-

ment, company. She had found him, yes, wounded at Gettysburg, dying in a hospital, and had followed him to the grave. And, she begged, would the President now give her the next one of her boys?

[22] As before he stood at the fireplace, hands behind him, head bent low, motionless. Slowly and almost as if talking to himself alone the words came and as before only those words:

[23] "I have two, and you have none."

[24] He crossed the room to his desk and began writing. As though nothing else was to do she followed, stood by his chair as he wrote, put her hand on the President's head, smoothed his thick and disorderly hair with motherly fingers. He signed an order giving her the next of her boys, stood up, put the priceless paper in her hand as he choked out the one word, "There!" and with long quick steps was gone from the room with her sobs and cries of thanks in his ears.

[25] Thus the Kentuckian, James Speed, gathered the incident and told it. By many strange ways Gettysburg was to Lincoln a fact in crimson mist. . . .

[26] Benjamin B. French, officer in charge of buildings in Washington, introduced the Honorable Edward Everett, orator of the day, who rose, bowed low to Lincoln, saying, "Mr. President." Lincoln responded, "Mr. Everett."

[27] The orator of the day then stood in silence before a crowd that stretched to limits that would test his voice. Beyond and around were the wheat fields, the meadows, the peach orchards, long slopes of land, and five and seven miles farther the contemplative blue ridge of a low mountain range. His eyes could sweep them as he faced the audience. He had taken note of it in his prepared and rehearsed address. "Overlooking these broad fields now reposing from the labors of the waning year, the mighty Alleghanies dimly towering before us, the graves of our brethren beneath our feet, it is with hesitation that I raise my poor voice to break the eloquent silence of God and Nature. But the duty to which you have called me must be performed;—grant me, I pray you, your indulgence and your sympathy." Everett proceeded, "It was appointed by law in Athens," and gave an extended sketch of the manner in which the Greeks cared for their dead who fell in battle. He spoke of the citizens assembled to consecrate the day. "As my eye ranges over the fields whose sods were so lately moistened by the blood of gallant and loyal men, I feel, as never before, how truly it was said of old that it is sweet and becoming to die for one's country."

[28] Northern cities would have been trampled in conquest but for "those who sleep beneath our feet," said the orator. He gave an outline of how the war began, traversed decisive features of the three days' battles at Gettysburg, discussed the doctrine of State sovereignty and denounced it, drew parallels from European history, and came to his peroration quoting Pericles on dead patriots: "The whole earth is the sepulchre of illustrious men." The men of nineteen sister States had stood side by side on the

perilous ridges. "Seminary Ridge, the Peach-Orchard, Cemetery, Culp, and Wolf Hill, Round Top, Little Round Top, humble names, henceforward dear and famous,—no lapse of time, no distance of space, shall cause you to be forgotten." He had spoken for an hour and fifty-seven minutes, some said a trifle over two hours, repeating almost word for word an address that occupied nearly two newspaper pages, as he had written it and as it had gone in advance sheets to many newspapers.

[29] Everett came to his closing sentence without a faltering voice: "Down to the latest period of recorded time, in the glorious annals of our common country there will be no brighter page than that which relates THE BATTLE OF GETTYSBURG." It was the effort of his life and embodied the perfections of the school of oratory in which he had spent his career. His erect form and sturdy shoulders, his white hair and flung-back head at dramatic points, his voice, his poise, and chiefly some quality of inside goodheartedness, held most of his audience to him, though the people in the front rows had taken their seats three hours before his oration closed.

[30] The Baltimore Glee Club sang an ode written for the occasion by Benjamin B. French, who had introduced Everett to the audience. The poets Longfellow, Bryant, Whittier, Lowell, George Boker, had been requested but none found time to respond with a piece to be set to music. The two closing verses of the ode by French immediately preceded the introduction of the President to the audience:

> Great God in Heaven!
> Shall all this sacred blood be shed?
> Shall we thus mourn our glorious dead?
> Oh, shall the end be wrath and woe,
> The knell of Freedom's overthrow,
> A country riven?
>
> It will not be!
> We trust, O God! thy gracious power
> To aid us in our darkest hour.
> This be our prayer—"O Father! save
> A people's freedom from its grave.
> All praise to Thee!"

[31] Having read Everett's address, Lincoln knew when the moment drew near for him to speak. He took out his own manuscript from a coat pocket, put on his steel-bowed glasses, stirred in his chair, looked over the manuscript, and put it back in his pocket. The Baltimore Glee Club finished. The specially chosen Ward Hill Lamon rose and spoke the words "The President of the United States," who rose, and holding in one hand the two sheets of paper at which he occasionally glanced, delivered the address in his high-pitched and clear-carrying voice. The *Cincinnati Commercial* reporter wrote, "The President rises slowly, draws from his pocket a paper, and, when commotion subsides, in a sharp, unmusical treble voice, reads

the brief and pithy remarks." Hay wrote in his diary, "The President, in a firm, free way, with more grace than is his wont, said his half dozen words of consecration." Charles Hale of the *Boston Advertiser,* also officially representing Governor Andrew of Massachusetts, had notebook and pencil in hand, took down the slow-spoken words of the President, as follows:

[31]   Fourscore and seven years ago, our fathers brought forth upon this continent a new nation, conceived in liberty and dedicated to the proposition that all men are created equal.

Now we are engaged in a great civil war, testing whether that nation—or any nation, so conceived and so dedicated—can long endure.

We are met on a great battle-field of that war. We are met to dedicate a portion of it as the final resting place of those who have given their lives that that nation might live.

It is altogether fitting and proper that we should do this.

But, in a larger sense, we cannot dedicate, we cannot consecrate, we cannot hallow, this ground. The brave men, living and dead, who struggled here, have consecrated it, far above our power to add or to detract.

The world will very little note nor long remember what we say here; but it can never forget what they did here.

It is for us, the living, rather, to be dedicated, here, to the unfinished work that they have thus far so nobly carried on. It is rather for us to be here dedicated to the great task remaining before us; that from these honored dead we take increased devotion to that cause for which they here gave the last full measure of devotion; that we here highly resolve that these dead shall not have died in vain; that the nation shall, under God, have a new birth of freedom, and that government of the people, by the people, for the people, shall not perish from the earth.

[32]   In a speech to serenaders just after the battle of Gettysburg four and a half months before, Lincoln had referred to the founding of the republic as taking place "eighty-odd years since." Then he had hunted up the exact date, which was eighty-seven years since, and phrased it "Fourscore and seven years ago" instead of "Eighty-seven years since." Also in the final copy Lincoln wrote "We have come" instead of the second "We are met" that Hale reported.

[33]   In the written copy of his speech from which he read Lincoln used the phrase "our poor power." In other copies of the speech which he wrote out later he again used the phrase "our poor power." So it was evident that he meant to use the word "poor" when speaking to his audience, but he omitted it. Also in the copy held in his hands while facing the audience he had not written the words "under God," though he did include those words in later copies which he wrote. Therefore the words "under God" were decided upon after he wrote the text the night before at the Wills residence.

[34]   The *New York Tribune* and many other newspapers indicated "[Applause.]" at five places in the address and "[Long continued applause.]" at the end. The applause, however, according to most of the responsible wit-

nesses, was formal and perfunctory, a tribute to the occasion, to the high office, to the array of important men of the nation on the platform, by persons who had sat as an audience for three hours. Ten sentences had been spoken in five minutes, and some were surprised that it should end before the orator had really begun to get his outdoor voice.

[35] A photographer had made ready to record a great historic moment, had bustled about with his dry plates, his black box on a tripod, and before he had his head under the hood for an exposure, the President had said "by the people, for the people" and the nick of time was past for a photograph.

[36] The *New York Times* reporter gave his summary of the program by writing: "The opening prayer by Reverend Mr. Stockton was touching and beautiful, and produced quite as much effect upon the audience as the classic sentences of the orator of the day. President Lincoln's address was delivered in a clear loud tone of voice, which could be distinctly heard at the extreme limits of the large assemblage. It was delivered (or rather read from a sheet of paper which the speaker held in his hand) in a very deliberate manner, with strong emphasis, and with a most business-like air."

[37] The *Philadelphia Press* man, John Russell Young, privately felt that Everett's speech was the performance of a great actor whose art was too evident, that it was "beautiful but cold as ice." The *New York Times* man noted: "Even while Mr. Everett was delivering his splendid oration, there were as many people wandering about the fields, made memorable by the fierce struggles of July, as stood around the stand listening to his eloquent periods. They seem to have considered, with President Lincoln, that it was not what was *said* here, but what was *done* here, that deserved their attention. . . . In wandering about these battlefields, one is astonished and indignant to find at almost every step of his progress the carcasses of dead horses which breed pestilence in the atmosphere. I am told that more than a score of deaths have resulted from this neglect in the village of Gettysburg the past summer; in the house in which I was compelled to seek lodgings, there are now two boys sick with typhoid fever attributed to this cause. Within a stone's throw of the whitewashed hut occupied as the headquarters of General Meade, I counted yesterday no less than ten carcasses of dead horses, lying on the ground where they were struck by the shells of the enemy."

[38] The audience had expected, as the printed program stipulated, "Dedicatory Remarks, by the President of the United States." No eloquence was promised. Where eloquence is in flow the orator must have time to get tuned up, to expatiate and expand while building toward his climaxes, it was supposed. The *New York Tribune* man and other like observers merely reported the words of the address with the one preceding sentence: "The dedicatory remarks were then delivered by the President." These reporters felt no urge to inform their readers about how Lincoln stood, what he did with his hands, how he moved, vocalized, or whether he emphasized or sub-

dued any parts of the address. Strictly, no address as such was on the program from him. He was down for just a few perfunctory "dedicatory remarks."

[39] According to Lamon, Lincoln himself felt that about all he had given the audience was ordinary garden-variety dedicatory remarks, for Lamon wrote that Lincoln told him just after delivering the speech that he had regret over not having prepared it with greater care. "Lamon, that speech won't *scour*. It is a flat failure and the people are disappointed." On the farms where Lincoln grew up as a boy when wet soil stuck to the mold board of a plow they said it didn't "scour."

[40] The near-by *Patriot and Union* of Harrisburg took its fling: "The President succeeded on this occasion because he acted without sense and without constraint in a panorama that was gotten up more for the benefit of his party than for the glory of the nation and the honor of the dead. . . . We pass over the silly remarks of the President; for the credit of the nation we are willing that the veil of oblivion shall be dropped over them and that they shall no more be repeated or thought of."

[41] The *Chicago Times* held that "Mr. Lincoln did most foully traduce the motives of the men who were slain at Gettysburg" in his reference to "a new birth of freedom," the *Times* saying, "They gave their lives to maintain the old government, and the only Constitution and Union." He had perverted history, misstated the cause for which they died, and with "ignorant rudeness" insulted the memory of the dead, the *Times* alleged: "Readers will not have failed to observe the exceeding bad taste which characterized the remarks of the President and Secretary of State at the dedication of the soldiers' cemetery at Gettysburg. The cheek of every American must tingle with shame as he reads the silly, flat, and dish-watery utterances of the man who has to be pointed out to intelligent foreigners as the President of the United States. And neither he nor Seward could refrain, even on that solemn occasion, from spouting their odious abolition doctrines. The readers of THE TIMES ought to know, too, that the valorous President did not dare to make this little journey to Gettysburg without being escorted by a bodyguard of soldiers. For the first time in the history of the country, the President of the United States, in traveling through a part of his dominions, on a peaceful, even a religious mission, had to be escorted by a bodyguard of soldiers . . . it was fear for his own personal safety which led the President to go escorted as any other military despot might go." In the pronouncement of a funeral sermon Mr. Lincoln had intruded an "offensive exhibition of boorishness and vulgarity," had alluded to tribal differences that an Indian orator eulogizing dead warriors would have omitted, "which he knew would excite unnecessarily the bitter prejudices of his hearers." Therefore the *Chicago Times* would inquire, "Is Mr. Lincoln less refined than a savage?"

[42] A Confederate outburst of war propaganda related to Lincoln and the Gettysburg exercises was set forth in a *Richmond Examiner* editorial, and probably written by its editor, Edward A. Pollard, taking a day off from

his merciless and occasionally wild-eyed criticism of President Jefferson Davis of the Confederacy. And the *Chicago Times,* which seldom let a day pass without curses on Lincoln for his alleged suppression of free speech and a free press, reprinted in full the long editorial from the *Examiner.* "The dramatic exhibition at Gettysburg is in thorough keeping with Yankee character, suited to the usual dignity of their chosen chief," ran part of the editorial scorn. "Stage play, studied attitudes, and effective points were carefully elaborated and presented to the world as the honest outpourings of a nation's heart. In spite of shoddy contracts, of universal corruption, and cruel thirst for southern blood, these people have ideas . . . have read of them in books . . . and determined accordingly to have a grand imitation of them. . . . Mr. Everett was equal to the occasion. He 'took down his Thucydides,' and fancied himself a Pericles commemorating the illustrious dead. The music, the eloquence, the bottled tears and hermetically sealed grief, prepared for the occasion, were all properly brought out in honor of the heroes, whom they crimp in Ireland, inveigle in Germany, or hunt down in the streets of New York.

[43] "So far the play was strictly classic. To suit the general public, however, a little admixture of the more irregular romantic drama was allowed. A vein of comedy was permitted to mingle with the deep pathos of the piece. This singular novelty, and deviation from classic propriety, was heightened by assigning this part to the chief personage. Kings are usually made to speak in the magniloquent language supposed to be suited to their elevated position. On the present occasion Lincoln acted the clown."

[44] This was in the customary tone of the *Chicago Times* and relished by its supporting readers. Its rival, the *Chicago Tribune,* however, had a reporter who telegraphed (unless some editor who read the address added his own independent opinion) a sentence: "The dedicatory remarks of President Lincoln will live among the annals of man."

[45] The *Cincinnati Gazette* reporter added after the text of the address, "That this was the right thing in the right place, and a perfect thing in every respect, was the universal encomium."

[46] The American correspondent of the *London Times* wrote that "the ceremony was rendered ludicrous by some of the sallies of that poor President Lincoln. . . . Anything more dull and commonplace it would not be easy to produce."

[47] Count Gurowski, the only man ever mentioned by Lincoln to Lamon as his possible assassin, wrote in a diary, "Lincoln spoke, with one eye to a future platform and to re-election."

[48] The *Philadelphia Evening Bulletin* said thousands who would not read the elaborate oration of Mr. Everett would read the President's few words "and not many will do it without a moistening of the eye and a swelling of the heart." The *Detroit Advertiser and Tribune* said Mr. Everett had nobly told the story of the battle, "but he who wants to take in the very spirit of the day, catch the unstudied pathos that animates a sincere but

simple-minded man, will turn from the stately periods of the professed orator to the brief speech of the President." The *Providence Journal* reminded readers of the saying that the hardest thing in the world is to make a good five-minute speech: "We know not where to look for a more admirable speech than the brief one which the President made at the close of Mr. Everett's oration. . . . Could the most elaborate and splendid oration be more beautiful, more touching, more inspiring, than those thrilling words of the President? They had in our humble judgment the charm and power of the very highest eloquence."

[49]   Later men were to find that Robert Toombs of Georgia had in 1850 opened a speech: "Sixty years ago our fathers joined together to form a more perfect Union and to establish justice. . . . We have now met to put that government on trial. . . . In my judgment the verdict is such as to give hope to the friends of liberty throughout the world."

[50]   Lincoln had spoken of an idea, a proposition, a concept, worth dying for, which brought from a Richmond newspaper a countering question and answer, "For what are we fighting? An abstraction."

[51]   The *Springfield Republican* had veered from its first opinion that Lincoln was honest but "a Simple Susan." Its comment ran: "Surpassingly fine as Mr. Everett's oration was in the Gettysburg consecration, the rhetorical honors of the occasion were won by President Lincoln. His little speech is a perfect gem; deep in feeling, compact in thought and expression, and tasteful and elegant in every word and comma. Then it has the merit of unexpectedness in its verbal perfection and beauty. We had grown so accustomed to homely and imperfect phrase in his productions that we had come to think it was the law of his utterance. But this shows he can talk handsomely as well as act sensibly. Turn back and read it over, it will repay study as a model speech. Strong feelings and a large brain were its parents—a little painstaking its *accoucheur*."

[52]   That scribbler of curious touch who signed himself "The Lounger" in *Harper's Weekly* inquired why the ceremony at Gettysburg was one of the most striking events of the war. "There are grave-yards enough in the land—what is Virginia but a cemetery?—and the brave who have died for us in this fierce war consecrate the soil from the ocean to the Mississippi. But there is peculiar significance in the field of Gettysburg, for there 'thus far' was thundered to the rebellion. . . . The President and the Cabinet were there, with famous soldiers and civilians. The oration by Mr. Everett was smooth and cold. . . . The few words of the President were from the heart to the heart. They can not be read, even, without kindling emotion. 'The world will little note nor long remember what we say here, but it can never forget what they did here.' It was as simple and felicitous and earnest a word as was ever spoken. . . . Among the Governors present was Horatio Seymour. He came to honor the dead of Gettysburg. But when they were dying he stood in New York sneeringly asking where was the victory prom-

ised for the Fourth of July? These men were winning that victory, and dying for us all; and now he mourns, *ex officio,* over their graves."

[53] Everett's opinion of the speech he heard Lincoln deliver was written in a note to Lincoln the next day and was more than mere courtesy: "I should be glad if I could flatter myself that I came as near to the central idea of the occasion in two hours as you did in two minutes." Lincoln's immediate reply was: "In our respective parts yesterday, you could not have been excused to make a short address, nor I a long one. I am pleased to know that, in your judgment, the little I did say was not entirely a failure."

[54] At Everett's request Lincoln wrote with pen and ink a copy of his Gettysburg Address, which manuscript was auctioned at a Sanitary Fair in New York for the benefit of soldiers. At the request of George Bancroft, the historian, he wrote another copy for a Soldiers' and Sailors' Fair at Baltimore. He wrote still another to be lithographed as a facsimile in a publication, *Autographed Leaves of Our Country's Authors.* For Mr. Wills, his host at Gettysburg, he wrote another. The first draft, written in Washington, and the second one, held while delivering it, went into John Hay's hands to be eventually presented to the Library of Congress.

[55] After the ceremonies at Gettysburg Lincoln lunched with Governor Curtin, Mr. Everett, and others at the Wills home, held a reception that had not been planned, handshaking nearly an hour, looking gloomy and listless but brightening sometimes as a small boy or girl came in line, and stopping one tall man for remarks as to just how high up he reached. At five o'clock he attended a patriotic meeting in the Presbyterian church, walking arm-in-arm with old John Burns, and listening to an address by Lieutenant Governor-elect Anderson of Ohio. At six-thirty he was on the departing Washington train. In the dining-car his secretary John Hay ate with Simon Cameron and Wayne MacVeagh. Hay had thought Cameron and MacVeagh hated each other, but he noted: "I was more than usually struck by the intimate, jovial relations that existed between men that hate and detest each other as cordially as do these Pennsylvania politicians."

[56] The ride to Washington took until midnight. Lincoln was weary, talked little, stretched out on one of the side seats in the drawing-room and had a wet towel laid across his eyes and forehead.

[57] He had stood that day, the world's foremost spokesman of popular government, saying that democracy was yet worth fighting for. He had spoken as one in mist who might head on deeper yet into mist. He incarnated the assurances and pretenses of popular government, implied that it could and might perish from the earth. What he meant by "a new birth of freedom" for the nation could have a thousand interpretations. The taller riddles of democracy stood up out of the address. It had the dream touch of vast and furious events epitomized for any foreteller to read what was to come. He did not assume that the drafted soldiers, substitutes, and bounty-paid privates had died willingly under Lee's shot and shell, in deliberate consecra-

tion of themselves to the Union cause. His cadences sang the ancient song that where there is freedom men have fought and sacrificed for it, and that freedom is worth men's dying for. For the first time since he became President he had on a dramatic occasion declaimed, howsoever it might be read, Jefferson's proposition which had been a slogan of the Revolutionary War—"All men are created equal"—leaving no other inference than that he regarded the Negro slave as a man. His outwardly smooth sentences were inside of them gnarled and tough with the enigmas of the American experiment.

[58] Back at Gettysburg the blue haze of the Cumberland Mountains had dimmed till it was a blur in a nocturne. The moon was up and fell with a bland golden benevolence on the new-made graves of soldiers, on the sepulchers of old settlers, on the horse carcasses of which the onrush of war had not yet permitted removal. The *New York Herald* man walked amid them and ended the story he sent his paper: "The air, the trees, the graves are silent. Even the relic hunters are gone now. And the soldiers here never wake to the sound of reveille."

[59] In many a country cottage over the land, a tall old clock in a quiet corner told time in a tick-tock deliberation. Whether the orchard branches hung with pink-spray blossoms or icicles of sleet, whether the outside news was seedtime or harvest, rain or drought, births or deaths, the swing of the pendulum was right and left and right and left in a tick-tock deliberation.

[60] The face and dial of the clock had known the eyes of a boy who listened to its tick-tock and learned to read its minute and hour hands. And the boy had seen years measured off by the swinging pendulum, and grown to man size, had gone away. And the people in the cottage knew that the clock would stand there and the boy never again come into the room and look at the clock with the query, "What is the time?"

[61] In a row of graves of the Unidentified the boy would sleep long in the dedicated final resting-place at Gettysburg. Why he had gone away and why he would never come back had roots in some mystery of flags and drums, of national fate in which individuals sink as in a deep sea, of men swallowed and vanished in a man-made storm of smoke and steel.

[62] The mystery deepened and moved with ancient music and inviolable consolation because a solemn Man of Authority had stood at the graves of the Unidentified and spoken the words "We cannot consecrate—we cannot hallow—this ground. The brave men, living and dead, who struggled here, have consecrated it far above our poor power to add or detract. . . . From these honored dead we take increased devotion to that cause for which they gave the last full measure of devotion."

[63] To the backward and forward pendulum swing of a tall old clock in a quiet corner they might read those cadenced words while outside the windows the first flurry of snow blew across the orchard and down over the meadow, the beginnings of winter in a gun-metal gloaming to be later arched with a star-flung sky.

COMMENT AND QUESTIONS

I. Most of this selection is objective reporting of verifiable facts, with the verification or documentation of the facts incorporated into the writing. There are few obvious devices for interest, no diluting or popularizing of the material to make it more appealing. But most readers find the packed, informative account very absorbing. What is the basis of its interest?

II. Is the delineation of Edward Everett generally favorable or unfavorable? Explain.

III. What is the purpose of including in the account Lincoln's visit to the photographer (paragraph 10)?

IV. What purpose is served by including the visits of the woman to Lincoln's office (paragraphs 17-24)? By what means does Sandburg make these visits vivid and dramatic?

V. How does Sandburg give the reader a sense of the setting in which the ceremonies at Gettysburg took place?

VI. Study the conflicting reports and judgments of the ceremonies at Gettysburg (paragraphs 34-53) in the light of what you know about charged language. What techniques were used by the reporters? What forces were operating to influence their judgments? Do you think that some of those who disregarded or condemned Lincoln's speech were sincere?

VII. How do the last seven paragraphs (57-63) differ from the rest of the account in attitude toward the subject and in style? What do they contribute to the selection? Can you summarize, in factual language, Sandburg's evaluation of the Gettysburg address?

VIII. What does Sandburg mean by saying that Lincoln's smooth sentences were "gnarled and tough with the enigmas of the American experiment" (paragraph 57)?

RACHEL L. CARSON

The Gray Beginnings[*]

Some two billion years of the history of earth and ocean are reconstructed in the following selection. Rachel L. Carson studied biology at Johns Hopkins University and the Marine Biological Laboratory at Woods Hole, is an aquatic biologist with the Fish and Wildlife Service, and is the author of *Under the Sea Wind, The Sea*

[*] From *The Sea Around Us* by Rachel L. Carson. Copyright 1950, 1951 by Rachel L. Carson. Reprinted by permission of Oxford University Press, Inc.

Around Us, and *The Edge of the Sea.* "The Gray Beginnings" is the first chapter of *The Sea Around Us,* winner of the 1951 National Book Award for non-fiction.

And the earth was without form, and void; and darkness was upon the face of the deep. GENESIS

[1] Beginnings are apt to be shadowy, and so it is with the beginnings of that great mother of life, the sea. Many people have debated how and when the earth got its ocean, and it is not surprising that their explanations do not always agree. For the plain and inescapable truth is that no one was there to see, and in the absence of eyewitness accounts there is bound to be a certain amount of disagreement. So if I tell here the story of how the young planet Earth acquired an ocean, it must be a story pieced together from many sources and containing many whole chapters the details of which we can only imagine. The story is founded on the testimony of the earth's most ancient rocks, which were young when the earth was young; on other evidence written on the face of the earth's satellite, the moon; and on hints contained in the history of the sun and the whole universe of star-filled space. For although no man was there to witness this cosmic birth, the stars and the moon and the rocks were there, and, indeed, had much to do with the fact that there is an ocean.

[2] The events of which I write must have occurred somewhat more than 2 billion years ago. As nearly as science can tell that is the approximate age of the earth, and the ocean must be very nearly as old. It is possible now to discover the age of the rocks that compose the crust of the earth by measuring the rate of decay of the radioactive materials they contain. The oldest rocks found anywhere on earth—in Manitoba—are about 2.3 billion years old. Allowing 100 million years or so for the cooling of the earth's materials to form a rocky crust, we arrive at the supposition that the tempestuous and violent events connected with our planet's birth occurred nearly $2\frac{1}{2}$ billion years ago. But this is only a minimum estimate, for rocks indicating an even greater age may be found at any time.

[3] The new earth, freshly torn from its parent sun, was a ball of whirling gases, intensely hot, rushing through the black spaces of the universe on a path and at a speed controlled by immense forces. Gradually the ball of flaming gases cooled. The gases began to liquefy, and Earth became a molten mass. The materials of this mass eventually became sorted out in a definite pattern: the heaviest in the center, the less heavy surrounding them, and the least heavy forming the outer rim. This is the pattern which persists today—a central sphere of molten iron, very nearly as hot as it was 2 billion years ago, an intermediate sphere of semi-plastic basalt, and a hard outer shell, relatively quite thin and composed of solid basalt and granite.

[4] The outer shell of the young earth must have been a good many millions of years changing from the liquid to the solid state, and it is believed that, before this change was completed, an event of the greatest importance

took place—the formation of the moon. The next time you stand on a beach at night, watching the moon's bright path across the water, and conscious of the moon-drawn tides, remember that the moon itself may have been born of a great tidal wave of earthly substance, torn off into space. And remember that if the moon was formed in this fashion, the event may have had much to do with shaping the ocean basins and the continents as we know them.

[5] There were tides in the new earth, long before there was an ocean. In response to the pull of the sun the molten liquids of the earth's whole surface rose in tides that rolled unhindered around the globe and only gradually slackened and diminished as the earthly shell cooled, congealed and hardened. Those who believe that the moon is a child of earth say that during an early stage of the earth's development something happened that caused this rolling, viscid tide to gather speed and momentum and to rise to unimaginable heights. Apparently the force that created these greatest tides the earth has ever known was the force of resonance, for at this time the period of the solar tides had come to approach, then equal, the period of the free oscillation of the liquid earth. And so every sun tide was given increased momentum by the push of the earth's oscillation, and each of the twice-daily tides was larger than the one before it. Physicists have calculated that, after 500 years of such monstrous, steadily increasing tides, those on the side toward the sun became too high for stability, and a great wave was torn away and hurled into space. But immediately, of course, the newly created satellite became subject to physical laws that sent it spinning in an orbit of its own about the earth. This is what we call the moon.

[6] There are reasons for believing that this event took place after the earth's crust had become slightly hardened, instead of during its partly liquid state. There is to this day a great scar on the surface of the globe. This scar or depression holds the Pacific Ocean. According to some geophysicists, the floor of the Pacific is composed of basalt, the substance of the earth's middle layer, while all other oceans are floored with a thin layer of granite, which makes up most of the earth's outer layer. We immediately wonder what became of the Pacific's granite covering and the most convenient assumption is that it was torn away when the moon was formed. There is supporting evidence. The mean density of the moon is much less than that of the earth (3.3 compared with 5.5), suggesting that the moon took away none of the earth's heavy core, but that it is composed only of the granite and some of the basalt of the outer layers.

[7] The birth of the moon probably helped shape other regions of the world's ocean besides the Pacific. When part of the crust was torn away, strains must have been set up in the remaining granite envelope. Perhaps the granite mass cracked open on the side opposite the moon scar. Perhaps, as the earth spun on its axis and rushed on its orbit through space, the cracks widened and the masses of granite began to drift apart, moving over a tarry, slowly hardening layer of basalt. Gradually the outer portions of the

basalt layer became solid and the wandering continents came to rest, frozen into place with oceans between them. In spite of theories to the contrary, the weight of geologic evidence seems to be that the locations of the major ocean basins and the major continental land masses are today much the same as they have been since a very early period of the earth's history.

[8] But this is to anticipate the story, for when the moon was born there was no ocean. The gradually cooling earth was enveloped in heavy layers of cloud, which contained much of the water of the new planet. For a long time its surface was so hot that no moisture could fall without immediately being reconverted to steam. This dense, perpetually renewed cloud covering must have been thick enough that no rays of sunlight could penetrate it. And so the rough outlines of the continents and the empty ocean basins were sculptured out of the surface of the earth in darkness, in a Stygian world of heated rock and swirling clouds and gloom.

[9] As soon as the earth's crust cooled enough, the rains began to fall. Never have there been such rains since that time. They fell continuously, day and night, days passing into months, into years, into centuries. They poured into the waiting ocean basins, or, falling upon the continental masses, drained away to become sea.

[10] That primeval ocean, growing in bulk as the rains slowly filled its basins, must have been only faintly salt. But the falling rains were the symbol of the dissolution of the continents. From the moment the rains began to fall, the lands began to be worn away and carried to the sea. It is an endless, inexorable process that has never stopped—the dissolving of the rocks, the leaching out of their contained minerals, the carrying of the rock fragments and dissolved minerals to the ocean. And over the eons of time, the sea has grown even more bitter with the salt of the continents.

[11] In what manner the sea produced the mysterious and wonderful stuff called protoplasm we cannot say. In its warm, dimly lit waters the unknown conditions of temperature and pressure and saltiness must have been the critical ones for the creation of life from non-life. At any rate they produced the result that neither the alchemists with their crucibles nor modern scientists in their laboratories have been able to achieve.

[12] Before the first living cell was created, there may have been many trials and failures. It seems probable that, within the warm saltiness of the primeval sea, certain organic substances were fashioned from carbon dioxide, sulphur, nitrogen, phosphorus, potassium, and calcium. Perhaps these were transition steps from which the complex molecules of protoplasm arose— molecules that somehow acquired the ability to reproduce themselves and begin the endless stream of life. But at present no one is wise enough to be sure.

[13] Those first living things may have been simple microorganisms rather like some of the bacteria we know today—mysterious borderline forms that were not quite plants, not quite animals, barely over the intangible line that separates the non-living from the living. It is doubtful that this first life

possessed the substance chlorophyll, with which plants in sunlight transform lifeless chemicals into the living stuff of their tissues. Little sunshine could enter their dim world, penetrating the cloud banks from which fell the endless rains. Probably the sea's first children lived on the organic substances then present in the ocean waters, or, like the iron and sulphur bacteria that exist today, lived directly on inorganic food.

[14] All the while the cloud cover was thinning, the darkness of the nights alternated with palely illumined days, and finally the sun for the first time shone through upon the sea. By this time some of the living things that floated in the sea must have developed the magic of chlorophyll. Now they were able to take the carbon dioxide of the air and the water of the sea and of these elements, in sunlight, build the organic substances they needed. So the first true plants came into being.

[15] Another group of organisms, lacking the chlorophyll but needing organic food, found they could make a way of life for themselves by devouring the plants. So the first animals arose, and from that day to this, every animal in the world has followed the habit it learned in the ancient seas and depends, directly or through complex food chains, on the plants for food and life.

[16] As the years passed, and the centuries, and the millions of years, the stream of life grew more and more complex. From simple, one-celled creatures, others that were aggregations of specialized cells arose, and then creatures with organs for feeding, digesting, breathing, reproducing. Sponges grew on the rocky bottom of the sea's edge and coral animals built their habitations in warm, clear waters. Jellyfish swam and drifted in the sea. Worms evolved, and starfish, and hard-shelled creatures with many-jointed legs, the arthropods. The plants, too, progressed, from the microscopic algae to branched and curiously fruiting seaweeds that swayed with the tides and were plucked from the coastal rocks by the surf and cast adrift.

[17] During all this time the continents had no life. There was little to induce living things to come ashore, forsaking their all-providing, all-embracing mother sea. The lands must have been bleak and hostile beyond the power of words to describe. Imagine a whole continent of naked rock, across which no covering mantle of green had been drawn—a continent without soil, for there were no plants to aid in its formation and bind it to the rocks with their roots. Imagine a land of stone, a silent land, except for the sound of the rains and winds that swept across it. For there was no living voice, and no living thing moved over the surface of the rocks.

[18] Meanwhile, the gradual cooling of the planet, which had first given the earth its hard granite crust, was progressing into its deeper layers; and as the interior slowly cooled and contracted, it drew away from the outer shell. This shell, accommodating itself to the shrinking sphere within it, fell into folds and wrinkles—the earth's first mountain ranges.

[19] Geologists tell us that there must have been at least two periods of mountain building (often called "revolutions") in that dim period, so long

ago that the rocks have no record of it, so long ago that the mountains themselves have long since been worn away. Then there came a third great period of upheaval and readjustment of the earth's crust, about a billion years ago, but of all its majestic mountains the only reminders today are the Laurentian hills of eastern Canada, and a great shield of granite over the flat country around Hudson Bay.

[20] The epochs of mountain building only served to speed up the processes of erosion by which continents were worn down and their crumbling rock and contained minerals returned to the sea. The uplifted masses of the mountains were prey to the bitter cold of the upper atmosphere and under the attacks of frost and snow and ice the rocks cracked and crumbled away. The rains beat with greater violence upon the slopes of the hills and carried away the substance of the mountains in torrential streams. There was still no plant covering to modify and resist the power of the rains.

[21] And in the sea, life continued to evolve. The earliest forms have left no fossils by which we can identify them. Probably they were soft-bodied, with no hard parts that could be preserved. Then, too, the rock layers formed in those early days have since been so altered by enormous heat and pressure, under the foldings of the earth's crust, that any fossils they might have contained would have been destroyed.

[22] For the past 500 million years, however, the rocks have preserved the fossil record. By the dawn of the Cambrian period, when the history of living things was first inscribed on rock pages, life in the sea had progressed so far that all the main groups of backboneless or invertebrate animals had been developed. But there were no animals with backbones, no insects or spiders, and still no plant or animal had been evolved that was capable of venturing onto the forbidding land. So for more than three-fourths of geologic time the continents were desolate and uninhabited, while the sea prepared the life that was later to invade them and make them habitable. Meanwhile, with violent tremblings of the earth and with the fire and smoke of roaring volcanoes, mountains rose and wore away, glaciers moved to and fro over the earth, and the sea crept over the continents and again receded.

[23] It was not until Silurian time, some 350 million years ago, that the first pioneer of land life crept out on the shore. It was an arthropod, one of the great tribe that later produced crabs and lobsters and insects. It must have been something like a modern scorpion, but, unlike some of its descendants, it never wholly severed the ties that united it to the sea. It lived a strange life, half-terrestrial, half-aquatic, something like that of the ghost crabs that speed along the beaches today, now and then dashing into the surf to moisten their gills.

[24] Fish, tapered of body and stream-molded by the press of running waters, were evolving in Silurian rivers. In times of drought, in the drying pools and lagoons, the shortage of oxygen forced them to develop swim bladders for the storage of air. One form that possessed an air-breathing

lung was able to survive the dry periods by burying itself in mud, leaving a passage to the surface through which it breathed.

[25] It is very doubtful that the animals alone would have succeeded in colonizing the land, for only the plants had the power to bring about the first amelioration of its harsh conditions. They helped make soil of the crumbling rocks, they held back the soil from the rains that would have swept it away, and little by little they softened and subdued the bare rock, the lifeless desert. We know very little about the first land plants, but they must have been closely related to some of the larger seaweeds that had learned to live in the coastal shallows, developing strengthened stems and grasping, rootlike holdfasts to resist the drag and pull of the waves. Perhaps it was in some coastal lowlands, periodically drained and flooded, that some such plants found it possible to survive, though separated from the sea. This also seems to have taken place in the Silurian period.

[26] The mountains that had been thrown up by the Laurentian revolution gradually wore away, and as the sediments were washed from their summits and deposited on the lowlands, great areas of the continents sank under the load. The seas crept out of their basins and spread over the lands. Life fared well and was exceedingly abundant in those shallow, sunlit seas. But with the later retreat of the ocean water into the deeper basins, many creatures must have been left stranded in shallow, landlocked bays. Some of these animals found means to survive on land. The lakes, the shores of the rivers, and the coastal swamps of those days were the testing grounds in which plants and animals either became adapted to the new conditions or perished.

[27] As the lands rose and the seas receded, a strange fishlike creature emerged on the land, and over the thousands of years its fins became legs, and instead of gills it developed lungs. In the Devonian sandstone this first amphibian left its footprint.

[28] On land and sea the stream of life poured on. New forms evolved; some old ones declined and disappeared. On land the mosses and the ferns and the seed plants developed. The reptiles for a time dominated the earth, gigantic, grotesque, and terrifying. Birds learned to live and move in the ocean of air. The first small mammals lurked inconspicuously in hidden crannies of the earth as though in fear of the reptiles.

[29] When they went ashore the animals that took up a land life carried with them a part of the sea in their bodies, a heritage which they passed on to their children and which even today links each land animal with its origin in the ancient sea. Fish, amphibian, and reptile, warm-blooded bird and mammal—each of us carries in our veins a salty stream in which the elements sodium, potassium, and calcium are combined in almost the same proportions as in sea water. This is our inheritance from the day, untold millions of years ago, when a remote ancestor, having progressed from the one-celled to the many-celled stage, first developed a circulatory system in which the fluid was merely the water of the sea. In the same way, our lime-

hardened skeletons are a heritage from the calcium-rich ocean of Cambrian time. Even the protoplasm that streams within each cell of our bodies has the chemical structure impressed upon all living matter when the first simple creatures were brought forth in the ancient sea. And as life itself began in the sea, so each of us begins his individual life in a miniature ocean within his mother's womb, and in the stages of his embryonic development repeats the steps by which his race evolved, from gill-breathing inhabitants of a water world to creatures able to live on land.

[30] Some of the land animals later returned to the ocean. After perhaps 50 million years of land life, a number of reptiles entered the sea about 170 million years ago, in the Triassic period. They were huge and formidable creatures. Some had oarlike limbs by which they rowed through the water; some were web-footed, with long, serpentine necks. These grotesque monsters disappeared millions of years ago, but we remember them when we come upon a large sea turtle swimming many miles at sea, its barnacle-encrusted shell eloquent of its marine life. Much later, perhaps no more than 50 million years ago, some of the mammals, too, abandoned a land life for the ocean. Their descendants are the sea lions, seals, sea elephants, and whales of today.

[31] Among the land mammals there was a race of creatures that took to an arboreal existence. Their hands underwent remarkable development, becoming skilled in manipulating and examining objects, and along with this skill came a superior brain power that compensated for what these comparatively small mammals lacked in strength. At last, perhaps somewhere in the vast interior of Asia, they descended from the trees and became again terrestrial. The past million years have seen their transformation into beings with the body and brain and spirit of man.

[32] Eventually man, too, found his way back to the sea. Standing on its shores, he must have looked out upon it with wonder and curiosity, compounded with an unconscious recognition of his lineage. He could not physically re-enter the ocean as the seals and whales had done. But over the centuries, with all the skill and ingenuity and reasoning powers of his mind, he has sought to explore and investigate even its most remote parts, so that he might re-enter it mentally and imaginatively.

[33] He built boats to venture out on its surface. Later he found ways to descend to the shallow parts of its floor, carrying with him the air that, as a land mammal long unaccustomed to aquatic life, he needed to breathe. Moving in fascination over the deep sea he could not enter, he found ways to probe its depths, he let down nets to capture its life, he invented mechanical eyes and ears that could re-create for his senses a world long lost, but a world that, in the deepest part of his subconscious mind, he had never wholly forgotten.

[34] And yet he has returned to his mother sea only on her own terms. He cannot control or change the ocean as, in his brief tenancy of earth, he has subdued and plundered the continents. In the artificial world of his

cities and towns, he often forgets the true nature of his planet and the long vistas of its history, in which the existence of the race of men has occupied a mere moment of time. The sense of all these things comes to him most clearly in the course of a long ocean voyage, when he watches day after day the receding rim of the horizon, ridged and furrowed by waves; when at night he becomes aware of the earth's rotation as the stars pass overhead; or when, alone in this world of water and sky, he feels the loneliness of his earth in space. And then, as never on land, he knows the truth that his world is a water world, a planet dominated by its covering mantle of ocean, in which the continents are but transient intrusions of land above the surface of the all-encircling sea.

COMMENT AND QUESTIONS

I. Rachel Carson states in her opening paragraph the problem of the historian of young earth and ocean: "For the plain and inescapable truth is that no one was there to see, and in the absence of eyewitness accounts there is bound to be a certain amount of disagreement." This statement is somewhat ironical—for even with eyewitness accounts there is often disagreement.[1] Nevertheless, the writer dealing with prehistory has a particular problem of evaluating what evidence there is, and choosing among conflicting theories or between one possibility and another. Cite examples of the choices Miss Carson makes. What kinds of evidence support her interpretations?

II. Does this account of "the gray beginnings" seem to you incompatible with the idea of a First Cause, or a Creator of the universe? Explain.

III. Like most historical narratives, this one follows a chronological pattern; but, because the material is complex, and because developments occur simultaneously, a simple time-sequence is not always possible. Leaf through the selection, looking at the first sentences of paragraphs, and noticing how many of them establish some sort of time-relationship between units of the material. What other transitional devices are most commonly used here to link a new paragraph to the preceding one?

IV. Miss Carson's subject-matter is not necessarily appealing to a general audience, but *The Sea Around Us* has been widely read and enjoyed. By what means does the author make her material interesting?

V. If you have read Carl Becker's "Everyman His Own Historian" you may be interested in considering this question: how might an honest and intelligent account of the early history of earth and ocean differ, in fact and in interpretation, from Rachel Carson's, if such an account were written in 1850? in 1900? in 2000?

[1] See, for example, Carl Sandburg's "Lincoln Speaks at Gettysburg," page 823.

CATHERINE DRINKER BOWEN

The Business of a Biographer[*]

In the following essay, a contemporary biographer recounts her experiences in preparing her book *John Adams and the American Revolution*. Using a chronological framework, Mrs. Bowen analyzes the procedure and the problems of the biographer, distinguishes between different types of biography, and suggests standards for judging this kind of prose. In addition to *John Adams and the American Revolution*, Catherine Drinker Bowen's books include *Beloved Friend*, a life of Tchaikovsky, *Yankee from Olympus*, a biography of Justice Oliver Wendell Holmes, and *The Lion and the Throne*, the life and times of Sir Edward Coke. The essay below was published in *The Atlantic Monthly* in 1951.

1

[1] Gertrude Stein once gave a talk before—oddly enough—the boys of Choate School. "It is the business of an artist," she told them, "to be exciting."

[2] It is the business also of an historian. History is, in its essence, exciting; to present it as dull is to my mind, stark and unforgivable misrepresentation. And if history be, as Webster has it, the story of nations, biography the story of men—then by that same token, biography should prove, intrinsically, more exciting even than history. Biography is more immediately comprehensible; it is something our experience lets us know, in the Keatsian phrase, upon our pulses.

[3] Choice of subject is, for the biographer, a vital part of the total creative effort. Sometimes it is not even an individual that lights the biographical spark, but only a period in history. Such was, for example, my own experience with my last book, *John Adams and the American Revolution*. I had published three biographies set in the nineteenth century, and each of them had spilled over, at its outset, into an earlier period. With each I had been given a glimpse, tantalizing, provocative, into the Century of Enlightenment, that Century of Reason—extraordinary and vivid time when our American world was young and yeasty, when men of faith, men of intellect and staunchest character, threw down a king and fashioned a government to their very liking. "When, before the present epocha," wrote John Adams to his friend Wythe in 1775, "had three millions of people full power and fair opportunity to form and establish the wisest and happiest government that human wisdom can contrive?"

[*] Copyright 1951, by the Atlantic Monthly Company, 8 Arlington Street, Boston 16, Massachusetts.

[4] Reading those words, I had felt a stirring at the roots of my hair. Exciting? . . . I remembered a young historian, the ink yet damp upon his doctoral thesis, who had said to me with all the vigor and confidence of his twenty-odd years, "Now I have my training, I'm going to write and make some money. I'm not going to teach. I plan to take—well, some period of history, and *hop it up* the way you biographers do."

[5] Hopping up, I learned, is done with morphine, marihuana. But we biographers do not hop up history!—I told my young friend quickly. Does one hop up the Rocky Mountains, or a hibiscus flower? On the contrary, we ourselves are moved by this astonishment of height, this redness of red; we desire to reproduce this astonishment, this good news granted by earth or sky. So it is with history, if one be history-minded, and so it was with me when first I read John Adams's letters, his essay *On the Canon and Feudal Law*, his legal brief in defense of the British soldiers on trial for their lives after the Boston Massacre. The life of any active man reflects his times, and with Adams this is peculiarly, startlingly true. Nothing that he said, nothing he did could have been said or done in any other era.

[6] Adams's philosophy, moreover, was extraordinarily pertinent to the times in which I found myself living at the moment. This was February, 1945, and America was fighting a war. To our deeply troubled minds there had already been introduced, that spring, ideological problems which were to come after the war: problems of government, of federation. What, we had begun to ask ourselves, is the meaning of sovereignty? I wanted to study history through the eyes of a man interested in these problems, a man conscious of the word federation—a word that may well bring states or nations from the constant fear of war to the joyful practice of peace.

[7] John Adams from his twentieth year was a student of law, a student of governments past and present. He was a constitution maker. Even before Independence was declared, he taught the various colonies how to compose their several state governments. Adams put, in short, a canvas bottom under the American Revolution, so that when the guy ropes to Britain were cast off, the colonies did not fall through to chaos, bloodshed, and a new paternalism.

[8] Casting about, before my choice was fully made, I read the published biographies of Adams. There are not many, only five or six. I looked up Adams in the biographical dictionaries; I paged through the nine large volumes called *Life and Works of John Adams,* edited in the 1850s by John's grandson, Charles Francis Adams, our Minister to England during the Civil War. I read such published letters as I could find, notably those to Benjamin Rush of Philadelphia, to John Winthrop of Massachusetts who was Adams's teacher of mathematics at Harvard in the 1750s. I read the superb correspondence with Thomas Jefferson when the two were old men, living in retirement. I lingered long over the little volume called *Familiar Letters of John Adams and his Wife, during the Revolution.* I read also the letters of John's daughter Abigail and the later letters of John's wife, written

during John's presidency. I went through most of the books written by John's descendants—and the Adamses of Massachusetts were a writing tribe. *The Education of Henry Adams* tells much about Braintree, where John's boyhood was spent; so do the biographies and autobiographies of the various Charles Francises and the eight-volume *Memoirs* written by John's eldest son, John Quincy Adams, sixth President of the United States.

[9] All doubts fled. I had chosen my hero—or more exactly, he had chosen me. I knew by now the basic facts of Adams's life; it would be for me as biographer to make the facts live. Should this high aim be achieved, I was aware it would be due not alone to the manner of presentation but to the manner of research. Reading hundreds of books and manuscripts, how does the biographer know which passages to copy down? He doesn't know, he guesses, and the instinct behind his guess can make or mar the finished product. It is laborious work, this copying in research libraries, hour after hour and day after day, using a soft pencil for the sake of one's wrist and begging the librarian for a table by the daylight.

[10] In this process of research, I employ no helpers, no apprentices, no Ph.D. students to do my reading for me, nor even the subsequent filing and cross-filing of notes. It would be dangerous; something vital might be overlooked. Painting a portrait, does the artist hire an apprentice to choose his colors, decide the pose in which the subject will sit or the texture of the frame in which the portrait will hang? This copying in libraries, this eventual choice of incident is half the biographical battle, perhaps more than half. While the biographer reads, he is actually in process of composition; he recites passages to his friends on the telephone, he talks continually of his great discoveries.

[11] Selection of material depends, of course, on the type of biography one intends to write. The choice here is plain. Either one desires to dig out and reveal hitherto unpublished material, thereby gaining kudos in the academic world (with a likely raise from assistant professor of history to a full professorship)—or one desires to write a book that will be bought and read. My ambition, quite frankly, was to introduce John Adams to as many people as I could. Repeatedly, during research, I reminded myself of this aim. Otherwise, I might be tempted into following false clues, spend precious hours copying some incident which, while it may have been historically "new," was patently not biographical *news*—a matter altogether different. Whatever did not stand as illustration of Adams's character or Adams's part in forming the American States, must be thrown out. There were times indeed, when I almost wept with vexation, putting broken manuscripts, faded newspaper columns from me on the library table, or turning them face down against temptation.

[12] So strongly did I hold to this purpose that in my first year of reading I wrote it out, filing it in the folder marked *Preface to Book:* "The facts on which my narrative is based are available to everyone. I do not scorn what the academic historian calls secondary material, or tertiary or septuagenary

—so long as it is proven authentic. I aim not to startle with new material but to persuade with old, and I shall use a narrative form because for me it is the most persuasive. Fictionalized biography is the current label; I myself do not admit a phrase which besides being doubtful English, does not express what I am trying to do. Call this book, rather, a 'portrait' of John Adams. I shall draw a portrait, and like Saint-Mémin with his profiles, I shall use the *physionotrace:* I shall find instruments with which to measure, and then go ahead and paint. In brief, I shall study the available evidence and on the basis of it, build pictures which to me are consistent with the evidence. All my reading, all my research will be directed toward two goals: the understanding of John Adams's character; and the understanding of how it felt to be a citizen of the Eighteenth Century."

2

[13] The contract with my publishers allowed me five years; I sat down and portioned carefully the time that remained. I would give myself two full reading years, then twelve months to write out what I call the *chronology* of my narrative—that is, a straight, unvarnished succession of facts, names, dates which trace my hero's movement from place to place. Knowing where one's hero is at each given week—if not each day—is the first necessity in biography, and by no means easy to achieve. There would be, I knew, gaps of weeks and even months when I should lose John Adams between Braintree and Boston as dismally as though he had journeyed to Samarcand.

[14] So much for three years. The remaining two, I could devote to brooding about John Adams. I could think of him as walking, talking, studying, riding circuit, arguing cases in court, or resting at Braintree with his family. I could determine upon those scenes which best would illustrate character and times; I could cease collecting facts and begin visualizing my subject in terms of action. My story would have a protagonist as well as a hero: the United States of America was my protagonist. Its birth, its growth moved parallel with Adams's own coming of age. I must weave and interweave, move from Adams to history, from history to Adams. . . . To accomplish this, twenty-four months seemed all too short—twenty-four months to write my book.

[15] My schedule determined, I ploughed into the second year of research, traveling about the country to interview Adamses when they would permit it, and to interview historians for the exchange of ideas concerning government practical and theoretical. In the end, I found myself the possessor of hundreds of slips of yellow paper, cut to half the size of ordinary typewriter paper and covered with writing, the source carefully copied on the upper left-hand corner. My first files were chronological, with the exception of certain large subjects such as *Boston, streets and buildings* . . . or, *Washington, George* . . . or, *Philadelphia, appearance of* . . . or, *Statistics of Population, 1700–1776.* Or, simply and quite terrifyingly, the file marked IDEAS.

[16] I began to cross-file again, narrowing my chronology from decades to years, then to months, weeks, days, meanwhile committing to memory as many facts as I could, in the hope they would pop up at the needed moment. (In 1774, the Province of New York ordered *Liberty and Prudence* as the watermark for its official letter paper. In 1745, New England men sent 9000 cannon balls into Louisburg before the fortress surrendered.) The work fell of itself into three divisions: (1) Research about *things*. That is, how did the streets of Braintree look in 1745, in '65, in '74? How did John Adams's mother dress, what did Harvard students of the mid-Eighteenth Century eat and drink, what outdoor games did they play? (2) Research about *people*, their characters, affiliations, actions, beliefs. And (3) research about *ideas*, those philosophies and principles by which the Eighteenth Century lived, wrote its books, and created its governments.

[17] For the physical scene I found it necessary to visit Braintree in all four seasons. In the small tidy farmhouse where John was born, I went up narrow stairs, looked out a boy's dormer window onto February snow. I walked by Black's Creek when November held the salt grass stiff. John's great-great-granddaughter walked with me to show how she too had gone smelting in childhood between those marshy banks. I climbed Penn's Hill in June as Abigail Adams had climbed it to see the Battle of Bunker Hill across the Bay. In Boston, the old State House still stands, and in Philadelphia, Independence Hall. All the bustle of the twentieth century cannot efface the spirits that walk within these walls.

3

[18] But I spent far less time on the physical scene than on that other, harder quest. The Eighteenth Century is not to be trifled with. What made that century different from our own was not man's clothing but his outlook, his view of body and soul—a view so altered by time that only deepest immersion, a deliberate, disciplined shutting of the eyes would bring it back. Later, I was to say so, in an essay on *Sources and Methods* that was included in my bibliography. I mailed it to my publishers with the completed manuscript. Back, in due time, came my galley proofs from Boston, with an editorial query on the margin, "Author: Don't you mean *opening* of the eyes?"

[19] I did not mean opening, and said so by return mail. I meant a closing of the eyes, a shutting out of our boasted scientific "progress." . . . In John Adams's day, Galen's four fluid humours still governed the body—the sanguine, the phlegmatic, the choleric, the melancholic. Harvard in 1751 debated the truth of Copernicus's theory. The narrowing of one's mind to this strange constriction is a struggle painful, almost impossible. The Age of Enlightenment has tales to tell that wash our world away. Gone are Pasteur, Lister, and the germ theory of disease. Gone is Darwin. Special creation, spontaneous generation rule the universe. Newton, Descartes, Bacon, Harvey have not yet obliterated the long medieval darkness. Over

our shoulders peer Ramus, Abélard and the schoolmen, with Fra Castoreus and Meister Eckhart.

[20] It is another world, and the biographer must somehow enter it. To help on that awful journey, I sought every avenue that offered, spending hours in the map rooms of libraries, to familiarize myself with old Braintree, old Boston, old Worcester, with the great Plymouth highway running down from the north and with the Connecticut River that divided Massachusetts of 1750 almost as the Mississippi divides our country today. Searching for the faces, the authentic features of my subjects, I combed museums, art reference libraries, print rooms, comparing an Adams nose by Copley with an Adams nose by Stuart and deciding, in the end, that Saint-Mémin's physionotrace was more trustworthy than the draughtsmanship of the masters. As for Eighteenth Century newspapers, that gossipy sheet called *The Boston Gazette* became more recognizable to me than the New York *Times* for 1950. I could even distinguish between the anonymous gentlemen who wrote for the newspapers (most of whom turned out to be Sam Adams).

[21] In the Boston Public Library, I found some three thousand volumes from John Adams's own collection. I took them from the shelves, read John's inked marginal notes, and what I read made me laugh aloud. An impudent scholar surely, this Adams, of the sort that Carlyle calls "original men, the first peculiarity of which is that they in some measure *converse with the universe at first hand."*

[22] Taking stock, I saw that I was done with the period of intensive reading; it was time to give shape to what I had found. Nevertheless I was troubled; it is a crisis which every writer longs for and every scholar fears. I wanted to read more, learn more, even copy more; the file marked *Things to do* was not exhausted by half. The temptation was great and insidious; I had witnessed historians who went on digging up facts until they grew too old to write their books at all. In a New England library I had met two learned professors, deep in manuscript and notebooks—beautiful, lined notebooks, with *Category A* and *Category B* traced in red ink and black. Each professor took me out to lunch, kindly showed me his notes, and confided with a sigh, "How I dread the day when I finish reading in libraries and have to put all this material together and write my book!"

[23] It is indeed, a common occupational disease of historians. When I feel it stealing over me, I remind myself of what Justice Holmes told one of his secretaries: "There comes a time, young feller, when a book has to be *written!"*

[24] For me the time had come.

4

[25] For the actual writing of my tale, modern biography offered two literary forms: the critical and the narrative. In the first, the author remains eternally present, telling the reader what to think and bolstering all pronouncements with quotations from the original source, or leaving a shrewd

margin for error by employing such phrases as, "We consider . . . the records tell us . . . it is probable that . . ."

[26] The bulk of my biography would have no such handy props. Choice of the narrative form had set upon me an extra burden, an extra technical procedure; I must make my characters three-dimensional instead of two. It was the artist's task as distinct from the scholar's—and *it is the business of an artist to be exciting.* The words went over in my mind, and there were hours when the cold hand of fear lay on me.

[27] I could not, for instance, employ the frank critical statement that my hero in youth was shy, nor quote a reminiscent Adams acquaintance in proof of shyness. The reminiscence was penned thirty years later, when Adams had become the reverse of shy. To quote it would destroy utterly the illusion of reality, the hard-won empathy, immediacy, the sense of being *there.* How then, could I convey to my reader the fact that John was shy? Only in one way: I must show him being shy. From John's *Autobiography,* written half a century after the event, I had learned briefly of that fateful day when the boy, at sixteen, journeyed ten miles from Braintree to take his examinations for Harvard College. Quite obviously, those were, for John, fearful and significant hours. I must transcribe them; I must translate them from reminiscence to reality. I must let my reader travel to Cambridge with John, walk invisible beside his pony, trudge with him across Harvard Yard and up the steps to face his four examiners and that large, handsome, distinguished, and terrifying individual, President Holyoke of Harvard College. It was not for me to write, "We can therefore imagine John's feelings as he confronted the President of Harvard." I must do more than that, I must stand with my reader before that polished desk; with John I must answer the questions put in Latin, with John freeze to paralysis when he cannot recall the Latin word for *morality.*

[28] And in my method will be no deception. The reader knows I am not God, knows I cannot actually be inside John's mind—and knows by now, I sincerely trust, that behind my narrative is historical source and historical evidence without which I would not presume to take young Adams to Harvard Hall or anywhere else. Should the evidence anywhere conflict, I shall sacrifice my narrative. Experience tells me I must forever be prepared for such sacrifice, not in large things—the facts of our Revolutionary history are by now well ascertained—but in those small descriptive details that bring a scene alive. When first I wrote of young Adams's journey to Cambridge, for instance, I had him walk the ten miles on foot, alone and frightened. The very act of walking seemed characteristic of his mood. When I discovered he had a pony, it altered somehow the very climate of the journey.

[29] In this connection, when five of my Adams chapters appeared serially in the *Atlantic,* I received a letter from a distinguished college professor, himself a biographer. He approved my chapters, he said cordially. "I wish," he went on, "to take advantage of your research. But I am puzzled. You

have written Adams's conversation in such a manner that I cannot tell which words he actually spoke. In the published volume, will your documentation support these conversations?"

[30] I told the professor that it would be for him rather than for me to say if my published bibliography proved adequate. My own conscience was clear. Each public utterance of John's, whether a speech in Congress, an essay in the *Boston Gazette,* or a legal brief used in court, was historical, actual, directly from source even if paraphrased. My ambition had been to persuade people to read historic documents such as Adams's essay *On the Canon and Feudal Law,* his *Instructions to the Braintree Representatives in 1765.* It was, indeed, more than an ambition with me; it was an obsession. Americans must know these glorious pages, these inspired paragraphs.

[31] Unfortunately for the biographer, readers will not suffer lengthy quotations. At sight of set-in paragraphs, readers flee; they are gone, lost, the book is closed. The thought was awful to me. I must devise ways, I must lend a hand to my readers. . . . Could not James Otis, sitting in the *Gazette* office, read aloud the best lines from some long-drawn page? Or John himself, riding down from circuit court in Falmouth, rehearse his forthcoming essay on the *Canon and Feudal Law?* Or Sam Adams, journeying with John in the coach to Philadelphia, could quote Hawley's shrewd letter of advice to the Congressional delegates from Massachusetts.

[32] So much for Adams's historical utterances. His private conversations were another matter. The sense of them, the emotional or critical content, I took from Adams's Diary or letters, then paraphrased into dialogue, taking care to have the sentences as brief as possible. Over even these insignificant phrases I labored long, testing words with the *Oxford English Dictionary* to make sure I fell into no anachronism. (Readers have demurred at my putting the word *propaganda* into Adams's mouth, yet the *Oxford English Dictionary* gives 1718 as the first date of use. Readers of *Yankee from Olympus* objected to my using *sabotage* in our Civil War era; it came direct from a Boston newspaper of 1861.)

[33] To reproduce the speech of a past era is impossible. Attempting to catch even the echo of a rhythm that is gone, I took to bed with me each night for years, some seventeenth or eighteenth century book and read myself to sleep . . . Burton, John Selden, Isaak Walton, Sir Thomas Browne, John Bunyan; I chose chatty, facile writers who were at home in the vernacular and who wrote, I felt sure, as they talked. *The Letters of George Third* were a treasury of conversational idiom, John Aubrey's *Brief Lives* (1680) a very mine of phrases: "They *culled out* their *greatest shillings* to lay in the scale against the tobacco." . . . Or, "He *addicted himself* but little to the study of the law, being a *great waster.*"

[34] The device even of private conversation I used as sparingly as possible and never for any purpose but one—to reveal character, emotion, the state of being of my subjects. In real life, people do talk, and had not Plutarch, Heroditus, Thucydides, Tacitus used dialogue to illuminate history?

[35] Academic historians, accustomed to write only in the critical form, are slow to recognize the difficulties of the straight narrative method. They are apt to call it "popularization," and their implication is not flattering. Yet among classic historians are those who acknowledge not only the difficulties but the value of historical narrative. In his brilliant essay, "The Muse of History," George Macaulay Trevelyan says:—

[36] "It is in narrative that modern historical writing is weakest, and to my thinking it is a very serious weakness—spinal in fact. Some writers would seem never to have studied the art of telling a story. There is no 'flow' to their events, which stand like ponds instead of running like streams. Yet history is, in its unchangeable essence, 'a tale.' Round the story, as flesh and blood round the bone, should be gathered many different things—character drawing, study of social and intellectual movements, speculations as to probable causes and effects, and whatever else the historian can bring to illustrate the past. But the art of history remains always the art of narrative. That is the bed rock."

5

[37] Acceptance of the narrative form was my first biographical step. But it was after all only an artistic decision, not a piece of writing. I had worked for three years; I had done my research, I had set down my chronology. Yet no character or place had actually been introduced to the reader. How then should the tale be opened, how closed? Was I to open with birth and close with death? It was at about this time that a novelist, a writer of detective stories, remarked to me, "What an easy time you biographers have, compared with us fiction writers! The shape of your book is laid out ready to hand, before you even begin to write."

[38] I said, "What shape, exactly?" The novelist told me it was self-evident:—"Birth, education, marriage, death."

[39] He could not have been more mistaken. Life has no shape, artistically speaking, any more than grief has a shape, or jealousy, or love, or any of those large angry things. It is for the writer to find a shape, find boundaries, a circumference within which he may freely move according to his abilities. If he tries to encompass the universe within his book, he will surely get lost, and getting lost is a sin the experienced writer can never permit himself. Nothing will repel the reader more quickly than an author who wanders from his tale. . . . John Adams lived for ninety years. Was I to tell the full story of those years? Should I write of Adams as lawyer, as political philosopher, as diplomat to France and Holland, as President? What particular bias would guide me? Why, in short, was I writing this book?

[40] Once more I asked myself the vital question—a question elementary, yet it would seem, neglected by writers of history. For my beginning, John Adams himself gave the philosophic clue; his story must open, not at his birth but when Adams was ten—the year, he told Dr. Rush much later, when he "first became a politician." This was 1745, the famous year of the

Louisburg victory, a moment of great significance both for hero and protagonist, for Adams and history.

[41] I went on, yet as I proceeded, it became plain my story was sickening from surfeit of material; I was not creating a living character as I had hoped to do. I was setting down a mere list of events, an Adams calendar, with no space to explain why things happened or how the men felt who brought these things to pass.

[42] In much perturbation of spirit, I made the decision to end in the year 1776, with the Declaration of Independence, when Adams was only forty. To sacrifice the Old John Adams was no easy decision. This was a glorious old man, as appealing at eighty as he was at thirty. I had looked forward to describing those years of retirement at Quincy, when an ex-President of the United States signed his letters so cheerfully, "The Farmer of Stony Fields." To end in 1776 would be to sacrifice the wonderful correspondence with Jefferson—above all, to sacrifice the most dramatic death scene in American history. What climax could possibly substitute for dying on the Fourth of July? Moreover, I am suspicious of a biography that skimps the death scene of its hero. "It imports us to know how great men die as to know how they live."

[43] History came to my rescue. The Declaration of Independence was itself a kind of death; it marked the end of an empire. There were Americans who recognized this fact in all its significance, and who greatly mourned, even as they rejoiced. The Fourth of July, 1776, would be an ending and—for America, my protagonist—a beginning. The Fourth of July was a death and a resurrection, the very Easter of our national spirit.

[44] Within my circle, within my stated circumference, I had room now to move, room to paint a scene or two, describe an incident to the full. I could let John Adams sit by his farmhouse window and *think*. Sitting and thinking was characteristic of Adams; again and again his Diary records, "At home, without company, thinking." I had space, now, to describe the room where John sat, describe the old Plymouth Road beyond his window, the hard-packed snow, the squeak of sled runners as neighbors hauled their wood by oxcart to the town. And when my "big" scenes fell due, such as for instance, the Boston Massacre, I could allow three entire chapters to Adams's defense of the British soldiers involved on that fateful night of March Fifth. I could print Adams's legal brief in its entirety, using every device in the calendar of biographical technique—describe the courtroom, the rain against long windows on those cold autumn days of 1770. I could have the sound of military bugles drift up from where British frigates lay armed and watchful in Boston Harbor down the hill.

[45] My circle was closed, my boundaries defined; I knew what my first scene would be and my last. My book had now an end and a beginning—but then so, for example, has Wednesday. On Wednesday the sun rises and sets. Yet if the world is to be interested in what one does on Wednesday, one has to meet with trouble on Wednesday—meet an obstacle and conquer it.

Or we can let the obstacle conquer, choosing tragedy for our Wednesday story.

[46] Conflict, the book trade calls it. Suspense. As biographer, I could not scorn this technique of the craft. My story needed it. John Adams was, all in all, a happy man. *"Les hommes heureux,"* say the French, *"n'ont pas d'histoires."* I myself do not hold with such cynicism. Surely, Wordsworth's Happy Warrior is the truly happy man? And to be a warrior, a man must have fought for something, fought with something—perhaps with the devil, perhaps with his own soul. Life that possesses no conflict possesses no victory.

[47] What then, was the conflict in John Adams's first forty years? What made those years exciting *for him?* What, in short, was my over-all plot? Once more, history herself gave answer and plot: *How John Adams brought America to Independence.*

[48] Herein lay personal conflict in plenty, though John Adams never carried a gun. When he took sides with the revolutionists, Adams sacrificed, or so he thought, every material thing that made life worth while. By 1770, he was the leading lawyer of Massachusetts; he was offered many more cases than he could handle. The law courts were royal courts, their judges crown-appointed. When they closed, John's means of livelihood was gone. John was greatly ambitious for his three sons, especially for the eldest, John Quincy, who, John wrote his wife, "has genius." It was Adams's ambition to send John Quincy to Harvard, then to London to study law at the Inner Temple. He desired John Quincy to know the world, not grow to manhood in the narrow atmosphere of farm and township. When Adams chose the patriot side, he took as it were his vow of poverty, relinquished consciously and with sadness all ambition for his son. There was no way he could know this same son would one day be President of the United States. "I am melancholy for the public," he wrote his wife Abigail in the summer of '74, "and anxious for my family. I go mourning in my heart all the day long, though I say nothing."

[49] I had now my conflict, my "plot." It was my hope that this general plot would suggest a separate, specialized plot for every one of my thirty-two chapters. I desired each chapter to be an entity, a tale that might be read aloud and the book laid down until next evening. I hoped to devise chapter endings that would lead the reader on. I had a writing motto: *Will the reader turn the page?* Traced on yellow cardboard the words hung over my desk, a terrible warning.

[50] Somebody asked Charles Dickens about his rules of composition, the artistic principles by which he proceeded. "I have only one artistic principle," he said. "That is, to rouse the emotions of my readers."

[51] Between novelist and biographer the difference is profound. The one invents situations that will rouse a reader's emotions; the other brings out the significance of situations that already exist. Both are concerned with *la recherche du temps perdu,* both wish to uncover the nature or motivations

of man. "It is the business of an artist to be exciting." A large order, an ambition high and difficult. *Will the reader turn the page?* Ours is a vocation which carries great hazard; Justice Holmes used to say that no author could become truly conceited because every two years or so he exposes himself anew to the ridicule of the public.

[52] There is no art that does not demand virtuosity. "If you own a hundred thousand francs' worth of craftsmanship," Degas told a pupil, "spend five sous to buy more." It is the business of a biographer to know his subject. And then, summoning such techniques as he has mastered through practice of his calling, he will settle upon literary form, upon circumference and plot—making it his business then to project his story with all the vigor his endowments will permit.

COMMENT AND QUESTIONS

I. What is the difference between critical biography and narrative biography as Mrs. Bowen uses the terms? What appear to be the advantages of the narrative form? What difficulties does it present to the writer?

II. It is not surprising that Mrs. Bowen objects to the label *fictionalized biography,* particularly when it is applied to her writing; the term suggests taking liberties with facts in the manner of the historical novelist, and, as this essay indicates, Mrs. Bowen's books grow out of painstaking research, and she is scrupulously careful not to contradict or ignore the evidence her research uncovers. The detail of John Adams' pony is one example; are other examples of this kind of faithfulness to factual detail implied in the essay?

The term *interpretive biography* (used to mean approximately what Mrs. Bowen means by *narrative biography*) is frequently applied to books like *John Adams and the American Revolution.* In what ways does the author interpret? To what extent does her biography of John Adams seem to be evaluative as well as informative?

III. Mrs. Bowen suggests, directly and indirectly, a number of standards by which the worth of a biography may be judged. What are these standards? Which ones are useful to a reader who has no knowledge of the subject of the biography except knowledge gained from the book he is trying to judge?

IV. In writing about the business of the biographer, Mrs. Bowen discusses various procedures and techniques which are applicable to other kinds of composition. For example, the author labels and classifies her notes; she selects material in accordance with a central purpose, rejecting what is interesting but not relevant to that purpose; she limits her subject so that she can deal with it fully; she remembers details to give the reader a sense of reality; she presents dramatically, instead of summarizing, important scenes. Can you think of other techniques or suggestions discussed in the essay which might be applied by the non-professional writer to his own work?

V. If you have read Carl Becker's "Everyman His Own Historian," you will see that Mr. Becker's philosophy of history and Mrs. Bowen's philosophy of biography have a good deal in common. The approach and the vocabulary of the two writers differ; but on what ideas about fact and interpretation, selection of materials, and the relationship of the past to the present are they in substantial agreement?

VIRGINIA WOOLF

Beau Brummell[*]

The Columbia Encyclopedia, 1942 edition, has this entry on Beau Brummell:

> Brummell, George Bryan (Beau Brummell) 1778–1840, Englishman of wealth, distinguished for exquisiteness of dress and manners. After a brief career at Oxford and in the army he became known as a man of fashion and as the intimate of the prince regent (later George IV). His finances could not stand reckless gambling, and heavy debt caused his flight to Calais, where he struggled on for 14 years. He held a sinecure consulate at Caen (1830–32) where he died in a hospital for the mendicant insane.

Virginia Woolf (1882–1941) was an English novelist and essayist whose works include *Mrs. Dalloway, To the Lighthouse, Orlando,* and *The Waves.* The following biographical essay is from *The Second Common Reader* published in 1932.

[1] When Cowper, in the seclusion of Olney, was roused to anger by the thought of the Duchess of Devonshire and predicted a time when "instead of a girdle there will be a rent, and instead of beauty, baldness," he was acknowledging the power of the lady he thought so despicable. Why, otherwise, should she haunt the damp solitudes of Olney? Why should the rustle of her silken skirts disturb those gloomy meditations? Undoubtedly the Duchess was a good haunter. Long after those words were written, when she was dead and buried beneath a tinsel coronet, her ghost mounted the stairs of a very different dwelling-place. An old man was sitting in his arm-chair at Caen. The door opened, and the servant announced, "The Duchess of Devonshire." Beau Brummell at once rose, went to the door and made a bow that would have graced the Court of St. James. Only, unfortunately, there was nobody there. The cold air blew up the staircase of an Inn. The Duchess was long dead, and Beau Brummell, in his old age and imbecility,

[*] From *The Second Common Reader* by Virginia Woolf, copyright, 1932, by Harcourt, Brace and Company, Inc.

was dreaming that he was back in London again giving a party. Cowper's curse had come true for both of them. The Duchess lay in her shroud, and Brummell, whose clothes had been the envy of kings, had now only one pair of much-mended trousers, which he hid as best he could under a tattered cloak. As for his hair, that had been shaved by order of the doctor.

[2] But though Cowper's sour predictions had thus come to pass, both the Duchess and the dandy might claim that they had had their day. They had been great figures in their time. Of the two, perhaps Brummell might boast the more miraculous career. He had no advantage of birth, and but little of fortune. His grandfather had let rooms in St. James's Street. He had only a moderate capital of thirty thousand pounds to begin with, and his beauty, of figure rather than of face, was marred by a broken nose. Yet without a single noble, important, or valuable action to his credit he cuts a figure; he stands for a symbol; his ghost walks among us still. The reason for this eminence is now a little difficult to determine. Skill of hand and nicety of judgment were his, of course; otherwise he would not have brought the art of tying neck-cloths to perfection. The story is, perhaps, too well known —how he drew his head far back and sunk his chin slowly down so that the cloth wrinkled in perfect symmetry, or if one wrinkle were too deep or too shallow, the cloth was thrown into a basket and the attempt renewed, while the Prince of Wales sat, hour after hour, watching. Yet skill of hand and nicety of judgment were not enough. Brummell owed his ascendancy to some curious combination of wit, of taste, of insolence, of independence —for he was never a toady—which it were too heavy handed to call a philosophy of life, but served the purpose. At any rate, ever since he was the most popular boy at Eton coolly jesting when they were for throwing a bargee into the river, "My good fellows, don't send him into the river; the man is evidently in a high state of perspiration, and it almost amounts to a certainty that he will catch cold," he floated buoyantly and gaily and without apparent effort to the top of whatever society he found himself among. Even when he was a captain in the Tenth Hussars and so scandalously inattentive to duty that he only knew his troop by "the very large blue nose" of one of the men, he was liked and tolerated. When he resigned his commission, for the regiment was to be sent to Manchester—and "I really could not go—think, your Royal Highness, Manchester!"—he had only to set up house in Chesterfield Street to become the head of the most jealous and exclusive society of his time. For example, he was at Almack's one night talking to Lord ——. The Duchess of —— was there, escorting her young daughter, Lady Louisa. The Duchess caught sight of Mr. Brummell, and at once warned her daughter that if that gentleman near the door came and spoke to them she was to be careful to impress him favorably, "for," and she sank her voice to a whisper, "he is the celebrated Mr. Brummell." Lady Louisa might well have wondered why a Mr. Brummell was celebrated, and why a Duke's daughter need take care to impress a Mr. Brummell. And then directly he began to move towards them the reason

of her mother's warning became apparent. The grace of his carriage was so astonishing; his bows were so exquisite. Everybody looked overdressed or badly dressed—some, indeed, looked positively dirty beside him. His clothes seemed to melt into each other with the perfection of their cut and the quiet harmony of their color. Without a single point of emphasis everything was distinguished—from his bow to the way he opened his snuff-box, with his left hand invariably. He was the personification of freshness and cleanliness and order. One could well believe that he had his chair brought into his dressing-room and was deposited at Almack's without letting a puff of wind disturb his curls or a spot of mud stain his shoes. When he actually spoke to her, Lady Louisa would be at first enchanted—no one was more agreeable, more amusing, had a manner that was more flattering and enticing—and then she would be puzzled. It was quite possible that before the evening was out he would ask her to marry him, and yet his manner of doing it was such that the most ingenuous débutante could not believe that he meant it seriously. His odd gray eyes seemed to contradict his lips; they had a look in them which made the sincerity of his compliments very doubtful. And then he said very cutting things about other people. They were not exactly witty; they were certainly not profound; but they were so skillful, so adroit—they had a twist in them which made them slip into the mind and stay there when more important phrases were forgotten. He had downed the Regent himself with his dexterous "Who's your fat friend?" and his method was the same with humbler people who snubbed him or bored him. "Why, what could I do, my good fellow, but cut the connection? I discovered that Lady Mary actually ate cabbage!"—so he explained to a friend his failure to marry a lady. And, again, when some dull citizen pestered him about his tour to the North, "Which of the lakes do I admire?" he asked his valet. "Windermere, sir." "Ah, yes—Windermere, so it is—Windermere." That was his style, flickering, sneering, hovering on the verge of insolence, skimming the edge of nonsense, but always keeping within some curious mean, so that one knew the false Brummell story from the true by its exaggeration. Brummell could never have said, "Wales, ring the bell," any more than he could have worn a brightly colored waistcoat or a glaring necktie. That "certain exquisite propriety" which Lord Byron remarked in his dress, stamped his whole being, and made him appear cool, refined, and debonair among the gentlemen who talked only of sport, which Brummell detested, and smelt of the stable, which Brummell never visited. Lady Louisa might well be on tenterhooks to impress Mr. Brummell favorably. Mr. Brummell's good opinion was of the utmost importance in the world of Lady Louisa.

[3] And unless that world fell into ruins his rule seemed assured. Handsome, heartless, and cynical, the Beau seemed invulnerable. His taste was impeccable, his health admirable; and his figure as fine as ever. His rule had lasted many years and survived many vicissitudes. The French Revolution had passed over his head without disordering a single hair. Empires had risen and fallen while he experimented with the crease of a neck-cloth

and criticized the cut of a coat. Now the battle of Waterloo had been fought and peace had come. The battle left him untouched; it was the peace that undid him. For some time past he had been winning and losing at the gaming-tables. Harriette Wilson had heard that he was ruined, and then, not without disappointment, that he was safe again. Now, with the armies disbanded, there was let loose upon London a horde of rough, ill-mannered men who had been fighting all those years and were determined to enjoy themselves. They flooded the gaming-houses. They played very high. Brummell was forced into competition. He lost and won and vowed never to play again, and then he did play again. At last his remaining ten thousand pounds was gone. He borrowed until he could borrow no more. And finally, to crown the loss of so many thousands, he lost the six-penny-bit with a hole in it which had always brought him good luck. He gave it by mistake to a hackney coachman: that rascal Rothschild got hold of it, he said, and that was the end of his luck. Such was his own account of the affair—other people put a less innocent interpretation on the matter. At any rate there came a day, 16th May, 1816, to be precise—it was a day upon which everything was precise—when he dined alone off a cold fowl and a bottle of claret at Watier's, attended the opera, and then took coach for Dover. He drove rapidly all through the night and reached Calais the day after. He never set foot in England again.

[4] And now a furious process of disintegration set in. The peculiar and highly artificial society of London had acted as a preservative; it had kept him in being; it had concentrated him into one single gem. Now that the pressure was removed, the odds and ends, so trifling separately, so brilliant in combination, which had made up the being of the Beau, fell asunder and revealed what lay beneath. At first his luster seemed undiminished. His old friends crossed the water to see him and made a point of standing him a dinner and leaving a little present behind them at his banker's. He held his usual levee at his lodgings; he spent the usual hours washing and dressing; he rubbed his teeth with a red root, tweezed out hairs with a silver tweezer, tied his cravat to admiration, and issued at four precisely as perfectly equipped as if the Rue Royale had been St. James's Street and the Prince himself had hung upon his arm. But the Rue Royale was not St. James's Street; the old French Countess who spat on the floor was not the Duchess of Devonshire; the good bourgeois who pressed him to dine off goose at four was not Lord Alvanley; and though he soon won for himself the title of Roi de Calais, and was known to workmen as "George, ring the bell," the praise was gross, the society coarse, and the amusements of Calais very slender. The Beau had to fall back upon the resources of his own mind. These might have been considerable. According to Lady Hester Stanhope, he might have been, had he chosen, a very clever man; and when she told him so, the Beau admitted that he had wasted his talents because a dandy's way of life was the only one "which could place him in a prominent light, and enable him to separate himself from the ordinary herd of men, whom

he held in considerable contempt." That way of life allowed of verse-making —his verses, called "The Butterfly's Funeral," were much admired; and of singing, and of some dexterity with the pencil. But now, when the summer days were so long and so empty, he found that such accomplishments hardly served to while away the time. He tried to occupy himself with writing his memoirs; he bought a screen and spent hours pasting it with pictures of great men and beautiful ladies whose virtues and frailties were symbolized by hyenas, by wasps, by profusions of cupids, fitted together with extraordinary skill; he collected Buhl furniture; he wrote letters in a curiously elegant and elaborate style to ladies. But these occupations palled. The resources of his mind had been whittled away in the course of years; now they failed him. And then the crumbling process went a little farther, and another organ was laid bare—the heart. He who had played at love all these years and kept so adroitly beyond the range of passion, now made violent advances to girls who were young enough to be his daughters. He wrote such passionate letters to Mademoiselle Ellen of Caen that she did not know whether to laugh or to be angry. She was angry, and the Beau, who had tyrannized over the daughters of Dukes, prostrated himself before her in despair. But it was too late—the heart after all these years was not a very engaging object even to a simple country girl, and he seems at last to have lavished his affections upon animals. He mourned his terrier Vick for three weeks; he had a friendship with a mouse; he became the champion of all the neglected cats and starving dogs in Caen. Indeed, he said to a lady that if a man and a dog were drowning in the same pond he would prefer to save the dog —if, that is, there were nobody looking. But he was still persuaded that everybody was looking; and his immense regard for appearances gave him a certain stoical endurance. Thus, when paralysis struck him at dinner he left the table without a sign; sunk deep in debt as he was, he still picked his way over the cobbles on the points of his toes to preserve his shoes, and when the terrible day came and he was thrown into prison he won the admiration of murderers and thieves by appearing among them as cool and courteous as if about to pay a morning call. But if he were to continue to act his part, it was essential that he should be supported—he must have a sufficiency of boot polish, gallons of eau-de-Cologne, and three changes of linen every day. His expenditure upon these items was enormous. Generous as his old friends were, and persistently as he supplicated them, there came a time when they could be squeezed no longer. It was decreed that he was to content himself with one change of linen daily, and his allowance was to admit of necessaries only. But how could a Brummell exist upon necessaries only? The demand was absurd. Soon afterwards he showed his sense of the gravity of the situation by mounting a black silk neck-cloth. Black silk neck-cloths had always been his aversion. It was a signal of despair, a sign that the end was in sight. After that everything that had supported him and kept him in being dissolved. His self-respect vanished. He would dine with anyone who would pay the bill. His memory weakened and he told the same story over and over again till even the burghers of Caen were bored. Then his manners degenerated. His extreme cleanliness lapsed into carelessness, and then into positive filth. People objected to his presence in the dining-room of the hotel. Then his mind went—he thought that the Duchess of Devonshire was coming up the stairs when it was only the wind. At last but one passion remained intact among the crumbled debris of so many—an immense greed. To buy Rheims biscuits he sacrificed the greatest treasure that remained to him—he sold his snuff-box. And then nothing was left but a heap of disagreeables, a mass of corruption, a senile and disgusting old man fit only for the charity of nuns and the protection of an asylum. There the clergyman begged him to pray. " 'I do try,' he said, but he added something which made me doubt whether he understood me." Certainly, he would try; for the clergyman wished it, and he had always been polite. He had been polite to thieves and to duchesses and to God Himself. But it was no use trying any longer. He could believe in nothing now except a hot fire, sweet biscuits and another cup of coffee if he asked for it. And so there was nothing for it but that the Beau who had been compact of grace and sweetness should be shuffled into the grave like any other ill-dressed, ill-bred, unneeded old man. Still, one must remember that Byron, in his moments of dandyism, "always pronounced the name of Brummell with a mingled emotion of respect and jealousy."

COMMENT AND QUESTIONS

I. Compare this biographical essay with the brief factual account in the note preceding it. What facts given in the encyclopedia article are omitted or minimized in the essay? What additional information is given by the essay? What different effect does the essay produce, and why?

II. What does Mrs. Woolf gain by first showing Beau Brummell in his old age and then going back for a chronological account of his career?

III. What details are particularly well chosen to give a sense of Brummell's personality?

IV. The episode involving Lady Louisa is more fully developed than any other single episode in the essay. What purposes does it serve, and why is it developed so fully?

V. Define as precisely as you can Mrs. Woolf's attitude toward her subject and the impression of Beau Brummell she leaves with the reader. For example, is there any admiration for Brummell? contempt? sympathy? pity? Would you say that the essay is an example of favorable, unfavorable, or balanced slanting?

VI. When we showed this essay to a college student and asked her if she found it morbid or depressing, she said, "Are you kidding? I think it's very *light* reading and cute. Who cares what happens to a man like that?" Do you agree or disagree? Why?

EDITORS OF *TIME*

An American Storyteller: Ernest Hemingway*

Chronological order, perhaps with some digression and flashback, is the natural organization for most biographical writing. The following article, which might be called a biographical report, illustrates a different technique. It is organized around two events: the award of the Nobel Prize for Literature to Ernest Hemingway in December, 1954, and the consequent visit to Hemingway of the writer assembling material for a cover story in the December 13, 1954, issue of *Time* magazine. The cover drawing of this issue of *Time* showed the head of Hemingway with a dark purple fish (to remind readers of *The Old Man and the Sea*) curved around his gray-white hair and beard; the caption read:

> NOVELIST HEMINGWAY
> The luck, she is still running good.
>
> Veteran out of the wars before he was twenty:
> Famous at twenty-five: thirty a master—
> Whittled a style for his time from a walnut stick
> In a carpenter's loft in a street of that April city.

[1] Thus Poet Archibald MacLeish recalls one of the great American writers in his days of early glory, back in the 1920s, when it always seemed to be April in Paris. Last week Ernest Hemingway was a long way from Paris and a long way from April. He was 55, but he looked older. He cruised in a black and green fishing boat off the coast of Cuba, near where the Gulf Stream draws a dark line on the seascape. The grey-white hair escaping from beneath a visored cap was unkempt, and the Caribbean glare induced a sea-squint in his brown, curious eyes set behind steel-rimmed spectacles. Most of his ruddy face was retired behind a clipped, white, patriarchal beard that gave him a bristled, Neptunian look. His leg muscles could have been halves of a split 16-lb. shot, welded there by years of tramping in Michigan, skiing in Switzerland, bullfighting in Spain, walking battlefronts and hiking uncounted miles of African safari. On his lap he held a board, and he bent over it with a pencil in one hand. He was still whittling away at his walnut prose.

[2] Five thousand miles away in Stockholm, a white-starched, tail-coated assembly of the Nobel Foundation was about to bestow literature's most distinguished accolade on the products of his pencil. This week, "for his

---

* From *Time*, "The Weekly Newsmagazine." Reprinted by permission. Copyright, Time Inc., 1954.

powerful, style-forming mastery of the art of modern narration," the Nobel Prize for Literature will be awarded to Ernest Miller Hemingway, originally of Oak Park, Ill. and later of most of the world's grand and adventurous places.

[3] Few would deny that Ernest Hemingway deserves the trumpets of fame. As an artist he broke the bounds of American writing, enriched U.S. literature with the century's hardest-hitting prose, and showed new ways to new generations of writers. He was imitated not only by other writers but by uncounted young men who, in fact or fancy, sought to live as dashingly as he. From Paris bistros to Chicago saloons, he is known as a character— not the sallow, writing type with an indoor soul, but a literary he-man. When his plane crashed on safari in Africa last winter and for nearly a day he was believed dead, even people who do not like his books felt a strange, personal sense of loss, and even people who never read novels were delighted when he walked out of the jungle carrying a bunch of bananas and a bottle of gin, and was quoted, possibly even correctly, as saying: "My luck, she is running very good."

[4] **Battered But Unbowed.** The hero of the great Hemingway legend was still not sufficiently recovered from his accident to travel to Stockholm for his latest, biggest honor (hitherto awarded only to five other American-born writers: Sinclair Lewis, Eugene O'Neill, Pearl Buck, T. S. Eliot and William Faulkner). Furthermore, the first announcement of the Nobel award and the bustle of publicity that followed had thrown Hemingway off his writing pace. He took to his boat in hopes of getting back to work on his new novel about Africa. "I was going real good, better than for a long time, when this came along," he said. "When you're a writer and you've got it you've got to keep going because when you've lost it you've lost it and God knows when you'll get it back."

[5] Hemingway's African injuries were a ruptured kidney, bad burns, cracked skull, two compressed vertebrae and one vertebra cracked clear through. These were added to scars that cover perhaps half his body surface, including half a dozen head wounds, 237 shrapnel scars in one leg, a shot-off kneecap, wounds in both feet, both arms, both hands and groin, all acquired in the two World Wars. By last week he was much improved, but his back was still bothering him. When he sat, he lined his chair with big flat picture books and a backboard. "I have to take so many pills," he said, "they have to fight among themselves if I take them too close together." His daily quota of alcohol, though still substantial enough to keep him in good standing among the alltime public enemies of the W.C.T.U., had fallen far below the old records. Gone were the uninhibited, wine-purpled, 100-proof, side-of-the-mouth bottle-swigging days of the swashbuckling young Ernest Hemingway who was "the bronze god of the whole literary experience in America," the lion-hunting, trophy-bagging, bullfight-loving Lord Byron of America. "I am a little beat up," Ernest Hemingway now admits, "but I assure you it is only temporary."

[6] **The Private World.** Even though held in by injury and age, Hemingway's life—on a small plantation ten miles outside of Havana, called *Finca Vigia,* or Lookout Farm—is still the special Hemingway blend of thought and action, artistry and nonconformity. The Hemingway of 1954 still has a bit of himself for the many sides of his life—and plenty left over to populate that private Hemingway world where the Hemingway heroes and heroines live their lives of pride and trouble, enduring with courage as long as they can, often destroyed but never defeated.

[7] For Ernest Hemingway, when he is writing, every day begins in that private world. As early as 5:30 in the morning, before any but some gabby bantams, a few insomniac cats and a cantankerous bird called "The Bitchy Owl" are awake, he goes to work in the big main bedroom of his villa. He writes standing up at the mantelpiece, using a pencil for narrative and description, a typewriter for dialogue "in order to keep up."

[8] Rising up from one side of his villa is a white tower from which he can gaze meditatively at Havana and the sea, or at his own domain—the *finca's* 13 acres, including flower and truck gardens, fruit trees, seven cows (which provide all the household's milk and butter), a large swimming pool, a temporarily defunct tennis court. In the 60-foot-long living room, heads of animals Hemingway shot in Africa stare glassy-eyed from the walls. But most imposing of all are Hemingway's books. He consumes books, newspapers and random printed matter the way a big fish gulps in plankton. One of the few top American writers alive who did not go to college, Hemingway read Darwin when he was ten, later taught himself Spanish so he could read *Don Quixote* and the bullfight journals. Hemingway has never slept well, and reading is his substitute. *Finca Vigia* holds 4,859 volumes of fiction, poetry, history, military manuals, biography, music, natural history, sports, foreign-language grammars and cookbooks.

[9] **The Perpetual Weekend.** For 15 years Hemingway has lived in Cuba. "I live here because I love Cuba—this does not imply a dislike for anyplace else—and because here I can get privacy when I write." But his life in Cuba is not quiet. Guests at the *finca* are apt to include friends from the wealthy sporting set, say Winston Guest or Alfred Gwynne Vanderbilt; pals from Hollywood, such as Gary Cooper or Ava Gardner; Spanish grandees, soldiers, sailors, Cuban politicians, prizefighters, barkeeps, painters and even fellow authors. It is open house for U.S. Air Force and Navy men, old Loyalists from the Spanish civil war, or for any of the eight Cubans, Spaniards and Americans who served with Hemingway on his boat, the *Pilar,* early in World War II when Hemingway and the *Pilar* cruised the Caribbean hunting for enemy submarines. And even if there are no guests, there is always the long-distance phone, which may carry the husky voice of Marlene Dietrich, calling to talk over a problem with "Papa."

[10] For Mary Welsh Hemingway, 46, an indefatigable former newspaper and magazine correspondent from Minnesota, it is a fortunate day when she

can reckon by 7 P.M. how many are staying for dinner and by 10 how many for the night. Life at *Finca Vigia* is, as she once reported it, a "perpetual weekend . . . involving time, space, motion, noise, animals and personalities, always approaching but seldom actually attaining complete uproar."

[11] In the past, when the routine at *Finca Vigia* grew too distracting, Hemingway found escape along grand avenues—a return to the plains below Tanganyika's Kilimanjaro or another trip to Venice, or a nightclub-and-museum-crawling trip to New York. But for the battered and mellowing Hemingway of today, the favorite refuge is his boat.

[12] **Reflections at Sea.** On a seagoing day (his first after winning the Nobel Prize), Hemingway's big Buick station wagon bounces through the suburbs along the Havana wharfsides by 9 A.M. The *Pilar* is a hardy, 42-foot craft with two Chrysler engines, built to Hemingway's specifications 20 years ago. Hemingway carefully supervises the provisioning of the *Pilar's* iceboxes for a hot day afloat—several brands of beer for his guest and the mate, some chilled tequila for Skipper Hemingway. He consults with his mate, an agile, creased Canary Islander named Gregorio Fuentes. Then Hemingway shucks off his shoes and socks, chins himself on the edge of the *Pilar's* flying bridge, throws one leg up, and, favoring his sore back, slowly raises himself to the roof to take the set of controls. The *Pilar* glides trimly past Morro Castle. Hemingway delightedly sniffs the sea-grape-scented air and gestures to the whole ocean. "It's the last free place there is, the sea."

[13] Gregorio deftly baits four lines and trails them from the stern. In fluid Spanish, Hemingway and the mate decide to fish the waters off Cojimar, the little fishing village near which Hemingway set *The Old Man and the Sea*.

[14] The air and the baking sun make him feel good. In the sea haze, from the blue water, amid the occasional flying fish, ideas seem to appear—Hemingway notions about how things are. "When a writer retires deliberately from life, or is forced out of it by some defect, his writing has a tendency to atrophy just like a limb of a man when it's not used." He slaps his growing midriff, which, in his enforced idleness, is spreading fore and aft. "Anyone who's had the fortune or misfortune to be an athlete has to keep his body in shape. I think body and mind are closely coordinated. Fattening of the body can lead to fattening of the mind. I would be tempted to say that it can lead to fattening of the soul, but I don't know anything about the soul."

[15] **The Soul & Traumas.** In a sense, Hemingway perhaps never fully faced up to the concept of soul in his writing. Religion is a subject he refuses to discuss at all. He is equally ill at ease in the world of the ruminative intellectual. But he recognizes that in that world there is much worth knowing. In the bright sun, Hemingway recalls the shut-in figure of Marcel Proust. "Because a man sees the world in a different way and sees more

diverse parts of the world does not make him the equal of a man like Marcel Proust," says Hemingway humbly. "Proust knew deeper and better than anyone the life of which he wrote."

[16]   Suddenly Gregorio cries out: "Feesh! Papa, feesh!"

[17]   Proust is gone. Hemingway reaches down, grabs one of the rods by its tip and pulls it to the roof. He jerks once to set the hook, then with slow, graceful movements he pumps the rod back, reels a few feet, pumps, reels. To protect his back, he lets his arms and one leg do the work. By the shivery feel on the line he can identify the catch. "Bonito," he tells Gregorio. "Good bonito." With smooth speed, he works the fish close to the stern. Gregorio grabs the wire leader and boats a blue-and-silver bonito of about 15 pounds. A broad, small-boy smile flashes through Hemingway's old-man whiskers. "Good," he says. "A fish on the boat before 10:30 is a good sign. Very good sign."

[18]   Gregorio takes the wheel and Hemingway lets himself down to the deck and sits down. His voice has an ordinary sound, but high-pitched for the big frame that produces it. For all his years away from his rootland, he speaks with an unmistakable Midwestern twang. Absent-mindedly he rubs a star-shaped scar near his right foot, one of the scars left by the mortar shell which gravely wounded him at Fossalta, Italy, in 1918 when he was a volunteer ambulance driver. Nick Adams, hero of many of Hemingway's short stories, was wounded at approximately the same place in much the same way. So was Lieut. Henry of *A Farewell to Arms;* so was Colonel Cantwell of *Across the River and Into the Trees.* A critic named Philip Young last year published a book attributing Hemingway's approach to life and his artistic creation mostly to the Fossalta wounding (plus some harsh sights witnessed when he was a boy in Michigan traveling with his doctor father on emergency calls). Hemingway does not think very highly of that book. "How would you like it if someone said that everything you've done in your life was done because of some trauma?" he says. "I don't want to go down as the Legs Diamond of Letters."

[19]   **Symbols & Style.** In the past, hardly anyone ever suspected Hemingway novels of symbolism. Then, in *The Old Man and the Sea,* people saw symbols—the old man stood for man's dignity, the big fish embodied nature, the sharks symbolized evil (or maybe just the critics).

[20]   "No good book has ever been written that has in it symbols arrived at beforehand and stuck in," says Hemingway. "That kind of symbol sticks out like raisins in raisin bread. Raisin bread is all right, but plain bread is better." He opens two bottles of beer and continues: "I tried to make a real old man, a real boy, a real sea and a real fish and real sharks. But if I made them good and true enough they would mean many things. The hardest thing is to make something really true and sometimes truer than true."

[21]   He looks ahead at some floating sargasso weed, where some flying fishes are skittering through the air. "Could be fish there," he says. A reel gives out a soft whine, and Hemingway goes into action again. "Beautiful!"

he cries. "Dolphin. They're beautiful." After landing his fish, shimmering blue, gold and green, Hemingway turns his attention to his guest. "Take him softly now," he croons. "Easy. Easy. Work him with style. That's it, up slowly with the rod, now reel in fast. *Suave*. With style. With style. Don't break his mouth." After the second fish at last flops onto the deck, Hemingway continues his reflections. "The right way to do it—style—is not just an idle concept," he says. "It is simply the way to get done what is supposed to be done. The fact that the right way also looks beautiful when it's done is just incidental."

[22] This feeling about style, perhaps more than anything else, has always been Hemingway's credo—whether it concerned the right way to kill a bull, track a wildebeest, serve Valpolicella or blow up a bridge. And it was usually the redeeming feature and ultimate triumph of his characters: they might die, but they died with style. They left behind them some aura of virtue, some defiant statement of this-is-the-way-it-should-be-done that amounted to a victory of sorts.

[23] **Judgment & Pride.** The matter of style reminds Hemingway of many things, including his Nobel Prize. He knows just what he would like to say if he went to Stockholm for the acceptance ceremony. He would like to talk about a half-forgotten poet and a great stylist—Ezra Pound. Poet Pound used to look over Hemingway's early manuscripts in Paris and returned them, mercilessly blue-penciled, the adjectives gone. Indicted for treason for his pro-Fascist broadcasts in Italy during World War II, Pound was declared "mentally incompetent" in 1946 and is now in Washington's St. Elizabeth's Hospital. "Ezra Pound is a great poet," says Hemingway fiercely, "and whatever he did he has been punished greatly and I believe should be freed to go and write poems in Italy where he is loved and understood. He was the master of T. S. Eliot. Eliot is a winner of the Nobel Prize. I believe it might well have gone to Pound . . . I believe this would be a good year to release both. There is a school of thought in America which, if encouraged far enough, could well believe that a man should be punished for the simple error against conformity of being a poet. Dante, by these standards, could well have spent his life in St. Elizabeth's Hospital for errors of judgment and of pride."

[24] Alongside the *Pilar*, the bait keeps bobbing and Dante gives way to the dolphins. In little time the *Pilar* boats 15 beauties. Excited as a boy, Hemingway overlooks a promise to quit early and take a late-afternoon nap. Not until almost dusk does the boat put in to harbor. The sun seems to be setting only a few yards off a corner of Havana, four miles distant, and Hemingway savors it as if it were his first sunset—or his last. "Look!" he exclaims. "Now watch it go down, and then you'll see a big green ball where it was." The sun falls as if jerked below the horizon, and for a long instant a big, green, sun-sized ball hangs in its place.

[25] As the *Pilar* turns the harbor mouth, Hemingway takes the controls. Ceremonially, Gregorio the mate hands up to him what remains of the

tequila and a fresh-cut half of lime. Hemingway does not actually drink the tequila, and the whole thing bears the appearance of a ritual, as if to ward off sea serpents. Only at the dock does he pass around the bottle. "We went out and had a good day and caught plenty fish and got pooped," he says. "Now we can relax for a while and talk and go to sleep." With a tired smile on his tired, grizzled face, he lumbers up the gangway and off to his car and home.

[26] **The Several Hemingways.** Tired or not, Hemingway is a man who likes to relax with memories. Once, he remembers, there was a battered old prizefighter in Key West who wanted to make a comeback and asked Hemingway to referee. "It was a Negro section," Hemingway recalls, "and they really introduced me in the ring: 'The referee for tonight's bouts, that world-famous millionaire sportsman and playboy, Mr. Ernest Hemingway!' Playboy was the greatest title they thought they could give a man. How can the Nobel Prize move a man who has heard plaudits like that?"

[27] While Hemingway was perhaps never a millionaire,[1] the playboy title often fitted him. Oak Park, Ill. (pop. 63,529) saw the earliest Hemingway—the versatile, outdoors-loving son of respected Dr. and Mrs. Clarence E. Hemingway. Later Oak Park's people wondered, as one of them put it, "how a boy brought up in Christian and Puritan nurture should know and write so well of the devil and the underworld." (He was born a Congregationalist, became a practicing Roman Catholic, now apparently does not go to church.) The city room of the Kansas City *Star* saw him fresh out of high school and itchy for excitement. He left after only seven months of covering "the short-stop run"—police, railroad station, hospital. He lied about his age (18) to join the Red Cross ambulance service. Soon, postcards came back from the Italian front. "Having a wonderful time," they said.

[28] The Hemingway who first stepped into Gertrude Stein's salon in postwar Paris was 22, "rather foreign looking, with passionately interested, rather than interesting eyes." But the Hemingway she remembered later, after they had parted company, was "yellow . . . just like the flatboat men on the Mississippi River as described by Mark Twain."

[29] In his Paris days, he often refused good newspaper assignments and lunched on five sous' worth of potatoes in order to write his stories his own way. Even before any of his work was published (1923), word of Hemingway's fresh new talent floated like tobacco smoke through Paris' expatriate cafés and salons. He impressed and became friends with many of the literary greats of the day, including James Joyce. "Once, in one of those casual conversations you have when you're drinking," recalls Hemingway, "Joyce said to me he was afraid his writing was too suburban and that maybe he should get around a bit and see the world. He was afraid of some things,

---

[1] Hemingway has undoubtedly taken in much more than $1,000,000 for his writing, says that he hasn't "the slightest idea" how much he has earned. For motion-picture rights alone, Hollywood has paid some $650,000, including $125,000 for *The Snows of Kilimanjaro*, the highest price ever paid for a short story.

lightning and things, but a wonderful man. He was under great discipline—his wife, his work and his bad eyes. His wife was there and she said, yes, his work was too suburban—'Jim could do with a spot of that lion hunting.' We would go out to drink and Joyce would fall into a fight. He couldn't even see the man so he'd say, 'Deal with him, Hemingway! Deal with him!' "

[30] The Hemingway of the late 1920s, prosperous and confident, dealt successfully with all comers. But he had his troubles. His first marriage, to Hadley Richardson of St. Louis, broke up in 1927, and his father committed suicide in 1928. Hemingway was later to marry two more St. Louisans: *Vogue* Writer Pauline Preiffer (1927) and Novelist Martha Gellhorn (1940). From his first marriage he has one son, John ("Bumby"), 32, a World War II soldier and OSS man who is now in a Portland, Oregon investment house. From his second he has two more sons, Patrick, 24, who has bought a plantation in Tanganyika, and Gregory, 22, who is completing premedical studies in Los Angeles.

[31] **Who's Hairy?** The Hemingway of *Death in the Afternoon* (1932) was passionate about bulls, matadors, violence and the art of risking death. Max Eastman, the pundit and critic, wrote in *Bull in the Afternoon* that Hemingway seemed to have "begotten . . . a literary style . . . of wearing false hair on the chest." One afternoon three years later, 54-year-old, relatively unhirsute Max Eastman was confronted in Scribner's New York office by bull-angry, 38-year-old Hemingway, who ripped open his shirt to prove that the chest hair was real. The scene culminated in the notorious scuffle whose true outcome has long since vanished in the fog of subjective claims and counterclaims.

[32] The Depression and the Spanish civil war produced the short-lived Political Hemingway. In *To Have and Have Not,* Hemingway's only full-length novel with a U.S. setting, he sounded vaguely socialist. Some critics, particularly the Communists, grasped at the death of the novel's hero, Harry Morgan, because he died insisting that "a man alone ain't got no . . . chance." One critic saw in the book a plea for some form of social collectivism. Hemingway wore his heart on his sleeve for the Loyalists in Spain, but *For Whom the Bell Tolls* clearly showed his contempt for the Communists. They, in turn, denounced his books for being militaristic and lacking social significance.

[33] The Hemingway of World War II wore a canteen of vermouth on one hip, a canteen of gin on the other, a helmet that he seldom used because he couldn't find one big enough. Accredited a foreign correspondent for *Collier's* (he jokingly called himself "Ernie Hemorrhoid, the poor man's Pyle"), he took part in more of the European war than many a soldier. With Colonel (now Major General) Charles T. Lanham's 22nd Infantry Regiment, he went through the Normandy breakthrough, Schnee Eifel, the Hürtgen Forest bloodletting and the defense of Luxembourg. Gathering 200 French irregulars around him, he negotiated huge allotments of am-

munition and alcohol and assisted in the liberation of Paris. Hemingway personally liberated the Ritz Hotel, posted a guard below to notify incoming friends: "Papa took good hotel. Plenty stuff in cellar."

[34] **Commander of the Chain.** The postwar Hemingway settled into another good hotel, the Gritti in Venice, to write "the big book" about World War II (a draft is now finished). But a piece of gun wadding went into his eye during a duck hunt and started an infection that doctors feared was going to kill him. Wanting to get one more story out of himself, he put the big book aside and batted out *Across the River and Into the Trees,* which most critics found a middle-aged love fantasy with an admixture of bad-tempered military shoptalk. Said Hemingway about the critics: "I have moved through plane geometry and algebra, and now I am in calculus. If they don't understand that, to hell with them."

[35] It is impossible to overlook the adolescent in Hemingway—his bravado, his emotional friendships, his vague but all-important code, his deep sentimentality about the good, the true, the straight, the beautiful, and occasionally the unprintable. But to preserve something of the adolescent through three decades in a world of literary critics, parodizers and cocktail-party highbrows takes a certain admirable courage. Above all, Hemingway can laugh at himself. Typical of Hemingway making fun of Hemingway is *El Ordine Militar, Nobile y Espirituoso do los Caballeros de Brusadelli*—which means, more or less, the Military Order of the Noble and Spirited Knights of Brusadelli. It was founded by Hemingway in Italy, and named, as he explains in *Across the River and Into the Trees,* "after a particularly notorious multi-millionaire taxpaying profiteer of Milan, who had . . . accused his young wife, publicly and legally through due process of law, of having deprived him of his judgment through her extraordinary sexual demands." As Commander of the Great Chain of the Order, Hemingway distributed knighthoods to friends; after his recovery he returned to Cuba, and mailed reports to fellow members. A sample, written just after he had finished writing *The Old Man and the Sea:* "Your Cuban representative has not been able to do much for the Order in the last year due to the deplorable necessity of writing a book . . . The book will be published on September 8th and all members of the Order will observe a moment of silence. The password will be: 'Don't cheer, boys. The poor readers are dying.'"

[36] **More Mature, Less Mannered.** How does Nobel Prizewinner Ernest Hemingway stand with his surviving readers? *The Sun Also Rises,* which offered an ironical threnody for the "lost generation," is today appealing mostly as a period piece. But even if Hemingway had stopped after the fine short stories written in the 1920s and *A Farewell to Arms,* he would have won a roomy place in American literature. Years later, when his style had become a fixture and when Hemingway prose occasionally dipped toward banality, the importance of the beginning was sometimes not considered. Much of his output of the '30s seems below par today, but *For Whom the Bell Tolls* (1940) was one of his best, and in *The Old Man and the Sea* he

is better than he ever was, more mature and less mannered. Unlike most American writers, who seemed inexplicably to wither after their triumphs (e.g., Sinclair Lewis, Joseph Hergesheimer, Thomas Wolfe), Ernest Hemingway has continued to grow.

[37] Almost from the beginning, critics have talked about Hemingway's obsession with death, all the dark and clinical tear and bleeding on the battlefields, in the bull rings, in the lunchroom where *The Killers* wait, with gloves on, for their victims. Yet somehow, in an atomic age, Hemingway seems much less macabre and violent than he did in the pacifist climate of the '30s. Hemingway still stands out from a pack of introspective and obscure writers with a dazzling simplicity, rarely politicking, never preaching, never using Freudian jargon.

[38] Some, including 1949's Nobel Prizewinner William Faulkner, think that his world is too narrow. "[Hemingway] has no courage," Faulkner once said. "[He] has never crawled out on a limb. He has never been known to use a word that might cause the reader to check with a dictionary to see if it is properly used." Hemingway has indeed remained in the carefully delineated, cut-to-the-bone world of simple, palpable acts. But at his best, Hemingway has a sense of fate recalling Melville, an American heartiness recalling Mark Twain (who never used big dictionary words either). Hemingway can carve icebergs of prose; only a few words on paper convey much more beneath the surface. The taut, economical style contains more than meets the casual eye—the dignity of man and also his imperfection, the recognition that there is a right way and a wrong, the knowledge that the redeeming things of life are measured in the profound satisfactions that come from struggle. Said Dr. Anders Österling, Permanent Secretary of the Swedish Academy, in Stockholm this week: "Courage is Hemingway's central theme—the bearing of one who is put to the test and who steels himself to meet the cold cruelty of existence without, by so doing, repudiating the great and generous moments . . ."

[39] John Donne provided Hemingway with the title of *For Whom the Bell Tolls*. "No man is an *Iland,* intire of it selfe," said Donne. Says Hemingway now: "A man both is and is not an island. Sometimes he has to be the strongest island there can be to be a part of the main. [I] am not good at stating metaphysics in a conversation, but I thought Santiago [the Old Man] was never alone because he had his friend and enemy the sea and the things that lived in the sea some of whom he loved and others that he hated."

[40] His lifetime has brought Ernest Hemingway recognition, distinction and reward that only death and passage of time bring to many others. Hemingway is satisfied. He would not change any of his life or of his writings—anyway, "not yet." He feels now as he did some years ago, and he is willing to rest on it: "You only have to do it once to get remembered by some people. But if you can do it year after year after year quite a lot of people remember and they tell their children and their children and their

grandchildren remember, and if it's books they can read them. And if it's good enough it lasts forever."

COMMENT AND QUESTIONS

I. The interestingly varied technique and structure of this article may be partially shown by the following informal outline of its content:

1. Hemingway at 55, Nobel Prize winner, "a little beat up" by old and recent injuries, but still unbowed (paragraphs 1–5)
2. His life in Cuba: work schedule, house, acres, library; his guests and friends; his wife (paragraphs 6–10)
3. Escape in his boat: a narrative of reflection, observation, and fishing during a day at sea (paragraphs 11–25)
4. The several Hemingways: a chronological account of different phases of his life and work (paragraphs 26–35)
5. Appraisals of the man and his work at the present time (paragraphs 36–40)

Notice the transitions between these large sections of the material, and point out other examples of skillful (or clever) transitions between smaller units in the report.

II. The section on the day at sea (paragraphs 11–25) offers a good study in narrative pace and other techniques of narration and description. It contains, too, a number of Hemingway's comments on writing and writers. Point out connections between the physical setting, the physical action, Hemingway's remarks, and the guest's remarks about Hemingway. How is Hemingway's concept of "style" illustrated in the day's activities?

III. In the chronological account of the several Hemingways, the World War I experience is barely mentioned. Why?

IV. To what extent is this article evaluative as well as informative? What dominant impression or impressions of Hemingway emerge from it? How would you define the attitude of the *Time* writers toward their subject?

READINGS

SECTION 5

Reading For Ideas and Values

JAMES HARVEY ROBINSON

Four Kinds of Thinking*

The following analysis of thinking is a selection from *The Mind in the Making*, a widely-read book published in 1921. James Harvey Robinson (1863–1936) was an American teacher and historian.[1]

[1] We do not think enough about thinking, and much of our confusion is the result of current illusions in regard to it. Let us forget for the moment any impressions we may have derived from the philosophers, and see what seems to happen in ourselves. The first thing that we notice is that our thought moves with such incredible rapidity that it is almost impossible to arrest any specimen of it long enough to have a look at it. When we are offered a penny for our thoughts we always find that we have recently had so many things in mind that we can easily make a selection which will not compromise us too nakedly. On inspection we shall find that even if we are not downright ashamed of a great part of our spontaneous thinking it is far too intimate, personal, ignoble or trivial to permit us to reveal more than a small part of it. I believe this must be true of everyone. We do not, of course, know what goes on in other people's heads. They tell us very little and we tell them very little. The spigot of speech, rarely fully opened, could never emit more than driblets of the ever renewed hogshead of thought—*noch grosser wie's Heidelberger Fass*. We find it hard to believe

---

* From *The Mind in the Making* by James Harvey Robinson. Copyright, 1921, by James Harvey Robinson; copyright, 1949, by Bankers Trust Company. Published by Harper & Brothers.

[1] See the portrayal of Robinson in Irwin Edman's essay "Former Teachers," p. 1098.

that other people's thoughts are as silly as our own, but they probably are.

[2]   We all appear to ourselves to be thinking all the time during our waking hours, and most of us are aware that we go on thinking while we are asleep, even more foolishly than when awake. When uninterrupted by some practical issue we are engaged in what is now known as *reverie*. This is our spontaneous and favorite kind of thinking. We allow our ideas to take their own course and this course is determined by our hopes and fears, our spontaneous desires, their fulfillment or frustration; by our likes and dislikes, our loves and hates and resentments. There is nothing else anything like so interesting to ourselves as ourselves. All thought that is not more or less laboriously controlled and directed will inevitably circle about the beloved Ego. It is amusing and pathetic to observe this tendency in ourselves and in others. We learn politely and generously to overlook this truth, but if we dare to think of it, it blazes forth like the noontide sun.

[3]   The reverie or "free association of ideas" has of late become the subject of scientific research. While investigators are not yet agreed on the results, or at least on the proper interpretation to be given to them, there can be no doubt that our reveries form the chief index to our fundamental character. They are a reflection of our nature as modified by often hidden and forgotten experiences. We need not go into the matter further here, for it is only necessary to observe that the reverie is at all times a potent and in many cases an omnipotent rival to every other kind of thinking. It doubtless influences all our speculations in its persistent tendency to self-magnification and self-justification, which are its chief preoccupations, but it is the last thing to make directly or indirectly for honest increase of knowledge. Philosophers usually talk as if such thinking did not exist or were in some way negligible. This is what makes their speculations so unreal and often worthless.

[4]   The reverie, as any of us can see for himself, is frequently broken and interrupted by the necessity of a second kind of thinking. We have to make practical decisions. Shall we write a letter or no? Shall we take the subway or a bus? Shall we have dinner at seven or half past? Shall we buy U.S. Rubber or a Liberty Bond? Decisions are easily distinguishable from the free flow of the reverie. Sometimes they demand a good deal of careful pondering and the recollection of pertinent facts; often, however, they are made impulsively. They are a more difficult and laborious thing than the reverie, and we resent having to "make up our mind" when we are tired, or absorbed in a congenial reverie. Weighing a decision, it should be noted, does not necessarily add anything to our knowledge, although we may, of course, seek further information before making it.

[5]   A third kind of thinking is stimulated when anyone questions our beliefs and opinions. We sometimes find ourselves changing our minds without any resistance or heavy emotion, but if we are told that we are wrong

we resent the imputation and harden our hearts. We are incredibly heedless in the formation of our beliefs, but find ourselves filled with an illicit passion for them when anyone proposes to rob us of their companionship. It is obviously not the ideas themselves that are dear to us, but our self-esteem, which is threatened. We are by nature stubbornly pledged to defend our own from attack, whether it be our person, our family, our property, or our opinion. A United States Senator once remarked to a friend of mine that God Almighty could not make him change his mind on our Latin-America policy. We may surrender, but rarely confess ourselves vanquished. In the intellectual world at least peace is without victory.

[6] Few of us take the pains to study the origin of our cherished convictions; indeed, we have a natural repugnance to so doing. We like to continue to believe what we have been accustomed to accept as true, and the resentment aroused when doubt is cast upon any of our assumptions leads us to seek every manner of excuse for clinging to them. *The result is that most of our so-called reasoning consists in finding arguments for going on believing as we already do.*

[7] I remember years ago attending a public dinner to which the Governor of the state was bidden. The chairman explained that His Excellency could not be present for certain "good" reasons; what the "real" reasons were the presiding officer said he would leave us to conjecture. This distinction between "good" and "real" reasons is one of the most clarifying and essential in the whole realm of thought. We can readily give what seem to us "good" reasons for being a Catholic or a Mason, a Republican or a Democrat, an adherent or opponent of the League of Nations. But the "real" reasons are usually on quite a different plane. Of course the importance of this distinction is popularly, if somewhat obscurely, recognized. The Baptist missionary is ready enough to see that the Buddhist is not such because his doctrines would bear careful inspection, but because he happened to be born in a Buddhist family in Tokio. But it would be treason to his faith to acknowledge that his own partiality for certain doctrines is due to the fact that his mother was a member of the First Baptist Church of Oak Ridge. A savage can give all sorts of reasons for his belief that it is dangerous to step on a man's shadow, and a newspaper editor can advance plenty of argument against the Bolsheviki. But neither of them may realize why he happens to be defending his particular opinion.

[8] The "real" reasons for our beliefs are concealed from ourselves as well as from others. As we grow up we simply adopt the ideas presented to us in regard to such matters as religion, family relations, property, business, our country, and the state. We unconsciously absorb them from our environment. They are persistently whispered in our ear by the group in which we happen to live. Moreover, as Mr. Trotter has pointed out, these judgments, being the product of suggestion and not of reasoning, have the quality of perfect obviousness, so that to question them

... is to the believer to carry skepticism to an insane degree, and will be met by contempt, disapproval, or condemnation, according to the nature of the belief in question. When, therefore, we find ourselves entertaining an opinion about the basis of which there is a quality of feeling which tells us that to inquire into it would be absurd, obviously unnecessary, unprofitable, undesirable, bad form, or wicked, we may know that that opinion is a nonrational one, and probably, therefore, founded upon inadequate evidence.[2]

[9] Opinions, on the other hand, which are the result of experience or of honest reasoning do not have this quality of "primary certitude." I remember when as a youth I heard a group of business men discussing the question of the immortality of the soul, I was outraged by the sentiment of doubt expressed by one of the party. As I look back now I see that I had at the time no interest in the matter, and certainly no least argument to urge in favor of the belief in which I had been reared. But neither my personal indifference to the issue, nor the fact that I had previously given it no attention, served to prevent an angry resentment when I heard *my* ideas questioned.

[10] This spontaneous and loyal support of our preconceptions—this process of finding "good" reasons to justify our routine beliefs—is known to modern psychologists as "rationalizing"—clearly only a new name for a very ancient thing. Our "good" reasons ordinarily have no value in promoting honest enlightenment, because, no matter how solemnly they may be marshaled, they are at bottom the result of personal preference or prejudice, and not of an honest desire to seek or accept new knowledge.

[11] In our reveries we are frequently engaged in self-justification, for we cannot bear to think ourselves wrong, and yet have constant illustrations of our weaknesses and mistakes. So we spend much time finding fault with circumstances and the conduct of others, and shifting on to them with great ingenuity the onus of our own failures and disappointments. *Rationalizing is the self-exculpation which occurs when we feel ourselves, or our group, accused of misapprehension or error.*

[12] The little word *my* is the most important one in all human affairs, and properly to reckon with it is the beginning of wisdom. It has the same force whether it is *my* dinner, *my* dog, and *my* house, or *my* faith, *my* country, and *my* God. We not only resent the imputation that our watch is wrong, or our car shabby, but that our conceptions of the canals of Mars, of the pronunciation of "Epictetus," of the medicinal value of salicine, or the date of Sargon I, are subject to revision.

[13] Philosophers, scholars, and men of science exhibit a common sensitiveness in all decisions in which their *amour propre* is involved. Thousands of argumentative works have been written to vent a grudge. However stately their reasoning, it may be nothing but rationalizing, stimulated by the most commonplace of all motives. A history of philosophy and theology could be written in terms of grouches, wounded pride, and aversions, and

[2] *Instincts of the Herd in Peace and War,* p. 44.

it would be far more instructive than the usual treatments of these themes. Sometimes, under Providence, the lowly impulse of resentment leads to great achievements. Milton wrote his treatise on divorce as a result of his troubles with his seventeen-year-old wife, and when he was accused of being the leading spirit in a new sect, the Divorcers, he wrote his noble *Areopagitica* to prove his right to say what he thought fit, and incidentally to establish the advantage of a free press in the promotion of Truth.

[14]   All mankind, high and low, thinks in all the ways which have been described. The reverie goes on all the time not only in the mind of the mill hand and the Broadway flapper, but equally in weighty judges and godly bishops. It has gone on in all the philosophers, scientists, poets, and theologians that have ever lived. Aristotle's most abstruse speculations were doubtless tempered by highly irrelevant reflections. He is reported to have had very thin legs and small eyes, for which he doubtless had to find excuses, and he was wont to indulge in very conspicuous dress and rings and was accustomed to arrange his hair carefully. Diogenes the Cynic exhibited the impudence of a touchy soul. His tub was his distinction. Tennyson in beginning his "Maud" could not forget his chagrin over losing his patrimony years before as the result of an unhappy investment in the Patent Decorative Carving Company. These facts are not recalled here as a gratuitous disparagement of the truly great, but to insure a full realization of the tremendous competition which all really exacting thought has to face, even in the minds of the most highly endowed mortals.

[15]   And now the astonishing and perturbing suspicion emerges that perhaps almost all that has passed for social science, political economy, politics, and ethics in the past may be brushed aside by future generations as mainly rationalizing. John Dewey has already reached this conclusion in regard to philosophy. Veblen and other writers have revealed the various unperceived presuppositions of the traditional political economy, and now comes an Italian sociologist, Vilfredo Pareto, who, in his huge treatise on general sociology, devotes hundreds of pages to substantiating a similar thesis affecting all the social sciences. This conclusion may be ranked by students of a hundred years hence as one of the several great discoveries of our age. It is by no means fully worked out, and it is so opposed to nature that it will be very slowly accepted by the great mass of those who consider themselves thoughtful. As a historical student I am personally fully reconciled to this newer view. Indeed, it seems to me inevitable that just as the various sciences of nature were, before the opening of the seventeenth century, largely masses of rationalizations to suit the religious sentiments of the period, so the social sciences have continued even to our own day to be rationalizations of uncritically accepted beliefs and customs.

[16]   *It will become apparent as we proceed that the fact that an idea is ancient and that it has been widely received is no argument in its favor, but should immediately suggest the necessity of carefully testing it as a probable instance of rationalization.*

[17] This brings us to another kind of thought which can fairly easily be distinguished from the three kinds described above. It has not the usual qualities of the reverie, for it does not hover about our personal complacencies and humiliations. It is not made up of the homely decisions forced upon us by everyday needs, when we review our little stock of existing information, consult our conventional preferences and obligations, and make a choice of action. It is not the defense of our own cherished beliefs and prejudices just because they are our own—mere plausible excuses for remaining of the same mind. On the contrary, it is that peculiar species of thought which leads us to *change* our mind.

[18] It is this kind of thought that has raised man from his pristine, sub-savage ignorance and squalor to the degree of knowledge and comfort which he now possesses. On his capacity to continue and greatly extend this kind of thinking depends his chance of groping his way out of the plight in which the most highly civilized peoples of the world now find themselves. In the past this type of thinking has been called Reason. But so many misapprehensions have grown up around the word that some of us have become very suspicious of it. I suggest, therefore, that we substitute a recent name and speak of "creative thought" rather than of Reason. *For this kind of meditation begets knowledge, and knowledge is really creative inasmuch as it makes things look different from what they seemed before and may indeed work for their reconstruction.*

[19] In certain moods some of us realize that we are observing things or making reflections with a seeming disregard of our personal preoccupations. We are not preening or defending ourselves; we are not faced by the necessity of any practical decision, nor are we apologizing for believing this or that. We are just wondering and looking and mayhap seeing what we never perceived before.

[20] Curiosity is as clear and definite as any of our urges. We wonder what is in a sealed telegram or in a letter in which some one else is absorbed, or what is being said in the telephone booth or in low conversation. This inquisitiveness is vastly stimulated by jealousy, suspicion, or any hint that we ourselves are directly or indirectly involved. But there appears to be a fair amount of personal interest in other people's affairs even when they do not concern us except as a mystery to be unraveled or a tale to be told. The reports of a divorce suit will have "news value" for many weeks. They constitute a story like a novel or play or moving picture. This is not an example of pure curiosity, however, since we readily identify ourselves with others, and their joys and despair then become our own.

[21] We also take note of, or "observe," as Sherlock Holmes says, things which have nothing to do with our personal interest and make no personal appeal either direct or by way of sympathy. This is what Veblen so well calls "idle curiosity." And it is usually idle enough. Some of us when we face the line of people opposite us in a subway train impulsively consider them in detail and engage in rapid inferences and form theories in regard to

them. On entering a room there are those who will perceive at a glance the degree of preciousness of the rugs, the character of the pictures, and the personality revealed by the books. But there are many, it would seem, who are so absorbed in their personal reverie or in some definite purpose that they have no bright-eyed energy for idle curiosity. The tendency to miscellaneous observation we come by honestly enough, for we note it in many of our animal relatives.

[22] Veblen, however, uses the term "idle curiosity" somewhat ironically, as is his wont. It is idle only to those who fail to realize that it may be a very rare and indispensable thing from which almost all distinguished human achievement proceeds, since it may lead to systematic examination and seeking for things hitherto undiscovered. For research is but diligent search which enjoys the high flavor of primitive hunting. Occasionally and fitfully idle curiosity thus leads to creative thought, which alters and broadens our own views and aspirations and may in turn, under highly favorable circumstances, affect the views and lives of others, even for generations to follow. An example or two will make this unique human process clear.

[23] Galileo was a thoughtful youth and doubtless carried on a rich and varied reverie. He had artistic ability and might have turned out to be a musician or painter. When he had dwelt among the monks at Valambrosa he had been tempted to lead the life of a religious. As a boy he busied himself with toy machines and he inherited a fondness for mathematics. All these facts are of record. We may safely assume also that, along with many other subjects of contemplation, the Pisan maidens found a vivid place in his thoughts.

[24] One day when seventeen years old he wandered into the cathedral of his native town. In the midst of his reverie he looked up at the lamps hanging by long chains from the high ceiling of the church. Then something very difficult to explain occurred. He found himself no longer thinking of the building, worshipers, or the services; of his artistic or religious interests; of his reluctance to become a physician as his father wished. He forgot the question of a career and even the *graziosissime donne*. As he watched the swinging lamps he was suddenly wondering if mayhap their oscillations, whether long or short, did not occupy the same time. Then he tested this hypothesis by counting his pulse, for that was the only timepiece he had with him.

[25] This observation, however remarkable in itself, was not enough to produce a really creative thought. Others may have noticed the same thing and yet nothing came of it. Most of our observations have no assignable results. Galileo may have seen that the warts on a peasant's face formed a perfect isosceles triangle, or he may have noticed with boyish glee that just as the officiating priest was uttering the solemn words, *ecce agnus Dei*, a fly lit on the end of his nose. To be really creative, ideas have to be worked up and then "put over," so that they become a part of man's social heritage. The highly accurate pendulum clock was one of the later results of Galileo's

discovery. He himself was led to reconsider and successfully to refute the old notions of falling bodies. It remained for Newton to prove that the moon was falling, and presumably all the heavenly bodies. This quite upset all the consecrated views of the heavens as managed by angelic engineers. The universality of the laws of gravitation stimulated the attempt to seek other and equally important natural laws and cast grave doubts on the miracles in which mankind had hitherto believed. In short, those who dared to include in their thought the discoveries of Galileo and his successors found themselves in a new earth surrounded by new heavens.

[26] On the 28th day of October, 1831, two hundred and fifty years after Galileo had noticed the isochronous vibrations of the lamps, creative thought and its currency had so far increased that Faraday was wondering what would happen if he mounted a disk of copper between the poles of a horseshoe magnet. As the disk revolved an electric current was produced. This would doubtless have seemed the idlest kind of an experiment to the stanch business men of the time, who, it happened, were just then denouncing the child-labor bills in their anxiety to avail themselves to the full of the results of earlier idle curiosity. But should the dynamos and motors which have come into being as the outcome of Faraday's experiment be stopped this evening, the business man of to-day, agitated over labor troubles, might, as he trudged home past lines of "dead" cars, through dark streets to an unlighted house, engage in a little creative thought of his own and perceive that he and his laborers would have no modern factories and mines to quarrel about had it not been for the strange practical effects of the idle curiosity of scientists, inventors, and engineers.

[27] The examples of creative intelligence given above belong to the realms of modern scientific achievement, which furnishes the most striking instances of the effects of scrupulous, objective thinking. But there are, of course, other great realms in which the recording and embodiment of acute observation and insight have wrought themselves into the higher life of man. The great poets and dramatists and our modern story-tellers have found themselves engaged in productive reveries, noting and artistically presenting their discoveries for the delight and instruction of those who have the ability to appreciate them.

[28] The process by which a fresh and original poem or drama comes into being is doubtless analogous to that which originates and elaborates so-called scientific discoveries; but there is clearly a temperamental difference. The genesis and advance of painting, sculpture, and music offer still other problems. We really as yet know shockingly little about these matters, and indeed very few people have the least curiosity about them. Nevertheless, creative intelligence in its various forms and activities is what makes man. Were it not for its slow, painful, and constantly discouraged operations through the ages man would be no more than a species of primate living on seeds, fruit, roots, and uncooked flesh, and wandering naked through the woods and over the plains like a chimpanzee.

[29] The origin and progress and future promotion of civilization are ill

understood and misconceived. These should be made the chief theme of education, but much hard work is necessary before we can reconstruct our ideas of man and his capacities and free ourselves from innumerable persistent misapprehensions. There have been obstructionists in all times, not merely the lethargic masses, but the moralists, the rationalizing theologians, and most of the philosophers, all busily if unconsciously engaged in ratifying existing ignorance and mistakes and discouraging creative thought. Naturally, those who reassure us seem worthy of honor and respect. Equally naturally those who puzzle us with disturbing criticisms and invite us to change our ways are objects of suspicion and readily discredited. Our personal discontent does not ordinarily extend to any critical questioning of the general situation in which we find ourselves. In every age the prevailing conditions of civilization have appeared quite natural and inevitable to those who grew up in them. The cow asks no questions as to how it happens to have a dry stall and a supply of hay. The kitten laps its warm milk from a china saucer, without knowing anything about porcelain; the dog nestles in the corner of a divan with no sense of obligation to the inventors of upholstery and the manufacturers of down pillows. So we humans accept our breakfasts, our trains and telephones and orchestras and movies, our national Constitution, or moral code and standards of manners, with the simplicity and innocence of a pet rabbit. We have absolutely inexhaustible capacities for appropriating what others do for us with no thought of a "thank you." We do not feel called upon to make any least contribution to the merry game ourselves. Indeed, we are usually quite unaware that a game is being played at all.

[30] We have now examined the various classes of thinking which we can readily observe in ourselves and which we have plenty of reasons to believe go on, and always have been going on, in our fellow-men. We can sometimes get quite pure and sparkling examples of all four kinds, but commonly they are so confused and intermingled in our reverie as not to be readily distinguishable. The reverie is a reflection of our longings, exultations, and complacencies, our fears, suspicions, and disappointments. We are chiefly engaged in struggling to maintain our self-respect and in asserting that supremacy which we all crave and which seems to us our natural prerogative. It is not strange, but rather quite inevitable, that our beliefs about what is true and false, good and bad, right and wrong, should be mixed up with the reverie and influenced by the same considerations which determine its character and course. We resent criticisms of our views exactly as we do of anything else connected with ourselves. Our notions of life and its ideals seem to us to be *our own* and as such necessarily true and right, to be defended at all costs.

[31] *We very rarely consider, however, the process by which we gained our convictions.* If we did so, we could hardly fail to see that there was usually little ground for our confidence in them. Here and there, in this department of knowledge or that, some one of us might make a fair claim to have taken some trouble to get correct ideas of, let us say, the situation in Russia,

the sources of our food supply, the origin of the Constitution, the revision of the tariff, the policy of the Holy Roman Apostolic Church, modern business organization, trade unions, birth control, socialism, the League of Nations, the excess-profits tax, preparedness, advertising in its social bearings; but only a very exceptional person would be entitled to opinions on all of even these few matters. And yet most of us have opinions on all these, and on many other questions of equal importance, of which we may know even less. We feel compelled, as self-respecting persons, to take sides when they come up for discussion. We even surprise ourselves by our omniscience. Without taking thought we see in a flash that it is most righteous and expedient to discourage birth control by legislative enactment, or that one who decries intervention in Mexico is clearly wrong, or that big advertising is essential to big business and that big business is the pride of the land. As godlike beings why should we not rejoice in our omniscience?

[32] It is clear, in any case, that our convictions on important matters are not the result of knowledge or critical thought, nor, it may be added, are they often dictated by supposed self-interest. Most of them are *pure prejudices* in the proper sense of that word. We do not form them ourselves. They are the whisperings of "the voice of the herd." We have in the last analysis no responsibility for them and need assume none. They are not really our own ideas, but those of others no more well informed or inspired than ourselves, who have got them in the same careless and humiliating manner as we. It should be our pride to revise our ideas and not to adhere to what passes for respectable opinion, for such opinion can frequently be shown to be not respectable at all. We should, in view of the considerations that have been mentioned, resent our supine credulity. As an English writer has remarked:

> If we feared the entertaining of an unverifiable opinion with the warmth with which we fear using the wrong implement at the dinner table, if the thought of holding a prejudice disgusted us as does a foul disease, then the dangers of man's suggestibility would be turned into advantages.

[33] The purpose of this essay [3] is to set forth briefly the way in which the notions of the herd have been accumulated. This seems to me the best, easiest, and least invidious educational device for cultivating a proper distrust for the older notions on which we still continue to rely.

COMMENT AND QUESTIONS

I. What is the point of the quotation from Mr. Trotter (paragraph 8)? Does Robinson appear to agree without qualification? Do you agree, or would you make some exceptions?

[3] Mr. Robinson is here referring to the whole of *The Mind in the Making*, not simply to this chapter.

II. What purposes are served by paragraph 18?

III. Define and distinguish between each of the four kinds of thinking. What seem to you the best examples of each in the essay?

IV. Does Robinson's analysis of the various kinds of thinking accord with your own self-examination and your observation? Cite examples from your own experience.

V. As Robinson uses the terms, what relationships exist between *idle curiosity* and *creative thought?* Between *reason* and *creative thinking?* Between *rationalization* and *real reasons?*

VI. At times, in paragraphs 14–16, 29, 32–33, for example, Robinson seems to belittle the thought and knowledge of the past. What grounds can you find for calling him a cynic? A pessimist? An optimist?

VII. This essay is in part informative and evaluative, in part persuasive. What attitudes or beliefs is Robinson attempting to persuade the reader to accept? What are his main arguments and his main appeals to the reader's emotions? Describe his tone in the essay. Is it well adapted to his purpose?

JOHN DEWEY

Does Human Nature Change?[*]

John Dewey (1859–1952) was an American philosopher and educator,[1] a follower of William James, and the founder of the progressive-school movement. "Does Human Nature Change?" is a selection from *Problems of Men,* published in 1946.

[1] I have come to the conclusion that those who give different answers to the question I have asked in the title of this article are talking about different things. This statement in itself, however, is too easy a way out of the problem to be satisfactory. For there is a real problem, and so far as the question is a practical one instead of an academic one, I think the proper answer is that human nature *does* change.

[2] By the practical side of the question, I mean the question whether or not important, almost fundamental, changes in the ways of human belief and action have taken place and are capable of still taking place. But to put this question in its proper perspective, we have first to recognize the sense in which human nature does not change. I do not think it can be shown that the innate needs of men have changed since man became man or that there is any evidence that they will change as long as man is on the earth.

---

[*] First published in *The Rotarian,* February, 1938. Reprinted by permission.
[1] See the portrayal of Dewey in Irwin Edman's essay "Former Teachers," p. 1098.

[3] By "needs" I mean the inherent demands that men make because of their constitution. Needs for food and drink and for moving about, for example, are so much a part of our being that we cannot imagine any condition under which they would cease to be. There are other things not so directly physical that seem to me equally engrained in human nature. I would mention as examples the need for some kind of companionship; the need for exhibiting energy, for bringing one's powers to bear upon surrounding conditions; the need for both coöperation with and emulation of one's fellows for mutual aid and combat alike; the need for some sort of aesthetic expression and satisfaction; the need to lead and to follow, etc.

[4] Whether my particular examples are well chosen or not does not matter so much as does recognition of the fact that there are some tendencies so integral a part of human nature that the latter would not be human nature if they changed. These tendencies used to be called instincts. Psychologists are now more chary of using that word than they used to be. But the word by which the tendencies are called does not matter much in comparison to the fact that human nature has its own constitution.

[5] Where we are likely to go wrong, after the fact is recognized that there is something unchangeable in the structure of human nature, is the inference we draw from it. We suppose that the manifestation of these needs is also unalterable. We suppose that the manifestations we have got used to are as natural and as unalterable as are the needs from which they spring.

[6] The need for food is so imperative that we call the persons insane who persistently refuse to take nourishment. But what kinds of food are wanted and used are a matter of acquired habit influenced by both physical environment and social custom. To civilized people today, eating human flesh is an entirely unnatural thing. Yet there have been peoples to whom it seemed natural because it was socially authorized and even highly esteemed. There are well-accredited stories of persons needing support from others who have refused palatable and nourishing foods because they were not accustomed to them; the alien foods were so "unnatural" they preferred to starve rather than eat them.

[7] Aristotle spoke for an entire social order as well as for himself when he said that slavery existed by nature. He would have regarded efforts to abolish slavery from society as an idle and utopian effort to change human nature where it was unchangeable. For according to him it was not simply the desire to be a master that was engrained in human nature. There were persons who were born with such an inherently slavish nature that it did violence to human nature to set them free.

[8] The assertion that human nature cannot be changed is heard when social changes are urged as reforms and improvements of existing conditions. It is always heard when the proposed changes in institutions or conditions stand in sharp opposition to what exists. If the conservative were wiser, he would rest his objections in most cases, not upon the unchangeability of human nature, but upon the inertia of custom; upon the resistance that

acquired habits offer to change after they are once acquired. It is hard to teach an old dog new tricks and it is harder yet to teach society to adopt customs which are contrary to those which have long prevailed. Conservatism of this type would be intelligent, and it would compel those wanting change not only to moderate their pace, but also to ask how the changes they desire could be introduced with a minimum of shock and dislocation.

[9] Nevertheless, there are few social changes that can be opposed on the ground that they are contrary to human nature itself. A proposal to have a society get along without food and drink is one of the few that are of this kind. Proposals to form communities in which there is no cohabitation have been made and the communities have endured for a time. But they are so nearly contrary to human nature that they have not endured long. These cases are almost the only ones in which social change can be opposed simply on the ground that human nature cannot be changed.

[10] Take the institution of war, one of the oldest, most socially reputable of all human institutions. Efforts for stable peace are often opposed on the ground that man is by nature a fighting animal and that this phase of his nature is unalterable. The failure of peace movements in the past can be cited in support of this view. In fact, however, war is as much a social pattern as is the domestic slavery which the ancients thought to be an immutable fact.

[11] I have already said that, in my opinion, combativeness is a constituent part of human nature. But I have also said that the manifestations of these native elements are subject to change because they are affected by custom and tradition. War does not exist because man has combative instincts, but because social conditions and forces have led, almost forced, these "instincts" into this channel.

[12] There are a large number of other channels in which the need for combat has been satisfied, and there are other channels not yet discovered or explored into which it could be led with equal satisfaction. There is war against disease, against poverty, against insecurity, against injustice, in which multitudes of persons have found full opportunity for the exercise of their combative tendencies.

[13] The time may be far off when men will cease to fulfill their need for combat by destroying each other and when they will manifest it in common and combined efforts against the forces that are enemies of all men equally. But the difficulties in the way are found in the persistence of certain acquired social customs and not in the unchangeability of the demand for combat.

[14] Pugnacity and fear are native elements of human nature. But so are pity and sympathy. We send nurses and physicians to the battlefield and provide hospital facilities as "naturally" as we charge bayonets and discharge machine guns. In early times there was a close connection between pugnacity and fighting, for the latter was done largely with the fists. Pugnacity plays a small part in generating wars today. Citizens of one country

do not hate those of another nation by instinct. When they attack or are attacked, they do not use their fists in close combat, but throw shells from a great distance at persons whom they have never seen. In modern wars, anger and hatred come after the war has started; they are effects of war, not the cause of it.

[15] It is a tough job sustaining a modern war; all the emotional reactions have to be excited. Propaganda and atrocity stories are enlisted. Aside from such extreme measures there has to be definite organization, as we saw in the two World Wars, to keep up the morale of even non-combatants. And morale is largely a matter of keeping emotions at a certain pitch; and unfortunately fear, hatred, suspicion, are among the emotions most easily aroused.

[16] I shall not attempt to dogmatize about the causes of modern wars. But I do not think that anyone will deny that they are social rather than psychological, though psychological appeal is highly important in working up a people to the point where they want to fight and in keeping them at it. I do not think, moreover, that anyone will deny that economic conditions are powerful among the social causes of war. The main point, however, is that whatever the sociological causes, they are affairs of tradition, custom, and institutional organization, and these factors belong among the changeable manifestations of human nature, not among the unchangeable elements.

[17] I have used the case of war as a typical instance of what is changeable and what is unchangeable in human nature, in their relation to schemes of social change. I have selected the case because it is an extremely difficult one in which to effect durable changes, not because it is an easy one. The point is that the obstacles in the way are put there by social forces which do change from time to time, not by fixed elements of human nature. This fact is also illustrated in the failures of pacifists to achieve their ends by appeal simply to sympathy and pity. For while, as I have said, the kindly emotions are also a fixed constituent of human nature, the channel they take is dependent upon social conditions.

[18] There is always a great outburst of these kindly emotions in time of war. Fellow feeling and the desire to help those in need are intense during war, as they are at every period of great disaster that comes home to observation or imagination. But they are canalized in their expression; they are confined to those upon our side. They occur simultaneously with manifestation of rage and fear against the other side, if not always in the same person, at least in the community generally. Hence the ultimate failure of pacifist appeals to the kindly elements of native human nature when they are separated from intelligent consideration of the social and economic forces at work.

[19] William James made a great contribution in the title of one of his essays, *The Moral Equivalent of War*. The very title conveys the point I am making. Certain basic needs and emotions are permanent. But they are

capable of finding expression in ways that are radically different from the ways in which they now currently operate.

[20] An even more burning issue emerges when any fundamental change in economic institutions and relations is proposed. Proposals for such sweeping change are among the commonplaces of our time. On the other hand, the proposals are met by the statement that the changes are impossible because they involve an impossible change in human nature. To this statement, advocates of the desired changes are only too likely to reply that the present system or some phase of it is contrary to human nature. The argument *pro* and *con* then gets put on the wrong ground.

[21] As a matter of fact, economic institutions and relations are among the manifestations of human nature that are most susceptible of change. History is living evidence of the scope of these changes. Aristotle, for example, held that paying interest is unnatural, and the Middle Ages reëchoed the doctrine. All interest was usury, and it was only after economic conditions had so changed that payment of interest was a customary and in that sense a "natural" thing, that usury got its present meaning.

[22] There have been times and places in which land was held in common and in which private ownership of land would have been regarded as the most monstrous of unnatural things. There have been other times and places when all wealth was possessed by an overlord and his subjects held wealth, if any, subject to his pleasure. The entire system of credit so fundamental in contemporary financial and industrial life is a modern invention. The invention of the joint-stock company with limited liability of individuals has brought about a great change from earlier facts and conceptions of property. I think the need of owning something is one of the native elements of human nature. But it takes either ignorance or a very lively fancy to suppose that the system of ownership that exists in the United States in 1946, with all its complex relations and its interweaving with legal and political supports, is a necessary and unchangeable product of an inherent tendency to appropriate and possess.

[23] Law is one of the most conservative of human institutions; yet through the cumulative effect of legislation and judicial decisions it changes, sometimes at a slow rate, sometimes rapidly. The changes in human relations that are brought about by changes in industrial and legal institutions then react to modify the ways in which human nature manifests itself, and this brings about still further changes in institutions, and so on indefinitely.

[24] It is for these reasons that I say that those who hold that proposals for social change, even of rather a profound character, are impossible and utopian because of the fixity of human nature confuse the resistance to change that comes from acquired habits with that which comes from original human nature. The savage, living in a primitive society, comes nearer to being a purely "natural" human being than does civilized man. Civilization itself is the product of altered human nature. But even the savage is bound

by a mass of tribal customs and transmitted beliefs that modify his original nature, and it is these acquired habits that make it so difficult to transform him into a civilized human being.

[25] The revolutionary radical, on the other hand, overlooks the force of engrained habits. He is right, in my opinion, about the indefinite plasticity of human nature. But he is wrong in thinking that patterns of desire, belief, and purpose do not have a force comparable to the inertia, the resistance to movement, possessed by these same objects when they are at rest. Habit, not original human nature, keeps things moving most of the time, about as they have moved in the past.

[26] If human nature is unchangeable, then there is no such thing as education and all our efforts to educate are doomed to failure. For the very meaning of education is modification of native human nature in formation of those new ways of thinking, of feeling, of desiring, and of believing that are foreign to raw human nature. If the latter were unalterable, we might have training but not education. For training, as distinct from education, means simply the acquisition of certain skills. Native gifts can be trained to a point of higher efficiency without that development of new attitudes and dispositions which is the goal of education. But the result is mechanical. It is like supposing that while a musician may acquire by practice greater technical ability, he cannot rise from one plane of musical appreciation and creation to another.

[27] The theory that human nature is unchangeable is thus the most depressing and pessimistic of all possible doctrines. If it were carried out logically, it would mean a doctrine of predestination from birth that would outdo the most rigid of theological doctrines. For according to it, persons are what they are at birth and nothing can be done about it, beyond the kind of training that an acrobat might give to the muscular system with which he is originally endowed. If a person is born with criminal tendencies, a criminal he will become and remain. If a person is born with an excessive amount of greed, he will become a person living by predatory activities at the expense of others; and so on. I do not doubt at all the existence of differences in natural endowment. But what I am questioning is the notion that they doom individuals to a fixed channel of expression. It is difficult indeed to make a silk purse out of a sow's ear. But the particular form which, say, a natural musical endowment will take depends upon the social influences to which one is subjected. Beethoven in a savage tribe would doubtless have been outstanding as a musician, but he would not have been the Beethoven who composed symphonies.

[28] The existence of almost every conceivable kind of social institution at some time and place in the history of the world is evidence of the plasticity of human nature. This fact does not prove that all these different social systems are of equal value, materially, morally, and culturally. The slightest observation shows that such is not the case. But the fact in prov-

ing the changeability of human nature indicates the attitude that should be taken toward proposals for social changes. The question is primarily whether they, in special cases, are desirable or not. And the way to answer that question is to try to discover what their consequences would be if they were adopted. Then if the conclusion is that they are desirable, the further question is how they can be accomplished with a minimum of waste, destruction, and needless dislocation.

[29] In finding the answer to this question, we have to take into account the force of existing traditions and customs; of the patterns of action and belief that already exist. We have to find out what forces already at work can be reinforced so that they move toward the desired change and how the conditions that oppose change can be gradually weakened. Such questions as these can be considered on the basis of fact and reason.

[30] The assertion that a proposed change is impossible because of the fixed constitution of human nature diverts attention from the question of whether or not a change is desirable and from the other question of how it shall be brought about. It throws the question into the arena of blind emotion and brute force. In the end, it encourages those who think that great changes can be produced offhand and by the use of sheer violence.

[31] When our sciences of human nature and human relations are anything like as developed as are our sciences of physical nature, their chief concern will be with the problem of how human nature is most effectively modified. The question will not be whether it is capable of change, but of how it is to be changed under given conditions. This problem is ultimately that of education in its widest sense. Consequently, whatever represses and distorts the processes of education that might bring about a change in human dispositions with the minimum of waste puts a premium upon the forces that bring society to a state of deadlock, and thereby encourages the use of violence as a means of social change.

COMMENT AND QUESTIONS

I. John Dewey bases his argument that human nature does change on an analysis of "human nature." What parts of it does he consider unchangeable? What parts are alterable? What examples does he give of each?

II. Dewey speaks several times of the strong opposition to proposed economic and social changes. How does he support his idea that profound changes in economic institutions and relations are not contrary to human nature? If not the fixity of human nature, then what accounts for the fact that changes in institutions are often difficult to bring about?

III. What relationships does Dewey, who devoted much of his life to education, see between education and the changeability of human nature?

IV. According to the philosophy of pragmatism, to which Dewey subscribed, the worth or validity of an action or idea is to be judged by the practical results it produces. What evidence can you see in this essay of Dewey's pragmatism?

V. Point out examples in the essay of the author's care in making distinctions and in avoiding sweeping generalizations.

PLATO

Apology*

In 399 B.C., Socrates, Greek philosopher and teacher, was accused of impiety and of corrupting the youth of Athens with false doctrines, and was tried and condemned to death by a court of 501 Athenian citizens. According to Athenian law, the accused acted as his own attorney and spoke to the court in his own behalf. If he was judged guilty of the charges, and if no punishment for the offense was established by Athenian law, his accusers proposed a penalty, and the defendant might propose an alternate penalty; the court then chose between them. The *Apology*, or *Defense* (the Greek word did not imply expression of regret, as our word *apology* may), is Socrates' speech to the court, reported by his pupil Plato. It gives us a picture of a human being, an almost legendary thinker, who has helped to shape Western thought, and whose voice still says over the centuries that wisdom and virtue come only from thought and inquiry, and that the unexamined life is not worth living.

[1] How you, O Athenians, have been affected by my accusers, I cannot tell; but I know that they almost made me forget who I was—so persuasively did they speak; and yet they have hardly uttered a word of truth. But of the many falsehoods told by them, there was one which quite amazed me;—I mean when they said that you should be upon your guard and not allow yourselves to be deceived by the force of my eloquence. To say this, when they were certain to be detected as soon as I opened my lips and proved myself to be anything but a great speaker, did indeed appear to me most shameless—unless by the force of eloquence they mean the force of truth; for if such is their meaning, I admit that I am eloquent. But in how different a way from theirs! Well, as I was saying, they have scarcely spoken the truth at all; but from me you shall hear the whole truth; not, however, delivered after their manner in a set oration duly ornamented with words and phrases. No, by heaven! but I shall use the words and arguments which occur to me at the moment; for I am confident in the justice of my cause: at my time of life I ought not to be appearing before you, O men of Athens, in the character of a juvenile orator—let no one expect it of me. And I must beg

* Translated by Benjamin Jowett.

of you to grant me a favour:—if I defend myself in my accustomed manner, and you hear me using the words which I have been in the habit of using in the agora, at the tables of the money-changers, or anywhere else, I would ask you not to be surprised, and not to interrupt me on this account. For I am more than seventy years of age, and appearing now for the first time in a court of law, I am quite a stranger to the language of the place; and therefore I would have you regard me as if I were really a stranger, whom you would excuse if he spoke in his native tongue, and after the fashion of his country:—Am I making an unfair request of you? Never mind the manner, which may or may not be good; but think only of the truth of my words, and give heed to that: let the speaker speak truly and the judge decide justly.

[2] And first, I have to reply to the older charges and to my first accusers, and then I will go on to the later ones. For of old I have had many accusers, who have accused me falsely to you during many years; and I am more afraid of them than of Anytus and his associates, who are dangerous, too, in their own way. But far more dangerous are the others, who began when you were children, and took possession of your minds with their falsehoods, telling of one Socrates, a wise man, who speculated about the heaven above, and searched into the earth beneath, and made the worse appear the better cause. The disseminators of this tale are the accusers whom I dread; for their hearers are apt to fancy that such enquirers do not believe in the existence of the gods. And they are many, and their charges against me are of ancient date, and they were made by them in the days when you were more impressible than you are now—in childhood, or it may have been in youth—and the cause when heard went by default, for there was none to answer. And hardest of all, I do not know and cannot tell the names of my accusers; unless in the chance case of a comic poet. All who from envy and malice have persuaded you—some of them having first convinced themselves—all this class of men are most difficult to deal with; for I cannot have them up here, and cross-examine them, and therefore I must simply fight with shadows in my own defence, and argue when there is no one who answers. I will ask you then to assume with me, as I was saying, that my opponents are of two kinds; one recent, the other ancient: and I hope that you will see the propriety of my answering the latter first, for these accusations you heard long before the others, and much oftener.

[3] Well, then, I must make my defence, and endeavour to clear away in a short time, a slander which has lasted a long time. May I succeed, if to succeed be for my good and yours, or likely to avail me in my cause! The task is not an easy one; I quite understand the nature of it. And so leaving the event with God, in obedience to the law I will now make my defence.

[4] I will begin at the beginning, and ask what is the accusation which has given rise to the slander of me, and in fact has encouraged Meletus to prefer this charge against me. Well, what do the slanderers say? They shall be my prosecutors, and I will sum up their words in an affidavit: "Socrates is an evildoer, and a curious person, who searches into things under the earth

and in heaven, and he makes the worse appear the better cause; and he teaches the aforesaid doctrines to others." Such is the nature of the accusation: it is just what you have yourselves seen in the comedy of Aristophanes, who has introduced a man whom he calls Socrates, going about and saying that he walks in air, and talking a deal of nonsense concerning matters of which I do not pretend to know either much or little—not that I mean to speak disparagingly of any one who is a student of natural philosophy. I should be very sorry if Meletus could bring so grave a charge against me. But the simple truth is, O Athenians, that I have nothing to do with physical speculations. Very many of those here present are witnesses to the truth of this, and to them I appeal. Speak then, you who have heard me, and tell your neighbours whether any of you have ever known me hold forth in few words or in many upon such matters. . . . You hear their answer. And from what they say of this part of the charge you will be able to judge of the truth of the rest.

[5] As little foundation is there for the report that I am a teacher and take money; this accusation has no more truth in it than the other. Although, if a man were really able to instruct mankind, to receive money for giving instruction would, in my opinion, be an honour to him. There is Gorgias of Leontium, and Prodicus of Ceos, and Hippias of Elis, who go the round of the cities, and are able to persuade the young men to leave their own citizens by whom they might be taught for nothing, and come to them whom they not only pay, but are thankful if they may be allowed to pay them. There is at this time a Parian philosopher residing in Athens, of whom I have heard; and I came to hear of him in this way:—I came across a man who has spent a world of money on the Sophists, Callias, the son of Hipponicus, and knowing that he had sons, I asked him: "Callias," I said, "if your two sons were foals or calves, there would be no difficulty in finding some one to put over them; we should hire a trainer of horses, or a farmer, probably, who would improve and perfect them in their own proper virtue and excellence; but as they are human beings, whom are you thinking of placing over them? Is there any one who understands human and political virtue? You must have thought about the matter, for you have sons; is there any one?" "There is," he said. "Who is he?" said I; "and of what country? and what does he charge?" "Evenus the Parian," he replied; "he is the man, and his charge is five minae." Happy is Evenus, I said to myself, if he really has this wisdom, and teaches at such a moderate charge. Had I the same, I should have been very proud and conceited; but the truth is that I have no knowledge of the kind.

[6] I dare say, Athenians, that some one among you will reply, "Yes, Socrates, but what is the origin of these accusations which are brought against you; there must have been something strange which you have been doing? All these rumours and this talk about you would never have arisen if you had been like other men: tell us, then, what is the cause of them, for

we should be sorry to judge hastily of you." Now, I regard this as a fair challenge, and I will endeavor to explain to you the reason why I am called wise and have such an evil fame. Please to attend then. And although some of you may think that I am joking, I declare that I will tell you the entire truth. Men of Athens, this reputation of mine has come of a certain sort of wisdom which I possess. If you ask me what kind of wisdom, I reply, wisdom such as may perhaps be attained by man, for to that extent I am inclined to believe that I am wise; whereas the persons of whom I was speaking have a superhuman wisdom, which I may fail to describe, because I have it not myself; and he who says that I have, speaks falsely, and is taking away my character. And here, O men of Athens, I must beg you not to interrupt me, even if I seem to say something extravagant. For the word which I will speak is not mine. I will refer you to a witness who is worthy of credit; that witness shall be the God of Delphi—he will tell you about my wisdom, if I have any, and of what sort it is. You must have known Chaerephon; he was early a friend of mine, and also a friend of yours, for he shared in the recent exile of the people, and returned with you. Well, Chaerephon, as you know, was very impetuous in all his doings, and he went to Delphi and boldly asked the oracle to tell him whether—as I was saying, I must beg you not to interrupt—he asked the oracle to tell him whether any one was wiser than I was, and the Pythian prophetess answered, that there was no man wiser. Chaerephon is dead himself; but his brother, who is in court, will confirm the truth of what I am saying.

[7] Why do I mention this? Because I am going to explain to you why I have such an evil name. When I heard the answer, I said to myself, What can the God mean? and what is the interpretation of his riddle? for I know that I have no wisdom, small or great. What then can he mean when he says that I am the wisest of men? And yet he is a god, and cannot lie; that would be against his nature. After long consideration, I thought of a method of trying the question. I reflected that if I could only find a man wiser than myself, then I might go to the god with a refutation in my hand. I should say to him, "Here is a man who is wiser than I am; but you said that I was the wisest." Accordingly I went to one who had the reputation of wisdom, and observed him—his name I need not mention; he was a politician whom I selected for examination—and the result was as follows: When I began to talk with him, I could not help thinking that he was not really wise, although he was thought wise by many, and still wiser by himself; and thereupon I tried to explain to him that he thought himself wise, but was not really wise; and the consequence was that he hated me, and his enmity was shared by several who were present and heard me. So I left him, saying to myself, as I went away: Well, although I do not suppose that either of us knows anything really beautiful and good, I am better off than he is,—for he knows nothing, and thinks that he knows; I neither know nor think that I know. In this latter particular, then, I seem to have slightly

the advantage of him. Then I went to another who had still higher pretensions to wisdom, and my conclusion was exactly the same. Whereupon I made another enemy of him, and of many others besides him.

[8] Then I went to one man after another, being not unconscious of the enmity which I provoked, and I lamented and feared this: but necessity was laid upon me,—the word of God, I thought, ought to be considered first. And I said to myself, Go I must to all who appear to know, and find out the meaning of the oracle. And I swear to you, Athenians, by the dog I swear!—for I must tell you the truth—the result of my mission was just this: I found that the men most in repute were all but the most foolish; and that others less esteemed were really wiser and better. I will tell you the tale of my wanderings and of the "Herculean" labours, as I may call them, which I endured only to find at last the oracle irrefutable. After the politicians, I went to the poets; tragic, dithyrambic, and all sorts. And there, I said to myself, you will be instantly detected; now you will find out that you are more ignorant than they are. Accordingly I took them some of the most elaborate passages in their own writings, and asked what was the meaning of them—thinking that they would teach me something. Will you believe me? I am almost ashamed to confess the truth, but I must say that there is hardly a person present who would not have talked better about their poetry than they did themselves. Then I knew that not by wisdom do poets write poetry, but by a sort of genius and inspiration; they are like diviners or soothsayers who also say many fine things, but do not understand the meaning of them. The poets appeared to me to be much in the same case; and I further observed that upon the strength of their poetry they believed themselves to be the wisest of men in other things in which they were not wise. So I departed, conceiving myself to be superior to them for the same reason that I was superior to the politicians.

[9] At last I went to the artisans. I was conscious that I knew nothing at all, as I may say, and I was sure that they knew many fine things; and here I was not mistaken, for they did know many things of which I was ignorant, and in this they certainly were wiser than I was. But I observed that even the good artisans fell into the same error as the poets;—because they were good workmen they thought that they also knew all sorts of high matters, and this defect in them overshadowed their wisdom; and therefore I asked myself on behalf of the oracle, whether I would like to be as I was, neither having their knowledge nor their ignorance, or like them in both; and I made answer to myself and to the oracle that I was better off as I was.

[10] This inquisition has led to my having many enemies of the worst and most dangerous kind, and has given occasion also to many calumnies. And I am called wise, for my hearers always imagine that I myself possess the wisdom which I find wanting in others; but the truth is, O men of Athens, that God only is wise; and by his answer he intends to show that the wisdom of men is worth little or nothing; he is not speaking of Socrates, he is only

using my name by way of illustration, as if he said, He, O men, is the wisest, who, like Socrates, knows that his wisdom is in truth worth nothing. And so I go about the world obedient to the god, and search and make enquiry into the wisdom of any one, whether citizen or stranger, who appears to be wise; and if he is not wise, then in vindication of the oracle I show him that he is not wise; and my occupation quite absorbs me, and I have no time to give either to any public matter of interest or to any concern of my own, but I am in utter poverty by reason of my devotion to the god.

[11] There is another thing:—young men of the richer classes, who have not much to do, come about me of their own accord; they like to hear the pretenders examined, and they often imitate me, and proceed to examine others; there are plenty of persons, as they quickly discover, who think that they know something, but really know little or nothing; and then those who are examined by them instead of being angry with themselves are angry with me: This confounded Socrates, they say; this villainous misleader of youth!—and then if somebody asks them, Why, what evil does he practise or teach? they do not know, and cannot tell; but in order that they may not appear to be at a loss, they repeat the ready-made charges which are used against all philosophers about teaching things up in the clouds and under the earth, and having no gods, and making the worse appear the better cause; for they do not like to confess that their pretence of knowledge has been detected—which is the truth; and as they are numerous and ambitious and energetic, and are drawn up in battle array and have persuasive tongues, they have filled your ears with their loud and inveterate calumnies. And this is the reason why my three accusers, Meletus and Anytus and Lycon, have set upon me; Meletus, who has a quarrel with me on behalf of the poets; Anytus, on behalf of the craftsmen and politicians; Lycon, on behalf of the rhetoricians: and, as I said at the beginning, I cannot expect to get rid of such a mass of calumny all in a moment. And this, O men of Athens, is the truth and the whole truth; I have concealed nothing, I have dissembled nothing. And yet, I know that my plainness of speech makes them hate me, and what is their hatred but a proof that I am speaking the truth? Hence has arisen the prejudice against me; and this is the reason of it, as you will find out either in this or in any future enquiry.

[12] I have said enough in my defence against the first class of my accusers; I turn to the second class. They are headed by Meletus, that good man and true lover of his country, as he calls himself. Against these, too, I must try to make a defence:—Let their affidavit be read: it contains something of this kind: It says that Socrates is a doer of evil, who corrupts the youth; and who does not believe in the gods of the State, but has other new divinities of his own. Such is the charge; and now let us examine the particular counts. He says that I am a doer of evil, and corrupt the youth; but I say, O men of Athens, that Meletus is a doer of evil, in that he pretends to be in earnest when he is only in jest, and is so eager to bring men

to trial from a pretended zeal and interest about matters in which he really never had the smallest interest. And the truth of this I will endeavour to prove to you.

[13] Come hither, Meletus, and let me ask a question of you. You think a great deal about the improvement of youth?

Yes, I do.

Tell the judges, then, who is their improver; for you must know, as you have taken the pains to discover their corrupter, and are citing and accusing me before them. Speak, then, and tell the judges who their improver is.—Observe, Meletus, that you are silent, and have nothing to say. But is not this rather disgraceful, and a very considerable proof of what I was saying, that you have no interest in the matter? Speak up, friend, and tell us who their improver is.

The laws.

But that, my good sir, is not my meaning. I want to know who the person is, who, in the first place, knows the laws.

The judges, Socrates, who are present in court.

What, do you mean to say, Meletus, that they are able to instruct and improve youth?

Certainly they are.

What, all of them, or some only and not others?

All of them.

By the goddess Here, that is good news! There are plenty of improvers, then. And what do you say of the audience,—do they improve them?

Yes, they do.

And the senators?

Yes, the senators improve them.

But perhaps the members of the assembly corrupt them?—or do they improve them?

They improve them.

Then every Athenian improves and elevates them; all with the exception of myself; and I alone am their corrupter? Is that what you affirm?

That is what I stoutly affirm.

I am very unfortunate if you are right. But suppose I ask you a question: How about horses? Does one man do them harm and all the world good? Is not the exact opposite the truth? One man is able to do them good, or at least not many;—the trainer of horses, that is to say, does them good, and others who have to do with them rather injure them? Is not that true, Meletus, of horses, or of any other animal? Most assuredly it is; whether you and Anytus say yes or no. Happy indeed would be the condition of youth if they had one corrupter only, and all the rest of the world were their improvers. But you, Meletus, have sufficiently shown that you never had a thought about the young: your carelessness is seen in your not caring about the very things which you bring against me.

And now, Meletus, I will ask you another question—by Zeus I will:

Which is better, to live among bad citizens, or among good ones? Answer, friend, I say; the question is one which may be easily answered. Do not the good do their neighbours good, and the bad do them evil?

Certainly.

And is there any one who would rather be injured than benefited by those who live with him? Answer, my good friend, the law requires you to answer—does any one like to be injured?

Certainly not.

And when you accuse me of corrupting and deteriorating the youth, do you allege that I corrupt them intentionally or unintentionally?

Intentionally, I say.

But you have just admitted that the good do their neighbours good, and the evil do them evil. Now, is that a truth which your superior wisdom has recognized thus early in life, and am I, at my age, in such darkness and ignorance as not to know that if a man with whom I have to live is corrupted by me, I am very likely to be harmed by him; and yet I corrupt him, and intentionally, too—so you say, although neither I nor any other human being is ever likely to be convinced by you. But either I do not corrupt them, or I corrupt them unintentionally; and on either view of the case you lie. If my offence is unintentional, the law has no cognizance of unintentional offences: you ought to have taken me privately, and warned and admonished me; for if I had been better advised, I should have left off doing what I only did unintentionally—no doubt I should; but you would have nothing to say to me and refused to teach me. And now you bring me up in this court, which is a place not of instruction, but of punishment.

It will be very clear to you, Athenians, as I was saying, that Meletus has no care at all, great or small, about the matter. But still I should like to know, Meletus, in what I am affirmed to corrupt the young. I suppose you mean, as I infer from your indictment, that I teach them not to acknowledge the gods which the State acknowledges, but some other new divinities or spiritual agencies in their stead. These are the lessons by which I corrupt the youth, as you say.

Yes, that I say emphatically.

Then, by the gods, Meletus, of whom we are speaking, tell me and the court, in somewhat plainer terms, what you mean! For I do not as yet understand whether you affirm that I teach other men to acknowledge some gods, and therefore that I do believe in gods, and am not an entire atheist—this you do not lay to my charge,—but only you say that they are not the same gods which the city recognizes—the charge is that they are different gods. Or, do you mean that I am an atheist simply, and a teacher of atheism?

I mean the latter—that you are a complete atheist.

What an extraordinary statement! Why do you think so, Meletus? Do you mean that I do not believe in the godhead of the sun or moon, like other men?

I assure you judges, that he does not: for he says that the sun is stone, and the moon earth.

Friend Meletus, you think that you are accusing Anaxagoras: and you have but a bad opinion of the judges, if you fancy them illiterate to such a degree as not to know that these doctrines are found in the books of Anaxagoras the Clazomenian, which are full of them. And so, forsooth, the youth are said to be taught them by Socrates, when there are not infrequently exhibitions of them at the theatre (price of admission one drachma at the most); and they might pay their money, and laugh at Socrates if he pretends to father these extraordinary views. And so, Meletus, you really think that I do not believe in any god?

I swear by Zeus that you believe absolutely in none at all.

Nobody will believe you, Meletus, and I am pretty sure that you do not believe yourself. I cannot help thinking, men of Athens, that Meletus is reckless and impudent, and that he has written this indictment in a spirit of mere wantonness and youthful bravado. Has he not compounded a riddle, thinking to try me? He said to himself:—I shall see whether the wise Socrates will discover my facetious contradiction, or whether I shall be able to deceive him and the rest of them. For he certainly does appear to me to contradict himself in the indictment as much as if he said that Socrates is guilty of not believing in the gods, and yet of believing in them—but this is not like a person who is in earnest.

I should like you, O men of Athens, to join me in examining what I conceive to be his inconsistency; and do you, Meletus, answer. And I must remind the audience of my request that they would not make a disturbance if I speak in my accustomed manner:

Did ever man, Meletus, believe in the existence of human things, and not of human beings? . . . I wish, men of Athens, that he would answer, and not be always trying to get up an interruption. Did ever any man believe in horsemanship, and not in horses? or in flute-playing, and not in flute-players? No, my friend; I will answer to you and to the court, as you refuse to answer for yourself. There is no man who ever did. But now please to answer the next question: Can a man believe in spiritual and divine agencies, and not in spirits or demigods?

He cannot.

How lucky I am to have extracted that answer, by the assistance of the court! But then you swear in the indictment that I teach and believe in divine or spiritual agencies (new or old, no matter for that); at any rate, I believe in spiritual agencies,—so you say and swear in the affidavit; and yet if I believe in divine beings, how can I help believing in spirits or demigods;—must I not? To be sure I must; and therefore I may assume that your silence gives consent. Now what are spirits or demigods? are they not either gods or the sons of gods?

Certainly they are.

But this is what I call the facetious riddle invented by you: the demigods or spirits are gods, and you say first that I do not believe in gods, and then again that I do believe in gods; that is, if I believe in demigods. For if the demigods are the illegitimate sons of gods, whether by the nymphs or by any other mothers, of whom they are said to be the sons—what human being will ever believe that there are no gods if they are the sons of Gods? You might as well affirm the existence of mules, and deny that of horses and asses. Such nonsense, Meletus, could only have been intended by you to make trial of me. You have put this into the indictment because you had nothing real of which to accuse me. But no one who has a particle of understanding will ever be convinced by you that the same men can believe in divine and superhuman things, and yet not believe that there are gods and demigods and heroes.

[14] I have said enough in answer to the charge of Meletus: any elaborate defence is unnecessary; but I know only too well how many are the enmities which I have incurred, and this is what will be my destruction if I am destroyed;—not Meletus, nor yet Anytus, but the envy and detraction of the world, which has been the death of many good men, and will probably be the death of many more; there is no danger of my being the last of them.

[15] Some one will say: And are you not ashamed, Socrates, of a course of life which is likely to bring you to an untimely end? To him I may fairly answer: There you are mistaken: a man who is good for anything ought not to calculate the chance of living or dying; he ought only to consider whether in doing anything he is doing right or wrong—acting the part of a good man or of a bad. Whereas, upon your view, the heroes who fell at Troy were not good for much, and the son of Thetis above all, who altogether despised danger in comparison with disgrace; and when he was so eager to slay Hector, his goddess mother said to him, that if he avenged his companion Patroclus, and slew Hector, he would die himself—"Fate," she said, in these or the like words, "waits for you next after Hector"; he, receiving this warning, utterly despised danger and death, and instead of fearing them, feared rather to live in dishonour, and not to avenge his friend. "Let me die forthwith," he replied, "and be avenged of my enemy, rather than abide here by the beaked ships, a laughingstock and a burden of the earth." Had Achilles any thought of death and danger? For wherever a man's place is, whether the place which he has chosen or that in which he has been placed by a commander, there he ought to remain in the hour of danger; he should not think of death or of anything but of disgrace. And this, O men of Athens, is a true saying.

[16] Strange, indeed, would be my conduct, O men of Athens, if I, who, when I was ordered by the generals whom you chose to command me at Potidaea and Amphipolis and Delium, remained where they placed me, like any other man, facing death—if now, when, as I conceive and imagine, God orders me to fulfill the philosopher's mission of searching into myself and other men, I were to desert my post through fear of death, or any other fear; that would indeed be strange, and I might justly be arraigned in court

for denying the existence of the gods, if I disobeyed the oracle because I was afraid of death, fancying that I was wise when I was not wise. For the fear of death is indeed the pretence of wisdom, and not real wisdom, being a pretence of knowing the unknown; and no one knows whether death, which men in their fear apprehend to be the greatest evil, may not be the greatest good. Is not this ignorance of a disgraceful sort, the ignorance which is the conceit that a man knows what he does not know? And in this respect only I believe myself to differ from men in general, and may perhaps claim to be wiser than they are:—that whereas I know but little of the world below, I do not suppose that I know: but I do know that injustice and disobedience to a better, whether God or man, is evil and dishonourable, and I will never fear or avoid a possible good rather than a certain evil. And therefore if you let me go now, and are not convinced by Anytus, who said that since I had been prosecuted I must be put to death; (or if not that I ought never to have been prosecuted at all); and that if I escape now, your sons will all be utterly ruined by listening to my words—if you say to me, Socrates, this time we will not mind Anytus, and you shall be let off, but upon one condition, that you are not to enquire and speculate in this way any more, and that if you are caught doing so again you shall die;—if this was the condition on which you let me go, I should reply: Men of Athens, I honour and love you; but I shall obey God rather than you, and while I have life and strength I shall never cease from the practice and teaching of philosophy, exhorting any one whom I meet and saying to him after my manner: You, my friend,—a citizen of the great and mighty and wise city of Athens,—are you not ashamed of heaping up the greatest amount of money and honour and reputation, and caring so little about wisdom and truth and the greatest improvement of the soul, which you never regard or heed at all? And if the person with whom I am arguing, says: Yes, but I do care; then I do not leave him or let him go at once; but I proceed to interrogate and examine and cross-examine him, and if I think that he has no virtue in him, but only says that he has, I reproach him with undervaluing the greater, and overvaluing the less. And I shall repeat the same words to every one whom I meet, young and old, citizen and alien, but especially to the citizens, inasmuch as they are my brethren. For know that this is the command of God; and I believe that no greater good has ever happened in the State than my service to the God. For I do nothing but go about persuading you all, old and young alike, not to take thought for your persons or your properties, but first and chiefly to care about the greatest improvement of the soul. I tell you that virtue is not given by money, but that from virtue comes money and every other good of man, public as well as private. This is my teaching, and if this is the doctrine which corrupts the youth, I am a mischievous person. But if any one says that this is not my teaching, he is speaking an untruth. Wherefore, O men of Athens, I say to you, do as Anytus bids or not as Anytus bids, and either acquit me or not; but whichever you do, understand that I shall never alter my ways, not even if I have to die many times.

[17] Men of Athens, do not interrupt, but hear me; there was an understanding between us that you should hear me to the end: I have something more to say, at which you may be inclined to cry out; but I believe that to hear me will be good for you, and therefore I beg that you will not cry out. I would have you know, that if you kill such an one as I am, you will injure yourselves more than you will injure me. Nothing will injure me, not Meletus nor yet Anytus—they cannot, for a bad man is not permitted to injure a better than himself. I do not deny that Anytus may, perhaps, kill him, or drive him into exile, or deprive him of civil rights; and he may imagine, and others may imagine, that he is inflicting a great injury upon him: but there I do not agree. For the evil of doing as he is doing—the evil of unjustly taking away the life of another—is greater far.

[18] And now, Athenians, I am not going to argue for my own sake, as you may think, but for yours, that you may not sin against the God by condemning me, who am his gift to you. For if you kill me you will not easily find a successor to me, who, if I may use such a ludicrous figure of speech, am a sort of gadfly, given to the State by God; and the State is a great and noble steed who is tardy in his motions owing to his very size, and requires to be stirred into life. I am that gadfly which God has attached to the State, and all day long and in all places am always fastening upon you, arousing and persuading and reproaching you. You will not easily find another like me, and therefore I would advise you to spare me. I dare say that you may feel out of temper (like a person who is suddenly awakened from sleep), and you think that you might easily strike me dead as Anytus advises, and then you would sleep on for the remainder of your lives, unless God in his care of you sent you another gadfly. When I say that I am given to you by God, the proof of my mission is this:—if I had been like other men, I should not have neglected all my own concerns or patiently seen the neglect of them during all these years, and have been doing yours, coming to you individually like a father or elder brother, exhorting you to regard virtue; such conduct, I say, would be unlike human nature. If I had gained anything, or if my exhortations had been paid, there would have been some sense in my doing so; but now, as you will perceive, not even the impudence of my accusers dares to say that I have ever exacted or sought pay of any one; of that they have no witness. And I have a sufficient witness to the truth of what I say—my poverty.

[19] Some one may wonder why I go about in private giving advice and busy myself with the concerns of others, but do not venture to come forward in public and advise the State. I will tell you why. You have heard me speak at sundry times and in divers places of an oracle or sign which comes to me, and is the divinity which Meletus ridicules in the indictment. This sign, which is a kind of voice, first began to come to me when I was a child;

it always forbids but never commands me to do anything which I am going to do. This is what deters me from being a politician. And rightly, as I think. For I am certain, O men of Athens, that if I had engaged in politics, I should have perished long ago, and done no good either to you or to myself. And do not be offended at my telling you the truth: for the truth is, that no man who goes to war with you or any other multitude, honestly striving against the many lawless and unrighteous deeds which are done in a state, will save his life; he who will fight for the right, if he would live even for a brief space, must have a private station and not a public one.

[20] I can give you convincing evidence of what I say, not words only, but what you value far more—actions. Let me relate to you a passage of my own life which will prove to you that I should never have yielded to injustice from any fear of death and that "as I should have refused to yield" I must have died at once. I will tell you a tale of the courts, not very interesting perhaps, but nevertheless true. The only office of State which I ever held, O men of Athens, was that of senator: the tribe Antiochis, which is my tribe, had the presidency at the trial of the generals who had not taken up the bodies of the slain after the battle of Arginusae; and you proposed to try them in a body, contrary to law, as you all thought afterwards; but at the time I was the only one of the Prytanes who was opposed to the illegality, and I gave my vote against you; and when the orators threatened to impeach and arrest me, and you called and shouted, I made up my mind that I would run the risk, having law and justice with me, rather than take part in your injustice because I feared imprisonment and death. This happened in the days of the democracy. But when the oligarchy of the Thirty was in power, they sent for me and four others into the rotunda, and bade us bring Leon the Salaminian from Salamis, as they wanted to put him to death. This was a specimen of the sort of comands which they were always giving with the view of implicating as many as possible in their crimes; and then I showed, not in word only but in deed, that, if I may be allowed to use such an expression, I cared not a straw for death, and that my great and only care was lest I should do an unrighteous or unholy thing. For the strong arm of that oppressive power did not frighten me into doing wrong; and when we came out of the rotunda the other four went to Salamis and fetched Leon, but I went quietly home. For which I might have lost my life, had not the power of the Thirty shortly afterwards come to an end. And many will witness to my words.

[21] Now, do you really imagine that I could have survived all these years, if I had led a public life, supposing that like a good man I had always maintained the right and had made justice, as I ought, the first thing? No, indeed, men of Athens, neither I nor any other man. But I have been always the same in all my actions, public as well as private, and never have I yielded any base compliance to those who are slanderously termed my disciples, or to any other. Not that I have any regular disciples. But if any one likes to come and hear me while I am pursuing my mission, whether he

be young or old, he is not excluded. Nor do I converse only with those who pay; but any one, whether he be rich or poor, may ask and answer me and listen to my words; and whether he turns out to be a bad man or a good one, neither result can be justly imputed to me; for I never taught or professed to teach him anything. And if any one says that he has ever learned or heard anything from me in private which all the world has not heard, let me tell you that he is lying.

[22] But I shall be asked, Why do people delight in continually conversing with you? I have told you already, Athenians, the whole truth about this matter: they like to hear the cross-examination of the pretenders to wisdom; there is amusement in it. Now, this duty of cross-examining other men has been imposed upon me by God; and has been signified to me by oracles, visions, and in every way in which the will of divine power was ever intimated to any one. This is true, O Athenians; or, if not true, would be soon refuted. If I am or have been corrupting the youth, those of them who are now grown up and have become sensible that I gave them bad advice in the days of their youth should come forward as accusers, and take their revenge; or if they do not like to come themselves, some of their relatives, fathers, brothers, or other kinsmen, should say what evil their families have suffered at my hands. Now is their time. Many of them I see in the court. There is Crito, who is of the same age and of the same deme with myself, and there is Critobulus his son, whom I also see. Then again there is Lysanias of Sphettus, who is the father of Aeschines—he is present; and also there is Antiphon of Cephisus, who is the father of Epigenes; and there are the brothers of several who have associated with me. There is Nicostratus the son of Theosdotides, and the brother of Theodotus (now Theodotus himself is dead, and therefore he, at any rate, will not seek to stop him); and there is Paralus the son of Demodocus, who had a brother Theages; and Adeimantus the son of Ariston, whose brother Plato is present; and Aeantodorus, who is the brother of Apollodorus, whom I also see. I might mention a great many others, some of whom Meletus should have produced as witnesses in the course of his speech; and let him still produce them, if he has forgotten—I will make way for him. And let him say, if he has any testimony of the sort which he can produce. Nay, Athenians, the very opposite is the truth. For all these are ready to witness on behalf of the corrupter, of the injurer of their kindred, as Meletus and Anytus call me; not the corrupted youth only—there might have been a motive for that—but their uncorrupted elder relatives. Why should they too support me with their testimony? Why, indeed, except for the sake of truth and justice, and because they know that I am speaking the truth, and that Meletus is a liar.

[23] Well, Athenians, this and the like of this is all the defence which I have to offer. Yet a word more. Perhaps there may be some one who is offended at me, when he calls to mind how he himself on a similar, or even a less serious occasion, prayed and entreated the judges with many tears, and how he produced his children in court, which was a moving

spectacle, together with a host of relations and friends; whereas I, who am probably in danger of my life, will do none of these things. The contrast may occur to his mind, and he may be set against me, and vote in anger because he is displeased at me on this account. Now, if there be such a person among you,—mind, I do not say that there is,—to him I may fairly reply: My friend, I am a man, and like other men, a creature of flesh and blood, and not "of wood or stone," as Homer says; and I have a family, yes, and sons, O Athenians, three in number, one almost a man, and two others who are still young; and yet I will not bring any of them hither in order to petition you for an acquittal. And why not? Not from any self-assertion or want of respect for you. Whether I am or am not afraid of death is another question, of which I will not now speak. But, having regard to public opinion, I feel that such conduct would be discreditable to myself, and to you, and to the whole State. One who has reached my years, and who has a name for wisdom, ought not to demean himself. Whether this opinion of me be deserved or not, at any rate the world has decided that Socrates is in some way superior to other men. And if those among you who are said to be superior in wisdom and courage, and any other virtue, demean themselves in this way, how shameful is their conduct! I have seen men of reputation, when they have been condemned, behaving in the strangest manner; they seem to fancy that they were going to suffer something dreadful if they died, and that they could be immortal if you only allowed them to live; and I think that such are a dishonour to the State, and that any stranger coming in would have said of them that the most eminent men of Athens, to whom the Athenians themselves give honour and command, are no better than women. And I say that these things ought not to be done by those of us who have a reputation; and if they are done, you ought not to permit them; you ought rather to show that you are far more disposed to condemn the man who gets up a doleful scene and makes the city ridiculous, than him who holds his peace.

[24] But, setting aside the question of public opinion, there seems to be something wrong in asking a favour of a judge, and thus procuring an acquittal, instead of informing and convincing him. For his duty is, not to make a present of justice, but to give judgment; and he has sworn that he will judge according to the laws, and not according to his own good pleasure; and we ought not to encourage you, nor should you allow yourselves to be encouraged, in this habit of perjury—there can be no piety in that. Do not then require me to do what I consider dishonourable and impious and wrong, especially now, when I am being tried for impiety on the indictment of Meletus. For if, O men of Athens, by force of persuasion and entreaty I could overpower your oaths, then I should be teaching you to believe that there are no gods, and in defending should simply convict myself of the charge of not believing in them. But that is not so—far otherwise. For I do believe that there are gods, and in a sense higher than that in

which any of my accusers believe in them. And to you and to God I commit my cause, to be determined by you as is best for you and me.

[*The vote is taken and Socrates is convicted.*]

[25] There are many reasons why I am not grieved, O men of Athens, at the vote of condemnation. I expected it, and am only surprised that the votes are so nearly equal; for I had thought that the majority against me would have been far larger; but now, had thirty votes gone over to the other side, I should have been acquitted. And I may say, I think, that I have escaped Meletus. I may say more; for without the assistance of Anytus and Lycon, any one may see that he would not have had a fifth part of the votes, as the law requires, in which case he would have incurred a fine of a thousand drachmae.

[26] And so he proposes death as the penalty. And what shall I propose on my part, O men of Athens? Clearly that which is my due. And what is my due? What returns shall be made to the man who has never had the wit to be idle during his whole life; but has been careless of what the many care for—wealth, and family interests, and military offices, and speaking in the assembly, and magistracies, and plots, and parties. Reflecting that I was really too honest a man to be a politician and live, I did not go where I could do no good to you or to myself; but where I could do the greatest good privately to every one of you, thither I went, and sought to persuade every man among you that he must look to himself, and seek virtue and wisdom before he looks to his private interests, and look to the State before he looks to the interests of the State; and that this should be the order which he observes in all his actions. What shall be done to such an one? Doubtless some good thing, O men of Athens, if he has his reward; and the good should be of a kind suitable to him. What would be a reward suitable to a poor man who is your benefactor, and who desires leisure that he may instruct you? There can be no reward so fitting as maintenance in the Prytaneum, O men of Athens, a reward which he deserves far more than the citizen who has won the prize at Olympia in the horse or chariot race, whether the chariots were drawn by two horses or by many. For I am in want, and he has enough; and he only gives you the appearance of happiness, and I give you the reality. And if I am to estimate the penalty fairly, I should say that maintenance in the Prytaneum is the just return.

[27] Perhaps you think that I am braving you in what I am saying now, as in what I said before about the tears and prayers. But this is not so. I speak rather because I am convinced that I never intentionally wronged any one, although I cannot convince you—the time has been too short; if there were a law at Athens, as there is in other cities, that a capital cause should not be decided in one day, then I believe that I should have convinced you. But I cannot in a moment refute great slanders; and, as I am convinced that I never wronged another, I will assuredly not wrong myself.

I will not say of myself that I deserve any evil, or propose any penalty. Why should I? Because I am afraid of the penalty of death which Meletus proposes? When I do not know whether death is a good or an evil, why should I propose a penalty which would certainly be an evil? Shall I say imprisonment? And why should I live in prison, and be the slave of the magistrate of the year—of the Eleven? Or shall the penalty be a fine, imprisonment until the fine is paid? There is the same objection. I should have to lie in prison, for money I have none, and cannot pay. And if I say exile (and this may possibly be the penalty which you will affix), I must indeed be blinded by the love of life, if I am so irrational as to expect that when you, who are my own citizens, cannot endure my discourses and words, and have found them so grievous and odious that you will have no more of them, others are likely to endure me. No, indeed, men of Athens, that is not very likely. And what a life should I lead, at my age, wandering from city to city, ever changing my place of exile, and always being driven out! For I am quite sure that wherever I go, there, as here, the young men will flock to me; and if I drive them away, their elders will drive me out at their request; and if I let them come, their fathers and friends will drive me out for their sakes.

[28] Some one will say: Yes, Socrates, but cannot you hold your tongue, and then you may go into a foreign city, and no one will interfere with you? Now, I have great difficulty in making you understand my answer to this. For if I tell you that to do as you say would be a disobedience to the God, and therefore that I cannot hold my tongue, you will not believe that I am serious; and if I say again that daily to discourse about virtue, and of those other things about which you hear me examining myself and others is the greatest good of man, and that the unexamined life is not worth living, you are still less likely to believe me. Yet I say what is true, although a thing of which it is hard for me to persuade you. Also, I have never been accustomed to think that I deserve to suffer any harm. Had I money I might have estimated the offence at what I was able to pay, and not have been much the worse. But I have none, and therefore I must ask you to proportion the fine to my means. Well, perhaps I could afford a mina, and therefore I propose that penalty: Plato, Crito, Critobulus, and Apollodorus, my friends here, bid me say thirty minae, and they will be the sureties. Let thirty minae be the penalty; for which sum they will be ample security to you.

[Socrates is condemned to death.]

[29] Not much time will be gained, O Athenians, in return for the evil name which you will get from the detractors of the city, who will say that you killed Socrates, a wise man; for they will call me wise, even though I am not wise, when they want to reproach you. If you had waited a little while, your desire would have been fulfilled in the course of nature. For I am far advanced in years, as you may perceive, and not far from death.

I am speaking now not to all of you, but only to those who have condemned me to death. And I have another thing to say to them: You think that I was convicted because I had no words of the sort which would have procured my acquittal—I mean, if I had thought fit to leave nothing undone or unsaid. Not so; the deficiency which led to my conviction was not of words—certainly not. But I had not the boldness or impudence or inclination to address you as you would have liked me to do, weeping and wailing and lamenting, and saying and doing many things which you have been accustomed to hear from others, and which, as I maintain, are unworthy of me. I thought at the time that I ought not to do anything common or mean when in danger: nor do I now repent of the style of my defence; I would rather die having spoken after my manner, than speak in your manner and live. For neither in war nor yet at law ought I or any man to use every way of escaping death. Often in battle there can be no doubt that if a man will throw away his arms, and fall on his knees before his pursuers, he may escape death; and in other dangers there are other ways of escaping death; if a man is willing to say and do anything. The difficulty, my friends, is not to avoid death, but to avoid unrighteousness; for that runs faster than death. I am old and move slowly, and the slower runner has overtaken me, and my accusers are keen and quick, and the faster runner, who is unrighteousness, has overtaken them. And now I depart hence condemned by you to suffer the penalty of death,—they too go their ways condemned by the truth to suffer the penalty of villainy and wrong; and I must abide by my award—let them abide by theirs. I suppose that these things may be regarded as fated,—and I think that they are well.

[30] And now, O men who have condemned me, I would fain prophesy to you; for I am about to die, and in the hour of death men are gifted with prophetic power. And I prophesy to you who are my murderers, that immediately after my departure punishment far heavier than you have inflicted on me will surely await you. Me you have killed because you wanted to escape the accuser, and not to give an account of your lives. But that will not be as you suppose: far otherwise. For I say that there will be more accusers of you than there are now; accusers whom hitherto I have restrained: and as they are younger they will be more inconsiderate with you, and you will be more offended at them. If you think that by killing men you can prevent some one from censuring your evil lives, you are mistaken; that is not a way of escape which is either possible or honourable; the easiest and the noblest way is not to be disabling others, but to be improving yourselves. This is the prophecy which I utter before my departure to the judges who have condemned me.

[31] Friends, who would have acquitted me, I would like also to talk with you about the thing which has come to pass, while the magistrates are busy, and before I go to the place at which I must die. Stay then a little, for we may as well talk with one another while there is time. You are my friends, and I should like to show you the meaning of this event which

has happened to me. O my judges—for you I may truly call judges—I should like to tell you of a wonderful circumstance. Hitherto the divine faculty of which the internal oracle is the source has constantly been in the habit of opposing me even about trifles, if I was going to make a slip or error in any matter; and now as you see there has come upon me that which may be thought, and is generally believed to be, the last and worst evil. But the oracle made no sign of opposition, either when I was leaving my house in the morning, or when I was on my way to the court, or while I was speaking, at anything which I was going to say; and yet I have often been stopped in the middle of a speech, but now in nothing I either said or did touching the matter in hand has the oracle opposed me. What do I take to be the explanation of this silence? I will tell you. It is an intimation that what has happened to me is a good, and that those of us who think that death is an evil are in error. For the customary sign would surely have opposed me had I been going to evil and not to good.

[32] Let us reflect in another way, and we shall see that there is great reason to hope that death is a good; for one of two things—either death is a state of nothingness and utter unconsciousness, or, as men say, there is a change and migration of the soul from this world to another. Now, if you suppose that there is no consciousness, but a sleep like the sleep of him who is undisturbed even by dreams, death will be an unspeakable gain. For if a person were to select the night in which his sleep was undisturbed even by dreams, and were to compare with this the other days and nights of his life, and then were to tell us how many days and nights he had passed in the course of his life better and more pleasantly than this one, I think that any man, I will not say a private man, but even the great king will not find many such days or nights, when compared with the others. Now, if death be of such a nature, I say that to die is gain; for eternity is then only a single night. But if death is the journey to another place, and there, as men say, all the dead abide, what good, O my friends and judges, can be greater than this? If, indeed, when the pilgrim arrives in the world below, he is delivered from the professors of justice in this world, and finds the true judges who are said to give judgment there, Minos and Rhadamanthus and Aeacus and Triptolemus, and other sons of God who were righteous in their own life, that pilgrimage will be worth making. What would not a man give if he might converse with Orpheus and Musaeus and Hesiod and Homer? Nay, if this be true, let me die again and again. I myself, too, shall have a wonderful interest in there meeting and conversing with Palamedes, and Ajax the son of Telamon, and any other ancient hero who has suffered death through an unjust judgment; and there will be no small pleasure, as I think, in comparing my own sufferings with theirs. Above all, I shall then be able to continue my search into true and false knowledge; as in this world, so also in the next; and I shall find out who is wise, and who pretends to be wise, and is not. What would not a man give, O judges, to be able to examine the leader of the great Trojan expedition; or Odysseus or Sisyphus,

or numberless others, men and women too! What infinite delight would there be in conversing with them and asking them questions! In another world they do not put a man to death for asking questions; assuredly not. For besides being happier than we are, they will be immortal, if what is said is true.

[33] Wherefore, O judges, be of good cheer about death, and know of a certainty, that no evil can happen to a good man, either in life or after death. He and his are not neglected by the gods; nor has my own approaching end happened by mere chance. But I see clearly that the time had arrived when it was better for me to die and be released from trouble; wherefore the oracle gave no sign. For which reason, also, I am not angry with my condemners, or with my accusers; they have done me no harm, although they did not mean to do me any good; and for this I may gently blame them.

[34] Still, I have a favour to ask of them. When my sons are grown up, I would ask you, O my friends, to punish them; and I would have you trouble them, as I have troubled you, if they seem to care about riches, or anything, more than about virtue; or if they pretend to be something when they are really nothing,—then reprove them, as I have reproved you, for not caring about that for which they ought to care, and thinking that they are something when they are really nothing. And if you do this, both I and my sons will have received justice at your hands.

[35] The hour of departure has arrived, and we go our ways—I to die, and you to live. Which is better God only knows.

COMMENT AND QUESTIONS

I. The opening paragraph of the *Apology* is an interesting study in speaker-audience relationship. What is Socrates' attitude toward his audience? What persuasive facts does he give about himself, and what impressions does he give of himself and of his accusers?

II. Socrates believes that more dangerous to him than the immediate accusations of Meletus, Anytus, and Lycon is the body of rumor and misapprehension about him which has grown over a period of time. What false ideas about himself does he attempt to correct in the opening section of his defense?

III. Exactly what did the oracle say about Socrates? What, according to Socrates, did the oracle mean? What is the special character of Socrates' wisdom?

IV. In the questioning of Meletus (paragraph 13 and the many short paragraphs following) does Socrates use any questionable reasoning in exposing this accuser? If so, where? Would tricky reasoning be justifiable under these circumstances?

V. Socrates asks Meletus who is the improver of the youth. What answer would you give to this question about the youth of the present day?

VI. What are the most important ideas in paragraphs 15-19 and paragraphs 28-29?

VII. What are Socrates' views about death? Do they seem reasonable to you? If you know anything of the Greek attitude toward death at this time, how does Socrates' attitude accord with or differ from it?

VIII. Consider the revelation of Socrates' character in the *Apology*. What admirable traits are revealed, and how? What faults, if any, does Socrates have? Justify your answer.

IX. John Stuart Mill, in "On the Liberty of Thought and Discussion" (page 950), speaks of the conviction of Socrates as one of "those dreadful mistakes which excite the astonishment and horror of posterity." If you had been a member of the jury hearing Socrates' speeches, how do you think you would have voted, and why?

X. Socrates lived some four hundred years before Jesus. In what ways are his ideas and values similar to and different from Christian ideas and values? See the "Sermon on the Mount," page 935.

PLATO

The Myth of the Cave*

The following selection from Book VII of *The Republic* by the Greek philosopher Plato (427-347 B.C.) is close to the center of Platonic thought. It touches on Plato's doctrine of Ideas or Forms—the theory that beyond the forms of the physical world there exist ideal Forms or Verities, of which the things of the visible world are only imperfect manifestations. And it discusses the education of Plato's philosopher-kings, the wise men and lovers of wisdom to whom the government of Plato's ideal Republic will be entrusted. Like all myths, "The Myth of the Cave" has a number of closely related applications: describing the education of the philosopher-kings, it also describes the ascent of the soul from the prison-house of the senses to the intellectual world of pure Being; and it may be read as a description of any process of education or enlightenment whereby one moves, at first with pain and confusion, from a world of familiar shadows into a brighter world of new concepts and realities.

And now, I said, let me show in a figure how far our nature is enlightened or unenlightened:—Behold! human beings living in an underground den, which has a mouth open towards the light and reaching all along the den; here they have been from their childhood, and have their legs and necks

* Translated by Benjamin Jowett.

chained so that they can not move, and can only see before them, being prevented by the chains from turning round their heads. Above and behind them a fire is blazing at a distance, and between the fire and the prisoners there is a raised way; and you will see, if you look, a low wall built along the way, like the screen which marionette players have in front of them, over which they show the puppets.

I see.

And do you see, I said, men passing along the wall carrying all sorts of vessels, and statues and figures of animals made of wood and stone and various materials, which appear over the wall? Some of them are talking, others silent.

You have shown me a strange image, and they are strange prisoners.

Like ourselves, I replied; and they see only their own shadows, or the shadows of one another, which the fire throws on the opposite wall of the cave?

True, he said; how could they see anything but the shadows if they were never allowed to move their heads?

And of the objects which are being carried in like manner they would only see the shadows?

Yes, he said.

And if they were able to converse with one another, would they not suppose that they were naming what was actually before them?

Very true.

And suppose further that the prison had an echo which came from the other side, would they not be sure to fancy when one of the passers-by spoke that the voice which they heard came from the passing shadow?

No question, he replied.

To them, I said, the truth would be literally nothing but the shadows of the images.

That is certain.

And now look again, and see what will naturally follow if the prisoners are released and disabused of their error. At first, when any of them is liberated and compelled suddenly to stand up and turn his neck round and walk and look towards the light, he will suffer sharp pains; the glare will distress him, and he will be unable to see the realities of which in his former state he had seen the shadows; and then conceive some one saying to him, that what he saw before was an illusion, but that now, when he is approaching nearer to being and his eye is turned towards more real existence, he has a clearer vision,—what will be his reply? And you may further imagine that his instructor is pointing to the objects as they pass and requiring him to name them,—will he not be perplexed? Will he not fancy that the shadows which he formerly saw are truer than the objects which are now shown to him?

Far truer.

And if he is compelled to look straight at the light, will he not have a pain in his eyes which will make him turn away to take refuge in the objects of vision which he can see, and which he will conceive to be in reality clearer than the things which are now being shown to him?

True, he said.

And suppose once more, that he is reluctantly dragged up a steep and rugged ascent, and held fast until he is forced into the presence of the sun himself, is he not likely to be pained and irritated? When he approaches the light his eyes will be dazzled, and he will not be able to see anything at all of what are now called realities.

Not all in a moment, he said.

He will require to grow accustomed to the sight of the upper world. And first he will see the shadows best, next the reflections of men and other objects in the water, and then the objects themselves; then he will gaze upon the light of the moon and the stars and the spangled heaven; and he will see the sky and the stars by night better than the sun or the light of the sun by day?

Certainly.

Last of all he will be able to see the sun, and not mere reflections of him in the water, but he will see him in his own proper place, and not in another; and he will contemplate him as he is.

Certainly.

He will then proceed to argue that this is he who gives the season and the years, and is the guardian of all that is in the visible world, and in a certain way the cause of all things which he and his fellows have been accustomed to behold.

Clearly, he said, he would first see the sun and then reason about him.

And when he remembered his old habitation, and the wisdom of the den and his fellow-prisoners, do you not suppose that he would felicitate himself on the change, and pity them?

Certainly, he would.

And if they were in the habit of conferring honors among themselves on those who were quickest to observe the passing shadows and to remark which of them went before, and which followed after, and which were together; and who were therefore best able to draw conclusions as to the future, do you think that he would care for such honors and glories, or envy the possessors of them? Would he not say with Homer,

> "Better to be the poor servant of a poor master,"

and to endure anything, rather than think as they do and live after their manner?

Yes, he said, I think that he would rather suffer anything than entertain these false notions and live in this miserable manner.

Imagine once more, I said, such an one coming suddenly out of the sun to be replaced in his old situation; would he not be certain to have his eyes full of darkness?

To be sure, he said.

And if there were a contest, and he had to compete in measuring the shadows with the prisoners who had never moved out of the den, while his sight was still weak, and before his eyes had become steady (and the time which would be needed to acquire this new habit of sight might be very considerable), would he not be ridiculous? Men would say of him that up he went and down he came without his eyes; and that it was better not even to think of ascending; and if any one tried to loose another and lead him up to the light, let them only catch the offender, and they would put him to death.

No question, he said.

This entire allegory, I said, you may now append, dear Glaucon, to the previous argument; the prisonhouse is the world of sight, the light of the fire is the sun, and you will not misapprehend me if you interpret the journey upwards to be the ascent of the soul into the intellectual world according to my poor belief, which, at your desire, I have expressed—whether rightly or wrongly God knows. But, whether true or false, my opinion is that in the world of knowledge the idea of good appears last of all, and is seen only with an effort; and, when seen, is also inferred to be the universal author of all things beautiful and right, parent of light and of the lord of light in this visible world, and the immediate source of reason and truth in the intellectual; and that this is the power upon which he who would act rationally either in public or private life must have his eye fixed.

I agree, he said, as far as I am able to understand you.

Moreover, I said, you must not wonder that those who attain to this beatific vision are unwilling to descend to human affairs; for their souls are ever hastening into the upper world where they desire to dwell; which desire of theirs is very natural, if our allegory may be trusted.

Yes, very natural.

And is there anything surprising in one who passes from divine contemplations to the evil state of man, misbehaving himself in a ridiculous manner; if, while his eyes are blinking and before he has become accustomed to the surrounding darkness, he is compelled to fight in courts of law, or in other places, about the images or the shadows of images of justice, and is endeavoring to meet the conceptions of those who have never yet seen absolute justice?

Anything but surprising, he replied.

Any one who has common sense will remember that the bewilderments of the eyes are of two kinds, and arise from two causes, either from coming out of the light or from going into the light, which is true of the mind's eye, quite as much as of the bodily eye; and he who remembers this when he sees any one whose vision is perplexed and weak, will not be too ready to laugh; he will first ask whether that soul of man has come out of the brighter life, and is unable to see because unaccustomed to the dark, or having turned from darkness to the day is dazzled by excess of light. And he will count the one happy in his condition and state of being, and he will pity the other; or, if he have a mind to laugh at the soul which comes from below into the light, there will be more reason in this than in the laugh which greets him who returns from above out of the light into the den.

That, he said, is a very just distinction.

But then, if I am right, certain professors of education must be wrong when they say that they can put a knowledge into the soul which was not there before, like sight into blind eyes.

They undoubtedly say this, he replied.

Whereas, our argument shows that the power and capacity of learning exists in the soul already; and that just as the eye was unable to turn from darkness to light without the whole body, so too the instrument of knowledge can only by the movement of the whole soul be turned from the world of becoming into that of being, and learn by degrees to endure the sight of being, and of the brightest and best of being, or in other words, of the good.

Very true.

And must there not be some art which will effect conversion in the easiest and quickest manner; not implanting the faculty of sight, for that exists already, but has been turned in the wrong direction, and is looking away from the truth?

Yes, he said, such an art may be presumed.

And whereas the other so-called virtues of the soul seem to be akin to bodily qualities, for even when they are not originally innate they can be implanted later by habit and exercise, the virtue of wisdom more than anything else contains a divine element which always remains, and by this conversion is rendered useful and profitable; or, on the other hand, hurtful and useless. Did you never observe the narrow intelligence flashing from the keen eye of a clever rogue—how eager he is, how clearly his paltry soul sees the way to his end; he is the reverse of blind, but his keen eye-sight is forced into the service of evil, and he is mischievous in proportion to his cleverness?

Very true, he said.

But what if there had been a circumcision of such natures in the days of their youth; and they had been severed from those sensual pleasures, such as eating and drinking, which, like leaden weights, were attached to them at their birth, and which drag them down and turn the vision of their souls upon the things that are below—if, I say, they had been released from these impediments and turned in the opposite direction, the very same faculty in them would have seen the truth as keenly as they see what their eyes are turned to now.

Very likely.

Yes, I said; and there is another thing which is likely, or rather a necessary inference from what has preceded, that neither the uneducated and uninformed of the truth, nor yet those who never make an end of their education, will be able ministers of State; not the former, because they have no single aim of duty which is the rule of all their actions, private as well as public; nor the latter, because they will not act at all except upon compulsion, fancying that they are already dwelling apart in the islands of the blest.

Very true, he replied.

Then, I said, the business of us who are the founders of the State will be to compel the best minds to attain that knowledge which we have already shown to be the greatest of all—they must continue to ascend until they arrive at the good; but when they have ascended and seen enough we must not allow them to do as they do now.

What do you mean?

I mean that they remain in the upper world: but this must not be allowed; they must be made to descend again among the prisoners in the den, and partake of their labors and honors, whether they are worth having or not.

But is not this unjust? he said; ought we to give them a worse life, when they might have a better?

You have again forgotten, my friend, I said, the intention of the legislator, who did not aim at making any one class in the State happy above the rest; the happiness was to be in the whole State, and he held the citizens together by persuasion and necessity, making them benefactors of the State, and therefore benefactors of one another; to this end he created them, not to please themselves, but to be his instruments in binding up the State.

True, he said, I had forgotten.

Observe, Glaucon, that there will be no injustice in compelling our philosophers to have a care and providence of others; we shall explain to them that in other States, men of their class are not obliged to share in the toils of politics: and this is reasonable, for they grow up at their own sweet will, and the government would rather not have them. Being self-taught, they can not be expected to show any gratitude for a culture which they have never received. But we have brought you into the world to be rulers of the hive, kings of yourselves and of the other citizens, and have educated you far better and more perfectly than they have been educated, and you are better able to share in the double duty. Wherefore each of you, when his turn comes, must go down to the general underground abode, and get the habit of seeing in the dark. When you have acquired the habit, you will see ten thousand times better than the inhabitants of the den, and you will know what the several images are, and what they represent, because you have seen the beautiful and just and good in their truth. And thus our State, which is also yours, will be a reality, and not a dream only, and will be administered in a spirit unlike that of other States, in which men fight with one another about shadows only and are distracted in the struggle for power, which in their eyes is a great good. Whereas the truth is that the State in which the rulers are most reluctant to govern is always the best and most quietly governed, and the State in which they are most eager, the worst.

Quite true, he replied.

COMMENT AND QUESTIONS

I. In this dialogue, Socrates, the principal speaker, leads Glaucon, by a series of planned steps and questions, to arrive at certain foreseen conclusions. This progressive question-answer mode of teaching and discussion, used by Socrates in his informal teaching and by Plato in his dialogues, is called "the Socratic method." How is it like or different from the methods of teaching to which you are accustomed? What are its advantages and disadvantages?

II. Listed on the left below are items from "The Myth of the Cave" which have symbolic meaning. Listed on the right, not in order, are meanings which the items represent. Think through the myth, and try to pair the symbols in the left-hand column with the ideas in the right-hand column. Does it seem to you that any of the symbolic meanings are unclear, or are inaccurately stated? Explain.

the prisoners	philosophers
the shadows of images seen by the prisoners	the process of education
	illusions, false notions
the firelight	unenlightened people
the steep ascent	the reality of the physical world
the upper world	the intellectual world of reality
the sun	the good, author of all things beautiful and right
freed prisoners who have become adjusted to the upper world	

III. What is the experience of the prisoner when he is first turned around and then dragged up out of the den?

IV. What is the reaction of the cave-dwellers to the freed prisoner when he first returns to the cave?

V. For what two reasons may one's vision be perplexed and weak?

VI. Why must the enlightened ones, in Plato's ideal State, descend to the den once more? What can they accomplish there?

VII. Can you apply the allegory of the cave to any intellectual or spiritual experience of your own?

VIII. If you have read John Dewey's "Does Human Nature Change?" do you think that Dewey and Plato are in agreement on the changeability of human nature? Do the two educators, separated in time by more than two thousand years, agree on the nature of the educative process? Explain.

PLATO

From the *Symposium**

The following excerpt from the *Symposium* (or Banquet) presents Plato's idea of love. Although the term "Platonic love" as it is generally used carries little of Plato's meaning, it is derived from his concept of love as a bridge between the material and the spiritual, by which one moves from the love of earthly objects to the love of absolute beauty. The situation that Plato establishes in the dialogue is this: Socrates and his friends, assembled for a banquet, decide to devote the evening to conversation and to speeches in honor of Love. When it is Socrates' turn to speak, he tells the company that he learned of love from a wise woman, Diotima of Mantineia, and that he will repeat what she said to him. In the dialogue that follows, Diotima asks the questions, and Socrates answers. (For a further note on Plato, see page 912.)

[1] "For there is nothing which men love but the good. Is there anything?" "Certainly, I should say, that there is nothing." "Then," she said, "the simple truth is, that men love the good." "Yes," I said. "To which must be added that they love the possession of the good?" "Yes, that must be added." "And not only the possession, but the everlasting possession of the good?" "That must be added too." "Then love," she said, "may be described generally as the love of the everlasting possession of the good?" "That is most true."

[2] "Then if this be the nature of love, can you tell me further," she said, "what is the manner of the pursuit? What are they doing who show all this eagerness and heat which is called love? and what is the object which they have in view? Answer me." "Nay, Diotima," I replied, "if I had known, I should not have wondered at your wisdom, neither should I have come to learn from you about this very matter." "Well," she said, "I will teach you:—The object which they have in view is birth in beauty, whether of body or soul." "I do not understand you," I said; "the oracle requires an explanation." "I will make my meaning clearer," she replied. "I mean to say, that all men are bringing to the birth in their bodies and in their souls. There is a certain age at which human nature is desirous of procreation —procreation which must be in beauty and not in deformity; and this procreation is the union of man and woman, and is a divine thing; for conception and generation are an immortal principle in the mortal creature, and in the inharmonious they can never be. But the deformed is always inharmonious with the divine, and the beautiful harmonious. Beauty, then,

* Translated by Benjamin Jowett.

is the destiny or goddess of parturition who presides at birth, and therefore, when approaching beauty, the conceiving power is propitious, and diffusive, and benign, and begets and bears fruit: at the sight of ugliness she frowns and contracts and has a sense of pain, and turns away, and shrivels up, and not without a pang refrains from conception. And this is the reason why, when the hour of conception arrives, and the teeming nature is full, there is such a flutter and ecstasy about beauty whose approach is the alleviation of the pain of travail. For love, Socrates, is not, as you imagine, the love of the beautiful only." "What then?" "The love of generation and of birth in beauty." "Yes," I said. "Yes, indeed," she replied. "But why of generation?" "Because to the mortal creature, generation is a sort of eternity and immortality," she replied; "and if, as has been already admitted, love is of the everlasting possession of the good, all men will necessarily desire immortality together with good: Wherefore love is of immortality."

[3] All this she taught me at various times when she spoke of love. And I remember her once saying to me, "What is the cause, Socrates, of love, and the attendant desire? See you not how all animals, birds, as well as beasts, in their desire of procreation, are in agony when they take the infection of love, which begins with the desire of union; whereto is added the care of offspring, on whose behalf the weakest are ready to battle against the strongest even to the uttermost, and to die for them, and will let themselves be tormented with hunger or suffer anything in order to maintain their young? Man may be supposed to act thus from reason; but why should animals have these passionate feelings? Can you tell me why?" Again I replied that I did not know. She said to me: "And do you expect ever to become a master in the art of love, if you do not know this?" "But I have told you already, Diotima, that my ignorance is the reason why I come to you; for I am conscious that I want a teacher; tell me then the cause of this and of the other mysteries of love." "Marvel not," she said, "if you believe that love is of the immortal, as we have several times acknowledged; for here again, and on the same principle too, the mortal nature is seeking as far as is possible to be everlasting and immortal: and this is only to be attained by generation, because generation always leaves behind a new existence in the place of the old. Nay, even in the life of the same individual there is succession and not absolute unity: a man is called the same, and yet in the short interval which elapses between youth and age, and in which every animal is said to have life and identity, he is undergoing a perpetual process of loss and reparation—hair, flesh, bones, blood, and the whole body are always changing. Which is true not only of the body, but also of the soul, whose habits, tempers, opinions, desires, pleasures, pains, fears, never remain the same in any one of us, but are always coming and going; and equally true of knowledge, and what is still more surprising to us mortals, not only do the sciences in general spring up and decay, so that in respect of them we are never the same; but each of them individually experiences a like change. For what is implied in the word 'recollection,' but the departure

of knowledge, which is ever being forgotten, and is renewed and preserved by recollection, and appears to be the same although in reality now, according to that law of succession by which all mortal things are preserved, not absolutely the same, but by substitution, the old worn-out mortality leaving another new and similar existence behind—unlike the divine, which is always the same and not another? And in this way, Socrates, the mortal body, or mortal anything, partakes of immortality; but the immortal in another way. Marvel not then at the love which all men have of their offspring; for that universal love and interest is for the sake of immortality."

[4] I was astonished at her words, and said: "Is this really true, O thou wise Diotima?" And she answered with all the authority of an accomplished Sophist: "Of that, Socrates, you may be assured;—think only of the ambition of men, and you will wonder at the senselessness of their ways, unless you consider how they are stirred by the love of an immortality of fame. They are ready to run all risks greater far than they would have run for their children, and to spend money and undergo any sort of toil, and even to die, for the sake of leaving behind them a name which shall be eternal. Do you imagine that Alcestis would have died to save Admetus, or Achilles to avenge Patroclus, or your own Codrus in order to preserve the kingdom for his sons, if they had not imagined that the memory of their virtues, which still survives among us, would be immortal? Nay," she said, "I am persuaded that all men do all things, and the better they are the more they do them, in hope of the glorious fame of immortal virtue; for they desire the immortal.

[5] "Those who are pregnant in the body only, betake themselves to women and beget children—this is the character of their love; their offspring, as they hope, will preserve their memory and give them the blessedness and immortality which they desire in the future. But souls which are pregnant—for there certainly are men who are more creative in their souls than in their bodies—conceive that which is proper for the soul to conceive or contain. And what are these conceptions?—wisdom and virtue in general. And such creators are poets and all artists who are deserving of the name inventor. But the greatest and fairest sort of wisdom by far is that which is concerned with the ordering of states and families, and which is called temperance and justice. And he who in youth has the seed of these implanted in him and is himself inspired, when he comes to maturity desires to beget and generate. He wanders about seeking beauty that he may beget offspring—for in deformity he will beget nothing—and naturally embraces the beautiful rather than the deformed body; above all, when he finds a fair and noble and well-nurtured soul, he embraces the two in one person, and to such an one he is full of speech about virtue and the nature and pursuits of a good man; and he tries to educate him; and at the touch of the beautiful which is ever present to his memory, even when absent, he brings forth that which he had conceived long before, and in company with him tends that which he brings forth; and they are married by a far nearer

tie and have a closer friendship than those who beget mortal children, for the children who are their common offspring are fairer and more immortal. Who, when he thinks of Homer and Hesiod and other great poets, would not rather have their children than ordinary human ones? Who would not emulate them in the creation of children such as theirs, which have preserved their memory and given them everlasting glory? Or who would not have such children as Lycurgus left behind him to be the saviours, not only of Lacedaemon, but of Hellas, as one may say? There is Solon, too, who is the revered father of Athenian laws; and many others there are in many other places, both among Hellenes and barbarians, who have given to the world many noble works, and have been the parents of virtue of every kind; and many temples have been raised in their honour for the sake of children such as theirs; which were never raised in honour of any one, for the sake of his mortal children.

[6] "These are the lesser mysteries of love, into which even you, Socrates, may enter; to the greater and more hidden ones which are the crown of these, and to which, if you pursue them in a right spirit, they will lead, I know not whether you will be able to attain. But I will do my utmost to inform you, and do you follow if you can. For he who would proceed aright in this matter should begin in youth to visit beautiful forms; and first, if he be guided by his instructor aright, to love one such form only— out of that he should create fair thoughts; and soon he will of himself perceive that the beauty of one form is akin to the beauty of another; and then if beauty of form in general is his pursuit, how foolish would he be not to recognize that the beauty in every form is one and the same! And when he perceives this he will abate his violent love of the one, which he will despise and deem a small thing, and will become a lover of all beautiful forms; in the next stage he will consider that the beauty of the mind is more honourable than the beauty of the outward form. So that if a virtuous soul have but a little comeliness, he will be content to love and tend him, and will search out and bring to the birth thoughts which may improve the young, until he is compelled to contemplate and see the beauty of institutions and laws, and to understand that the beauty of them all is of one family, and that personal beauty is a trifle; and after laws and institutions he will go on to the sciences, that he may see their beauty, being not like a servant in love with the beauty of one youth or man or institution, himself a slave mean and narrow-minded, but drawing towards and contemplating the vast sea of beauty, he will create many fair and noble thoughts and notions in boundless love of wisdom; until on that shore he grows and waxes strong, and at last the vision is revealed to him of a single science, which is the science of beauty everywhere. To this I will proceed; please to give me your very best attention:

[7] "He who has been instructed thus far in the things of love, and who has learned to see the beautiful in due order and succession, when he comes towards the end will suddenly perceive a nature of wondrous beauty (and

this, Socrates, is the final cause of all our former toils)—a nature which in the first place is everlasting, not growing and decaying, or waxing and waning; secondly, not fair in one point of view and foul in another, or at one time or in one relation or at one place fair, at another time or in another relation or at another place foul, as if fair to some and foul to others, or in the likeness of a face or hands or any other part of the bodily frame, or in any form of speech or knowledge, or existing in any other being, as, for example, in an animal, or in heaven, or in earth, or in any other place but beauty absolute, separate, simple, and everlasting, which without diminution and without increase, or any change, is imparted to the ever-growing and perishing beauties of all other things. He who from these ascending under the influence of true love, begins to perceive that beauty, is not far from the end. And the true order of going, or being led by another, to the things of love, is to begin from the beauties of earth and mount upwards for the sake of that other beauty, using these as steps only, and from one going on to two, and from two to all fair forms, and from fair forms to fair practices, and from fair practices to fair notions, until from fair notions he arrives at the notion of absolute beauty, and at last knows what the essence of beauty is. This, my dear Socrates," said the stranger of Mantineia, "is that life above all others which man should live, in the contemplation of beauty absolute; a beauty which if you once beheld, you would see not to be after the measure of gold, and garments, and fair boys and youths, whose presence now entrances you; and you and many an one would be content to live seeing them only and conversing with them without meat or drink, if that were possible—you only want to look at them and to be with them. But what if man had eyes to see the true beauty—the divine beauty, I mean, pure and clear and unalloyed, not clogged with the pollutions of mortality and all the colours and vanities of human life—thither looking, and holding converse with the true beauty simple and divine? Remember how in that communion only, beholding beauty with the eye of the mind, he will be enabled to bring forth, not images of beauty, but realities (for he has hold not of an image but of a reality), and bringing forth and nourishing true virtue to become the friend of God and be immortal, if mortal man may. Would that be an ignoble life?"

COMMENT AND QUESTIONS

In the pages of the *Symposium* preceding the excerpt printed here, Diotima has told Socrates that love is a spirit who mediates between gods and men, that love is the offspring of Poverty and Plenty, and that love is love of the beautiful and good. In the selection printed here, the wise woman further explains that since love is of the everlasting possession of the beautiful and good, it is necessarily of the love of immortality, or of generation and birth in beauty, which to mortal creatures is a sort of eternity and immortality. The creative body inspired by love will produce children who provide one kind of immortality; the creative soul inspired by love will produce works of art and works of wisdom and virtue, fairer and more immortal than mortal children. All these things, Diotima says, are the lesser mysteries of love. The greater mystery and the highest experience of love is the experience of moving upward from the love of material objects to the love of spiritual things and finally to a perception of perfect Beauty and Good.

Below are four translations of the short passage in which Diotima summarizes the ascent, step-by-step, to the highest vision of love. Reading it in somewhat different language may help to clarify this key idea:

1. And the true order of going, or being led by another to the things of love is to begin from the beauties of earth and mount upwards for the sake of that other beauty, using these as steps only, and from one going on to two, and from two to all fair forms, and from fair forms to fair practices, and from fair practices to fair notions, until from fair notions he arrives at the notion of absolute beauty, and at last knows what the essence of beauty is.

2. For such as discipline themselves upon this system, or are conducted by another begin to ascend through these transitory objects which are beautiful, towards that which is beauty itself, proceeding as on steps from the love of one form to that of two, and from that of two, to that of all forms which are beautiful; and from beautiful forms to beautiful habits and institutions, and from institutions to beautiful doctrines; until, from the meditation of many doctrines, they arrive at that which is nothing else than the doctrine of the supreme beauty itself, in the knowledge and contemplation of which at length they repose.

3. For let me tell you, the right way to approach the things of love, or to be led there by another, is this: beginning from these beautiful things, to mount for that beauty's sake ever upwards, as by a flight of steps, from one to two, and from two to all beautiful bodies, and from beautiful bodies to beautiful pursuits and practices, and from practices to beautiful learnings, so that from learnings he may come at last to that perfect learning which is the learning solely of that beauty itself, and may know at last that which is the perfection of beauty.

4. Those who learn the order of love, or are led by another, beginning with beautiful objects will move upward to beauty itself, proceeding as by steps from one fair form to all fair forms, from all fair forms to all fair actions, from all fair actions to all fair ideas, and thence, from the contemplation of fair ideas, to the knowledge of the very essence of beauty.

I. When Plato's idea is clear to you, give concrete examples of each of the steps or stages in this progression of love.

II. If you have read Plato's "Myth of the Cave," what parallels and what differences do you see between the ascent from the cave and the ascent, through love, to a knowledge of perfect beauty?

EPICURUS

Letter to a Friend*

Epicurus (340?–270 B.C.) was a Greek philosopher who founded the Epicurean school. The following letter expresses and explains the central idea of his philosophy, that happiness or pleasure is the greatest good of life—an idea simplified and corrupted by followers who called themselves Epicureans.

[1] We must consider that of desires some are natural, others empty; that of the natural some are necessary, others not; and that of the necessary some are necessary for happiness, others for bodily comfort, and others for life itself. A right understanding of these facts enables us to direct all choice and avoidance toward securing the health of the body and tranquility of the soul; this being the final aim of a blessed life. For the aim of all actions is to avoid pain and fear; and when this is once secured for us the tempest of the soul is entirely quelled, since the living animal no longer needs to wander as though in search of something he lacks, hunting for that by which he can fulfill some need of soul or body. We feel a need of pleasure only when we grieve over its absence; when we stop grieving we are in need of pleasure no longer. Pleasure, then, is the beginning and end of the blessed life.[1] For we recognize it as a good which is both primary and kindred to us. From pleasure we begin every act of choice and avoidance; and to pleasure we return again, using the feeling as the standard by which to judge every good.

[2] Now since pleasure is the good that is primary and most natural to us, for that very reason we do not seize all pleasures indiscriminately; on the contrary we often pass over many pleasures, when greater discomfort accrues to us as a result of them. Similarly we not infrequently judge pains better than pleasures, when the long endurance of a pain yields us a greater pleasure in the end. Thus every pleasure because of its natural kinship to us is good, yet not every pleasure is to be chosen; just as every pain also is an evil, yet that does not mean that all pains are necessarily to be shunned. It is by a scale of comparison and by the consideration of advantages and disadvantages that we must form our judgment on these matters. On particular occasions we may have reason to treat the good as bad, and the bad as good.

* From Epicurus' Letter to Menoecius, preserved in Diogenes Laertius, *Lives of the Philosophers*, Bk. X. Translated by Philip Wheelwright in *The Way of Philosophy* (Odyssey Press), pp. 511–13.

[1] I.e., since it is a product of that health of body and tranquility of soul mentioned above.

[3] Independence of circumstances we regard as a great good: not because we wish to dispense altogether with external advantages, but in order that, if our possessions are few, we may be content with what we have, sincerely believing that those enjoy luxury most who depend on it least, and that natural wants are easily satisfied if we are willing to forego superfluities. Plain fare yields as much pleasure as a luxurious table, provided the pain of real want is removed; bread and water can give exquisite delight to hungry and thirsty lips. To form the habit of a simple and modest diet, therefore, is the way to health: it enables us to perform the needful employments of life without shrinking, it puts us in better condition to enjoy luxuries when they are offered, and it renders us fearless of fortune.

[4] Accordingly, when we argue that pleasure is the end and aim of life, we do not mean the pleasure of prodigals and sensualists, as some of our ignorant or prejudiced critics persist in mistaking us. We mean the pleasure of being free from pain of body and anxiety of mind. It is not a continual round of drunken debauches and lecherous delights, nor the enjoyment of fish and other delicacies of a wealthy table, which produce a pleasant life; but sober reasoning, searching out the motives of choice and avoidance, and escaping the bondage of opinion, to which the greatest disturbances of spirit are due.

[5] The first step and the greatest good is prudence—a more precious thing than philosophy even, for all the other virtues are sprung from it. By prudence we learn that we can live pleasurably only if we live prudently, honorably, and justly, while contrariwise to live prudently, honorably, and justly guarantees a life that is pleasurable as well. The virtues are by nature bound up with a pleasant life, and a pleasant life is inseparable from them in turn.

[6] Is there any better and wiser man than he who holds reverent beliefs about the gods, is altogether free from the fear of death, and has serenely contemplated the basic tendencies of natural law? Such a man understands that the limit of good things is easy to attain, and that evils are slight either in duration or in intensity. He laughs at Destiny, which so many accept as all-powerful. Some things, he observes, occur of necessity, others by chance, and still others through our own agency. Necessity is irresponsible, chance is inconstant, but our own actions are free, and it is to them that praise and blame are properly attached. It would be better even to believe the myths about the gods than to submit to the Destiny which the natural philosophers teach. For the old superstitions at least offer some faint hope of placating the gods by worship, but the Necessity of the scientific philosophers is absolutely unyielding. As to chance, the wise man does not deify it as most men do; for if it were divine it would not be without order. Nor will he accept the view that it is a universal cause even though of a wavering kind; for he believes that what chance bestows is not the good and evil that determine a man's blessedness in life, but the starting-points from which each person can arrive at great good or great evil. He esteems the misfortune of

the wise above the prosperity of a fool; holding it better that well chosen courses of action should fail than that ill chosen ones should succeed by mere chance.

[7] Meditate on these and like precepts day and night, both privately and with some companion who is of kindred disposition. Thereby shall you never suffer disturbance, waking or asleep, but shall live like a god among men. For a man who lives constantly among immortal blessings is surely more than mortal.

COMMENT AND QUESTIONS

I. Read each sentence in paragraph 1 thoughtfully, deciding whether you agree or disagree with each statement made. For example, do you agree that "the final aim of a blessed life" is "securing the health of the body and the tranquility of the soul"? Are you satisfied with the statement that "the aim of all actions is to avoid pain and fear," or do you believe there are other aims? If so, what are they? If you have read the "Sermon on the Mount," what different aim or aims are implicit in it?

II. Under what circumstances, according to Epicurus, should we choose to endure pain or deny ourselves pleasure? Can you illustrate from your own experience?

III. What does Epicurus have to say about reason, about prudence, about external advantages (money, power, etc.), about necessity, chance, and freedom of the will?

IV. The *New World Dictionary* defines *epicure* as follows: "1. a person who enjoys and has a discriminating taste for foods and liquors. 2. a person who is especially fond of luxury and sensuous pleasures." It defines the adjective *Epicurean:* "1. of Epicurus or his philosophy. 2. fond of luxury and sensuous pleasure, especially that of eating and drinking. 3. suited to or characteristic of an epicure."

Compare these definitions with Epicurus' own statement of his beliefs.

V. If you have read the *Apology,* compare and contrast the ideas of Epicurus and of Socrates. Do you think Epicurus would have approved of the speech and actions of Socrates?

VI. If you have read the selection from Epictetus, what conflicts and what points of agreement do you find between him and Epicurus?

EPICTETUS

The Quiet Mind[*]

The Stoic philosophy, represented in the following selection, holds that pleasure, pain, and all external things are matters of indifference; that virtue and perfection of soul are the greatest good of man; and that the virtuous man, freed of all passion and desire, is also the happy man. Epictetus was a Greek Stoic philosopher who lived and taught in Rome in the first century A.D. Like Socrates, he left no writing, but his teaching was recorded by his pupil Flavius Arrianus. *The Manual,* from which this selection is taken, sets down a brief, sometimes overlapping statement of the main doctrines of Epictetus' philosophy.

Of all existing things some are in our power, and others are not in our power. In our power are thought, impulse, will to get and will to avoid, and, in a word, everything which is our own doing. Things not in our power include the body, property, reputation, office, and, in a word, everything which is not our own doing. Things in our power are by nature free, unhindered, untrammelled; things not in our power are weak, servile, subject to hindrance, dependent on others. Remember then that if you imagine that what is naturally slavish is free and what is naturally another's is your own, you will be hampered, you will mourn, you will be put to confusion, you will blame gods and men; but if you think that only your own belongs to you, and that what is another's is indeed another's, no one will ever put compulsion or hindrance on you, you will blame none, you will accuse none, you will do nothing against your will, no one will harm you, you will have no enemy, for no harm can touch you.

1. Aiming then at these high matters, you must remember that to attain them requires more than ordinary effort; you will have to give up some things entirely, and put off others for the moment. And if you would have these also—office and wealth—it may be that you will fail to get them, just because your desire is set on the former, and you will certainly fail to attain those things which alone bring freedom and happiness.

Make it your study then to confront every harsh impression with the words, 'You are but an impression, and not at all what you seem to be.' Then test it by those rules that you possess; and first by this—the chief test of all—"Is it concerned with what is in our power or with what is not in our power?" And if it is concerned with what is not in our power, be ready with the answer that it is nothing to you.

[*] From *The Manual* of Epictetus, translated by P. E. Matheson. Reprinted with permission of Clarendon Press.

2. Remember that the will-to-get promises attainment of what you will, and the will-to-avoid promises escape from what you avoid; and he who fails to get what he wills is unfortunate, and he who does not escape what he wills to avoid is miserable. If then you try to avoid only what is unnatural in the region within your control, you will escape from all that you avoid; but if you try to avoid disease or death or poverty you will be miserable.

Therefore let your will-to-avoid have no concern with what is not in man's power; direct it only to things in man's power that are contrary to nature. But for the moment you must utterly remove the will-to-get; for if you will to get something not in man's power you are bound to be unfortunate; while none of the things in man's power that you could honourably will to get is yet within your reach. Impulse to act and not to act, these are your concern; yet exercise them gently and without strain, and provisionally.

3. When anything, from the meanest thing upwards, is attractive or serviceable or an object of affection, remember always to say to yourself, "What is its nature?" If you are fond of a jug, say you are fond of a jug; then you will not be disturbed if it be broken. If you kiss your child or your wife, say to yourself that you are kissing a human being, for then if death strikes it you will not be disturbed.

4. When you are about to take something in hand, remind yourself what manner of thing it is. If you are going to bathe put before your mind what happens in the bath—water pouring over some, others being jostled, some reviling, others stealing; and you will set to work more securely if you say to yourself at once: "I want to bathe, and I want to keep my will in harmony with nature," and so in each thing you do; for in this way, if anything turns up to hinder you in your bathing, you will be ready to say, "I did not want only to bathe, but to keep my will in harmony with nature, and I shall not so keep it, if I lose my temper at what happens."

5. What disturbs men's minds is not events but their judgments on events. For instance, death is nothing dreadful, or else Socrates would have thought it so. No, the only dreadful thing about it is men's judgment that it is dreadful. And so when we are hindered, or disturbed, or distressed, let us never lay the blame on others, but on ourselves, that is, on our own judgments. To accuse others for one's own misfortunes is a sign of want of education; to accuse oneself shows that one's education has begun; to accuse neither oneself nor others shows that one's education is complete.

6. Be not elated at an excellence which is not your own. If the horse in his pride were to say, "I am handsome," we could bear with it. But when you say with pride, "I have a handsome horse," know that the good horse is the ground of your pride. You ask then what you can call your own. The answer is—the way you deal with your impressions. Therefore when you deal with your impressions in accord with nature, then you may be proud indeed, for your pride will be in a good which is your own.

7. When you are on a voyage, and your ship is at anchorage, and you

disembark to get fresh water, you may pick up a small shellfish or a truffle by the way, but you must keep your attention fixed on the ship, and keep looking towards it constantly, to see if the Helmsman calls you; and if he does, you have to leave everything, or be bundled on board with your legs tied like a sheep. So it is in life. If you have a dear wife or child given you, they are like the shellfish or the truffle, they are very well in their way. Only, if the Helmsman call, run back to your ship, leave all else, and do not look behind you. And if you are old, never go far from the ship, so that when you are called you may not fail to appear.

8. Ask not that events should happen as you will, but let your will be that events should happen as they do, and you shall have peace.

9. Sickness is a hindrance to the body, but not to the will, unless the will consent. Lameness is a hindrance to the leg, but not to the will. Say this to yourself at each event that happens, for you shall find that though it hinders something else, it will not hinder you.

10. When anything happens to you, always remember to turn to yourself and ask what faculty you have to deal with it. If you see a beautiful boy or a beautiful woman, you will find continence the faculty to exercise there; if trouble is laid on you, you will find endurance; if ribaldry, you will find patience. And if you train yourself in this habit your impressions will not carry you away.

11. Never say of anything, "I lost it," but say, "I gave it back." Has your child died? It was given back. Has your wife died? She was given back. Has your estate been taken from you? Was not this also given back? But you say, "He who took it from me is wicked." What does it matter to you through whom the Giver asked it back? As long as He gives it you, take care of it, but not as your own; treat it as passers-by treat an inn.

12. If you wish to make progress, abandon reasonings of this sort: "If I neglect my affairs I shall have nothing to live on"; "If I do not punish my son, he will be wicked." For it is better to die of hunger, so that you be free from pain and free from fear, than to live in plenty and be troubled in mind. It is better for your son to be wicked than for you to be miserable. Wherefore begin with little things. Is your drop of oil spilt? Is your sup of wine stolen? Say to yourself, "This is the price paid for freedom from passion, this is the price of a quiet mind." Nothing can be had without a price. When you call your slave-boy, reflect that he may not be able to hear you, and if he hears you, he may not be able to do anything you want. But he is not so well off that it rests with him to give you peace of mind.

13. If you wish to make progress, you must be content in external matters to seem a fool and a simpleton; do not wish men to think you know anything, and if any should think you to be somebody, distrust yourself. For know that it is not easy to keep your will in accord with nature and at the same time keep outward things; if you attend to one you must needs neglect the other.

14. It is silly to want your children and your wife and your friends to live

for ever, for that means that you want what is not in your control to be in your control, and what is not your own to be yours. In the same way if you want your servant to make no mistakes, you are a fool, for you want vice not to be vice but something different. But if you want not to be disappointed in your will to get, you can attain to that.

Exercise yourself then in what lies in your power. Each man's master is the man who has authority over what he wishes or does not wish, to secure the one or to take away the other. Let him then who wishes to be free not wish for anything or avoid anything that depends on others; or else he is bound to be a slave.

15. Remember that you must behave in life as you would at a banquet. A dish is handed round and comes to you; put out your hand and take it politely. It passes you; do not stop it. It has not reached you; do not be impatient to get it, but wait till your turn comes. Bear yourself thus towards children, wife, office, wealth, and one day you will be worthy to banquet with the gods. But if when they are set before you, you do not take them but despise them, then you shall not only share the gods' banquet, but shall share their rule. For by so doing Diogenes and Heraclitus and men like them were called divine and deserved the name.

16. When you see a man shedding tears in sorrow for a child abroad or dead, or for loss of property, beware that you are not carried away by the impression that it is outward ills that make him miserable. Keep this thought by you: "What distresses him is not the event, for that does not distress another, but his judgment on the event." Therefore do not hesitate to sympathize with him so far as words go, and if it so chance, even to groan with him; but take heed that you do not also groan in your inner being.

17. Remember that you are an actor in a play, and the Playwright chooses the manner of it: if he wants it short, it is short; if long, it is long. If he wants you to act a poor man you must act the part with all your powers; and so if your part be a cripple or a magistrate or a plain man. For your business is to act the character that is given you and act it well; the choice of the cast is Another's.

18. When a raven croaks with evil omen, let not the impression carry you away, but straightway distinguish in your own mind and say, "These portents mean nothing to me; but only to my bit of a body or my bit of property or name, or my children or my wife. But for me all omens are favourable if I will, for, whatever the issue may be, it is in my power to get benefit therefrom."

19. You can be invincible, if you never enter on a contest where victory is not in your power. Beware then that when you see a man raised to honour or great power or high repute you do not let your impression carry you away. For if the reality of good lies in what is in our power, there is no room for envy or jealousy. And you will not wish to be praetor, or prefect or consul, but to be free; and there is but one way to freedom—to despise what is not in our power.

20. Remember that foul words or blows in themselves are no outrage, but your judgment that they are so. So when any one makes you angry, know that it is your own thought that has angered you. Wherefore make it your first endeavour not to let your impressions carry you away. For if once you gain time and delay, you will find it easier to control yourself.

21. Keep before your eyes from day to day death and exile and all things that seem terrible, but death most of all, and then you will never set your thoughts on what is low and will never desire anything beyond measure.

22. If you set your desire on philosophy you must at once prepare to meet with ridicule and the jeers of many who will say, "Here he is again, turned philosopher. Where has he got these proud looks?" Nay, put on no proud looks, but hold fast to what seems best to you, in confidence that God has set you at this post. And remember that if you abide where you are, those who first laugh at you will one day admire you, and that if you give way to them, you will get doubly laughed at.

23. If it ever happen to you to be diverted to things outside, so that you desire to please another, know that you have lost your life's plan. Be content then always to be a philosopher; if you wish to be regarded as one too, show yourself that you are one and you will be able to achieve it.

24. Let not reflections such as these afflict you: "I shall live without honour, and never be of any account"; for if lack of honour is an evil, no one but yourself can involve you in evil any more than in shame. Is it your business to get office or to be invited to an entertainment?

Certainly not.

Where then is the dishonour you talk of? How can you be "of no account anywhere," when you ought to count for something in those matters only which are in your power, where you may achieve the highest worth?

"But my friends," you say, "will lack assistance."

What do you mean by "lack assistance"? They will not have cash from you and you will not make them Roman citizens. Who told you that to do these things is in our power, and not dependent upon others? Who can give to another what is not his to give?

"Get them then," says he, "that we may have them."

If I can get them and keep my self-respect, honour, magnanimity, show the way and I will get them. But if you call on me to lose the good things that are mine, in order that you may win things that are not good, look how unfair and thoughtless you are. And which do you really prefer? Money, or a faithful, modest friend? Therefore help me rather to keep these qualities, and do not expect from me actions which will make me lose them.

"But my country," says he, "will lack assistance, so far as lies in me."

Once more I ask, What assistance do you mean? It will not owe colonnades or baths to you. What of that? It does not owe shoes to the blacksmith or arms to the shoemaker; it is sufficient if each man fulfils his own function. Would you do it no good if you secured to it another faithful and modest citizen?

"Yes."

Well, then, you would not be useless to it.

"What place then shall I have in the city?"

Whatever place you can hold while you keep your character for honour and self-respect. But if you are going to lose these qualities in trying to benefit your city, what benefit, I ask, would you have done her when you attain to the perfection of being lost to shame and honour?

25. Has some one had precedence of you at an entertainment or a levée or been called in before you to give advice? If these things are good you ought to be glad that he got them; if they are evil, do not be angry that you did not get them yourself. Remember that if you want to get what is not in your power, you cannot earn the same reward as others unless you act as they do. How is it possible for one who does not haunt the great man's door to have equal shares with one who does, or one who does not go in his train equality with one who does; or one who does not praise him with one who does? You will be unjust then and insatiable if you wish to get these privileges for nothing, without paying their price. What is the price of a lettuce? An obol perhaps. If then a man pays his obol and gets his lettuces, and you do not pay and do not get them, do not think you are defrauded. For as he has the lettuces so you have the obol you did not give. The same principle holds good too in conduct. You were not invited to some one's entertainment? Because you did not give the host the price for which he sells his dinner. He sells it for compliments, he sells it for attentions. Pay him the price then, if it is to your profit. But if you wish to get the one and yet not give up the other, nothing can satisfy you in your folly.

What! you say, you have nothing instead of the dinner?

Nay, you have this, you have not praised the man you did not want to praise, you have not had to bear with the insults of his doorstep.

26. It is in our power to discover the will of Nature from those matters on which we have no difference of opinion. For instance, when another man's slave has broken the wine-cup we are very ready to say at once, "Such things must happen." Know then that when your own cup is broken, you ought to behave in the same way as when your neighbour's was broken. Apply the same principle to higher matters. Is another's child or wife dead? Not one of us but would say, "Such is the lot of man"; but when one's own dies, straightway one cries, "Alas! miserable am I." But we ought to remember what our feelings are when we hear it of another.

27. As a mark [1] is not set up for men to miss it, so there is nothing intrinsically evil in the world.

COMMENT AND QUESTIONS

Because this selection, which we have entitled "The Quiet Mind," is a series of separate teachings or maxims, it has no particular organization, and the numbered sections frequently repeat and overlap. In reviewing the

[1] That is, happiness, the result of virtue, is the mark set up for men to aim at.

934 READING FOR IDEAS AND VALUES

selection, you should consider what the main ideas are, and how they could be expressed in a related, organized way.

I. What does Epictetus mean in the first sentence of section 1 by "these high matters"?

II. What is the meaning of the word *impression* as Epictetus uses it in the second paragraph of section 1? What is the meaning of the sentence (section 5), "What disturbs men's minds is not events but their judgments on events"? Are the two ideas, about impressions and about judgments on events similar, or are they the same? Explain.

III. According to Epictetus, with what, in general, is the wise man not concerned? What are some of the particular things and events by which he is not disturbed? What methods does he use to keep himself undisturbed?

IV. How does the closing statement of the selection, that there is nothing intrinsically evil in the world, follow logically from the preceding material?

V. It has been said that the coldness and austerity of Stoicism make it a philosophy few men can live by; that it makes almost impossible demands on human nature. What examples or statements of Epictetus would seem to you to support that view? On the other hand, do you find in Epictetus any basic wisdom which might be useful to all men?

VI. Another great Stoic philosopher was the Roman Emperor Marcus Aurelius (121–180), referred to in Mill's essay "On the Liberty of Thought and Discussion," page 958. Matthew Arnold called Marcus Aurelius "perhaps the most beautiful figure in history," and said that while the sentences of Epictetus fortify the character, the sentences of Marcus Aurelius touch the soul with the "gentleness and sweetness" of his morality. Below are some short passages from the *Meditations* which Marcus Aurelius addressed to himself for the purpose of guiding his own conduct:

One man, when he has done a service to another, is ready to set it down to his account as a favor conferred. Another is not ready to do this, but still in his own mind he thinks of the man as his debtor, and he knows what he has done. A third in a manner does not even know what he has done, *but he is like a vine which has produced grapes, and seeks for nothing more after it has once produced its proper fruit.* As a horse when he has run, a dog when he has caught the game, a bee when it has made its honey, so a man when he has done a good act, does not call out for others to come and see, but he goes on to another act, as a vine goes on to produce again the grapes in season. Must a man, then, be one of these, who in a manner acts thus without observing it? Yes. . . .

Thou sayest, "Men cannot admire the sharpness of thy wits." Be it so; but there are many other things of which thou canst not say, "I am not formed for them by nature." Show those qualities, then, which are altogether in thy power,—sincerity, gravity, endurance of labor, aversion to pleasure, contentment with thy portion and with few things, benevolence, frankness, no love of superfluity, freedom from trifling, magnanimity. Dost thou not see how many qualities thou art at once able to exhibit, as to which there is no excuse of natural incapacity and unfitness, and yet thou still remainest voluntarily below the mark? . . .

Thou wilt not cease to be miserable till thy mind is in such a condition, that, what luxury is to those who enjoy pleasure, such shall be to thee, in every matter which presents itself, the doing of the things which are conformable to man's constitution; for a man ought to consider as an enjoyment everything which it is in his power to do according to his own nature,—and it is in his power everywhere. . . .

When thou wishest to delight thyself, think of the virtues of those who live with thee; for instance, the activity of one, and the modesty of another, and the liberality of a third, and some other good quality of a fourth. . . .

Short is the little which remains to thee of life. Live as on a mountain. Let men see, let them know, a real man, who lives as he was meant to live. If they cannot endure him, let them kill him. For that is better than to live as men do.

Do any of these statements of Marcus Aurelius seem to you incompatible with the ideas of Epictetus? Do they seem to you to have more "gentleness and sweetness" than the doctrines of Epictetus? Explain.

VII. If you have read the selections surrounding this one, would you say that there are any elements which might be called Stoic in the teaching of Socrates? Of Epicurus? Of Jesus? Explain.

JESUS

Sermon on the Mount

A headnote which attempted to state the importance and meaning of the Sermon on the Mount would be presumptuous and unnecessary. We shall merely say that it is the fullest single statement in the Bible of the basic doctrines of Jesus. According to the *New Standard Bible Dictionary,* the Sermon on the Mount is "at any rate in large measure, a compilation of the sayings of Jesus . . . gradually collected and massed in the present elaborate composition," and it constitutes "a general summary of what Matthew understands to have been Jesus' teachings about the disciple's relationship to duty and to God." The translation presented here is that of the King James version; students who prefer to read another version can find this passage in Matthew, chapters 5, 6, and 7.

CHAPTER 5

And seeing the multitudes, he went up into a mountain: and when he was set, his disciples came unto him:

2 And he opened his mouth, and taught them, saying,

3 Blessed *are* the poor in spirit: for theirs is the kingdom of heaven.

4 Blessed *are they* that mourn: for they shall be comforted.

5 Blessed *are* the meek: for they shall inherit the earth.

6 Blessed *are* they which do hunger and thirst after righteousness: for they shall be filled.

7 Blessed *are* the merciful: for they shall obtain mercy.

8 Blessed *are* the pure in heart: for they shall see God.

9 Blessed *are* the peacemakers: for they shall be called the children of God.

10 Blessed *are* they which are persecuted for righteousness' sake: for theirs is the kingdom of heaven.

11 Blessed are ye, when *men* shall revile you, and persecute *you,* and shall say all manner of evil against you falsely, for my sake.

12 Rejoice, and be exceeding glad: for great *is* your reward in heaven: for so persecuted they the prophets which were before you.

13 Ye are the salt of the earth: but if the salt have lost his savour, wherewith shall it be salted? it is thenceforth good for nothing, but to be cast out, and to be trodden under foot of men.

14 Ye are the light of the world. A city that is set on an hill cannot be hid.

15 Neither do men light a candle, and put it under a bushel, but on a candlestick; and it giveth light unto all that are in the house.

16 Let your light so shine before men, that they may see your good works, and glorify your Father which is in heaven.

17 Think not that I am come to destroy the law, or the prophets: I am not come to destroy, but to fulfil.

18 For verily I say unto you, Till heaven and earth pass, one jot or one tittle shall in no wise pass from the law, till all be fulfilled.

19 Whosoever therefore shall break one of these least commandments, and shall teach men so, he shall be called the least in the kingdom of heaven: but whosoever shall do and teach *them,* the same shall be called great in the kingdom of heaven.

20 For I say unto you, That except your righteousness shall exceed *the righteousness* of the scribes and Pharisees, ye shall in no case enter into the kingdom of heaven.

21 Ye have heard that it was said by them of old time, Thou shalt not kill; and whosoever shall kill shall be in danger of the judgment:

22 But I say unto you, That whosoever is angry with his brother without a cause shall be in danger of the judgment: and whosoever shall say to his brother, Raca, shall be in danger of the council: but whosoever shall say, Thou fool, shall be in danger of hell fire.

23 Therefore if thou bring thy gift to the altar, and there rememberest that thy brother hath ought against thee;

24 Leave there thy gift before the altar, and go thy way; first be reconciled to thy brother, and then come and offer thy gift.

25 Agree with thine adversary quickly, whiles thou art in the way with him; lest at any time the adversary deliver thee to the judge, and the judge deliver thee to the officer, and thou be cast into prison.

26 Verily I say unto thee, Thou shalt by no means come out thence, till thou hast paid the uttermost farthing.

27 Ye have heard that it was said by them of old time, Thou shalt not commit adultery:

28 But I say unto you, That whosoever looketh on a woman to lust after her hath committed adultery with her already in his heart.

29 And if thy right eye offend thee, pluck it out, and cast *it* from thee: for it is profitable for thee that one of thy members should perish, and not *that* thy whole body should be cast into hell.

30 And if thy right hand offend thee, cut it off, and cast *it* from thee: for it is profitable for thee that one of thy members should perish, and not *that* thy whole body should be cast into hell.

31 It hath been said, Whosoever shall put away his wife, let him give her a writing of divorcement:

32 But I say unto you, That whosoever shall put away his wife, saving for the cause of fornication, causeth her to commit adultery: and whosoever shall marry her that is divorced committeth adultery.

33 Again, ye have heard that it hath been said by them of old time, Thou shalt not forswear thyself, but shalt perform unto the Lord thine oaths:

34 But I say unto you, Swear not at all; neither by heaven; for it is God's throne:

35 Nor by the earth; for it is his footstool: neither by Jerusalem; for it is the city of the great King.

36 Neither shalt thou swear by thy head, because thou canst not make one hair white or black.

37 But let your communication be, Yea, yea; Nay, nay: for whatsoever is more than these cometh of evil.

38 Ye have heard that it hath been said, An eye for an eye, and a tooth for a tooth:

39 But I say unto you, That ye resist not evil: but whosoever shall smite thee on thy right cheek, turn to him the other also.

40 And if any man will sue thee at the law, and take away thy coat, let him have *thy* cloke also.

41 And whosoever shall compel thee to go a mile, go with him twain.

42 Give to him that asketh thee, and from him that would borrow of thee turn not thou away.

43 Ye have heard that it hath been said, Thou shalt love thy neighbour, and hate thine enemy.

44 But I say unto you, Love your enemies, bless them that curse you, do good to them that hate you, and pray for them which despitefully use you, and persecute you;

45 That ye may be the children of your Father which is in heaven: for he maketh his sun to rise on the evil and on the good, and sendeth rain on the just and on the unjust.

46 For if ye love them which love you, what reward have ye? do not even the publicans the same?

47 And if ye salute your brethren only, what do ye more *than others*? do not even the publicans so?

48 Be ye therefore perfect, even as your Father which is in heaven is perfect.

CHAPTER 6

Take heed that ye do not your alms before men, to be seen of them: otherwise ye have no reward of your Father which is in heaven.

2 Therefore when thou doest *thine* alms, do not sound a trumpet before thee, as the hypocrites do in the synagogues and in the streets, that they may have glory of men. Verily I say unto you, They have their reward.

3 But when thou doest alms, let not thy left hand know what thy right hand doeth:

4 That thine alms may be in secret: and thy Father which seeth in secret himself shall reward thee openly.

5 And when thou prayest, thou shalt not be as the hypocrites *are:* for they love to pray standing in the synagogues and in the corners of the streets, that they may be seen of men. Verily I say unto you, They have their reward.

6 But thou, when thou prayest, enter into thy closet, and when thou hast shut thy door, pray to thy Father which is in secret; and thy Father which seeth in secret shall reward thee openly.

7 But when ye pray, use not vain repetitions, as the heathen *do:* for they think that they shall be heard for their much speaking.

8 Be not ye therefore like unto them: for your Father knoweth what things ye have need of, before ye ask him.

9 After this manner therefore pray ye: Our Father which art in heaven, Hallowed be thy name.

10 Thy kingdom come. Thy will be done in earth, as *it is* in heaven.

11 Give us this day our daily bread.

12 And forgive us our debts, as we forgive our debtors.

13 And lead us not into temptation, but deliver us from evil: For thine is the kingdom, and the power, and the glory, for ever. Amen.

14 For if ye forgive men their trespasses, your heavenly Father will also forgive you:

15 But if ye forgive not men their trespasses, neither will your Father forgive your trespasses.

16 Moreover when ye fast, be not, as the hypocrites, of a sad countenance: for they disfigure their faces, that they may appear unto men to fast. Verily I say unto you, They have their reward.

17 But thou, when thou fastest, anoint thine head, and wash thy face;

18 That thou appear not unto men to fast, but unto thy Father which is in secret: and thy Father, which seeth in secret, shall reward thee openly.

19 Lay not up for yourselves treasures upon earth, where moth and rust doth corrupt, and where thieves break through and steal:

20 But lay up for yourselves treasures in heaven, where neither moth nor rust doth corrupt, and where thieves do not break through nor steal:

21 For where your treasure is, there will your heart be also.

22 The light of the body is the eye: if therefore thine eye be single, thy whole body shall be full of light.

23 But if thine eye be evil, thy whole body shall be full of darkness. If therefore the light that is in thee be darkness, how great *is* that darkness!

24 No man can serve two masters: for either he will hate the one, and love the other; or else he will hold to the one, and despise the other. Ye cannot serve God and mammon.

25 Therefore I say unto you, Take no thought for your life, what ye shall eat, or what ye shall drink; nor yet for your body, what ye shall put on. Is not the life more than meat, and the body than raiment?

26 Behold the fowls of the air: for they sow not, neither do they reap, nor gather into barns; yet your heavenly Father feedeth them. Are ye not much better than they?

27 Which of you by taking thought can add one cubit unto his stature?

28 And why take ye thought for raiment? Consider the lilies of the field, how they grow; they toil not, neither do they spin:

29 And yet I say unto you, That even Solomon in all his glory was not arrayed like one of these.

30 Wherefore, if God so clothe the grass of the field, which to day is, and to morrow is cast into the oven, *shall he* not much more *clothe* you, O ye of little faith?

31 Therefore take no thought, saying, What shall we eat? or, What shall we drink? or, Wherewithal shall we be clothed?

32 (For after all these things do the Gentiles seek:) for your heavenly Father knoweth that ye have need of all these things.

33 But seek ye first the kingdom of God, and his righteousness; and all these things shall be added unto you.

34 Take therefore no thought for the morrow: for the morrow shall take thought for the things of itself. Sufficient unto the day *is* the evil thereof.

CHAPTER 7

Judge not, that ye be not judged.

2 For with what judgment ye judge, ye shall be judged: and with what measure ye mete, it shall be measured to you again.

3 And why beholdest thou the mote that is in thy brother's eye, but considerest not the beam that is in thine own eye?

4 Or how wilt thou say to thy brother, Let me pull out the mote out of thine eye; and, behold, a beam *is* in thine own eye?

5 Thou hypocrite, first cast out the beam out of thine own eye; and then shalt thou see clearly to cast out the mote out of thy brother's eye.

6 Give not that which is holy unto the dogs, neither cast ye your pearls before swine, lest they trample them under their feet, and turn again and rend you.

7 Ask, and it shall be given you; seek, and ye shall find; knock, and it shall be opened unto you:

8 For every one that asketh receiveth; and he that seeketh findeth; and to him that knocketh it shall be opened.

9 Or what man is there of you, whom if his son ask bread, will he give him a stone?

10 Or if he ask a fish, will he give him a serpent?

11 If ye then, being evil, know how to give good gifts unto your children, how much more shall your Father which is in heaven give good things to them that ask him?

12 Therefore all things whatsoever ye would that men should do to you, do ye even so to them: for this is the law and the prophets.

13 Enter ye in at the strait gate: for wide *is* the gate, and broad *is* the way, that leadeth to destruction, and many there be which go in thereat:

14 Because strait *is* the gate, and narrow *is* the way, which leadeth unto life, and few there be that find it.

15 Beware of false prophets, which come to you in sheep's clothing, but inwardly they are ravening wolves.

16 Ye shall know them by their fruits. Do men gather grapes of thorns, or figs of thistles?

17 Even so every good tree bringeth forth good fruit; but a corrupt tree bringeth forth evil fruit.

18 A good tree cannot bring forth evil fruit, neither *can* a corrupt tree bring forth good fruit.

19 Every tree that bringeth not forth good fruit is hewn down, and cast into the fire.

20 Wherefore by their fruits ye shall know them.

21 Not every one that saith unto me, Lord, Lord, shall enter into the kingdom of heaven; but he that doeth the will of my Father which is in heaven.

22 Many will say to me in that day, Lord, Lord, have we not prophesied in thy name? and in thy name have cast out devils? and in thy name done many wonderful works?

23 And then will I profess unto them, I never knew you: depart from me, ye that work iniquity.

24 Therefore whosoever heareth these sayings of mine, and doeth them, I will liken him unto a wise man, which built his house upon a rock:

25 And the rain descended, and the floods came, and the winds blew, and beat upon that house; and it fell not: for it was founded upon a rock.

26 And every one that heareth these sayings of mine, and doeth them not, shall be likened unto a foolish man, which built his house upon the sand:

27 And the rain descended, and the floods came, and the winds blew, and beat upon that house; and it fell: and great was the fall of it.

28 And it came to pass, when Jesus had ended these sayings, the people were astonished at his doctrine:

29 For he taught them as *one* having authority, and not as the scribes.

COMMENT AND QUESTIONS

Richard G. Moulton, editor of *The Modern Reader's Bible*, states that the Sermon on the Mount, like many sections in the Bible, has a sevenfold structure and "follows a literary form prominent in the Hebrew philosophy we call wisdom literature." Each of these sections consists, he says, of a maxim supported by comment. Students who wish to follow this pattern may find the following outline useful.

Section 1. Matt. 5:3–12; the maxim is 3.
Section 2. Matt. 5:13; the maxim is "Ye are the salt of the earth."
Section 3. Matt. 5:14–16; the maxim is "Ye are the light of the world."
Section 4. Matt. 5:17–48; the maxim is 17.
Section 5. Matt. 6:1–18; the maxim is 1.
Section 6. Matt. 6:19–34; the maxim is 19–20.
Section 7. Matt. 7:1–29 (i.e., the whole of 7); the maxim is 1. Mr. Moulton points out that this seventh section is miscellaneous (another characteristic feature of wisdom literature) and that the number of sayings in it is seven.

I. It has been said that the expression "poor in spirit" (5:3) is a general expression clarified by the statements that follow it. Just what do you take the expression to mean?

II. In 5:13–15 Jesus is using figures of speech to clarify an idea. Explain the figures of speech and their meaning. Whom is Jesus addressing with the pronoun *ye* in these lines?

III. In 5:17–20 Jesus refers to "the law," "the prophets," "the commandments." What specific laws, prophets and commandments do you think may be referred to? If you have read "The Jew and the Christian," page 1022, what statements made by Mr. Ballou are supported by this passage?

IV. In 5:25 Jesus says, "Agree with thine adversary quickly." Does this imply that one should deny his own principles in order to avoid disagreement and suffering, or that one should not quarrel over material possessions? Does the reading of 5:38–48 help you to answer this question?

V. In 6:22–23 Jesus is again using figurative language. What is the literal meaning?

VI. In 6:24 it is stated that "Ye cannot serve God and mammon." What is the relationship between this statement and 6:19–21? How does your dictionary define mammon? How would you define what is meant by mammon in terms of modern life?

VII. John Stuart Mill in "On the Liberty of Thought and Discussion," pages 967–969, comments at some length on Christian morality. Do you think that what Mill says there is true of the Sermon on the Mount? Explain.

VIII. In your opinion, which of the precepts of Jesus are most difficult to follow in modern living? If you were to follow these precepts strictly, what changes would you have to make in your present way of life?

IX. If you have read the selections from Epicurus and Epictetus, you are now familiar with the basic concepts of three views of life—the Epicurean, the Stoic, and the Christian. Which of these three philosophies do you think it would be most difficult to live by? Which would be most deeply rewarding?

JOHN HENRY NEWMAN

Enlargement of Mind

Students come to college, we say, to get an education. But what should the nature of this education be? To this question, from the time of Plato to the present, there have been many answers. In *The Idea of a University,* originally a series of lectures given in 1852, John Henry Newman (1801–1890) analyzed the scope and nature of university education; Walter Pater called his work "the perfect handling of a theory." The following excerpt from Newman's sixth lecture, "Knowledge Viewed in Relation to Learning," defines what he considers the essence, the *sine qua non,* of a liberal education.

Churchman, theologian, educator, leader of the Oxford Movement in the Anglican Church and later cardinal in the Roman Catholic Church, Newman was one of the intellectual leaders in the nineteenth century and was perhaps the greatest prose stylist in a period of great writers of prose. The good reader will attend not only to what Newman has to say but to his manner of saying it.

[1] I suppose the *primâ-facie* view which the public at large would take of a University, considering it as a place of Education, is nothing more or less than a place for acquiring a great deal of knowledge on a great many subjects. Memory is one of the first developed of mental faculties; a boy's business when he goes to school is to learn, that is, to store up things in his memory. For some years his intellect is little more than an instrument for taking in facts, or a receptacle for storing them; he welcomes them as fast as they come to him; he lives on what is without; he has his eyes ever about him; he has a lively susceptibility of impressions; he imbibes information of every kind; and little does he make his own in a true sense of the word, living rather upon his neighbors all around him. He has opinions, religious,

political, and literary, and, for a boy, is very positive in them and sure about them; but he gets them from his schoolfellows, or his masters, or his parents, as the case may be. Such as he is in his other relations, such also is he in his school exercises; his mind is observant, sharp, ready, retentive; he is almost passive in the acquisition of knowledge. I say this in no disparagement of the idea of a clever boy. Geography, chronology, history, language, natural history, he heaps up the matter of these studies as treasures for a future day. It is the seven years of plenty with him; he gathers in by handfuls, like the Egyptians, without counting; and though, as time goes on, there is exercise for his argumentative powers in the Elements of Mathematics, and for his taste in the Poets and Orators, still, while at school, or at least, till quite the last years of his time, he acquires, and little more; and when he is leaving for the University, he is mainly the creature of foreign influences and circumstances, and made up of accidents, homogeneous or not, as the case may be. Moreover, the moral habits, which are a boy's praise, encourage and assist this result; that is, diligence, assiduity, regularity, despatch, persevering application; for these are the direct conditions of acquisition, and naturally lead to it. Acquirements, again, are emphatically producible, and at a moment; they are a something to show, both for master and scholar; an audience, even though ignorant themselves of the subjects of an examination, can comprehend when questions are answered and when they are not. Here again is a reason why mental culture is in the minds of men identified with the acquisition of knowledge.

[2] The same notion possesses the public mind, when it passes on from the thought of a school to that of a University: and with the best of reasons so far as this, that there is no true culture without acquirements, and that philosophy presupposes knowledge. It requires a great deal of reading, or a wide range of information, to warrant us in putting forth our opinions on any serious subject; and without such learning the most original mind may be able indeed to dazzle, to amuse, to refute, to perplex, but not to come to any useful result or any trustworthy conclusion. There are indeed persons who profess a different view of the matter, and even act upon it. Every now and then you will find a person of vigorous or fertile mind, who relies upon his own resources, despises all former authors, and gives the world, with the utmost fearlessness, his views upon religion, or history, or any other popular subject. And his works may sell for a while; he may get a name in his day; but this will be all. His readers are sure to find in the long run that his doctrines are mere theories, and not the expression of facts, that they are chaff instead of bread, and then his popularity drops as suddenly as it rose.

[3] Knowledge then is the indispensable condition of expansion of mind, and the instrument of attaining to it; this cannot be denied; it is ever to be insisted on; I begin with it as a first principle; however, the very truth of it carries men too far, and confirms to them the notion that it is the whole of the matter. A narrow mind is thought to be that which contains little knowledge; and an enlarged mind, that which holds a great deal; and what

seems to put the matter beyond dispute is, the fact of the great number of studies which are pursued in a University, by its very profession. Lectures are given on every kind of subject; examinations are held; prizes awarded. There are moral, metaphysical, physical Professors; Professors of languages, of history, of mathematics, of experimental science. Lists of questions are published, wonderful for their range and depth, variety and difficulty; treatises are written, which carry upon their very face the evidence of extensive reading or multifarious information; what then is wanting for mental culture to a person of large reading and scientific attainments? what is grasp of mind but acquirement? where shall philosophical repose be found, but in the consciousness and enjoyment of large intellectual possessions?

[4] And yet this notion is, I conceive, a mistake, and my present business is to show that it is one, and that the end of a Liberal Education is not mere knowledge, or knowledge considered in its *matter;* and I shall best attain my object, by actually setting down some cases, which will be generally granted to be instances of the process of enlightenment or enlargement of mind, and others which are not, and thus, by the comparison, you will be able to judge for yourselves, Gentlemen, whether Knowledge, that is, acquirement, is after all the real principle of the enlargement, or whether that principle is not rather something beyond it.

[5] For instance, let a person, whose experience has hitherto been confined to the more calm and unpretending scenery of these islands, . . . go for the first time into parts where physical nature puts on her wilder and more awful forms, whether at home or abroad, as into mountainous districts; or let one, who has ever lived in a quiet village, go for the first time to a great metropolis,—then I suppose he will have a sensation which perhaps he never had before. He has a feeling not in addition or increase of former feelings, but of something different in its nature. He will perhaps be borne forward, and find for a time that he has lost his bearings. He has made a certain progress, and he has a consciousness of mental enlargement; he does not stand where he did, he has a new centre, and a range of thoughts to which he was before a stranger.

[6] Again, the view of the heavens which the telescope opens upon us, if allowed to fill and possess the mind, may almost whirl it round and make it dizzy. It brings in a flood of ideas, and is rightly called an intellectual enlargement, whatever is meant by the term.

[7] And so again, the sight of beasts of prey and other foreign animals, their strangeness, the originality (if I may use the term) of their forms and gestures and habits and their variety and independence of each other, throw us out of ourselves into another creation, and as if under another Creator, if I may so express the temptation which may come on the mind. We seem to have new faculties, or a new exercise for our faculties, by this addition to our knowledge; like a prisoner, who, having been accustomed to wear manacles or fetters, suddenly finds his arms and legs free.

[8] Hence Physical Science generally, in all its departments, as bringing

before us the exuberant riches and resources, yet the orderly course of the Universe, elevates and excites the student, and at first, I may say, almost takes away his breath, while in time it exercises a tranquilizing influence upon him.

[9] Again, the study of history is said to enlarge and enlighten the mind, and why? because, as I conceive, it gives it a power of judging of passing events, and of all events, and a conscious superiority over them, which before it did not possess.

[10] And in like manner, what is called seeing the world, entering into active life, going into society, travelling, gaining acquaintance with the various classes of the community, coming into contact with the principles and modes of thought of various parties, interests, and races, their views, aims, habits and manners, their religious creeds and forms of worship,—gaining experience how various yet how alike men are, how low-minded, how bad, how opposed, yet how confident in their opinions; all this exerts a perceptible influence upon the mind, which it is impossible to mistake, be it good or be it bad, and is popularly called its enlargement.

[11] And then again, the first time the mind comes across the arguments and speculations of unbelievers, and feels what a novel light they cast upon what he has hitherto accounted sacred; and still more, if it gives into them and embraces them, and throws off as so much prejudice what it has hitherto held, and, as if waking from a dream, begins to realize to its imagination that there is now no such thing as law and the transgression of law, that sin is a phantom, and punishment a bugbear, that it is free to sin, free to enjoy the world and the flesh; and still further, when it does enjoy them, and reflects that it may think and hold just what it will, that "the world is all before it where to choose," and what system to build up as its own private persuasion; when this torrent of wilful thoughts rushes over and inundates it, who will deny that the fruit of the tree of knowledge, or what the mind takes for knowledge, has made it one of the gods, with a sense of expansion and elevation,—an intoxication in reality, still, so far as the subjective state of the mind goes, an illumination? Hence the fanaticism of individuals or nations, who suddenly cast off their Maker. Their eyes are opened; and, like the judgment-stricken king in the Tragedy, they see two suns, and a magic universe, out of which they look back upon their former state of faith and innocence with a sort of contempt and indignation, as if they were then but fools, and the dupes of imposture.

[12] On the other hand, Religion has its own enlargement, and an enlargement, not of tumult, but of peace. It is often remarked of uneducated persons, who have hitherto thought little of the unseen world, that, on their turning to God, looking into themselves, regulating their hearts, reforming their conduct, and meditating on death and judgment, heaven and hell, they seem to become, in point of intellect, different beings from what they were. Before, they took things as they came, and thought no more of one thing than another. But now every event has a meaning; they have their own

estimate of whatever happens to them; they are mindful of times and seasons, and compare the present with the past; and the world, no longer dull, monotonous, unprofitable, and hopeless, is a various and complicated drama, with parts and an object, and an awful moral.

[13] Now from these instances, to which many more might be added, it is plain, first, that the communication of knowledge certainly is either a condition or the means of that sense of enlargement or enlightenment, of which at this day we hear so much in certain quarters: this cannot be denied; but next, it is equally plain, that such communication is not the whole of the process. The enlargement consists, not merely in the passive reception into the mind of a number of ideas hitherto unknown to it, but in the mind's energetic and simultaneous action upon and towards and among those new ideas, which are rushing in upon it. It is the action of a formative power, reducing to order and meaning the matter of our acquirements; it is a making the objects of our knowledge subjectively our own, or, to use a familiar word, it is a digestion of what we receive, into the substance of our previous state of thought; and without this no enlargement is said to follow. There is no enlargement, unless there be a comparison of ideas one with another, as they come before the mind, and a systematizing of them. We feel our minds to be growing and expanding *then,* when we not only learn, but refer what we learn to what we know already. It is not the mere addition to our knowledge that is the illumination; but the locomotion, the movement onwards, of that mental centre, to which both what we know, and what we are learning, the accumulating mass of our acquirements, gravitates. And therefore a truly great intellect, and recognized to be such by the common opinion of mankind, such as the intellect of Aristotle, or of St. Thomas, or of Newton, or of Goethe, . . . is one which takes a connected view of old and new, past and present, far and near, and which has an insight into the influence of all these one on another; without which there is no whole, and no centre. It possesses the knowledge, not only of things, but also of their mutual and true relations; knowledge, not merely considered as acquirement but as philosophy.

[14] Accordingly, when this analytical, distributive, harmonizing process is away, the mind experiences no enlargement, and is not reckoned as enlightened or comprehensive, whatever it may add to its knowledge. For instance, a great memory, as I have already said, does not make a philosopher, any more than a dictionary can be called a grammar. There are men who embrace in their minds a vast multitude of ideas, but with little sensibility about their real relations towards each other. These may be antiquarians, annalists, naturalists; they may be learned in the law; they may be versed in statistics; they are most useful in their own place; I should shrink from speaking disrespectfully of them; still, there is nothing in such attainments to guarantee the absence of narrowness of mind. If they are nothing more than well-read men, or men of information, they

have not what specially deserves the name of culture of mind, or fulfills the type of Liberal Education.

[15] In like manner, we sometimes fall in with persons who have seen much of the world, and of the men who, in their day, have played a conspicuous part in it, but who generalize nothing, and have no observation, in the true sense of the word. They abound in information, in detail, curious and entertaining, about men and things; and, having lived under the influence of no very clear or settled principles, religious or political, they speak of every one and every thing, only as so many phenomena, which are complete in themselves, and lead to nothing, not discussing them, or teaching any truth, or instructing the hearer, but simply talking. No one would say that these persons, well informed as they are, had attained to any great culture of intellect or to philosophy.

[16] The case is the same still more strikingly where the persons in question are beyond dispute men of inferior powers and deficient education. Perhaps they have been much in foreign countries, and they receive, in a passive, otiose, unfruitful way, the various facts which are forced upon them there. Seafaring men, for example, range from one end of the earth to the other; but the multiplicity of external objects, which they have encountered, forms no symmetrical and consistent picture upon their imagination; they see the tapestry of human life, as it were on the wrong side, and it tells no story. They sleep, and they rise up, and they find themselves, now in Europe, now in Asia; they see visions of great cities and wild regions; they are in the marts of commerce, or amid the islands of the South; they gaze on Pompey's Pillar, or on the Andes; and nothing which meets them carries them forward or backward, to any idea beyond itself. Nothing has a drift or relation; nothing has a history or a promise. Every thing stands by itself, and comes and goes in its turn, like the shifting scenes of a show, which leave the spectator where he was. Perhaps you are near such a man on a particular occasion, and expect him to be shocked or perplexed at something which occurs; but one thing is much the same to him as another, or, if he is perplexed, it is as not knowing what to say, whether it is right to admire, or to ridicule, or to disapprove, while conscious that some expression of opinion is expected from him; for in fact he has no standard of judgment at all, and no landmarks to guide him to a conclusion. Such is mere acquisition, and, I repeat, no one would dream of calling it philosophy.

[17] Instances, such as these, confirm, by the contrast, the conclusion I have already drawn from those which preceded them. That only is true enlargement of mind which is the power of viewing many things at once as one whole, of referring them severally to their true place in the universal system, of understanding their respective values, and determining their mutual dependence. Thus is that form of Universal Knowledge, of which I have on a former occasion spoken, set up in the individual intellect,

and constitutes its perfection. Possessed of this real illumination, the mind never views any part of the extended subject-matter of Knowledge without recollecting that it is but a part, or without the associations which spring from this recollection. It makes every thing in some sort lead to every thing else; it would communicate the image of the whole to every separate portion, till that whole becomes in imagination like a spirit, every where pervading and penetrating its component parts, and giving them one definite meaning. Just as our bodily organs, when mentioned, recall their function in the body, as the word "creation" suggests the Creator, and "subjects" a sovereign, so, in the mind of the Philosopher, as we are abstractedly conceiving of him, the elements of the physical and moral world, sciences, arts, pursuits, ranks, offices, events, opinions, individualities, are all viewed as one, with correlative functions, and as gradually by successive combinations converging, one and all, to the true centre.

[18] To have even a portion of this illuminative reason and true philosophy is the highest state to which nature can aspire, in the way of intellect; it puts the mind above the influences of chance and necessity, above anxiety, suspense, unsettlement, and superstition, which is the lot of the many. Men whose minds are possessed with some one object, take exaggerated views of its importance, are feverish in the pursuit of it, make it the measure of things which are utterly foreign to it, and are startled and despond if it happens to fail them. They are ever in alarm or in transport. Those on the other hand who have no object or principle whatever to hold by, lose their way, every step they take. They are thrown out, and do not know what to think or say, at every fresh juncture; they have no view of persons, or occurrences, or facts, which come suddenly upon them, and they hang upon the opinion of others, for want of internal resources. But the intellect which has been disciplined to the perfection of its powers, which knows, and thinks while it knows, which has learned to leaven the dense mass of facts and events with the elastic force of reason, such an intellect cannot be partial, cannot be exclusive, cannot be impetuous, cannot be at a loss, cannot but be patient, collected, and majestically calm, because it discerns the end in every beginning, the origin in every end, the law in every interruption, the limit in each delay; because it ever knows where it stands, and how its path lies from one point to another. It is the τετράγωνος of the Peripatetic,[1] and has the "nil admirari"[2] of the Stoic,—

>Felix qui potuit rerum cognoscere causas,
>Atque metus omnes, et inexorabile fatum
>Subjecit pedibus, strepitumque Acherontis avari.[3]

[1] An allusion to Aristotle's *Ethics*—the good and *foursquare* man.
[2] To be amazed at nothing.
[3] Happy the man who can understand the causes of things, and thus spurn all fear and inexorable fate and the roar of greedy Acheron.

There are men who, when in difficulties, originate at the moment vast ideas or dazzling projects; who, under the influence of excitement, are able to cast a light, almost as if from inspiration, on a subject or course of action which comes before them; who have a sudden presence of mind equal to any emergency, rising with the occasion, and an undaunted magnanimous bearing, and an energy and keenness which is but made intense by opposition. This is genius, this is heroism; it is the exhibition of a natural gift, which no culture can teach, at which no Institution can aim; here, on the contrary, we are concerned, not with mere nature, but with training and teaching. That perfection of the Intellect, which is the result of Education, and its *beau ideal,* to be imparted to individuals in their respective measures, is the clear, calm, accurate vision and comprehension of all things, as far as the finite mind can embrace them, each in its place, and with its own characteristics upon it. It is almost prophetic from its knowledge of history; it is almost heart-searching from its knowledge of human nature; it has almost supernatural charity from its freedom from littleness and prejudice; it has almost the repose of faith, because nothing can startle it; it has almost the beauty and harmony of heavenly contemplation, so intimate is it with the eternal order of things and the music of the spheres.

COMMENT AND QUESTIONS

In this selection Newman's essential purpose is to define an abstract concept—what he calls mental enlargement, mental illumination, or philosophical knowledge—and to persuade the reader that the achieving of such mental enlargement is the true end of education.

I. Earlier in this book we have discussed the techniques of extended definition. Like brief definitions, extended definitions put the subject into a genus or class, and differentiate it from other members of its class with which it might be confused. Extended definitions also clarify the subject in one or more of these ways: (1) by giving examples; (2) by comparing the subject with something familiar to the reader; (3) by comparing and contrasting it with related subjects; (4) by tracing its history or development; (5) by negating or excluding—showing what it does not mean or does not include as the author is using it; (6) by restating in different words the essentials of the definition; (7) by analyzing—breaking the subject into its components, and examining each part.

Which of these methods of definition has Newman used? Where, in your judgment, has he used one or more of the methods most effectively?

II. Do you agree that enlargement of mind should be the chief end of education? What other aims or ends might be considered equally important?

950   READING FOR IDEAS AND VALUES

III. To see Newman's skill in organizing his thought, read the first sentences only in paragraphs 1, 2, 3, 13, 14, 17, 18. Note that these sentences provide the framework upon which the development rests and also supply a kind of sentence outline and summary of the essay.

IV. Now look at the development more closely by examining paragraphs 5 through 12. What makes these paragraphs a unit? How has the author secured transitions from one paragraph to another? Newman is famous for his ability to see various sides of a question—an ability illustrated in paragraphs 11 and 12. Considering his strong religious beliefs, do you see a reason why paragraph 12 follows rather than precedes paragraph 11? Is paragraph 12 more effective because it is preceded by paragraph 11? Explain your answer.

V. Follow in detail the development of the thought in paragraphs 13 through 17. What is the unifying idea? What purpose is served by each paragraph?

VI. In the last paragraph (18) Newman makes certain claims for the kind of education he has been describing and also admits that there are some powers which are beyond the reach of such an education. Just what claims does he make? Do the admissions add to or detract from his whole argument in favor of liberal education?

VII. Some aspects of Newman's style which are particularly worthy of notice are his use of sustained parallelism to make his long sentences perfectly clear, his use of balance and antithesis and climactic arrangement, the varied pace and rhythm of his sentences, the subtle use of alliteration, the choice of figures of speech (the tapestry figure in paragraph 16, for example). Can you find examples of these stylistic traits in this selection?

VIII. Plato in "The Myth of the Cave" is also writing about education. What are the major points of agreement and disagreement between Newman and Plato?

JOHN STUART MILL

On the Liberty of Thought and Discussion

The following selection is a sustained logical argument in favor of freedom of thought and opinion. Although most students will need to spend at least three hours on the essay in order to follow the close reasoning and understand the clear but very complex structure of the argument, the time will be well spent. John Stuart Mill (1806–1873) was an English writer, economist, and logician who has been called "the saint of rationalism." "On the Liberty of Thought and Discussion" is Chapter Two of his famous essay *On Liberty*, published in 1859.

[1] The time, it is to be hoped, is gone by, when any defence would be necessary of the "liberty of the press" as one of the securities against corrupt or tyrannical government. No argument, we may suppose, can now be needed, against permitting a legislature or an executive, not identified in interest with the people, to prescribe opinions to them, and determine what doctrines or what arguments they shall be allowed to hear. This aspect of the question, besides, has been so often and so triumphantly enforced by preceding writers, that it needs not be specially insisted on in this place. Though the law of England, on the subject of the press, is as servile to this day as it was in the time of the Tudors, there is little danger of its being actually put in force against political discussion, except during some temporary panic, when fear of insurrection drives ministers and judges from their propriety; and, speaking generally, it is not, in constitutional countries, to be apprehended that the government, whether completely responsible to the people or not, will often attempt to control the expression of opinion, except when in doing so it makes itself the organ of the general intolerance of the public. Let us suppose, therefore, that the government is entirely at one with the people, and never thinks of exerting any power of coercion unless in agreement with what it conceives to be their voice. But I deny the right of the people to exercise such coercion, either by themselves or by their government. The power itself is illegitimate. The best government has no more title to it than the worst. It is as noxious, or more noxious, when exerted in accordance with public opinion, than when in opposition to it. If all mankind minus one were of one opinion, and only one person were of the contrary opinion, mankind would be no more justified in silencing that one person, than he, if he had the power, would be justified in silencing mankind. Were an opinion a personal possession of no value except to the owner; if to be obstructed in the enjoyment of it were simply a private injury, it would make some difference whether the injury was inflicted only on a few persons or on many. But the peculiar evil of silencing the expression of an opinion is, that it is robbing the human race; posterity as well as the existing generation; those who dissent from the opinion, still more than those who hold it. If the opinion is right, they are deprived of the opportunity of exchanging error for truth: if wrong, they lose, what is almost as great a benefit, the clearer perception and livelier impression of truth, produced by its collision with error.

[2] It is necessary to consider separately these two hypotheses, each of which has a distinct branch of the argument corresponding to it. We can never be sure that the opinion we are endeavouring to stifle is a false opinion; and if we were sure, stifling it would be an evil still.

[3] First: the opinion which it is attempted to suppress by authority may possibly be true. Those who desire to suppress it, of course deny its truth; but they are not infallible. They have no authority to decide the

question for all mankind, and exclude every other person from the means of judging. To refuse a hearing to an opinion, because they are sure that it is false, is to assume that *their* certainty is the same thing as *absolute* certainty. All silencing of discussion is an assumption of infallibility. Its condemnation may be allowed to rest on this common argument, not the worse for being common.

[4] Unfortunately for the good sense of mankind, the fact of their fallibility is far from carrying the weight in their practical judgment which is always allowed to it in theory; for while every one well knows himself to be fallible, few think it necessary to take any precautions against their own fallibility, or admit the supposition that any opinion, of which they feel very certain, may be one of the examples of the error to which they acknowledge themselves to be liable. Absolute princes, or others who are accustomed to unlimited deference, usually feel this complete confidence in their own opinions on nearly all subjects. People more happily situated, who sometimes hear their opinions disputed, and are not wholly unused to be set right when they are wrong, place the same unbounded reliance only on such of their opinions as are shared by all who surround them, or to whom they habitually defer; for in proportion to a man's want of confidence in his own solitary judgment, does he usually repose, with implicit trust, on the infallibility of "the world" in general. And the world, to each individual, means the part of it with which he comes in contact; his party, his sect, his church, his class of society; the man may be called, by comparison, almost liberal and large-minded to whom it means anything so comprehensive as his own country or his own age. Nor is his faith in this collective authority at all shaken by his being aware that other ages, countries, sects, churches, classes, and parties have thought, and even now think, the exact reverse. He devolves upon his own world the responsibility of being in the right against the dissentient worlds of other people; and it never troubles him that mere accident has decided which of these numerous worlds is the object of his reliance, and that the same causes which make him a Churchman in London, would have made him a Buddhist or a Confucian in Pekin. Yet it is as evident in itself, as any amount of argument can make it, that ages are no more infallible than individuals; every age having held many opinions which subsequent ages have deemed not only false but absurd; and it is as certain that many opinions now general will be rejected by future ages, as it is that many, once general, are rejected by the present.

[5] The objection likely to be made to this argument would probably take some such form as the following. There is no greater assumption of infallibility in forbidding the propagation of error, than in any other thing which is done by public authority on its own judgment and responsibility. Judgment is given to men that they may use it. Because it may be used erroneously, are men to be told that they ought not to use it at all? To prohibit what they think pernicious, is not claiming exemption from error,

but fulfilling the duty incumbent on them, although fallible, of acting on their conscientious conviction. If we were never to act on our opinions, because those opinions may be wrong, we should leave all our interests uncared for, and all our duties unperformed. An objection which applies to all conduct can be no valid objection to any conduct in particular. It is the duty of governments, and of individuals, to form the truest opinions they can; to form them carefully, and never impose them upon others unless they are quite sure of being right. But when they are sure (such reasoners may say), it is not conscientiousness but cowardice to shrink from acting on their opinions, and allow doctrines which they honestly think dangerous to the welfare of mankind, either in this life or in another, to be scattered abroad without restraint, because other people, in less enlightened times, have persecuted opinions now believed to be true. Let us take care, it may be said, not to make the same mistake: but governments and nations have made mistakes in other things, which are not denied to be fit subjects for the exercise of authority: they have laid on bad taxes, made unjust wars. Ought we therefore to lay on no taxes, and, under whatever provocation, make no wars? Men, and governments, must act to the best of their ability. There is no such thing as absolute certainty, but there is assurance sufficient for the purposes of human life. We may, and must, assume our opinion to be true for the guidance of our own conduct: and it is assuming no more when we forbid bad men to pervert society by the propagation of opinions which we regard as false and pernicious.

[6] I answer, that it is assuming very much more. There is the greatest difference between presuming an opinion to be true, because, with every opportunity for contesting it, it has not been refuted, and assuming its truth for the purpose of not permitting its refutation. Complete liberty of contradicting and disproving our opinion is the very condition which justifies us in assuming its truth for purposes of action; and on no other terms can a being with human faculties have any rational assurance of being right.

[7] When we consider either the history of opinion, or the ordinary conduct of human life, to what is it to be ascribed that the one and the other are no worse than they are? Not certainly to the inherent force of the human understanding; for, on any matter not self-evident, there are ninety-nine persons totally incapable of judging of it for one who is capable; and the capacity of the hundredth person is only comparative; for the majority of the eminent men of every past generation held many opinions now known to be erroneous, and did or approved numerous things which no one will now justify. Why is it, then, that there is on the whole a preponderance among mankind of rational opinions and rational conduct? If there really is this preponderance—which there must be unless human affairs are, and have always been, in an almost desperate state—it is owing to a quality of the human mind, the source of everything respectable in man either as an intellectual or as a moral being, namely, that his errors are corrigible. He is

capable of rectifying his mistakes, by discussion and experience. Not by experience alone. There must be discussion, to show how experience is to be interpreted. Wrong opinions and practices gradually yield to fact and argument; but facts and arguments, to produce any effect on the mind, must be brought before it. Very few facts are able to tell their own story, without comments to bring out their meaning. The whole strength and value, then, of human judgment, depending on the one property, that it can be set right when it is wrong, reliance can be placed on it only when the means of setting it right are kept constantly at hand. In the case of any person whose judgment is really deserving of confidence, how has it become so? Because he has kept his mind open to criticism of his opinions and conduct. Because it has been his practice to listen to all that could be said against him; to profit by as much of it as was just, and expound to himself, and upon occasion to others, the fallacy of what was fallacious. Because he has felt, that the only way in which a human being can make some approach to knowing the whole of a subject, is by hearing what can be said about it by persons of every variety of opinion, and studying all modes in which it can be looked at by every character of mind. No wise man ever acquired his wisdom in any mode but this; nor is it in the nature of human intellect to become wise in any other manner. The steady habit of correcting and completing his own opinion by collating it with those of others, so far from causing doubt and hesitation in carrying it into practice, is the only stable foundation for a just reliance on it: for, being cognizant of all that can, at least obviously, be said against him, and having taken up his position against all gainsayers—knowing that he has sought for objections and difficulties, instead of avoiding them, and has shut out no light which can be thrown upon the subject from any quarter—he has a right to think his judgment better than that of any person, or any multitude, who have not gone through a similar process.

[8] It is not too much to require that what the wisest of mankind, those who are best entitled to trust their own judgment, find necessary to warrant their relying on it, should be submitted to by that miscellaneous collection of a few wise and many foolish individuals, called the public. The most intolerant of churches, the Roman Catholic Church, even at the canonisation of a saint, admits, and listens patiently to, a "devil's advocate." The holiest of men, it appears, cannot be admitted to posthumous honours, until all that the devil could say against him is known and weighed. If even the Newtonian philosophy were not permitted to be questioned, mankind could not feel as complete assurance of its truth as they now do. The beliefs which we have most warrant for have no safeguard to rest on, but a standing invitation to the whole world to prove them unfounded. If the challenge is not accepted, or is accepted and the attempt fails, we are far enough from certainty still; but we have done the best that the existing state of human reason admits of; we have neglected nothing that could give the truth a chance of reaching us: if the lists are kept open, we may

hope that if there be a better truth, it will be found when the human mind is capable of receiving it; and in the meantime we may rely on having attained such approach to truth as is possible in our own day. This is the amount of certainty attainable by a fallible being, and this the sole way of attaining it.

[9] Strange it is, that men should admit the validity of the arguments for free discussion, but object to their being "pushed to an extreme"; not seeing that unless the reasons are good for an extreme case, they are not good for any case. Strange that they should imagine that they are not assuming infallibility, when they acknowledge that there should be free discussion on all subjects which can possibly be *doubtful,* but think that some particular principle or doctrine should be forbidden to be questioned because it is so *certain,* that is, because *they are certain* that it is certain. To call any proposition certain, while there is any one who would deny its certainty if permitted, but who is not permitted, is to assume that we ourselves, and those who agree with us, are the judges of certainty, and judges without hearing the other side.

[10] In the present age—which has been described as "destitute of faith, but terrified at scepticism"—in which people feel sure, not so much that their opinions are true, as that they should not know what to do without them—the claims of an opinion to be protected from public attack are rested not so much on its truth, as on its importance to society. There are, it is alleged, certain beliefs so useful, not to say indispensable, to well-being that it is as much the duty of governments to uphold those beliefs, as to protect any other of the interests of society. In a case of such necessity, and so directly in the line of their duty, something less than infallibility may, it is maintained, warrant, and even bind, governments to act on their own opinion, confirmed by the general opinion of mankind. It is also often argued, and still oftener thought, that none but bad men would desire to weaken these salutary beliefs; and there can be nothing wrong, it is thought, in restraining bad men, and prohibiting what only such men would wish to practise. This mode of thinking makes the justification of restraints on discussion not a question of the truth of doctrines, but of their usefulness; and flatters itself by that means to escape the responsibility of claiming to be an infallible judge of opinions. But those who thus satisfy themselves, do not perceive that the assumption of infallibility is merely shifted from one point to another. The usefulness of an opinion is itself a matter of opinion: as disputable, as open to discussion, and requiring discussion as much as the opinion itself. There is the same need of an infallible judge of opinions to decide an opinion to be noxious, as to decide it to be false, unless the opinion condemned has full opportunity of defending itself. And it will not do to say that the heretic may be allowed to maintain the utility or harmlessness of his opinion, though forbidden to maintain its truth. The truth of an opinion is part of its utility. If we would know whether or not it is desirable that a proposition should be

believed, is it possible to exclude the consideration of whether or not it is true? In the opinion, not of bad men, but of the best men, no belief which is contrary to truth can be really useful: and can you prevent such men from urging that plea, when they are charged with culpability for denying some doctrine which they are told is useful, but which they believe to be false? Those who are on the side of received opinions never fail to take all possible advantage of this plea; you do not find *them* handling the question of utility as if it could be completely abstracted from that of truth: on the contrary, it is, above all, because their doctrine is "the truth," that the knowledge or the belief of it is held to be so indispensable. There can be no fair discussion of the question of usefulness when an argument so vital may be employed on one side, but not on the other. And in point of fact, when law or public feeling do not permit the truth of an opinion to be disputed, they are just as little tolerant of a denial of its usefulness. The utmost they allow is an extenuation of its absolute necessity, or of the positive guilt of rejecting it.

[11] In order more fully to illustrate the mischief of denying a hearing to opinions because we, in our own judgment, have condemned them, it will be desirable to fix down the discussion to a concrete case; and I choose, by preference, the cases which are least favourable to me—in which the argument against freedom of opinion, both on the score of truth and on that of utility, is considered the strongest. Let the opinions impugned be the belief in a God and in a future state, or any of the commonly received doctrines of morality. To fight the battle on such ground gives a great advantage to an unfair antagonist; since he will be sure to say (and many who have no desire to be unfair will say it internally), Are these the doctrines which you do not deem sufficiently certain to be taken under the protection of law? Is the belief in a God one of the opinions to feel sure of which you hold to be assuming infallibility? But I must be permitted to observe, that it is not the feeling sure of a doctrine (be it what it may) which I call an assumption of infallibility. It is the undertaking to decide that question *for others,* without allowing them to hear what can be said on the contrary side. And I denounce and reprobate this pretension not the less, if put forth on the side of my most solemn convictions. However positive any one's persuasion may be, not only of the falsity but of the pernicious consequences—not only of the pernicious consequences, but (to adopt expressions which I altogether condemn) the immorality and impiety of an opinion; yet if, in pursuance of that private judgment, though backed by the public judgment of his country or his contemporaries, he prevents the opinion from being heard in its defence, he assumes infallibility. And so far from the assumption being less objectionable or less dangerous because the opinion is called immoral or impious, this is the case of all others in which it is most fatal. These are exactly the occasions on which the men of one generation commit those dreadful mistakes which excite the astonishment and horror of posterity. It is

among such that we find the instances memorable in history, when the arm of the law has been employed to root out the best men and the noblest doctrines; with deplorable success as to the men, though some of the doctrines have survived to be (as if in mockery) invoked in defence of similar conduct towards those who dissent from *them,* or from their received interpretation.

[12] Mankind can hardly be too often reminded, that there was once a man named Socrates, between whom and the legal authorities and public opinion of his time there took place a memorable collision. Born in an age and country abounding in individual greatness, this man has been handed down to us by those who best knew both him and the age, as the most virtuous man in it; while *we* know him as the head and prototype of all subsequent teachers of virtue, the source equally of the lofty inspiration of Plato and the judicious utilitarianism of Aristotle, *"i maëstri di color che sanno,"* the two headsprings of ethical as of all other philosophy. This acknowledged master of all the eminent thinkers who have since lived—whose fame, still growing after more than two thousand years, all but outweighs the whole remainder of the names which make his native city illustrious—was put to death by his countrymen, after a judicial conviction, for impiety and immorality. Impiety, in denying the gods recognised by the State; indeed his accuser asserted (see the "Apologia") that he believed in no gods at all. Immorality, in being, by his doctrines and instructions, a "corrupter of youth." Of these charges the tribunal, there is every ground for believing, honestly found him guilty, and condemned the man who probably of all then born had deserved best of mankind to be put to death as a criminal.

[13] To pass from this to the only other instance of judicial iniquity, the mention of which, after the condemnation of Socrates, would not be an anti-climax: the event which took place on Calvary rather more than eighteen hundred years ago. The man who left on the memory of those who witnessed his life and conversation such an impression of his moral grandeur that eighteen subsequent centuries have done homage to him as the Almighty in person, was ignominiously put to death, as what? As a blasphemer. Men did not merely mistake their benefactor; they mistook him for the exact contrary of what he was, and treated him as that prodigy of impiety which they themselves are now held to be for their treatment of him. The feelings with which mankind now regard these lamentable transactions, especially the latter of the two, render them extremely unjust in their judgment of the unhappy actors. These were, to all appearance, not bad men—not worse than men commonly are, but rather the contrary; men who possessed in a full, or somewhat more than a full measure, the religious, moral, and patriotic feelings of their time and people: the very kind of men who, in all times, our own included, have every chance of passing through life blameless and respected. The high-priest who rent his garments when the words were pronounced, which,

according to all the ideas of his country, constituted the blackest guilt, was in all probability quite as sincere in his horror and indignation as the generality of respectable and pious men now are in the religious and moral sentiments they profess; and most of those who now shudder at his conduct, if they had lived in his time, and been born Jews, would have acted precisely as he did. Orthodox Christians who are tempted to think that those who stoned to death the first martyrs must have been worse men than they themselves are, ought to remember that one of those persecutors was Saint Paul.

[14] Let us add one more example, the most striking of all, if the impressiveness of an error is measured by the wisdom and virtue of him who falls into it. If ever any one, possessed of power, had grounds for thinking himself the best and most enlightened among his contemporaries, it was the Emperor Marcus Aurelius. Absolute monarch of the whole civilized world, he preserved through life not only the most unblemished justice, but what was less to be expected from his Stoical breeding, the tenderest heart. The few failings which are attributed to him, were all on the side of indulgence: while his writings, the highest ethical product of the ancient mind, differ scarcely perceptibly, if they differ at all, from the most characteristic teachings of Christ. This man, a better Christian in all but the dogmatic sense of the word, than almost any of the ostensibly Christian sovereigns who have since reigned, persecuted Christianity. Placed at the summit of all the previous attainments of humanity, with an open, unfettered intellect, and a character which led him of himself to embody in his moral writings the Christian ideal, he yet failed to see that Christianity was to be a good and not an evil to the world, with his duties to which he was so deeply penetrated. Existing society he knew to be in a deplorable state. But such as it was, he saw, or thought he saw, that it was held together, and prevented from being worse, by belief and reverence of the received divinities. As a ruler of mankind, he deemed it his duty not to suffer society to fall in pieces; and saw not how, if its existing ties were removed, any others could be formed which could again knit it together. The new religion openly aimed at dissolving these ties: unless, therefore, it was his duty to adopt that religion, it seemed to be his duty to put it down. Inasmuch then as the theology of Christianity did not appear to him true or of divine origin; inasmuch as this strange history of a crucified God was not credible to him, and a system which purported to rest entirely upon a foundation to him so wholly unbelievable, could not be foreseen by him to be that renovating agency which, after all abatements, it has in fact proved to be; the gentlest and most amiable of philosophers and rulers, under a solemn sense of duty, authorized the persecution of Christianity. To my mind this is one of the most tragical facts in all history. It is a bitter thought, how different a thing the Christianity of the world might have been, if the Christian faith had been adopted as the religion of the empire under the auspices of Marcus Aurelius instead of those of Constantine. But it would be equally unjust to him and

false to truth, to deny, that no one plea which can be urged for punishing anti-Christian teaching, was wanting to Marcus Aurelius for punishing, as he did, the propagation of Christianity. No Christian more firmly believes that Atheism is false, and tends to the dissolution of society, than Marcus Aurelius believed the same things of Christianity; he who, of all men then living, might have been thought the most capable of appreciating it. Unless any one who approves of punishment for the promulgation of opinions, flatters himself that he is a wiser and better man than Marcus Aurelius—more deeply versed in the wisdom of his time, more elevated in his intellect above it—more earnest in his search for truth, or more singleminded in his devotion to it when found; let him abstain from that assumption of the joint infallibility of himself and the multitude, which the great Antoninus made with so unfortunate a result. . . .

[15] But, indeed, the dictum that truth always triumphs over persecution is one of those pleasant falsehoods which men repeat after one another till they pass into commonplaces, but which all experience refutes. History teems with instances of truth put down by persecution. If not suppressed for ever, it may be thrown back for centuries. To speak only of religious opinions: the Reformation broke out at least twenty times before Luther, and was put down. Arnold of Brescia was put down. Fra Dolcino was put down. Savonarola was put down. The Albigeois were put down. The Vaudois were put down. The Lollards were put down. The Hussites were put down. Even after the era of Luther, whatever persecution was persisted in, it was successful. In Spain, Italy, Flanders, the Austrian empire, Protestantism was rooted out; and, most likely, would have been so in England, had Queen Mary lived, or Queen Elizabeth died. Persecution has always succeeded, save where the heretics were too strong a party to be effectually persecuted. No reasonable person can doubt that Christianity might have been extirpated in the Roman Empire. It spread, and became predominant, because the persecutions were only occasional, lasting but a short time, and separated by long intervals of almost undisturbed propagandism. It is a piece of idle sentimentality that truth, merely as truth, has any inherent power denied to error of prevailing against the dungeon and the stake. Men are not more zealous for truth than they often are for error, and a sufficient application of legal or even of social penalties will generally succeed in stopping the propagation of either. The real advantage which truth has consists in this, that when an opinion is true, it may be extinguished once, twice, or many times, but in the course of ages there will generally be found persons to rediscover it, until some one of its reappearances falls on a time when from favourable circumstances it escapes persecution until it has made such head as to withstand all subsequent attempts to suppress it. . . .

[16] Let us now pass to the second division of the argument, and dismissing the supposition that any of the received opinions may be false,

let us assume them to be true, and examine into the worth of the manner in which they are likely to be held, when their truth is not freely and openly canvassed. However unwillingly a person who has a strong opinion may admit the possibility that his opinion may be false, he ought to be moved by the consideration that, however true it may be, if it is not fully, frequently, and fearlessly discussed, it will be held as a dead dogma, not a living truth.

[17] There is a class of persons (happily not quite so numerous as formerly) who think it enough if a person assents undoubtingly to what they think true, though he has no knowledge whatever of the grounds of the opinion, and could not make a tenable defence of it against the most superficial objections. Such persons, if they can once get their creed taught from authority, naturally think that no good, and some harm, comes of its being allowed to be questioned. Where their influence prevails, they make it nearly impossible for the received opinion to be rejected wisely and considerately, though it may still be rejected rashly and ignorantly; for to shut out discussion entirely is seldom possible, and when it once gets in, beliefs not grounded on conviction are apt to give way before the slightest semblance of an argument. Waiving, however, this possibility—assuming that the true opinion abides in the mind, but abides as a prejudice, a belief independent of, and proof against, argument—this is not the way in which truth ought to be held by a rational being. This is not knowing the truth. Truth, thus held, is but one superstition the more, accidentally clinging to the words which enunciate a truth.

[18] If the intellect and judgment of mankind ought to be cultivated, a thing which Protestants at least do not deny, on what can these faculties be more appropriately exercised by any one, than on the things which concern him so much that it is considered necessary for him to hold opinions on them? If the cultivation of the understanding consists in one thing more than in another, it is surely in learning the grounds of one's own opinions. Whatever people believe, on subjects on which it is of the first importance to believe rightly, they ought to be able to defend against at least the common objections. But, some one may say, "Let them be *taught* the grounds of their opinions. It does not follow that opinions must be merely parroted because they are never heard controverted. Persons who learn geometry do not simply commit the theorems to memory, but understand and learn likewise the demonstrations; and it would be absurd to say that they remain ignorant of the grounds of geometrical truths, because they never hear any one deny, and attempt to disprove them." Undoubtedly: and such teaching suffices on a subject like mathematics, where there is nothing at all to be said on the wrong side of the question. The peculiarity of the evidence of mathematical truths is that all the argument is on one side. There are no objections, and no answers to objections. But on every subject on which difference of opinion is possible, the truth depends on a balance to be struck between two sets of conflicting reasons.

Even in natural philosophy, there is always some other explanation possible of the same facts; some geocentric theory instead of heliocentric, some phlogiston instead of oxygen; and it has to be shown why that other theory cannot be the true one: and until this is shown, and until we know how it is shown, we do not understand the grounds of our opinion. But when we turn to subjects infinitely more complicated, to morals, religion, politics, social relations, and the business of life, three-fourths of the arguments for every disputed opinion consist in dispelling the appearances which favour some opinion different from it. The greatest orator, save one, of antiquity, has left it on record that he always studied his adversary's case with as great, if not still greater, intensity than even his own. What Cicero practised as the means of forensic success requires to be imitated by all who study any subject in order to arrive at the truth. He who knows only his own side of the case, knows little of that. His reasons may be good, and no one may have been able to refute them. But if he is equally unable to refute the reasons on the opposite side; if he does not so much as know what they are, he has no ground for preferring either opinion. The rational position for him would be suspension of judgment, and unless he contents himself with that, he is either led by authority, or adopts, like the generality of the world, the side to which he feels most inclination. Nor is it enough that he should hear the arguments of adversaries from his own teachers, presented as they state them, and accompanied by what they offer as refutations. That is not the way to do justice to the arguments, or bring them into real contact with his own mind. He must be able to hear them from persons who actually believe them; who defend them in earnest, and do their very utmost for them. He must know them in their most plausible and persuasive form; he must feel the whole force of the difficulty which the true view of the subject has to encounter and dispose of; else he will never really possess himself of the portion of truth which meets and removes that difficulty. Ninety-nine in a hundred of what are called educated men are in this condition; even of those who can argue fluently for their opinions. Their conclusion may be true, but it might be false for anything they know: they have never thrown themselves into the mental position of those who think differently from them, and considered what such persons may have to say; and consequently they do not, in any proper sense of the word, know the doctrine which they themselves profess. They do not know those parts of it which explain and justify the remainder; the considerations which show that a fact which seemingly conflicts with another is reconcilable with it, or that, of two apparently strong reasons, one and not the other ought to be preferred. All that part of the truth which turns the scale, and decides the judgment of a completely informed mind, they are strangers to; nor is it ever really known, but to those who have attended equally and impartially to both sides, and endeavoured to see the reasons of both in the strongest light. So essential is this discipline to a real understanding of moral and human subjects, that if opponents of all important truths do not exist, it is indispensable to imagine them, and supply them with the strongest arguments which the most skilful devil's advocate can conjure up.

[19] To abate the force of these considerations, an enemy of free discussion may be supposed to say, that there is no necessity for mankind in general to know and understand all that can be said against or for their opinions by philosophers and theologians. That it is not needful for common men to be able to expose all the misstatements or fallacies of an ingenious opponent. That it is enough if there is always somebody capable of answering them, so that nothing likely to mislead uninstructed persons remains unrefuted. That simple minds, having been taught the obvious grounds of the truths inculcated on them, may trust to authority for the rest, and being aware that they have neither knowledge nor talent to resolve every difficulty which can be raised, may repose in the assurance that all those which have been raised have been or can be answered, by those who are specially trained to the task.

[20] Conceding to this view of the subject the utmost that can be claimed for it by those most easily satisfied with the amount of understanding of truth which ought to accompany the belief of it; even so, the argument for free discussion is no way weakened. For even this doctrine acknowledges that mankind ought to have a rational assurance that all objections have been satisfactorily answered; and how are they to be answered if that which requires to be answered is not spoken? or how can the answer be known to be satisfactory, if the objectors have no opportunity of showing that it is unsatisfactory? If not the public, at least the philosophers and theologians who are to resolve the difficulties, must make themselves familiar with those difficulties in their most puzzling form; and this cannot be accomplished unless they are freely stated, and placed in the most advantageous light which they admit of. The Catholic Church has its own way of dealing with this embarrassing problem. It makes a broad separation between those who can be permitted to receive its doctrines on conviction, and those who must accept them on trust. Neither, indeed, are allowed any choice as to what they will accept; but the clergy, such at least as can be fully confided in, may admissibly and meritoriously make themselves acquainted with the arguments of opponents, in order to answer them, and may, therefore, read heretical books; the laity, not unless by special permission, hard to be obtained. This discipline recognises a knowledge of the enemy's case as beneficial to the teachers, but finds means, consistent with this, of denying it to the rest of the world: thus giving to the *élite* more mental culture, though not more mental freedom, than it allows to the mass. By this device it succeeds in obtaining the kind of mental superiority which its purposes require; for though culture without freedom never made a large and liberal mind, it can make a clever *nisi prius* advocate of a cause. But in countries professing Protestantism, this resource is denied; since Protestants hold, at least in theory, that the responsibility for the choice of a religion must be

borne by each for himself, and cannot be thrown off upon teachers. Besides, in the present state of the world, it is practically impossible that writings which are read by the instructed can be kept from the uninstructed. If the teachers of mankind are to be cognizant of all that they ought to know, everything must be free to be written and published without restraint.

[21] If, however, the mischievous operation of the absence of free discussion, when the received opinions are true, were confined to leaving men ignorant of the grounds of those opinions, it might be thought that this, if an intellectual, is no moral evil, and does not affect the worth of the opinions, regarded in their influence on the character. The fact, however, is, that not only the grounds of the opinion are forgotten in the absence of discussion, but too often the meaning of the opinion itself. The words which convey it cease to suggest ideas, or suggest only a small portion of those they were originally employed to communicate. Instead of a vivid conception and a living belief, there remain only a few phrases retained by rote; or, if any part, the shell and husk only of the meaning is retained, the finer essence being lost. The great chapter in human history which this fact occupies and fills, cannot be too earnestly studied and meditated on.

[22] It is illustrated in the experience of almost all ethical doctrines and religious creeds. They are all full of meaning and vitality to those who originate them, and to the direct disciples of the originators. Their meaning continues to be felt in undiminished strength, and is perhaps brought out into even fuller consciousness, so long as the struggle lasts to give the doctrine or creed an ascendancy over other creeds. At last it either prevails, and becomes the general opinion, or its progress stops; it keeps possession of the ground it has gained, but ceases to spread further. When either of these results has become apparent, controversy on the subject flags, and gradually dies away. The doctrine has taken its place, if not as a received opinion, as one of the admitted sects or divisions of opinion: those who hold it have generally inherited, not adopted it; and conversion from one of these doctrines to another, being now an exceptional fact, occupies little place in the thoughts of their professors. Instead of being, as at first, constantly on the alert either to defend themselves against the world, or to bring the world over to them, they have subsided into acquiescence, and neither listen, when they can help it, to arguments against their creed, nor trouble dissentients (if there be such) with arguments in its favour. From this time may usually be dated the decline in the living power of the doctrine. We often hear the teachers of all creeds lamenting the difficulty of keeping up in the minds of believers a lively apprehension of the truth which they nominally recognise, so that it may penetrate the feelings, and acquire a real mastery over the conduct. No such difficulty is complained of while the creed is still fighting for its existence: even the weaker combatants then know and feel what they are fighting for, and the difference between it and other doctrines; and in that period of every creed's existence, not a

few persons may be found, who have realised its fundamental principles in all the forms of thought, have weighed and considered them in all their important bearings, and have experienced the full effect on the character which belief in that creed ought to produce in a mind thoroughly imbued with it. But when it has come to be an hereditary creed, and to be received passively, not actively—when the mind is no longer compelled, in the same degree as at first, to exercise its vital powers on the questions which its belief presents to it, there is a progressive tendency to forget all of the belief except the formularies, or to give it a dull and torpid assent, as if accepting it on trust dispensed with the necessity of realising it in consciousness, or testing it by personal experience, until it almost ceases to connect itself at all with the inner life of the human being. Then are seen the cases, so frequent in this age of the world as almost to form the majority, in which the creed remains as it were outside the mind, incrusting and petrifying it against all other influences addressed to the higher parts of our nature; manifesting its power by not suffering any fresh and living conviction to get in, but itself doing nothing for the mind or heart except standing sentinel over them to keep them vacant.

[23] To what an extent doctrines intrinsically fitted to make the deepest impression upon the mind may remain in it as dead beliefs, without being ever realized in the imagination, the feelings, or the understanding, is exemplified by the manner in which the majority of believers hold the doctrines of Christianity. By Christianity I here mean what is accounted such by all churches and sects—the maxims and precepts contained in the New Testament. These are considered sacred, and accepted as laws, by all professing Christians. Yet it is scarcely too much to say that no one Christian in a thousand guides or tests his individual conduct by reference to those laws. The standard to which he does refer it, is the custom of his nation, his class, or his religious profession. He has thus, on the one hand, a collection of ethical maxims, which he believes to have been vouchsafed to him by infallible wisdom as rules for his government; and on the other, a set of everyday judgments and practices, which go a certain length with some of those maxims, not so great a length with others, stand in direct opposition to some, and are, on the whole, a compromise between the Christian creed and the interests and suggestions of worldly life. To the first of these standards he gives his homage; to the other his real allegiance. All Christians believe that the blessed are the poor and humble, and those who are ill-used by the world; that it is easier for a camel to pass through the eye of a needle than for a rich man to enter the kingdom of heaven; that they should judge not, lest they be judged; that they should swear not at all; that they should love their neighbor as themselves; that if one take their cloak, they should give him their coat also; that they should take no thought for the morrow; that if they would be perfect, they should sell all that they have and give it to the poor. They are not insincere when they say that they believe these things. They do believe them, as people believe what they have always heard lauded

and never discussed. But in the sense of that living belief which regulates conduct, they believe these doctrines just up to the point to which it is usual to act upon them. The doctrines in their integrity are serviceable to pelt adversaries with; and it is understood that they are to be put forward (when possible) as the reasons for whatever people do that they think laudable. But any one who reminded them that the maxims require an infinity of things which they never even think of doing, would gain nothing but to be classed among those very unpopular characters who affect to be better than other people. The doctrines have no hold on ordinary believers—are not a power in their minds. They have an habitual respect for the sound of them, but no feeling which spreads from the words to the things signified, and forces the mind to take *them* in, and make them conform to the formula. Whenever conduct is concerned, they look round for Mr. A and B to direct them how far to go in obeying Christ. . . .

[24] It still remains to speak of one of the principal causes which make diversity of opinion advantageous, and will continue to do so until mankind shall have entered a stage of intellectual advancement which at present seems at an incalculable distance. We have hitherto considered only two possibilities: that the received opinion may be false, and some other opinion, consequently, true; or that, the received opinion being true, a conflict with the opposite error is essential to a clear apprehension and deep feeling of its truth. But there is a commoner case than either of these; when the conflicting doctrines, instead of being one true and the other false, share the truth between them; and the nonconforming opinion is needed to supply the remainder of the truth, of which the received doctrine embodies only a part. Popular opinions, on subjects not palpable to sense, are often true, but seldom or never the whole truth. They are a part of the truth; sometimes a greater, sometimes a smaller part, but exaggerated, distorted, and disjointed from the truths by which they ought to be accompanied and limited. Heretical opinions, on the other hand, are generally some of these suppressed and neglected truths, bursting the bonds which kept them down, and either seeking reconciliation with the truth contained in the common opinion, or fronting it as enemies, and setting themselves up, with similar exclusiveness, as the whole truth. The latter case is hitherto the most frequent, as, in the human mind, one-sidedness has always been the rule, and many-sidedness the exception. Hence, even in revolutions of opinion, one part of the truth usually sets while another rises. Even progress, which ought to superadd, for the most part only substitutes, one partial and incomplete truth for another; improvement consisting chiefly in this, that the new fragment of truth is more wanted, more adapted to the needs of the time, than that which it displaces. Such being the partial character of prevailing opinions, even when resting on a true foundation, every opinion which embodies somewhat of the portion of truth which the common opinion omits, ought to be considered precious, with whatever amount of error and confusion

that truth may be blended. No sober judge of human affairs will feel bound to be indignant because those who force on our notice truths which we should otherwise have overlooked, overlook some of those which we see. Rather, he will think that so long as popular truth is one-sided, it is more desirable than otherwise that unpopular truth should have one-sided assertors too; such being usually the most energetic, and the most likely to compel reluctant attention to the fragment of wisdom which they proclaim as if it were the whole.

[25] Thus, in the eighteenth century, when nearly all the instructed, and all those of the uninstructed who were led by them, were lost in admiration of what is called civilisation, and of the marvels of modern science, literature, and philosophy, and while greatly overrating the amount of unlikeness between the men of modern and those of ancient times, indulged the belief that the whole of the difference was in their own favour; with what a salutary shock did the paradoxes of Rousseau explode like bombshells in the midst, dislocating the compact mass of one-sided opinion, and forcing its elements to recombine in a better form and with additional ingredients. Not that the current opinions were on the whole farther from the truth than Rousseau's were; on the contrary, they were nearer to it; they contained more of positive truth, and very much less of error. Nevertheless there lay in Rousseau's doctrine, and has floated down the stream of opinion along with it, a considerable amount of exactly those truths which the popular opinion wanted; and these are the deposit which was left behind when the flood subsided. The superior worth of simplicity of life, the enervating and demoralising effect of the trammels and hypocrisies of artificial society, are ideas which have never been entirely absent from cultivated minds since Rousseau wrote; and they will in time produce their due effect, though at present needing to be asserted as much as ever, and to be asserted by deeds, for words, on this subject, have nearly exhausted their power.

[26] In politics, again, it is almost a commonplace, that a party of order or stability, and a party of progress or reform, are both necessary elements of a healthy state of political life; until the one or the other shall have so enlarged its mental grasp as to be a party equally of order and of progress, knowing and distinguishing what is fit to be preserved from what ought to be swept away. Each of these modes of thinking derives its utility from the deficiencies of the other; but it is in a great measure the opposition of the other that keeps each within the limits of reason and sanity. Unless opinions favourable to democracy and to aristocracy, to property and to equality, to co-operation and to competition, to luxury and to abstinence, to sociality and individuality, to liberty and discipline, and all the other standing antagonisms of practical life, are expressed with equal freedom, and enforced and defended with equal talent and energy, there is no chance of both elements obtaining their due; one scale is sure to go up, and the other down. Truth, in the great practical concerns of life, is so much a question of the reconciling and combining of opposites, that very few have minds

sufficiently capacious and impartial to make the adjustment with an approach to correctness, and it has to be made by the rough process of a struggle between combatants fighting under hostile banners. On any of the great open questions just enumerated, if either of the two opinions has a better claim than the other, not merely to be tolerated, but to be encouraged and countenanced, it is the one which happens at the particular time and place to be in a minority. That is the opinion which, for the time being, represents the neglected interests, the side of human well-being which is in danger of obtaining less than its share. I am aware that there is not, in this country, any intolerance of differences of opinion on most of these topics. They are adduced to show, by admitted and multiplied examples, the universality of the fact, that only through diversity of opinion is there, in the existing state of human intellect, a chance of fair play to all sides of the truth. When there are persons to be found who form an exception to the apparent unanimity of the world on any subject, even if the world is in the right, it is always probable that dissentients have something worth hearing to say for themselves, and that truth would lose something by their silence.

[27] It may be objected, "But *some* received principles, especially on the highest and most vital subjects, are more than half-truths. The Christian morality, for instance, is the whole truth on that subject, and if any one teaches a morality which varies from it, he is wholly in error." As this is of all cases the most important in practice, none can be fitter to test the general maxim. But before pronouncing what Christian morality is or is not, it would be desirable to decide what is meant by Christian morality. If it means the morality of the New Testament, I wonder that any one who derives his knowledge of this from the book itself, can suppose that it was announced, or intended, as a complete doctrine of morals. The Gospel always refers to a pre-existing morality, and confines its precepts to the particulars in which that morality was to be corrected, or superseded by a wider and higher; expressing itself, moreover, in terms most general, often impossible to be interpreted literally, and possessing rather the impressiveness of poetry or eloquence than the precision of legislation. To extract from it a body of ethical doctrine, has never been possible without eking it out from the Old Testament, that is, from a system elaborate indeed, but in many respects barbarous, and intended only for a barbarous people. St. Paul, a declared enemy to this Judaical mode of interpreting the doctrine and filling up the scheme of his Master, equally assumes a pre-existing morality, namely that of the Greeks and Romans; and his advice to Christians is in a great measure a system of accommodation to that; even to the extent of giving an apparent sanction to slavery. What is called Christian, but should rather be termed theological, morality, was not the work of Christ or the Apostles, but is of much later origin, having been gradually built up by the Catholic Church of the first five centuries, and though not implicitly adopted by moderns and Protestants, has been much less modified

by them than might have been expected. For the most part, indeed, they have contented themselves with cutting off the additions which had been made to it in the Middle Ages, each sect supplying the place by fresh additions, adapted to its own character and tendencies. That mankind owe a great debt to this morality, and to its early teachers, I should be the last person to deny; but I do not scruple to say of it that it is, in many important points, incomplete and one-sided, and that unless ideas and feelings, not sanctioned by it, had contributed to the formation of European life and character, human affairs would have been in a worse condition than they now are. Christian morality (so called) has all the characters of a reaction; it is, in great part, a protest against Paganism. Its ideal is negative rather than positive; passive rather than active; Innocence rather than Nobleness; Abstinence from Evil, rather than energetic Pursuit of Good; in its precepts (as has been well said) "thou shalt not" predominates unduly over "thou shalt." In its horror of sensuality, it made an idol of asceticim, which has been gradually compromised away into one of legality. It holds out the hope of heaven and the threat of hell, as the appointed and appropriate motives to a virtuous life: in this falling far below the best of the ancients, and doing what lies in it to give to human morality an essentially selfish character, by disconnecting each man's feelings of duty from the interests of his fellow-creatures, except so far as a self-interested inducement is offered to him for consulting them. It is essentially a doctrine of passive obedience; it inculcates submission to all authorities found established; who indeed are not to be actively obeyed when they command what religion forbids, but who are not to be resisted, far less rebelled against, for any amount of wrong to ourselves. And while, in the morality of the best Pagan nations, duty to the State holds even a disproportionate place, infringing on the just liberty of the individual; in purely Christian ethics, that grand department of duty is scarcely noticed or acknowledged. It is in the Koran, not the New Testament, that we read the maxim—"A ruler who appoints any man to an office, when there is in his dominions another man better qualified for it, sins against God and against the State." What little recognition the idea of obligation to the public obtains in modern morality is derived from Greek and Roman sources, not from Christian; as, even in the morality of private life, whatever exists of magnanimity, highmindedness, personal dignity, even the sense of honour, is derived from the purely human, not the religious part of our education, and never could have grown out of a standard of ethics in which the only worth, professedly recognised, is that of obedience.

[28] I am as far as any one from pretending that these defects are necessarily inherent in the Christian ethics in every manner in which it can be conceived, or that the many requisites of a complete moral doctrine which it does not contain do not admit of being reconciled with it. Far less would I insinuate this of the doctrines and precepts of Christ himself. I believe that the sayings of Christ are all that I can see any evidence of their having

no absolute truth

been intended to be; that they are irreconcilable with nothing which a comprehensive morality requires; that everything which is excellent in ethics may be brought within them, with no greater violence to their language than has been done to it by all who have attempted to deduce from them any practical system of conduct whatever. But it is quite consistent with this to believe that they contain, and were meant to contain, only a part of the truth; that many essential elements of the highest morality are among the things which are not provided for, nor intended to be provided for, in the recorded deliverances of the Founder of Christianity, and which have been entirely thrown aside in the system of ethics erected on the basis of those deliverances by the Christian Church. And this being so, I think it a great error to persist in attempting to find in the Christian doctrine that complete rule for our guidance which its author intended it to sanction and enforce, but only partially to provide. I believe, too, that this narrow theory is becoming a grave practical evil, detracting greatly from the moral training and instruction which so many well-meaning persons are now at length exerting themselves to promote. I much fear that by attempting to form the mind and feelings on an exclusively religious type, and discarding those secular standards (as for want of a better name they may be called) which heretofore coexisted with and supplemented the Christian ethics, receiving some of its spirit, and infusing into it some of theirs, there will result, and is even now resulting, a low, abject, servile type of character, which, submit itself as it may to what it deems the Supreme Will, is incapable of rising to or sympathising in the conception of Supreme Goodness. I believe that other ethics than any which can be evolved from exclusively Christian sources, must exist side by side with Christian ethics to produce the moral regeneration of mankind; and that the Christian system is no exception to the rule, that in an imperfect state of the human mind the interests of truth require a diversity of opinions. It is not necessary that in ceasing to ignore the moral truths not contained in Christianity men should ignore any of those which it does contain. Such prejudice, or oversight, when it occurs, is altogether an evil; but it is one from which we cannot hope to be always exempt, and must be regarded as the price paid for an inestimable good. The exclusive pretension made by a part of the truth to be the whole, must and ought to be protested against; and if a reactionary impulse should make the protestors unjust in their turn, this one-sidedness, like the other, may be lamented, but must be tolerated. If Christians would teach infidels to be just to Christianity, they should themselves be just to infidelity. It can do truth no service to blink the fact, known to all who have the most ordinary acquaintance with literary history, that a large portion of the noblest and most valuable moral teaching has been the work, not only of men who did not know, but of men who knew and rejected, the Christian faith.

[29] I do not pretend that the most unlimited use of the freedom of enunciating all possible opinions would put an end to the evils of religious or

philosophical sectarianism. Every truth which men of narrow capacity are in earnest about, is sure to be asserted, inculcated, and in many ways even acted on, as if no other truth existed in the world, or at all events none that could limit or qualify the first. I acknowledge that the tendency of all opinions to become sectarian is not cured by the freest discussion, but is often heightened and exacerbated thereby; the truth which ought to have been, but was not, seen, being rejected all the more violently because proclaimed by persons regarded as opponents. But it is not on the impassioned partisan, it is on the calmer and more disinterested bystander, that this collision of opinions works its salutary effect. Not the violent conflict between parts of the truth, but the quiet suppression of half of it, is the formidable evil; there is always hope when people are forced to listen to both sides; it is when they attend only to one that errors harden into prejudices, and truth itself ceases to have the effect of truth, by being exaggerated into falsehood. And since there are few mental attributes more rare than that judicial faculty which can sit in intelligent judgment between two sides of a question, of which only one is represented by an advocate before it, truth has no chance but in proportion as every side of it, every opinion which embodies any fraction of the truth, not only finds advocates, but is so advocated as to be listened to.

[30] We have now recognised the necessity to the mental well-being of mankind (on which all their other well-being depends) of freedom of opinion, and freedom of the expression of opinion, on four distinct grounds; which we will now briefly recapitulate.

[31] First, if any opinion is compelled to silence, that opinion may, for aught we can certainly know, be true. To deny this is to assume our own infallibility.

[32] Secondly, though the silenced opinion be an error, it may, and very commonly does, contain a portion of truth; and since the general or prevailing opinion on any subject is rarely or never the whole truth, it is only by the collision of adverse opinions that the remainder of the truth has any chance of being supplied.

[33] Thirdly, even if the received opinion be not only true, but the whole truth; unless it is suffered to be, and actually is, vigorously and earnestly contested, it will, by most of those who receive it, be held in the manner of a prejudice, with little comprehension or feeling of its rational grounds. And not only this, but, fourthly, the meaning of the doctrine itself will be in danger of being lost, or enfeebled, and deprived of its vital effect on the character and conduct: the dogma becoming a mere formal profession, inefficacious for good, but cumbering the ground, and preventing the growth of any real and heartfelt conviction, from reason or personal experience. . . .

COMMENT AND QUESTIONS

In the first paragraph, which should be read very carefully, Mill limits the subject, states his point of view, and indicates the main divisions of the essay. Then he proceeds to support his opinion by presenting arguments in favor of it and by anticipating and refuting objections which might be raised. In the last paragraphs of this selection he summarizes his case.

I. The following rough outline was written by an able student. Not intended to be a model outline, it illustrates the kind of notes an intelligent reader may take as an aid to understanding the development and main ideas of a complex piece of writing. Such notes are of value, too, when one wishes to review material previously read. The outline is printed here to illustrate one type of note-taking, and to give a general view of the content of the essay. As you read it, recall the detailed development of each point, and read again parts of the essay that you remember only vaguely.

Evil of silencing opinion is that it robs the human race. If opinion is right, people are deprived of opportunity of exchanging error for truth. If opinion is wrong, they lose the clearer perception of truth produced by collision with error.

I. Opinion to be suppressed may be true.
   A. People who want to suppress it say it is false, but people and ages are not infallible.
   B. Man is capable of rectifying his mistakes only through experience and discussion.
      1. Beliefs can be relied on only when there has been a standing invitation to prove them wrong.
      2. Even RC church has devil's advocate.
      3. The lists must be kept open, to give a chance of receiving a better truth.
   C. Poor argument that "useful" beliefs should be protected.
      1. Usefulness of an opinion is itself a matter of opinion.
      2. Truth of an opinion is part of its utility.
   D. Illustrations of mischief of denying a hearing to opinions because we condemn them. When the opinion is called impious or immoral, men of one generation most often make dreadful mistakes which horrify posterity.
      1. Socrates—impiety and immorality.
      2. Jesus—blasphemy.
      3. Christianity itself—dissolution of society.
   E. Idea that truth triumphs over persecution is false. It can be put down. Truth has only this advantage—in the course of ages it will generally be rediscovered in more favorable circumstances.
II. Opinion to be suppressed may not be true; but consider how beliefs are held if discussion on them is not allowed.
   A. If not fearlessly discussed, a belief becomes a dead dogma.
   B. Blind belief, proof against argument, is prejudice, superstition; this is not the way truth should be held by a rational being.

C. He who knows only his side of the case knows little of that. One really knows a doctrine by knowing the arguments against it.
D. Not knowing grounds of opinion is a moral evil as well as an intellectual one: in the absence of discussion, not only the grounds of the belief but the meaning of it is forgotten. New creeds have meaning in the lives and characters of members; later, when hereditary and passively accepted, the belief is outside the mind, encrusting it against other perhaps more vital influences. Doctrines of Christianity used as an example here.

III. Conflicting doctrines often share the truth between them.
A. We should consider precious, dissenting doctrines which contain some portion of the truth.
B. Since popular truth is one-sided, unpopular truth should have one-sided assertors too.
C. Rousseau in 18th century emphasized a neglected side of truth.
D. Minority opinion needs to be heard; it represents neglected interests.
E. Argument that Christian morality is not the whole truth of morality.
  1. What is it?
    a. New Testament refers to pre-existent morality of Old Testament, in many respects barbarous.
    b. St. Paul assumes pre-existing morality of Greece and Rome (slavery).
    c. Morality actually built up by Catholic Church in first five centuries.
  2. Christian morality is negative, passive, obedient, selfish—not social.
  3. Sayings of Christ contain and were meant to contain only part of truth.
  4. Ethics derived from other sources must exist with Christian ethics for moral regeneration of mankind.
F. There is always hope when people are forced to listen to both sides; when they hear only one, error hardens into prejudice and truth is exaggerated into falsehood.

IV. Conclusion.
A. Opinion compelled to silence may be true. To deny this is to assume infallibility.
B. Though silenced opinion be error, it may contain a portion of the truth.
C. Even if popular opinion is true, without discussion it will be held as prejudice, with no comprehension of rational grounds.
D. The meaning of the uncontested doctrine will be lost or enfeebled, deprived of any vital effect on character or conduct.

II. In the last sentence of paragraph 4, Mill speaks of opinions once generally accepted and now thought false. What examples of such opinions can you give from your knowledge of history, science, and the like?

III. How is Mill's discussion of the canonization of a saint (paragraph 8) relevant to his argument?

IV. What distinction does Mill make between feeling sure of a doctrine and assuming infallibility? What is his attitude toward each?

V. What fact is Mill attempting to establish in his discussion of Socrates (paragraph 12) and of Jesus (paragraph 13)? Has Mill chosen effective examples to prove his point? Explain. Comment on the last sentence in paragraph 13.

VI. What further or different fact is he illustrating in his discussion (paragraph 14) of Marcus Aurelius? Has he shown skill in choosing an example? See the last sentence of the paragraph and comment on it as a specimen of argument. Can you reduce this sentence to a syllogism?

VII. In paragraph 15, how does Mill prove that truth does not always triumph over persecution? How does he explain the survival of persecuted truth?

VIII. In paragraph 16, what does Mill mean by "received opinions"? What are examples of received opinions in our own society?

IX. In paragraphs 22–23, Mill discusses the "decline in the living power of [an uncontested] doctrine." Just what does he mean? What example does he give? Can you suggest other examples?

X. In paragraph 25, Mill speaks favorably of Rousseau. Why? And how is Rousseau related to Mill's main argument?

XI. What, according to Mill (paragraph 26), is the value of the two-party system of government?

XII. What views about Christian morality does Mill express in paragraphs 27–28? See the "Sermon on the Mount," page 935. Do you find evidence that Mill has been unfair in his comment? Explain.

XIII. What is the major premise for Mill's whole argument? (See Mill's summary, paragraphs 30–33.) Depending on how you phrase it, you may find one major premise, or more than one.

XIV. To what extent do you agree with Mill's argument in favor of complete freedom of thought and expression? If you disagree with, or have reservations about, any parts of Mill's position, exactly where do you disagree, and how would you justify the position you hold?

RALPH WALDO EMERSON

Self-Reliance

The following essay is an assertion of the importance of the individual and a plea for independent, non-conformist thought and action. Many students will find its statements extreme, its advice almost impossible to put into practice in complex present-day society. The good reader, however, will bear in mind the historical context of the essay (the United States in 1840), and also, realizing that the colorful, dramatic overstatement is a technique of emphasis, will look through the sometimes-extravagant expression to the solid core of what the author has to say to any generation. Ralph Waldo Emerson (1803–1882) was an American essayist and poet, and a leader in the Transcendentalist movement of the nineteenth century. "Self-Reliance" was published in *Essays* in 1841.

[1] I read the other day some verses written by an eminent painter which were original and not conventional. The soul always hears an admonition in such lines, let the subject be what it may. The sentiment they instil is of more value than any thought they may contain. To believe your own thought, to believe that what is true for you in your private heart is true for all men,—that is genius. Speak your latent conviction, and it shall be the universal sense; for the inmost in due time becomes the outmost,—and our first thought is rendered back to us by the trumpets of the Last Judgment. Familiar as the voice of the mind is to each, the highest merit we ascribe to Moses, Plato, and Milton is, that they set at naught books and traditions, and spoke not what men, but what *they* thought. A man should learn to detect and watch that gleam of light which flashes across his mind from within, more than the lustre of the firmament of bards and sages. Yet he dismisses without notice his thought, because it is his. In every work of genius we recognize our own rejected thoughts: they come back to us with a certain alienated majesty. Great works of art have no more affecting lesson for us than this. They teach us to abide by our spontaneous impression with good-humored inflexibility then most when the whole cry of voices is on the other side. Else to-morrow a stranger will say with masterly good sense precisely what we have thought and felt all the time, and we shall be forced to take with shame our own opinion from another.

[2] There is a time in every man's education when he arrives at the conviction that envy is ignorance; that imitation is suicide; that he must take himself for better, for worse, as his portion; that though the wide universe is full of good, no kernel of nourishing corn can come to him but through his toil bestowed on that plot of ground which is given to him to till. The power which resides in him is new in nature, and none but he knows what that is which he can do, nor does he know until he has tried. Not for nothing one face, one character, one fact, makes much impression on him, and another none. This sculpture in the memory is not without pre-established harmony. The eye was placed where one ray should fall, that it might testify of that particular ray. We but half express ourselves, and are ashamed of that divine idea which each of us represents. It may be safely trusted as proportionate and of good issues, so it be faithfully imparted, but God will not have his work made manifest by cowards. A man is relieved and gay when he has put his heart into his work and done his best; but what he has said or done otherwise, shall give him no peace. It is a deliverance which does not deliver. In the attempt his genius deserts him; no muse befriends; no invention, no hope.

[3] Trust thyself; every heart vibrates to that iron string. Accept the place the divine providence has found for you, the society of your contemporaries, the connection of events. Great men have always done so, and confided themselves childlike to the genius of their age, betraying their perception that the absolutely trustworthy was seated at their heart, working through their hands, predominating in all their being. And we are now men, and

must accept in the highest mind the same transcendent destiny; and not minors and invalids in a protected corner, not cowards fleeing before a revolution, but guides, redeemers, and benefactors, obeying the Almighty effort, and advancing on Chaos and the Dark.

[4] What pretty oracles nature yields us on this text, in the face and behavior of children, babes, and even brutes! That divided and rebel mind, that distrust of a sentiment because our arithmetic has computed the strength and means opposed to our purpose, these have not. Their mind being whole, their eye is as yet unconquered, and when we look in their faces, we are disconcerted. Infancy conforms to nobody: all conform to it, so that one babe commonly makes four or five out of the adults who prattle and play to it. So God has armed youth and puberty and manhood no less with its own piquancy and charm, and made it enviable and gracious and its claims not to be put by, if it will stand by itself. Do not think the youth has no force, because he cannot speak to you and me. Hark! in the next room his voice is sufficiently clear and emphatic. It seems he knows how to speak to his contemporaries. Bashful or bold, then, he will know how to make us seniors very unnecessary.

[5] The nonchalance of boys who are sure of a dinner, and would disdain as much as a lord to do or say aught to conciliate one, is the healthy attitude of human nature. A boy is in the parlor what the pit is in the playhouse; independent, irresponsible, looking out from his corner on such people and facts as pass by, he tries and sentences them on their merits, in the swift, summary way of boys, as good, bad, interesting, silly, eloquent, troublesome. He cumbers himself never about consequences, about interests; he gives an independent, genuine verdict. You must court him: he does not court you. But the man is, as it were, clapped into jail by his consciousness. As soon as he has once acted or spoken with *éclat,* he is a committed person, watched by the sympathy or the hatred of hundreds, whose affections must now enter into his account. There is no Lethe for this. Ah, that he could pass again into his neutrality! Who can thus avoid all pledges, and having observed, observe again from the same unaffected, unbiassed, unbribable, unaffrighted innocence, must always be formidable. He would utter opinions on all passing affairs, which being seen to be not private, but necessary, would sink like darts into the ear of men, and put them in fear.

[6] These are the voices which we hear in solitude, but they grow faint and inaudible as we enter into the world. Society everywhere is in conspiracy against the manhood of every one of its members. Society is a joint-stock company, in which the members agree, for the better securing of his bread to each shareholder, to surrender the liberty and culture of the eater. The virtue in most request is conformity. Self-reliance is its aversion. It loves not realties and creators, but names and customs.

[7] Whoso would be a man must be a non-conformist. He who would gather immortal palms must not be hindered by the name of goodness, but must explore if it be goodness. Nothing is at last sacred but the integrity

of your own mind. Absolve you to yourself, and you shall have the suffrage of the world. I remember an answer which when quite young I was prompted to make to a valued adviser, who was wont to importune me with the dear old doctrines of the church. On my saying, "What have I to do with the sacredness of traditions, if I live wholly from within?" my friend suggested: "But these impulses may be from below, not from above." I replied: "They do not seem to me to be such; but if I am the Devil's child, I will live then from the Devil." No law can be sacred to me but that of my nature. Good and bad are but names very readily transferable to that or this; the only right is what is after my constitution, the only wrong what is against it. A man is to carry himself in the presence of all opposition, as if everything were titular and ephemeral but him. I am ashamed to think how easily we capitulate to badges and names, to large societies and dead institutions. Every decent and well-spoken individual affects and sways me more than is right. I ought to go upright and vital, and speak the rude truth in all ways. If malice and vanity wear the coat of philanthropy, shall that pass? If an angry bigot assumes this bountiful cause of Abolition, and comes to me with his last news from Barbadoes, why should I not say to him: "Go love thy infant; love thy wood-chopper: be good-natured and modest: have that grace; and never varnish your hard, uncharitable ambition with this incredible tenderness for black folk a thousand miles off. Thy love afar is spite at home." Rough and graceless would be such greeting, but truth is handsomer than the affectation of love. Your goodness must have some edge to it,—else it is none. The doctrine of hatred must be preached as the counteraction of the doctrine of love when that pules and whines. I shun father and mother and wife and brother, when my genius calls me. I would write on the lintels of the door-post, *Whim.* I hope it is somewhat better than whim at last, but we cannot spend the day in explanation. Expect me not to show cause why I seek or why I exclude company. Then, again, do not tell me, as a good man did to-day, of my obligation to put all poor men in good situations. Are they *my* poor? I tell thee, thou foolish philanthropist, that I grudge the dollar, the dime, the cent, I give to such men as do not belong to me and to whom I do not belong. There is a class of persons to whom by all spiritual affinity I am bought and sold; for them I will go to prison, if need be; but your miscellaneous popular charities; the education at college of fools; the building of meeting-houses to the vain end to which many now stand; alms to sots; and the thousand-fold Relief Societies; —though I confess with shame I sometimes succumb and give the dollar, it is a wicked dollar which by and by I shall have the manhood to withhold. . . .

[8] What I must do is all that concerns me, not what the people think. This rule, equally arduous in actual and in intellectual life, may serve for the whole distinction between greatness and meanness. It is the harder, because you will always find those who think they know what is your duty better than you know it. It is easy in the world to live after the world's

opinion; it is easy in solitude to live after our own; but the great man is he who in the midst of the crowd keeps with perfect sweetness the independence of solitude.

[9] The objection to conforming to usages that have become dead to you is, that it scatters your force. It loses your time and blurs the impression of your character. If you maintain a dead church, contribute to a dead Bible society, vote with a great party either for the government or against it, spread your table like base housekeepers,—under all these screens I have difficulty to detect the precise man you are. And, of course, so much force is withdrawn from your proper life. But do your work, and I shall know you. Do your work, and you shall reinforce yourself. A man must consider what a blind-man's-buff is this game of conformity. If I know your sect, I anticipate your argument. I hear a preacher announce for his text and topic the expediency of one of the institutions of his church. Do I not know beforehand that not possibly can he say a new and spontaneous word? Do I not know that, with all this ostentation of examining the grounds of the institution, he will do no such thing? Do I not know that he is pledged to himself not to look but at one side,—the permitted side, not as a man, but as a parish minister? He is a retained attorney, and these airs of the bench are the emptiest affectation. Well, most men have bound their eyes with one or another handkerchief, and attached themselves to some one of these communities of opinion. This conformity makes them not false in a few particulars, authors of a few lies, but false in all particulars. Their every truth is not quite true. Their two is not the real two, their four is not the real four; so that every word they say chagrins us, and we know not where to begin to set them right. Meantime nature is not slow to equip us in the prison-uniform of the party to which we adhere. We come to wear one cut of face and figure, and acquire by degrees the gentlest asinine expression. There is a mortifying experience in particular, which does not fail to wreak itself also in the general history; I mean "the foolish face of praise," the forced smile which we put on in company where we do not feel at ease in answer to conversation which does not interest us. The muscles, not spontaneously moved, but moved by a low usurping wilfulness, grow tight about the outline of the face with the most disagreeable sensation.

[10] For non-conformity the world whips you with its displeasure. And therefore a man must know how to estimate a sour face. The by-standers look askance on him in the public street or in the friend's parlor. If this aversion had its origin in contempt and resistance like his own, he might well go home with a sad countenance; but the sour faces of the multitude, like their sweet faces, have no deep cause, but are put on and off as the wind blows and a newspaper directs. Yet is the discontent of the multitude more formidable than that of the senate and the college. It is easy enough for a firm man who knows the world to brook the rage of the cultivated classes. Their rage is decorous and prudent, for they are timid as being very vulnerable themselves. But when to their feminine rage the indignation of

the people is added, when the ignorant and the poor are aroused, when the unintelligent brute force that lies at the bottom of society is made to growl and mow, it needs the habit of magnanimity and religion to treat it godlike as a trifle of no concernment.

[11] The other terror that scares us from self-trust is our consistency; a reverence for our past act or word, because the eyes of others have no other data for computing our orbit than our past acts, and we are loath to disappoint them.

[12] But why should you keep your head over your shoulder? Why drag about this corpse of your memory, lest you contradict somewhat you have stated in this or that public place? Suppose you should contradict yourself; what then? It seems to be a rule of wisdom never to rely on your memory alone, scarcely even in acts of pure memory, but to bring the past for judgment into the thousand-eyed present, and live ever in a new day. In your metaphysics you have denied personality to the Deity: yet when the devout motions of the soul come, yield to them heart and life, though they should clothe God with shape and color. Leave your theory, as Joseph his coat in the hand of the harlot, and flee.

[13] A foolish consistency is the hobgoblin of little minds, adored by little statesmen and philosophers and divines. With consistency a great soul has simply nothing to do. He may as well concern himself with his shadow on the wall. Speak what you think now in hard words and to-morrow speak what to-morrow thinks in hard words again, though it contradict everything you said to-day.—"Ah, so you shall be sure to be misunderstood?"—Is it so bad, then, to be misunderstood? Pythagoras was misunderstood, and Socrates, and Jesus, and Luther, and Copernicus, and Galileo, and Newton, and every pure and wise spirit that ever took flesh. To be great is to be misunderstood.

[14] I suppose no man can violate his nature. All the sallies of his will are rounded in by the law of his being, as the inequalities of Andes and Himmaleh are insignificant in the curve of the sphere. Nor does it matter how you gauge and try him. A character is like an acrostic or Alexandrian stanza;—read it forward, backward, or across, it still spells the same thing. In this pleasing, contrite wood-life which God allows me, let me record day by day my honest thought without prospect or retrospect, and, I cannot doubt, it will be found symmetrical, though I mean it not and see it not. My book should smell of pines and resound with the hum of insects. The swallow over my window should interweave that thread or straw he carries in his bill into my web also. We pass for what we are. Character teaches above our wills. Men imagine that they communicate their virtue or vice only by overt actions, and do not see that virtue or vice emit a breath every moment.

[15] There will be an agreement in whatever variety of actions, so they be each honest and natural in their hour. For of one will, the actions will be harmonious, however unlike they seem. These varieties are lost sight of at

a little distance, at a little height of thought. One tendency unites them all. The voyage of the best ship is a zigzag line of a hundred tacks. See the line from a sufficient distance, and it straightens itself to the average tendency. Your genuine action will explain itself, and will explain your other genuine actions. Your conformity explains nothing. Act singly, and what you have already done singly will justify you now. . . .

[16] I hope in these days we have heard the last of conformity and consistency. Let the words be gazetted and ridiculous henceforward. Instead of the gong for dinner, let us hear a whistle from the Spartan fife. Let us never bow and apologize more. A great man is coming to eat at my house. I do not wish to please him; I wish that he should wish to please me. I will stand here for humanity, and though I would make it kind, I would make it true. Let us affront and reprimand the smooth mediocrity and squalid contentment of the times, and hurl in the face of custom, and trade, and office, the fact which is the upshot of all history, that there is a great responsible Thinker and Actor working wherever a man works; that a true man belongs to no other time or place, but is the centre of things. Where he is, there is nature. He measures you, and all men, and all events. Ordinarily, everybody in society reminds us of somewhat else, or of some other person. Character, reality, reminds you of nothing else; it takes place of the whole creation. The man must be so much, that he must make all circumstances indifferent. Every true man is a cause, a country, and an age; requires infinite spaces and numbers and time fully to accomplish his design;—and posterity seems to follow his steps as a train of clients. A man Cæsar is born, and for ages after we have a Roman Empire. Christ is born, and millions of minds so grow and cleave to his genius, that he is confounded with virtue and the possible of man. An institution is the lengthened shadow of one man; as Monachism, of the Hermit Antony; the Reformation, of Luther; Quakerism, of Fox; Methodism, of Wesley; Abolition, of Clarkson. Scipio, Milton called "the height of Rome"; and all history resolves itself very easily into the biography of a few stout and earnest persons.

[17] Let a man then know his worth, and keep things under his feet. Let him not peep or steal, or skulk up and down with the air of a charity-boy, a bastard, or an interloper, in the world which exists for him. But the man in the street, finding no worth in himself which corresponds to the force which built a tower or sculptured a marble god, feels poor when he looks on these. To him a palace, a statue, or a costly book have an alien and forbidding air, much like a gay equipage, and seem to say like that, "Who are you sir?" Yet they all are his suitors for his notice, petitioners to his faculties that they will come out and take possession. The picture waits for my verdict: it is not to command me, but I am to settle its claims to praise. That popular fable of the sot who was picked up dead drunk in the street, carried to the duke's house, washed and dressed and laid in the duke's bed, and, on his waking, treated with all obsequious ceremony like the duke, and assured that he had been insane, owes its popularity to the fact, that it

symbolizes so well the state of man, who is in the world a sort of sot, but now and then wakes up, exercises his reason and finds himself a true prince.

[18] Our reading is mendicant and sycophantic. In history, our imagination plays us false. Kingdom and lordship, power and estate, are a gaudier vocabulary than private John and Edward in a small house and common day's work; but the things of life are the same to both; the sum total of both are the same. Why all this deference to Alfred, and Scanderbeg, and Gustavus? Suppose they were virtuous; did they wear out virtue? As great a stake depends on your private act to-day, as followed their public and renowned steps. When private men shall act with original views, the lustre will be transferred from the actions of kings to those of gentlemen. . . .

[19] The magnetism which all original action exerts is explained when we inquire the reason of self-trust. Who is the Trustee? What is the aboriginal Self, on which a universal reliance may be grounded? What is the nature and power of that science-baffling star, without parallax, without calculable elements, which shoots a ray of beauty even into trivial and impure actions, if the least mark of independence appear? The inquiry leads us to that source, at once the essence of genius, of virtue, and of life, which we call Spontaneity or Instinct. We denote this primary wisdom as Intuition, whilst all later teachings are tuitions. In that deep force, the last fact behind which analysis cannot go, all things find their common origin. For, the sense of being which in calm hours rises, we know not how, in the soul, is not diverse from things, from space, from light, from time, from man, but one with them, and proceeds obviously from the same source whence their life and being also proceed. We first share the life by which things exist, and afterwards see them as appearances in nature, and forget that we have shared their cause. Here is the fountain of action and of thought. Here are the lungs of that inspiration which giveth man wisdom, and which cannot be denied without impiety and atheism. We lie in the lap of immense intelligence, which makes us receivers of its truth and organs of its activity. When we discern justice, when we discern truth, we do nothing of ourselves, but allow a passage to its beams. If we ask whence this comes, if we seek to pry into the soul that causes, all philosophy is at fault. Its presence or its absence is all we can affirm. Every man discriminates between the voluntary acts of his mind, and his involuntary perceptions, and knows that to his involuntary perceptions a perfect faith is due. He may err in the expression of them, but he knows that these things are so, like day and night, not to be disputed. My wilful actions and acquisitions are but roving;—the idlest revery, the faintest native emotion, command my curiosity and respect. Thoughtless people contradict as readily the statements of perceptions as of opinions, or rather much more readily; for, they do not distinguish between perception and notion. They fancy that I choose to see this or that thing. But perception is not whimsical, it is fatal. If I see a trait, my children will see it after me, and in course of time, all mankind,—

although it may chance that no one has seen it before me. For my perception of it is as much a fact as the sun.

[20] The relations of the soul to the divine spirit are so pure, that it is profane to seek to interpose helps. It must be that when God speaketh he should communicate, not one thing, but all things; should fill the world with his voice; should scatter forth light, nature, time, souls, from the centre of the present thought; and new date and new create the whole. Whenever a mind is simple, and receives a divine wisdom, old things pass away,—means, teachers, texts, temples, fall; it lives now, and absorbs past and future into the present hour. All things are made sacred by relation to it,—one as much as another. All things are dissolved to their centre by their cause, and, in the universal miracle, petty and particular miracles disappear. If, therefore, a man claims to know and speak of God, and carries you backward to the phraseology of some old mouldered nation in another country, in another world, believe him not. Is the acorn better than the oak which is its fulness and completion? Is the parent better than the child into whom he has cast his ripened being? Whence, then, this worship of the past? The centuries are conspirators against the sanity and authority of the soul. Time and space are but physiological colors which the eye makes, but the soul is light; where it is, is day; where it was, is night; and history is an impertinence and an injury, if it be anything more than a cheerful apologue or parable of my being and becoming.

[21] Man is timid and apologetic; he is no longer upright; he dares not say, "I think," "I am," but quotes some saint or sage. He is ashamed before the blade of grass or the blowing rose. These roses under my window make no reference to former roses or to better ones; they are for what they are; they exist with God to-day. There is no time to them. There is simply the rose; it is perfect in every moment of its existence. Before a leaf-bud has burst, its whole life acts; in the full-blown flower there is no more; in the leafless root there is no less. Its nature is satisfied, and it satisfies nature, in all moments alike. But man postpones or remembers; he does not live in the present, but with reverted eye laments the past, or, heedless of the riches that surround him, stands on tiptoe to foresee the future. He cannot be happy and strong until he too lives with nature in the present, above time.

[22] This should be plain enough. Yet see what strong intellects dare not yet hear God himself, unless he speak the phraseology of I know not what David, or Jeremiah, or Paul. We shall not always set so great a price on a few texts, on a few lives. We are like children who repeat by rote the sentences of grandames and tutors, and, as they grow older, of the men of talents and character they chance to see,—painfully recollecting the exact words they spoke; afterwards, when they come into the point of view which those had who uttered these sayings, they understand them, and are willing to let the words go; for, at any time, they can use words as good when occasion comes. If we live truly, we shall see truly. It is as easy for the strong

man to be strong, as it is for the weak to be weak. When we have new perception, we shall gladly disburden the memory of its hoarded treasures as old rubbish. When a man lives with God, his voice shall be as sweet as the murmur of the brook and the rustle of the corn.

[23] And now at last the highest truth on this subject remains unsaid: probably cannot be said; for all that we say is the far-off remembering of the intuition. That thought, by what I can now nearest approach to say it, is this. When good is near you, when you have life in yourself, it is not by any known or accustomed way; you shall not discern the footprints of any other; you shall not see the face of man; you shall not hear any name; the way, the thought, the good, shall be wholly strange and new. It shall exclude example and experience. You take the way from man, not to man. All persons that ever existed are its forgotten ministers. Fear and hope are alike beneath it. There is somewhat low even in hope. In the hour of vision, there is nothing that can be called gratitude, nor properly joy. The soul raised over passion beholds identity and eternal causation, perceives the self-existence of Truth and Right, and calms itself with knowing that all things go well. Vast spaces of nature, the Atlantic Ocean, the South Sea,—long intervals of time, years, centuries,—are of no account. This which I think and feel underlay every former state of life and circumstances, as it does underlie my present, and what is called life, and what is called death.

[24] Life only avails, not the having lived. Power ceases in the instant of repose; it resides in the moment of transition from a past to a new state, in the shooting of the gulf, in the darting to an aim. This one fact the world hates, that the soul *becomes;* for that forever degrades the past, turns all riches to poverty, all reputation to a shame, confounds the saint with the rogue, shoves Jesus and Judas equally aside. Why, then, do we prate of self-reliance? Inasmuch as the soul is present, there will be power not confident but agent. To talk of reliance is a poor external way of speaking. Speak rather of that which relies, because it works and is. Who has more obedience than I masters me, though he should not raise his finger. Round him I must revolve by the gravitation of spirits. We fancy it rhetoric, when we speak of eminent virtue. We do not yet see that virtue is Height, and that a man or a company of men, plastic and permeable to principles, by the law of nature must overpower and ride all cities, nations, kings, rich men, poets, who are not.

[25] This is the ultimate fact which we so quickly reach on this, as on every topic, the resolution of all into the ever-blessed ONE. Self-existence is the attribute of the Supreme Cause, and it constitutes the measure of good by the degree in which it enters into all lower forms. All things real are so by so much virtue as they contain. Commerce, husbandry, hunting, whaling, war, eloquence, personal weight, are somewhat, and engage my respect as examples of its presence and impure action. I see the same law working in nature for conservation and growth. Power is in nature the essential measure of right. Nature suffers nothing to remain in her kingdoms which

cannot help itself. The genesis and maturation of a planet, its poise and orbit, the bended tree recovering itself from the strong wind, the vital resources of every animal and vegetable, are demonstrations of the self-sufficing, and, therefore, self-relying soul.

[26] Thus all concentrates; let us not rove; let us sit at home with the cause. Let us stun and astonish the intruding rabble of men and books and institutions, by a simple declaration of the divine fact. Bid the invaders take the shoes from off their feet, for God is here within. Let our simplicity judge them, and our docility to our own law demonstrate the poverty of nature and fortune beside our native riches. . . .

[27] The populace think that your rejection of popular standards is a rejection of all standard, and mere antinomianism; and the bold sensualist will use the name of philosophy to gild his crimes. But the law of consciousness abides. There are two confessionals, in one or the other of which we must be shriven. You may fulfil your round of duties by clearing yourself in the *direct,* or in the *reflex* way. Consider whether you have satisfied your relations to father, mother, cousin, neighbor, town, cat, and dog; whether any of these can upbraid you. But I may also neglect this reflex standard, and absolve me to myself. I have my own stern claims and perfect circle. It denies the name of duty to many offices that are called duties. But if I can discharge its debts, it enables me to dispense with the popular code. If any one imagines that this law is lax, let him keep its commandment one day.

[28] And truly it demands something godlike in him who has cast off the common motives of humanity, and has ventured to trust himself for a taskmaster. High be his heart, faithful his will, clear his sight, that he may in good earnest be doctrine, society, law, to himself, that a simple purpose may be to him as strong as iron necessity is to others!

[29] If any man consider the present aspects of what is called by distinction *society*, he will see the need of these ethics. The sinew and heart of man seem to be drawn out, and we are become timorous, desponding whimperers. We are afraid of truth, afraid of fortune, afraid of death, and afraid of each other. Our age yields no great and perfect persons. We want men and women who shall renovate life and our social state, but we see that most natures are insolvent, cannot satisfy their own wants, have an ambition out of all proportion to their practical force, and do lean and beg day and night continually. Our housekeeping is mendicant, our arts, our occupations, our marriages, our religion, we have not chosen, but society has chosen for us. We are parlor soldiers. We shun the rugged battle of fate, where strength is born.

[30] If our young men miscarry in their first enterprises, they lose all heart. If the young merchant fails, men say he is *ruined*. If the finest genius studies at one of our colleges, and is not installed in an office within one year afterwards in the cities or suburbs of Boston or New York, it seems to his friends and to himself that he is right in being disheartened, and in complaining the rest of his life. A sturdy lad from New Hampshire or Vermont, who in turn tries all the professions, who *teams it, farms it, peddles,* keeps a school,

preaches, edits a newspaper, goes to Congress, buys a township, and so forth, in successive years, and always, like a cat, falls on his feet, is worth a hundred of these city dolls. He walks abreast with his days, and feels no shame in not "studying a profession," for he does not postpone his life, but lives already. He has not one chance, but a hundred chances. Let a Stoic open the resources of man, and tell men they are not leaning willows, but can and must detach themselves; that with the exercise of self-trust, new powers shall appear; that a man is the word made flesh, born to shed healing to the nations, that he should be ashamed of our compassion, and that the moment he acts from himself, tossing the laws, the books, idolatries, and customs out of the window, we pity him no more, but thank and revere him,—and that teacher shall restore the life of man to splendor, and make his name dear to all history.

[31] It is easy to see that a greater self-reliance must work a revolution in all the offices and relations of men; in their religion; in their education; in their pursuits; their modes of living; their association; in their property; in their speculative views.

1. In what prayers do men allow themselves! That which they call a holy office is not so much as brave and manly. Prayer looks abroad and asks for some foreign addition to come through some foreign virtue, and loses itself in endless mazes of natural and supernatural, and mediatorial and miraculous. Prayer that craves a particular commodity,—anything less than all good,—is vicious. Prayer is the contemplation of the facts of life from the highest point of view. It is the soliloquy of a beholding and jubilant soul. It is the spirit of God pronouncing his works good. But prayer as a means to effect a private end is meanness and theft. It supposes dualism and not unity in nature and consciousness. As soon as the man is at one with God, he will not beg. He will then see prayer in all action. The prayer of the farmer kneeling in his field to weed it, the prayer of the rower kneeling with the stroke of his oar, are true prayers heard throughout nature, though for cheap ends. Caratach, in Fletcher's *Bonduca,* when admonished to inquire the mind of the god Audate, replies,—

> His hidden meaning lies in our endeavors;
> Our valors are our best gods.

[32] Another sort of false prayers are our regrets. Discontent is the want of self-reliance: it is infirmity of will. Regret calamities, if you can thereby help the sufferer: if not, attend your own work, and already the evil begins to be repaired. Our sympathy is just as base. We come to them who weep foolishly, and sit down and cry for company, instead of imparting to them truth and health in rough electric shocks, putting them once more in communication with their own reason. The secret of fortune is joy in our hands. Welcome evermore to gods and men is the self-helping man. For him all doors are flung wide: him all tongues greet, all honors crown, all eyes follow with desire. Our love goes out to him and embraces him, because he did not

need it. We solicitously and apologetically caress and celebrate him, because he held on his way and scorned our disapprobation. The gods love him because men hated him. "To the persevering mortal," said Zoroaster, "the blessed Immortals are swift."

[33] As men's prayers are a disease of the will, so are their creeds a disease of the intellect. They say with those foolish Israelites, "Let not God speak to us lest we die. Speak thou, speak any man with us, and we will obey." Everywhere I am hindered of meeting God in my brother, because he has shut his own temple doors, and recites fables merely of his brother's or his brother's brother's God. Every new mind is a new classification. If it prove a mind of uncommon activity and power, a Locke, a Lavoisier, a Hutton, a Bentham, a Fourier, it imposes its classification on other men, and lo! a new system. In proportion to the depth of the thought, and so to the number of the objects it touches and brings within reach of the pupil, is his complacency. But chiefly is this apparent in creeds and churches, which are also classifications of some powerful mind acting on the elemental thought of duty, and man's relation to the Highest. Such is Calvinism, Quakerism, Swedenborgism. The pupil takes the same delight in subordinating everything to the new terminology, as a girl who has just learned botany in seeing a new earth and new seasons thereby. It will happen for a time, that the pupil will find his intellectual power has grown by the study of his master's mind. But in all unbalanced minds, the classification is idolized, passes for the end, and not for a speedily exhaustible means, so that the walls of the system blend to their eye in the remote horizon with the walls of the universe; the luminaries of heaven seem to them hung on the arch their master built. They cannot imagine how you aliens have any right to see,—how you can see; "it must be somehow that you stole the light from us." They do not yet perceive, that light, unsystematic, indomitable, will break into any cabin, even into theirs. Let them chirp awhile and call it their own. If they are honest and do well, presently their neat new pinfold will be too strait and low, will crack, will lean, will rot and vanish, and the immortal light, all young and joyful, million-orbed, million-colored, will beam over the universe as on the first morning.

2. It is for want of self-reliance that the superstition of Travelling, whose idols are Italy, England, Egypt, retains its fascination for all educated Americans. They who made England, Italy, or Greece venerable in the imagination did so by sticking fast where they were, like an axis of the earth. In manly hours, we feel that duty is our place. The soul is no traveller; the wise man stays at home, and when his necessities, his duties, on any occasion, call him from his house, or into foreign lands, he is at home still, and shall make men sensible, by the expression of his countenance, that he goes the missionary of wisdom and virtue, and visits cities and men like a sovereign, and not like an interloper or a valet.

[34] I have no churlish objection to the circumnavigation of the globe, for the purposes of art, of study, and benevolence, so that the man is first

domesticated, or does not go abroad with the hope of finding somewhat greater than he knows. He who travels to be amused, or to get somewhat which he does not carry, travels away from himself, and grows old even in youth among old things. In Thebes, in Palmyra, his will and mind have become old and dilapidated as they. He carries ruins to ruins.

[35] Travelling is a fool's paradise. Our first journeys discover to us the indifference of places. At home I dream that at Naples, at Rome, I can be intoxicated with beauty, and lose my sadness. I pack my trunk, embrace my friends, embark on the sea, and at last wake up in Naples, and there beside me is the stern fact, the sad self, unrelenting, identical, that I fled from. I seek the Vatican, and the palaces. I affect to be intoxicated with sights and suggestions, but I am not intoxicated. My giant goes with me wherever I go.

3. But the rage of travelling is a symptom of a deeper unsoundness affecting the whole intellectual action. The intellect is vagabond, and our system of education fosters restlessness. Our minds travel when our bodies are forced to stay at home. We imitate; and what is imitation but the travelling of the mind? Our houses are built with foreign taste; our shelves are garnished with foreign ornaments; our opinions, our tastes, our faculties, lean, and follow the Past and the Distant. The soul created the arts wherever they have flourished. It was in his own mind that the artist sought his model. It was an application of his own thought to the thing to be done and the conditions to be observed. And why need we copy the Doric or the Gothic model? Beauty, convenience, grandeur of thought, and quaint expression are as near to us as to any, and if the American artist will study with hope and love the precise thing to be done by him, considering the climate, the soil, the length of the day, the wants of the people, the habit and form of the government, he will create a house in which all these will find themselves fitted, and taste and sentiment will be satisfied also.

[36] Insist on yourself; never imitate. Your own gift you can present every moment with the cumulative force of a whole life's cultivation; but of the adopted talent of another, you have only an extemporaneous, half possession. That which each can do best, none but his Maker can teach him. No man yet knows what it is, nor can, till that person has exhibited it. Where is the master who could have taught Shakespeare? Where is the master who could have instructed Franklin, or Washington, or Bacon, or Newton? Every great man is a unique. The Scipionism of Scipio is precisely that part he could not borrow. Shakespeare will never be made by the study of Shakespeare. Do that which is assigned you, and you cannot hope too much or dare too much. There is at this moment for you an utterance brave and grand as that of the colossal chisel of Phidias, or trowel of the Egyptians, or the pen of Moses, or Dante, but different from all these. Not possibly will the soul all rich, all eloquent, with thousand-cloven tongue, deign to repeat itself; but if you can hear what these patriarchs say, surely you can reply to them in the same pitch of voice; for the ear and the tongue are two organs

let others do thinking for us

of one nature. Abide in the simple and noble regions of thy life, obey thy heart, and thou shalt reproduce the Foreworld again.

4. As our Religion, our Education, our Art look abroad, so does our spirit of society. All men plume themselves on the improvement of society, and no man improves. . . .

[37] The civilized man has built a coach, but has lost the use of his feet. He is supported on crutches, but lacks so much support of muscle. He has a fine Geneva watch, but he fails of the skill to tell the hour by the sun. A Greenwich nautical almanac he has, and so being sure of the information when he wants it, the man in the street does not know a star in the sky. The solstice he does not observe, the equinox he knows as little; and the whole bright calendar of the year is without a dial in his mind. His note-books impair his memory; his libraries overload his wit; the insurance office increases the number of accidents; and it may be a question whether machinery does not encumber; whether we have not lost by refinement some energy, by a Christianity intrenched in establishments and forms, some vigor of wild virtue. For every Stoic was a Stoic; but in Christendom where is the Christian? . . .

[38] The reliance on Property, including the reliance on governments which protect it, is the want of self-reliance. Men have looked away from themselves and at things so long, that they have come to esteem the religious, learned, and civil institutions as guards of property, and they deprecate assaults on these, because they feel them to be assaults on property. They measure their esteem of each other by what each has, and not by what each is. But a cultivated man becomes ashamed of his property, out of new respect for his nature. Especially he hates what he has, if he see that it is accidental,—came to him by inheritance, or gift, or crime; then he feels that it is not having; it does not belong to him, has no root in him, and merely lies there, because no revolution or no robber takes it away. But that which a man is, does always by necessity acquire, and what the man acquires is living property, which does not wait the beck of rulers, or mobs, or revolutions, or fire, or storm, or bankruptcies, but perpetually renews itself wherever the man breathes. . . .

[39] Nothing can bring you peace but yourself. Nothing can bring you peace but the triumph of principles.

COMMENT AND QUESTIONS

In thinking about this essay, it may be helpful to know something of the philosophical and literary movement called transcendentalism, for which Emerson was an important spokesman. Not a systematic philosophy, transcendentalism was compounded of many elements, including Platonism, Hebraism and Christianity, and ideas from Eastern philosophies and religions. Its tenets and expression differed with different writers, but transcendentalists held in common two closely related beliefs: that knowledge transcends the senses ("We denote this primary wisdom as Intuition," Emerson says), and that an embracing divinity dwells in all things—in everything in nature and in the individual souls of men. Man could feel the indwelling God in the laws and beauty of nature, and he could fulfill his part in the divine unity by listening to and acting on the promptings of his individual soul which was one with the world-soul. Optimism, self-trust, and reliance on intuition rather than on outside authority and tradition were therefore natural corollaries of the transcendentalist philosophy. To it Emerson added his own boundless faith in the worth and potentiality of each individual, and in the individual genius of this country.

I. "Self-Reliance," like much of Emerson's writing, is loosely organized; we have cut the essay without injury to the continuity of ideas, and it would be possible in a number of places to rearrange the paragraphs without loss. Emerson's power lies not in the organization and structure of the whole essay, but in separate paragraphs, and chiefly in pithy, picturesque, hard-hitting individual sentences. Vivid concrete language, often figurative, accounts for much of the quality of his style. Analyze the writing in paragraphs 12-13, 21, 34-35, and 37, particularly for concrete language and techniques of emphasis. Point out other passages in the essay in which the phrasing is memorable.

II. Think about the following quotations from "Self-Reliance." Which ones seem to you wholly true or sound? Which ones partially true? With which ones can you not agree?

"In every work of genius we recognize our own rejected thoughts."

"We but half express ourselves, and are ashamed of the divine idea which each of us represents."

"Society everywhere is in conspiracy against the manhood of every one of its members."

"Whoso would be a man must be a non-conformist."

"What I must do is all that concerns me, not what the people think."

"A foolish consistency is the hobgoblin of little minds, adored by little statesmen and philosophers and divines."

"As men's prayers are a disease of the will, so are their creeds a disease of the intellect."

"Travelling is a fool's paradise."

"Insist on yourself; never imitate."

III. Emerson frequently acted with the independence and indifference to public opinion advocated in "Self-Reliance." At the same time, he was personally kind, gentle, courteous, sociable, generous and helpful to others. Do you see any evidence in the essay of such kindness and gentleness?

IV. A college student, after reading this essay, remarked that Emerson was recommending an easy, self-indulgent sort of life—just following your impulses and doing as you please. Emerson did not so regard the principles of self-reliance; he speaks of the "stern duties" imposed by being true to one's own nature, and says, "If any one imagines that this law is lax, let him keep its commandments one day." What would you do—precisely how would you act—if you followed the commandments of self-reliance for a day? Would it be easy?

V. If you have read Stuart Chase's "The Luxury of Integrity," compare the ideas of Emerson and Chase. To what extent are they saying the same thing, and in what ways do they differ?

HENRY DAVID THOREAU

From *Walden*

Henry David Thoreau (1817–1862) was a friend of Emerson, influenced by Emerson's doctrine of self-reliance and by the transcendentalist attitude toward nature.[1] Believing that "the mass of men lead lives of quiet desperation," that they are slaves to their property, and are distracted by superfluities and complexities and petty details from the real business of living, Thoreau went to live for two years (1845–1847) in the woods by Walden Pond, near Concord, Massachusetts. Here he hoped "so to love wisdom as to live according to its dictates, a life of simplicity, independence, magnanimity, and trust . . . to solve some of the problems of life, not only theoretically, but practically." The following selection from the book *Walden* gives some of Thoreau's philosophy and some of the experience of his sojourn in the woods.

[1] I was seated by the shore of a small pond, about a mile and a half south of the village of Concord and somewhat higher than it, in the midst of an extensive wood between that town and Lincoln, and about two miles south of that our only field known to fame, Concord Battle Ground; but I was so low in the woods that the opposite shore, half a mile off, like the rest, covered with wood, was my most distant horizon. For the first week, whenever I looked out on the pond it impressed me like a tarn high up on the side of a mountain, its bottom far above the surface of other lakes, and, as the sun arose, I saw it throwing off its nightly clothing of mist, and here and there, by degrees, its soft ripples or its smooth reflecting surface was revealed, while the mists, like ghosts, were stealthily withdrawing in every direction into the woods, as at the breaking up of some nocturnal con-

[1] See Emerson's "Self-Reliance," page 973, and the comment on transcendentalism, page 987f.

venticle. The very dew seemed to hang upon the trees later into the day than usual, as on the sides of mountains.

[2] This small lake was of most value as a neighbor in the intervals of a gentle rain-storm in August, when, both air and water being perfectly still, but the sky overcast, midafternoon had all the serenity of evening, and the wood thrush sang around, and was heard from shore to shore. A lake like this is never smoother than at such a time; and the clear portion of the air above it being shallow and darkened by clouds, the water, full of light and reflections, becomes a lower heaven itself so much the more important. From a hilltop near by, where the wood had been recently cut off, there was a pleasing vista southward across the pond, through a wide indentation in the hills which form the shore there, where their opposite sides sloping toward each other suggested a stream flowing out in that direction through a wooded valley, but stream there was none. That way I looked between and over the near green hills to some distant and higher ones in the horizon, tinged with blue. Indeed, by standing on tiptoe I could catch a glimpse of some of the peaks of the still bluer and more distant mountain ranges in the northwest, those true-blue coins from heaven's own mint, and also of some portion of the village. But in other directions, even from this point, I could not see over or beyond the woods which surrounded me. It is well to have some water in your neighborhood, to give buoyancy to and float the earth. One value even of the smallest well is, that when you look into it you see that earth is not continent but insular. This is as important as that it keeps butter cool. When I looked across the pond from this peak toward the Sudbury meadows, which in time of flood I distinguished elevated perhaps by a mirage in their seething valley, like a coin in a basin, all the earth beyond the pond appeared like a thin crust insulated and floated even by this small sheet of intervening water, and I was reminded that this on which I dwelt was but *dry land*.

[3] Though the view from my door was still more contracted, I did not feel crowded or confined in the least. There was pasture enough for my imagination. The low shrub oak plateau to which the opposite shore arose stretched away toward the prairies of the West and the steppes of Tartary, affording ample room for all the roving families of men. "There are none happy in the world but beings who enjoy freely a vast horizon,"—said Damodara, when his herds required new and larger pastures.

[4] Both place and time were changed, and I dwelt nearer to those parts of the universe and to those eras in history which had most attracted me. Where I lived was as far off as many a region viewed nightly by astronomers. We are wont to imagine rare and delectable places in some remote and more celestial corner of the system, behind the constellation of Cassiopeia's Chair, far from noise and disturbance. I discovered that my house actually had its site in such a withdrawn, but forever new and unprofaned, part of the universe. If it were worth the while to settle in those parts near to the Pleiades or the Hyades, to Aldebaran or Altair, then I was really there,

or at an equal remoteness from the life which I had left behind, dwindled and twinkling with as fine a ray to my nearest neighbor, and to be seen only in moonless nights by him. Such was that part of creation where I had squatted;—

> There was a shepherd that did live,
> And held his thoughts as high
> As were the mounts whereon his flocks
> Did hourly feed him by.

What should we think of the shepherd's life if his flocks always wandered to higher pastures than his thoughts?

[5] Every morning was a cheerful invitation to make my life of equal simplicity, and I may say innocence, with Nature herself. I have been as sincere a worshipper of Aurora as the Greeks. I got up early and bathed in the pond; that was a religious exercise, and one of the best things which I did. They say that characters were engraven on the bathing tub of King Tching-thang to this effect: "Renew thyself completely each day; do it again, and again, and forever again." I can understand that. Morning brings back the heroic ages. I was as much affected by the faint hum of a mosquito making its invisible and unimaginable tour through my apartment at earliest dawn, when I was sitting with door and windows open, as I could be by any trumpet that ever sang of fame. It was Homer's requiem; itself an Iliad and Odyssey in the air, singing its own wrath and wanderings. There was something cosmical about it; a standing advertisement, till forbidden, of the everlasting vigor and fertility of the world. The morning, which is the most memorable season of the day, is the awakening hour. Then there is least somnolence in us; and for an hour, at least, some part of us awakes which slumbers all the rest of the day and night. Little is to be expected of that day, if it can be called a day, to which we are not awakened by our Genius, but by the mechanical nudgings of some servitor, are not awakened by our own newly acquired force and aspirations from within, accompanied by the undulations of celestial music, instead of factory bells, and a fragrance filling the air—to a higher life than we fell asleep from; and thus the darkness bear its fruit, and prove itself to be good, no less than the light. That man who does not believe that each day contains an earlier, more sacred, and auroral hour than he has yet profaned, has despaired of life, and is pursuing a descending and darkening way. After a partial cessation of his sensuous life, the soul of man, or its organs rather, are reinvigorated each day, and his Genius tries again what noble life it can make. All memorable events, I should say, transpire in morning time and in a morning atmosphere. The Vedas say, "All intelligences awake with the morning." Poetry and art, and the fairest and most memorable of the actions of men, date from such an hour. All poets and heroes, like Memnon, are the children of Aurora, and emit their music at sunrise. To him whose elastic and vigorous thought keeps pace with the sun, the day is a perpetual morning.

It matters not what the clocks say or the attitudes and labors of men. Morning is when I am awake and there is a dawn in me. Moral reform is the effort to throw off sleep. Why is it that men give so poor an account of their day if they have not been slumbering? They are not such poor calculators. If they had not been overcome with drowsiness, they would have performed something. The millions are awake enough for physical labor; but only one in a million is awake enough for effective intellectual exertion, only one in a hundred millions to a poetic or divine life. To be awake is to be alive. I have never yet met a man who was quite awake. How could I have looked him in the face?

[6] We must learn to reawaken and keep ourselves awake, not by mechanical aids, but by an infinite expectation of the dawn, which does not forsake us in our soundest sleep. I know of no more encouraging fact than the unquestionable ability of man to elevate his life by a conscious endeavor. It is something to be able to paint a particular picture, or to carve a statue, and so to make a few objects beautiful; but it is far more glorious to carve and paint the very atmosphere and medium through which we look, which morally we can do. To affect the quality of the day, that is the highest of arts. Every man is tasked to make his life, even in its details, worthy of the contemplation of his most elevated and critical hour. If we refused, or rather used up, such paltry information as we get, the oracles would distinctly inform us how this might be done.

[7] I went to the woods because I wished to live deliberately, to front only the essential facts of life, and see if I could not learn what it had to teach, and not, when I came to die, discover that I had not lived. I did not wish to live what was not life, living is so dear; nor did I wish to practise resignation, unless it was quite necessary. I wanted to live deep and suck out all the marrow of life, to live so sturdily and Spartan-like as to put to rout all that was not life, to cut a broad swath and shave close, to drive life into a corner, and reduce it to its lowest terms, and, if it proved to be mean, why then to get the whole and genuine meanness of it, and publish its meanness to the world; or if it were sublime, to know it by experience, and be able to give a true account of it in my next excursion. For most men, it appears to me, are in a strange uncertainty about it, whether it is of the devil or of God, and have *somewhat hastily* concluded that it is the chief end of man here to "glorify God and enjoy him forever."

[8] Still we live meanly, like ants; though the fable tells us that we were long ago changed into men; like pygmies we fight with cranes; it is error upon error, and clout upon clout, and our best virtue has for its occasion a superfluous and evitable wretchedness. Our life is frittered away by detail. An honest man has hardly need to count more than his ten fingers, or in extreme cases he may add his ten toes, and lump the rest. Simplicity, simplicity, simplicity! I say, let your affairs be as two or three, and not a hundred or a thousand; instead of a million count half a dozen, and keep your accounts on your thumb-nail. In the midst of this chopping sea of civilized

life, such are the clouds and storms and quicksands and thousand-and-one items to be allowed for, that a man has to live, if he would not founder and go to the bottom and not make his port at all, by dead reckoning, and he must be a great calculator indeed who succeeds. Simplify, simplify. Instead of three meals a day, if it be necessary eat but one; instead of a hundred dishes, five; and reduce other things in proportion. Our life is like a German Confederacy, made up of petty states, with its boundary forever fluctuating, so that even a German cannot tell you how it is bounded at any moment. The nation itself, with all its so-called internal improvements, which, by the way, are all external and superficial, is just such an unwieldy and overgrown establishment, cluttered with furniture and tripped up by its own traps, ruined by luxury and heedless expense, by want of calculation and a worthy aim, as the million households in the land; and the only cure for it, as for them, is in a rigid economy, a stern and more than Spartan simplicity of life and elevation of purpose. It lives too fast. Men think that it is essential that the *Nation* have commerce, and export ice, and talk through a telegraph, and ride thirty miles an hour, without a doubt, whether *they* do or not; but whether we should live like baboons or like men, is a little uncertain. If we do not get out sleepers, and forge rails, and devote days and nights to the work, but go to tinkering upon our *lives* to improve *them,* who will build railroads? And if railroads are not built, how shall we get to Heaven in season? But if we stay at home and mind our business, who will want railroads? We do not ride on the railroad; it rides upon us. Did you ever think what those sleepers are that underlie the railroad? Each one is a man, an Irishman, or a Yankee man. The rails are laid on them, and they are covered with sand, and the cars run smoothly over them. They are sound sleepers, I assure you. And every few years a new lot is laid down and run over; so that, if some have the pleasure of riding on a rail, others have the misfortune to be ridden upon. And when they run over a man that is walking in his sleep, a supernumerary sleeper in the wrong position, and wake him up, they suddenly stop the cars, and make a hue and cry about it, as if this were an exception. I am glad to know that it takes a gang of men for every five miles to keep the sleepers down and level in their beds as it is, for this is a sign that they may sometime get up again.

[9] Why should we live with such hurry and waste of life? We are determined to be starved before we are hungry. Men say that a stitch in time saves nine, and so they take a thousand stitches to-day to save nine tomorrow. As for *work,* we haven't any of any consequence. We have the Saint Vitus' dance, and cannot possibly keep our heads still. If I should only give a few pulls at the parish bell-rope, as for a fire, that is, without setting the bell, there is hardly a man on his farm in the outskirts of Concord, notwithstanding that press of engagements which was his excuse so many times this morning, nor a boy, nor a woman, I might almost say, but would forsake all and follow that sound, not mainly to save property from the flames, but, if we will confess the truth, much more to see it burn, since burn

it must, and we, be it known, did not set it on fire,—or to see it put out, and have a hand in it, if that is done as handsomely; yes, even if it were the parish church itself. Hardly a man takes a half-hour's nap after dinner, but when he wakes he holds up his head and asks, "What's the news?" as if the rest of mankind had stood his sentinels. Some give directions to be waked every half-hour, doubtless for no other purpose; and then, to pay for it, they tell what they have dreamed. After a night's sleep the news is as indispensable as the breakfast. "Pray tell me anything new that has happened to a man anywhere on this globe,"—and he reads it over his coffee and rolls, that a man has had his eyes gouged out this morning on the Wachito River; never dreaming the while that he lives in the dark unfathomed mammoth cave of this world, and has but the rudiment of an eye himself.

[10] For my part, I could easily do without the post-office. I think that there are very few important communications made through it. To speak critically, I never received more than one or two letters in my life—I wrote this some years ago—that were worth the postage. The penny-post is, commonly, an institution through which you seriously offer a man that penny for his thoughts which is so often safely offered in jest. And I am sure that I never read any memorable news in a newspaper. If we read of one man robbed, or murdered, or killed by accident, or one house burned, or one vessel wrecked, or one steamboat blown up, or one cow run over on the Western Railroad, or one mad dog killed, or one lot of grasshoppers in the winter,—we never need read of another. One is enough. If you are acquainted with the principle, what do you care for a myriad instances and applications? To a philosopher all *news*, as it is called, is gossip, and they who edit and read it are old women over their tea. Yet not a few are greedy after this gossip. There was such a rush, as I hear, the other day at one of the offices to learn the foreign news by the last arrival, that several large squares of plate glass belonging to the establishment were broken by the pressure,—news which I seriously think a ready wit might write a twelvemonth, or twelve years, beforehand with sufficient accuracy. As for Spain, for instance, if you know how to throw in Don Carlos and the Infanta, and Don Pedro and Seville and Granada, from time to time in the right proportions,—they may have changed the names a little since I saw the papers,—and serve up a bull-fight when other entertainments fail, it will be true to the letter, and give us as good an idea of the exact state or ruin of things in Spain as the most succinct and lucid reports under this head in the newspapers: and as for England, almost the last significant scrap of news from that quarter was the revolution of 1649; and if you have learned the history of her crops for an average year, you never need attend to that thing again, unless your speculations are of a merely pecuniary character. If one may judge who rarely looks into the newspapers, nothing new does ever happen in foreign parts, a French revolution not excepted.

[11] What news! how much more important to know what that is which was never old! "Kieou-he-yu (great dignitary of the state of Wei) sent a

man to Khoung-tseu to know his news. Khoung-tseu caused the messenger to be seated near him, and questioned him in these terms: What is your master doing? The messenger answered with respect: My master desires to diminish the number of his faults, but he cannot come to the end of them. The messenger being gone, the philosopher remarked: What a worthy messenger! What a worthy messenger!" The preacher, instead of vexing the ears of drowsy farmers on their day of rest at the end of the week,—for Sunday is the fit conclusion of an ill-spent week, and not the fresh and brave beginning of a new one,—with this one other draggle-tail of a sermon, should shout with thundering voice, "Pause! Avast! Why so seeming fast, but deadly slow?"

[12] Shams and delusions are esteemed for soundest truths, while reality is fabulous. If men would steadily observe realities only, and not allow themselves to be deluded, life, to compare it with such things as we know, would be like a fairy tale and the Arabian Nights' Entertainments. If we respected only what is inevitable and has a right to be, music and poetry would resound along the streets. When we are unhurried and wise, we perceive that only great and worthy things have any permanent and absolute existence, that petty fears and petty pleasures are but the shadow of the reality. This is always exhilarating and sublime. By closing the eyes and slumbering, and consenting to be deceived by shows, men establish and confirm their daily life of routine and habit everywhere, which still is built on purely illusory foundations. Children, who play life, discern its true law and relations more clearly than men, who fail to live it worthily, but who think that they are wiser by experience, that is, by failure. I have read in a Hindoo book, that "there was a king's son, who, being expelled in infancy from his native city, was brought up by a forester, and, growing up to maturity in that state, imagined himself to belong to the barbarous race with which he lived. One of his father's ministers having discovered him, revealed to him what he was, and the misconception of his character was removed, and he knew himself to be a prince. So soul," continues the Hindoo philosopher, "from the circumstances in which it is placed, mistakes its own character, until the truth is revealed to it by some holy teacher, and then it knows itself to be *Brahme*." I perceive that we inhabitants of New England live this mean life that we do because our vision does not penetrate the surface of things. We think that that *is* which *appears* to be. If a man should walk through this town and see only the reality, where, think you, would the "Mill-dam" go to? If he should give us an account of the realities he beheld there, we should not recognize the place in his description. Look at a meeting-house, or a court-house, or a jail, or a shop, or a dwelling-house, and say what that thing really is before a true gaze, and they would all go to pieces in your account of them. Men esteem truth remote, in the outskirts of the system, behind the farthest star, before Adam and after the last man. In eternity there is indeed something true and sublime. But all these times and places and occasions are now and

here. God himself culminates in the present moment, and will never be more divine in the lapse of all the ages. And we are enabled to apprehend at all what is sublime and noble only by the perpetual instilling and drenching of the reality that surrounds us. The universe constantly and obediently answers to our conceptions; whether we travel fast or slow, the track is laid for us. Let us spend our lives in conceiving then. The poet or the artist never yet had so fair and noble a design but some of his posterity at least could accomplish it.

[13] Let us spend one day as deliberately as Nature, and not be thrown off the track by every nutshell and mosquito's wing that falls on the rails. Let us rise early and fast, or break fast, gently and without perturbation; let company come and let company go, let the bells ring and the children cry,— determined to make a day of it. Why should we knock under and go with the stream? Let us not be upset and overwhelmed in that terrible rapid and whirlpool called a dinner, situated in the meridian shallows. Weather this danger and you are safe, for the rest of the way is down hill. With unrelaxed nerves, with morning vigor, sail by it, looking another way, tied to the mast like Ulysses. If the engine whistles, let it whistle till it is hoarse for its pains. If the bell rings, why should we run? We will consider what kind of music they are like. Let us settle ourselves, and work and wedge our feet downward through the mud and slush of opinion, and prejudice, and tradition, and delusion, and appearance, that alluvion which covers the globe, through Paris and London, through New York and Boston and Concord, through Church and State, through poetry and philosophy and religion, till we come to a hard bottom and rocks in place, which we can call *reality*, and say, This is, and no mistake; and then begin, having a *point d'appui*, below freshet and frost and fire, a place where you might found a wall or a state, or set a lamp-post safely, or perhaps a gauge, not a Nilometer, but a Realometer, that future ages might know how deep a freshet of shams and appearances had gathered from time to time. If you stand right fronting and face to face to a fact, you will see the sun glimmer on both its surfaces, as if it were a cimeter, and feel its sweet edge dividing you through the heart and marrow, and so you will happily conclude your mortal career. Be it life or death, we crave only reality. If we are really dying, let us hear the rattle in our throats and feel cold in the extremities; if we are alive, let us go about our business.

[14] Time is but the stream I go a-fishing in. I drink at it; but while I drink I see the sandy bottom and detect how shallow it is. Its thin current slides away, but eternity remains. I would drink deeper; fish in the sky, whose bottom is pebbly with stars. I cannot count one. I know not the first letter of the alphabet. I have always been regretting that I was not as wise as the day I was born. The intellect is a cleaver; it discerns and rifts its way into the secret of things. I do not wish to be any more busy with my hands than is necessary. My head is hands and feet. I feel all my best faculties concentrated in it. My instinct tells me that my head is an organ for

burrowing, as some creatures use their snout and fore paws, and with it I would mine and burrow my way through these hills. I think that the richest vein is somewhere hereabouts; so by the divining-rod and thin rising vapors I judge; and here I will begin to mine.

COMMENT AND QUESTIONS

I. Thoreau says that he "wished to live deliberately, to front only the essential facts of life." What does he appear to mean by the essential facts of life? What things does he regard as superficial or non-essential? What things, in his opinion, are actually detrimental to a good life?

II. Early in *Walden,* Thoreau, who seldom left the town in which he was born, says, "I have travelled a good deal in Concord." In what ways does he also travel a good deal at Walden Pond? In what ways does he settle, and "live deep"? Do the two terms, "travel" and "live deep" have the same meaning?

III. "It is something to be able to paint a particular picture, or to carve a statue, and so to make a few objects beautiful; but it is far more glorious to carve and paint the very atmosphere and medium through which we look, which morally we can do. To affect the quality of the day, that is the highest of arts." Do you agree with this statement? Would one who devoted himself to this "highest of arts" live solely for himself, and not for others?

IV. Thoreau's style is highly individual. Point out examples of irony; of humor; of exaggeration for effect; of good figures of speech.

V. If you have read the selection from Epictetus, page 928, what similarities and dissimilarities do you find between the basic ideas of Epictetus and Thoreau?

ALBERT EINSTEIN

Science and Religion *

Albert Einstein (1879–1955), German-born, naturalized-American theoretical physicist, is well known for his theory of relativity and his later generalized theory of gravitation. The following selection, first printed in 1941, has been reprinted as Part II of a longer essay "Science and Religion" in *Out of My Later Years,* a collection of Dr. Einstein's essays and addresses published in 1950.

* From *Out of My Later Years*. Reprinted by permission of The Philosophical Library, Inc.

[1] It would not be difficult to come to an agreement as to what we understand by science. Science is the century-old endeavor to bring together by means of systematic thought the perceptible phenomena of this world into as thoroughgoing an association as possible. To put it boldly, it is the attempt at the posterior reconstruction of existence by the process of conceptualization. But when asking myself what religion is, I cannot think of the answer so easily. And even after finding an answer which may satisfy me at this particular moment, I still remain convinced that I can never under any circumstances bring together, even to a slight extent, all those who have given this question serious consideration.

[2] At first, then, instead of asking what religion is, I should prefer to ask what characterizes the aspirations of a person who gives me the impression of being religious: a person who is religiously enlightened appears to me to be one who has, to the best of his ability, liberated himself from the fetters of his selfish desires and is preoccupied with thoughts, feelings, and aspirations to which he clings because of their super-personal value. It seems to me that what is important is the force of this super-personal content and the depth of the conviction concerning its overpowering meaningfulness, regardless of whether any attempt is made to unite this content with a Divine Being, for otherwise it would not be possible to count Buddha and Spinoza as religious personalities. Accordingly, a religious person is devout in the sense that he has no doubt of the significance and loftiness of those super-personal objects and goals which neither require nor are capable of rational foundation. They exist with the same necessity and matter-of-factness as he himself. In this sense religion is the age-old endeavor of mankind to become clearly and completely conscious of these values and goals and constantly to strengthen and extend their effects. If one conceives of religion and science according to these definitions then a conflict between them appears impossible. For science can only ascertain what *is*, but not what should be, and outside of its domain value judgments of all kinds remain necessary. Religion, on the other hand, deals only with evaluations of human thought and action; it cannot justifiably speak of facts and relationships between facts. According to this interpretation, the well-known conflicts between religion and science in the past must all be ascribed to a misapprehension of the situation which has been described.

[3] For example, a conflict arises when a religious community insists on the absolute truthfulness of all statements recorded in the Bible. This means an intervention on the part of religion into the sphere of science; this is where the struggle of the Church against the doctrines of Galileo and Darwin belongs. On the other hand, representatives of science have often made an attempt to arrive at fundamental judgments with respect to values and ends on the basis of scientific method, and in this way have set themselves in opposition to religion. These conflicts have all sprung from fatal errors.

[4] Now, even though the realms of religion and science in themselves are clearly marked off from each other, nevertheless there exist between the

two, strong reciprocal relationships and dependencies. Though religion may be that which determines the goal, it has, nevertheless, learned from science, in the broadest sense, what means will contribute to the attainment of the goals it has set up. But science can only be created by those who are thoroughly imbued with the aspiration towards truth and understanding. This source of feeling, however, springs from the sphere of religion. To this there also belongs the faith in the possibility that the regulations valid for the world of existence are rational, that is comprehensible to reason. I cannot conceive of a genuine scientist without that profound faith. The situation may be expressed by an image: science without religion is lame, religion without science is blind.

[5] Though I have asserted above, that in truth a legitimate conflict between religion and science cannot exist, I must nevertheless qualify this assertion once again on an essential point, with reference to the actual content of historical religions. This qualification has to do with the concept of God. During the youthful period of mankind's spiritual evolution, human fantasy created gods in man's own image, who, by the operations of their will were supposed to determine, or at any rate to influence, the phenomenal world. Man sought to alter the disposition of these gods in his own favor by means of magic and prayer. The idea of God in the religions taught at present is a sublimation of that old conception of the gods. Its anthropomorphic character is shown, for instance, by the fact that men appeal to the Divine Being in prayers and plead for the fulfilment of their wishes.

[6] Nobody, certainly, will deny that the idea of the existence of an omnipotent, just and omnibeneficent personal God is able to accord man solace, help, and guidance; also, by virtue of its simplicity the concept is accessible to the most undeveloped mind. But, on the other hand, there are decisive weaknesses attached to this idea in itself, which have been painfully felt since the beginning of history. That is, if this Being is omnipotent, then every occurrence, including every human action, every human thought, and every human feeling and aspiration is also His work; how is it possible to think of holding men responsible for their deeds and thoughts before such an Almighty Being? In giving out punishment and rewards He would to a certain extent be passing judgment on himself. How can this be combined with the goodness and righteousness ascribed to Him?

[7] The main source of the present-day conflicts between the spheres of religion and of science lies in this concept of a personal God. It is the aim of science to establish general rules which determine the reciprocal connection of objects and events in time and space. For these rules, or laws of nature, absolutely general validity is required—not proven. It is mainly a program, and faith in the possibility of its accomplishment in principle is only founded on partial success. But hardly anyone could be found who would deny these partial successes and ascribe them to human self-deception. The fact that on the basis of such laws we are able to predict the temporal behavior of phenomena in certain domains with great precision and cer-

tainty, is deeply embedded in the consciousness of the modern man, even though he may have grasped very little of the contents of those laws. He need only consider that planetary courses within the solar system may be calculated in advance with great exactitude on the basis of a limited number of simple laws. In a similar way, though not with the same precision, it is possible to calculate in advance the mode of operation of an electric motor, a transmission system, or of a wireless apparatus, even when dealing with a novel development.

[8] To be sure, when the number of factors coming into play in a phenomenological complex is too large, scientific method in most cases fails us. One need only think of the weather, in which case prediction even for a few days ahead is impossible. Nevertheless no one doubts that we are confronted with a causal connection whose causal components are in the main known to us. Occurrences in this domain are beyond the reach of exact prediction because of the variety of factors in operation, not because of any lack of order in nature.

[9] We have penetrated far less deeply into the regularities obtaining within the realm of living things, but deeply enough nevertheless to sense at least the rule of fixed necessity. One need only think of the systematic order in heredity, and in the effect of poisons, as for instance alcohol on the behavior of organic beings. What is still lacking here is a grasp of connections of profound generality, but not a knowledge of order in itself.

[10] The more a man is imbued with the ordered regularity of all events, the firmer becomes his conviction that there is no room left by the side of this ordered regularity for causes of a different nature. For him neither the rule of human nor the rule of Divine Will exists as an independent cause of natural events. To be sure, the doctrine of a personal God interfering with natural events could never be *refuted,* in the real sense, by science, for this doctrine can always take refuge in those domains in which scientific knowledge has not yet been able to set foot.

[11] But I am persuaded that such behavior on the part of the representatives of religion would not only be unworthy but also fatal. For a doctrine which is able to maintain itself not in clear light but only in the dark, will of necessity lose its effect on mankind, with incalculable harm to human progress. In their struggle for the ethical good, teachers of religion must have the stature to give up the doctrine of a personal God, that is, give up that source of fear and hope which in the past placed such vast power in the hands of priests. In their labors they will have to avail themselves of those forces which are capable of cultivating the Good, the True, and the Beautiful in humanity itself. This is, to be sure, a more difficult but an incomparably more worthy task. After religious teachers accomplish the refining process indicated, they will surely recognize with joy that true religion has been ennobled and made more profound by scientific knowledge.

[12] If it is one of the goals of religion to liberate mankind as far as

possible from the bondage of egocentric cravings, desires, and fears, scientific reasoning can aid religion in yet another sense. Although it is true that it is the goal of science to discover rules which permit the association and foretelling of facts, this is not its only aim. It also seeks to reduce the connections discovered to the smallest possible number of mutually independent conceptual elements. It is in this striving after the rational unification of the manifold that it encounters its greatest successes, even though it is precisely this attempt which causes it to run the greatest risk of falling a prey to illusions. But whoever has undergone the intense experience of successful advances made in this domain, is moved by profound reverence for the rationality made manifest in existence. By way of the understanding he achieves a far-reaching emancipation from the shackles of personal hopes and desires, and thereby attains that humble attitude of mind towards the grandeur of reason incarnate in existence, which, in its profoundest depths, is inaccessible to man. This attitude, however, appears to me to be religious, in the highest sense of the word. And so it seems to me that science not only purifies the religious impulse of the dross of its anthropomorphism, but also contributes to a religious spiritualization of our understanding of life.

[13] The further the spiritual evolution of mankind advances, the more certain it seems to me that the path to genuine religiosity does not lie through the fear of life, and the fear of death, and blind faith, but through striving after rational knowledge. In this sense I believe that the priest must become a teacher if he wishes to do justice to his lofty educational mission.

COMMENT AND QUESTIONS

I. The ability to grasp the essentials of a piece of writing and to summarize it in precise, packed language is very useful to a college student. As a test of your reading and capacity for exact expression, think through the development of Einstein's essay, and then write a summary of it (150 words or more) in which you include all the important ideas. Write your summary before you read the next question.

II. Now read, and compare with your own summary, the two printed below. Each was written on a quiz in class, in fifteen minutes, by an able student.

[1] Science is the attempt to associate and explain the phenomena of the world; religion is harder to define. The religiously enlightened man is concerned with and convinced of the importance of super-personal thoughts and goals which neither have nor need a rational basis. The understanding of these thoughts and the achievement of these goals is, then, the purpose of religion.

Viewed thus, science, which deals with what *is*, and religion, which deals with what *should be*, cannot conflict except through the overstepping of their limits. This occurs when religion tries to assume full truth for the Bible and conflicts with, for instance, Darwin, or when science attempts value judgments.

Although religion and science are strictly divided, they are interdependent. Religion needs science to point the way to the achievement of its goals; science needs the desire for truth and the faith in future success that religion gives.

In spite of theoretical absence of conflict, the actual content of present religions presents a great conflict in the doctrine of a personal God, which developed from the ancient conception of one or many almighty beings controlling the world. This idea gives comfort and aid and is easily conceived, but it is logically weak. How can God control the thoughts and actions of all beings, yet hold them responsible for these very thoughts and actions? He is judging Himself.

As science has pursued the determining of natural laws (rules interrelating objects and events in time and space), it has failed only through number and variety of factors, not through lack of order in nature. This increasingly manifest logic rules out control of the world by any other factor, human or Divine. Religious teachers must courageously abandon the powerful doctrine of a personal God, utilizing instead the forces for good extant within humanity itself.

Since the purpose of science is also to reduce natural laws to a few basic concepts, it helps religion in another way, for such achievement brings profound respect for the logic of existence and a resulting uplift to the super-personal thoughts and ideals which are the goal of religion.

Science, then, not only purifies religion by disproving the false concept of a personal God, but also contributes to religious spiritualization in the understanding of the phenomenal world. The road to true religion lies not through blind faith, but through science, the search for rational knowledge.

[2] Science deals with what is—the facts of the physical world and their relationship. Religion is concerned with what should be—super-personal ideals and values. Defined this way, science and religion should not conflict, but should be mutually helpful—religion providing the goals, and science the way of attaining the religious values. They conflict only when one wrongly intrudes into the other's proper realm. At present such conflict occurs when religious groups insist on the idea of a personal anthropomorphic God who intervenes and changes natural law in answer to prayer. Scientific knowledge reveals a great ordered regularity in the universe which allows no room for such independent causes or interference. Religious leaders should therefore give up the idea of the personal God and should work, with the aid of science, to teach reverence for the great rationality manifest in existence, and to cultivate the True, Good and Beautiful in humanity itself.

Both of these summaries are good. Which seems to you better, and why?

III. It is also useful to a student to be able to phrase very briefly the central idea of a piece of writing. Write a single, concentrated sentence which does this for the Einstein essay.

IV. State as clearly as you can what you think Einstein's intentions were in writing this essay. He has deliberately given a somewhat unusual definition to the word "religion" and to the expression "religious person." Is he justified in doing so in the light of his intentions? Would you define these terms differently? If so, how?

V. If you have read Newman's "Belief in One God," compare Newman's and Einstein's views on the idea of a personal God. Do you think that each writer supports his views convincingly?

THOMAS HENRY HUXLEY

Agnosticism and Christianity*

Thomas Henry Huxley (1825–1895) was a distinguished English biologist and teacher, known particularly for his defense of Darwin's theory of evolution, and for his lectures and writings explaining science to general audiences. The following selection is part of the essay "Agnosticism and Christianity," first printed in 1889.

[1]   The present discussion has arisen out of the use, which has become general in the last few years, of the terms "Agnostic" and "Agnosticism."
[2]   The people who call themselves "Agnostics" have been charged with doing so because they have not the courage to declare themselves "Infidels." It has been insinuated that they have adopted a new name in order to escape the unpleasantness which attaches to their proper denomination. To this wholly erroneous imputation, I have replied by showing that the term "Agnostic" did, as a matter of fact, arise in a manner which negatives it; and my statement has not been, and cannot be refuted. Moreover, speaking for myself, and without impugning the right of any other person to use the term in another sense, I further say that Agnosticism is not properly described as a "negative" creed, nor indeed as a creed of any kind, except in so far as it expresses absolute faith in the validity of a principle which is as much ethical as intellectual. This principle may be stated in various ways, but they all amount to this: that it is wrong for a man to say that he is certain of the objective truth of any proposition unless he can produce evidence which logically justifies that certainty. This is what Agnosticism asserts; and, in my opinion, it is all that is essential to Agnosticism. That which Agnostics deny and repudiate, as immoral, is the contrary doctrine, that there are propositions which men ought to believe, without logically satisfactory evidence; and that reprobation ought to attach to the profession of disbelief in such inadequately supported propositions. The justification of the Agnostic principle lies in the success which follows upon its application, whether in the field of natural, or in that of civil, history; and in the fact that, so far as these topics are concerned, no sane man thinks of denying its validity.
[3]   Still speaking for myself, I add, that though Agnosticism is not, and cannot be, a creed, except in so far as its general principle is concerned; yet

* From *Science and Christian Tradition* by Thomas Henry Huxley. Published by Appleton-Century-Crofts, Inc.

that the application of that principle results in the denial of, or the suspension of judgment concerning, a number of propositions respecting which our contemporary ecclesiastical "gnostics" profess entire certainty. And, in so far as these ecclesiastical persons can be justified in their old-established custom (which many nowadays think more honoured in the breach than the observance) of using opprobrious names to those who differ from them, I fully admit their right to call me and those who think with me "Infidels"; all I have ventured to urge is that they must not expect us to speak of ourselves by that title.

[4] The extent of the region of the uncertain, the number of the problems the investigation of which ends in a verdict of not proven, will vary according to the knowledge and the intellectual habits of the individual Agnostic. I do not very much care to speak of anything as "unknowable." What I am sure about is that there are many topics about which I know nothing; and which, so far as I can see, are out of reach of my faculties. But whether these things are knowable by any one else is exactly one of those matters which is beyond my knowledge, though I may have a tolerably strong opinion as to the probabilities of the case. Relatively to myself, I am quite sure that the region of uncertainty—the nebulous country in which words play the part of realities—is far more extensive than I could wish. Materialism and Idealism; Theism and Atheism; the doctrine of the soul and its mortality or immortality—appear in the history of philosophy like the shades of Scandinavian heroes, eternally slaying one another and eternally coming to life again in a metaphysical "Nifelheim." It is getting on for twenty-five centuries, at least, since mankind began seriously to give their minds to these topics. Generation after generation, philosophy has been doomed to roll the stone uphill; and, just as all the world swore it was at the top, down it has rolled to the bottom again. All this is written in innumerable books; and he who will toil through them will discover that the stone is just where it was when the work began. Hume saw this; Kant saw it; since their time, more and more eyes have been cleaned of the films which prevented them from seeing it; until now the weight and number of those who refuse to be the prey of verbal mystifications has begun to tell in practical life.

[5] It was inevitable that a conflict should arise between Agnosticism and Theology; or rather, I ought to say, between Agnosticism and Ecclesiasticism. For Theology, the science, is one thing; and Ecclesiasticism, the championship of a foregone conclusion as to the truth of a particular form of Theology, is another. With scientific Theology, Agnosticism has no quarrel. On the contrary, the Agnostic, knowing too well the influence of prejudice and idiosyncrasy, even on those who desire most earnestly to be impartial, can wish for nothing more urgently than that the scientific theologian should not only be at perfect liberty to thresh out the matter in his own fashion; but that he should, if he can, find flaws in the Agnostic position; and, even if demonstration is not to be had, that he should put, in their full

force, the grounds of the conclusions he thinks probable. The scientific theologian admits the agnostic principle, however widely his results may differ from those reached by the majority of Agnostics.

[6] But, as between Agnosticism and Ecclesiasticism, or, as our neighbours across the Channel call it, Clericalism, there can be neither peace nor truce. The Cleric asserts that it is morally wrong not to believe certain propositions, whatever the results of a strict scientific investigation of the evidence of these propositions. He tells us that "religious error is, in itself, of an immoral nature." He declares that he has prejudged certain conclusions, and looks upon those who show cause for arrest of judgment as emissaries of Satan. It necessarily follows that, for him, the attainment of faith, not the ascertainment of truth, is the highest aim of mental life. And, on careful analysis of the nature of this faith, it will too often be found to be, not the mystic process of unity with the Divine, understood by the religious enthusiast; but that which the candid simplicity of a Sunday scholar once defined it to be. "Faith," said this unconscious plagiarist of Tertullian, "is the power of saying you believe things which are incredible."

[7] Now I, and many other Agnostics, believe that faith, in this sense, is an abomination; and though we do not indulge in the luxury of self-righteousness so far as to call those who are not of our way of thinking hard names, we do feel that the disagreement between ourselves and those who hold this doctrine is even more moral than intellectual. It is desirable there should be an end of any mistakes on this topic. If our clerical opponents were clearly aware of the real state of the case, there would be an end of the curious delusion, which often appears between the lines of their writings, that those whom they are so fond of calling "Infidels" are people who not only ought to be, but in their hearts are, ashamed of themselves. It would be discourteous to do more than hint the antipodal opposition of this pleasant dream of theirs to facts.

[8] The clerics and their lay allies commonly tell us, that if we refuse to admit that there is good ground for expressing definite convictions about certain topics, the bonds of human society will dissolve and mankind lapse into savagery. There are several answers to this assertion. One is that the bonds of human society were formed without the aid of their theology; and, in the opinion of not a few competent judges, have been weakened rather than strengthened by a good deal of it. Greek science, Greek art, the ethics of old Israel, the social organisation of old Rome, contrived to come into being, without the help of any one who believed in a single distinctive article of the simplest of the Christian creeds. The science, the art, the jurisprudence, the chief political and social theories, of the modern world have grown out of those of Greece and Rome—not by favour of, but in the teeth of, the fundamental teachings of early Christianity, to which science, art, and any serious occupation with the things of this world, were alike despicable.

[9] Again, all that is best in the ethics of the modern world, in so far as it

has not grown out of Greek thought, or Barbarian manhood, is the direct development of the ethics of old Israel. There is no code of legislation, ancient or modern, at once so just and so merciful, so tender to the weak and poor, as the Jewish law; and, if the Gospels are to be trusted, Jesus of Nazareth himself declared that he taught nothing but that which lay implicitly, or explicitly, in the religious and ethical system of his people.

And the scribe said unto him, Of a truth, Teacher, thou hast well said that he is one; and there is none other but he and to love him with all the heart, and with all the understanding, and with all the strength, and to love his neighbour as himself, is much more than all the whole burnt offerings and sacrifices. (Mark xii:32, 33.)

[10] Here is the briefest of summaries of the teaching of the prophets of Israel of the eighth century; does the Teacher, whose doctrine is thus set forth in his presence, repudiate the exposition? Nay; we are told, on the contrary, that Jesus saw that he "answered discreetly," and replied, "Thou are not far from the kingdom of God."

[11] So that I think that even if the creeds, from the so-called "Apostles'" to the so-called "Athanasian," were swept into oblivion; and even if the human race should arrive at the conclusion that, whether a bishop washes a cup or leaves it unwashed, is not a matter of the least consequence, it will get on very well. The causes which have led to the development of morality in mankind, which have guided or impelled us all the way from the savage to the civilized state, will not cease to operate because a number of ecclesiastical hypotheses turn out to be baseless. And, even if the absurd notion that morality is more the child of speculation than of practical necessity and inherited instinct, had any foundation; if all the world is going to thieve, murder, and otherwise misconduct itself as soon as it discovers that certain portions of ancient history are mythical; what is the relevance of such arguments to any one who holds by the Agnostic principle?

[12] Surely, the attempt to cast out Beelzebub by the aid of Beelzebub is a hopeful procedure as compared to that of preserving morality by the aid of immorality. For I suppose it is admitted that an Agnostic may be perfectly sincere, may be competent, and may have studied the question at issue with as much care as his clerical opponents. But, if the Agnostic really believes what he says, the "dreadful consequence" argufier (consistently, I admit, with his own principles) virtually asks him to abstain from telling the truth, or to say what he believes to be untrue, because of the supposed injurious consequences to morality. "Beloved brethren, that we may be spotlessly moral, before all things let us lie," is the sum total of many an exhortation addressed to the "Infidel." Now, as I have already pointed out, we cannot oblige our exhorters. We leave the practical application of the convenient doctrines of "Reserve" and "Non-natural interpretation" to those who invented them.

[13] I trust that I have now made amends for any ambiguity, or want of fulness, in my previous exposition of that which I hold to be the essence

of the Agnostic doctrine. Henceforward, I might hope to hear no more of the assertion that we are necessarily Materialists, Idealists, Atheists, Theists, or any other ists, if experience had led me to think that the proved falsity of a statement was any guarantee against its repetition. And those who appreciate the nature of our position will see, at once, that when Ecclesiasticism declares that we ought to believe this, that, and the other, and are very wicked if we don't, it is impossible for us to give any answer but this: We have not the slightest objection to believe anything you like, if you will give us good grounds for belief; but, if you cannot, we must respectfully refuse, even if that refusal should wreck morality and insure our own damnation several times over. We are quite content to leave that to the decision of the future. The course of the past has impressed us with the firm conviction that no good ever comes of falsehood, and we feel warranted in refusing even to experiment in that direction.

COMMENT AND QUESTIONS

I. The agnostic principle, Huxley says, is "that it is wrong for a man to say that he is certain of the objective truth of any proposition unless he can produce evidence which logically justifies that certainty." What is the importance of the word *objective* in this statement of the agnostic position? How does agnosticism differ from atheism? From infidelism?

II. Give examples of the "propositions" and "topics" about which opponents of agnosticism express certainty, and about which Huxley feels that he knows nothing.

III. What distinction does Huxley make between theology and ecclesiasticism? Why does agnosticism have no quarrel with the former? Why must it be at war with the latter?

IV. What is Huxley's answer to the assertion that mankind would lapse into savagery if certain ecclesiastical propositions were abandoned?

V. In what sense is the agnostic position a moral and ethical one?

VI. Does Huxley (without using the terms) make a distinction between inside and outside knowledge? For which kind of knowledge would he appear to have greater respect?

VII. The tone of this essay differs from the tone of most of the persuasive pieces in this section, in that Huxley is openly combative and impatient with his opposition. Can you see reasons for the tone he uses?

WILLIAM JAMES

Religious Faith *

William James (1842–1910) was an American psychologist, philosopher, and distinguished teacher at Harvard. "Religious Faith" is an excerpt from *The Will to Believe,* a collection of essays and lectures published in 1897.

[1] And now, in turning to what religion may have to say to the question,[1] I come to what is the soul of my discourse. Religion has meant many things in human history; but when from now onward I use the word I mean to use it in the supernaturalist sense, as declaring that the so-called order of nature, which constitutes this world's experience, is only one portion of the total universe, and that there stretches beyond this visible world an unseen world of which we now know nothing positive, but in its relation to which the true significance of our present mundane life consists. A man's religious faith (whatever more special items of doctrine it may involve) means for me essentially his faith in the existence of an unseen order of some kind in which the riddles of the natural order may be found explained. In the more developed religions the natural world has always been regarded as the mere scaffolding or vestibule of a truer, more eternal world, and affirmed to be a sphere of education, trial, or redemption. In these religions, one must in some fashion die to the natural life before one can enter into life eternal. The notion that this physical world of wind and water, where the sun rises and the moon sets, is absolutely and ultimately the divinely aimed-at and established thing, is one which we find only in very early religions, such as that of the most primitive Jews. It is this natural religion (primitive still, in spite of the fact that poets and men of science whose goodwill exceeds their perspicacity keep publishing it in new editions tuned to our contemporary ears) that, as I said a while ago, has suffered definitive bankruptcy in the opinion of a circle of persons, among whom I must count myself, and who are growing more numerous every day. For such persons the physical order of nature, taken simply as science knows it, cannot be held to reveal any one harmonious spiritual intent. It is mere *weather,* as Chauncey Wright called it, doing and undoing without end.

[2] Now, I wish to make you feel, if I can in the short remainder of this hour, that we have a right to believe the physical order to be only a partial order; that we have a right to supplement it by an unseen spiritual order

---

* From *The Will to Believe* by William James. Published by Longmans, Green & Co., Inc.

[1] The question of the meaning of life.

which we assume on trust, if only thereby life may seem to us better worth living again. But as such a trust will seem to some of you sadly mystical and execrably unscientific, I must first say a word or two to weaken the veto which you may consider that science opposes to our act.

[3] There is included in human nature an ingrained naturalism and materialism of mind which can only admit facts that are actually tangible. Of this sort of mind the entity called "science" is the idol. Fondness for the word "scientist" is one of the notes by which you may know its votaries; and its short way of killing any opinion that it disbelieves in is to call it "unscientific." It must be granted that there is no slight excuse for this. Science has made such glorious leaps in the last three hundred years, and extended our knowledge of nature so enormously both in general and in detail; men of science, moreover, have as a class displayed such admirable virtues,—that it is no wonder if the worshippers of science lose their head. In this very University, accordingly, I have heard more than one teacher say that all the fundamental conceptions of truth have already been found by science, and that the future has only the details of the picture to fill in. But the slightest reflection on the real conditions will suffice to show how barbaric such notions are. They show such a lack of scientific imagination, that it is hard to see how one who is actively advancing any part of science can make a mistake so crude. Think how many absolutely new scientific conceptions have arisen in our own generation, how many new problems have been formulated that were never thought of before, and then cast an eye upon the brevity of science's career. It began with Galileo, not three hundred years ago. Four thinkers since Galileo, each informing his successor of what discoveries his own lifetime had seen achieved, might have passed the torch of science into our hands as we sit here in this room. Indeed, for the matter of that, an audience much smaller than the present one, an audience of some five or six score people, if each person in it could speak for his own generation, would carry us away to the black unknown of the human species, to days without a document or monument to tell their tale. Is it credible that such a mushroom knowledge, such a growth overnight as this, *can* represent more than the minutest glimpse of what the universe will really prove to be when adequately understood? No! our science is a drop, our ignorance a sea. Whatever else be certain, this at least is certain,—that the world of our present natural knowledge *is* enveloped in a larger world of *some* sort of whose residual properties we at present can frame no positive idea.

[4] Agnostic positivism, of course, admits this principle theoretically in the most cordial terms, but insists that we must not turn it to any practical use. We have no right, this doctrine tells us, to dream dreams, or suppose anything about the unseen part of the universe, merely because to do so may be for what we are pleased to call our highest interests. We must always wait for sensible evidence for our beliefs; and where such evidence is inaccessible we must frame no hypotheses whatever. Of course this is a

safe enough position *in abstracto*. If a thinker had no stake in the unknown, no vital needs, to live or languish according to what the unseen world contained, a philosophic neutrality and refusal to believe either one way or the other would be his wisest cue. But, unfortunately, neutrality is not only inwardly difficult, it is also outwardly unrealizable, where our relations to an alternative are practical and vital. This is because, as the psychologists tell us, belief and doubt are living attitudes, and involve conduct on our part. Our only way, for example, of doubting or refusing to believe, that a certain thing *is*, is continuing to act as if it were *not*. If, for instance, I refuse to believe that the room is getting cold, I leave the windows open and light no fire just as if it still were warm. If I doubt that you are worthy of my confidence, I keep you uninformed of all my secrets just as if you were *un*worthy of the same. If I doubt the need of insuring my house, I leave it uninsured as much as if I believed there were no need. And so if I must not believe that the world is divine, I can only express that refusal by declining ever to act distinctively as if it were so, which can only mean acting on certain critical occasions as if it were *not* so, or in an irreligious way. There are, you see, inevitable occasions in life when inaction is a kind of action, and must count as action, and when not to be for is to be practically against; and in all such cases strict and consistent neutrality is an unattainable thing.

[5] And, after all, is not this duty of neutrality, where only our inner interests would lead us to believe, the most ridiculous of commands? Is it not sheer dogmatic folly to say that our inner interests can have no real connection with the forces that the hidden world may contain? In other cases divinations based on inner interests have proved prophetic enough. Take science itself! Without an imperious inner demand on our part for ideal logical and mathematical harmonies, we should never have attained to proving that such harmonies lie hidden between all the chinks and interstices of the crude natural world. Hardly a law has been established in science, hardly a fact ascertained, which was not first sought after, often with sweat and blood, to gratify an inner need. Whence such needs come from we do not know: we find them in us, and biological psychology so far only classes them with Darwin's "accidental variations." But the inner need of believing that this world of nature is a sign of something more spiritual and eternal than itself is just as strong and authoritative in those who feel it, as the inner need of uniform laws of causation ever can be in a professionally scientific head. The toil of many generations has proved the latter need prophetic. Why *may* not the former one be prophetic, too? And if needs of ours outrun the visible universe, why *may* not that be a sign that an invisible universe is there? What, in short, has authority to debar us from trusting our religious demands? Science as such assuredly has no authority, for she can only say what is, not what is not; and the agnostic "thou shalt not believe without coercive sensible evidence" is simply an expression

(free to any one to make) of private personal appetite for evidence of a certain peculiar kind.

[6] Now, when I speak of trusting our religious demands, just what do I mean by "trusting"? Is the word to carry with it license to define in detail an invisible world, and to anathematize and excommunicate those whose trust is different? Certainly not! Our faculties of belief were not primarily given us to make orthodoxies and heresies withal; they were given us to live by. And to trust our religious demands means first of all to live in the light of them, and to act as if the invisible world which they suggest were real. It is a fact of human nature, that men can live and die by the help of a sort of faith that goes without a single dogma of definition. The bare assurance that this natural order is not ultimate but a mere sign or vision, the eternal staging of a many-storied universe, in which spiritual forces have the last word and are eternal,—this bare assurance is to such men enough to make life seem worth living in spite of every contrary presumption suggested by its circumstances on the natural plane. Destroy this inner assurance, however, vague as it is, and all the light and radiance of existence is extinguished for these persons at a stroke. Often enough the wild-eyed look at life—the suicidal mood—will then set in.

[7] And now the application comes directly home to you and me. Probably to almost everyone of us here the most adverse life would seem well worth living, if we only could be *certain* that our bravery and patience with it were terminating and eventuating and bearing fruit somewhere in an unseen spiritual world. By granting we are not certain, does it then follow that a bare trust in such a world is a fool's paradise and lubberland, or rather that it is a living attitude in which we are free to indulge? Well, we are free to trust at our own risks anything that is not impossible, and that can bring analogies to bear in its behalf. That the world of physics is probably not absolute, all the converging multitude of arguments that make in favor of idealism tend to prove; and that our whole physical life may lie soaking in a spiritual atmosphere, a dimension of being that we at present have no organ for apprehending, is vividly suggested to us by the analogy of our domestic animals. Our dogs, for example, are in our human life but not of it. They witness hourly the outward body of events whose inner meaning cannot, by any possible operation, be revealed to their intelligence,—events in which they themselves often play the cardinal part. My terrier bites a teasing boy, and the father demands damages. The dog may be present at every step of the negotiations, and see the money paid, without an inkling of what it all means, without a suspicion that it has anything to do with *him;* and he never *can* know in his natural dog's life. Or take another case which used greatly to impress me in my medical-student days. Consider a poor dog whom they are vivisecting in a laboratory. He lies strapped on a board and shrieking at his executioners, and to his own dark consciousness is literally in a sort of hell. He cannot see a

single redeeming ray in the whole business; and yet all these diabolical-seeming events are often controlled by human intentions with which, if his poor benighted mind could only be made to catch a glimpse of them, all that is heroic in him would religiously acquiesce. Healing truth, relief to future sufferings of beast and man, are to be bought by them. It may be genuinely a process of redemption. Lying on his back on the board there he may be performing a function incalculably higher than any that prosperous canine life admits of; and yet, of the whole performance, this function is the one portion that must remain absolutely beyond his ken.

[8] Now turn from this to the life of man. In the dog's life we see the world invisible to him because we live in both worlds. In human life, although we only see our world, and his within it, yet encompassing both these worlds a still wider world may be there, as unseen by us as our world is by him; and to believe in that world *may* be the most essential function that our lives in this world have to perform. But "*may* be! *may* be!" one now hears the positivist contemptuously exclaim; "what use can a scientific life have for maybes?" Well, I reply, the "scientific" life itself has much to do with maybes, and human life at large has everything to do with them. So far as man stands for anything, and is productive or originative at all, his entire vital function may be said to have to deal with maybes. Not a victory is gained, not a deed of faithfulness or courage is done, except upon a maybe; not a service, not a sally of generosity, not a scientific exploration or experiment or text-book, that may not be a mistake. It is only by risking our persons from one hour to another that we live at all. And often enough our faith beforehand in an uncertified result *is the only thing that makes the result come true.* Suppose, for instance, that you are climbing a mountain, and have worked yourself into a position from which the only escape is by a terrible leap. Have faith that you can successfully make it, and your feet are nerved to its accomplishment. But mistrust yourself, and think of all the sweet things you have heard the scientists say of *maybes,* and you will hesitate so long that, at last, all unstrung and trembling, and launching yourself in a moment of despair, you roll in the abyss. In such a case (and it belongs to an enormous class), the part of wisdom as well as of courage is to *believe what is in the line of your needs,* for only by such belief is the need fulfilled. Refuse to believe, and you shall indeed be right, for you shall irretrievably perish. But believe, and again you shall be right, for you shall save yourself. You make one or the other of two possible universes true by your trust or mistrust,—both universes having been only *maybes,* in this particular, before you contributed your act.

[9] Now, it appears to me that the question whether life is worth living is subject to conditions logically much like these. It does, indeed, depend on you *the liver.* If you surrender to the nightmare view and crown the evil edifice by your own suicide, you have indeed made a picture totally black. Pessimism, completed by your act, is true beyond a doubt, so far as your world goes. Your mistrust of life has removed whatever worth your

own enduring existence might have given to it; and now, throughout the whole sphere of possible influence of that existence, the mistrust has proved itself to have had divining power. But suppose, on the other hand, that instead of giving way to the nightmare view, you cling to it that this world is not the *ultimatum*. Suppose you find yourself a very wellspring, as Wordsworth says, of—

> Zeal and the virtue to exist by faith
> As soldiers live by courage; as, by strength
> Of heart, the sailor fights with roaring seas.

Suppose, however thickly evils crowd upon you, that your unconquerable subjectivity proves to be their match, and that you find a more wonderful joy than any passive pleasure can bring in trusting ever in the larger whole. Have you not now made life worth living on these terms? What sort of a thing would life really be, with your qualities ready for a tussle with it, if it only brought fair weather and gave these higher faculties of yours no scope? Please remember that optimism and pessimism are definitions of the world, and that our own reactions on the world, small as they are in bulk, are integral parts of the whole thing, and necessarily help to determine the definition. They may even be the decisive elements in determining the definition. A large mass can have its unstable equilibrium overturned by the addition of a feather's weight; a long phrase may have its sense reversed by the addition of the three letters *n-o-t*. This life *is* worth living, we can say, *since it is what we make it, from the moral point of view;* and we are determined to make it from that point of view, so far as we have anything to do with it, a success.

[10] Now, in this description of faiths that verify themselves I have assumed that our faith in an invisible order is what inspires those efforts and that patience which make this visible order good for moral men. Our faith in the seen world's goodness (goodness now meaning fitness for successful moral and religious life) has verified itself by leaning on our faith in the unseen world. But will our faith in the unseen world similarly verify itself? Who knows?

[11] Once more it is a case of *maybe;* and once more *maybes* are the essence of the situation. I confess that I do not see why the very existence of an invisible world may not in part depend on the personal response which any one of us may make to the religious appeal. God himself, in short, may draw vital strength and increase of very being from our fidelity. For my own part, I do not know what the sweat and blood and tragedy of this life mean, if they mean anything short of this. If this life be not a real fight, in which something is eternally gained for the universe by success, it is no better than a game of private theatricals from which one may withdraw at will. But it *feels* like a real fight,—as if there were something really wild in the universe which we, with all our idealities and faithfulnesses, are needed to redeem; and first of all to redeem our own hearts from atheisms

and fears. For such a half-wild, half-saved universe our nature is adapted. The deepest thing in our nature is this *Binnenleben* (as a German doctor lately has called it), this dumb region of the heart in which we dwell alone with our willingnesses and unwillingnesses, our faiths and fears. As through the cracks and crannies of caverns those waters exude from the earth's bosom which then form the fountain-heads of springs, so in these crepuscular depths of personality the sources of all our outer deeds and decisions take their rise. Here is our deepest organ of communication with the nature of things; and compared with all these concrete movements of our soul all abstract statements and scientific arguments—the veto, for example, which the strict positivist pronounces upon our faith—sound to us like mere chatterings of the teeth. For here possibilities, not finished facts, are the realities with which we have acutely to deal; and to quote my friend William Salter, of the Philadelphia Ethical Society, "as the essence of courage is to stake one's life on a possibility, so the essence of faith is to believe that the possibility exists."

[12] These, then, are my last words to you: Be *not* afraid of life. Believe that life *is* worth living, and your belief will help create the fact. The "scientific proof" that you are right may not be clear before the day of judgment (or some stage of being which that expression may serve to symbolize) is reached. But the faithful fighters of this hour, or the beings that then and there will represent them, may turn to the faint-hearted, who here decline to go on, with words like those with which Henry IV greeted the tardy Crillon after a great victory had been gained: "Hang yourself, brave Crillon! we fought at Arques, and you were not there."

COMMENT AND QUESTIONS

A pragmatic philosophy—the position that the worth of an idea depends on its practical effects—underlies this argument for faith in an unseen order. If belief in an unknown spiritual world will satisfy a vital need, and will give meaning to this life, James is saying, then we have a right to such belief.

I. If you have read Thomas Huxley's "Agnosticism and Christianity," you will see that Huxley and James disagree about religious faith; indeed, paragraph 4 of James' essay is a direct argument against the agnostic position defended by Huxley. What are James' arguments against (1) agnostic neutrality; (2) reliance on scientific evidence alone? Is there an area of agreement between James and Huxley in their attitudes toward religious orthodoxy? Do they agree on any other matters about science and religion?

II. William James is very skillful in the use of persuasive example and analogy. What point is he making by means of each of the following: the man who does not believe the room is getting cold; the dog on the operating table; the mountain climber faced with a jump over an abyss?

III. James is chiefly concerned with the idea that faith in an unseen world makes life worth living. Examine the further idea, discussed in paragraph 11, that the invisible world itself may be strengthened by the faith of humanity. What concept of God does James appear to hold?

IV. Study the sentence structures and rhythms in paragraph 8, and try to determine by what techniques James achieves a vivid, forceful style.

JOHN HENRY NEWMAN

Belief in One God

The following selection is difficult reading, not because Newman writes obscurely, but because the subject itself is a difficult one to clarify. The reader may follow Newman more easily if he keeps the following points in mind: Newman is here trying to explain how he, one of the great religious thinkers, arrives at his sense of the reality and immediacy of the existence of God. He is not so much trying to *prove* the existence of God as he is trying to make clear the source and the means of his own perceptions of divinity. After mentioning the theological and rational grounds for belief, he goes on to show that his own belief is essentially intuitive, and to argue for the validity of a belief so arrived at. This selection is an excerpt from *The Grammar of Assent,* published in 1870, a work in which Newman makes a penetrating examination of the relationship between reason and faith. For further information on Newman see the note on page 942.

[1] There is one God, such and such in Nature and Attributes.
[2] I say "such and such," for, unless I explain what I mean by "one God," I use words which may mean anything or nothing. I may mean a mere *anima mundi;*[1] or an initial principle which once was in action and now is not; or collective humanity. I speak then of the God of the Theist and of the Christian: a God who is numerically One, who is Personal; the Author, Sustainer, and Finisher of all things, the life of Law and Order, the Moral Governor; One who is Supreme and Sole; like Himself, unlike all things besides Himself which all are but His creatures; distinct from, independent of them all; One who is self-existing, absolutely infinite, who has ever been and ever will be, to whom nothing is past or future; who is all perfection, and the fulness and archetype of every possible excellence, the Truth Itself, Wisdom, Love, Justice, Holiness; One who is All-powerful, All-knowing, Omnipresent, Incomprehensible. These are some of the distinctive prerogatives which I ascribe unconditionally and unreservedly to the great Being whom I call God.
[3] This being what Theists mean when they speak of God, their assent

[1] soul of the world.

to this truth admits without difficulty of being what I have called a notional assent. It is an assent following upon acts of inference, and other purely intellectual exercises; and it is an assent to a large development of predicates, correlative to each other, or at least intimately connected together, drawn out as if on paper, as we might map a country which we had never seen, or construct mathematical tables, or master the methods of discovery of Newton or Davy, without being geographers, mathematicians, or chemists ourselves.

[4] So far is clear; but the question follows, Can I attain to any more vivid assent to the Being of a God, than that which is given merely to notions of the intellect? Can I enter with a personal knowledge into the circle of truths which make up that great thought? Can I rise to what I have called an imaginative apprehension of it? Can I believe as if I saw? Since such a high assent requires a present experience or memory of the fact, at first sight it would seem as if the answer must be in the negative; for how can I assent as if I saw, unless I have seen? but no one in this life can see God. Yet I conceive a real assent is possible, and I proceed to show how.

[5] When it is said that we cannot see God, this is undeniable; but still in what sense have we a discernment of His creatures, of the individual beings which surround us? The evidence which we have of their presence lies in the phenomena which address our senses, and our warrant for taking these for evidence is our instinctive certitude that they are evidence. By the law of our nature we associate those sensible phenomena or impressions with certain units, individuals, substances, whatever they are to be called, which are outside and out of the reach of sense, and we picture them to ourselves in those phenomena. The phenomena are as if pictures; but at the same time they give us no exact measure or character of the unknown things beyond them;—for who will say there is any uniformity between the impressions which two of us would respectively have of some third thing, supposing one of us had only the sense of touch, and the other only the sense of hearing? Therefore, when we speak of our having a picture of the things which are perceived through the senses, we mean a certain representation, true as far as it goes, but not adequate.

[6] And so of those intellectual and moral objects which are brought home to us through our senses:—that they exist, we know by instinct; that they are such and such, we apprehend from the impressions which they leave upon our minds. Thus the life and writings of Cicero or Dr. Johnson, of St. Jerome or St. Chrysostom, leave upon us certain impressions of the intellectual and moral character of each of them, *sui generis*,[2] and unmistakable. We take up a passage of Chrysostom or a passage of Jerome; there is no possibility of confusing the one with the other; in each case we see the man in his language. And so of any great man whom we may have known: that he is not a mere impression on our senses, but a real being, we

---

[2] of its own kind; in a class by itself.

know by instinct; that he is such and such, we know by the matter or quality of that impression.

[7] Now certainly the thought of God, as Theists entertain it, is not gained by an instinctive association of His presence with any sensible phenomena; but the office which the senses directly fulfill as regards creation devolves indirectly on certain of our mental phenomena as regards the Creator. Those phenomena are found in the sense of moral obligation. As from a multitude of instinctive perceptions, acting in particular instances, of something beyond the senses, we generalize the notion of an external world, and then picture that world in and according to those particular phenomena from which we started, so from the perceptive power which identifies the intimations of conscience with the reverberations or echoes (so to say) of an external admonition, we proceed on to the notion of a Supreme Ruler and Judge, and then again we image Him and His attributes in those recurring intimations, out of which, as mental phenomena, our recognition of His existence was originally gained. And, if the impressions which His creatures make on us through our senses oblige us to regard those creatures as *sui generis* respectively, it is not wonderful that the notices, which He indirectly gives us through our conscience, of His own nature are such as to make us understand that He is like Himself and like nothing else.

[8] I have already said I am not proposing here to prove the Being of a God; yet I have found it impossible to avoid saying where I look for the proof of it. For I am looking for that proof in the same quarter as that from which I would commence a proof of His attributes and character,—by the same means as those by which I show how we apprehend Him, not merely as a notion, but as a reality. The last indeed of these three investigations alone concerns me here, but I cannot altogether exclude the two former from my consideration. However, I repeat, what I am directly aiming at, is to explain how we gain an image of God and give a real assent to the proposition that He exists. And next, in order to do this, of course I must start from some first principle;—and that first principle, which I assume and shall not attempt to prove, is that which I should also use as a foundation in those other two inquiries, viz. that we have by nature a conscience.

[9] I assume, then, that Conscience has a legitimate place among our mental acts; as really so, as the action of memory, of reasoning, of imagination, or as the sense of the beautiful; that, as there are objects which, when presented to the mind, cause it to feel grief, regret, joy, or desire, so there are things which excite in us approbation or blame, and which we in consequence call right or wrong; and which, experienced in ourselves, kindle in us that specific sense of pleasure or pain, which goes by the name of a good or bad conscience. This being taken for granted, I shall attempt to show that in this special feeling, which follows on the commission of what we call right or wrong, lie the materials for the real apprehension of a Divine Sovereign and Judge.

[10] The feeling of conscience (being, I repeat, a certain keen sensibility,

pleasant or painful,—self-approval and hope, or compunction and fear,—attendant on certain of our actions, which in consequence we call right or wrong) is twofold:—it is a moral sense, and a sense of duty; a judgment of the reason and a magisterial dictate. Of course its act is indivisible; still it has these two aspects, distinct from each other, and admitting of a separate consideration. Though I lost my sense of the obligation which I lie under to abstain from acts of dishonesty, I should not in consequence lose my sense that such actions were an outrage offered to my moral nature. Again, though I lost my sense of their moral deformity, I should not therefore lose my sense that they were forbidden to me. Thus conscience has both a critical and a judicial office, and though its promptings, in the breasts of the millions of human beings to whom it is given, are not in all cases correct, that does not necessarily interfere with the force of its testimony and of its sanction: its testimony that there is a right and a wrong, and its sanction to that testimony conveyed in the feelings which attend on right or wrong conduct. Here I have to speak of conscience in the latter point of view, not as supplying us, by means of its various acts, with the elements of morals, such as may be developed by the intellect into an ethical code, but simply as the dictate of an authoritative monitor bearing upon the details of conduct as they come before us, and complete in its several acts, one by one.

[11] Let us then thus consider conscience, not as a rule of right conduct, but as a sanction of right conduct. This is its primary and most authoritative aspect; it is the ordinary sense of the word. Half the world would be puzzled to know what was meant by the moral sense; but everyone knows what is meant by a good or bad conscience. Conscience is ever forcing on us by threats and by promises that we must follow the right and avoid the wrong; so far it is one and the same in the mind of everyone, whatever be its particular errors in particular minds as to the acts which it orders to be done or to be avoided; and in this respect it corresponds to our perception of the beautiful and deformed. As we have naturally a sense of the beautiful and graceful in nature and art, though tastes proverbially differ, so we have a sense of duty and obligation, whether we all associate it with the same certain actions in particular or not. Here, however, Taste and Conscience part company: for the sense of beautifulness, as indeed the Moral Sense, has no special relations to persons, but contemplates objects in themselves; conscience, on the other hand, is concerned with persons primarily, and with actions mainly as viewed in their doers, or rather with self alone and one's own actions, and with others only indirectly and as if in association with self. And further, taste is its own evidence, appealing to nothing beyond its own sense of the beautiful or the ugly, and enjoying the specimens of the beautiful simply for their own sake; but conscience does not repose on itself, but vaguely reaches forward for something beyond self, and dimly discerns a sanction higher than self for its decisions, as is evidenced in that keen sense of obligation and responsibility which informs them. And hence it is that we are accustomed to speak of conscience as a voice, a term which

we should never think of applying to the sense of the beautiful; and moreover a voice, or the echo of a voice, imperative and constraining, like no other dictate in the whole of our experience.

[12] And again, in consequence of this prerogative of dictating and commanding, which is of its essence, Conscience has an intimate bearing on our affections and emotions, leading us to reverence and awe, hope and fear, especially fear, a feeling which is foreign for the most part, not only to Taste, but even to the Moral Sense, except in consequence of accidental associations. No fear is felt by anyone who recognizes that his conduct has not been beautiful, though he may be mortified at himself, if perhaps he has thereby forfeited some advantage; but, if he has been betrayed into any kind of immorality, he has a lively sense of responsibility and guilt, though the act be no offence against society,—of distress and apprehension, even though it may be of present service to him,—of compunction and regret, though in itself it be most pleasurable,—of confusion of face, though it may have no witnesses. These various perturbations of mind which are characteristic of a bad conscience, and may be very considerable,—self-reproach, poignant shame, haunting remorse, chill dismay at the prospect of the future,—and their contraries, when the conscience is good, as real though less forcible, self-approval, inward peace, lightness of heart, and the like,—these emotions constitute a specific difference between conscience and our other intellectual senses,—common sense, good sense, sense of expedience, taste, sense of honour, and the like,—as indeed they would also constitute between conscience and the moral sense, supposing these two were not aspects of one and the same feeling, exercised upon one and the same subject-matter.

[13] So much for the characteristic phenomena, which conscience presents, nor is it difficult to determine what they imply. I refer once more to our sense of the beautiful. This sense is attended by an intellectual enjoyment, and is free from whatever is of the nature of emotion, except in one case, viz. when it is excited by personal objects; then it is that the tranquil feeling of admiration is exchanged for the excitement of affection and passion. Conscience too, considered as a moral sense, an intellectual sentiment, is a sense of admiration and disgust, of approbation and blame: but it is something more than a moral sense; it is always, what the sense of the beautiful is only in certain cases; it is always emotional. No wonder then that it always implies what that sense only sometimes implies; that it always involves the recognition of a living object, towards which it is directed. Inanimate things cannot stir our affections; these are correlative with persons. If, as is the case, we feel responsibility, are ashamed, are frightened, at transgressing the voice of conscience, this implies that there is One to whom we are responsible, before whom we are ashamed, whose claims upon us we fear. If, on doing wrong, we feel the same tearful, broken-hearted sorrow which overwhelms us on hurting a mother; if, on doing right, we enjoy the same sunny serenity of mind, the same soothing, satisfactory delight which

follows on our receiving praise from a father, we certainly have within us the image of some person, to whom our love and veneration look, in whose smile we find our happiness, for whom we yearn, towards whom we direct our pleadings, in whose anger we are troubled and waste away. These feelings in us are such as require for their exciting cause an intelligent being: we are not affectionate towards a stone, nor do we feel shame before a horse or a dog; we have no remorse or compunction on breaking mere human law: yet, so it is, conscience excites all these painful emotions, confusion, foreboding, self-condemnation; and on the other hand it sheds upon us a deep peace, a sense of security, a resignation, and a hope, which there is no sensible, no earthly object to elicit. "The wicked flees, when no one pursueth"; then why does he flee? whence his terror? Who is it that he sees in solitude, in darkness, in the hidden chambers of his heart? If the cause of these emotions does not belong to this visible world, the Object to which his perception is directed must be Supernatural and Divine; and thus the phenomena of Conscience, as a dictate, avail to impress the imagination with the picture of a Supreme Governor, a Judge, holy, just, powerful, all-seeing, retributive, and Conscience is the creative principle of religion, as the Moral Sense is the principle of ethics. . . .

[14] To a mind thus carefully formed upon the basis of its natural conscience, the world, both of nature and of man, does but give back a reflection of those truths about the One Living God, which have been familiar to it from childhood. Good and evil meet us daily as we pass through life, and there are those who think it philosophical to act towards the manifestations of each with some sort of impartiality, as if evil had as much right to be there as good, or even a better, as having more striking triumphs and a broader jurisdiction. And because the course of things is determined by fixed laws, they consider that those laws preclude the present agency of the Creator in the carrying out of particular issues. It is otherwise with the theology of a religious imagination. It has a living hold on truths which are really to be found in the world, though they are not upon the surface. It is able to pronounce by anticipation, what it takes a long argument to prove—that good is the rule, and evil the exception. It is able to assume that, uniform as are the laws of nature, they are consistent with a particular Providence. It interprets what it sees around it by this previous inward teaching, as the true key of that maze of vast complicated disorder; and thus it gains a more and more consistent and luminous vision of God from the most unpromising materials. Thus conscience is a connecting principle between the creature and his Creator; and the firmest hold of theological truths is gained by habits of personal religion. When men begin all their works with the thought of God, acting for His sake, and to fulfill His will, when they ask His blessing on themselves and their life, pray to Him for the objects they desire, and see Him in the event, whether it be according

to their prayers or not, they will find everything that happens tends to confirm them in the truths about Him which live in their imagination, varied and unearthly as those truths may be. Then they are brought into His presence as that of a Living Person, and are able to hold converse with Him, and that with a directness and simplicity, with a confidence and intimacy, *mutatis mutandis*,[3] which we use towards an earthly superior; so that it is doubtful whether we realize the company of our fellowmen with greater keenness than these favoured minds are able to contemplate and adore the Unseen, Incomprehensible Creator. . . .

COMMENT AND QUESTIONS

I. In paragraphs 3 and 4 Newman distinguishes between two kinds of assent. What does he mean by assent and how do the two kinds differ? Can you supply examples from your own experience of each kind of assent?

II. Express in terms of inside and outside knowledge what Newman is saying in paragraph 7. If you were asked how you know of the existence and the character traits of some *person* close to you, your best friend, for example, how would you answer?

III. What is the most important idea in paragraph 9?

IV. In paragraph 10 Newman states that the promptings of conscience "are not in all cases correct." Do you think this damages his argument that we can depend on the conscience to give us knowledge of God?

V. In paragraphs 11, 12, and 13 what similarities and differences does Newman find in comparing taste or sense of beauty with conscience? What conclusions does the comparison lead him to? Think of your own experience with taste and conscience. Is it similar to Newman's account?

VI. If you want to test your capacity as a reader and a thinker, write down *before you read the statement below,* your own statement (about 150 words) of the core of Newman's argument and then compare the two.

In terms of inside and outside knowledge Newman is saying something like this: Our outside knowledge is not direct knowledge: we believe the reports that our senses give us, and on the basis of data supplied by the senses we form our picture of the material or phenomenal world. But, Newman says, we have another kind of knowledge, inside knowledge, the kind of knowledge given us by intuition, by our sense of beauty, for example, and our moral sense. If we build up our picture of the physical world on the basis of the data that come to us through our senses (outside knowledge) why should we not construct our image of God on the basis of the data supplied by the moral sense and conscience (inside knowledge)? And if we trust the inside knowledge that is thus given us and build our lives on it, we will come to a more intimate knowledge of God—will believe as if we saw—and will confirm by the whole of our experience (inside and outside) the divine truths which we know through intuition or inside knowledge.

[3] necessary changes having been made.

VII. Einstein in "Science and Religion" argues against belief in a personal God. If you have read the Einstein essay, what comment do you think Einstein might make on Newman's ideas and what comment might Newman make on Einstein's?

ROBERT O. BALLOU

The Jew and the Christian*

The following informative and evaluative account of the development of the Judeo-Christian faith might logically have been included in the preceding section of readings, "History and Biography: Information and Evaluation." We have placed it here because it so clearly deals with ideas as well as facts, and because it is closely related to the surrounding essays on religious values. Robert O. Ballou (1892–   ), an American writer and publisher, is the editor of *The Bible of the World* and *The Portable World Bible,* a condensation of *The Bible of the World,* published in 1944. The aim of *The Portable World Bible,* from which this selection is taken, is to present compactly the central ideas of the world's eight great religions—Hinduism, Buddhism, Zoroastrianism, Judeo-Christianity, Mohammedanism, Confucianism, and Taoism. "The Jew and the Christian" is Mr. Ballou's introduction to selections from the Old and New Testaments.

[1]   Out of the land of Egypt, out of a swamp of bulrushes, out of the loins of a slave woman 1200 years before the birth of Christ, came the child who was to become the supreme lawmaker of all time. The religion of Judaism, for which he laid the foundation, and that of Christianity, which was its child, are to-day the strong bases of Western religious culture.

[2]   There is no story of the miraculous conception or birth of Moses such as those which record the origins of Jesus, of Gautama Buddha, and of Zarathushtra. There were no voices of angels singing to herald the coming of the great Hebrew leader, no moving star or other phenomena of nature to lead shepherds and wise men to the bed of the child, no bending down of trees over the mother, as in the story of the birth of the Buddha, no luminosity about the place of *accouchement,* such as that which we are told shone about Zarathushtra's birthplace three days before his birth. There were no prophets either at his birth or during his childhood to proclaim his divinity. Nor did Moses ever claim for himself any divine qualities which set him apart from other mortals.

[3]   The greatest of all the leaders of the Jews was a child of his people, hidden at birth in the bulrushes on the bank of an Egyptian river by his

* From *The Portable World Bible,* edited by Robert O. Ballou. Copyright, 1939, 1944, by Robert O. Ballou. Reprinted by permission of The Viking Press, Inc.

mother in order that he might escape the edict of Pharaoh that every child of the Hebrews should be killed. And though we are told that he later saw God, talked with him, and received directly from the omnipotent hand the stone tablets containing the Ten Commandments, he remained a man of his people to the day of his death and beyond.

[4] From time immemorial the Jews had prophesied the coming of a Messiah. Christians believe that the prophecy was fulfilled in the birth of Jesus. The orthodox Jews' dissension from this belief does not arise from protestation that Moses was this long-heralded Messiah. They still await a divine leader in human form, and are content to regard one of the world's most dramatic stories—that of the life of Moses—as the narrative of a natural phenomenon and Moses as a thoroughly human being. They are satisfied to say, in the words of Deuteronomy, "There arose not a prophet since in Israel like unto Moses, whom the Lord knew face to face."

[5] Yet if a religion which is swayed by so many cross currents and has so many leaders in it as has Judaism may be said to have a personal founder, surely that man is Moses. With Aaron as his lieutenant, he led the Children of Israel out of their bondage in Egypt and during forty years of wandering held them together, strengthened them in their heart-breaking discouragements, instructed them, laid down laws for them which he enforced with an iron hand, and gave them the Ten Commandments in the form recognized to-day by both Jew and Christian. By pleading, demonstration, threats, denunciations, and even ruthless slaughter of the recalcitrant, he induced them to worship only Jehovah, thus paving the way for the monotheism which is the basis of Western theology.

[6] To understand the complex pattern of the Jewish religion, it is necessary to look back to times long prior to the birth of Moses, to a time probably before the Iranian branch of Indo-Europeans migrated to Persia.

[7] The Jews were then a group of Semitic tribes wandering on the Arabian desert and slowly drifting towards Palestine, constantly seeking better pastures for their herds of sheep and goats.

[8] There is evidence that even at this early date they recognized a code of laws enunciated in ten sentences which they called "the Ten Commands." Some of these are identical in meaning with edicts of the Ten Commandments. Some are not. But they are undoubtedly the parent of the later code. (See *The Bible of the World*, p. 1368.) The stories of the origins of the earth and of man may already have been established much as we have them today in Genesis. The story of Adam and Eve in its essentials may, or may not, have had some relation to a basic legend believed by that other great race of religious men, the Indo-Europeans, who told the story of Mashya and Mashyoi in Persia and that of Yama and Yami in India. The story of the flood and the ark which Noah built appears in its essential details in the earlier Babylonian *Epic of Gilgamish*. (See *The Bible of the World*, pp. 1366, 1367.) Some of the laws later enunciated in the Old Testament (notably those of exact retaliation) are from the Code of Hammurabai, a

Babylonian king who ruled about 2250 B.C. who is probably identical with the King Amraphel of Genesis 14, 1. According to the Babylonian story this code, inscribed on tablets, was given to Hammurabai by the sun god himself, an almost exact parallel to the story of Jehovah giving Moses the Ten Commandments.

[9] Obviously, then, Judaism owes much to earlier religions. But it has contributed to the present much more than it has borrowed from the past.

[10] That contribution began even before the birth of Moses when, about 2000 B.C., the Jews wandered from "Ur of the Chaldees" westward to found a nation. Because in their migration they crossed the Euphrates River, they were called "Hebrews" from a word which means "to cross over." Genesis tells us that they were led by the patriarch Abraham.

[11] Some scholars now question the existence of the individual man Abraham, believing rather that this was the designation of a tribe, but the name stands in Jewish belief for one of the greatest of all the early patriarchs, the first of the strong Jewish leaders whose names have been preserved, the "father of the faithful," and the "friend of God."

[12] At the time of Abraham his people believed in many gods. These gods had been given names after first having been worshipped merely as natural phenomena or objects. The Hebrews accorded their worship to individual deities as their fancies—or their beliefs in relative godly strengths—dictated. But the God of Abraham was *Yaweh,* Yaweh the strong, Yaweh whose power, so Abraham said, was far greater than the combined strength of all the other gods. Abraham and Yaweh had made a compact whereby the great god had agreed to accept the Hebrews as his chosen people, to take a special interest in them, and to further their well-being so long as they acknowledged him alone as their god, gave no homage to other gods, and did his will.

[13] Now the doing of his will was a complex matter. Sacrifices, burnt offerings heaped upon an altar, prayers and incantations—these he wanted, but they were not in themselves enough. The will of Yaweh was that the people of Abraham should, in their daily lives, follow a course of conduct which had in view the well-being and happiness of their fellow tribesmen. Thus an ethical pattern was woven into the religion along with its rites and ceremonies. It did not yet include the concept of world brotherhood. Ethical conduct towards members of the tribe of Abraham was one thing— that to others, another. But even here was the beginning of an ethical code which later was to dominate the Western World.

[14] Abraham's compact with Yaweh did not constitute the monotheism, the belief that there is one God only, which Judaism and its child Christianity accept to-day, but was rather "henotheism," the worship of one god, while recognizing others. Until long after the death of Moses the existence of other gods was believed in by the Jews. The first commandment did not say "Thou shalt believe that there are no other gods but me,"

but rather "Thou shalt have no other gods before me." This tacit recognition of the existence of other gods was reinforced by such admonitions as "Revile not the gods." When God appeared to Moses in the burning bush he did not say, "I am the only God," nor did he apparently feel that the simple words "I am God" were enough to make him known. He identified himself among the gods by saying "I am the God of thy father, the God of Abraham, the God of Isaac, and the God of Jacob." Even years later, when Moses' leadership had ended with his death and Joshua, having led his people through a long lifetime, was about to die, he urged them to "put away the strange gods which are among you, and incline your hearts unto the Lord God of Israel."

[15] Directly descended from Abraham, through his son Isaac, was Jacob, twin brother of Esau. Jacob, whose name later became Israel, was the father of twelve sons who became heads of the twelve tribes of Israel. Esau meanwhile headed another tribe near Canaan who became known as the Edomites.

[16] The story of the twelve sons of Jacob—how one of them, Joseph, was sold by his brothers and carried into Egypt, how Joseph rose to leadership under the powerful Pharaoh, of how he brought his people to live there in a land of plenty, how he and his master died, and how another Pharaoh enslaved the Hebrews—is told in the later part of Genesis and the first part of Exodus.

[17] Then arose the mighty figure of Moses, the son of a Hebrew slave named Levi, who was adopted by the daughter of Pharaoh when she found him hidden in the bulrushes. As a son of the royal household he might have cast his lot in with the Egyptian overlords. But the Pharaoh's daughter had engaged Moses' own mother (who had thrust herself forward through subterfuge) to nurse him, and from her he must have been well schooled in the manner of his birth and the history of his people. When as a young man he saw the burdens laid upon the Hebrews, he was overcome with sadness. This rapidly grew into anger and drove Moses to kill an Egyptian who was beating a Jew. Escaping from the wrath of the Pharaoh, he went into the land of Midian where he married and had the first of several encounters with Yaweh who, speaking from the midst of a burning bush, said that his name was "I Am" (just as, in the later Hinduist *Upanishads,* Yama tells Nachiketas that God can be named only by the words "He Is"). Reaffirming the ancient covenant with Abraham, Yaweh said that he had come to strengthen his people. With Moses acting as his spokesman and executive, he would lead them out of their captivity.

[18] How Moses courageously faced the Pharaoh, demanding and finally accomplishing the release of the Hebrews (with the help of "I Am" and the plagues he sent upon the Egyptians), how he led them across the Red Sea and to the very edge of the Promised Land with the fire by night and the cloud by day which Yaweh sent to guide them, is told in the magnificent story of Exodus. This story is of primary importance in the belief of devout

Jews to this day, for they have not forgotten Yaweh's ancient covenant with Abraham, and God's help in their deliverance from Egypt is one of the basic evidences that he fulfilled his part of that compact.

[19] After the death of Moses the Hebrew people passed through centuries of vicissitudes as a nation. These are important from a religious point of view only in so far as the changing circumstances influenced their religious, and therefore, their ethical concepts—those two forces which, as early as Abraham, were becoming so strongly enmeshed with tribal feeling that the three were to become one. Their attitude towards God, their attitude towards themselves as a united and exclusive people, and their standards of ethical conduct merged in the one mighty phenomenon of Judaism.

[20] For nearly a century in the time of the kings they enjoyed prosperity and peace. Then, during the reign of Rehoboam, when the nation was in the throes of political dissension and revolt against high taxation, once more the people were divided. Now the two groups became a northern and a southern kingdom, "Israel" and "Judah." In both kingdoms prosperity brought luxury and with it a falling away from the ancient worship of Yaweh. Many adopted the licentious practices of the Canaanitish religion and worshipped the Canaanitish gods. Their covenant with Yaweh forgotten, an increase in the commercial spirit brought with it exploitation, extortion, the selling of the poor into slavery for debts, immorality, and wars.

[21] Rising to the need of the times came a succession of great leaders. They have been called prophets, but perhaps it would be more accurate to call them sociologists and religious truth-tellers. For their teachings were based upon a deep understanding of the human heart and mind, a keen knowledge of the ills and needs of their people, and an exalted vision of righteous justice.

[22] One can only speculate on how much or how little they were influenced by other similar religious phenomena which were occurring throughout the world. This great age of religious awakening took place a little more than half a millennium before the birth of Christ and gave the *Upanishads* with their conception of the supreme Brahma, Gautama Buddha, and Mahavira to India, Confucius and Lao Tze to China, and the great monotheistic and work-revering Zarathushtra to Persia. In Greece men sought elevation of the human soul through beauty in one of the world's greatest periods of art. Rome was spreading its civilization through conquest and leaving its mark indelibly upon world society through the Roman genius in law making.

[23] In Israel these seers and moral leaders saw the threatened disintegration of national unity and morality, and reminded their people over and over of their covenant with Yaweh and their debt to him for their deliverance from slavery. They warned them that greed, dishonesty, cruelty, intolerance, lasciviousness, materialism, and sloth were the instruments of national suicide. Perhaps they were strongly influenced by contemporary Zoroastrianism, for whereas Jehovah had previously been represented as

the source of all things, both good and evil, he was now credited only with good while Satan (parallel of the Zoroastrian Angra Mainyu) was thought to create evil. Other evidences point to possible extensive borrowing of concepts from the fertile and vital religion of the great Persian.

[24] But regardless of how much Judaism may have taken from Zoroastrianism or other religions, its own utterances at this time were vastly more important. It was combining, with such force, conviction, and practicality as had never before been achieved, a theology and a social code. It was building an ethical religion in which man was to achieve salvation through co-operation with the one God, omnipotent Lord of the universe and loving, merciful father of us all, in whose godhead we could participate through righteousness and love in the service of our fellow-men.

[25] Considering the later prophets and the earlier leaders as one group, no other religious history has within it such an assembly of giants—Abraham and Moses, Elijah (who is reported to have raised a man from the dead and miraculously filled a widow's pitcher with milk centuries before Christ was said to have performed similar miracles), Elisha, Amos, Hosea, Joel, Micah, the dour and sorrowful Jeremiah (first to suggest that others besides Jews might share in the blessings of Jehovah-worship), Nahum, Habbakuk, Zephaniah, Ezekiel, Job of the many trials and great faith, Isaiah to whose loving Father-God all men were equal regardless of race, colour, or time or place of their births, and the deep-throated Daniel, saved by faith from the jaws of lions, who could dream and sing while he told of the holiness of Jehovah, and the glory which slept in the souls of men, waiting only for a reign of human righteousness to awaken it and vivify the human world.

[26] But no nation has ever realized the visions of greatness seen by its spiritual leaders. Century by century the moral and religious practices of the Jews declined until, like coins which become so worn that their original values cannot be deciphered, they had little in common with the teachings of the great prophets. It was time for a new vision and a new leader.

[27] Twelve hundred years after the death of Moses, about the time when Krishna in the *Bhagavad Gita* was calling India to righteous living and devotion to God, when Buddhism was flooding eastward into China and Japan, and Zoroastrianism was falling away from the greatness which its founder had brought to it, there was born in Bethlehem of Judea a Jew who was to descend upon the Hebrew congregation like a storm from heaven. Crying for repentance and rededication to God, he offered salvation in holy loving kindness to all who would follow him.

[28] Jesus of Nazareth was well versed in the religion of his fathers and dedicated, as were those great religious leaders whose concepts he carried on, to worship of "the God of Abraham, the God of Isaac, and the God of Jacob," Jehovah, who was now seen as the one God, omnipotent ruler of the universe and loving father of mankind. As he grew to manhood Jesus saw a Hebrew nation whose religious life consisted largely in external observ-

ances, in rituals and sacrifices, in petty dietary laws and other domestic rules, rather than in that spiritual co-operation with God through humility, social righteousness, and faith of which the later prophets spoke. He saw a priestly class who hypocritically held themselves above others—as the priests of Hinduism did at the time of Gautama's birth—and a people who believed that they were the chosen of God and thus the superiors of all other peoples. Intolerance, bigotry, hypocrisy, and materialism were like acid poisons eating away the soul of Israel.

[29] There were other great Jewish leaders who saw these things, others who were carrying on and advancing the religious thought of the prophets. One of the most notable of these, the incomparable Rabbi Hillel, was still living when Jesus was born. He preached the Golden Rule of Reciprocity (which Confucius had taught in China and Gautama Buddha in India more than half a millennium before) and other principles of humility, worship of the one God, and universal brotherhood, which became such essential parts of Christ's doctrine. But the Hebrew nation as a whole heeded these exhortations as little as they had those of Isaiah—as little as the Christian nations of the twentieth century heed the doctrines of Jesus Christ.

[30] The mission which Jesus set for himself was essentially no different from that to which Isaiah, Amos, Jeremiah, Ezekiel, Hillel, and the other great Jewish leaders had devoted their lives. Each of these and Jesus tried to bring understanding and a reawakened consciousness of the need of righteousness to his people, just as Confucius and Lao Tze in China, Gautama Buddha in India, and Zarathushtra in Persia had done. It was no part of the intention or effort of any one of these to overthrow the religion of his fathers and set up a new religion in its place. Many of Christ's most forceful admonitions, including his great commandments—"The Lord thy God is one God. Thou shalt love the Lord thy God with all thy heart, and thy neighbour as thyself"—were direct quotations from the Old Testament. The Golden Rule he quoted (with a slight change to make it positive instead of negative) from Hillel. He announced his purpose (Luke 4:18–19) in the words of an Old Testament prophet: "The Lord anointed me to preach good tidings to the poor. He hath sent me to proclaim release to the captives and recovering of sight to the blind, to set at liberty them that are bruised, to proclaim the acceptable year of the Lord." (Isaiah 61:1–2.) He said that he had come not to destroy, but to fulfil, the Jewish laws. He at all times observed the Jewish religious ceremonies rigorously. Even his cry of despair on the cross, "My God, my God, why hast thou forsaken me?" evidenced his preoccupation with Hebrew religious texts, for it is a direct quotation from an Old Testament Psalm.

[31] Racially and religiously Christ was born, lived, and died a loyal Jew, He sought merely to strengthen observance of the Jewish law and widen his people's understanding of the merciful, loving, Father-God whose Lordship was attested by the Jewish spiritual leaders who preceded him. He wanted to impress upon his people the doctrine that devotion to God was

meaningless unless it was expressed first of all in devotion to one's fellowmen.

[32] The life of Jesus is shrouded in mystery and mysticism. As in the earlier stories of Gautama Buddha and Zarathushtra, the scriptural story tells of the miraculous conception of Jesus, of homage paid to him at birth by wise men (probably Zoroastrian priests) who recognized his divinity, of his temptation by Satan (as Buddha was tempted by Mara and Zarathushtra assaulted by a personification of evil), of many miracles which he performed during his ministry, and, as a last proof of his divinity, of his resurrection after death.

[33] Jesus' reception during his life was a stormy one. The multitudes, drawn by his tremendous personal magnetism and his never failing understanding and kindness, flocked to him, proclaimed his goodness and greatness, and many of them acknowledged him as the Son of God and the long-awaited Messiah. But powerful forces in the Jewish congregation, jealous of his popularity, incensed by his denunciation of some of them, and bitterly critical of his disregard for formalism, his willingness to violate some of the minor laws of the Jews, and his heretical claim that he was the Son of God, repudiated him, conspired to kill him, saw him crucified, and, after his death, persecuted his followers.

[34] It is probably to that persecution that we owe the spread of Judeo-Christianity to the West and its influence upon modern life, for reaction from it produced the ministry of Paul. In the beginning those who followed the doctrines of Jesus, the Jew from Nazareth, were thought of merely as the representatives of a new Jewish sect, just as the first Buddhists were merely representatives of a new sect in Hinduism. There was nothing startling or revolutionary in the appearance of one more sect. Judaism had survived many divisions and the infusions of many interpretations. But the doctrine of Jesus, after his death, was singularly unsuccessful among the Jews. It was only when the convert, Paul, turned from the persecuting Jews and began his almost fanatic proselytizing among the Gentiles that the doctrine spread into Greece and Rome and thence to the rest of the Western World.

[35] During Paul's ministry, in the first century after the death of Jesus, the followers of Christ's doctrine (or more properly the followers of Christ's doctrine as interpreted by Paul and his colleagues) definitely left the Jewish congregation, called themselves Christians, and established the Christian Church at Antioch. Thus occurred the greatest and most tragic schism in the religious history of the Western World, and one which Christ himself never intended and never foresaw.

[36] None of the story of Jesus in any form which is now extant was recorded during his lifetime. The earliest writings of the New Testament are in the Acts of the Apostles and the Pauline Epistles, written A.D. 50–65. The four Gospels, which tell the story of Christ's life, were written A.D. 65–150. The three called "the Synoptics" because they "see together" or

present substantially the same point of view (Matthew, Mark, and Luke) were written first. The last, the Gospel of John, was written much later and presents a somewhat different theological concept which has much that relates it to the religions of India and China. "In the beginning was the Word," John writes, "and the Word was with God, and the Word was God." Thus he was presenting a concept which was very like that of the Tao in Taoism and the Brahman of the *Upanishads*. Indeed, Chinese translations of the Gospel of John begin, "In the beginning was the *Tao*, and the *Tao* was with God, and the *Tao* was God," repeating the concept of one of the verses of the *Tao-Te King*, basic scripture of Taoism.

[37] There are logical questions to be asked, pertinent to contemporary social problems, in view of the history of New Testament writing. Would the Gospels, and thus the story of the life of Christ, ever have been written at all and preserved for us had it not been for the passionate ministry of Paul and his colleagues? How much of the point of view in the Gospels, the Acts of the Apostles, and the Epistles, how much of the point of view of the Christian Church to-day, and how much of the separation between Jew and Gentile to-day, rise directly from Paul's point of view rather than from the doctrines of Christ himself? These questions have been asked many times and no attempt to answer them will be made here. They are raised simply because they are healthy questions for the mind of any one approaching the subject of Christ's place in the religious history of the Western World or the subject of a world emerging from the most destructive war in history and hoping for a society based upon the brotherhood of man. They are raised because they emphasize once more the indisputable fact that Jesus (regardless of the question of his special divinity, which Christians assert and Jews deny) was one in a long line of great Jewish spiritual leaders who together gave the world the religious and ethical foundations of Western civilization which are threatened to-day by a vast complex of international antagonisms.

[38] The Christan cannot, if he wishes to understand his own beliefs, separate Christ from his predecessors, nor can the Jew, if he wishes to understand the full flowering of the religious thought of his Old Testament prophets, ignore its logical development in the doctrine of Jesus Christ. That there should ever have been any separation between the doctrines of Israel and those of Christianity is a sad commentary on the Jew's lack of understanding of Isaiah, Ezekiel, Hillel, and his other great leaders, and the Christian's lack of understanding of the Jew whom he calls Saviour.

[39] The sacred books of the Jew and the Christian are contained in what the Western World calls the Holy Bible, of which the Old Testament only is acknowledged by the orthodox Jew, while the Christian Church has added to it the New Testament containing the Gospels, the Pauline writings, and certain other books. During the early years of the Christian Church there was a movement by the Christians to abolish the Old Testament entirely and to accept only the New as the Christian Bible. For-

tunately it failed, else Christianity would have been robbed of far the greater part of its scriptures, including the scriptural bases on which Christ built his doctrine.

[40] The Old Testament of Judaism contains 24 books arranged in three groups known as the Law (the first five books, called the *Torah* by Jews and the *Pentateuch* by Christians), the Prophets, and the Writings. These books are still read in the original (Hebrew, with the exception of about half the book of Daniel, parts of Ezra, and one verse of Jeremiah, which are in Aramaic) in all orthodox Jewish synagogues. In the Christian Bible they have been rearranged into 39 books. The New Testament consists of 27 books which were originally written in Greek during the first century of the Christian era.

[41] There are also other books, which are considered apocryphal by many. But those of the Old Testament Apocrypha are still included in the Bibles of the Greek and Roman Catholic Churches, which also take some of their traditions from the New Testament Apocrypha, though they do not include the books of this group in their Bible.

COMMENT AND QUESTIONS

Mr. Ballou's essay was written before the discovery in 1947 of the Dead Sea Scrolls. It may be worth noting here that the study of the Scrolls tends to underline and clarify the close linkage of Judaic and Christian ideas, chiefly by suggesting that Christianity may have been an offspring of the form of Judaism called Essenism. A recent writer on the world's religions, discussing the new light thrown by the Dead Sea Scrolls on the beliefs and practices of the Essenes, says:

> In the light of these facts it is understandable that scholars have recently revived the theory of Renan that Christianity grew out of Essenism. The Essenes were that Jewish sect which most specifically anticipated the character and teachings of John the baptizer and of Jesus. This does not mean that John and Jesus had no originality, but only that their teachings were more an outgrowth of Essenism than of any other form of Judaism. Many of the Christian traditions were enigmatic before this theory was understood. Now they have become clear.[1]

I. How, according to Ballou's account, did ethical and social principles come to be interwoven with the religious rites of Judaism?

II. What was the mission Jesus set for himself, and what did it have in common with the mission of other Jewish leaders?

III. How does Ballou support the statement that "racially and religiously, Christ was born, lived, and died a loyal Jew"?

IV. What was the importance of Paul in the history of Judeo-Christianity?

[1] Quinter Marcellus Lyon, *The Great Religions* (New York, The Odyssey Press, Inc., 1957), p. 605.

V. What lack of understanding by Christians and by Jews does Ballou see in the split between Christianity and Judaism?

VI. If you have read Aldous Huxley's discussion of the perennial philosophy, does it seem to you that what Ballou has to say about the evolution of Judeo-Christianity strengthens or dims the possibility that men might agree on a perennial philosophy?

VII. In what specific ways does Ballou's discussion support or refute Thomas Huxley's contention (in "Agnosticism and Christianity") that the bonds of human society and morality were formed without the aid of Christian theology?

VIII. Consider the statements and implications in this essay about the debt of Judaism to other religions, the debt of Christianity to Judaism, and the recurrence of similar traditions and ideas in the world's various religions. Does a knowledge of such debts, dependencies, and interrelationships seem to you to detract from the validity of a particular religious faith, or does it seem to you to enrich it? Explain your attitude.

ALDOUS HUXLEY

The Bhagavad-Gita and the Perennial Philosophy[*]

The *Bhagavad-Gita,* or Song of God, is the epic and gospel of the Hindu faith. The following essay, written by Aldous Huxley as an introduction to a translation of the *Bhagavad-Gita* by Swami Prabhavananda and Christopher Isherwood,[1] is largely a discussion of the elements which the author believes all the great religions of the world have in common. Aldous Huxley (1894–   ) is an English novelist and essayist, among whose works are *Antic Hay, Point Counter Point, Brave New World,* and *The Perennial Philosophy.*

[1]   More than twenty-five centuries have passed since that which has been called the Perennial Philosophy was first committed to writing; and in the course of those centuries it has found expression, now partial, now complete, now in this form, now in that, again and again. In Vedanta and Hebrew prophecy, in the Tao Teh King and the Platonic dialogues, in the Gospel according to St. John and Mahayana theology, in Plotinus and the Areopagite, among the Persian Sufis and the Christian

[*] Introduction to the *Bhagavad-Gita,* translated by Swami Prabhavananda and Christopher Isherwood. Copyright, 1944, 1951, by The Vedanta Society of Southern California.
[1] This translation of the *Bhagavad-Gita* is available in an inexpensive Mentor Edition.

mystics of the Middle Ages and the Renaissance—the Perennial Philosophy has spoken almost all the languages of Asia and Europe and has made use of the terminology and traditions of every one of the higher religions. But under all this confusion of tongues and myths, of local histories and particularist doctrines, there remains a Highest Common Factor, which is the Perennial Philosophy in what may be called its chemically pure state. This final purity can never, of course, be expressed by any verbal statement of the philosophy, however undogmatic that statement may be, however deliberately syncretistic. The very fact that it is set down at a certain time by a certain writer, using this or that language, automatically imposes a certain sociological and personal bias on the doctrines so formulated. It is only in the act of contemplation, when words and even personality are transcended, that the pure state of the Perennial Philosophy can actually be known. The records left by those who have known it in this way make it abundantly clear that all of them, whether Hindu, Buddhist, Hebrew, Taoist, Christian or Mohammedan, were attempting to describe the same essentially indescribable Fact.

[2] The original scriptures of most religions are poetical and unsystematic. Theology, which generally takes the form of a reasoned commentary on the parables and aphorisms of the scriptures, tends to make its appearance at a later stage of religious history. The Bhagavad-Gita occupies an intermediate position between scripture and theology; for it combines the poetical qualities of the first with the clear cut methodicalness of the second. The book may be described, writes Ananda K. Coomaraswamy in his admirable *Hinduism and Buddhism,* 'as a compendium of the whole Vedic doctrine to be found in the earlier Vedas, Brahmanas and Upanishads, and being therefore the basis of all the later developments, it can be regarded as the focus of all Indian religion.' But this 'focus of Indian religion' is also one of the clearest and most comprehensive summaries of the Perennial Philosophy ever to have been made. Hence its enduring value, not only for Indians, but for all mankind.

[3] At the core of the Perennial Philosophy we find four fundamental doctrines.

[4] First: the phenomenal world of matter and of individualized consciousness—the world of things and animals and men and even gods—is the manifestation of a Divine Ground within which all partial realities have their being, and apart from which they would be nonexistent.

[5] Second: human beings are capable not merely of knowing *about* the Divine Ground by inference; they can also realize its existence by a direct intuition, superior to discursive reasoning. This immediate knowledge unites the knower with that which is known.

[6] Third: man possesses a double nature, a phenomenal ego and an eternal Self, which is the inner man, the spirit, the spark of divinity within the soul. It is possible for a man, if he so desires, to identify himself with the

spirit and therefore with the Divine Ground, which is of the same or like nature with the spirit.

[7] Fourth: man's life on earth has only one end and purpose: to identify himself with his eternal Self and so to come to unitive knowledge of the Divine Ground.

[8] In Hinduism the first of these four doctrines is stated in the most categorical terms. The Divine Ground is Brahman, whose creative, sustaining and transforming aspects are manifested in the Hindu trinity. A hierachy of manifestations connects inanimate matter with man, gods, High Gods and the undifferentiated Godhead beyond.

[9] In Mahayama Buddhism the Divine Ground is called Mind or the Pure Light of the Void, the place of the High Gods is taken by the Dhyani-Buddhas.

[10] Similar conceptions are perfectly compatible with Christianity and have in fact been entertained, explicitly or implicitly, by many Catholic and Protestant mystics, when formulating a philosophy to fit facts observed by super-rational intuition. Thus, for Eckhart and Ruysbroeck, there is an Abyss of Godhead underlying the Trinity, just as Brahman underlies Brahma, Vishnu and Shiva. Suso has even left a diagrammatic picture of the relations subsisting between Godhead, triune God and creatures. In this very curious and interesting drawing, a chain of manifestation connects the mysterious symbol of the Divine Ground with the three Persons of the Trinity, and the Trinity in turn is connected in a descending scale with angels and human beings. These last, as the drawing vividly shows, may make one of two choices. They can either lead the life of the outer man, the life of separative selfhood; in which case they are lost (for, in the words of the Theologia Germanica, 'nothing burns in hell but the self'). Or else they can identify themselves with the inner man, in which case it becomes possible for them, as Suso shows, to ascend again, through unitive knowledge, to the Trinity and even, beyond the Trinity, to the ultimate Unity of the Divine Ground.

[11] Within the Mohammedan tradition such a rationalization of the immediate mystical experience would have been dangerously unorthodox. Nevertheless, one has the impression, while reading certain Sufi texts, that their authors did in fact conceive of *al haqq*, the Real, as being the Divine Ground or Unity of Allah, underlying the active and personal aspects of the Godhead.

[12] The second doctrine of the Perennial Philosophy—that it is possible to know the Divine Ground by a direct intuition higher than discursive reasoning—is to be found in all the great religions of the world. A philosopher who is content merely to know about the ultimate Reality—theoretically and by hearsay—is compared by Buddha to a herdsman of other men's cows. Mohammed uses an even homelier barnyard metaphor. For him the philosopher who has not realized his metaphysics is just an ass bearing a load of books. Christian, Hindu and Taoist teachers wrote no

less emphatically about the absurd pretensions of mere learning and analytical reasoning. In the words of the Anglican Prayer Book, our eternal life, now and hereafter, 'stands in the knowledge of God'; and this knowledge is not discursive but 'of the heart,' a super-rational intuition, direct, synthetic and timeless.

[13] The third doctrine of the Perennial Philosophy, that which affirms the double nature of man, is fundamental in all the higher religions. The unitive knowledge of the Divine Ground has, as its necessary condition, self-abnegation and charity. Only by means of self-abnegation and charity can we clear away the evil, folly and ignorance which constitute the thing we call our personality and prevent us from becoming aware of the spark of divinity illuminating the inner man. But the spark within is akin to the Divine Ground. By identifying ourselves with the first we can come to unitive knowledge of the second. These empirical facts of the spiritual life have been variously rationalized in terms of the theologies of the various religions. The Hindus categorically affirm that thou art That—that the indwelling Atman is the same as Brahman. For orthodox Christianity there is not an identity between the spark and God. Union of the human spirit with God takes place—union so complete the word 'deification' is applied to it; but it is not the union of identical substances. According to Christian theology, the saint is 'deified,' not because Atman *is* Brahman, but because God has assimilated the purified human spirit into the divine substance by an act of grace. Islamic theology seems to make a similar distinction. The Sufi, Mansur, was executed for giving to the words 'union' and 'deification' the literal meaning which they bear in the Hindu tradition. For our present purposes, however, the significant fact is that these words are actually used by Christians and Mohammedans to describe the empirical facts of metaphysical realization by means of direct, super-rational intuition.

[14] In regard to man's final end, all the higher religions are in complete agreement. The purpose of human life is the discovery of Truth, the unitive knowledge of the Godhead. The degree to which this unitive knowledge is achieved here on earth determines the degree to which it will be enjoyed in the posthumous state. Contemplation of truth is the end, action the means. In India, in China, in ancient Greece, in Christian Europe, this was regarded as the most obvious and axiomatic piece of orthodoxy. The invention of the steam engine produced a revolution, not merely in industrial techniques, but also and much more significantly in philosophy. Because machines could be made progressively more and more efficient, western man came to believe that men and societies would automatically register a corresponding moral and spiritual improvement. Attention and allegiance came to be paid, not to Eternity, but to the Utopian future. External circumstances came to be regarded as more important than states of mind about external circumstances, and the end of human life was held to be action, with contemplation as a means to that end. These false and, historically, aberrant and heretical doctrines are now systematically taught

in our schools and repeated, day in, day out, by those anonymous writers of advertising copy who, more than any other teachers, provide European and American adults with their current philosophy of life. And so effective has been the propaganda that even professing Christians accept the heresy unquestioningly and are quite unconscious of its complete incompatibility with their own or anybody else's religion.

[15] These four doctrines constitute the Perennial Philosophy in its minimal and basic form. A man who can practise what the Indians call Jnana yoga (the metaphysical discipline of discrimination between the Real and the apparent) asks for nothing more. This simple working hypothesis is enough for his purposes. But such discrimination is exceedingly difficult and can hardly be practised, at any rate in the preliminary stages of the spiritual life, except by persons endowed with a particular kind of mental constitution. That is why most statements of the Perennial Philosophy have included another doctrine, affirming the existence of one or more human Incarnations of the Divine Ground, by whose mediation and grace the worshipper is helped to achieve his goal—that unitive knowledge of the Godhead, which is man's eternal life and beatitude. The Bhagavad-Gita is one such statement. Here, Krishna is an Incarnation of the Divine Ground in human form. Similarly, in Christian and Buddhist theology, Jesus and Gotama are Incarnations of divinity. But whereas in Hinduism and Buddhism more than one Incarnation of the Godhead is possible (and is regarded as having in fact taken place), for Christians there has been and can be only one.

[16] An Incarnation of the Godhead and, to a lesser degree, any theocentric saint, sage or prophet is a human being who knows Who he is and can therefore effectively remind other human beings of what they have allowed themselves to forget: namely, that if they choose to become what potentially they already are, they too can be eternally united with the Divine Ground.

[17] Worship of the Incarnation and contemplation of his attributes are for most men and women the best preparation for unitive knowledge of the Godhead. But whether the actual knowledge itself can be achieved by this means is another question. Many Catholic mystics have affirmed that, at a certain stage of that contemplative prayer in which, according to the most authoritative theologians, the life of Christian perfection ultimately consists, it is necessary to put aside all thoughts of the Incarnation as distracting from the higher knowledge of that which has been incarnated. From this fact have arisen misunderstandings in plenty and a number of intellectual difficulties. Here, for example, is what Abbot John Chapman writes in one of his admirable Spiritual Letters: 'The problem of *reconciling* (not merely uniting) mysticism with Christianity is more difficult. The Abbot (Abbot Marmion) says that St John of the Cross is like a sponge full of Christianity. You can squeeze it all out, and the full mystical theory remains. Consequently, for fifteen years or so, I hated St John of the

Cross and called him a Buddhist. I loved St Teresa, and read her over and over again. She is first a Christian, only secondarily a mystic. Then I found that I had wasted fifteen years, so far as prayer was concerned.' And yet, he concludes, in spite of its 'Buddhistic' character, the practice of mysticism (or, to put it in other terms, the realization of the Perennial Philosophy) makes good Christians. He might have added that it also makes good Hindus, good Buddhists, good Taoists, good Moslems and good Jews.

[18] The solution to Abbot Chapman's problem must be sought in the domain, not of philosophy, but of psychology. Human beings are not born identical. There are many different temperaments and constitutions; and within each psycho-physical class one can find people at very different stages of spiritual development. Forms of worship and spiritual discipline which may be valuable for one individual may be useless or even positively harmful for another belonging to a different class and standing, within that class, at a lower or higher level of development. All this is clearly set forth in the Gita, where the psychological facts are linked up with general cosmology by means of the postulate of the *gunas*. Krishna, who is here the mouthpiece of Hinduism in all its manifestations, finds it perfectly natural that different men should have different methods and even apparently different objects of worship. All roads lead to Rome—provided, of course, that it is Rome and not some other city which the traveller really wishes to reach. A similar attitude of charitable inclusiveness, somewhat surprising in a Moslem, is beautifully expressed in the parable of Moses and the Shepherd, told by Jalaluddin Rumi in the second book of the Masnavi. And within the more exclusive Christian tradition these problems of temperament and degree of development have been searchingly discussed in their relation to the way of Mary and the way of Martha in general, and in particular to the vocation and private devotion of individuals.

[19] We now have to consider the ethical corollaries of the Perennial Philosophy. 'Truth,' says St Thomas Aquinas, 'is the last end for the entire universe, and the contemplation of truth is the chief occupation of wisdom.' The moral virtues, he says in another place, belong to contemplation, not indeed essentially, but as a necessary predisposition. Virtue, in other words, is not the end, but the indispensable means to the knowledge of divine reality. Shankara, the greatest of the Indian commentators on the Gita, holds the same doctrine. Right action is the way to knowledge; for it purifies the mind, and it is only to a mind purified from egotism that the intuition of the Divine Ground can come.

[20] Self-abnegation, according to the Gita, can be achieved by the practice of two all-inclusive virtues—love and non-attachment. The latter is the same thing as that 'holy indifference,' on which St François de Sales is never tired of insisting. 'He who refers every action to God,' writes Camus, summarizing his master's teaching, 'and has no aims save His Glory, will find rest everywhere, even amidst the most violent commotions.' So long as we practise this holy indifference to the fruits of action, 'no lawful occupation will

separate us from God; on the contrary, it can be made a means of closer union.' Here the word 'lawful' supplies a necessary qualification to a teaching which, without it, is incomplete and even potentially dangerous. Some actions are intrinsically evil or inexpedient; and no good intentions, no conscious offering of them to God, no renunciation of the fruits can alter their essential character. Holy indifference requires to be taught in conjunction not merely with a set of commandments prohibiting crimes, but also with a clear conception of what in Buddha's Eightfold Path is called 'right livelihood.' Thus, for the Buddhist, right livelihood was incompatible with the making of deadly weapons and of intoxicants; for the mediæval Christian, with the taking of interest and with various monopolistic practices which have since come to be regarded as legitimate good business. John Woolman, the American Quaker, provides a most enlightening example of the way in which a man may live in the world, while practising perfect non-attachment and remaining acutely sensitive to the claims of right livelihood. Thus, while it would have been profitable and perfectly lawful for him to sell West Indian sugar and rum to the customers who came to his shop, Woolman refrained from doing so, because these things were the products of slave labour. Similarly, when he was in England, it would have been both lawful and convenient for him to travel by stage coach. Nevertheless, he preferred to make his journeys on foot. Why? Because the comforts of rapid travel could only be bought at the expense of great cruelty to the horses and the most atrocious working conditions for the post-boys. In Woolman's eyes, such a system of transportation was intrinsically undesirable, and no amount of personal non-attachment could make it anything but undesirable. So he shouldered his knapsack and walked.

[21] In the preceding pages I have tried to show that the Perennial Philosophy and its ethical corollaries constitute a Highest Common Factor, present in all the major religions of the world. To affirm this truth has never been more imperatively necessary than at the present time. There will never be enduring peace unless and until human beings come to accept a philosophy of life more adequate to the cosmic and psychological facts than the insane idolatries of nationalism and the advertising man's apocalyptic faith in Progress towards a mechanized New Jerusalem. All the elements of this philosophy are present, as we have seen, in the traditional religions. But in existing circumstances there is not the slightest chance that any of the traditional religions will obtain universal acceptance. Europeans and Americans will see no reason for being converted to Hinduism, say, or Buddhism. And the people of Asia can hardly be expected to renounce their own traditions for the Christianity professed, often sincerely, by the imperialists who, for four hundred years and more, have been systematically attacking, exploiting and oppressing, and are now trying to finish off the work of destruction by 'educating' them. But happily there is the Highest Common Factor of all religions, the Perennial Philosophy which has always and

everywhere been the metaphysical system of the prophets, saints and sages. It is perfectly possible for people to remain good Christians, Hindus, Buddhists or Moslems and yet to be united in full agreement on the basic doctrines of the Perennial Philosophy.

[22] The Bhagavad-Gita is perhaps the most systematic scriptural statement of the Perennial Philosophy. To a world at war, a world that, because it lacks the intellectual and spiritual prerequisites to peace, can only hope to patch up some kind of precarious armed truce, it stands pointing, clearly and unmistakably, to the only road of escape from the self-imposed necessity of self-destruction.

COMMENT AND QUESTIONS

I. Restate in your own words the main ideas of the first paragraph.

II. State as clearly as you can the four fundamental doctrines (paragraphs 4–14) of the Perennial Philosophy. Compare these with the doctrines of the church in which you were brought up, or with those of any church whose doctrines are familiar to you.

III. What, according to Huxley (paragraphs 19–20), are the ethical corollaries of the Perennial Philosophy?

IV. Why, according to Huxley (paragraphs 21–22), is the Perennial Philosophy important at the present time?

V. State what you think Huxley's intentions were in writing this introduction to the *Bhagavad-Gita*. Is he simply informing or is he also evaluating and persuading? Justify your answer.

VI. Aldous Huxley is a grandson of Thomas Huxley. If you have read the latter's essay "Agnosticism and Christianity," can you see any common ground in the points of view of the two men? How many of the writers on religion and ethics whom you have read (for example, Plato, Epicurus, Einstein, James, Newman, Emerson, Sartre) do you think would agree wholly or in part with the doctrines and ethical corollaries of the Perennial Philosophy? Explain.

JEAN-PAUL SARTRE

Existentialism*

The following discussion of existentialism, originally a lecture, is taken from *Existentialism and Humanism,* published in 1948. Jean-Paul Sartre (1905–), French novelist, playwright, and philosopher, is a leading spokesman for the philosophy which he is explaining and defending in this selection. Assuming a universe without purpose, in which the individual alone determines what he will be, Sartre considers existentialism a philosophy not of pessimism and passivity, but of optimism and action.

[1] What, then, is this that we call existentialism? Most of those who are making use of this word would be highly confused if required to explain its meaning. For since it has become fashionable, people cheerfully declare that this musician or that painter is "existentialist." A columnist in *Clartés* signs himself "The Existentialist," and, indeed, the word is now so loosely applied to so many things that it no longer means anything at all. It would appear that, for the lack of any novel doctrine such as that of surrealism, all those who are eager to join in the latest scandal or movement now seize upon this philosophy in which, however, they can find nothing to their purpose. For in truth this is of all teachings the least scandalous and the most austere: it is intended strictly for technicians and philosophers. All the same, it can easily be defined.

[2] The question is only complicated because there are two kinds of existentialists. There are, on the one hand, the Christians, amongst whom I shall name Jaspers and Gabriel Marcel, both professed Catholics; and on the other the existential atheists, amongst whom we must place Heidegger as well as the French existentialists and myself. What they have in common is simply the fact that they believe that *existence* comes before *essence*—or, if you will, that we must begin from the subjective. What exactly do we mean by that?

[3] If one considers an article of manufacture—as, for example, a book or a paper-knife—one sees that it has been made by an artisan who had a conception of it; and he has paid attention, equally, to the conception of a paper-knife and to the pre-existent technique of production which is a part of that conception and is, at bottom, a formula. Thus the paper-knife is at the same time an article producible in a certain manner and one which, on the other hand, serves a definite purpose, for one cannot suppose

* From *Existentialism and Humanism,* by Jean-Paul Sartre, translated by Philip Mairet. Reprinted with permission of Methuen and Co., Ltd., and Les Éditions Nagel.

that a man would produce a paper-knife without knowing what it was for. Let us say, then, of the paper-knife that its essence—that is to say the sum of the formulae and the qualities which made its production and its definition possible—precedes its existence. The presence of such-and-such a paper-knife or book is thus determined before my eyes. Here, then, we are viewing the world from a technical standpoint, and we can say that production precedes existence.

[4] When we think of God as the creator, we are thinking of him, most of the time, as a supernal artisan. Whatever doctrine we may be considering, whether it be a doctrine like that of Descartes, or of Leibnitz himself, we always imply that the will follows, more or less, from the understanding or at least accompanies it, so that when God creates he knows precisely what he is creating. Thus, the conception of man in the mind of God is comparable to that of the paper-knife in the mind of the artisan: God makes man according to a procedure and a conception, exactly as the artisan manufactures a paper-knife, following a definition and a formula. Thus each individual man is the realization of a certain conception which dwells in the divine understanding. In the philosophic atheism of the eighteenth century, the notion of God is suppressed, but not, for all that, the idea that essence is prior to existence; something of that idea we still find everywhere, in Diderot, in Voltaire and even in Kant. Man possesses a human nature; that "human nature," which is the conception of human being, is found in every man; which means that each man is a particular example of a universal conception, the conception of Man. In Kant, this universality goes so far that the wild man of the woods, man in the state of nature and the bourgeois are all contained in the same definition and have the same fundamental qualities. Here again, the essence of man precedes that historic existence which we confront in experience.

[5] Atheistic existentialism, of which I am a representative, declares with greater consistency that if God does not exist there is at least one being whose existence comes before its essence, a being which exists before it can be defined by any conception of it. That being is man or, as Heidegger has it, the human reality. What do we mean by saying that existence precedes essence? We mean that man first of all exists, encounters himself, surges up in the world—and defines himself afterwards. If man as the existentialist sees him is not definable, it is because to begin with he is nothing. He will not be anything until later, and then he will be what he makes of himself. Thus, there is no human nature, because there is no God to have a conception of it. Man simply is. Not that he is simply what he conceives himself to be, but he is what he wills, and as he conceives himself after already existing—as he wills to be after that leap towards existence. Man is nothing else but that which he makes of himself. That is the first principle of existentialism. And this is what people call its "subjectivity," using the word as a reproach against us. But what do we mean to say by this, but that man is of a greater dignity than a stone or a table? For we mean to say that man

primarily exists—that man is, before all else, something which propels itself towards a future and is aware that it is doing so. Man is, indeed, a project which possesses a subjective life, instead of being a kind of moss, or a fungus or a cauliflower. Before that projection of the self nothing exists; not even in the heaven of intelligence: man will only attain existence when he is what he purposes to be. Not, however, what he may wish to be. For what we usually understand by wishing or willing is a conscious decision taken—much more often than not—after we have made ourselves what we are. I may wish to join a party, to write a book or to marry—but in such a case what is usually called my will is probably a manifestation of a prior and more spontaneous decision. If, however, it is true that existence is prior to essence, man is responsible for what he is. Thus, the first effect of existentialism is that it puts every man in possession of himself as he is, and places the entire responsibility for his existence squarely upon his own shoulders. And, when we say that man is responsible for himself, we do not mean that he is responsible only for his own individuality, but that he is responsible for all men. The word "subjectivism" is to be understood in two senses, and our adversaries play upon only one of them. Subjectivism means, on the one hand, the freedom of the individual subject and, on the other, that man cannot pass beyond human subjectivity. It is the latter which is the deeper meaning of existentialism. When we say that man chooses himself, we do mean that every one of us must choose himself; but by that we also mean that in choosing for himself he chooses for all men. For in effect, of all the actions a man may take in order to create himself as he wills to be, there is not one which is not creative, at the same time, of an image of man such as he believes he ought to be. To choose between this or that is at the same time to affirm the value of that which is chosen; for we are unable ever to choose the worse. What we choose is always the better; and nothing can be better for us unless it is better for all. If, moreover, existence precedes essence and we will to exist at the same time as we fashion our image, that image is valid for all and for the entire epoch in which we find ourselves. Our responsibility is thus much greater than we had supposed, for it concerns mankind as a whole. If I am a worker, for instance, I may choose to join a Christian rather than a Communist trade union. And if, by that membership, I choose to signify that resignation is, after all, the attitude that best becomes a man, that man's kingdom is not upon this earth, I do not commit myself alone to that view. Resignation is my will for everyone, and my action is, in consequence, a commitment on behalf of all mankind. Or if, to take a more personal case, I decide to marry and to have children, even though this decision proceeds simply from my situation, from my passion or my desire, I am thereby committing not only myself, but humanity as a whole, to the practice of monogamy. I am thus responsible for myself and for all men, and I am creating a certain image of man as I would have him to be. In fashioning myself I fashion man.

[6] This may enable us to understand what is meant by such terms—per-

haps a little grandiloquent—as anguish, abandonment and despair. As you will soon see, it is very simple. First, what do we mean by anguish? The existentialist frankly states that man is in anguish. His meaning is as follows —When a man commits himself to anything, fully realizing that he is not only choosing what he will be, but is thereby at the same time a legislator deciding for the whole of mankind—in such a moment a man cannot escape from the sense of complete and profound responsibility. There are many, indeed, who show no such anxiety. But we affirm that they are merely disguising their anguish or are in flight from it. Certainly, many people think that in what they are doing they commit no one but themselves to anything: and if you ask them, "What would happen if everyone did so?" they shrug their shoulders and reply, "Everyone does not do so." But in truth, one ought always to ask oneself what would happen if everyone did as one is doing; nor can one escape from that disturbing thought except by a kind of self-deception. The man who lies in self-excuse, by saying "Everyone will not do it" must be ill at ease in his conscience, for the act of lying implies the universal value which it denies. By its very disguise his anguish reveals itself. This is the anguish that Kierkegaard called "the anguish of Abraham." You know the story: An angel commanded Abraham to sacrifice his son: and obedience was obligatory, if it really was an angel who had appeared and said, "Thou, Abraham, shalt sacrifice thy son." But anyone in such a case would wonder, first, whether it was indeed an angel and secondly, whether I am really Abraham. Where are the proofs? A certain mad woman who suffered from hallucinations said that people were telephoning to her, and giving her orders. The doctor asked, "But who is it that speaks to you?" She replied: "He says it is God." And what, indeed, could prove to her that it was God? If an angel appears to me, what is the proof that it is an angel; or, if I hear voices, who can prove that they proceed from heaven and not from hell, or from my own subconsciousness or some pathological condition? Who can prove that they are really addressed to me?

[7] Who, then, can prove that I am the proper person to impose, by my own choice, my conception of man upon mankind? I shall never find any proof whatever; there will be no sign to convince me of it. If a voice speaks to me, it is still I myself who must decide whether the voice is or is not that of an angel. If I regard a certain course of action as good, it is only I who choose to say that it is good and not bad. There is nothing to show that I am Abraham: nevertheless I also am obliged at every instant to perform actions which are examples. Everything happens to every man as though the whole human race had its eyes fixed upon what he is doing and regulated its conduct accordingly. So every man ought to say, "Am I really a man who has the right to act in such a manner that humanity regulates itself by what I do." If a man does not say that, he is dissembling his anguish. Clearly, the anguish with which we are concerned here is not one that could lead to quietism or inaction. It is anguish pure and simple, of the kind

well known to all those who have borne responsibilities. When, for instance, a military leader takes upon himself the responsibility for an attack and sends a number of men to their death, he chooses to do it and at bottom he alone chooses. No doubt he acts under a higher command, but its orders, which are more general, require interpretation by him and upon that interpretation depends the life of ten, fourteen or twenty men. In making the decision, he cannot but feel a certain anguish. All leaders know that anguish. It does not prevent their acting, on the contrary it is the very condition of their action, for the action presupposes that there is a plurality of possibilities, and in choosing one of these, they realize that it has value only because it is chosen. Now it is anguish of that kind which existentialism describes, and moreover, as we shall see, makes explicit through direct responsibility towards other men who are concerned. Far from being a screen which could separate us from action, it is a condition of action itself.

[8] And when we speak of "abandonment"—a favorite word of Heidegger—we only mean to say that God does not exist, and that it is necessary to draw the consequences of his absence right to the end. The existentialist is strongly opposed to a certain type of secular moralism which seeks to suppress God at the least possible expense. Towards 1880, when the French professors endeavored to formulate a secular morality, they said something like this:—God is a useless and costly hypothesis, so we will do without it. However, if we are to have morality, a society and a law-abiding world, it is essential that certain values should be taken seriously; they must have an *à priori* existence ascribed to them. It must be considered obligatory *à priori* to be honest, not to lie, not to beat one's wife, to bring up children and so forth; so we are going to do a little work on this subject, which will enable us to show that these values exist all the same, inscribed in an intelligible heaven although, of course, there is no God. In other words—and this is, I believe, the purport of all that we in France call radicalism—nothing will be changed if God does not exist; we shall rediscover the same norms of honesty, progress and humanity, and we shall have disposed of God as an out-of-date hypothesis which will die away quietly of itself. The existentialist, on the contrary, finds it extremely embarrassing that God does not exist, for there disappears with Him all possibility of finding values in an intelligible heaven. There can no longer be any good *à priori*, since there is no infinite and perfect consciousness to think it. It is nowhere written that "the good" exists, that one must be honest or must not lie, since we are now upon the plane where there are only men. Dostoevsky once wrote "If God did not exist, everything would be permitted"; and that, for existentialism, is the starting point. Everything is indeed permitted if God does not exist, and man is in consequence forlorn, for he cannot find anything to depend upon either within or outside himself. He discovers forthwith, that he is without excuse. For if indeed existence precedes essence, one will never be able to explain one's action by reference to a given and specific human nature; in other words, there is no determinism—man is free, man *is*

freedom. Nor, on the other hand, if God does not exist, are we provided with any values or commands that could legitimize our behavior. Thus we have neither behind us, nor before us in a luminous realm of values, any means of justification or excuse. We are left alone, without excuse. That is what I mean when I say that man is condemned to be free. Condemned, because he did not create himself, yet is nevertheless at liberty, and from the moment that he is thrown into this world he is responsible for everything he does. The existentialist does not believe in the power of passion. He will never regard a grand passion as a destructive torrent upon which a man is swept into certain actions as by fate, and which, therefore, is an excuse for them. He thinks that man is responsible for his passion. Neither will an existentialist think that a man can find help through some sign being vouchsafed upon earth for his orientation: for he thinks that the man himself interprets the sign as he chooses. He thinks that every man, without any support or help whatever, is condemned at every instant to invent man. As Ponge has written in a very fine article, "Man is the future of man." That is exactly true. Only, if one took this to mean that the future is laid up in Heaven, that God knows what it is, it would be false, for then it would no longer even be a future. If, however, it means that, whatever man may now appear to be, there is a future to be fashioned, a virgin future that awaits him—then it is a true saying. But in the present one is forsaken.

[9] As an example by which you may the better understand this state of abandonment, I will refer to the case of a pupil of mine, who sought me out in the following circumstances. His father was quarrelling with his mother and was also inclined to be a "collaborator"; [1] his elder brother had been killed in the German offensive of 1940 and this young man, with a sentiment somewhat primitive but generous, burned to avenge him. His mother was living alone with him, deeply afflicted by the semi-treason of his father and by the death of her eldest son, and her one consolation was in this young man. But he, at this moment, had the choice between going to England to join the Free French Forces or of staying near his mother and helping her to live. He fully realized that this woman lived only for him and that his disappearance—or perhaps his death—would plunge her into despair. He also realized that, concretely and in fact, every action he performed on his mother's behalf would be sure of effect in the sense of aiding her to live, whereas anything he did in order to go and fight would be an ambiguous action which might vanish like water into sand and serve no purpose. For instance, to set out for England he would have to wait indefinitely in a Spanish camp on the way through Spain; or, on arriving in England or in Algiers he might be put into an office to fill up forms. Consequently, he found himself confronted by two very different modes of action; the one concrete, immediate, but directed towards only one individual; and the other an action addressed to an end infinitely greater, a national collectivity, but for that very reason ambiguous—and it might be frustrated

[1] A Frenchman who cooperated with the Germans in World War II.

on the way. At the same time, he was hesitating between two kinds of morality; on the one side the morality of sympathy, of personal devotion and, on the other side, a morality of wider scope but of more debatable validity. He had to choose between those two. What could help him to choose? Could the Christian doctrine? No. Christian doctrine says: Act with charity, love your neighbour, deny yourself for others, choose the way which is hardest, and so forth. But which is the harder road? To whom does one owe the more brotherly love, the patriot or the mother? Which is the more useful aim, the general one of fighting in and for the whole community, or the precise aim of helping one particular person to live? Who can give an answer to that *à priori?* No one. Nor is it given in any ethical scripture. The Kantian ethic says, Never regard another as a means, but always as an end. Very well; if I remain with my mother, I shall be regarding her as the end and not as a means: but by the same token I am in danger of treating as means those who are fighting on my behalf; and the converse is also true, that if I go to the aid of the combatants I shall be treating them as the end at the risk of treating my mother as a means.

[10] If values are uncertain, if they are still too abstract to determine the particular, concrete case under consideration, nothing remains but to trust in our instincts. That is what this young man tried to do; and when I saw him he said, "In the end, it is feeling that counts; the direction in which it is really pushing me is the one I ought to choose. If I feel that I love my mother enough to sacrifice everything else for her—my will to be avenged, all my longings for action and adventure—then I stay with her. If, on the contrary, I feel that my love for her is not enough, I go." But how does one estimate the strength of a feeling? The value of his feeling for his mother was determined precisely by the fact that he was standing by her. I may say that I love a certain friend enough to sacrifice such or such a sum of money for him, but I cannot prove that unless I have done it. I may say, "I love my mother enough to remain with her," if actually I have remained with her. I can only estimate the strength of this affection if I have performed an action by which it is defined and ratified. But if I then appeal to this affection to justify my action, I find myself drawn into a vicious circle.

[11] Moreover, as Gide has very well said, a sentiment which is play-acting and one which is vital are two things that are hardly distinguishable one from another. To decide that I love my mother by staying beside her, and to play a comedy the upshot of which is that I do so—these are nearly the same thing. In other words, feeling is formed by the deeds that one does; therefore I cannot consult it as a guide to action. And that is to say that I can neither seek within myself for an authentic impulse to action, nor can I expect, from some ethic, formulae that will enable me to act. You may say that the youth did, at least, go to a professor to ask for advice. But if you seek counsel—from a priest, for example—you have selected that priest; and at bottom you already knew, more or less, what he would advise. In other

words, to choose an adviser is nevertheless to commit oneself by that choice. If you are a Christian, you will say, Consult a priest; but there are collaborationists, priests who are resisters and priests who wait for the tide to turn: which will you choose? Had this young man chosen a priest of the resistance, or one of the collaboration, he would have decided beforehand the kind of advice he was to receive. Similarly, in coming to me, he knew what advice I should give him, and I had but one reply to make. You are free, therefore choose—that is to say, invent. No rule of general morality can show you what you ought to do: no signs are vouchsafed in this world. The Catholics will reply, "Oh, but they are!" Very well; still, it is I myself, in every case, who have to interpret the signs. While I was imprisoned,[2] I made the acquaintance of a somewhat remarkable man, a Jesuit, who had become a member of that order in the following manner. In his life he had suffered a succession of rather severe setbacks. His father had died when he was a child, leaving him in poverty, and he had been awarded a free scholarship in a religious institution, where he had been made continually to feel that he was accepted for charity's sake, and, in consequence, he had been denied several of those distinctions and honors which gratify children. Later, about the age of eighteen, he came to grief in a sentimental affair; and finally, at twenty-two—this was a trifle in itself, but it was the last drop that overflowed his cup—he failed in his military examination. This young man, then, could regard himself as a total failure: it was a sign—but a sign of what? He might have taken refuge in bitterness or despair. But he took it—very cleverly for him—as a sign that he was not intended for secular successes, and that only the attainments of religion, those of sanctity and of faith, were accessible to him. He interpreted his record as a message from God, and became a member of the Order. Who can doubt but that this decision as to the meaning of the sign was his, and his alone? One could have drawn quite different conclusions from such a series of reverses—as, for example, that he had better become a carpenter or a revolutionary. For the decipherment of the sign, however, he bears the entire responsibility. That is what "abandonment" implies, that we ourselves decide our being. And with this abandonment goes anguish.

[12] As for "despair," the meaning of this expression is extremely simple. It merely means that we limit ourselves to a reliance upon that which is within our wills, or within the sum of the probabilities which render our action feasible. Whenever one wills anything, there are always these elements of probability. If I am counting upon a visit from a friend, who may be coming by train or by tram, I presuppose that the train will arrive at the appointed time, or that the tram will not be derailed. I remain in the realm of possibilities; but one does not rely upon any possibilities beyond those that are strictly concerned in one's action. Beyond the point at which the possibilities under consideration cease to affect my action, I ought to disinterest myself. For there is no God and no prevenient design, which

---

[2] As a German prisoner of war in World War II.

can adapt the world and all its possibilities to my will. When Descartes said, "Conquer yourself rather than the world," what he meant was, at bottom, the same—that we should act without hope.

[13] Marxists, to whom I have said this, have answered: "Your action is limited, obviously, by your death; but you can rely upon the help of others. That is, you can count both upon what the others are doing to help you elsewhere, as in China and in Russia, and upon what they will do later, after your death, to take up your action and carry it forward to its final accomplishment which will be the revolution. Moreover you must rely upon this; not to do so is immoral." To this I rejoin, first, that I shall always count upon my comrades-in-arms in the struggle, in so far as they are committed, as I am, to a definite, common cause; and in the unity of a party or a group which I can more or less control—that is, in which I am enrolled as a militant and whose movements at every moment are known to me. In that respect, to rely upon the unity and the will of the party is exactly like my reckoning that the train will run to time or that the tram will not be derailed. But I cannot count upon men whom I do not know, I cannot base my confidence upon human goodness or upon man's interest in the good of society, seeing that man is free and that there is no human nature which I can take as foundational. I do not know where the Russian revolution will lead. I can admire it and take it as an example in so far as it is evident, today, that the proletariat plays a part in Russia which it has attained in no other nation. But I cannot affirm that this will necessarily lead to the triumph of the proletariat: I must confine myself to what I can see. Nor can I be sure that comrades-in-arms will take up my work after my death and carry it to the maximum perfection, seeing that those men are free agents and will freely decide, tomorrow, what man is then to be. Tomorrow, after my death, some men may decide to establish Fascism, and the others may be so cowardly or so slack as to let them do so. If so, Fascism will then be the truth of man, and so much the worse for us. In reality, things will be such as men have decided they shall be. Does that mean that I should abandon myself to quietism? No. First I ought to commit myself and then act my commitment, according to the time-honored formula that "one need not hope in order to undertake one's work." Nor does this mean that I should not belong to a party, but only that I should be without illusion and that I should do what I can. For instance, if I ask myself "Will the social ideal as such, ever become a reality?" I cannot tell, I only know that whatever may be in my power to make it so, I shall do; beyond that, I can count upon nothing.

[14] Quietism is the attitude of people who say, "let others do what I cannot do." The doctrine I am presenting before you is precisely the opposite of this, since it declares that there is no reality except in action. It goes further, indeed, and adds, "Man is nothing else but what he purposes, he exists only in so far as he realizes himself, he is therefore nothing else but the sum of his actions, nothing else but what his life is." Hence we

can well understand why some people are horrified by our teaching. For many have but one resource to sustain them in their misery, and that is to think, "Circumstances have been against me, I was worthy to be something much better than I have been. I admit I have never had a great love or a great friendship; but that is because I never met a man or a woman who were worthy of it; if I have not written any very good books, it is because I had not the leisure to do so; or, if I have had no children to whom I could devote myself it is because I did not find the man I could have lived with. So there remains within me a wide range of abilities, inclinations and potentialities, unused but perfectly viable, which endow me with a worthiness that could never be inferred from the mere history of my actions." But in reality and for the existentialist, there is no love apart from the deeds of love; no potentiality of love other than that which is manifested in loving; there is no genius other than that which is expressed in works of art. The genius of Proust is the totality of the works of Proust; the genius of Racine is the series of his tragedies, outside of which there is nothing. Why should we attribute to Racine the capacity to write yet another tragedy when that is precisely what he did not write? In life, a man commits himself, draws his own portrait and there is nothing but that portrait. No doubt this thought may seem comfortless to one who has not made a success of his life. On the other hand, it puts everyone in a position to understand that reality alone is reliable; that dreams, expectations and hopes serve to define a man only as deceptive dreams, abortive hopes, expectations unfulfilled; that is to say, they define him negatively, not positively. Nevertheless, when one says, "You are nothing else but what you live," it does not imply that an artist is to be judged solely by his works of art, for a thousand other things contribute no less to his definition as a man. What we mean to say is that a man is no other than a series of undertakings, that he is the sum, the organization, the set of relations that constitute these undertakings.

COMMENT AND QUESTIONS

I. Explain clearly each of the following existentialist beliefs:

1. That existence precedes essence.
2. That man makes himself.
3. That man is responsible for all men.
4. That one should accept anguish, abandonment, and despair.
5. That there is no reality except in action.

II. In paragraph 2 and particularly in paragraph 5, Sartre equates the idea that "existence precedes essence" with the idea of "subjectivity." What does the term *subjectivity* mean in this context?

III. Explain the statement, "In fashioning myself I fashion man."

IV. How do *anguish, abandonment,* and *despair,* as Sartre uses the words, differ in meaning? Could one term be used to convey all three meanings? Explain.

V. What does Sartre mean by saying that man is condemned to be free?

VI. In what sense is existentialism an optimistic philosophy? In what sense does it dignify man?

VII. If you have read the selection from Epictetus (page 928), do you find points of agreement between Epictetus and Sartre?

VIII. If you have read the selections from Plato printed in this book, what contrasts do you see between the Platonic and the existentialist view of man? Are there any parallels or similarities between the two philosophies?

IX. After saying (in paragraph 2) that there are two kinds of existentialists, the religious and the atheistic, Sartre is principally concerned in this essay with what he calls the atheistic existentialist position. Can you see any way in which the fundamental principles of existentialism could be reconciled with belief in the existence of God?

WILLIAM FAULKNER

Remarks on Receiving the Nobel Prize *

William Faulkner (1897–), winner of the 1949 Nobel Prize for Literature, is regarded by many critics as the most brilliant living American short-story writer and novelist. Among his novels are *The Sound and the Fury; As I Lay Dying; Light in August; Absalom, Absalom; Intruder in the Dust;* and *A Fable.* Mr. Faulkner gave the following short address in Stockholm, Sweden, in December, 1950, when he accepted the award of the Nobel Prize.

[1] I feel that this award was not made to me as a man but to my work—a life's work in the agony and sweat of the human spirit, not for glory and least of all for profit, but to create out of the materials of the human spirit something which did not exist before. So this award is only mine in trust. It will not be difficult to find a dedication for the money part of it commensurate with the purpose and significance of its origin. But I would like to do the same with the acclaim too, by using this moment as a pinnacle from which I might be listened to by the young men and women already dedicated to the same anguish and travail, among whom is already that one who will some day stand here where I am standing.

[2] Our tragedy today is a general and universal physical fear so long sustained by now that we can even bear it. There are no longer problems of the spirit. There is only the question: when will I be blown up? Because

* Used with permission of Random House, Inc.

of this, the young man or woman writing today has forgotten the problems of the human heart in conflict with itself which alone can make good writing because only that is worth writing about, worth the agony and the sweat.

[3] He must learn them again. He must teach himself that the basest of all things is to be afraid; and, teaching himself that, forget it forever, leaving no room in his workshop for anything but the old verities and truths of the heart, the old universal truths lacking which any story is ephemeral and doomed—love and honor and pity and pride and compassion and sacrifice. Until he does so he labors under a curse. He writes not of love but of lust, of defeats in which nobody loses anything of value, of victories without hope, and worst of all, without pity or compassion. His griefs grieve on no universal bones, leaving no scars. He writes not of the heart but of the glands.

[4] Until he relearns these things he will write as though he stood alone and watched the end of man. I decline to accept the end of man. It is easy enough to say that man is immortal simply because he will endure; that when the last ding-dong of doom has clanged and faded from the last worthless rock hanging tideless in the last red and dying evening, that even then there will still be one more sound: that of his puny inexhaustible voice, still talking. I refuse to accept this. I believe that man will not merely endure: he will prevail. He is immortal, not because he alone among creatures has an inexhaustible voice, but because he has a soul, a spirit capable of compassion and sacrifice and endurance. The poet's, the writer's, duty is to write about these things. It is his privilege to help man endure by lifting his heart, by reminding him of the courage and honor and hope and pride and compassion and pity and sacrifice which have been the glory of his past. The poet's voice need not merely be the record of man, it can be one of the props, the pillars to help him endure and prevail.

COMMENT AND QUESTIONS

I. In what phrases in the first two paragraphs does Faulkner stress the suffering a writer must endure? What is the nature of this suffering, and what should be its purpose?

II. According to Faulkner, what is the duty and the privilege of the writer?

III. Faulkner is addressing his remarks to young men and women who are dedicated to writing. What does he say about human life and values that is of concern to the non-writer?

IV. Do you think Faulkner could agree with Epicurus (see page 925) that "pleasure is the beginning and end of the blessed life"?

W. MACNEILE DIXON

The Human Situation *

The following selection is part of a book called *The Human Situation,* which was originally delivered as the Gifford Lectures in the University of Glasgow, 1935–37. This book, now available in an inexpensive edition, is one that we should like to recommend to all thoughtful college students. W. Macneile Dixon (1886–1946) was Professor of English Language and Literature in the University of Glasgow, and is the author of a number of books including *Tragedy, The Englishman,* and *An Apology for the Arts.*

[1] The first and fundamental wonder is existence itself. That I should be alive, conscious, a person, a part of the whole, that I should have emerged out of nothingness, that the Void should have given birth not merely to things, but to me. Among the many millions who throughout the centuries have crossed the stage of time, probably not more than a handful have looked about them with astonishment, or found their own presence within the visible scene in any way surprising. Our immediate impressions and requirements, the daily doings, comings and goings of others like ourselves absorb in the years of infancy all our attention. Life steals imperceptibly upon us, without any sudden shock or sense of strangeness. How quietly we accommodate ourselves to the situation! In our early years, when all is fresh and new, we take the miracle for granted, and find abundant occupation and endless variety of interest. We are busy looking about us, and grow accustomed to living, and nothing appears startling to which we are accustomed. Thus it is that in the existence of the world or ourselves there appears for most of us no cause for amazement. So far from asking with Coleridge the unanswerable question, "Why should there be anything at all, any world at all?" we accept life without wonder and without curiosity. One might almost imagine that we were here on well-known ground, and but revisiting a country with which we had a previous acquaintance. Yet let the mind once awake—and distress of mind is the great awakener of mind—and this emergence from the womb of the immeasurable universe rises to its full significance, to tower above all other thoughts, the wonder of wonders, beyond digestion into speech. To find oneself a member of a particular family and society, among innumerable other families and societies, engaged in a round of activities, to feel, think, love, hate, to eat, drink, sleep, to be involved in all these multitudinous affairs, not knowing

* From *The Human Situation* by W. Macneile Dixon. Reprinted with permission of Edward Arnold, Ltd., and St. Martin's Press.

in the least why this state of things should be ours, how we came into possession of this peculiar nature, acquired these needs, powers and passions, how or why we were launched upon this most extraordinary adventure—once give way to thoughts like these, and you are a prisoner for life, the prisoner of philosophy. But you will remain one of a negligible minority. And if it be a delusion to suppose that many human beings have been concerned with such musings, it is equally a delusion to suppose they have been spiritually minded, anxious about the state of their souls, eager for communion with God. All but the slenderest of minorities have been immersed in a struggle for existence, for material satisfactions, have sought the pleasures of the senses, or followed after power or wealth. Most have died, whatever their pursuits, in the full vigour of their sensuality, and all in the full tide of their ignorance. If there has been one God, universally acknowledged, universally worshipped, in all ages and countries, it is money.

> What is here?
> 'Gold? yellow, precious, glittering gold?'

The inhabitants of Norwich in 1650 petitioned Parliament to grant them the land and other materials "of that vast and altogether useless cathedral of Norwich" towards the building of a workhouse and repairing piers.

[2] However it came about, here we find ourselves, and in many and most delicately balanced ways, adjusted to the business in hand. Had the adjustment been perfect, had the whole worked without friction, as the earth moves through the heavens without a disturbing ripple, our lives like those of the plants, without desire or pain, possibly a dim sense of happiness, a gentle, unruffled dream might have been ours. Nature appears to have begun, if she ever did begin, her great undertaking with insensate things, and it mattered not at all what she did with them. Whirling suns, seas, mountains, even plants, trees, flowers of all varieties might have come into and passed out of existence without disturbance of the great calm of eternity. But with the entrance upon the scene of that disturbing visitor, the soul, that singular entity which suffers and enjoys, with the coming of beings capable of sharp pains and acute desires, there arose a formidable situation. These entities sought satisfaction for their wishes and avoidance of suffering. They became struggling creatures, in possession of life, but not the life they desired. Every man goes about arm in arm with disappointment. They discovered a harsh limit to their power over things. They found an enemy in the field, an evil thing, figured in all religions as the Adversary, the Opponent, the ἀντίθεόν, Ahriman in the Persian system, Lucifer or Satan in the Christian.

[3] How unfortunate, some theologians tell us, that man gave way to mental curiosity, and so forfeited his happy lot in the Garden of Eden, rising to a level of intelligence above the lowlier, unaspiring animals, content with pasture, with satisfactions of food and sex. They fared better,

and ours, but for the great aboriginal catastrophe, would have been a like existence, without expectations or searchings of heart, without souls embittered by fruitless desires. The knowledge of good and evil was the fatal departure from the original design—Nature's error, or, as in the Christian view, the fault of man himself. The pursuit of wisdom brought misery, and to intelligence was attached a penalty.

[4] There is a saying that nature does nothing in vain. Yet if she created automatic machines, and some thinkers like the behaviourists insist we are no more, why did she proceed to the blunder, for assuredly a blunder it was, of conferring upon them an unnecessary sensitivity to pain and pleasure? Without sensitivity machines work very well. How much better had she been content with insensate things. But we are not stones or trees, and in making sensitive beings nature went clean out of her way. Consciousness is an unpardonable blot upon her scheme, and for this philosophy an inexplicable enigma. So it is that, in the midst of nature, man appears not as her child, but as a changeling. Exiled from his native home of innocence, elevated to kingly rank in the creation, the bond between mother and son was snapped. She reared a disappointed and rebellious child, a critic of his parent, judging her morals detestable, counselling, as did Huxley, resistance to her rule and defiance of her authority. Cosmic nature, he declares, is "no school of virtue," but the headquarters of its enemy.

[5] That the world is not to their mind has never ceased to surprise, if not to exasperate the philosophers. Its pattern displeases them, and they would remould it nearer to their hearts' desire. Some religions think it past mending, but the passion for reforming the world and one's neighbours has afflicted all the schools of thought, nor has it yet been abandoned. Yet the patterns they would substitute have never been divulged. The most dissatisfied are chary of offering alternative and superior worlds, nor does it appear that they know of any with which our own unfavourably compares. By some natural talent they perceive its deficiencies, but the plan of operations is kept a secret. Alfonso the Wise of Spain, indeed, remarked that "he could have suggested improvements in the universe had the Creator consulted him." Unfortunately at that moment a terrible thunderstorm burst over the Alcazar, and there is no record of his proposals, if he had any.

[6] The world has been called *theatrum Dei*, God's theatre. And if we were merely players on the stage, repeating words put into our mouths, performing actions assigned to us, and like them really unconcerned, appearing to suffer and yet not suffering, the situation were beyond rebuke. It is unhappily quite otherwise. Feeling entered the world and let loose a torrent of ills—the sick heart, the ailing body, the distressed mind.

> All thoughts that rive the heart are here, and all are vain,
> Horror, and scorn, and hate, and fear, and indignation.

[7] It is a curious speculation, yet not irrelevant to our enquiry, how human lots are cast, so strangely varied they are. You are born and no

reasons given, a man or a woman, an Arab or an Andaman islander, an African pygmy or an Egyptian Pharaoh, a Chinese coolie or an English gentleman, a St. Thomas or an Ivan the Terrible. You are ushered into the world in the Stone Age, the fifth or fifteenth century, a vegetarian or a cannibal, of base or noble stock, the child of half-witted parents or of Viking breed, an imbecile or a fanatic. You inherit, according to the accident of your birth, a family blood-feud, a belief in Voodoo and a string of fantastic fetishes, or a Christian creed of love and charity. You are a warrior or a serf as Heaven decrees, are exposed as an infant born in ancient Sparta, die in middle life bitten by a poisonous snake in India, or live a respectable German merchant to a ripe old age. One of a million million possible lots is yours. Is it accidental, an act of God, or, as some have conjectured, a selection made by yourself in a previous state? How profound a mystery lies behind these so manifestly unequal conditions of human existence! And what justice is it, if one man languishes most of his life on a bed of sickness, and another enjoys health and happiness or sits upon an imperial throne? Nature strews these inequalities of place, time, heredity, circumstances with a monstrous partiality. On what principles you are allotted good looks, a musical ear, a sunny temper, an affectionate disposition, a talent for figures, or denied these qualities does not appear. We are, the maxim runs, as God made us, and there the matter perforce must end.

[8] Nor is it only our nature and disposition that we inherit, but the habits and traditions of some community, a Pagan, a Buddhistic or a Mohammedan creed, the *mos majorum,* the custom of our ancestors; and, with few exceptions, by these our lives are governed. These bodies of ours, as it would seem at haphazard distributed, are not negligible, or to be treated with cavalier indifference. From their tiresome demands and complaints there is no escape. They do very much as they please with us, often lame our best intentions and enforce our most sensual. To keep them in repair is a constant anxiety. What a despot is the stomach, whose caprices make us moody or cheerful, bland or irritable. Listen to the enormous laughter of Rabelais while he recounts the indignities to which the body subjects the mind, making indecency an intimate part of our lives. He mocks at nature, which delights in shaming us. Our pride revolts, we are nauseated by ourselves, as was Swift, or nervously and shamefacedly avert our eyes from the dishonours we must endure.

[9] If nature gave us logic, she appears to be singularly lacking in what she bestows. For she herself drives no straight furrow, and exhibits an inconsistency which in a man would be accounted madness. Her habit is to turn upon herself, wound and afflict herself, undoing with her left hand what she has done with her right. What more inharmonious than that she should send hailstones to the destruction of her own blossoms and fruits, tempests upon the crops she has herself ripened to the harvest? The meteorite that, in 1908, fell in Siberia, about 100 tons in weight, destroyed the forest

in which it fell for a radius of about forty miles. The lightning splits the tree, and sets the forest aflame. The sand of the desert or the encroaching sea turns fertile fields into barren wastes, and reduces whole populations to distress or starvation. It is her own features which nature thus rends and mangles. Wild beasts destroy 3000 persons every year in India, and 20,000 die of snake-bite. There are 700 million sufferers from malaria in the world. Forty per cent of the children born in Central China perish from cold or famine before they are a year old.

[10] When people talk of nature, what do they mean? Is it the immensity, the sublimity, the grandeur, or the indifference, the inhumanity she exhibits, of which they are thinking? We know her wonders and splendours, we know also her disorders, her cataclysms, her tempests. Nature is everything we admire and fear, everything we love, and everything we hate. She is "the sum of all phenomena." A perfectly ordered world, exact as a geometrical pattern, is the world desired by the logical mind. But how different the reality. Before its irrationalities reason trembles. The eruption of Krakatoa, in 1783, destroyed 40,000 human beings; the Quito, in 1797, also 40,000; the Lisbon earthquake, in 1755, twice that number. Is human life a bubble? Within the present century, in 1908, and again, in 1920, similar disturbances in Sicily and China eliminated half a million lives in sixty seconds. The eruption of Mount Pelé, in less than a quarter of an hour, laid the capital of Martinique in ruins, with the loss of 30,000 lives. During the Yangtse floods in 1931 over a million perished by drowning. Etna wakes and Messina perishes. Islands are submerged with their human freights, like ships at sea. In 1929 Ninaforu, in the Pacific, simply disappeared with all its inhabitants into the ocean depths. Would these things be "if the King of the universe were our friend"? The larks are not always in the sky on an April morning.

[11] Professor Bosanquet thought it exceedingly improbable that an earthquake would destroy London. His reason for thinking so was not a geological one. It would be, he believed, contrary to "the world-wisdom." Such a preference by nature for London over Tokio or California is indeed very flattering to us as a nation, and very comforting. But what are we to think of a philosopher who says such things? You say nothing: you close his book.

[12] Nature does not seem to know her own mind, or else she speaks an equivocal language. Are her powers, perhaps, limited, and hers an imperium divided among satraps, or governors, not wholly in subordination to her central authority? For if not, why should there be a discord between her animate and inanimate provinces? The human mind looks for unity, yet everywhere in nature's realm contending powers are in conflict. You have the physical world indifferent to living things, unconcerned whether they exist or do not exist. In its turn, upon the insecure foundation of the body, the living organism, rises the mind, incapable, it would seem, of any independent existence. So that thought, love, hope, the soul and its affections,

the whole intellectual structure of human life, are perilously poised in a trembling insecurity upon the material elements, themselves in continual flux.

[13]   Were nature constant in her intentions we might hope to understand them, but how at odds with herself this Lady Bountiful, mother of all living, when she counsels one species of her own creation, providing an armoury the most ingenious, claws and fangs and suckers, instruments of death, that one tribe of her offspring might the better murder the members of another, a device, to our poor uninstructed vision, neither lovely nor divine. Nature is no believer in disarmament. The bird preys upon the insect and the worm, the glow-worm feeds upon the snail, the ichneumon lays its eggs upon the caterpillar, which, when the grubs emerge, will serve as their food. There are animals which seem an incarnation of malice, like that dweller in darkness, the blood-sucking vampire bat. How difficult to think of Christ as the son of the God of nature! Nature encourages internecine strife. Nor has she any favourites among her creatures, unless it be the insect tribe. There are not less than ten million varieties of them in existence. "In India alone the loss of crops, of timber, and of animal products by insect damage is estimated at over 150 million pounds annually, and the death roll due to insect-borne diseases at over a million and a half lives."[1]

[14]   Life is one throughout the universe, yet its parts are in conflict. Nature has her racks and thumbscrews. You cannot instruct her in any of the torturer's or executioner's arts. There is no kindness in the sea, no benevolence in the forest. If you complain that men are a cruel breed, you need not enquire whence they derived the propensity. It is inherited, and from the mother's side.

[15]   Perhaps these things should not be mentioned. Truth is a thorny rose. Sentimental writers do not dwell upon this theme. These star-gazers do not remind us of the *bellum omnium contra omnes*.[2] How tiresome are the one-eyed philosophies. There will be brave men born after us who will not attempt to build up their spiritual lives on a diet of lies. All forms of life, all organisms in which it is manifested, are engaged in an unceasing struggle to maintain themselves against the disintegrating forces of nature. All are in conflict with each other for the means of life, clan against clan, individual against individual. Each exists at the expense of others, and keeps its foothold only by success over the rest. Here is a telegram from South Australia, dated Nov. 6, 1934. "It is estimated that the farmers in Adelaide will lose at least three-quarters of their crops through the depredations of grass-hoppers, which are advancing in uncontrollable swarms on a front of 250 miles." How deep it goes, this warfare, you may conjecture if you remind yourself that the very trees of the forest are battling with each other for the light of the sun, and that the plants have their defensive

---

[1] *The World of Nature*, by H. C. Knapp-Fisher, p. 295.
[2] war of all against all.

armour, the rose and thistle their thorns, the nettle its sting. Make your heart iron within you, when you remember that to live you must kill, either plants or animals. "To live, my Lucilius, is to make war." Hunger for food, hunger for life, of which war is merely the continuation, are the presiding issues.

[16] It is no doubt necessary to think in terms of right and wrong, yet how much more convincing would be our moralists if they began at the beginning, if they could bring themselves to think first in terms of life and death. Who is ignorant that good and evil go everywhere hand in hand, in the closest, indeed inseparable, partnership? The misfortunes of one community make the fortunes of another. If England secures the world markets, they are lost to Germany. If oil becomes the necessary and universal fuel, the oil-producing districts flourish at the expense of those which have none. Among the competitors for a post, or the hand of a lady, one only can prove successful, and not invariably the most deserving. The magistrate and police depend for their livelihood on the swindler and the burglar, the physician upon the sick and disabled. Scarcity of food brings destitution to the poor and high prices to the farmer, and the higher a nation's standard of intellect and skill the worse for the incapable and unintelligent.

[17] We are not sure of what best nourishes, or what damages, the delicate machinery of nerve and brain. We guess at the causes of our physical lassitude. Poisons circulate in our blood from origins unknown. We are surrounded by unseen foes. Nor are our souls less vulnerable than our bodies. Affections spring up in us only to be thwarted or forbidden, or we discover too late that they have been foolishly misplaced and are betrayed. Our very sympathies lead us astray. We are imposed upon by falsehoods and depressed by misunderstandings. The whole region of the emotions is subject to doubts, misgivings, confusion, and those who have shallow natures, feeling little, appear to be best suited for life. Instinct and desire point one way and mature reflection another. Duties conflict not merely with our wishes, but with opposing duties, so that we are in doubt where our loyalty is first due, which cause we should espouse, to which of the arguing voices we should give ear. And, do what we will, to live at all without inflicting injuries upon others is well-nigh, if not altogether impossible. "A terrible thing is life," says Socrates in the *Gorgias*. He thought it a disease, and left with his friend, Crito, a commission to sacrifice a cock as a thank-offering for his deliverance.

[18] Yet within this "odious scene of violence and cruelty," as Mill, rising to a moral superiority over the universe, called it, there runs a counter current. So that in nature's speech there is an equivocation, an irony, an irony clearly discerned, with that unclouded vision of theirs, by the Greeks, and even by the simpler peoples of the earth. A recent traveller reports the philosophy of an African tribe: "They said that although God is good, and wishes good for everybody, unfortunately he has a half-witted brother, who is always interfering with what he does. This half-witted brother keeps on obtruding

himself, and does not give God a chance." How kindly a view of Satan! And what is irony? It is a double-speaking, it is language which, since it is open to two interpretations, hides the speaker's meaning, in which a sense is wrapped other than the obvious sense, language which says one thing and yet means another. There is the irony, too, of circumstances, promising what they do not perform, or it may be performing what they do not promise, or by the event baffling confident expectation. For this ironical language nature has a fondness. Observe that this nature which wars upon herself is the nature which constructs the exquisite fabric of the living organism, and with a physician's arts ministers to the diseases she inflicts, produces in the body anti-toxins to defeat the toxins, administers anaesthetics, and exercises a *vis medicatrix* [3] all her own. How difficult to recognise in the ferocities we see around us the subtle power which made the brain, which elaborated with consummate exactness the mechanism of the heart and lungs, all the devices by which the body maintains its existence! That nature should create a world full of difficulties and dangers, and thereupon proceed to place within it fabrics of an infinite delicacy and complexity to meet these very dangers and difficulties is a contradiction that baffles the understanding. With a cunning past all human thought she solves the problems she has, as it were, absent-mindedly set herself. The flood and the earthquake have no consideration for the plant or animal, yet nature which sends the flood and earthquake has provided, with foresight or in a dream, for the living things they destroy. She both smiles and frowns upon her own creation, and is at once friendly and unfriendly. Like a scarlet thread it runs through her dominion, this inconsistency. Side by side with the undeniable and admirable adjustment between things organic and inorganic, you have the hostility, the discordance. What wonder that men, bewildered by this inexplicable procedure, have supposed her governments distributed among a hierarchy of squabbling deities, persecuting or protecting this or that race of men—Zeus the Greeks, Jehovah the Jews? What wonder they supposed even the trees to be the better of protecting deities, the olive Athena, the vine Dionysus? Ah, nature! subtle beyond all human subtlety, enigmatic, profound, life-giver and life-destroyer, nourishing mother and assassin, inspirer of all that is best and most beautiful, of all that is most hideous and forbidding!

[19] That the world is a unity the philosophers and men of science reiterate with a wearisome persistence. That it is united, they have the sense not to proclaim. How the world became disunited they have not told us. Yet in this procession of time and tears it is not so much the rivers of blood which flow through history, it is the broken hearts that appal us. What elicits human horror and indignation is not so much the suffering that the strong may with courage endure as the suffering at random inflicted upon the weak and innocent and defenceless. I read not long since of a child, who trustingly looked up the chimney to see the coming of Santa Claus.

[3] healing power.

Her clothing took fire, and she was burnt to death. A painful world we might school ourselves to combat, were it only rational, but the conjunction of pain and senselessness is hard to bear. Nor would the heroic race of men, "toil-worn since being began," shrink from grief and wounds were it only assigned a noble task. But nature prescribes no tasks. She calls for no volunteers for a great essay. For the asking she might have millions. She points willing climbers to no Everest. The discovery of the goal—by far the most difficult task—she leaves to us. We are mountaineers by nature, but born blind, and must find for ourselves the Himalayan peak, if there be any peak, we are built to ascend, or else while away the time till the great axe falls, and the futilities are done with. Go where you will through nature, you find no directions for travellers. You choose your path, uncounselled and at your own peril, and the unlikely track may prove to be the best. To be clear-sighted is often to be short-sighted, as when the molluscs and crustaceans, protecting themselves with heavy defensive armour, entered with all their care and caution a blind alley, while naked, unaccommodated man, selecting the more dangerous path, advanced to the headship of living creatures.

[20] Life is a unique experience. There is nothing with which to compare it, no measure of its value in terms of some other thing, and money will not purchase it. Yet with this pearl of price we know not what to do. Schopenhauer loves to dwell, in illustration of his pessimistic thesis, upon the boredom of life, and cites card-playing, a kill-time device, as "quite peculiarly an indication of the miserable side of humanity." That mortals should desire immortality, and yet find difficulty in passing an afternoon—if you have a fancy for paradoxes, here is a pretty one. We contemplate eternity without horror, and find an hour of our own society intolerable. "How dreary it is to be alive, gentlemen!" And how poverty-stricken is the human soul, which, even when armed with supernatural powers, can find no occupation for itself. Marlowe's Faustus, with Mephistopheles to gratify his every wish, can make nothing of his transcendent opportunity.

[21] Tacitus draws a terrible picture of the *taedium vitae*[4] which in imperial times descended upon the Roman aristocracy:

> In his cool hall, with haggard eyes,
>   The Roman noble lay:
> He drove abroad, in furious guise,
>   Along the Appian Way.
>
> He made a feast, drank fierce and fast,
>   And crown'd his head with flowers—
> No easier nor no quicker pass'd
>   The impracticable hours.

Or if, by good fortune, we inherit a nature abundant in resource, which finds every moment full of charm, and think the world a divine playground,

---

[4] weariness of life.

another shadow darkens the windows of the soul. As the child, enchanted with the fairy spectacle upon the stage, the joyous bustle and the glittering lights, whispered to its mother—"Mother, this is not going to end soon, is it?" we are startled to discover that

> in the very temple of delight
> Veil'd melancholy has her sovran shrine.

To foresee the end of happiness poisons the springs of happiness. It will end, and soon. We are permitted an hour at the pageant and the curtain falls.

[22] It may be that, although appearances are against her, nature meant well by us, that her powers were limited. She has done what she could, giving us a "second best," since the best was beyond her. It lay within her strength to confer life, but not to preserve it. Yet one cannot refrain from asking, was it necessary that man's superiority should prove his bane, that his aspirations should end in the grave? To create immortal longings in the ephemeral being of an hour, to implant in him passions never to be gratified, for knowledge never to be attained, for understanding never to be fulfilled, to give him imagination, a fatal dowry, poverty of his possessions with the abundance of his cravings—was this necessary? It appears either a refinement of malicious irony, or a promise of fulfilment, but which? The gods are silent.

> Or is it that some Force, too wise, too strong,
> Even for yourselves to conjure or beguile,
> Sweeps earth, and heaven, and men, and gods along,
> Like the broad volume of the insurgent Nile?
> And the great powers we serve, themselves may be
> Slaves of a tyrannous necessity? . . .
>
> Oh, wherefore cheat our youth, if thus it be,
> Of one short joy, one lust, one pleasant dream?
> Stringing vain words of powers we cannot see,
> Blind divinations of a will supreme;
> Lost labour! when the circumambient gloom
> But hides, if Gods, Gods careless of our doom?

[23] There is, among her inconsistencies, another persuasive artifice of nature, for which, by any mechanical philosophy it is difficult, indeed, to account—the artifice by which she induced men to interest in a future they could not hope to see. She persuades them to self-sacrifice, to loss of life for their offspring, for their race, their country, to martyrdom for their faiths, for shadowy, intangible notions, less substantial than gossamer. By what arrangement of cranks, wheels and levers did she cozen this creature of a day to look beyond his own instant profit, his obvious gain? Why should hope have a place, heroism a place, renunciation a place in this automaton? Is cajolery among her talents? Manifestly the Spartans at Thermopylae were flattered to their ruin by a ridiculous pride of race.

[24] View life as a whole, exert all your powers of fancy, take all history into your account, the embarrassing contradiction remains. On all sides it raises its sphinx-like, ironical countenance. Another and final illustration will suffice. At the heart of existence there lies an undeniable sweetness, which no philosophy has fathomed, and no railing accusation against life can dislodge. The complaints against it are legion. In all ages and societies goes up the bitter cry, "Vanity of vanities, all is vanity." "All that exists," wrote Leopardi, "is evil, that anything exists is an evil; everything exists only to achieve evil; existence itself is an evil, and destined to evil. There is no other good than nonexistence."

[25] So much for life: not a pennyworth of value anywhere. Yet the doctrines and religions, and they are numerous, which condemn existence, offer no adequate explanation of the clinging attraction for a state they censure and profess to despise. From this so undesirable a possession their adherents are, for the most part, curiously unwilling to part. "What sort of a pessimist is this," asks Nietzsche, "who plays the flute?" The pessimists are not alone in vilifying life. They have the support of Christian preachers. "The whole world," says Donne, "is but a universal churchyard, but our common grave." Christianity has little good to say of life, yet how reluctant the best Christians are to become angels. Like the worldlings they, too, are intoxicated with the pleasures of sense. They marry and are given in marriage. They succumb at times to song and laughter. Cheerfulness keeps lurking in odd corners of the horrid gloom. There is some magic at work here. Is it possible that something may be said for this vale of sorrows? Though not to be compared with the ineffable bliss we demand, yet as an alternative to nothing a case for existence can be stated. In fairness to nature you must enter this natural sweetness in the ledger of your account with her. The ecstasy of lovers, the joy in activity, the glow, the radiance, the sunlight, the perfume—omit these, and it is a caricature you have drawn, not the landscape. There is a music in the air.

> Riding adown the country lanes;
>   The larks sang high—
> O heart, for all thy griefs and pains
>   Thou shalt be loath to die.

[26] Many philosophers have been defeatists. Diogenes and Zeno, Epictetus and Marcus Aurelius, Schopenhauer and Spinoza. Ἀπάθεια, ἀταραξία, nil admirari, indifference, impassivity, passionlessness, they are all one. Stoicism, Epicureanism, Taoism, how many creeds and doctrines are in their essence, withdrawals from life? For them it is not an adventure but a weary pilgrimage. They take no pleasure in it. Sick of time, they take refuge in eternity. And we seem forced to the strange conclusion that Paganism suits world conditions better. Perhaps it should, indeed, be expected. For why should the haters of life be more at home in it than its lovers? The creed of the Northmen, for example, left room for activity and prowess, for skill and enterprise, for courage and adventure. They had a liking for the risks and

dangers of existence, which gave a zest to living, and for a worthy antagonist, who put them on their mettle.

[27] Life is like the sea, never at rest, untamed, moody, capricious, perilous. Many a man who knows the sea has sworn, and sworn again, that once on land he would never more embark upon so inclement, so treacherous, so hateful an element. And few who have so sworn have not heard with aching hearts her call, and longed for her bitter and incomparable society. Like life she lays a spell upon them, a spell not resident in her smiles, though smile she can, nor in her calm, though, like life, she, too, has her seasons of calm, her sheltered lagoons and quiet havens. Men are said to love flattery. The sea never flatters. They are said to love ease. She offers toil. Like life, she deals in every form of danger, and many modes of death—famine, thirst, fire, cold, shipwreck. Like life she strips men of their pretentions and vanities, exposes the weakness of the weak and the folly of the fool. Wherein then lies the fascination, against which the soft Lydian airs cannot with men that are men prevail? It flings a challenge and human nature rises to a challenge. Men are by nature striving creatures, heroically stubborn, as is the mind itself.

> Still nursing the unconquerable hope,
> Still clutching the inviolable shade.

They love best what they do for themselves, for what they themselves make they have a great affection; what is given them out of charity they value less. The world seems somehow so made as to suit best the adventurous and courageous, the men who, like Nelson, wear all their stars, like Napoleon's marshals their most splendid uniforms, not that they may be less but more conspicuous and incur greater dangers than their fellows. Leonidas at Thermopylae, resolved to stand and die for his country's cause, wished to save two lads by sending them home with a message to Sparta. He was met by the answer, "We are not here to carry messages, but to fight." However it comes about, such men are more inspiring figures than the defeatists.

[28] Matthew Arnold quotes with admiration Pope's rendering of the passage in Homer in which Sarpedon urges his friend Glaucus into the fight, the passage which in the original Lord Granville quoted on his death-bed.

> Could all our care elude the gloomy grave
> Which claims no less the fearful than the brave,
> For lust of fame I should not vainly dare
> In fighting fields, nor urge thy soul to war;
> But since, alas! ignoble age must come,
> Disease, and death's inexorable doom;
> The life which others pay, let us bestow,
> And give to fame what we to nature owe.

Cogito, ergo sum, said Descartes. "I think, therefore I am." He desired a platform, or rather an undeniable proposition as the foundation of his philosophic thought. His successors have not found it either undeniable or sufficient. They have rejected, too, such alternatives as "I act, therefore I am." "I desire, therefore I am." Let me suggest still another. No philosophers, or men of science, have so far had the hardihood, as far as I know, to deny us our pains. They relieve us of all else. They have taken from us our personality, our freedom, our souls, our very selves. They have, however, left us our sorrows. Let us take, then, as our foundation the proposition "I suffer, therefore I am." And let us add to it the converse and equally true statement, "I am, therefore I suffer." The privilege, if it be a privilege, of existence is ours and we have paid the price required. We have discharged our debts. We have not had something for nothing. We have free minds, and can look around us with a smile. Nothing can any longer intimidate us.

COMMENT AND QUESTIONS

I. The human situation, as Mr. Dixon sees it, is full of irony, paradox, contradiction. What irony or irrationality does he find in each of the following: the fact that man has imagination, and is sensitive to pleasure and pain; the existence of natural phenomena such as floods, earthquakes, and volcanic eruptions; the relationship of the mind and the body; the relationship between species of living things; the fact that nature cures and heals; the human desire for immortality; human self-sacrifice for race or country or a faith; the sweetness of life?

II. The passages below express attitudes toward nature that were very common in the nineteenth century.

The indescribable innocence and beneficence of Nature,—of sun and wind and rain, of summer and winter,—such health, such cheer, they afford forever! and such sympathy have they ever with our race, that all Nature would be affected and the sun's brightness fade, and the winds would sigh humanely, and the clouds rain tears, and the woods shed their leaves and put on mourning in midsummer, if any man should ever for a just cause grieve.—HENRY DAVID THOREAU, *Walden*

>   And I have felt
> A presence that disturbs me with the joy
> Of elevated thoughts; a sense sublime
> Of something far more deeply interfused,
> Whose dwelling is the light of setting suns,
> And the round ocean and the living air,
> And the blue sky, and in the mind of man:
> A motion and a spirit, that impels
> All thinking things, all objects of all thought,
> And rolls through all things. Therefore am I still
> A lover of the meadows and the woods,
> And mountains; and of all that we behold
> From this green earth; of all the mighty world

>   Of eye, and ear,—both what they half create,
>   And what perceive; well pleased to recognise
>   In nature and the language of the sense
>   The anchor of my purest thoughts, the nurse,
>   The guide, the guardian of my heart, and soul
>   Of all my moral being.—WILLIAM WORDSWORTH,
>   "Lines Composed a Few Miles Above Tintern Abbey"

Compare Dixon's view of nature with the views held by Thoreau and Wordsworth. Which view are you inclined to hold? Which seems to you more nearly true?

III. "Every man goes about arm in arm with disappointment," the author says. Do you agree or disagree with this statement? Do you think that intelligent men are likely to feel more or less disappointment than unintelligent men; or do you think intelligence has no relevance to disappointment?

IV. In paragraph 22, Dixon restates an idea he has touched on earlier: "It may be that, although appearances are against her, nature meant well by us, that her powers were limited." A more conventional idea is that nature (or God) is all-powerful. Does one of these ideas seem to you more satisfying than the other? If so, why?

V. Do you think the author is implying that life is purposeless? Do you think he is implying that it is not worth living? Explain.

VI. Given the human situation presented in the essay, what attitudes toward life does the author think an intelligent human being should hold? How should he live?

IRWIN EDMAN

A Reasonable Life in a Mad World*

Irwin Edman (1896–1954) was a professor of philosophy at Columbia University; author of *Four Ways of Philosophy, Philosopher's Holiday, Candle in the Dark, Arts and the Man;* and a contributor to *The New Yorker* as well as to scholarly journals. He is one of the most readable and one of the most rewarding of modern writers-on-philosophy. The following essay was published in *The Atlantic Monthly* in 1949.

[1] That the world is mad has been the judgment of self-denominated sane philosophers from the Greeks to the present day. It is not a discovery of our own age that both the public and private lives of human beings are

---

* Copyright, 1949, by The Atlantic Monthly Company, 8 Arlington Street, Boston 16, Massachusetts.

dominated by folly and stupidity. Philosophers pressing the point have brought such charges not against human nature only—that is, the world of human relations—but against that larger universe in which the world of human relations is set. As far back as the Book of Job and probably much further back, for there must have been at least gruntingly articulate Jobs in prehistory, it is not only men who have been declared mad: by any standards of rationality the universe itself has been called irrational, pointless, meaningless, with incidental, unintended overtones of cruelty and injustice.

[2] With the provincialism of each generation, ours imagines that the causes of cynicism and despair are new in our time. There have, of course, been modern improvements and refinements of stupidity and folly. No previous generation has been by way of organizing itself with insane efficiency for blowing the whole race to smithereens. It does not take a particularly logical mind at the present moment to discover that the world is quite mad, though a great many critics apparently think that the cruel absurdity of technical efficiency combined with moral bankruptcy is a discovery that it took great wit on their part to turn up.

[3] Reputations are being made by reiterating, to the extent of four or five hundred pages, that collective modern man is a technical genius merged with a moral imbecile.

[4] The first encouragement I can bring is the reminder that the kind of madness which we all realize to be the present state of the world is not something new. It is, just like everything else in the modern world, bigger and more streamlined, if not better. It is a pity some of the great satirists are dead; Swift and Voltaire would have given their eyeteeth for the present situation. And Aristophanes would scarcely have believed it. But the essential charges they would bring against the present time and the essential absurdities they would show up are not different in essence now from what they were.

[5] Neither nature nor man appears reasonable by reasonable human standards. So acutely does this seem to many people to be true that in almost exuberant desperation they decide to march crazily in the insane procession. Existentialists make a cult of anxiety and despair and find a kind of wry comfort in saying, Since the world is absurd, let absurdity and irony be our standards. There are others who say—and the currency of an ersatz theological literature shows how epidemic they are—that since the world and mankind at present seem so palpably absurd it simply can't be true, and history, as Toynbee [1] now assures us, moves delightfully and progressively to fulfillment in the Church of God—a kind of quiet, English Church incorporating the best features of Islam, Buddhism, Confucianism, and a little, even, of the Hebrew prophets and the secular sciences.

[6] The excitements and confused urgencies of the present time may seem to make hysteria or mystical narcosis or hedonistic excitement tantamount to a philosophy. But the still, small voice of rationality persists. And the

---

[1] Arnold J. Toynbee, contemporary English historian and author of *A Study of History*.

question still remains the same as that propounded by the Greeks long ago: How, in a world certainly not at first acquaintance rational-appearing, is it possible to lead a rational life?

[7] It seems mad now to say that anyone could believe, as the Fabians [2] did (including such unsentimental people as George Bernard Shaw and Sidney and Beatrice Webb and Graham Wallas and later H. G. Wells), that the world could be transformed into a livable, beautiful, reasonable place by the co-operation of reasonable men. It is not simply that the violent external events of the past generation have revealed to us how precarious were security and comfort, and for how few it obtained at all.

[8] But the psychological sciences have revealed to us the deep sources of violence, confusion, hysteria, and madness in ourselves. What perhaps a generation ago seemed a melodramatic aphorism when Santayana uttered it seems now to be a hitting of the nail on the head: "The normal man holds a lunatic in leash." The definition needs to be amended. In the light of the past twenty-five years, the normal man no longer *does* hold a lunatic in leash. The fact that even talk about a third world war has become standard has practically made lunacy respectable. It is now become a stamp of madness to talk as if one seriously believed that a peaceful and just world were possible.

[9] And yet the sentiment of rationality persists and the hope persists also that it is not impossible, at least in imagination, to dream and in organized effort to work for what seems "an ordered, coherent world society." The most ardent workers for such a world, however, realize that there is plenty of madness left, out of which a third world war may come.

II

[10] The persistence of power politics, the greed for privilege, the insane clutching of wealth, the pathological tribalisms of nations, of class, and of race; it is this world in which we are actually living, and the human problem for anyone in it is to discover what is a reasonable life in such a world.

[11] Is it to forget as far as possible and to live only in the moment and to make that moment as brief and bright as possible? Is it to surrender any hope for pleasure or happiness now and give one's dedicated and ruthless devotion to work for a more reasonable world? Is it to seek Nirvana or to seek some salvation in another world? There seems to be some sense in each answer, but which answer one chooses will depend ultimately on how one answers a basic question: Is the world always and necessarily mad? Is it completely mad now, and is it possible even now to understand the madness and, through understanding, to endure or change it?

[12] Let us try as simply as possible to deal with some of these questions. First, is the world always and necessarily mad? By "the world," of course, one means both the processes of nature and the activities of human beings.

[2] English socialists who aimed to reform society gradually, avoiding revolutionary methods.

1068 READING FOR IDEAS AND VALUES

For "world" in the first sense one had perhaps better use the word "universe." A thoroughly rational universe would be one which was achieving a purpose set down in advance, a purpose which in human terms made sense and which by human standards made moral sense. A rational universe might be one such as the Deists conceived in the eighteenth century, in which nature was simply reason incarnate or reason embodied in the vast machinery of things.

[13] In one respect at least the advance of knowledge of the physical world has not made the world seem more irrational. It has made it seem orderly and regular. But in another respect an understanding of the causes and consequences of nature by conventional standards made nature seem wholly irrational. "I am what I am," said Jehovah in the Old Testament, as if that announcement were sufficient explanation of his wrathful ways. "It is what it is and it does what it does" may be said to be the conclusions of empirical physical science. It is maddening to rational creatures to discover they were born into a world which is not particularly interested in human purposes, which perhaps permits and sustains these purposes but is innocent of any solicitude concerning them. The rain notoriously falls on the just and the unjust, and the just feel highly put upon. Death is no respecter of persons; plagues fell the virtuous. The most generous and devoted enterprises are washed away by floods along with the conspiracies of the sinister and hateful.

[14] Theologians have spent a good deal of time trying to gloss away the irrationalities of the universe, explaining that God moves in a mysterious or at least salutary way, his morally therapeutic wonders to perform. Job was not greatly impressed by his comforters, and neither are we. But if exasperated humans have criticized the world in general, they have been especially critical of the madness of their fellow men. Voltaire found his greatest weapon of satire in treating cruelty, barbarism, and superstition not as evil but as absurd.

[15] The most serious and damaging charge we can bring against civilization is that by the very standards of civilization it is a ridiculous failure. It takes a high degree of sophistication and technical resources to make such an international shambles as we seem fated to do. It takes something like genius in folly to have millions starving in the midst of plenty, to have technological magic whose fruits are poverty, squalor, anarchy, and death; it takes a refinement of absurdity to use the most generous aphorism of the highest religions to justify or rationalize intolerance, violence, and our established international disorder.

[16] Now about the first irrationality: that of the universe itself. Perhaps the only reasonable attitude is that of resignation and endurance of it. Perhaps it is only the persistence of our childhood wishes and expectations that has led us to an assumption that the universe must conform to human purposes and that it is shockingly unreasonable of it not so to conform. We can, within the limits of a world not made for us, make it conform to ideals and values which flower out of nature itself. Part of the life of reason is a

contemplation of the unchanging and unchangeable elements in the world of nature; part of it is a sedulous attempt to discover the ways of changing the world in the interest of human values.

[17] With respect to the world of human activities there has been an accelerated desperation at the present time. In the old days when humor could still flourish in Central Europe it used to be said that the difference between the temper of Berlin and Vienna could be stated as follows: In Berlin when things went wrong it was remarked: "The situation is serious but not hopeless"; in Vienna with smiling deprecation the Viennese used to say: "The situation is hopeless but not serious." The Berlin version seems of late more greatly to have impressed the world.

[18] Though Existentialism may be said to describe the world as being both hopeless and trivial, if one so conceives the realm of human affairs the Epicurean prescription for a reasonable life is perhaps the best that one can find. However clouded and uncertain the future, there is at least possible for the lucky and the prudent a brief, bright interval in which they may find luster and to which their refined sensibilities may give luster. In a world without meaning they may find exquisite nuances of meaning in the arts, in friendship, in love.

[19] The trouble with the Epicurean solution and abdication is that it is always haunted by a scruple of conscience and the shadow of despair. There is something already tarnished in a brightness that declares itself both ultimately meaningless and transient. Sorrow and inhibition and regret dog the footsteps of the Epicurean in a world where folly is no longer a joke but a terrifying threat to all mankind.

[20] There are those, therefore, in our own age who jump to the other extreme. One insists that one *must* give up any hope for present happiness and give one's dedicated and ruthless devotion to work for a better world. I have friends, especially in social or government work or in the social sciences, who regard humor, irony, urbanity, or relaxation with something of the same moral impatience with which a missionary might watch the natives of the Fiji Islands dance or lounge in the sun. There is so little time; it is later than you think; there is no time for comedy. Urbanity is a form of evasion, and laughter is a form of bourgeois or decadent callousness. Let us gird our loins and work together rapidly for the common good or we shall all in common be destroyed. The psychiatric departments of hospitals number among their patients a good many people who in their earnest haste to save the world from destruction ended up by destroying their equilibrium and almost themselves. The tension of moral earnestness, the refusal to permit the enjoyment of even such goods as are possible in a chaotic world, is one of the diseases of our civilization, not a sign of its health. If Epicureanism leads to dismay, unrelieved moral dedication leads to fanaticism. Neither the playboy nor the zealot is a true or adequate incarnation of the life of reason.

[21] Those who recognize the disillusion of a pleasure philosophy or the

destructiveness of a moral fanaticism have begun in our age, as they have in other ages, to turn to otherworldly philosophies. They have tried to seek an inward light unquenchable by external circumstances. They have tried in spirit to follow the Indian saint into the wilderness or the monk into his cell or the mystic into his remote meditation. They have sought Nirvana, or a Oneness with the One, or an Aloneness with the Alone. The follies of society are not cured by the incantations of pure mysticism, and the search for oblivion is really a pathological attempt simply to become oblivious to the actual and remediable conflicts and disorders in society.

[22]   There are still others than the pleasure-lovers, the Nirvana-seekers, the devotees of such mystics, who have sought to make a prescription for a reasonable life. Among those others now epidemic are followers of historians and zoologists who with the theological wave of a wand discover that a palpably absurd world is somehow moving toward a cozy fulfillment where, as I heard Mr. Toynbee say, "God is Love." It would seem a strange moment to detect the course of history as the operations of universal love when the world is being filled with universal hate.

[23]   No, I do not think any of these ersatz solutions will do. The pressure of events simply confirms again what the life of reason does consist in: a brave contemplation of what things are discoverably like and a resolute attempt to improve the lot of man in the conditions into which he finds himself born. The life of reason must always have a stoic element because there is no sign that either the follies of humanity or the uncaring order of nature will ever be magically transformed.

[24]   The life of reason must also contain an element of hope, for it is quite clear, as the history of every improvement in man's estate has shown us, that human intelligence accompanied by human goodwill may profoundly improve the life of mankind. The life of reason must include the pleasure principle also, for what else gives life meaning if not joy and delight of life, and what a folly it would be not to cherish and embrace, not to nourish then, even in a sick society, that which yields the fruit of a quickened, multiplied awareness, the substance of vision and of joy. The universe may be pointless, but there are many good points in it. Our urgencies may be intense, but the world does not end with us or even with our own civilization; nor, if we do not quench intelligence and generosity in ourselves, is it a foregone conclusion that our civilization must end. And the best insurance, perhaps, of maintaining both is to reaffirm the quality of life itself, of its possibility of beauty and its intimations of order and of justice.

COMMENT AND QUESTIONS

I. Mr. Edman assumes that his readers agree that the world is mad. Do you agree? In the essay, what aspects of the world and of human relations are mentioned in support of the assumption of madness?

II. Supply concrete examples of what the author is talking about in the last sentence of paragraph 7, and in the first half of the single sentence of paragraph 10.

III. What seems to be Edman's answer to the question "Is the world always and necessarily mad"?

IV. What are the various prescriptions for a reasonable life which the author rejects as "ersatz solutions"? Why does he reject each one?

V. If you have read Sartre's essay on existentialism, Epicurus' "Letter to a Friend," and the discussion of mysticism in Aldous Huxley's essay on the perennial philosophy, you are in a better position to judge what Edman is saying. Do you agree with his attitudes toward existentialism, Epicureanism, and mysticism?

VI. State in your own words the concept of the reasonable life presented in the last two paragraphs of the essay. Does the author's conclusion follow logically from the ideas and details presented earlier in the essay? To what extent do you agree or disagree with Edman's idea of the reasonable life?

READINGS

SECTION 6

Simple Narrative, Autobiograpy, and Informal Essays

LINCOLN STEFFENS

I Get a Colt to Break In*

The following autobiographical narrative presents a series of episodes in a single phase (probably a year) of a boy's life. Lincoln Steffens (1866–1936) was a prominent American journalist and editor, best known in the early twentieth century for his exposés of corruption in business and government. "I Get a Colt to Break In" is one of the early chapters of his well-written and interesting *Autobiography*, published in 1931.

Colonel Carter gave me a colt. I had my pony, and my father meanwhile had bought a pair of black carriage horses and a cow, all of which I had to attend to when we had no "man." And servants were hard to get and to keep in those days; the women married, and the men soon quit service to seize opportunities always opening. My hands were pretty full, and so was the stable. But Colonel Carter seemed to think that he had promised me a horse. He had not; I would have known it if he had. No matter. He thought he had, and maybe he did promise himself to give me one. That was enough. The kind of man that led immigrant trains across the continent and delivered them safe, sound, and together where he promised would keep his word. One day he drove over from Stockton, leading a two-year-old which he brought to our front door and turned over to me as mine. Such a horse!

She was a cream-colored mare with a black forelock, mane, and tail and a

---

* From *The Autobiography of Lincoln Steffens*, copyright, 1931, by Harcourt, Brace and Company, Inc.

black stripe along the middle of her back. Tall, slender, high-spirited, I thought then—I think now—that she was the most beautiful of horses. Colonel Carter had bred and reared her with me and my uses in mind. She was a careful cross of a mustang mare and thoroughbred stallion, with the stamina of the wild horse and the speed and grace of the racer. And she had a sense of fun. As Colonel Carter got down out of his buggy and went up to her, she snorted, reared, flung her head high in the air, and, coming down beside him, tucked her nose affectionately under his arm.

"I have handled her a lot," he said. "She is as kind as a kitten, but she is as sensitive as a lady. You can spoil her by one mistake. If you ever lose your temper, if you ever abuse her, she will be ruined forever. And she is unbroken. I might have had her broken to ride for you, but I didn't want to. I want you to do it. I have taught her to lead, as you can see; had to, to get her over here. But here she is, an unbroken colt; yours. You take and you break her. You're only a boy, but if you break this colt right, you'll be a man—a young man, but a man. And I'll tell you how."

Now, out West, as everyone knows, they break in a horse by riding out to him in his wild state, lassoing, throwing, and saddling him; then they let him up, frightened and shocked, with a yelling broncho-buster astride of him. The wild beast bucks, the cowboy drives his spurs into him, and off they go, jumping, kicking, rearing, falling, till by the weight of the man, the lash, and the rowels, the horse is broken—in body and spirit. This was not the way I was to break my colt.

"You must break her to ride without her ever knowing it," Colonel Carter said. "You feed and you clean her—you; not the stable man. You lead her out to water and to walk. You put her on a long rope and let her play, calling her to you and gently pulling on the rope. Then you turn her loose in the grass lot there and, when she has romped till tired, call her. If she won't come, leave her. When she wants water or food, she will run to your call, and you will pet and feed and care for her." He went on for half an hour, advising me in great detail how to proceed. I wanted to begin right away. He laughed. He let me lead her around to the stable, water her, and put her in the stable and feed her.

There I saw my pony. My father, sisters, and Colonel Carter saw me stop and look at my pony.

"What'll you do with him?" one of my sisters asked. I was bewildered for a moment. What should I do with the little red horse? I decided at once.

"You can have him," I said to my sisters.

"No," said Colonel Carter, "not yet. You can give your sisters the pony by and by, but you'll need him till you have taught the colt to carry you and a saddle—months; and you must not hurry. You must learn patience, and you will if you give the colt time to learn it, too. Patience and control. You can't control a young horse unless you can control yourself. Can you shoot?" he asked suddenly.

I couldn't. I had a gun and I had used it some, but it was a rifle, and I could not bring down with it such game as there was around Sacramento—birds and hares. Colonel Carter looked at my father, and I caught the look. So did my father. I soon had a shotgun. But at the time Colonel Carter turned to me and said:

"Can't shoot straight, eh? Do you know what that means? That means that you can't control a gun, and that means you can't control yourself, your eye, your hands, your nerves. You are wriggling now. I tell you that a good shot is always a good man. He may be a 'bad man' too, but he is quiet, strong, steady in speech, gait, and mind. No matter, though. If you break in this colt right, if you teach her her paces, she will teach you to shoot and be quiet."

He went off downtown with my father, and I started away with my colt. I fed, I led, I cleaned her, gently, as if she were made of glass; she was playful and willing, a delight. When Colonel Carter came home with my father for supper, he questioned me.

"You should not have worked her today," he said. "She has come all the way from Stockton and must be tired. Yes, yes, she would not show her fatigue; too fine for that, and too young to be wise. You have got to think for her, consider her as you would your sisters."

Sisters! I thought; I had never considered my sisters. I did not say that, but Colonel Carter laughed and nodded to my sisters. It was just as if he had read my thought. But he went on to draw on my imagination a centaur; the colt as a horse's body—me, a boy, as the head and brains of one united creature. I liked that. I would be that. I and the colt: a centaur.

After Colonel Carter was gone home I went to work on my new horse. The old one, the pony, I used only for business: to go to fires, to see my friends, run errands, and go hunting with my new shotgun. But the game that had all my attention was the breaking in of the colt, the beautiful cream-colored mare, who soon knew me—and my pockets. I carried sugar to reward her when she did right, and she discovered where I carried it; so did the pony, and when I was busy they would push their noses into my pockets, both of which were torn down a good deal of the time. But the colt learned. I taught her to run around a circle, turn and go the other way at a signal. My sisters helped me. I held the long rope and the whip (for signaling), while one of the girls led the colt; it was hard work for them, but they took it in turns. One would lead the colt round and round till I snapped the whip; then she would turn, turning the colt, till the colt did it all by herself. And she was very quick. She shook hands with each of her four feet. She let us run under her, back and forth. She was slow only to carry me. Following Colonel Carter's instructions, I began by laying my arm or a surcingle over her back. If she trembled, I drew it slowly off. When she could abide it, I tried buckling it, tighter and tighter. I laid over her, too, a blanket, folded at first, then open, and, at last, I slipped up on her myself, sat there a second, and as she trembled, slid off. My sisters held her for me, and when I could get up and sit there a moment or two, I tied her at a block, and we, my sisters and I, made a procession of mounting and dismounting. She soon got used to this, and would let us slide off over her rump, but it was a long, long time before she would carry me.

That we practiced by leading her along a high curb where I could get on as she walked, ride a few steps, and then, as she felt me and crouched, slip off. She never did learn to carry a girl on her back; my sisters had to lead her while I rode. This was not purposeful. I don't know just how it happened, but I do remember the first time I rode on my colt all the way round the lot and how, when I put one of the girls up, she refused to repeat. She shuddered, shook and frightened them off.

While we were breaking in the colt a circus came to town. The ring was across the street from our house. Wonderful! I lived in that circus for a week. I saw the show but once, but I marked the horse-trainers, and in the mornings when they were not too busy I told them about my colt, showed her to them, and asked them how to train her to do circus tricks. With their hints I taught the colt to stand up on her hind legs, kneel, lie down, and balance on a small box. This last was easier than it looked. I put her first on a low big box and taught her to turn on it; then got a little smaller box upon which she repeated what she did on the big one. By and by we had her so that she would step up on a high box so small that her four feet were almost touching, and there also she would turn.

The circus man gave me one hint that was worth all the other tricks put together. "You catch her doing something of herself that looks good," he said, "and then you keep her at it." It was thus that I taught her to bow to people. The first day I rode her out on to the streets was a proud one for me and for the colt, too, apparently. She did not walk, she danced; perhaps she was excited, nervous; anyhow I liked the way she threw up her head, champed at the bit, and went, dancing, prancing down the street. Everybody stopped to watch us, and so, when she began to sober down, I picked her up again with heel and rein, saying, "Here's people, Lady," and she would show off to my delight. By constant repetition I had her so trained that she would single-foot, head down, along a country road till we came to a house or a group of people. Then I'd say, "People, Lady," and up would go her head, and her feet would dance.

But the trick that set the town talking was her bowing to anyone I spoke to. "Lennie Steffens' horse bows to you," people said, and she did. I never told how it was done; by accident. Dogs used to run out at us and the colt enjoyed it; she kicked at them sometimes with both hind hoofs. I joined her in the game, and being able to look behind more conveniently than she could, I watched the dogs until they were in range, then gave the colt a signal to kick. "Kick, gal," I'd say, and tap her ribs with my heel. We used to get dogs together that way; the colt would kick them over and over and leave them yelping in the road. Well, one day when I met a girl I knew I lifted my hat, probably muttered a "Good day," and I must have touched the colt with my heel. Anyway, she dropped her head and kicked—not much; there was no dog near, so she had responded to my unexpected signal by what looked like a bow. I caught the idea and kept her at it. Whenever I wanted to bow to a girl or anyone else, instead of saying "Good day," I muttered "Kick, gal," spurred her lightly, and—the whole centaur bowed and was covered with glory and conceit.

Yes, conceit. I was full of it, and the colt was quite as bad. One day my chum Hjalmar came into town on his Black Bess, blanketed. She had had a great fistula cut out of her shoulder and had to be kept warm. I expected to see her weak and dull, but no, the good old mare was champing and dancing, like my colt.

"What is it makes her so?" I asked, and Hjalmar said he didn't know, but he thought she was proud of the blanket. A great idea. I had a gaudy horse blanket. I put it on the colt, and I could hardly hold her. We rode down the main street together, both horses, and both boys, so full of vanity that everybody stopped to smile. We thought they admired, and maybe they did. But some boys on the street gave us another angle. They, too, stopped and looked, and as we passed, one of them said, "Think you're hell, don't you?"

Spoilsport!

We did, as a matter of fact; we thought we were hell. The recognition of it dashed us for a moment; not for long, and the horses paid no heed. We pranced, the black and the yellow, all the way down J Street, up K Street, and agreed that we'd do it again, often. Only I said, we wouldn't use blankets. If the horses were proud of a blanket, they'd be proud of anything unusually conspicuous. We tried a flower next time. I fixed a big rose on my colt's bridle just under her ear and it was great—she pranced downtown with her head turned, literally, to show off her flower. We had to change the decorations from time to time, put on a ribbon, or a bell, or a feather, but, really, it was not necessary for my horse. Old Black Bess needed an incentive to act up, but all I had to do to my horse was to pick up the reins, touch her with my heel, and say, "People"; she would dance from one side of the street to the other, asking to be admired. As she was. As we were.

I would ride down to my father's store, jump off my prancing colt in the middle of the street, and run up into the shop. The colt, free, would stop short, turn, and follow me right up on the sidewalk, unless I bade her wait. If anyone approached her while I was gone, she would snort, rear, and strike. No stranger could get near her. She became a frightened, frightening animal, and yet when I came into sight, she would run up to me, put her head down, and as I straddled her neck, she would throw up her head and pitch me into my seat, facing backwards, of course. I whirled around right, and off we'd go, the vainest boy and the proudest horse in the State.

"Hey, give me a ride, will you?" some boy would ask.

"Sure," I'd say, and jump down and watch the boy try to catch and mount my colt. He couldn't. Once a cowboy wanted to try her, and he caught her; he dodged her forefeet, grabbed the reins, and in one spring was on her back. I never did that again. My colt reared, then bucked, and, as the cowboy kept his seat, she shuddered, sank to the ground, and rolled over. He slipped aside and would have risen with her, but I was alarmed and begged him not to. She got up at my touch and followed me so close that she stepped on my heel and hurt me. The cowboy saw the point.

"If I were you, kid," he said, "I'd never let anybody mount that colt. She's too good."

That, I think, was the only mistake I made in the rearing of Colonel Carter's gift-horse. My father differed from me. He discovered another error or sin, and thrashed me for it. My practice was to work hard on a trick, privately, and when it was perfect, let him see it. I would have the horse out in our vacant lot doing it as he came home to supper. One evening, as he approached the house, I was standing, whip in hand, while the colt, quite free, was stepping carefully over the bodies of a lot of girls, all my sisters and all their girl friends. (Grace Gallatin, later Mrs. Thompson-Seton, was among them.) My father did not express the admiration I expected; he was frightened and furious. "Stop that," he called, and he came running around into the lot, took the whip, and lashed me with it. I tried to explain; the girls tried to help me explain.

I had seen in the circus a horse that stepped thus over a row of prostrate clowns. It looked dangerous for the clowns, but the trainer had told me how to do it. You begin with logs, laid out a certain distance apart; the horse walks over them under your lead, and whenever he touches one you rebuke him. By and by he will learn to step with such care that he never trips. Then you substitute clowns. I had no clowns, but I did get logs, and with the girls helping, we taught the colt to step over the obstacles even at a trot. Walking, she touched nothing. All ready thus with the logs, I had my sisters lie down in the grass, and again and again the colt stepped over them. None was ever touched. My father would not listen to any of this; he just walloped me, and when he was tired or satisfied and I was in tears, I blubbered a short excuse: "They were only girls." And he whipped me some more.

My father was not given to whipping; he did it very seldom, but he did it hard when he did it at all. My mother was just the opposite. She did not whip me, but she often smacked me, and she had a most annoying habit of thumping me on the head with her thimbled finger. This I resented more than my father's thoroughgoing thrashings, and I can tell why now. I would be playing Napoleon and as I was reviewing my Old Guard, she would crack my skull with that thimble. No doubt I was in the way; it took a lot of furniture and sisters to represent properly a victorious army; and you might think as my mother did that a thimble is a small weapon. But imagine Napoleon at the height of his power, the ruler of the world on parade, getting a sharp rap on his crown from a woman's thimble. No. My father's way was more appropriate. It was hard. "I'll attend to you in the morning," he would say, and I lay awake wondering which of my crimes he had discovered. I know what it is to be sentenced to be shot at sunrise. And it hurt, in the morning, when he was not angry but very fresh and strong. But you see, he walloped me in my own person; he never humiliated Napoleon or my knighthood, as my mother did. And I learned something from his discipline, something useful.

I learned what tyranny is and the pain of being misunderstood and wronged, or, if you please, understood and set right; they are pretty much the same. He and most parents and teachers do not break in their boys as carefully as I broke in my colt. They haven't the time that I had, and they have not some other incentives I had. I saw this that day when I rubbed my sore legs. He had to explain to my indignant mother what had happened. When he had told it his way, I gave my version: how long and cautiously I had been teaching my horse to walk over logs and girls. And having shown how sure I was of myself and the colt, while my mother was boring into his silence with one of her reproachful looks, I said something that hit my father hard.

"I taught the colt that trick, I have taught her all that you see she knows, without whipping her. I have never struck her; not once. Colonel Carter said I mustn't, and I haven't."

And my mother, backing me up, gave him a rap: "There," she said, "I told you so." He walked off, looking like a thimble-rapped Napoleon.

COMMENT AND QUESTIONS

I. This selection may be called a narrative essay as well as a simple narrative. What central idea emerges from the story of Steffens and his colt?

II. In what ways does Steffens' experience with the colt widen his perception?

III. What is the reason for presenting so fully Colonel Carter's advice about handling the colt?

IV. How would you characterize Steffens' attitude toward himself in the narrative?

V. How does he make clear, before the closing paragraphs, that he has never whipped the colt?

VI. What is the meaning of "rap" in the last paragraph?

VII. Lincoln Steffens writes very well. The paragraph in which Colonel Carter draws in his imagination the centaur (page 1074) is one example of effective expression. Analyze the structure and movement of sentences to determine what makes this passage effective. Point out other examples of particularly good writing in the selection.

CLARENCE DAY

Father Opens My Mail*

The following account of a father-son relationship has been classified as an essay and as autobiography. It is both. It is also a simple narrative in that it relates a sequence of events in time-order. Clarence Day (1874–1935) is best known for his humorous autobiographical works, *God and My Father, Life With Father, Life With Mother,* and *Father and I.* "Father Opens My Mail" is a chapter of *Life With Father,* which was published in 1935 and dramatized in 1939.

There was a time in my boyhood when I felt that Father had handicapped me severely in life by naming me after him, "Clarence." All literature, so far as I could see, was thronged with objectionable persons named Clarence. Percy was bad enough, but there had been some good fighters named Percy. The only Clarence in history was a duke who did something dirty at Tewkesbury, and who died a ridiculous death afterwards in a barrel of malmsey.

As for the Clarences in the fiction I read, they were horrible. In one story, for instance, there were two brothers, Clarence and Frank. Clarence was a "vain, disagreeable little fellow" who was proud of his curly hair and fine clothes, while Frank was a "rollicking boy who was ready to play games with anybody." Clarence didn't like to play games, of course. He just minced around looking on.

One day when the mother of these boys had gone out, this story went on, Clarence "tempted" Frank to disobey her and fly their kite on the roof. Frank didn't want to, but Clarence kept taunting him and daring him until Frank was stung into doing it. After the two boys went up to the roof, Frank got good and dirty, running up and down and stumbling over scuttles, while Clarence sat there, giving him orders, and kept his natty clothes tidy. To my horror, he even spread out his handkerchief on the trapdoor to sit on. And to crown it all, this sneak told on Frank as soon as their mother came in.

This wasn't an exceptionally mean Clarence, either. He was just run-of-the-mill. Some were worse.

So far as I could ever learn, however, Father had never heard of these stories, and had never dreamed of there being anything objectionable in his name. Quite the contrary. And yet as a boy he had lived a good rough-and-tumble boy's life. He had played and fought on the city streets, and kept a

* Reprinted from *Life with Father* by Clarence Day, by permission of Alfred A. Knopf, Inc. Copyright, 1934, 1935, by Clarence Day.

dog in Grandpa's stable, and stolen rides to Greenpoint Ferry on the high, lurching bus. In the summer he had gone to West Springfield and had run down Shad Lane through the trees to the house where Grandpa was born, and had gone barefoot and driven the cows home just as though he had been named Tom or Bill.

He had the same character as a boy, I suppose, that he had as a man, and he was too independent to care if people thought his name fancy. He paid no attention to the prejudices of others, except to disapprove of them. He had plenty of prejudices himself, of course, but they were his own. He was humorous and confident and level-headed, and I imagine that if any boy had tried to make fun of him for being named Clarence, Father would simply have laughed and told him he didn't know what he was talking about.

I asked Mother how this name had ever happened to spring up in our family. She explained that my great-great-grandfather was Benjamin Day, and my great-grandfather was Henry, and consequently my grandfather had been named Benjamin Henry. He in turn had named his eldest son Henry and his second son Benjamin. The result was that when Father was born there was no family name left. The privilege of choosing a name for Father had thereupon been given to Grandma, and unluckily for the Day family she had been reading a novel, the hero of which was named Clarence.

I knew that Grandma, though very like Grandpa in some respects, had a dreamy side which he hadn't, a side that she usually kept to herself, in her serene, quiet way. Her romantic choice of this name probably made Grandpa smile, but he was a detached sort of man who didn't take small matters seriously, and who drew a good deal of private amusement from the happenings of everyday life. Besides, he was partly to blame in this case, because that novel was one he had published himself in his magazine.

I asked Mother, when she had finished, why I had been named Clarence too.

It hadn't been her choice, Mother said. She had suggested all sorts of names to Father, but there seemed to be something wrong with each one. When she had at last spoken of naming me after him, however, he had said at once that that was the best suggestion yet—he said it sounded just right.

Father and I would have had plenty of friction in any case. This identity of names made things worse. Every time that I had been more of a fool than he liked, Father would try to impress on me my responsibilities as his eldest son, and above all as the son to whom he had given his name, as he put it. A great deal was expected, it seemed to me, of a boy who was named after his father. I used to envy my brothers, who didn't have anything expected of them on this score at all.

I envied them still more after I was old enough to begin getting letters. I then discovered that when Father "gave" me his name he had also, not unnaturally, I had to admit, retained it himself, and when anything came for Clarence S. Day he opened it, though it was sometimes for me.

He also opened everything that came addressed to Clarence S. Day, Jr.

He didn't do this intentionally, but unless the "Jr." was clearly written, it looked like "Esq.," and anyhow Father was too accustomed to open all Clarence Day letters to remember about looking carefully every time for a "Jr." So far as mail and express went, I had no name at all of my own.

For the most part nobody wrote to me when I was a small boy except firms whose advertisements I had read in the *Youth's Companion* and to whom I had written requesting them to send me their circulars. These circulars described remarkable bargains in magicians' card outfits, stamps and coins, pocket knives, trick spiders, and imitation fried eggs, and they seemed interesting and valuable to me when I got them. The trouble was that Father usually got them and at once tore them up. I then had to write for such circulars again, and if Father got the second one too, he would sometimes explode with annoyance. He became particularly indignant one year, I remember, when he was repeatedly urged to take advantage of a special bargain sale of false whiskers. He said he couldn't understand why these offerings kept pouring in. I knew why, in this case, but at other times I was often surprised myself at the number he got, not realizing that as a result of my postcard requests my or our name had been automatically put on several large general mailing lists.

During this period I got more of my mail out of Father's wastebasket than I did from the postman.

At the age of twelve or thirteen, I stopped writing for these childish things and turned to a new field. Father and I, whichever of us got at the mail first, began then to receive not merely circulars but personal letters beginning:

Dear Friend Day:

In reply to your valued request for one of our Mammoth Agents' Outfits, kindly forward postoffice order for $1.49 to cover cost of postage and packing, and we will put you in a position to earn a large income in your spare time with absolutely no labor on your part, by taking subscriptions for *The Secret Handbook of Mesmerism,* and our *Tales of Blood* series.

And one spring, I remember, as the result of what I had intended to be a secret application on my part, Father was assigned "the exclusive rights for Staten Island and Hoboken of selling the Gem Home Popper for Pop Corn. Housewives buy it at sight."

After Father had stormily endured these afflictions for a while, he and I began to get letters from girls. Fortunately for our feelings, these were rare, but they were ordeals for both of us. Father had forgotten, if he ever knew, how silly young girls sound, and I got my first lesson in how unsystematic they were. No matter how private and playful they meant their letters to be, they forgot to put "Jr." on the envelope every once in so often. When Father opened these letters, he read them all the way through, sometimes twice, muttering to himself over and over: "This is very peculiar. I don't understand this at all. Here's a letter to me from some person I never heard of. I can't see what it's all about." By the time it had occurred to him that possibly the letter might be for me, I was red and embarrassed and even angrier at the girl than at Father. And on days when he had read some of the phrases aloud to the family, it nearly killed me to claim it.

Lots of fellows whom I knew had been named after their fathers without having such troubles. But although Father couldn't have been kinder-hearted or had any better intentions, when he saw his name on a package or envelope it never dawned on him that it might not be for him. He was too active in his habits to wait until I had a chance to get at it. And as he was also single-minded and prompt to attend to unfinished business, he opened everything automatically and then did his best to dispose of it.

This went on even after I grew up until I had a home of my own. Father was always perfectly decent about it, but he never changed. When he saw I felt sulky, he was genuinely sorry and said so, but he couldn't see why all this should annoy me, and he was surprised and amused that it did. I used to get angry once in a while when something came for me which I particularly hadn't wished him to see and which I would find lying, opened, on the hall table marked "For Jr.?" when I came in; but nobody could stay angry with Father—he was too utterly guiltless of having meant to offend.

He often got angry himself, but it was mostly at things, not at persons, and he didn't mind a bit (as a rule) when persons got angry at him. He even declared, when I got back from college, feeling dignified, and told him I wished he'd be more careful, that he suffered from these mistakes more than I did. It wasn't *his* fault, he pointed out, if my stupid correspondents couldn't remember my name, and it wasn't any pleasure to him to be upset at his breakfast by finding that a damned lunatic company in Battle Creek had sent him a box of dry bread crumbs, with a letter asserting that this rubbish would be good for his stomach. "I admit I threw it into the fireplace, Clarence, but what else could I do? If you valued this preposterous concoction, my dear boy, I'm sorry. I'll buy another box for you today, if you'll tell me where I can get it. Don't feel badly! I'll buy you a barrel. Only I hope you won't eat it."

In the days when Mrs. Pankhurst and her friends were chaining themselves to lamp posts in London, in their campaign for the vote, a letter came from Frances Hand trustfully asking "Dear Clarence" to do something to help Woman Suffrage—speak at a meeting, I think. Father got red in the face. "Speak at one of their meetings!" he roared at Mother. "I'd like nothing better! You can tell Mrs. Hand that it would give me great pleasure to inform all those crackpots in petticoats exactly what I think of their antics."

"Now, Clare," Mother said, "you mustn't talk that way. I like that nice Mrs. Hand, and anyhow this letter must be for Clarence."

One time I asked Father for his opinion of a low-priced stock I'd been watching. His opinion was that it was not worth a damn. I thought this over, but still wished to buy it, so I placed a scale order with another firm instead of with Father's office, and said nothing about it. At the end of the month this other firm sent me a statement setting forth each of my little transactions in full, and of course they forgot to put the "Jr." at the end of my name. When Father opened the envelope, he thought at first in his excitement that this firm had actually opened an account for him without being asked. I found him telling Mother that he'd like to wring their damned necks.

"That must be for me, Father," I said, when I took in what had happened.

We looked at each other.

"You bought this stuff?" he said incredulously. "After all I said about it?"

"Yes, Father."

He handed over the statement and walked out of the room.

Both he and I felt offended and angry. We stayed so for several days, too, but then we made up.

Once in a while when I got a letter that I had no time to answer I used to address an envelope to the sender and then put anything in it that happened to be lying around on my desk—a circular about books, a piece of newspaper, an old laundry bill—anything at all, just to be amiable, and yet at the same time to save myself the trouble of writing. I happened to tell several people about this private habit of mine at a dinner one night— a dinner at which Alice Duer Miller and one or two other writers were present. A little later she wrote me a criticism of Henry James and ended by saying that I needn't send her any of my old laundry bills because she wouldn't stand it. And she forgot to put on the "Jr."

"In the name of God," Father said bleakly, "this is the worst yet. Here's a woman who says I'd better not read *The Golden Bowl*, which I have no intention whatever of doing, and she also warns me for some unknown reason not to send her my laundry bills."

The good part of all these experiences, as I realize now, was that in the end they drew Father and me closer together. My brothers had only chance battles with him. I had a war. Neither he nor I relished its clashes, but they made us surprisingly intimate.

COMMENT AND QUESTIONS

I. "Father Opens My Mail" has at first a rambling organization, partly because it is one chapter of a book on the author's experiences with his father, and partly because an informal, conversational style is part of its tone. Does the discussion of the name "Clarence" and the author's feeling about it have any direct bearing on the narrative of Father's opening Clarence, Jr.'s mail? What is the purpose of this introductory discussion?

II. Into what main stages or periods does the struggle between Clarence Day and his father fall?

III. The narrative pace of this selection is worth study. Because the account covers a long period of time, the author necessarily summarizes much of the material, but he is very skillful in breaking and illustrating his summary with the presentation of little scenes or parts of scenes. Could any of the presented material have been summarized without loss?

IV. What characteristics of Father are revealed in this selection? What characteristics of Clarence Day, Jr.? Does it seem natural—or at least believable—that they should have warred over the mail?

V. Select two or three parts of this narrative which seem to you particularly good, and analyze those parts. Are they good because of the basic material, or because of skill in expression or presentation?

COLETTE

My Mother and the Animals*

The following autobiographical selection is concentrated in time. The author recalls a brief experience (her return to her country home after a visit in Paris) in which immediate impressions called up associated memories. Colette (1873-1954) was a French novelist whose work has long been acclaimed in her native country, and who in recent years has been widely read in this country too; she was the first woman to be elected to the Académie Goncourt, a French literary society consisting of ten members. Among her short novels which have been translated into English are *The Vagabond, The Cat, Gigi, Julie de Carneilhan, Chéri,* and *The Last of Chéri.* "My Mother and the Animals" is a chapter of *La Maison de Claudine,* first published in 1922, and published in this country in 1953 under the title *My Mother's House.*

A succession of harsh sounds, made by the train, cabs, and omnibuses, is all that my memory retains of a brief visit to Paris when I was six years old. Of a week in Paris five years later I remember nothing but arid heat, panting thirst, feverish fatigue and fleas in a hotel bedroom in the Rue St. Roch.

I remember also that I kept on gazing upwards, vaguely oppressed by the height of the houses, and that a photographer won my heart by calling me, as he doubtless called every child, a "wonder."

Five years in the country followed without so much as a thought of Paris.

But when I was sixteen, on returning to Puisaye after a fortnight of

---

* From *My Mother's House* by Colette, copyright, 1953, by Farrar, Straus and Young, Inc. Used by permission of the publishers, Farrar, Straus and Cudahy, Inc., and Martin Secker and Warburg, Ltd.

theatres, museums and shops, I brought home with me, among memories of finery and greediness, mixed with hopes, regrets, and feelings of scorn, as innocent and awkward as myself, the surprise and the melancholy aversion aroused in me by what I called houses without animals.

Mere cubes without gardens, flowerless abodes where no cat mews behind the dining-room door, where one never treads near the fireside on some part of a dog sprawling like a rug; rooms devoid of familiar spirits, wherein the hand seeking a friendly caress encounters only inanimate wood, or marble, or velvet; I left all these with famished senses, with a vehement need to touch once again fleeces and leaves, warm feathers and the exciting dewiness of flowers.

As if I were discovering them all together again, I extended my composite greeting to my mother, the garden and the circle of animals.

My return coincided with the watering of the garden, and I still cherish happy memories of the sixth hour of the evening, the green watering-can soaking the blue sateen frock, the strong smell of leaf-mould, and the afterglow that cast a pink reflection on the pages of a forgotten book, the white petals of the tobacco flowers and the white fur of the cat in her basket.

Nonoche the tortoiseshell had had kittens two days earlier, and Bijou her daughter the following evening, and as for Musette, the Havanese bitch, perennial breeder of bastards. . . .

"Minet-Chéri, go and see Musette's puppy!"

So I went off to the kitchen where Musette was engaged in feeding an ash-colored monster, still half blind and nearly as big as herself. Fathered by some local gun-dog, he tugged like a calf at the delicate teats, strawberry-pink against the silver-pale fur, and trampled rhythmically with extended claws a silky belly that would have suffered severely if . . . if my mother had not cut out and sewed for him, from an old pair of white gloves, suede mittens reaching to his elbows. I never saw a ten days' pup look so much like a gendarme.

How many treasures had bloomed in my absence! I ran to the great basket overflowing with indistinguishable cats. That orange ear certainly belonged to Nonoche, but that plume of a black angora tail could only belong to her daughter Bijou, intolerant as a pretty woman. One long slim dry paw, like that of a black rabbit, threatened the heavens; and a tiny kitten spotted like a civet-cat, slumbering replete and prostrate on its back in the middle of this disorder, looked as though it has been assassinated.

I set to work happily to disentangle the mass of nurses and well-licked nurslings from which arose a pleasant smell of new-mown hay, fresh milk and well-tended fur, and I discovered that Bijou, four times a mother in three years, from whose teats hung a chaplet of newborn offspring, was herself engaged in noisily sucking, with an over-large tongue and a purring not unlike the roar of a log fire, the milk of the aged Nonoche, who lay inert with comfort, one paw across her eyes. Bending nearer, I listened to the double purring, treble and bass, that is the mysterious prerogative of the feline race; a rumbling as of a distant factory, a whirring as of a captive moth, a frail mill whose profound slumber stops its grinding. I was not surprised at the chain of mutually suckling cats. To those who live in the country and use their eyes everything becomes alike miraculous and simple. We had long considered it natural that a bitch should nourish a kitten, that a cat should select as her lair the top of the cage wherein trustful green canaries sang happily, their beaks from time to time plucking from the sleeper an occasional silky hair for nesting purposes.

A whole year of my childhood was devoted to the task of capturing, in the kitchen or the cow-house, the rare flies of winter for the benefit of two swallows, October nestlings thrown down to us by a gale. Was it not essential to preserve them and to find provender for their insatiable beaks that disdained any but living prey?

It was thanks to them that I learned how infinitely a tame swallow can surpass, in insolent sociability, even the most pampered of dogs. Our two swallows spent their time perching on a shoulder or a head, nestling in the work-basket, running about under the table like chickens, pecking at the nonplussed dog or chirping in the very face of the disconcerted cat. They came to school in my pocket and returned home by air. As soon as the shining sickle of their wings grew and sharpened, they would vanish at any time into the vault of the spring sky, but a single shrill call of "Ti-i-inies" would bring them cleaving the wind like two arrows, to alight in my hair, to which they would cling with all the strength of their little curved black steel claws.

All was faery and yet simple among the fauna of my early home. You could never believe that a cat could eat strawberries? And yet, because I have seen him so many times, I know that Babou, that black Satan, interminable and as sinuous as an eel, would carefully select in Madame Pomié's kitchen garden the ripest of the Royal Sovereigns or the Early Scarlets. He it was, too, who would be discovered poetically absorbed in smelling newly-opened violets.

Have you ever heard tell of Pelisson's spider that so passionately loved music? I for one am ready to believe it and also to add, as my slender contribution to the sum of human knowledge, the story of the spider that my mother kept—as my father expressed it—on her ceiling, in that year that ushered in my sixteenth spring. A handsome garden spider she was, her belly like a clove of garlic emblazoned with an ornate cross. In the daytime she slept, or hunted in the web that she had spun across the bedroom ceiling. But during the night, towards three o'clock in the morning, at the moment when her chronic insomnia caused my mother to relight the lamp and open her bedside book, the great spider would also wake, and after a careful survey would lower herself from the ceiling by a thread, directly above the little oil lamp upon which a bowl of chocolate simmered through the night. Slowly she would descend, swinging limply to and fro like a big bead, and grasping the edge of the cup with all her eight legs, she would bend over head foremost and drink to satiety. Then she would draw herself ceilingwards again, heavy with creamy chocolate, her ascent punctuated by the pauses and meditations imposed by an overloaded stomach, and would resume her post in the centre of her silken rigging.

Still wearing my travelling coat, I sat dreaming, weary, enchanted and re-enslaved in the midst of my kingdom.
"Where is your spider, mother?"
My mother's grey eyes, magnified by her glasses, clouded:
"Have you come back from Paris only to ask for news of the spider, you ungrateful child?"
I hung my head, awkward in my affection, ashamed of that which was best in me:
"I couldn't help remembering sometimes, at night, at the spider's hour, when I couldn't sleep. . . ."
"Minet-Chéri, you couldn't sleep? Was your bed uncomfortable? The spider's in her web, I suppose. But do come and see if my caterpillar is hibernating. I really think she's going to become a chrysalis, and I've given her a little box of dry sand. She's an Emperor moth caterpillar and I think a bird must have pecked her stomach but she's quite well again now."

The caterpillar was perhaps asleep, moulded to the form of a supporting twig of box thorn. The ravages around her testified to her vitality. There were nothing but shreds of leaves, gnawed stems and barren shoots. Plump, as thick as my thumb and over four inches long, she swelled the fat rolls of her cabbage-green body, adorned at intervals with hairy warts of turquoise blue. I detached her gently from her twig and she writhed in anger, exposing her paler stomach and all her spiky little paws that clung leech-like to the branch to which I returned her.
"But, mother, she has devoured everything!"
The grey eyes behind the spectacles wavered perplexedly from the denuded twigs to the caterpillar and thence to my face:
"But what can I do about it? And after all, the box thorn she's eating, you know, is the one that strangles honeysuckle."
"Yes, but won't the caterpillar eat the honeysuckle too?"
"I don't know. But in any case, what can I do about it? I can hardly kill the creature."

The scene is before me as I write, the garden with its sun-warmed walls, the last of the black cherries hanging on the tree, the sky webbed with long pink clouds. I can feel again beneath my fingers the vigorous resentment of the caterpillar, the wet. leathery hydrangea leaves, and my mother's little work-worn hand.
I can evoke the wind at will and make it rustle the stiff papery blades

1088   NARRATIVE, AUTOBIOGRAPHY, ESSAYS

of the bamboos and sing, through the comb-like leaves of the yew, as a worthy accompaniment to the voice that on that day and on all the other days, even to the final silence, spoke words that had always the same meaning.

"That child must have proper care. Can't we save that woman? Have those people got enough to eat? I can hardly kill the creature."

COMMENT AND QUESTIONS

I. This recollection offers good examples of the techniques of description. Close observation recorded in exact concrete language accounts for much of the vivid quality of Colette's writing. Point out phrases or passages which you think are particularly effective in enabling the reader to visualize what the author saw.

II. We have said earlier that good description vitalizes a scene and appeals to various senses. Point out examples of this principle in operation in "My Mother and the Animals."

III. What is the dominant impression of Colette's home, and what details best contribute to it? What is the dominant impression of her mother, and how is it established?

JAMES THURBER

Which*

James Thurber (1894–   ) is well known, particularly to readers of *The New Yorker*, for his witty and satiric prose pieces and drawings. His books include *My Life and Hard Times, The Middle-Aged Man on the Flying Trapeze, Let Your Mind Alone, Fables for Our Time, My World—and Welcome to It, Thurber Country*, and *Alarms and Diversions*. "Which" is a section of "Ladies' and Gentlemen's Guide to English Usage," published in 1929 in *The New Yorker*. The reference to Fowler in the opening sentences is to H. W. Fowler, whose excellent and readable *Dictionary of Modern English Usage* Mr. Thurber is quoting.

[1] The relative pronoun "which" can cause more trouble than any other word, if recklessly used. Foolhardy persons sometimes get lost in which-clauses and are never heard of again. My distinguished contemporary, Fowler, cites several tragic cases, of which the following is one: "It was rumoured that Beaconsfield intended opening the Conference with a speech in French,

* From *Ladies' and Gentlemen's Guide to Modern English Usage* by James Thurber. Reprinted by permission.

his pronunciation of which language leaving everything to be desired . . ." That's as much as Mr. Fowler quotes because, at his age, he was afraid to go any farther. The young man who originally got into that sentence was never found. His fate, however, was not as terrible as that of another adventurer who became involved in a remarkable which-mire. Fowler has followed his devious course as far as he safely could on foot: "Surely what applies to games should also apply to racing, the leaders of which being the very people from whom an example might well be looked for . . ." Not even Henry James could have successfully emerged from a sentence with "which," "whom," and "being" in it. The safest way to avoid such things is to follow in the path of the American author, Ernest Hemingway. In his youth he was trapped in a which-clause one time and barely escaped with his mind. He was going along on solid ground until he got into this: "It was the one thing of which, being very much afraid—for whom has not been warned to fear such things—he . . ." Being a young and powerfully built man, Hemingway was able to fight his way back to where he had started, and begin again. This time he skirted the treacherous morass in this way: "He was afraid of one thing. This was the one thing. He had been warned to fear such things. Everybody has been warned to fear such things." Today Hemingway is alive and well, and many happy writers are following along the trail he blazed.

[2] What most people don't realize is that one "which" leads to another. Trying to cross a paragraph by leaping from "which" to "which" is like Eliza crossing the ice. The danger is in missing a "which" and falling in. A case in point is this: "He went up to a pew which was in the gallery, which brought him under a colored window which he loved and always quieted his spirit." The writer, worn out, missed the last "which"—the one that should come just before "always" in that sentence. But supposing he had got it in! We would have: "He went up to a pew which was in the gallery, which brought him under a colored window which he loved and which always quieted his spirit." Your inveterate whicher in this way gives the effect of tweeting like a bird or walking with a crutch, and is not welcome in the best company.

[3] It is well to remember that one "which" leads to two and that two "whiches" multiply like rabbits. You should never start out with the idea that you can get by with one "which." Suddenly they are all around you. Take a sentence like this: "It imposes a problem which we either solve, or perish." On a hot night, or after a hard day's work, a man often lets himself get by with a monstrosity like that, but suppose he dictates that sentence bright and early in the morning. It comes to him typed out by his stenographer and he instantly senses that something is the matter with it. He tries to reconstruct the sentence, still clinging to the "which," and gets something like this: "It imposes a problem which we either solve, or which, failing to solve, we must perish on account of." He goes to the water cooler, gets a drink, sharpens his pencil, and grimly tries again. "It imposes a problem

1090 NARRATIVE, AUTOBIOGRAPHY, ESSAYS

which we either solve or which we don't solve and . . ." He begins once more: "It imposes a problem which we either solve, or which we do not solve, and from which . . ." The more times he does it the more "whiches" he gets. The way out is simple: "We must either solve this problem, or perish." Never monkey with "which." Nothing except getting tangled up in a typewriter ribbon is worse.

COMMENT AND QUESTIONS

I. Concrete figurative language is an important part of James Thurber's style. Point out the expressed and implied comparisons used in this selection. What does each one contribute to the total effect and meaning?

II. In paragraph 3 Mr. Thurber shifts to direct address to the reader and imperative mood. Why do you think he makes this shift?

III. Revise the following "which-mire":

This article, which comes from "Ladies' and Gentlemen's Guide to English Usage," which was published in 1929, was written by James Thurber, who is a contributor to *The New Yorker* in which magazine appear many of his stories and drawings which depict human beings who are caught in a society which is frustrating.

E. B. WHITE

Calculating Machine*

E. B. White (1899–), one of the best of contemporary American essayists, wrote regularly for *Harper's Magazine* for a number of years, and is a contributing editor to *The New Yorker*. His essays have been collected in *One Man's Meat* and *The Second Tree from the Corner;* the following short piece is taken from the second of those volumes, published in 1951.

A publisher in Chicago has sent us a pocket calculating machine by which we may test our writing to see whether it is intelligible. The calculator was developed by General Motors, who, not satisfied with giving the world a Cadillac, now dream of bringing perfect understanding to men. The machine (it is simply a celluloid card with a dial) is called the Reading Ease Calculator and shows four grades of "reading ease"—Very Easy, Easy, Hard, and Very Hard. You count your words and syllables, set the dial, and

* From *The Second Tree from the Corner*, copyright, 1951, by E. B. White, published by **Harper & Brothers**.

an indicator lets you know whether anybody is going to understand what you have written. An instruction book came with it, and after mastering the simple rules we lost no time in running a test on the instruction book itself, to see how *that* writer was doing. The poor fellow! His leading essay, the one on the front cover, tested Very Hard.

Our next step was to study the first phrase on the face of the calculator: "How to test Reading-Ease of written matter." There is, of course, no such things as reading ease of written matter. There is the ease with which matter can be read, but that is a condition of the reader, not of the matter. Thus the inventors and distributors of this calculator get off to a poor start, with a Very Hard instruction book and a slovenly phrase. Already they have one foot caught in the brier patch of English usage.

Not only did the author of the instruction book score badly on the front cover, but inside the book he used the word "personalize" in an essay on how to improve one's writing. A man who likes the word "personalize" is entitled to his choice, but we wonder whether he should be in the business of giving advice to writers. "Whenever possible," he wrote, "personalize your writing by directing it to the reader." As for us, we would as lief Simonize our grandmother as personalize our writing.

In the same envelope with the calculator, we received another training aid for writers—a booklet called "How to Write Better," by Rudolf Flesch. This, too, we studied, and it quickly demonstrated the broncolike ability of the English language to throw whoever leaps cocksurely into the saddle. The language not only can toss a rider but knows a thousand tricks for tossing him, each more gay than the last. Dr. Flesch stayed in the saddle only a moment or two. Under the heading "Think Before You Write," he wrote, "The main thing to consider is your *purpose* in writing. Why are you sitting down to write?" And echo answered: Because, sir, it is more comfortable than standing up.

Communication by the written word is a subtler (and more beautiful) thing than Dr. Flesch and General Motors imagine. They contend that the "average reader" is capable of reading only what tests Easy, and that the writer should write at or below this level. This is a presumptuous and degrading idea. There is no average reader, and to reach down toward this mythical character is to deny that each of us is on the way up, is ascending. ("Ascending," by the way, is a word Dr. Flesch advises writers to stay away from. Too unusual.)

It is our belief that no writer can improve his work until he discards the dulcet notion that the reader is feeble-minded, for writing is an act of faith, not a trick of grammar. Ascent is at the heart of the matter. A country whose writers are following a calculating machine downstairs is not ascending—if you will pardon the expression—and a writer who questions the capacity of the person at the other end of the line is not a writer at all, merely a schemer. The movies long ago decided that a wider communication could be achieved by a deliberate descent to a lower level, and they walked proudly down until they reached the cellar. Now they are groping for the light switch, hoping to find the way out.

We have studied Dr. Flesch's instructions diligently, but we return for guidance in these matters to an earlier American, who wrote with more patience, more confidence. "I fear chiefly," he wrote, "lest my expression may not be *extra-vagant* enough, may not wander far enough beyond the narrow limits of my daily experience, so as to be adequate to the truth of which I have been convinced . . . Why level downward to our dullest perception always, and praise that as common sense? The commonest sense is the sense of men asleep, which they express by snoring."

Run that through your calculator! It may come out Hard, it may come out Easy. But it will come out whole, and it will last forever.

COMMENT AND QUESTIONS

I. This essay illustrates a method frequently used by E. B. White, and also by other informal essayists—the method of starting with a small, particular observation or event, and proceeding to its larger implications. For all the humor and lightness of tone in "Calculating Machine," what serious things is Mr. White saying about language and about contemporary society?

II. The quotation near the end of the essay is from Thoreau. Another expression of E. B. White's admiration for Thoreau and the reason for his feeling about the earlier American will be found in "Walden, 1939" in the following pages.

E. B. WHITE

Walden, 1939*

This personal essay, written after a visit to the woods and pond where Thoreau had lived nearly a hundred years before, is a tribute by one writer to another, and a commentary on modern society. For a note on E. B. White, see page 1090.

Miss Nims, take a letter to Henry David Thoreau.

[1] Dear Henry: I thought of you the other afternoon as I was approaching Concord doing fifty on Route 62. That is a high speed at which to hold a philosopher in one's mind, but in this century we are a nimble bunch.

[2] On one of the lawns in the outskirts of the village a woman was cutting

---

*From *One Man's Meat*, copyright, 1939, by E. B. White, published by Harper & Brothers.

the grass with a motorized lawn mower. What made me think of you was that the machine had rather got away from her, although she was game enough, and in the brief glimpse I had of the scene it appeared to me that the lawn was mowing the lady. She kept a tight grip on the handles, which throbbed violently with every explosion of the one-cylinder motor, and as she sheered around bushes and lurched along at a reluctant trot behind her impetuous servant, she looked like a puppy who had grabbed something that was too much for him. Concord hasn't changed much, Henry; the farm implements and the animals still have the upper hand.

[3] I may as well admit that I was journeying to Concord with the deliberate intention of visiting your woods; for although I have never knelt at the grave of a philosopher nor placed wreaths on moldy poets, and have often gone a mile out of my way to avoid some place of historical interest, I have always wanted to see Walden Pond. The account which you left of your sojourn there is, you will be amused to learn, a document of increasing pertinence; each year it seems to gain a little headway, as the world loses ground. We may all be transcendental yet, whether we like it or not. As our common complexities increase, any tale of individual simplicity (and yours is the best written and the cockiest) acquires a new fascination; as our goods accumulate, but not our well-being, your report of an existence without material adornment takes on a certain awkward credibility.

[4] My purpose in going to Walden Pond, like yours, was not to live cheaply or to live dearly there, but to transact some private business with the fewest obstacles. Approaching Concord, doing forty, forty-five, doing fifty, the steering wheel held snug in my palms, the highway held grimly in my vision, the crown of the road now serving me (on the righthand curves), now defeating me (on the lefthand curves), I began to rouse myself from the stupefaction which a day's motor journey induces. It was a delicious evening, Henry, when the whole body is one sense, and imbibes delight through every pore, if I may coin a phrase. Fields were richly brown where the harrow, drawn by the stripped Ford, had lately sunk its teeth; pastures were green; and overhead the sky had that same everlasting great look which you will find on Page 144 of the Oxford pocket edition. I could feel the road entering me, through tire, wheel, spring, and cushion; shall I not have intelligence with earth too? Am I not partly leaves and vegetable mold myself?—a man of infinite horsepower, yet partly leaves.

[5] Stay with me on 62 and it will take you into Concord. As I say, it was a delicious evening. The snake had come forth to die a bloody S on the highway, the wheel upon its head, its bowels flat now and exposed. The turtle had come up too to cross the road and die in the attempt, its hard shell smashed under the rubber blow, its intestinal yearning (for the other side of the road) forever squashed. There was a sign by the wayside which announced that the road had a "cotton surface." You wouldn't know what that is, but neither, for that matter, did I. There is a cryptic ingredient in many of our modern improvements—we are awed and pleased without

knowing quite what we are enjoying. It is something to be traveling on a road with a cotton surface.

[6] The civilization round Concord to-day is an odd distillation of city, village, farm, and manor. The houses, yards, fields look not quite suburban, not quite rural. Under the bronze beech and the blue spruce of the departed baron grazes the milch goat of the heirs. Under the porte-cochère stands the reconditioned station wagon; under the grape arbor sit the puppies for sale. (But why do men degenerate ever? What makes families run out?)

[7] It was June and everywhere June was publishing her immemorial stanza; in the lilacs, in the syringa, in the freshly edged paths and the sweetness of moist beloved gardens, and the little wire wickets that preserve the tulips' front. Farmers were already moving the fruits of their toil into their yards, arranging the rhubarb, the asparagus, the strictly fresh eggs on the painted stands under the little shed roofs with the patent shingles. And though it was almost a hundred years since you had taken your ax and started cutting out your home on Walden Pond, I was interested to observe that the philosophical spirit was still alive in Massachusetts; in the center of a vacant lot some boys were assembling the framework of a rude shelter, their whole mind and skill concentrated in the rather inauspicious helter-skeleton of studs and rafters. They too were escaping from town, to live naturally, in a rich blend of savagery and philosophy.

[8] That evening, after supper at the inn, I strolled out into the twilight to dream my shapeless transcendental dreams and see that the car was locked up for the night (first open the right front door, then reach over, straining, and pull up the handles of the left rear and the left front till you hear the click, then the handle of the right rear, then shut the right front but open it again, remembering that the key is still in the ignition switch, remove the key, shut the right front again with a bang, push the tiny keyhole cover to one side, insert key, turn, and withdraw). It is what we all do, Henry. It is called locking the car. It is said to confuse thieves and keep them from making off with the laprobe. Four doors to lock behind one robe. The driver himself never uses a laprobe, the free movement of his legs being vital to the operation of the vehicle; so that when he locks the car it is a pure and unselfish act. I have in my life gained very little essential heat from laprobes, yet I have ever been at pains to lock them up.

[9] The evening was full of sounds, some of which would have stirred your memory. The robins still love the elms of New England villages at sundown. There is enough of the thrush in them to make song inevitable at the end of day, and enough of the tramp to make them hang round the dwellings of men. A robin, like many another American, dearly loves a white house with green blinds. Concord is still full of them.

[10] Your fellow-townsmen were stirring abroad—not many afoot, most of them in their cars; and the sound which they made in Concord at evening was a rustling and a whispering. The sound lacks steadfastness and is wholly unlike that of a train. A train, as you know who lived so near the Fitchburg

line, whistles once or twice sadly and is gone, trailing a memory in smoke, soothing to ear and mind. Automobiles, skirting a village green, are like flies that have gained the inner ear—they buzz, cease, pause, start, shift, stop, halt, brake, and the whole effect is a nervous polytone curiously disturbing.

[11]   As I wandered along, the toc toc of ping pong balls drifted from an attic window. In front of the Reuben Brown house a Buick was drawn up. At the wheel, motionless, his hat upon his head, a man sat, listening to Amos and Andy on the radio (it is a drama of many scenes and without an end). The deep voice of Andrew Brown, emerging from the car, although it originated more than two hundred miles away, was unstrained by distance. When you used to sit on the shore of your pond on Sunday morning, listening to the church bells of Acton and Concord, you were aware of the excellent filter of the intervening atmosphere. Science has attended to that, and sound now maintains its intensity without regard for distance. Properly sponsored, it goes on forever.

[12]   A fire engine, out for a trial spin, roared past Emerson's house, hot with readiness for public duty. Over the barn roofs the martins dipped and chittered. A swarthy daughter of an asparagus grower, in culottes, shirt, and bandanna, pedaled past on her bicycle. It was indeed a delicious evening, and I returned to the inn (I believe it was your house once) to rock with the old ladies on the concrete veranda.

[13]   Next morning early I started afoot for Walden, out Main Street and down Thoreau, past the depot and the Minuteman Chevrolet Company. The morning was fresh, and in a bean field along the way I flushed an agriculturist, quietly studying his beans. Thoreau Street soon joined Number 126, an artery of the State. We number our highways nowadays, our speed being so great we can remember little of their quality or character and are lucky to remember their number. (Men have an indistinct notion that if they keep up this activity long enough all will at length ride somewhere, in next to no time.) Your pond is on 126.

[14]   I knew I must be nearing your woodland retreat when the Golden Pheasant lunchroom came into view—Sealtest ice cream, toasted sandwiches, hot frankfurters, waffles, tonics, and lunches. Were I the proprietor, I should add rice, Indian meal, and molasses—just for old time's sake. The Pheasant, incidentally, is for sale: a chance for some nature lover who wishes to set himself up beside a pond in the Concord atmosphere and live deliberately, fronting only the essential facts of life on Number 126. Beyond the Pheasant was a place called Walden Breezes, an oasis whose porch pillars were made of old green shutters sawed into lengths. On the porch was a distorting mirror, to give the traveler a comical image of himself, who had miraculously learned to gaze in an ordinary glass without smiling. Behind the Breezes, in a sun-parched clearing, dwelt your philosophical descendants in their trailers, each trailer the size of your hut, but all grouped together for the sake of congeniality. Trailer people leave the city, as you did, to discover

solitude and in any weather, at any hour of the day or night, to improve the nick of time; but they soon collect in villages and get bogged deeper in the mud than ever. The camp behind Walden Breezes was just rousing itself to the morning. The ground was packed hard under the heel, and the sun came through the clearing to bake the soil and enlarge the wry smell of cramped housekeeping. Cushman's bakery truck had stopped to deliver an early basket of rolls. A camp dog, seeing me in the road, barked petulantly. A man emerged from one of the trailers and set forth with a bucket to draw water from some forest tap.

[15] Leaving the highway I turned off into the woods toward the pond, which was apparent through the foliage. The floor of the forest was strewn with dried old oak leaves and *Transcripts*. From beneath the flattened popcorn wrapper (*granum explosum*) peeped the frail violet. I followed a footpath and descended to the water's edge. The pond lay clear and blue in the morning light, as you have seen it so many times. In the shallows a man's waterlogged shirt undulated gently. A few flies came out to greet me and convoy me to your cove, past the No Bathing signs on which the fellows and the girls had scrawled their names. I felt strangely excited suddenly to be snooping around your premises, tiptoeing along watchfully, as though not to tread by mistake upon the intervening century. Before I got to the cove I heard something which seemed to me quite wonderful: I heard your frog, a full clear *troonk,* guiding me, still hoarse and solemn, bridging the years as the robins had bridged them in the sweetness of the village evening. But he soon quit, and I came on a couple of young boys throwing stones at him.

[16] Your front yard is marked by a bronze tablet set in a stone. Four small granite posts, a few feet away, show where the house was. On top of the tablet was a pair of faded blue bathing trunks with a white stripe. Back of it is a pile of stones, a sort of cairn, left by your visitors as a tribute I suppose. It is a rather ugly little heap of stones, Henry. In fact the hillside itself seems faded, browbeaten; a few tall skinny pines, bare of lower limbs, a smattering of young maples in suitable green, some birches and oaks, and a number of trees felled by the last big wind. It was from the bole of one of these fallen pines, torn up by the roots, that I extracted the stone which I added to the cairn—a sentimental act in which I was interrupted by a small terrier from a nearby picnic group, who confronted me and wanted to know about the stone.

[17] I sat down for a while on one of the posts of your house to listen to the bluebottles and the dragonflies. The invaded glade sprawled shabby and mean at my feet, but the flies were tuned to the old vibration. There were the remains of a fire in your ruins, but I doubt that it was yours; also two beer bottles trodden into the soil and become part of earth. A young oak had taken root in your house, and two or three ferns, unrolling like the ticklers at a banquet. The only other furnishings were a DuBarry pattern sheet, a page torn from a picture magazine, and some crusts in wax paper.

[18] Before I quit I walked clear round the pond and found the place where you used to sit on the northeast side to get the sun in the fall, and the beach where you got sand for scrubbing your floor. On the eastern side of the pond, where the highway borders it, the State has built dressing rooms for swimmers, a float with diving towers, drinking fountains of porcelain, and rowboats for hire. The pond is in fact a State Preserve, and carries a twenty-dollar fine for picking wild flowers, a decree signed in all solemnity by your fellow-citizens Walter C. Wardwell, Erson B. Barlow, and Nathaniel I. Bowditch. There was a smell of creosote where they had been building a wide wooden stairway to the road and the parking area. Swimmers and boaters were arriving; bodies plunged vigorously into the water and emerged wet and beautiful in the bright air. As I left, a boatload of town boys were splashing about in mid-pond, kidding and fooling, the young fellows singing at the tops of their lungs in a wild chorus:

> Amer-ica, Amer-i-ca, God shed his grace on thee,
> And crown thy good with brotherhood
> From sea to shi-ning sea!

[19] I walked back to town along the railroad, following your custom. The rails were expanding noisily in the hot sun, and on the slope of the roadbed the wild grape and the blackberry sent up their creepers to the track.

[20] The expense of my brief sojourn in Concord was:

Canvas shoes	$1.95
Baseball bat	.25 } gifts to take back to a boy
Left-handed fielder's glove	1.25
Hotel and meals	4.25
In all	$7.70

As you see, this amount was almost what you spent for food for eight months. I cannot defend the shoes or the expenditure for shelter and food: they reveal a meanness and grossness in my nature which you would find contemptible. The baseball equipment, however, is the kind of impediment with which you were never on even terms. You must remember that the house where you practiced the sort of economy which I respect was haunted only by mice and squirrels. You never had to cope with a shortstop.

COMMENT AND QUESTIONS

This essay will have more meaning if you have read the selection from Thoreau's *Walden* on page 989. To one familiar with the whole of *Walden*, E. B. White's essay is rich in allusions to and echoes of Thoreau's work. For example, the end of paragraph 4 echoes a passage in which Thoreau, writing about the beneficence of Nature and his sense of oneness with

Nature, asks, "Shall I not have intelligence with the earth? Am I not partly leaves and vegetable mould myself?" And E. B. White's record of his expenses in paragraph 20 recalls Thoreau's meticulous records in *Walden* —in all, a cost of $28.12½ for building his house; a profit of $8.71½ from his beans, etc.

I. What does Mr. White gain by writing his essay in the form of a letter to Thoreau?

II. Why do you think he has included each of the following in the letter: the woman and the lawn mower (paragraph 2); the death of the snake and the turtle (paragraph 5); the "cotton surface" of the road (paragraph 5); the business of locking the car (paragraph 8); the numbering of the highways (paragraph 13); the lunch room and trailer camp (paragraph 14)?

III. What passages best convey E. B. White's judgment of present-day civilization and progress? How would you describe his tone and attitude in the essay? Is he sad, cynical, bitter, good-humored, resigned, nostalgic for a way of life no longer possible; or is he communicating a combination of some of these feelings?

IV. When Mr. White speaks in the last paragraph of "the sort of economy which I respect," what might he mean besides economy with money?

IRWIN EDMAN

Former Teachers*

In the following essay, a philosopher and teacher looks back on his own student days and comments on the personalities, methods, and ideas of those who taught him. "Former Teachers" is Chapter Twelve of *Philosopher's Holiday* (1938), and is preceded by a chapter entitled "Former Students." For a further note on Irwin Edman, see page 1065.

[1] By an easy transition I am led from reflection about former students to meditation on former teachers. For I have had teachers as well as pupils, and in considering what effect one has had, or failed to have, on one's one-time students, I cannot help looking back on teachers who, though they might be embarrassed to acknowledge it, or insistent on denying it, had an influence over me. I shall leave out my early love for Miss Foley in 4A, or Miss Carpendale in 7B, whom I feared horribly, partly because she taught me the impossible subject of arithmetic, and partly because of her immense height and blazing red hair and unrelenting expression and deep

* From *Philosopher's Holiday* by Irwin Edman, copyright, 1938, by Irwin Edman. Reprinted by permission of The Viking Press, Inc., New York.

mannish voice. I felt rather sorry for the trim little teacher of shopwork (another impossible subject) when I heard Miss Carpendale had married him. I was sure even then that that was the way it had happened.

[2] I shall begin rather with high school, for I don't remember that in grade school anybody aroused my mind and imagination. That event came in my first term at Townsend Harris Hall, the preparatory school, called at the time the academic department, of the College of the City of New York. The man involved was named Michael J. Kelleher, an enthusiastic, curly-haired Irishman, who, at the top of his voice but with a winning cadence, dragooned us into liking *The Ancient Mariner* and *Ivanhoe*. He also dragooned some of us into liking our own writing. He was the first one, save, perhaps, Miss Foley, to make me think I could write. Miss Foley's observation had been based on one sentence. I had written a self-portrait of a camel. The last sentence was: "I do not need water for days at a time; I have it with me." She said that was very good and very well informed. Mr. Michael Kelleher wrote in a large bold hand on a theme of mine: "This has the sweet breath of the country about it." It was an essay on Central Park.

[3] But I recall Mr. Michael Kelleher chiefly because he gave us the contagious impression of so liking poetry that he simply had to tell us about it. Since we were the fourth class he had each morning, it occurred to me even then that it was very remarkable that he should be able to care so deeply and vividly about Rebecca and Rowena still. But he did. It was, I found out, the first year he had taught. I have often thought since it might be well to have a big turn-over in the teaching profession. But that is not really necessary. For, years later, finding myself in the neighbourhood of my old school, I decided to hunt out my old teacher. It was not quite the end of the hour and I heard the powerful cadenced voice of Mr. Kelleher still making clear to fourteen-year-olds the wonder and mystery of *The Ancient Mariner*. I could hear him and even see his figure outlined through the transparent glass of the door:

> "Alone, alone, all, all alone,
> Alone on a wide, wide sea,
> And never a saint took pity on
> My soul in agony. . . ."

The remembered shiver went up my spine. Mr. Kelleher was a born teacher of poetry. He did not explain it; he communicated it by contagion.

[4] There were three other high school teachers I remember. One was the beautifully dressed, slim Mr. Knickerbocker who taught us French. His technique belied his debonair appearance. There was no languid elegance about his methods. He spent the first fifteen minutes of each hour rapidly going around the class making certain that we knew the new words in each lesson. It was a martinet method, but it worked. One did not twice come to class unprepared, to have Mr. Knickerbocker's clear blue eyes briefly

stare one into humiliation if one guessed, or could not even guess, the meaning of a word. There was not much about appreciation of French literature, and I presume such methods now would be regarded as unimaginative drill. But one knew a great many words with precision before the term was over.

[5] My third debt to my high school teachers is to Bird W. Stair, now a professor in the College of the City of New York. He had just come to New York from Indiana; he used the English class as an introduction to ideas, and I suspect my feeling that literature was the vehicle, sensuous and imaginative, of ideas came from him. After three terms with him I had learned once and for all that books, even old ones, were distillations of life, and began to think less of literature with a capital L. As I look back on it now, I am quite sure that Mr. Stair found Burke's Speech on Conciliation and *Macbeth* the springboards for various ideas that had a rather tenuous connexion with them. "English" became at his hands an introduction to philosophy, manners, contemporary political ideas, journalism, and love. These ideas were not always directly germane to the text; but they were ideas, and though their accent and their origin were Middle-Western— Middle Western *revolte*—they were an introduction to the great world and to the realm of mind.

[6] The fourth teacher I recall in high school is one who, if he still lives, may possibly remember me. If he does, he recalls me as the worst student of mathematics he ever had. Rumour circulated in the school that Mr. Powell, an urbane, sad man who looked like a banker, was a very wealthy man who taught simply to occupy his time. I never believed it; no one would, I thought, teach solid geometry for amusement. If I were rich, I kept on thinking during the class, I should buy a yacht; I should go around the world. I should, if I must teach, teach English. Mr. Powell noticed my mind wandering; he also noticed when I came up to the blackboard for a demonstration that mathematics was not my *forte*. He called me to him once at the end of the hour. "You do not seem stupid," he said, "but mathematics seems a lot of hocus pocus to you." For the most part, it still does; and I regret it very much. For I am told on good authority that in the logistic symbols of the newer mathematics lies hid the secret of the universe. I recall also that Plato said a gift for mathematics was essential to a philosopher. But it is too late to do anything about it now; it was too late then. And when it came to trigonometry, I, too, was "alone on a wide, wide sea," and Mr. Powell I always remember as the only teacher of mathematics ever to take pity on my soul in agony.

[7] When one speaks of one's old teachers, it is generally to one's college teachers that one refers. For it is then, if one is lucky, that one comes in contact with men who communicate and articulate the things and ideas which become the seeds of one's later intellectual and imaginative life. Every college has five or six men who in essence are its educational system.

I was very lucky. For during my undergraduate days at Columbia, there was a galaxy of teachers available to the student who in their respective ways and as a group would be hard to duplicate at any college in any period. As a freshman straight from high school, I heard Charles A. Beard lecture on American Government; as a sophomore—and in 1914—I heard Carlton Hayes lecture on European History; as a junior I heard John Erskine talk on Shakespeare, and was in a small class where he taught us, really taught us, writing; and in my senior year I had the unique and irrecoverable experience of traversing the history of philosophy with Frederick J. E. Woodbridge. It was not until my graduate study that I came to know John Dewey.

[8] Charles A. Beard illustrates something very remarkable about the art of teaching. Today everybody, even the literary youngsters, are interested in government. For even literature seems less in the Ivory Tower than it did in 1913. But the study of government, then officially known at Columbia as "Politics," did not, to most of us addicted to poetry and music, seem to be our meat, and there was nothing in the dark blue tome, Beard's *American Government and Politics,* that seemed arresting. There were endless details about the mechanisms and structure of State and Federal government. It was not the Beard of the *Economic Interpretation of the Constitution.*

[9] But his lectures were another matter. The lanky figure leaning against the wall, drawling wittily with half-closed eyes, made the questions of government seem the most vital that anyone could broach, and touched matters that lay far deeper than the mere forms of constitutional government.

[10] Every good teacher has his own special art; with some, it is a genius for a clarity that sometimes is more lucid than the complexities of the subject justify. Sometimes it is a talent for apophthegm or leading suggestion, a word that evokes a vista or an idea that opens a world. I cannot now quite remember what Professor Beard's special technique was. He was clear, he was suggestive, he was witty. But none of these things could quite account for the hold he had on the smug and the rebels alike, on both the pre-lawyers and pre-poets. I suspect it was a certain combination of poetry, philosophy, and honesty in the man himself, a sense he communicated that politics mattered far beyond the realm commonly called political, and an insight he conveyed into the life that forms of government furthered or betrayed. One morning he came into class as usual, stood against the wall, and, half-closing his eyes, said:

[11] "Gentlemen, today we are to discuss the budget system in State government. I am sure that must seem to you a dull subject. But if you will tell me, gentlemen, how much *per capita* a nation spends on its Army, on its Navy, on education, on public works, I shall be able to tell you, I think, as much about that nation as if you gave me the works of its poets and philosophers."

[12] We listened with revised and revived attention to an exposition, full

of figures and detail, of the State budget system. Charles A. Beard showed us what politics had to do with the life beyond it and which it made possible. And he taught us, too, the difference between the forms of government and the living substance of its operations. Under his easy, drawling manner, we sensed a passionate concern for an understanding of the realities of government, the economic forces and the interested persons involved in it, and the ideal of government: the liberation of the energies of men. Nobody who has ever listened to Beard can disdain the study of politics in favour of the study of "higher things." He has been too well taught, as tragic world events have since shown, how government may nourish or destroy "higher things."

[13] Up to the autumn of 1914 Europe seemed to most American college students a solar system away. In the autumn of 1914, when the war had been going on two months, Europe came for the first time in the imagination of many Americans to be vivid and near. European history ceased to be the anthropology and the archaeology of distant peoples who spoke remote languages. It became as alive as yesterday's events: it was what explained today's news. It was, therefore, no wonder that at the beginning of the college year Carlton Hayes's course in "Europe since 1815" had become the most popular course in Columbia College. But it was not only the war that accounted for that. Carlton Hayes had for some time been one of the most popular professors in the college. His lectures were the most famous dramatic spectacle on the campus. Nor was it as a performance alone that they were famous. Everyone had heard that Hayes could actually make clear French political parties; I have never met anybody since who could or can.

[14] The complicated history of Germany in the second half of the nineteenth century took shape as well as drama under his presentation of it. And in the midst of being taught and taught clearly, one had the incidental and additional pleasure of hearing a man to whom the great catastrophe of war had its roots in a past he knew, in the traditions of nations among whom he had lived familiarly, and in the desperate mythologies of nationalism, to which he had given special study and concern. One was treated, besides, to unforgettable vignettes of Disraeli dropping his morning walking stick as the cannons boomed noon at Gibraltar; of the Manchester school of economists, the "spiritual advisers" to the robber barons of early nineteenth-century industrial England; of the black walnut furniture of the Victorian period; of the times and the manners of Louis Napoleon; of the studies that produced the *Communist Manifesto*. One was shaken out of the smugness of the middle-class world in which most students were brought up and out of the provincial Americanism in which most of us had lived.

[15] It did not matter, it served only as spice, that some of the barbs delivered in a dry voice by this baldish, sharp-featured man in his thirties were directed at us, at our very smugness, at our laziness, or at our fathers: when he was explaining the attitude of the manufacturers of the early

Industrial Revolution, he reminded us that we all knew manufacturers; "some of your fathers," he drawled, "are manufacturers." It did matter a little to some of us that he mocked poetry and philosophy (this *in re* Shelley and Godwin) . . . "philosophy is what is taught in Philosophy Hall . . ." But it did not matter much. For during a whole year, we sat through a whole century of European history, and Bismarck, Garibaldi, Social Legislation in England, Benevolent Tories like Shaftesbury and reformers like Cobden and Bright, "nationalism"—what devastating force Carlton Hayes put and can still put into the word—democracy, the Third Republic, became familiar parts of our imagination. In the midst of cries of "pro-German" and "pro-Ally," "preparedness" and "pacifism," during the three years before America went into the war, we knew somewhat better than many of our older compatriots what had brought the tornado about. Carlton Hayes had brought European history, as Charles Beard had brought American government, from the abstraction of a textbook to an experience lived and a problem to be faced. And it always surprised some of us that, in the midst of the lectures—first-rate theatrical performances, words shot out for emphasis, silences sustained for a moment, gestures and movements deployed like those of a good actor—when we looked down at our notes, they were as ordered and clear as if we had listened to a scholastic metronome . . . I confess with shame that I achieved only a B.

[16] You were allowed, if you had a fairly good academic record, to take in the senior year a graduate course that was at the time one of the famous academic enterprises of the period. It was James Harvey Robinson's course in the History of the Intellectual Classes in Western Europe. Everyone who had gone to high school knew the two volumes of Robinson and Beard's *Development of Modern Europe*. But the Robinson we came to know as a legend and a rumour by the time we were sophomores was the Robinson who had invented the "new history"—the history of causes and consequences, the history that treated politics as the surface of more fundamental matters, economic and social and cultural, and that regarded the date of the invention of the steam engine as more important than the dates of a king, and the industrial use of steam as more significant than monarchies and dynasties. We had also heard of Robinson, along with Dewey and Beard, as among the intellectual-liberal forces that were making our university famous in some quarters, notorious in others. And, finally, we had heard of the remarkable brilliance of the lectures in History 72.

[17] The latter was a graduate course to which undergraduates, a handful of us, were admitted on sufferance. The majority of the class of over two hundred were graduate students of history, many of them women high school teachers from all over the country, particularly the West and South. Professor Robinson was a short man, with thin, greying hair and a deprecating, half-tired, half-amused, drawling voice. He seemed to be having a half-weary good time examining the origins of human stupidity, and those

vestigial remains of our culture that blocked the free and hopeful functioning of human intelligence. It took us a few weeks in the course to get to the beginnings of *intellectual* history. For Robinson, with saturnine delight, liked to show us the mind of the child, the slave, and the animal still functioning in us. Once he brought in a leading editorial from the New York *Times* to illustrate the theme, and another time quoted from a batch of Sunday sermons reported in that journal the next day. The course was not a course in intellectual heroes, but a course in the changing fashions of adult follies taken seriously in various ages. It only gradually became clear what intellectual heroes were presiding over the whole story as he gave it. They were Freud and Marx and Dewey and the anthropologists, and H. G. Wells, the prophet, then, of intelligence reshaping the world. There were only two or three gods of the past left unbesmirched, or whose clay feet were not recognized. They were Lucretius, who saw the diabolism of religion; Francis Bacon, who saw the human possibilities of science; Voltaire, who exhibited the foolishness of superstition. Plato was a man who believed in Truth, Goodness, and Beauty because he saw the actual world as a chaos which, Robinson loved to remind us, he compared to "a man with a running nose. . . ." Aristotle's science was childish (Robinson did not know how soon again it was to be fashionable and how more fundamental than fashion it is); St. Augustine was a most amusingly and scandalously human saint. It was not until the enlightenment of the eighteenth century that anybody, so most of us gathered from the course, was very enlightened.

[18] Many of the graduate students were shocked, especially by the treatment of religion. The undergraduates from Columbia College had heard much of this before and had no faith (as did some of the graduate students) to have taken away. One of the young women complained to Professor Robinson: "You are taking away my faith." He looked at her oddly. "But if I took away a headache," he said simply, "you would not complain."

[19] We undergraduates enjoyed the sallies, the freshness, the irreverence, and enjoyed, too, the fundamental feeling that lay at the basis of it all—that man, if he took his own intelligence into his hands—could make the world less a shambles and an idiocy than it had so often been. It was in the great days of the liberal faith when trust in intelligence was in the ascendant. If Robinson made the world appear a satire to intelligent observation, he made it seem a lyric hope to generosity and understanding. Dixon Ryan Fox, now President of Union College, was the young instructor who took the third quiz hour with the undergraduates. He felt it his special obligation to let us see the other side. And after a week, when he knew Robinson had been "*exposing*" modern Protestantism, he called in the chaplain as a counterweight. He need not have bothered; we had our own grains of salt. One of the reasons we had grains of salt was that some of us had been studying with a man who will go down, I am quite certain, as one of the great philosophical teachers of our generation. His slender

published writings will live, but they will live for a small circle of students. But Frederick J. E. Woodbridge had educated a whole generation of students in philosophy; and a whole circle of them scattered over the country, including Morris Cohen and Sidney Hook and J. H. Randall, Jr., and Herbert Schneider (to mention only a few), are living testimonies to his influence and his power. In my college days, the great thing was to have taken his course in the History of Philosophy. Some of us were taking it at the same time that we took Robinson's History of the Intellectual Classes in Western Europe. It was rather a different story we were told. It was not a story, but a succession of experiences of philosophers whose importance lay "not in their truth but in their power." It was a shock that turned into a liberation for those of us who had come to philosophy looking for *the* Truth with a dogmatic capital letter. There were other shocks, too. Much that was said in the textbooks we never heard in class, or we heard the contrary. Professor Woodbridge, who looked like a bishop and would have made a very eloquent one, talked like a poet whose theme happened to be the human mind. He talked most like a poet on the days when he was most interested; one remembers what days those were: the early Greeks, Plato, Aristotle, Marcus Aurelius, Lucretius, Spinoza with his sovereign detachment, and Locke with his sovereign common sense. He was not an unprejudiced observer and we rather liked the frankness and the brevity with which he dismissed the Germans and Rousseau. But what one was most moved by was the things by which he himself was most moved: the Plato who was the son of Apollo, the poet and the dramatist of ideas; Marcus Aurelius, the disillusioned statesman whistling to keep up his comical courage; Lucretius looking out with dramatic sympathy and equable understanding on the eternal nature of things. We were impressed by a mind whose maturity had not dulled its enthusiasms, and an understanding uncorrupted by the technical controversies of the academy, by the routine of the classroom, by the burden of administration of an elder statesman, for Woodbridge was graduate Dean of the University. He taught a whole generation of students of philosophy to keep their eye on the object, to see a thinker in his own terms, to cease to raise foolish and irrelevant questions, and above all, to raise the central and relevant ones about a man's teaching. On Aristotle's metaphysics, he began by reminding us that Aristotle was asking the simple and the ultimate question: "What does it mean to be? . . ." We found ourselves astonished to be reminded that the Middle Ages were in their own time not the Middle Ages at all. We were made aware of Locke's simple English attempt to be sensible, tolerant, and direct, and learned to understand what Spinoza meant and why he saw it as a liberation to see all things under the form of eternity. For in that wonderful class, as Will Durant (sitting next to me in alphabetical order) remarked, we were listening not to a professor of philosophy but to philosophy itself. It was impossible to feel you were listening to a doctrine; Professor Woodbridge has never founded a school. You were hearing philosophy itself and came to understand it as an attempt to speak in the categories of mind of the categories of things.

[20] I did not—I think not many of us did—understand it all. But we began to understand what understanding meant, in words that had eloquence without rhetoric. We heard great things nobly uttered. We learnt no doctrine but we grasped the significance of intellectual procedure; and to a whole generation of philosophers, though Professor Woodbridge has long since ceased to be their teacher, he remains their teacher still. He made us understand as none else had done, to use one of his own phrases, "the enterprise of learning."

[21] A figure more widely known outside purely academic circles was and is John Dewey. In 1915 his name was already, if not a household, certainly a schoolroom word. His *How We Think* was used in all the normal schools of the country, and even fashionable ladies dipped into his far from easy books. I had read almost all of Dewey I could get hold of by the time I was a senior, but it was not until my first year as a graduate student that I heard, or, I believe, saw him. His familiar figure and speech, seeming at first that of a Vermont farmer, the casual gait, the keen but often absent eyes, seem so familiar now that I can scarcely believe I did not know them before.

[22] I admit the first lecture was quite a shock, a shock of dullness and confusion, if that can be said. It was at any rate a disappointment. I had not found Dewey's prose easy, but I had learned that its difficulty lay for the most part in its intellectual honesty, which led him to qualify an idea in one sentence half a page long. In part also it lay in the fact that this profoundly original philosopher was struggling to find a vocabulary to say what had never been said in philosophy before, to find a diction that would express with exactness the reality of change and novelty, philosophical words having been used for centuries to express the absolute and the fixed. Once one had got used to the long sentences, with their string of qualifying clauses, to the sobriety, to the lack of image and of colour, one sensed the liberating force of this philosophy. Here was not an answer but a quest for light in the living movement of human experience; in the very precariousness of experience there lay open to the perplexed human creature the possibilities that peril itself provocatively suggested. I had found here, as have so many of my generation, a philosophy that, instead of laying down a diagram of an ideal universe that had nothing to do with the one of actual human doings and sufferings, opened a vision of conscious control of life, of a democracy operating through creative intelligence in the liberation of human capacities and natural goods. In *How We Think* I had learned that thinking itself was simply a discipline of the animal habit of trial and error, and of the possible human habit of imagination and foresight. In *Democracy and Education* I had gathered that it was not in the forms of democratic government that true democracy lay, but in the substance of intelligent co-operation, largely dependent on education. Dewey was not easy,

but once one had mastered his syntax, a vision of a liberal and liberated commonwealth was one's reward, and a philosophy that was not only a vision but a challenge.

[23] I was naturally prepared, therefore, to expect something of intellectual excitement from the lectures in "Psychological Ethics." Intellectual excitement was the last term to describe what I experienced that September afternoon. The course came, in the first place, directly after lunch. It was well attended; there were even some fashionably dressed society ladies, for Dewey had become a vogue. But this famous philosopher who had written so much on "Interest in Education" as the essence of the educational process could not, save by a radical distortion of the term, be said at first hearing to sound interesting. He had none of the usual tricks or gifts of the effective lecturer. He sat at his desk, fumbling with a few crumpled yellow sheets and looking abstractedly out the window. He spoke very slowly in a Vermont drawl. He looked both very kindly and very abstracted. He hardly seemed aware of the presence of a class. He took little pains to underline a phrase, or emphasize a point, or, so at first it seemed to me, to make any. Occasionally he would apparently realize that people in the back of the room might not hear his quiet voice: he would then accent the next word, as likely as not a preposition or a conjunction. He seemed to be saying whatever came into his head next, and at one o'clock on an autumn afternoon to at least one undergraduate what came next did not always have or seem to have a very clear connexion with what had just gone before. The end of the hour finally came and he simply stopped; it seemed to me he might have stopped anywhere. But I soon found that it was my mind that had wandered, not John Dewey's. I began very soon to do what I had seldom done in college courses—to take notes. It was then a remarkable discovery to make on looking over my notes to find that what had seemed so casual, so rambling, so unexciting, was of an extraordinary coherence, texture, and brilliance. I had been listening to a man actually *thinking* in the presence of a class. As one became accustomed to Dewey's technique, it was this last aspect of his teaching that was most impressive—and educative. To attend a lecture of John Dewey was to participate in the actual business of thought. Those pauses were delays in creative thinking, when the next step was really being considered, and for the glib dramatics of the teacher-actor was substituted the enterprise, careful and candid, of the genuine thinker. Those hours came to seem the most arresting educational experiences, almost, I have ever had. One had to be scrupulously attentive and one learned to be so. Not every day or in every teacher does one overhear the palpable processes of thought. One came to enjoy and appreciate the homely metaphor, "the fork in the road," the child and his first attempts to speak, the New England town meeting, instead of the classical images one had been accustomed to from more obviously eloquent lips. Moreover, if one listened attentively one discovered apophthegm and epigram delivered as casually and sleepily as if they were clichés. I remember one instance. It had been

rather a long lecture designed to show that the crucial tests of the morals of a group came in what that group regarded as violations of its conventions. The bell rang. Professor Dewey began to crumple up his notes. "And so," he said, "I think sometimes one can tell more about the morals of our society from the inmates of its jails than from the inmates of its universities." The student next to me who had been semi-dozing stirred in half-alarmed surprise.

[24] I learned later in a seminar to see Dewey's greatest gift as a teacher, that of initiating inquiry rather than that of disseminating a doctrine. The subject matter of the seminar was innocent enough and removed from the immediacies of current controversy. It was a year's course, meeting every Tuesday afternoon, on "The Logic of John Stuart Mill." The seminar remains in my memory, it must be added, not simply for John Dewey or John Stuart Mill. It consisted, looking back on it and indeed as it appeared then, of a very remarkable group. It included two now well-known professors of philosophy, Brand Blandshard of Swathmore College and Sterling Lamprecht of Amherst, Paul Blanshard, later to become Commissioner of Accounts under Mayor LaGuardia, and Albert C. Barnes, the inventor and manufacturer of Argyrol and collector of French paintings, even then a grey-haired man who used to come up from Philadelphia every week with his secretary expressly to study philosophy with his friend John Dewey.

[25] I do not suppose Professor Dewey said more than five percent of the words actually uttered in that seminar. For the latter consisted largely of papers presented by various members of the group. But one remembered what he said. The subject matter was obviously close to him, for had not Mill been one of the great nineteenth century leaders of the empirical school of thought; had he not been, in his way, a pragamatist and, like Dewey himself, a liberal? But one noticed particularly Dewey's gift for pointing to the exact difficulty or the exact limitations of a man or a paper; his capacity for sympathetically seeing what a student was driving at, even when he did not quite succeed in saying it, and Dewey's candid expression of his own position or his own prejudices.

[26] One instance of Dewey's frankness comes to my mind. There was among the group a young lady who had come from England where she had studied philosophy with Bertrand Russell at Cambridge. She listened patiently for weeks to Dewey's varied insistence that the truth of an idea was tested by its use. One day she burst out toward the close of the seminar in the sharp, clipped speech of the educated Englishwoman: "But, professor, I have been taught to believe that true means true; that false means false, that good means good and bad means bad; I don't understand all this talk about more or less true, more or less good. Could you explain more exactly?"

[27] Professor Dewey looked at her mildly for a moment and said: "Let me tell you a parable. Once upon a time in Philadelphia there was a paranoiac. He thought he was dead. Nobody could convince him he was

alive. Finally, one of the doctors thought of an ingenious idea. He pricked the patient's finger. 'Now,' he said, 'are you dead?' 'Sure,' said the paranoiac, 'that proves that dead men bleed. . . .' Now I'll say true or false if you want me to, but I'll mean better or worse."

[28] There are all kinds of talents that go to make up a great teacher. Among those not commonly noted in the textbooks are simplicity and candour. These qualities in Dewey even an undergraduate could recognize and understand.

[29] I cannot say that John Erskine seemed to me a great man in the sense that Woodbridge and Dewey did and do, nor did *The Private Life of Helen of Troy*, for all its bright entertainment, lead me to think I had been obtuse on this point as an undergraduate. But I am convinced he was a very remarkable teacher and it has always seemed to me a pity that he gave up the profession of distinguished teaching for that of the popular novelist. Erskine's quality as a teacher was that of communication by contagion; you felt the quality of the authors he talked about and books seemed to have something to do with life rather than libraries.

[30] Literature was an exercise in imagination, not in archaeology, and there must be thousands of students besides myself who learned to read authors in their own terms, to enjoy them for their own sakes, from John Erskine's famous course in Elizabethan Literature. It is true that one enjoyed Professor Erskine for other reasons. He had wit—often malicious—in his own right, and, when he was in the vein, poetry and philosophy, too. He obviously loved poetry and it seemed to him both to matter and a matter of course that we should love it, too. One felt about him something of the prima donna lecturer; it was evidenced by the pointed silence that would occur while some unfortunate late-comer found his way to his seat. It was clear, too, from the way in which, not infrequently, Shakespeare or Marlowe or Castiglione would be the springboards for little bravura lectures by our teacher on the importance of love or of being a cultivated gentleman, the latter one of his favourite themes. But if he was sometimes the prima donna, he always respected the materials he taught, and for many years no one at Columbia was a more devoted servant to the art and to the love of literature than he. And not the least of his services to that art were, first, the noble and musical way in which he read poetry itself; and secondly, the pains he took to encourage signs of that art among undergraduates. Other teachers might make literature seem a set of documents to be investigated; no one quite knew why. Erskine made it an art to be lived and loved.

[31] It is occasionally said that a good student needs no teachers and that all that he does need is a library and leisure. Neither the poor nor the good student needs bad teachers or bored ones; he is better off without them. But he is very fortunate indeed if he can look back on his college days and enumerate half a dozen men who, by their passion for ideas, their clarity about them, their love for the communication of them, their exemplifica-

tion in their own being of intellectual discipline and candour, have given a meaning to facts that, even with leisure and libraries, he would not have been as likely to find by himself.

[32] I feel my college generation at Columbia was very fortunate. Half a dozen good teachers in a college are enough to make it distinguished. We had more than half a dozen very exceptional ones. But then I think current undergraduates at Columbia, if they are discerning, will, looking back, be able to say the same.

COMMENT AND QUESTIONS

The kind of writing found in "Former Teachers" is not easy to imitate. It is a product of wide knowledge, sharp observation, deep and lively interest in people and ideas, and careful attention to style. Such writing is not produced by mechanical application of techniques. By examining it closely, however, you can learn much that can be applied in your own writing.

I. Edman's handling of the writer-reader relationship, particularly through subtle shifts in pronouns (sometimes "I," sometimes "we," sometimes "you"), is worth studying. See paragraph 15, which at first uses "we" and later "I," and paragraph 16, which starts with "you" and shifts back to "we." What reasons can you find for these changes? Glance through the essay to see other similar changes, and try to state the reasons for each.

II. Leaf through the essay looking only at the first sentence in each paragraph, and notice the unobtrusive but effective way in which the organization is made clear and the paragraphs are joined by transitions. Notice also how many of the paragraphs begin with topic sentences.

III. Read paragraphs 9–11 and point out examples of Edman's way of vitalizing people by describing them, showing them in action, and telling anecdotes about them. Where else in the essay do you find him using these techniques with particular success?

IV. For what reasons does Edman admire Frederick J. E. Woodbridge (paragraphs 19–20)? Has he communicated his reasons meaningfully to the reader? If so, how? Notice also the style and sentence structure in these paragraphs.

V. Edman's treatment of John Dewey in paragraphs 21–23 produces a kind of suspense. What is the nature of this suspense, and how is it achieved?

VI. Has Edman enjoyed his courses more than most college students do? If so, is it simply because he has had such good teachers?

VII. What characteristics do Edman's best teachers appear to have in common?

VIII. If your instructor finds the topic acceptable, write an essay similar to Edman's about two or three of your own former teachers. Try to imitate Edman's techniques of vitalizing people. Your essay, like Edman's, should contain reflective comment and evaluation.

ROBERT LOUIS STEVENSON

The Lantern-Bearers*

The following reflective essay is built on a personal experience which becomes the symbol of a larger idea. Robert Louis Stevenson (1850–1894), Scottish novelist, essayist, and poet, was one of the distinguished stylists of the late nineteenth century. He is probably best known today for his stories of fantasy and romantic adventure, among them *Treasure Island, Kidnapped, The Master of Ballantrae,* and *The Strange Case of Dr. Jekyll* and *Mr. Hyde.* "The Lantern-Bearers" was published in 1888.

I

[1] These boys congregated every autumn about a certain easterly fisher-village, where they tasted in a high degree the glory of existence. The place was created seemingly on purpose for the diversion of young gentlemen. A street or two of houses, mostly red and many of them tiled; a number of fine trees clustered about the manse and the kirkyard, and turning the chief street into a shady alley; many little gardens more than usually bright with flowers; nets a-drying, and fisher-wives scolding in the backward parts; a smell of fish, a genial smell of seaweed; whiffs of blowing sand at the street-corners; shops with golf-balls and bottled lollipops; another shop with penny pickwicks (that remarkable cigar) and the *London Journal,* dear to me for its startling pictures, and a few novels, dear for their suggestive names: such, as well as memory serves me, were the ingredients of the town. These, you are to conceive posted on a spit between two sandy bays, and sparsely flanked with villas—enough for the boys to lodge in with their subsidiary parents, not enough (not yet enough) to cocknify the scene: a haven in the rocks in front: in front of that, a file of gray islets: to the left, endless links and sandwreaths, a wilderness of hiding-holes, alive with popping rabbits and soaring gulls: to the right, a range of seaward crags, one rugged brow beyond another; the ruins of a mighty and ancient fortress on the brink of one; coves between—now charmed into sunshine quiet, now whistling with wind and clamorous with bursting surges; the dens and sheltered hollows redolent of thyme and southernwood, the air at the cliff's edge brisk and clean and pungent of the sea—in front of all, the Bass Rock, tilted seaward like a doubtful bather, the surf ringing it with white, the solan-geese hanging round its summit like a great and glittering smoke. This choice piece of seaboard was sacred, besides, to the wrecker; and the Bass, in the eye of fancy, still flew the colors of King James; and in the ear of fancy the arches

* Published by Charles Scribner's Sons.

of Tantallon still rang with horseshoe iron, and echoed to the commands of Bell-the-Cat.

[2] There was nothing to mar your days, if you were a boy summering in that part, but the embarrassment of pleasure. You might golf if you wanted; but I seem to have been better employed. You might secrete yourself in the Lady's Walk, a certain sunless dingle of elders, all mossed over by the damp as green as grass, and dotted here and there by the stream-side with roofless walls, the cold homes of anchorites. To fit themselves for life, and with a special eye to acquire the art of smoking, it was even common for the boys to harbor there; and you might have seen a single penny pickwick, honestly shared in lengths with a blunt knife, bestrew the glen with these apprentices. Again, you might join our fishing-parties, where we sat perched as thick as solan-geese, a covey of little anglers, boy and girl, angling over each other's heads, to the much entanglement of lines and loss of podleys and consequent shrill recrimination—shrill as the geese themselves. Indeed, had that been all, you might have done this often; but though fishing be a fine pastime, the podley is scarce to be regarded as a dainty for the table; and it was a point of honor that a boy should eat all that he had taken. Or again, you might climb the Law, where the whale's jawbone stood landmark in the buzzing wind, and behold the face of many counties, and the smokes and spires of many towns, and the sails of distant ships. You might bathe, now in the flaws of fine weather, that we pathetically call our summer, now in a gale of wind, with the sand scourging your bare hide, your clothes thrashing abroad from underneath their guardian stone, the froth of the great breakers casting you headlong ere it had drowned your knees. Or you might explore the tidal rocks, above all in the ebb of springs, when the very roots of the hills were for the nonce discovered; following my leader from one group to another, groping in slippery tangle for the wreck of ships, wading in pools after the abominable creatures of the sea, and ever with an eye cast backward on the march of the tide and the menaced line of your retreat. And then you might go Crusoeing, a word that covers all extempore eating in the open air; digging perhaps a house under the margin of the links, kindling a fire of the sea-ware, and cooking apples there—if they were truly apples, for I sometimes suppose the merchant must have played us off with some inferior and quite local fruit, capable of resolving, in the neighborhood of fire, into mere sand and smoke and iodine; or perhaps pushing to Tantallon, you might lunch on sandwiches and visions in the grassy court, while the wind hummed in the crumbling turrets; or clambering along the coast, eat geans [1] (the worst, I must suppose, in Christendom) from an adventurous gean-tree that had taken root under a cliff, where it was shaken with an ague of east wind, and silvered after gales with salt, and grew so foreign among its bleak surroundings that to eat of its produce was an adventure in itself.

[3] There are mingled some dismal memories with so many that were

[1] Wild cherries.

joyous. Of the fisher-wife, for instance, who had cut her throat at Canty Bay; and of how I ran with the other children to the top of the Quadrant, and beheld a posse of silent people escorting a cart, and on the cart, bound in a chair, her throat bandaged, and the bandage all bloody—horror!— the fisher-wife herself, who continued thenceforth to hag-ride my thoughts, and even to-day (as I recall the scene) darkens daylight. She was lodged in the little old jail in the chief street; but whether or no she died there, with a wise terror of the worst, I never inquired. She had been tippling; it was but a dingy tragedy; and it seems strange and hard that, after all these years, the poor crazy sinner should be still pilloried on her cart in the scrap-book of my memory. Nor shall I readily forget a certain house in the Quadrant where a visitor died, and a dark old woman continued to dwell alone with the dead body; nor how this old woman conceived a hatred to myself and one of my cousins, and in the dread hour of the dusk, as we were clambering on the garden-walls, opened a window in that house of mortality and cursed us in a shrill voice and with a marrowy choice of language. It was a pair of very colorless urchins that fled down the lane from this remarkable experience! But I recall with a more doubtful sentiment, compounded out of fear and exultation, the coil of equinoctial tempests; trumpeting squalls, scouring flaws of rain; the boats with their reefed lugsails scudding for the harbor mouth, where danger lay, for it was hard to make when the wind had any east in it; the wives clustered with blowing shawls at the pier-head, where (if fate was against them) they might see boat and husband and sons—their whole wealth and their whole family—engulfed under their eyes; and (what I saw but once) a troop of neighbors forcing such an unfortunate homeward, and she squalling and battling in their midst, a figure scarcely human, a tragic Maenad.

[4] These are things that I recall with interest; but what my memory dwells upon the most, I have been all this while withholding. It was a sport peculiar to the place, and indeed to a week or so of our two months' holiday there. Maybe it still flourishes in its native spot; for boys and their pastimes are swayed by periodic forces inscrutable to man; so that tops and marbles reappear in their due season, regular like the sun and moon; and the harmless art of knucklebones has seen the fall of the Roman empire and the rise of the United States. It may still flourish in its native spot, but nowhere else, I am persuaded; for I tried myself to introduce it on Tweedside, and was defeated lamentably; its charm being quite local, like a country wine that cannot be exported.

[5] The idle manner of it was this:—

[6] Toward the end of September, when school-time was drawing near and the nights were already black, we would begin to sally from our respective villas, each equipped with a tin bull's eye lantern. The thing was so well known that it had worn a rut in the commerce of Great Britain; and the grocers, about the due time, began to garnish their windows with our particular brand of luminary. We wore them buckled to the waist upon a

cricket belt, and over them, such was the rigor of the game, a buttoned topcoat. They smelled noisomely of blistered tin; they never burned aright, though they would always burn our fingers; their use was naught; the pleasure of them merely fanciful; and yet a boy with a bull's-eye under his top-coat asked for nothing more. The fishermen used lanterns about their boats, and it was from them, I suppose, that we had got the hint; but theirs were not bull's-eyes, nor did we ever play at being fishermen. The police carried them at their belts, and we had plainly copied them in that; yet we did not pretend to be policemen. Burglars, indeed, we may have had some haunting thoughts of; and we had certainly an eye to past ages when lanterns were more common, and to certain storybooks in which we had found them to figure very largely. But take it for all in all, the pleasure of the thing was substantive; and to be a boy with a bull's-eye under his top-coat was good enough for us.

[7] When two of these asses met, there would be an anxious "Have you got your lantern?" and a gratified "Yes!" That was the shibboleth, and very needful too; for, as it was the rule to keep our glory contained, none could recognize a lantern-bearer, unless (like the polecat) by the smell. Four or five would sometimes climb into the belly of a ten-man lugger, with nothing but the thwarts above them—for the cabin was usually locked, or choose out some hollow of the links where the wind might whistle overhead. There the coats would be unbuttoned and the bull's-eye discovered, and in the checkering glimmer, under the huge windy hall of the night, and cheered by a rich steam of toasting tinware, these fortunate young gentlemen would crouch together in the cold sand of the links or on the scaly bilges of the fishing-boat, and delight themselves with inappropriate talk. Woe is me that I may not give some specimens—some of their foresights of life, or deep inquiries into the rudiments of man and nature, these were so fiery and so innocent, they were so richly silly, so romantically young. But the talk, at any rate, was but a condiment; and these gatherings themselves only accidents in the career of the lantern-bearer. The essence of this bliss was to walk by yourself in the black night; the slide shut, the top-coat buttoned; not a ray escaping, whether to conduct your footsteps or to make your glory public: a mere pillar of darkness in the dark; and all the while, deep down in the privacy of your fool's heart, to know you had a bull's-eye at your belt, and to exult and sing over the knowledge.

II

[8] It is said that a poet has died young in the breast of the most stolid. It may be contended, rather, that this (somewhat minor) bard in almost every case survives, and is the spice of life to his possessor. Justice is not done to the versatility and the unplumbed childishness of man's imagination. His life from without may seem but a rude mound of mud; there will be some golden chamber at the heart of it, in which he dwells delighted;

and for as dark as his pathway seems to the observer, he will have some kind of bull's-eye at his belt.

[9] It would be hard to pick out a career more cheerless than that of Dancer, the miser, as he figures in the "Old Bailey Reports," a prey to the most sordid persecutions, the butt of his neighborhood; betrayed by his hired man, his house beleaguered by the impish schoolboy, and he himself grinding and fuming and impotently fleeing to the law against these pin-pricks. You marvel at first that any one should willingly prolong a life so destitute of charm and dignity; and then you call to memory that had he chosen, had he ceased to be a miser, he could have been freed at once from these trials, and might have built himself a castle and gone escorted by a squadron. For the love of more recondite joys, which we cannot estimate, which, it may be, we should envy, the man had willingly foregone both comfort and consideration. "His mind to him a kingdom was"; and sure enough, digging into that mind, which seems at first a dust-heap, we unearth some priceless jewels. For Dancer must have had the love of power and the disdain of using it, a noble character in itself; disdain of many pleasures, a chief part of what is commonly called wisdom; disdain of the inevitable end, that finest trait of mankind; scorn of men's opinions, another element of virtue; and at the back of all, a conscience just like yours and mine, whining like a cur, swindling like a thimble-rigger, but still pointing (there or thereabout) to some conventional standard. Here was a cabinet portrait to which Hawthorne perhaps had done justice; and yet not Hawthorne either, for he was mildly minded, and it lay not in him to create for us that throb of the miser's pulse, his fretful energy of gusto, his vast arms of ambition clutching in he knows not what: insatiable, insane, a god with a muck-rake. Thus, at least, looking in the bosom of the miser, consideration detects the poet in the full tide of life, with more, indeed, of the poetic fire than usually goes to epics; and tracing that mean man about his cold hearth, and to and fro in his discomfortable house, spies within him a blazing bonfire of delight. And so with others, who do not live by bread alone, but by some cherished and perhaps fantastic pleasure; who are meat salesmen to the external eye, and possibly to themselves are Shakespeares, Napoleons, or Beethovens; who have not one virtue to rub against another in the field of active life, and yet perhaps, in the life of contemplation, sit with the saints. We see them on the street, and we can count their buttons; but Heaven knows in what they pride themselves! Heaven knows where they have set their treasure!

[10] There is one fable that touches very near the quick of life: the fable of the monk who passed into the woods, heard a bird break into song, hearkened for a trill or two, and found himself on his return a stranger at his convent gates; for he had been absent fifty years, and of all his comrades there survived but one to recognize him. It is not only in the woods that this enchanter carols, though perhaps he is native there. He sings in the most doleful places. The miser hears him and chuckles, and the days are moments. With no more

apparatus than an ill-smelling lantern I have evoked him on the naked links. All life that is not merely mechanical is spun out of two strands: seeking for that bird and hearing him. And it is just this that makes life so hard to value, and the delight of each so incommunicable. And just a knowledge of this, and a remembrance of those fortunate hours in which the bird has sung to us, that fills us with such wonder when we turn the pages of the realist. There, to be sure, we find a picture of life in so far as it consists of mud and of old iron, cheap desires and cheap fears, that which we are ashamed to remember and that which we are careless whether we forget; but of the note of that time-devouring nightingale we hear no news.

[11] The case of these writers of romance is most obscure. They have been boys and youths; they have lingered outside the window of the beloved, who was then most probably writing to some one else; they have sat before a sheet of paper, and felt themselves mere continents of congested poetry, not one line of which would flow; they have walked alone in the woods, they have walked in cities under the countless lamps; they have been to sea, they have hated, they have feared, they have longed to knife a man and maybe done it; the wild taste of life has stung their palate. Or, if you deny them all the rest, one pleasure at least they have tasted to the full—their books are there to prove it—the keen pleasure of successful literary composition. And yet they fill the globe with volumes, whose cleverness inspires me with despairing admiration, and whose consistent falsity to all I care to call existence, with despairing wrath. If I had no better hope than to continue to revolve among the dreary and petty businesses, and to be moved by the paltry hopes and fears with which they surround and animate their heroes, I declare I would die now. But there has never an hour of mine gone quite so dully yet; if it were spent waiting at a railway junction, I would have some scattering thoughts, I could count some grains of memory, compared to which the whole of one of these romances seems but dross.

[12] These writers would retort (if I take them properly) that this was very true; that it was the same with themselves and other persons of (what they call) the artistic temperament; that in this we were exceptional, and should apparently be ashamed of ourselves; but that our works must deal exclusively with (what they call) the average man, who was a prodigious dull fellow, and quite dead to all but the paltriest considerations. I accept the issue. We can only know others by ourselves. The artistic temperament (a plague on the expression!) does not make us different from our fellow-men, or it would make us incapable of writing novels; and the average man (a murrain on the word!) is just like you and me, or he would not be average. It was Whitman who stamped a kind of Birmingham sacredness upon the latter phrase; but Whitman knew very well, and showed very nobly, that the average man was full of joys and full of a poetry of his own. And this harping on life's dulness and man's meanness is a loud profession of incompetence; it is one of two things: the cry of the blind eye, *I cannot see,* or the complaint of the dumb tongue, *I cannot utter.* To draw a life without delights is to prove that I have not real-

ized it. To picture a man without some sort of poetry—well, it goes near to prove my case, for it shows an author may have little enough. To see Dancer only as a dirty, old, small-minded, impotently fuming man, in a dirty house, besieged by Harrow boys, and probably beset by small attorneys, is to show myself as keen an observer as . . . the Harrow boys. But these young gentlemen (with a more becoming modesty) were content to pluck Dancer by the coat-tails; they did not suppose they had surprised his secret or could put him living in a book: and it is there my error would have lain. Or say that in the same romance—I continue to call these books romances, in the hope of giving pain—say that in the same romance which now begins really to take shape, I should leave to speak of Dancer, and follow instead the Harrow boys; and say that I came on some such business as that of my lantern-bearers on the links; and described the boys as very cold, spat upon by flurries of rain, and drearily surrounded, all of which they were; and their talk as silly and indecent, which it certainly was. I might upon these lines, and had I Zola's genius, turn out, in a page or so, a gem of literary art, render the lantern-light with the touches of a master, and lay on the indecency with the ungrudging hand of love; and when all was done, what a triumph would my picture be of shallowness and dulness! how it would have missed the point! how it would have belied the boys! To the ear of the stenographer, the talk is merely silly and indecent; but ask the boys themselves, and they are discussing (as it is highly proper they should) the possibilities of existence. To the eye of the observer they are wet and cold and drearily surrounded; but ask themselves, and they are in the heaven of a recondite pleasure, the ground of which is an ill-smelling lantern.

III

[13] For, to repeat, the ground of a man's joy is often hard to hit. It may hinge at times upon a mere accessory, like the lantern, it may reside, like Dancer's, in the mysterious inwards of psychology. It may consist with perpetual failure, and find exercise in the continued chase. It has so little bond with externals (such as the observer scribbles in his note-book) that it may even touch them not; and the man's true life, for which he consents to live, lie altogether in the field of fancy. The clergyman, in his spare hours, may be winning battles, the farmer sailing ships, the banker reaping triumph in the arts; all leading another life, plying another trade from that they choose; like the poet's housebuilder, who, after all is cased in stone,

> "By his fireside, as impotent fancy prompts,
> Rebuilds it to his liking."

In such a case the poetry runs underground. The observer (poor soul, with his documents!) is all abroad. For to look at the man is but to court deception. We shall see the trunk from which he draws his nourishment; but he himself is above and abroad in the green dome of foliage, hummed through by winds and nested in by nightingales. And the true realism were that of the poets, to climb up after him like a squirrel, and catch some glimpse of the heaven for which he lives. And the true realism, always and everywhere, is that of the poets: to find out where joy resides, and give it a voice far beyond singing.

[14] For to miss the joy is to miss all. In the joy of the actors lies the sense of any action. That is the explanation, that the excuse. To one who has not the secret of the lanterns, the scene upon the links is meaningless. And hence the haunting and truly spectral unreality of realistic books. Hence, when we read the English realists, the incredulous wonder with which we observe the hero's constancy under the submerging tide of dulness, and how he bears up with his jibbing sweetheart, and endures the chatter of idiot girls, and stands by his whole unfeatured wilderness of an existence, instead of seeking relief in drink or foreign travel. Hence in the French, in that meat-market of middle-aged sensuality, the disgusted surprise with which we see the hero drift sidelong, and practically quite untempted, into every description of misconduct and dishonor. In each, we miss the personal poetry, the enchanted atmosphere, that rainbow work of fancy that clothes what is naked and seems to ennoble what is base; in each, life falls dead like dough, instead of soaring away like a balloon into the colors of the sunset; each is true, each inconceivable; for no man lives in the external truth, among salts and acids, but in the warm, phantasmagoric chamber of his brain, with the painted windows and the storied walls.

[15] Of this falsity we have had a recent example from a man who knows far better—Tolstoi's *Powers of Darkness*. Here is a piece full of force and truth, yet quite untrue. For before Mikita was led into so dire a situation he was tempted, and temptations are beautiful at least in part; and a work which dwells on the ugliness of crime and gives no hint of any loveliness in the temptation, sins against the modesty of life, and even when a Tolstoi writes it, sinks to melodrama. The peasants are not understood; they saw their life in fairer colors; even the deaf girl was clothed in poetry for Mikita, or he had never fallen. And so, once again, even an Old Bailey melodrama, without some brightness of poetry and lustre of existence, falls into the inconceivable and ranks with fairy tales.

IV

[16] In nobler books we are moved with something like the emotions of life; and this emotion is very variously provoked. We are so moved when Levine labors in the field, when Andre sinks beyond emotion, when Richard Feverel and Lucy Desborough meet beside the river, when Antony, "not cowardly, puts off his helmet," when Kent has infinite pity on the dying Lear, when, in Dostoieffsky's *Despised and Rejected*, the uncomplaining hero drains his cup of suffering and virtue. These are notes that please the great heart of man. Not only love, and the fields, and the bright face of danger, but sacrifice and death and unmerited suffering humbly supported, touch in us the vein of the poetic. We love to think of them, we long to try them, we are humbly hopeful that we may prove heroes also.

[17]   We have heard, perhaps, too much of lesser matters. Here is the door, here is the open air. *Itur in antiquam silvam.*[2]

COMMENT AND QUESTIONS

This reflective essay—rich (perhaps too rich) in concrete detail, in language, and in its picture of human life—requires careful reading. First you need to follow its general development. In paragraphs 1–3 Stevenson describes his boyhood experiences as he remembers them; the reasons for the fullness and variety of details become evident later. In paragraphs 4–7 he introduces the bull's-eye lantern, then tells what it is and how the boys feel about it. In Section II, paragraphs 8 and 9, he further clarifies the meaning or symbolism of the lantern and shows that the miser, Dancer, has his lantern too. In paragraph 10 he introduces another symbol, the bird's song, which you will need to interpret. In the same paragraph he begins his attack on writers of realistic fiction by saying that they portray only the mud and fears of life. In paragraphs 11 and 12 he continues to argue against what he considers the false picture of life that realists present. At the end of Section II he returns to his lantern figure to show what realists fail to include in their writings. In Section III he continues to discuss the mysterious inner life of man and the deceptive appearance of man's outer life. In Section IV he deals with the way life is presented in what he calls "noble books," and the spirit and the view of life that they contain.

Much of this essay may appear to be mere description, or mere argument, sometimes intemperately stated, against a type of literature which Stevenson, himself an avowed romanticist, did not like. A critical reader may question the amount of descriptive detail, and may disagree with Stevenson's opinions of the realistic novelists; but he will also see that Stevenson is dealing with things more significant than bull's-eye lanterns and literary differences.

I. State in a sentence what you take to be the central idea of the essay.

II. Explain just what use Stevenson has made of the lantern figure in order to make this idea clear. Is the figure a good one for his purposes?

III. Can you see any reason why Stevenson wrote three long paragraphs before he introduced the boys and the lanterns? What details in these paragraphs show not the pleasantness but the unpleasantness and even the sordidness of life? Why did Stevenson include these details?

IV. Comment on Stevenson's interpretation of Dancer's character (paragraph 9).

V. How does Stevenson interpret the fable of the monk and the bird song, and how is the fable related to the main idea of the essay? Do you think that the essay would have been equally clear and effective if Stevenson had omitted the fable and had been content to use only the lantern figure?

VI. From paragraph 10 to the end of the essay Stevenson is stating his own

---

[2] One goes into the ancient forest.

view of life and is attacking the view of "realistic" novelists. Do you find places where Stevenson's reasoning seems questionable? In what passages do you find the most heavily charged language? (Students who have read such writers as Zola and Flaubert will be in a position to judge for themselves Stevenson's indictment of what he calls "realism.")

VII. Consider Stevenson's choice of words, the movement and rhythm of his sentences, his use of details and of figures of speech, especially in paragraphs 3, 6, 10, 13, and 14. Do you see why he is regarded as one of the distinguished prose writers of the nineteenth century?

VIII. Study the description-of-a-place in paragraph 1. What techniques of description are used?

IX. When you think of the essay as a whole, what is your judgment of it? Why?

X. If your instructor approves, write a reflective personal essay based on one or more of your own childhood experiences.

HOWARD MUMFORD JONES

The Attractions of Stupidity*

Howard Mumford Jones (1892–) is an American writer, scholar, and professor of English at Harvard. "The Attractions of Stupidity" was a Commencement address given at Tufts University in 1944.

[1] The object of a college education is supposed to be the training of the mind. We hold that a student who presents himself at the door of one of our institutions and who remains with us long enough, is bound to go out that door a better and brainier man than when he went in. He is supposed, among other things, to be better prepared to enter upon the profession or occupation of his choice.

[2] But it is curious that those who pursue such an occupation—let us say, journalism—though they may acclaim the virtues of college education in other fields, are sceptical about it in their own, and hold to the philosophy that the young graduate, once he has had the nonsense knocked out of him, may amount to something in spite of his college education. Or they argue that, to be sure, a B.S. in blacksmithing is better than no B.S. at all; but better than a B.S. in blacksmithing is a bachelor's degree in nothing in particular. They argue this way because they suppose that a college education gives a general training to the mind superior to specific training in skills.

[3] When you try to pin these people down to what it is that is learned in

* Reprinted through the courtesy of Howard Mumford Jones and *The Tuftonian*.

college, they elude you. Will a course in chemistry give you this mysterious general training? Well, they say, a course in chemistry is a very good thing in its way, but of course unless you are going to be a professional chemist, you will soon forget your chemistry. Well, you ask, is a course in English desirable? Yes, they will respond, a course in literature is a very good thing. Of course, people don't generally read the classics except when they have to, so that, if you are going to lead a busy life, you had better read the classics in college, for otherwise you will never read them. If you press the point, if you ask some alumnus whether he still reads the classics, he will look uncomfortable, and probably say something about enjoying Professor So-and-So's course in Shakespeare—but he hasn't kept up his reading, though he remembers the course with pleasure.

[4] All this suggests that no specific subject furnishes the essence of what people get out of college. Is there, then, some residue which courses leave in the mind and which constitutes a general education? What is this residue? There are the pleasant memories of Professor So-and-So's course which the alumnus retains. Unfortunately one doesn't have to go to college to acquire pleasant memories, since there are more interesting people outside college walls than there are in them. Is there some mysterious effect upon the mind, some impalpable essence engendered in college, some thing of which everybody admits the existence, though nobody knows its definition? If there be such a thing, it will scarcely help us, since one cannot define the indefinable. Moreover, as we look about among our friends on the campus, few of them seem distinguished by any impalpable essence, or, for that matter, any extraordinary amount of intellect. There are always a few who prefer books to activity, but the general run of students pay only that decent regard to their lessons which represents the last-ditch stand of the faculty. In truth, if a college education means no more than is represented by an alumni meeting, why bother about it? Perhaps we are in the center of a good-natured conspiracy in which everybody refuses to call things by their right names.

[5] Now I am going to venture upon an explanation of this dilemma. I have lately been reading the essays of Walter Bagehot, and in his letters on the *coup d'etat* of Louis Napoleon, Bagehot suggests that the English people are protected against any such violent upheavals as a French revolution by their superior stupidity. He compares the English to the Romans as a great political people. Of the Romans he says: "Is not a certain dullness of mind their most visible characteristic? What is the history of their speculative mind? A blank. What their literature? A copy. They have not left a single discovery in any abstract science, not a single perfect or well-formed work of high imagination." He points out that the Greeks, in contrast, who invented almost everything worth inventing, succumbed to the Romans at last, and that in general the stupid people win and the clever people lose. Such are the attractions of stupidity.

[6] This is an illuminating theory. It sheds a good deal of light on the colleges. Take, for example, the classroom. The classroom may be described

as a scene of polite warfare between the professors and the undergraduates. A hundred years ago that warfare often broke out in actual violence, but we have changed to more civilized forms of conflict. In that warfare the faculty are on the side of the Greeks and the students are on the side of the Romans. It is the business of the faculty to transmit to the students a body of culture, and it is the business of the Romans to resist as long as they can. It is obvious, on Bagehot's theory, that the Romans—that is to say, the stupid majority—will always win. That they do win is amply evident. For example, the faculty has to bring instruction down to the level of the students; they seldom succeed in lifting the students up to the level of the Greeks. Again, the standards set in any college are inevitably the standards of the average—that is to say, of the great middle body of the stupid as compared with the minority of clever people. If you raise the standards too high, you fail almost everybody, and the trustees complain; if you sink them too low, you let almost everybody in.

[7] Perhaps there is a great law of nature at work in these matters, against which we struggle in vain. There is something fresh, sound, and admirable about stupidity. This has been remarked by numerous philosophers, including Carlyle, and confirmed in our time by mental tests invented by educators. Not to know too much, not to think too much, not to ask too many questions—these are the conditions of a normal or median existence. Let us have men about us who are fat, sleek-headed men, and men that sleep o'night. Perhaps the great body of American undergraduates are following right instinct in resisting instruction as capably as they do. Last year I taught freshmen and sophomores, and I was delighted to find them writing the same hazy ideas in the same bad sentences they used when I began teaching 25 years ago. There was something refreshing in this discovery. Time stood still while I renewed my youth.

[8] On the other hand, the colleges have set their faces against the universal law. They continue to battle on the side of the Greeks. They seem to think the great law of the survival value of stupidity can somehow be got around. When they can lure a student into deserting the Romans for the Greeks, they are quite shameless in their treason. This suggests that the student may, if he likes, desert the ranks of the Romans; and because the ranks of the Romans are so large, perhaps he is not missed. What attracts the student to this remarkable act of treason?

[9] If he remains among the Romans, who were, you will recall, a great political people, he will have the solid satisfaction of belonging to a large majority. If he looks around him in college, he will discern, as far as the eye can see, the serried ranks of the Roman battalions drawn up to protect him and themselves from the inroads of the Greeks. When he graduates, he will graduate into the world of the Romans—a world of comfortable conformity, of conventional interests, of tried and solid satisfactions. He will become one of the great average of American citizens, good, respectable, worthy; he will marry and rear his children in the way of the Romans; he may join a luncheon club and a country club, living very much as his father did. It will not

be an exciting life—at least from the Greek point of view—but it will be a natural, conformable sort of existence.

[10] What have the Greeks to offer? Not very much. In the first place, the student will have to abandon his natural place in the ranks of the Romans, and strike out for himself. From the Roman point of view, he is a deserter, and stupidity is always expert in this, that it knows how to punish desertion. If he gives himself up to intellectual adventure, if he tries to do his own thinking, if he attempts to reach conclusions for himself, if he announces and stands by his convictions, he may rest assured his friends will begin by looking at him askance, and probably end by abandoning him altogether. He may find a few acquaintances among the Greeks, but the Greeks have ever been a queer sort of people, more remarkable for their eccentricities than otherwise. They hold to the philosophy (I do not say they practise it) that every tub should stand on its own bottom. The undergraduate who deserts the ranks of the stupid has, from the Roman point of view, queered himself. He fits into no campus pigeon hole. The Romans cannot think of him as a member of the faculty, for he is clearly of an age with themselves; and they cannot think of him as one of themselves, for he thinks, in some respects, like a member of the faculty.

[11] Our young friend is, then, likely to have a painful time. He will find even the faculty unsympathetic, for the Greeks have a polity of their own, which has no assured place for the converted barbarian. He will read books, and disagree with them; he will take courses, and find the courses designed and taught for the Romans. If he writes out what he thinks, he will discover that nobody has much patience with manuscripts. And when he graduates, he will graduate into the world of the Romans, which has no use for the non-Romans except to assimilate them.

[12] Will he have any durable satisfactions? I can think of only one. He will be master of his own intellectual house. His thoughts will be his own thoughts, and not borrowed ones—the Romans, you remember, were great borrowers. He will have his own point of view, his own scale of values, his own philosophy. And he is headed for an interesting, if painful, life, a life of incessant conflict with the ideas and standards of the Romans. The Apostle Paul, who was something of a Greek, wrote to the church in Corinth that he had been "in stripes, in imprisonments, in tumults, in labours, in watchings, in fastings." He led, in other words, the life of a nonconformist. The incessant struggle of the mind to be true to itself, to absorb new truths, to grow, to overcome pressures—these are the painful portion of the independent thinker. Almost his sole reward is the satisfaction of integrity.

[13] He may not even have that—as the Romans have it. The Calvinists used to struggle with themselves to discover whether they were saved; just when they had a comforting sense of salvation, a voice whispered that this satisfaction might be a lure of the old deluder. The kind of intellectual integrity the Greeks have is of this sort. It does not generalize from insufficient instances. When it receives proof that an opinion is false, it yields. It is humble before

the vast ocean of ignorance, and modest in respect to its own minute attainments. It allows a considerable margin for the possibility of being self-deceived. On one point, and on one point only, it continually insists: its thoughts are its own thoughts, its conclusions its own conclusions, based upon information, analysis, and belief.

[14]   Despite the superior attractions of stupidity, it happens from time to time that college students really choose the difficult way of intellectual life. I suppose it is due in some degree to the lamentable influence of the faculty upon them. I suppose it is due to the lingering truth of John Stuart Mill's statement that it is better to be Socrates dissatisfied than a pig satisfied. Whatever the cause, it is the occasional appearance of a convert to the Greeks that causes these flutters of alarm among the solid and conservative members of the community. They awake to the fact that colleges do really offer an opportunity to live the intellectual life provided anybody wants to live it.

[15]   I do not know how many at Tufts College have chosen the Roman, and how many have chosen the Greek way of life in this unhistorical history, but I seem to see a number of the Greek persuasion before me; and if there are others present, if there are those who are wavering, let me quote to you and to them in conclusion this famous quatrain of Montrose:

> He either fears his faith too much
> Or his deserts are small
> Who fears to put it to the touch,
> To win or lose it all.

If you have any capacity which may fit you for the life of the Greeks, and should you choose to conceal it and live among the Romans, nobody will be any the wiser. Even if you elect the Greek way, your choice may be wrong because you may lack the intellectual fortitude to go it alone. But if your choice is made, if you have deserted the Romans, I can at least promise you an uncertain, an uncomfortable, possibly an inglorious, but most surely and emphatically a crowded, interesting, and exciting career.

COMMENT AND QUESTIONS

I. A combination of humorous overstatement and ironical statement gives this essay much of its flavor. Point out examples of each kind of statement.

II. To what extent do you agree with what Mr. Jones says in paragraph 4 about the majority of college students? To what extent do you agree with his picture in paragraph 6 of the warfare between faculty and students?

III. What is the relevance of the first four paragraphs to the main idea of the essay?

IV. What, according to Mr. Jones, are "the superior attractions of stupidity"? Does he make them sound superior and attractive to you?

V. Phrase in a sentence the rewards of the "Greek way of life" that Mr.

Jones would like his audience to choose. Do you think that he weakens his case for it by applying to it words like "painful," "difficult," uncertain," "uncomfortable," "inglorious"? Explain.

EDWARD WEEKS

How Big Is One[*]

The following informal essay raises a question of concern to many Americans: as our production, our society, and our government become bigger and bigger, what happens to the individual? Edward Weeks (1898–), writer, lecturer, and literary critic, has been editor of *The Atlantic Monthly* since 1938. "How Big Is One" was originally delivered as a lecture to the American Unitarian Association, and was published in *The Atlantic* of August, 1958.

[1] My late friend, the French writer Raoul de Roussy de Sales, who knew America intimately, used to tease me about our infatuation with bigness. "It's in your blood," he would say. "When I listen to Americans talking on shipboard, or in a Paris restaurant, or here in New York, it is only a question of time before someone will come out with that favorite boast of yours—*'the biggest in the world!'* The New York skyline, or the Washington Monument, or the Chicago Merchandise Mart—the biggest in the world. You say it without thinking what it means." How right he was, yet until he prodded me about it, I had never realized that this was indeed our national boast. We take pride in being big, and in a youthful way we used to think that bigness was our own special prerogative. But now we know better; now we find ourselves confronted with nations or with groups of nations which are quite as big as we are and which have the potential of being considerably bigger. This calls for a new orientation; indeed, I think it might be timely if we examine this concept of bigness and try to determine how it has affected our private lives and our thinking.

[2] We have been in love with bigness ever since the adolescence of our democracy. The courtship began on the frontier: the uncut virgin forests, so dense and terrifying; the untamed flooding rivers; the limitless prairies; the almost impassable Sierras—to overcome obstacles like these, man, so puny in comparison, had to outdo himself. He had to be bigger than Hercules. The English live on a small, contained island, and English humor is naturally based on understatement; but an American when he is having fun always exaggerates.

[*] Copyright 1958, by The Atlantic Monthly Company, 8 Arlington Street, Boston 16, Massachusetts.

[3] Our first hero of the frontier was a superman, Davy Crockett, who could outshoot, outfight, and outwoo anyone. One day he sauntered into the forest for an airing but forgot to take his thunderbolt along. This made it embarrassing when he came face to face with a panther. The scene is described in the old almanac, as Howard Mumford Jones says, "in metaphoric language which has all the freshness of dawn." The panther growled and Crockett growled right back—"He grated thunder with his teeth"—and so the battle began. In the end, the panther, tamed, goes home with Davy, lights the fire on a dark night with flashes from his eyes, brushes the hearth every morning with his tail, and rakes the garden with his claws. Davy did the impossible, and listening to the legends of his prowess made it easier for the little guy on the frontier to do the possible.

[4] Davy Crockett had a blood brother in Mike Fink, the giant of the river boatmen, and first cousins in Tony Beaver and Paul Bunyan of the North Woods and Pecos Bill of the Southwest. They were ringtailed roarers, and everything they did had an air of gigantic plausibility. Prunes are a necessary part of the lumberjack's diet, and Paul Bunyan's camp had such a zest for prunes that the prune trains which hauled the fruit came in with two engines, one before and one behind pushing. "Paul used to have twenty flunkies sweepin' the prunestones out from under the tables, but even then they'd get so thick we had to wade through 'em up over our shoes sometimes on our way in to dinner. They'd be all over the floor and in behind the stove and piled up against the windows where they'd dumped 'em outside so the cook couldn't see out at all hardly. . . . In Paul's camp back there in Wisconsin the prunestones used to get so thick they had to have twenty ox-teams haulin' 'em away, and they hauled 'em out in the woods, and the chipmunks ate 'em and grew so big the people shot 'em for tigers." Only an American could have invented that build-up, and I am grateful to Esther Shephard for having recaptured the legend so accurately in her *Paul Bunyan*.

[5] Texas, with its fondness for bigness, preferred the living man to the legend: it provided the space for men like Richard King, the founder of the King Ranch. Richard King's story as told by Tom Lea is Horatio Alger multiplied by a thousand. The son of Irish immigrants, he ran off to sea at the age of eleven; a river boat captain in his twenties, he came ashore, married the parson's daughter, bought 15,000 acres of desert at two cents an acre, and went into the cattle business. His close friend and adviser was Lieutenant Colonel Robert E. Lee of the Second United States Cavalry, and it was Lee who gave King what has come to be the family slogan: "Buy land; and never sell." The King Ranch has grown to 700,000 acres in Texas with big offshoots in Kentucky, Pennsylvania, Australia, Cuba, and Brazil, and those of us who dwell in cities and suburbia have developed a kind of Mount Vernon reverence for this vast domain. It is just about as big, we think, as a good ranch ought to be.

[6] I entered publishing in the summer of 1923 as a book salesman in New York. As I look back over the thirty-five years of my working life, I recognize

that a significant change has taken place in our business community. The motorcars which I used to covet as a young bachelor, the Stutz Bearcat, the Mercer, the Simplex, the Locomobile, the Pierce Arrow—all these beauties and hundreds of the lesser breeds, like the Hupmobile, the Maxwell, the Franklin, the Stanley Steamer, and the Moon—are museum pieces today. The beauty and the originality which went into their design have been melted down and vulgarized in the models of the five major companies which survive.

[7] In the days I am speaking of, Mr. Potts was our family grocer, and he knew the exact cuts of roast beef and lamb which would bring joy to my father's heart, just as he was prepared for my mother's remonstrance when there was too much gristle. There used to be a family grocer, like Mr. Potts, in every American community. Then some genius in Memphis, Tennessee, came up with the Piggly-Wiggly, the first gigantic cash and carry where the customer waited on himself, and in no time there were chains of these super markets stretching across the country. Such consolidation as this has been going on in every aspect of business, and at a faster and faster tempo.

[8] When I was a book salesman, an American book publisher who sold a million dollars' worth of his books in one year was doing quite a prosperous business. Today a publisher who sells only a million dollars' worth of books a year cannot afford to remain in business; he has to join forces with another and larger publisher so that their combined production will carry them over the break-even point.

[9] In the nineteen-twenties almost every American city had two newspapers, and the larger ones had four or five, and there is no doubt that this competition for ideas, for the truth was a healthy thing for the community. Today most American communities are being served by a single paper.

[10] Of the daily papers that were being published in this country in 1929, 45 per cent have either perished or been consolidated. This consolidation, this process of making big ones out of little ones, is a remorseless thing, and it may be a harmful thing if it tends to regiment our thinking.

[11] We Americans have a remarkable capacity for ambivalence. On the one hand we like to enjoy the benefits of mass production, and on the other we like to assert our individual taste. Ever since the Civil War we have been exercising our genius to build larger and larger combines. Experience has taught us that when these consolidations grow to the size of a giant octopus, we have got to find someone to regulate them. When our railroads achieved almost insufferable power, we devised the Interstate Commerce Commission, and we eventually found in Joseph Eastman a regulator of impeccable integrity who knew as much as any railroad president. We have not had such good luck with our other regulatory agencies, as the recent ignoble record of the FCC makes clear. What troubles me even more than the pliancy of FCC commissioners to political pressure is their willingness to favor the pyramiding under a single ownership of television channels, radio stations, and newspapers. Isn't this the very monopoly they were supposed to avoid?

[12] The empire builders, who were well on their way to a plutocracy, were

brought within bounds by the first Roosevelt. Then under the second Roosevelt it was labor's turn, and in their bid for power they have raised the challenge of what regulations can be devised which will bring them to a clearer recognition of their national responsibility. In the not far future we can see another huge decision looming up: When atomic energy is harnessed for industrial use, will it be in the hands of a few private corporations or in a consolidation which the government will control? My point is that in the daily exposure to such bigness the individual is made to feel smaller than he used to be, smaller and more helpless than his father and grandfather before him.

[13] I realize, of course, that twice in this century our capacity to arm on an enormous scale has carried us to victory with a speed which neither the Kaiser nor Hitler believed possible. But it is my anxiety that, in a cold war which may last for decades, the maintenance of bigness, which is necessary to cope with the U.S.S.R., may regiment the American spirit.

[14] In his book, *Reflections on America,* Jacques Maritain, the French philosopher, draws a sharp distinction "between the spirit of the American people and the logic of the superimposed structure or ritual of civilization." He speaks of "the state of tension, of hidden conflict, between this spirit of the people and this logic of the structure; the steady, latent rebellion of the spirit of the people against the logic of the structure." Maritain believes that the spirit of the American people is gradually overcoming and breaking the logic of their materialistic civilization. I should like to share his optimism, but first we have some questions to answer, questions about what the pressure of bigness is doing to American integrity and to American taste.

[15] Henry Wallace has called this the century of the Common Man. Well, the longer I live in it the more I wonder whether we are producing the Uncommon Man in sufficient quantity. No such doubts were entertained a century ago. When Ralph Waldo Emerson delivered his famous address on "The American Scholar" to the Phi Beta Kappa Society of Harvard in 1837, he was in a mood of exhilaration, not doubt, and he heralded among other things a change which had taken place in American literature. It was a change in the choice of subject matter; it was a change in approach, and it showed that we had thrown off the leading strings of Europe. Here is how he described it:

The elevation of what was called the lowest class in the state assumed in literature a very marked and benign an aspect. Instead of the sublime and beautiful, the near, the low, the common, was explored and poetized. . . . The literature of the poor, the feelings of the child, the philosophy of the street, the meaning of household life, are the topics of the time. It is a great stride. It is a sign—is it not?—of new vigor when the extremities are made active, when currents of warm life run into the hands and the feet. . . . This writing is blood-warm. Man is surprised to find that things near are not less beautiful and wondrous than things remote. The near explains the far. The drop is a small ocean. A man is related to all nature. This perception of the worth of the vulgar is fruitful in discoveries.

[16] This change from the appreciation of the elite to the appreciation of the commonplace, or as Emerson called it, the vulgar, has been increasingly magnified under the pressure of numbers. But were Emerson able to return to us for a short visit, I am not sure that he would be altogether happy about what we have done to elevate the vulgar in literature or in television.

[17] In contemporary literature, new books—the best we can produce—are still published in hard covers and sold to a discriminating body of readers. If I had to guess, I should say that there are about one million discriminating readers in this country today, and what disturbs me as an editor is that this number has not increased with the population; it has not increased appreciably since the year 1920. What has increased is the public for comic books, for murder mysteries, for sex and sadism. This debasement, especially in fiction, was most noticeable in the early stages of our paperbacks, when the racks in any drugstore were crowded with lurid, large-bosomed beauties who were being either tortured or pursued. Recently there has been an improvement, both in quantity and in seriousness, thanks to the editors of Anchor Books and the New American Library, thanks also to a feeling of outrage which was expressed in many communities. But it still seems to me regrettable that after a hundred years of public education we have produced such a demand for the lowest common denominator of emotionalism.

[18] Am I, I sometimes wonder, a minority of one when I shudder at certain photographs in our pictorial magazines? The picture of a Negro being lynched; the picture of an airliner which has crashed and burned, with that naked body to the left identified as an opera singer whose voice we have all heard and loved; the picture of a grieving mother whose child has just been crushed in an automobile accident? Am I a minority of one in thinking that these are invasions of privacy, indecent and so shocking that we cringe from the sight?

[19] Television, for which we once had such high hope, is constantly betrayed by the same temptation. It can rise magnificently to the occasion, as when it brought home to us the tragedy in Hungary, yet time and again its sponsored programs sink to a sodden level of brutality, shooting, and torture. And is there any other country in the world which would suffer through such incredible singing commercials as are flung at us? Does the language always have to be butchered for popular appeal, as when we are adjured to "live modern" and "smoke for real"? Am I a minority of one in thinking that the giveaway programs, by capitalizing on ignorance, poverty, and grief, are a disgrace? These are deliberate efforts to reduce a valuable medium to the level of the bobby-soxers.

[20] There was a time when the American automobiles led the world in their beauty, diversity, and power, but the gaudy gondolas of today are an insult to the intelligence. In an era of close crowding when parking is an insoluble problem, it was sheer arrogance on the part of the Detroit designers to produce a car which was longer than the normal garage, so wasteful of gasoline, so laden with useless chromium and fantails that it costs a small fortune to

have a rear fender repaired. I saw in a little Volkswagen not long ago a sign in the windshield reading, "Help Stamp out Cadillacs!" There speaks the good-natured but stubborn resistance of the American spirit against the arrogance of Detroit.

[21] Is it inevitable in mass production that when you cater to the many, something has to give, and what gives is quality? I wonder if this has to be. I wonder if the great majority of the American people do not have more taste than they are credited with. The phenomenal increase in the sale of classical music recordings the moment they became available at mass production prices tells me that Americans will support higher standards when they are given the chance. I stress the aberration of taste in our time because I think it is something that does not have to be. The republic deserves better standards, not only for the elect, but straight across the board.

[22] I wish that our directors of Hollywood, the heads of our great networks, and those who, like the automobile designers in Detroit, are dependent upon American taste—I wish that such arbiters would remember what Alexis de Tocqueville wrote a hundred and twenty-five years ago in his great book, *Democracy in America*. "When the conditions of society are becoming more equal," said Tocqueville, "and each individual man becomes more like all the rest, more weak and more insignificant, a habit grows up of ceasing to notice the citizens to consider only the people, and of overlooking individuals to think only of their kind."

[23] It seems to me that our tastemakers have been guilty of this fallacy ever since the close of World War II. They have ceased to notice the citizens and consider only the people, just as Tocqueville warned. They no longer plan for the differences in individual taste, but think only of people in the mass.

[24] In the years that followed the crash of 1929, Americans began to transfer their trust from big business to big government; if big business and banking, so ran the reasoning, could not be trusted to keep us out of depressions, perhaps big government could. Gradually in this emergency we began to shape up our version of the welfare state, a concept which was evolving in many parts of the Western world and to which both Democrats and Republicans are now committed.

[25] A welfare state requires a big government with many bureaus, just as big government in its turn requires big taxes. We embarked on big government with the idea of safeguarding those segments of American society which were most in jeopardy, and now after twenty-five years of experimentation we are beginning to learn that the effects of big government upon the individual are both good and bad. It is good to provide the individual with security, and to give him the chance to adjust his special claims; another and perhaps unsuspected asset has been dramatized by Edwin O'Connor in his novel, *The Last Hurrah*, in which he showed us how President Roosevelt had diminished and destroyed the sovereignty of the city boss. It is Washington, not Ward Eight, that has the big patronage to give today.

[26] The maleffects of big government are more subtle. Consider, for instance, the debilitating effect of heavy taxation. I remember a revealing talk I had with Samuel Zemurray when he was president of the United Fruit Company. Born in Russia, Zemurray made his start here by pushing a fruit cart through the streets of Gadsden, Alabama. Then he set up his own business as a banana jobber by selling the bunches of bananas the fruit company didn't want. He sold out to United Fruit and continued to acquire shares until he controlled the majority of the stock. In the autumn of F.D.R.'s second term, when we were sitting in adjoining Pullman seats on the long run to Washington, Mr. Zemurray began talking about the President's promises to "the forgotten man." "He made three promises," Zemurray said, "and he has kept two of them: the promise to labor and that to the farmer. The promise he has not kept is to the little businessman. Under today's taxes it would be quite impossible for a young man to do as I did—he would never be able to accumulate enough capital."

[27] Some years after this talk, in 1946 to be exact, I was on a plane flying West from Chicago. It was a Sunday morning and the man who sat beside me at the window seat had the big bulk of the Chicago *Tribune* spread open on his knees, but out of politeness' sake he gave me the proverbial greeting, "Hello, where are you from?" And when I said, "From Boston," his face lit up. "Do they still have good food at the Automat?" he asked. "Boy, that's where I got my start and it certainly seems a lifetime ago." And then in a rush out poured his life story in one of those sudden confidences with which Americans turn to one another: How he had become a salesman of bedroom crockery, and how his Boston boss had refused to raise him to thirty dollars a week. In his anger he had switched to the rival company, and under their encouragement he had simply plastered Cape Cod with white washbowls, pitchers, soap dishes, and tooth mugs. "Seven carloads I sold in the first year," he told me. The company called him back to its head office in Chicago, and then came the crash. The company owned a bank and lake shore real estate, and when the smoke had cleared away and recovery was possible, he found himself running the whole shebang. His wife hadn't been able to keep up with it all, he said, shaking his head sadly. He had had his first coronary, and what kept him alive today was his hope for his two sons, who had just come out of the Navy. "But, you know," he said to me, his eyes widening, "they neither of them want to come in with me. They don't seem to want to take the chances that I took. They want to tie up with a big corporation. I just don't get it."

[28] Security for the greatest number is a modern shibboleth, but somebody still has to set the pace and take the risk. And if we gain security, but sacrifice first venture and then initiative, we may find, as the Labor Party in England did, that we end with all too little incentive. As I travel this country since the war, I have the repeated impression that fewer and fewer young men are venturing into business on their own. More and more of them seek the safety of the big corporations. There are compelling reasons for this, the ever-shrinking margin of operating profit being the most insistent. But if we keep on trading

independence and initiative for security, I wonder what kind of American enterprise will be left fifty years from now.

[29] A subtle conditioning of the voter has been taking place during the steady build-up of big government. During the depression and recovery we took our directives from Washington almost without question; so too during the war, when we were dedicated to a single purpose and when the leadership in Washington in every department was the best the nation could supply. And for almost twenty years local authority and the ability to test our political initiative in the home county and state has dwindled. About the only common rally which is left to us is the annual drive for the community fund. Too few of our ablest young men will stand for local office. Their jobs come first, and they console themselves with the thought that if they succeed they may be called to Washington in maturity. We used to have a spontaneous capacity for rallying; we could be inflamed, and our boiling point was low. Our present state of lethargy, our tendency to let George do it in Washington, is not only regrettable, it is bad for our system.

[30] I remember one of the last talks I had with Wendell Willkie. He was still showing the exhaustion of defeat, and he spoke with concern as he said, "One of the weaknesses in our democracy is our tendency to delegate. During an election year we will work our hearts out, and then when the returns are in, we think we have done our part. For the next three years what happens to the party is the responsibility of the national committeemen. Have you ever looked at them?"

[31] The decision having been made to drop the atomic bomb on Hiroshima, President Truman tells us that he retired and slept soundly. But those in authority in these days are less sure. The delegation of so much authority to those in Washington and the difficulties of dealing with an opponent so ruthless and enigmatic as Russia seem to have developed in our most responsible officials a secretiveness and an uncertainty which make it hard for the citizen to follow. This administration has practiced a policy of nondisclosure toward the press and the electorate which has left the average citizen in a state of constant uncertainty. I have nothing but admiration for the dedication and stamina of Secretary Dulles, but I wish with all my heart that he had made our purpose and our commitments clearer for our allies and for our own people to understand. When we pulled that dam out from under Nasser's feet, we projected a crisis which must have come as a great shock to France and Britain. And how can we blame the young leaders of Hungary for misunderstanding the words "dynamic liberation" when we at home had no clear notion of what they meant? It was inexcusable not to have warned the American people that the Sputniks were coming and that greater exertions must be expected of us. This is no time for remoteness or for lulling slogans or for the avoidance of hard truths. The volume of material, the thousands of articles dealing with the great issues of today which are pouring into my office from unknown, unestablished writers, testifies to the conscientiousness and the courage of

American thinking. The pity of it is that such people have not been taken more fully into the confidence of their own government.

[32] I have said that the concept of bigness has been an American ideal since our earliest times. I pointed to our propensity to build larger and larger combines ever since the Civil War, and how the process of consolidation has speeded up during the past thirty-five years. I suggested that we cannot have the fruits of mass production without suffering the effects of regimentation. And I ask that we look closely at what the pressure of bigness has done to American taste and opinion. Is the individual beginning to lose self-confidence and his independence? In short, how big is one?

[33] Surely, in an atomic age self-reliance and self-restraint are needed as they have never been before. See with what force Van Wyck Brooks expresses this truth in his *Writer's Notebook:*

Unless humanity is intrinsically decent, heaven help the world indeed, for more and more we are going to see man naked. There is no stopping the world's tendency to throw off imposed restraints, the *religious* authority that is based on the ignorance of the many, the *political* authority that is based on the knowledge of the few. The time is coming when there will be nothing to restrain men except what they find in their own bosoms; and what hope is there for us then unless it is true that, freed from fear, men are naturally predisposed to be upright and just?

[34] As we look about us, what evidence can we find that in an atmosphere overshadowed by Russia and made murky by the distrust of McCarthyism there are citizens who will still stand forth, upright and ready to speak the hard truth for the public good? How big is one?

[35] One is as big as George F. Kennan, who believes that we cannot continue to live in this state of frozen belligerency in Europe. We do not have to accept all of his proposals before applauding his thoughtful, audacious effort to break up the ice.

[36] One is as big as Omer Carmichael, the superintendent of schools in Louisville, Kentucky, who led the movement for voluntary integration in his border state; as big as Harry Ashmore, the editor of the Little Rock, Arkansas, *Gazette,* for his fearless and reasonable coverage of the Faubus scandal.

[37] One is as big as Frank Laubach, who believes in teaching the underdeveloped nations how to read their own languages, and then in supplying them with reading matter which will aid them to develop their farming and health.

[38] One is as big as Linus Pauling, Harold C. Urey, Robert Oppenheimer, and the other editors and sponsors of the *Bulletin of the Atomic Scientists,* who have never underestimated Russian scientific capacities, who have always believed in the peaceful value of scientific exchange and never ceased to struggle against fanaticism in secrecy and security.

[39] One is as big as Edith Hamilton, the classicist, the lover of Greece and

of moderation; and as Alice Hamilton, her younger sister, who pioneered in the dangerous field of industrial medicine.

[40] One is as big as Sheldon and Eleanor Glueck, who for years have been guiding lights in the resistant field of juvenile delinquency.

[41] One is as big as Ralph Bunche and Eleanor Roosevelt.

[42] One is as big as Louis M. Lyons, whose interpretation of the news and whose judgment of the popular press have provided, in the words of the Lauterbach Award, "a conscience for a whole profession."

[43] One is as big as I. I. Rabi, a brilliant scientist and a passionate humanist, who, on being asked how long it would it would take us to catch up to Russia and to safeguard our long-range future, replied, "A generation. You know how long it takes to change a cultural pattern. The growing general awareness of this need will help us, but nevertheless we will have to work hard to succeed in a generation."

[44] One is as big as Frederick May Eliot, president for twenty-one years of the American Unitarian Association, who worked himself to the bone for the deepening of faith and for reconciliation.

[45] One is as big as you yourself can make it.

COMMENT AND QUESTIONS

I. This essay has five parts, each one developed largely by concrete instances and examples: (1) the American ideal of bigness; (2) the accelerated growth of bigness in the last thirty-five years; (3) big mass production and the loss of quality and taste; (4) big government and its effects; (5) the position of the individual in all this bigness. What sub-points is Mr. Weeks making in each of the five sections, and what examples can you recall from each section? Can you add from your own experience further illustrations of the points he is making?

II. The essay ends optimistically, with final emphasis on the possible bigness of one. What preparation for this ending, or what suggestions of optimism, can you find in the earlier sections?

III. Published in the late summer of 1958, "How Big Is One" makes a number of references to current or recently-current affairs and to people an educated audience of that time would identify. Some of these references will not carry exact meaning after a few years. Do you think that this fact will then seriously damage the clarity and the effect of the essay?

IV. Judging by what Mr. Weeks says and by the examples he gives, what modifications of our bigness do you think he would like to see? What kind of spirit would he like individual Americans to have? Do you agree with the author?

Glossary: A Brief Rhetoric

ABSTRACT WORDS. See CONCRETE AND ABSTRACT EXPRESSION.

ALLEGORY. Symbolic narrative, in which people, objects, and events have another meaning and are used to present an idea. In *Pilgrim's Progress,* Christian, the hero, and his companion, Hopeful, escape the dungeon of the Giant Despair in Doubting Castle by the use of the key of Promise (i.e., the promise of salvation for the faithful).

ALLITERATION. The repetition of consonant sounds, usually at the beginning of words: "The *f*urrow *f*ollowed *f*ree"; ". . . we do not, properly speaking, *l*ove *l*ife at all, but *l*iving."

ANALOGY. A sustained comparison of two ideas or situations. For a note on analogies, see page 737.

ANALYSIS. A method of organization and development which consists of dividing a complex subject into its main parts, examining each of those parts, and showing their relationship to one another and to the whole. When a writer says, "There are three distinct areas of conflict in the Middle East," or "The problem created by fraternities is fourfold," he is introducing an analysis of a subject complex enough to require division.

ANALYSIS OF A CONCEPT. See ANALYSIS. The analysis of a concept or a problem often starts with a clear statement of the idea or problem, indicates the logical divisions into which it falls, discusses each division, and concludes with a summary of the material or a suggested solution for the problem.

ANALYSIS OF A MECHANISM. See ANALYSIS. The analysis of a mechanism (an electric razor, a gasoline engine, a door chime, etc.) usually falls into three large divisions: (1) the description of the whole mechanism; (2) the analysis of its main functional parts; (3) the operation of the mechanism.

ANTICLIMAX. See CLIMACTIC ARRANGEMENT.

ANTITHESIS. A stylistic arrangement of opposed elements to heighten the contrast between them: "I wish to preach not the doctrine of ignoble ease, but the doctrine of the strenuous life."

ATTITUDINAL AND FACTUAL MEANING. See INSIDE AND OUTSIDE KNOWLEDGE; also ATTITUDINAL LANGUAGE.

ATTITUDINAL LANGUAGE. Language which expresses the feelings or attitudes of a communicator toward himself, his subject, and his audience. If one says, "This girl weighs a hundred and ten pounds," he is using non-attitudinal, factual language. If he says, "This girl is slim and lovely," or "Isn't it too bad your date's so skinny?" he is using attitudinal language. See also, SLANTING, CHARGED LANGUAGE, and INSIDE AND OUTSIDE KNOWLEDGE.

BALANCE. See PARALLELISM. When parallel expressions are similar in length and rhythm as well as in grammatical construction, they are said to be *balanced:* "The world will little note nor long remember what we say here; but it can never forget what they did here."

BALANCED SLANTING. See SLANTING.

CAUSE-AND-EFFECT ARRANGEMENT. A pattern of organization in which a writer discusses the causes of an event or situation, and then the effects—for example, the causes of limited college admissions, and the present effects and probable future effects of a situation in which not all able young men and women can be educated. Sometimes a writer reverses the order, starting with the effects of a development or event, and then discussing its causes.

CHARGED WORDS AND CHARGED LANGUAGE. Words which carry strong emotional (i.e., attitudinal) meaning are called charged words, and language which carries strong attitudinal meaning (i.e., which produces or is intended to produce a series of emotional charges—attractions or repulsions—in the hearer or reader) is called charged language. Charged words and charged language vary in the amount of charge they have and in their effect on different people.

Words may be relatively uncharged, as in the scientific use of language—*amoeba, transformer;* lightly charged—*slender, agile;* or heavily charged—*friend, traitor, coward, love, honor, heroism.* The degree of charge a word carries depends on its accepted meaning and associations and the whole context in which it is used.

Charged language is a product of slanting. It may be more fully defined as the selection (slanting) of words or facts or emphasis in a way that significantly influences feelings toward, or judgment of, a subject. Although charged language is more subject to misuse and misinterpretation than the language of factual communication, it is essential for expression of inside knowledge and the communication of attitudinal meaning.

Factual language: Miss Anita Welsh has announced her engagement to Mr. Arnold Lloyd.

Charged language: Charming Anita Welsh to wed wealthy socialite.

Charged language: Fickle Anita Welsh to try matrimony for a fourth time with playboy Arnold Lloyd.

See INSIDE AND OUTSIDE KNOWLEDGE, SLANTING, CONTEXT.

CHRONOLOGICAL ARRANGEMENT. A pattern of organization which records events in the time-order in which they occur. It is the arrangement naturally used in the writing of history, in biography, in simple narratives, and in articles which trace the development of a movement, institution, or situation. It is also used in giving instructions or following a simple process from beginning to end.

CLIMACTIC ARRANGEMENT. The arrangement of sentence elements to build to a climax or strong ending. In the following examples, parallel elements are arranged in an order of increasing importance:

> And now abideth faith, hope, charity, these three; but the greatest of these is charity.

> A jug of wine, a loaf of bread—and thou
> Beside me singing in the wilderness.

Violation of the natural order of climax robs a sentence of its force, unless the anticlimax is used deliberately for humor. An example of thoughtless anticlimax is: "It was a stupendous performance, and very good."

Paragraphs and whole compositions, like sentences, should build to strong endings.

CONCRETE AND ABSTRACT EXPRESSION. Abstract words generally name qualities (*intelligence, honor*), concepts (*evolution, scientific method*), and conditions (*poverty, insanity*). Concrete words generally refer to things that exist in the physical world and can be perceived by the senses: *chair, apple, light bulb, rose bush.* If writing is too concrete—something that seldom occurs—the reader tends to be lost in a welter of particulars; if writing is too abstract—as is more often the case—the reader may lose the meaning because he has not been given enough tangible information to relate to the world of his own experience. The good writer communicates his meaning by judicious choice and combination of concrete and abstract expressions. Some of the principles that guide him in his choice are stated below.

1. Abstract words (*truth, right, justice, religion, wealth, democracy, freedom,* for example) frequently do not have the same meaning for different people. They are necessary in language for expressing general ideas and arriving at judgments and conclusions; and they are powerful words, carrying as they so often do a heavy emotional charge. But because of their multiple meanings and emotional associations, they often confuse rather than clarify; at best, unless they are defined by concrete

illustration, they leave only a vague impression of what the writer had in mind when he used them. Concrete words, on the other hand, point to things which have existence in the physical world, on the nature and meaning of which people can agree. Concrete words like *horse, tree, typewriter* call up an image of the object named. It is true, of course, that there are different kinds of horses, trees, and typewriters; still, in a context, the label carries a reasonably definite meaning. Concrete words, therefore, communicate more exactly the image or idea which the writer had in mind.

2. In striving for definite expression, the writer often needs to choose, not simply between abstract and concrete words, but between fairly concrete and more concrete words. Words are more concrete (or less abstract) as they give more particulars about the thing they refer to: *palomino* is more concrete than *horse, white birch* more concrete than *tree.*

3. Concrete words and details convey clearer information than abstract statement because they give supporting facts, statistics, reasons, and examples, and answer such questions as: What kind? What color? How large? How far? How many? In what way?

4. Concrete words and details also evoke more definite feelings than abstract statements. Charged abstract words often produce a strong emotional response; but that response may be a confused cloud of feeling aroused by the word, unfocused on any particular situation, and possibly far removed from the idea in the communicator's mind. With concrete words the feeling is different. Compare "The little left tackle broke his collar bone" with "One of the players received an injury." Since concrete words refer to more definite things, the emotion they evoke will be a sharper, more focused emotion as the reader reacts to the image of particular things called up by the words. Concrete communication gives the reader the sense of being present in the situation or experience; of seeing what the writer saw, touching and smelling and hearing as the writer did. He comes closer, therefore, to sharing the writer's inside knowledge.

CONCRETE WORDS AND DETAILS. See CONCRETE AND ABSTRACT EXPRESSION.

CONTEXT. The surrounding words or surrounding circumstances which establish the meaning of a particular word or of a larger unit of expression. In the sentences "A fire glowed on the hearth" and "A fire raged through the North End," the exact meaning of the word *fire* (and our response to the word) is determined by the context in which it is used. Since context determines meaning, the quoting of words outside of their context is often misleading.

DEFINITION. Exact definition of terms which a reader may not know, or which have different meanings for different people, is vital to clear communication. Extended definition, in which a writer devotes several pages or an entire article or book to clarifying a term, is a common pattern in informative writing. For a note on the techniques of such definition, see page 949, Question I.

DOMINANT IMPRESSION. In descriptive writing, the unified effect or central idea to which the descriptive details contribute. A mere accumulation of particulars about a person or a place may give the reader a blurred, conglomerate picture instead of a sharply drawn image. The writer therefore selects particulars which produce a central or dominant impression—for example, an impression of disorder, or gaiety, or calm, or nervous activity.

DRAMATIC NARRATION. A term used in two ways. It may mean the vivid and suspenseful presentation of material, which gives the reader a sense of action and conflict. In fiction, *dramatic narration* is the technique of letting action and dialogue tell the story (as in a play) without interpretive comment by the author.

ECONOMY. The briefest expression is not always the best, but in effective prose, every word counts. Economical and concise expression, probably the most striking trait of good English, is the result of choosing words which work, and so warrant the space they take on the page. Related ways of achieving economy are:

1. Avoiding unnecessary words and verbose expressions:

    Wordy: He spoke to me in regard to the matter of the accident.
    Revised: He spoke to me about the accident.

    Wordy: I think in my own mind that we should leave at six P.M. in the evening.
    Revised: I think we should leave at six P.M. (*or,* at six in the evening).

    Wordy: She rendered a vocal selection.
    Revised: She sang.

2. Cutting weak clauses to phrases or to single words:

    The wind which blew through the cracks made a whistling sound. [two clauses]
    Revised: The wind whistled through the cracks. [one clause; an exact verb cuts out five words]

    The children were happy and gay; they played in the street which was wet with rain. [three clauses]
    Revised: The children, happy and gay, played in the rain-wet street. [one clause; apposed adjectives (*happy and gay*) and a compound adjective (*rain-wet*) cut two clauses]

3. Using exact words:

    Wordy and inexact: She planted some bulbs of those little yellow and purple flowers that bloom in the spring.
    Revised: She planted some crocus bulbs.

Wordy: The conductor lifted the stick that he uses to direct the orchestra.
Revised: The conductor lifted his baton.

4. Selecting the material necessary for one's purpose and leaving out irrelevant material and unimportant details.

It is important to remember, however, that concrete details which clarify or vivify a general statement, and repetition for desired emphasis are *not* wordiness. Economy and precision, properly understood, are not achieved simply by brevity, and never by sacrificing words and details that convey significant shades of meaning or are necessary for exact factual communication. Economy comes from removing a clutter of purposeless circumlocution, weak clauses, and irrelevancies, and replacing it with clear, strong, working words.

EMPHASIS. Able writers seldom depend upon mechanical devices such as underlining and capitalizing, or intensives like *very, so, most, frightfully* as ways of achieving emphasis; they get emphasis by choice of exact words, appropriate sentence form, and careful construction. The entry on ECONOMY deals in part with the choice of exact, emphatic words. Here we shall discuss four other techniques of emphasis: the use of proportion, pause, arrangement and structure in sentences, and skillful repetition.

1. Emphasis by proportion. In a whole composition, main ideas are emphasized by fuller development than is accorded less significant ideas.

2. Emphasis by pause. Pauses created by chapter divisions, paragraph breaks, and marks of punctuation throw emphasis on material immediately preceding and following the pause. The concluding sentences in the passage below, which could have been written as one sentence, are made emphatic by the period pauses:

With no more than six inches of looking glass and a pair of old candles to help him, he had thrust on crimson breeches, lace collar, waistcoat of taffeta, and shoes with rosettes on them as big as double dahlias in less than ten minutes by the stable clock. He was ready. He was flushed. He was excited. But he was terribly late.—Virginia Woolf, *Orlando*

3. Emphasis by arrangement and structure. Since pauses create positions of emphasis, the beginnings and ends of sentences and of paragraphs naturally receive the greatest emphasis; those positions are occupied by words and ideas which the writer wishes to stress. Occasional inversion, or changing of the normal sentence order, is a device for emphasis. In the sentences below, an adverb and two nouns (objects) are emphasized by being taken out of their normal position and put at the beginning of the sentence:

Sorrowfully she turned and walked down the road.

John I admire; *his brother* I detest.

The end of the sentence is a position even more emphatic than the beginning, partly because it is followed by the period stop, and partly because there is a well-established general expectation that important things come last. Strong sentences, therefore, build to strong endings. (See Climactic Arrangement.)

Skillful subordination is another structural technique of emphasis: main ideas are emphasized by being expressed in main clauses, with less significant ideas expressed in dependent clauses, or phrases, or words.

Here are two unemphatic sentences about Leonardo da Vinci's *Last Supper:*

> When Leonardo painted the Last Supper, the damp wall of the refectory was oozing with mineral salts. The effort to see the Eucharist as one taking leave of his friends, not as the pale Host of the altar, was strange after all the mystic developments of the Middle Age.

Walter Pater, in *The Renaissance,* wrote them this way:

> On the damp wall of the refectory, oozing with mineral salts, Leonardo painted the Last Supper. . . . Strange, after all the mystic developments of the Middle Age, was the effort to see the Eucharist, not as the pale Host of the altar, but as one taking leave of his friends.

In Pater's first sentence, the main idea is emphasized by being stated in the main clause, and further emphasized by the position of that clause at the end. In the second sentence, the two important ideas, "strange" and "as one taking leave of his friends," are given emphasis by an unusual sentence arrangement which puts them at beginning and end.

4. Emphasis by repetition. Skillfully used, repetition of words, phrases, and sentence structures can create emotional effects, bind together sentences in a paragraph, and effectively emphasize key words and ideas:

> This great nation *will endure* as it has *endured, will* survive and *will* prosper. So, first of all, let me assert my firm belief that the only thing we have to *fear* is *fear* itself. . . .

> *We shall fight* on the beaches, *we shall fight* on the landing grounds, *we shall fight* in the fields and in the streets, *we shall fight* in the hills. . . ."

Evaluation. The evaluative or critical use of language is similar to the informative use (see Informative Writing) in that it requires knowledge of as many facts as possible and sound reasoning about facts; but the critic's conclusions go beyond the realm of verifiable fact into the realm of values. In some respects, too, evaluation is similar to persuasion, since persuasion also deals with values and judgments, and since the critic's judgments may influence the opinions of his readers. But evaluation at its best is objective and non-partisan; the critic's primary purpose is not to influence his readers but to arrive at and express the truest judgment to which his knowledge and his standards lead him.

1142   GLOSSARY: A BRIEF RHETORIC

FIGURATIVE LANGUAGE. Figurative language is language in which words are used non-literally. The basis of most figurative language is comparison or association of two ordinarily separate things or ideas. Figurative language contributes more to good prose than most people realize. For examples see the selection from *Walden,* page 989ff. The most common figures of speech are:

1. *Simile:* a non-literal comparison usually introduced by *like* or *as,* of two things unlike in most respects but similar in others:

Still we live meanly, *like ants.*

2. *Metaphor:* an implied non-literal comparison:

Time is *but the stream I go fishing in.*

3. *Analogy:* a sustained comparison of two ideas or situations.
(For a fully developed analogy see Vannevar Bush, "The Builders," page 731ff.)

FLASHBACK. A device used in narrative writing. A flashback is a character's recollection of past events, usually a full recollection of a scene from the past.

FORMAL AND INFORMAL STYLE. Since style, like dress, varies with time and occasion, and the intention of the writer, effective styles may range from very formal and academic to familiar and colloquial, and may even extend into vulgate expression.

Vulgate, the least literate level of language—nearly always spoken, seldom written in published form except in fiction which reproduces this type of speech—is the English used by people with little or no education.

Formal English, more often written than spoken, used by highly educated people addressing an audience of their peers, is likely to have the following characteristics: long sentences, often in parallel and balanced construction, often with modifiers interrupting the normal order; periodic sentences—sentences with meaning suspended until the end; triads—three parallel phrases or clauses; and allusions—brief references to literature or history which only a well educated audience would understand. Formal English is likely to be impersonal rather than personal in its style. Contractions *(can't, don't)* are avoided in formal English. An important characteristic of formal English is a wide and exact vocabulary, frequently specialized or technical. (For an example of formal English that illustrates most of the characteristics listed, see the paragraph quoted from Carl Becker on page 759.)

Informal English, the English most commonly spoken and written by educated people, lies between formal English and vulgate English and overlaps both levels. Informal English, particularly written informal English, uses a wider and more exact vocabulary than is typical of vulgate English, but a less formal and specialized vocabulary than that of formal

English. It is, in sentence style, less elaborate than formal English; its sentences are likely to be shorter and to have the rhythms and uncomplicated constructions of speech. It is more often personal than impersonal; that is, the writer includes himself and his feelings and attitudes in his communication. Allusions in informal English are usually to widely understood current events rather than to the historical and literary events of which formal English assumes understanding. (Most of the selections in this text are examples of informal English. For a single passage that illustrates many of the characteristics of informal style, see the first few paragraphs of Lincoln Steffens, "I Get a Colt to Break In," pages 1072–3.)

GENERAL-TO-PARTICULAR ARRANGEMENT. A pattern of organization frequently used in paragraphs and in longer pieces of writing. In a paragraph developed in this pattern, the topic sentence, a summary statement of the idea, stands at or near the beginning of the paragraph and is followed by facts, statistics, instances, details, or examples which support and clarify it.

Particular-to-general arrangement is a less common pattern than general-to-particular. Sometimes, though, a writer starts with particular details or examples and builds to a more general idea at the end.

IMPERSONAL STYLE. See PERSONAL AND IMPERSONAL STYLE.

INFORMATIVE WRITING. The function of purely informative writing is to convey verifiable facts and ideas as objectively as possible. Informative communication presents, explains, and interprets factual meaning. It answers such questions as: What is it? Who is it? How is it done? How does it operate? How did it develop? What are the facts? What do the facts mean?

Although expressions of attitude and personal judgment are excluded from writing intended to convey *only* factual meaning, a writer's intention is often complex, and a communication primarily informative may have secondary and supporting purposes. Thus a writer may entertain or use other devices of persuasion to make his information more palatable or of more immediate concern to the audience; or his interpretation of facts may lead him to evaluations.

INSIDE AND OUTSIDE KNOWLEDGE (ATTITUDINAL MEANING AND FACTUAL MEANING). If we use *knowledge* in its broadest sense, we can say that every meaning that language can communicate is some kind of knowledge. In this book we refer to two different kinds of knowledge, inside and outside knowledge. What one knows about what is going on inside his own mind or what he learns or conjectures about what is going on inside the minds of others is inside knowledge; what he knows or conjectures about the world outside is outside knowledge. The distinction between the two kinds of knowledge can be a very important one. Some concrete examples will help to make it clear.

If I tell you I am sad, I communicate inside knowledge or meaning; if I say there is a red truck in the driveway, I communicate outside knowledge. In the first statement I am talking about something that only I can know about at first hand, the actual *feeling* of sadness that is *inside* me. In the sentence about the red truck I am talking about objects in the outside world—the truck and the driveway; by looking at the truck you too can have first-hand knowledge of it, by which you can check my statement. If you tell me that what I called a truck is really a stationwagon, I can look again and see that I should have said stationwagon.

One more example. If I say, "I am sad because I don't own the beautiful red stationwagon that is in the driveway," I communicate outside information about the ownership and color and location of the stationwagon, and I also communicate my inside knowledge about the stationwagon when I call it beautiful and say that I feel sad about not owning it. Most of the time, as in the example just given, language communicates a combination of outside and inside knowledge, of fact and attitude.

Meaning that conveys knowledge (facts and ideas about facts) concerning the outside world is *factual meaning*. It consists of what one knows or conjectures about the world that the senses—sight, hearing, taste, etc.—report to us. Meaning that conveys knowledge (feelings, attitudes, value judgments, beliefs) of the subjective, inside world is *attitudinal meaning*. Attitudinal meaning includes all forms of inside, first-person knowledge. If I look into my own consciousness I find there at different times all kinds of states of mind which are parts of inside knowledge—emotions, moods, desires, fears, wishes, sympathies, hopes, likes and dislikes, tastes, judgments, doubts, beliefs. Will and conscience are also parts of inside knowledge, for I can *feel* my will tell me to do something and feel my conscience tell me not to do it. Some things shock me, some sadden me, some delight me . . . When I put into words any of these bits of inside knowledge, they become the attitudinal meaning that I communicate.

INTENTION. The purpose the communicator has in mind—the effect that he wishes to produce by his communication. Although in some communications the intention may be complex and changing, in general a communicator has one of four primary intentions: (1) he wants simply to communicate factual knowledge as clearly as he can (i.e., *to inform*); (2) he wants to communicate factual knowledge and to pass judgment (i.e., *to evaluate* or *criticize*); (3) he wants to communicate (or to appear to communicate) knowledge *and* to influence the attitudes, ideas, or actions of the audience (i.e., *to persuade* or *convince*); or (4) he wants *to communicate experience*—to enable others to share his feelings, attitudes, states of mind, or at any rate to cause others to experience certain feelings, attitudes, states of mind.

INTEREST. For a brief analysis of techniques commonly used for making writing interesting see item I under Comment and Questions, page 734.

IRONY. The word *irony* is derived from the Greek *eironeia,* meaning dissimulation or understatement. Verbal irony is now a figure of speech in which the real meaning is different from, sometimes the opposite of, the apparent or literal meaning. Examples of verbal irony are "A delightful examination, wasn't it?" and "We had a lovely time; it didn't matter a bit that he sent me pink roses for my orange dress and walked me six blocks in the rain."

Different types of irony (dramatic irony, the irony of fate) have in common with verbal irony the element of contrast—between what is said and what is meant, between what is not understood and what is realized, between what is expected and what occurs; contrast, in short, between what things seem to be and what they actually are.

For an example of sustained irony and some analysis of ironic techniques see George Orwell's "The Principles of Newspeak," page 737, and the comment and questions that follow the Orwell selection.

LOGICAL ARGUMENT. The closely organized logical argument usually follows a basic plan of this kind: (1) The writer or speaker states the question clearly and fairly, defining any terms that might be ambiguous, and limiting the argument to the specific issues which he regards as important; he may in this preliminary step of his argument consider the history of the question and its present significance. (2) He states his position and supports that position by citing facts and authorities, and by reasoning from the evidence he presents. (3) He recognizes and refutes any outstanding arguments against his ideas. (4) He summarizes his argument and emphasizes the merits of his position or his proposal. Less formal arguments are likely to include these four steps, too, but to follow a more personal, less orderly plan.

MAJOR PREMISE. See SYLLOGISM.

NARRATIVE ESSAY. An essay which communicates an idea or makes a comment on life by telling a true or fictitious story.

OBJECTIVE STYLE. A style in which the author reports facts, and either excludes expressions of personal feeling and value judgments, or attempts to give a fair account by the use of balanced slanting. See PERSONAL AND IMPERSONAL STYLE.

ORGANIZATION. Organization, or the planned and orderly arrangement of ideas, should be determined by the nature of the material. For some patterns of organization commonly used (alone or in combination) in informative writing, see the entries on ANALYSIS, CAUSE-AND-EFFECT ARRANGEMENT, CHRONOLOGICAL ARRANGEMENT, DEFINITION, GENERAL-TO-PARTICULAR ARRANGEMENT, QUESTION-TO-ANSWER. For other suggestions about organization, see DOMINANT IMPRESSION, LOGICAL ARGUMENT, and TRANSITIONS.

PACE. The movement of narrative writing, which depends on the balance between summary and presentation of material. Summary is general statement which gives the net result of action: "They talked for an hour and arrived at no decision." Presentation is the full and dramatic development of scenes of action—for example, the actual conversation summarized above, or parts of it, with perhaps some details about the setting and the characters involved. In general, presentation is more effective than summary because it takes the reader into the scene; the full presentation of trivial or repetitious scenes, however, is likely to bore the reader. In a narrative which covers a long period of time, the skillful writer usually quickens his pace by summarizing unimportant events, but slows his pace to present significant actions or experiences.

PARALLELISM. The principle of usage which requires that coordinate elements in a compound construction be given the same grammatical form. Words, phrases, clauses, and even sentences may be expressed in parallel form. Skillful parallelism is an element of style: it is a means of packing a number of closely related ideas and details into a single sentence and keeping their relationship clear; it may also be used for emphasis, and for rhythmical effects which are part of the total meaning of a passage. The following paragraph illustrates effective parallelism:

> But if men forget that the future will some day be a present, they forget, too, that the present is already here, and that even in a dark time some of the brightness for which they long is open to the responsive senses, the welcoming heart, and the liberated mind. The moments as they pass even now have their tang and character. They may yield even now the contagious joy of feeling and perception. Here are the familiar flowers, the music we love, the poetry by which we are moved. Here are the books and companions, the ideas and the relaxations, the gaieties and the co-operative tasks of our familiar world. These things may be threatened, they may be precarious, they may be ours only by the grace of God, or of geographical or economic accident. But undeniably, beckoningly, along with the portents and alarms, here they are. Here, in all tragic times, they always have been, affording challenge and delight to the senses, solace and nourishment for the affections, and friendly stimulus to the understanding.
> —Irwin Edman, *Candle in the Dark*

PERSONAL AND IMPERSONAL STYLE. In personal style the writer generally writes in the first person (using *I* or *we*) and does not hesitate to write freely about his own ideas, feelings, and experiences. In impersonal style the writer is concerned with his subject; he generally avoids the use of the first person and attempts to keep himself and his feelings out of his writing. A good friendly letter, or an essay of Charles Lamb, will serve as an example of personal style; an article in the *Encyclopaedia Britannica* as an example of impersonal style. The degree of intimacy that a writer permits himself varies, or should vary, with his intention. See INTENTION.

PERSUASION. In persuasive writing the communicator has the primary intention of influencing the ideas, attitudes and/or actions of his audience. The three chief means of persuasion are (1) persuasion by logical argument (see LOGICAL ARGUMENT); (2) persuasion by appeal to emotion (see SLANTING, CHARGED WORDS AND CHARGED LANGUAGE); and (3) persuasion by irony and ridicule (see IRONY).

For an example of different techniques of persuasive writing see:

J. S. Mill, "On the Liberty of Thought and Discussion" (primarily persuasion by logical argument), page 950ff.

Winston Churchill, "Dunkirk" (persuasion by appeal to emotion, along with some logical argument), page 800ff.

George Orwell, "The Principles of Newspeak" (in parts, persuasion by irony and ridicule), page 737ff.

PRINCIPLE OF SELECTION. Before it is expressed in words, our knowledge, both inside and outside, is influenced by the principle of selection. What we know or observe depends on what we notice; that is, what we select, consciously or unconsciously, as worthy of notice or attention. As we observe, the principle of selection determines which facts we take in, choosing some and omitting others.

Suppose, for example, that a lumberjack, a tree surgeon, and an artist were all asked to examine a large tree in a forest and to write a full and true description of it. Although the three true descriptions would agree in some details, they would differ in others because each man would select the facts in the light of his special knowledge and interest. And the principle of selection applies, too, to what one remembers; a student embarrassed in class by an unexpected question or comment from the instructor may well miss or fail to remember the next ten minutes of a lecture. In both noticing and remembering, the principle of selection applies; it is influenced not only by our special interests and point of view but by our whole mental state at the moment. Thus the principle of selection serves as a kind of sieve or screen which chooses and sifts out the knowledge that comes to us.

What is true of the direct knowledge that comes to us is at least doubly true of the knowledge that comes to us through others, for their knowledge first went through the sifting process of their principle of selection and then through a second sifting process (see SLANTING) as they chose what details they would communicate and what words they would express them in.

A reader who is aware of the principle of selection knows that he seldom or never knows all the facts about any fairly complicated subject, and he realizes too that the information that he gets from reading has been sifted before, by other minds, and so may be distorted even though it comes from people who are giving the whole truth as they know it. He is likely to be aware, too, of the importance of thinking about a writer's intention and the way that intention has affected the whole communication. (See INTENTION.)

QUESTION-TO-ANSWER. A pattern of organization in which the writer starts with a question or questions and then supplies answers. This pattern is frequently used in analyses of current problems; for example, Is mass culture resulting in mediocrity? Is the four day week desirable? Do college fraternities gain or lose by national affiliations? Question-to-answer articles are often evaluative: on the basis of the facts he assembles, the writer arrives at a judgment.

REPETITION. Thoughtless or awkward repetition of sounds, words, and sentence patterns is a mark of immature writing. Controlled repetition, however, is an effective means of emphasizing important words and ideas, of binding together the sentences in a passage, and of creating emotional effects. See RHYTHM and "Emphasis by repetition" under EMPHASIS.

RHYTHM. Rhythm, which means measured movement and flow, is more marked in poetry than in prose, but prose rhythms may be of great importance in giving stress to ideas and in conveying and inspiring feeling. The good reader is aware not only of the sense, but also of the sound and movement of what he reads, for these are part of the meaning. Parallel constructions and controlled repetition are frequently used in markedly rhythmical prose, as they are in the passages below. In the first passage, the movement of sentences suggests the pendulum of the clock; in the second, parallel clauses mount in a periodic structure; in the third, the complex, cumulative rhythms communicate feeling as well as thought about the kind of intellect the author is describing.

In many a country cottage over the land, a tall old clock in a quiet corner told time in a tick-tock deliberation. Whether the orchard branches hung with pink-spray blossoms or icicles of sleet, whether the outside news was seedtime or harvest, rain or drought, births or deaths, the swing of the pendulum was right and left and right and left in a tick-tock deliberation.—CARL SANDBURG, "Lincoln Speaks at Gettysburg"

Finally, brethren, whatsoever things are true, whatsoever things are honest, whatsoever things are just, whatsoever things are pure, whatsoever things are of good report; if there be any virtue, and if there be any praise, think on these things.—The Epistle of Paul to the Philippians

But the intellect which has been disciplined to the perfection of its powers, which knows, and thinks while it knows, which has learned to leaven the dense mass of facts and events with the elastic force of reason, such an intellect cannot be partial, cannot be exclusive, cannot be impetuous, cannot be at a loss, cannot but be patient, collected, and majestically calm, because it discerns the end in every beginning, the origin in every end, the law in every interruption, the limit in each delay; because it ever knows where it stands, and how its path lies from one point to another.—John Henry Newman, *The Idea of a University*

SELECTION. See PRINCIPLE OF SELECTION, and SLANTING.

SIMPLE NARRATIVE. A short, uncomplicated story in which events are set down in natural time-order.

SLANTING. Slanting may be defined as the process of selecting (1) knowledge (facts and ideas); (2) words; and (3) emphasis, to achieve the intentions of the communicator. Slanting is present in some degree in all communication; one may *slant for* (favorable slanting), *slant against* (unfavorable slanting) or *slant both ways* (balanced slanting).

The favorable or unfavorable or balanced slanting of the subject matter is determined, as we have said, by the intention of the communicator: he selects the knowledge, the words, and the emphasis, and he adapts them to fit his intention and to achieve his purpose. Sometimes he slants his material consciously and deliberately; sometimes, especially in spontaneous or impulsive uses of language, he is unaware that he is making a choice, and after he has spoken, he may be surprised at what he has said. In such spontaneous utterances, slanting still occurs and is still controlled by intention, but the intention operates on a subconscious rather than a conscious level.

The subject of slanting is a large and important one, too large to be treated fully in a brief article. The following examples will illustrate some of the effects of slanting:

1. Slanting by selection of knowledge. Suppose these facts are known about Mr. Jackson: He is an honor student; he hasn't shaved for a week; he owns a convertible; and he has not paid his laundry bill for two months. By slanting (i.e., selecting from these facts) in different ways, a writer could give different impressions of Mr. Jackson:

Favorable slanting: Jackson is an honor student and he owns a convertible.

Unfavorable slanting: Jackson hasn't shaved for a week and hasn't paid his laundry bill for two months.

Balanced slanting: Although Jackson is an honor student he hasn't paid his laundry bill for two months.
   or
Although Jackson hasn't paid his laundry bill . . . he is an honor student.

2. Slanting by selection of charged words:

Unslanted factual statement: Jeanette is five feet six, weighs one hundred and five pounds and has platinum colored hair.

Slanted favorably: Jeanette is a slender blonde.

Slanted unfavorably: Jeanette is a skinny girl with peroxided hair.

3. Slanting by use of emphasis:

Favorable: (emphasizes strength) Although Ajax is awkward, he is very strong.

Unfavorable: (emphasizes awkwardness) Although Ajax is strong, he is quite awkward.

For articles in this glossary related to the subject of slanting see Intention, The Principle of Selection, Emphasis, Charged Words, Inside and Outside Knowledge. For a good example of various devices of slanting see Deems Taylor's "The Monster," page 780ff. In "The Monster" paragraphs 1–11 illustrate unfavorable slanting or slanting against, and paragraphs 12–14 illustrate favorable slanting. The article as a whole comes close to balanced slanting.

1150   GLOSSARY: A BRIEF RHETORIC

SPEAKER-AUDIENCE RELATIONSHIP. See WRITER-READER RELATIONSHIP.

STYLE. A hard-to-define quality of excellence or distinction. There is, of course, no single "good style" or "right style," for style is highly individual. It is compounded of many elements, including the writer's personality, his way of thinking, his intention, his conscious or unconscious slanting, his tone, his choice of words, his arrangement of words, the length and rhythm of his sentences. In analyzing a writer's style, it is helpful to have in mind the principles and techniques discussed in the following entries: CONCRETE AND ABSTRACT EXPRESSION, ECONOMY, EMPHASIS, FIGURATIVE LANGUAGE, FORMAL AND INFORMAL STYLE, INTENTION, PARALLELISM, PERSONAL AND IMPERSONAL STYLE, REPETITION, RHYTHM, SUBORDINATION, TONE, VARIETY IN SENTENCES.

SUBORDINATION. Expressing in dependent clauses, or phrases, or single words, ideas which are not significant enough to be expressed in a main clause or an independent sentence.

> The quarterback was tired. He was also battered. He was determined to win.
>
> *Subordinated:* The quarterback, though tired and battered, was determined to win.

By means of subordination, mature writers achieve emphasis, economy, and clarity: emphasis, because the important idea is expressed in a main clause, and less important ideas are subordinated to it; economy, because whole sentences can often be reduced to single words; and clarity, because subordination and subordinating conjunctions work together to show exact relationships between unequal parts of the sentence. The degree of subordination a writer uses is an aspect of his style, and is determined by his material and by the total effect he wants his writing to produce.

SUMMARY AND PRESENTATION. See PACE.

SYLLOGISM. In formal logic, the pattern in which a deductive argument is expressed. A syllogism consists of three statements—a major premise, a minor premise, and a conclusion. It contains three and only three main terms, each of which appears twice, but not twice in the same statement. The "middle term" appears in both premises.

There are four patterns or "figures" of the syllogism, in which the terms have different positions. In the following examples, the middle term is printed in capital letters to show its position in the four figures:

> *Figure 1:* ALL DOGS are carnivorous.
> My cocker is a DOG.
> Therefore my cocker is carnivorous.
>
> *Figure 2:* No thief CAN BE TRUSTED.
> All good men CAN BE TRUSTED.
> Therefore no good men are thieves.

Figure 3: Every COLLEGE STUDENT has great opportunities.
Some COLLEGE STUDENTS are poor.
Therefore some poor people have great opportunities.

Figure 4: Most people devote themselves to MATERIAL GAIN.
MATERIAL GAIN is not a worthy goal in life.
Therefore most people do not devote themselves to a worthy goal in life.

When a syllogism has any of these four relationships between terms and between premises and conclusion, its argument is said to be "valid." When the two premises are true, and the argument is valid, the conclusion of the syllogism can be accepted as true.

SYMBOLISM. A symbol is a particular object or person or experience which stands for, or is associated with, some larger relationship or idea. Symbolism is therefore a method of communicating simultaneously a particular meaning and a deeper associated meaning.

Symbolic meaning is intricately woven into the fabric of everyday life and thought. Hundreds of symbols like wedding rings, fraternity pins, Phi Beta Kappa keys, trophies, flags, military decorations, and religious emblems derive meaning not from their intrinsic worth, but from the larger concept of which they are the concrete token. Similarly, in literature, a symbol is any concrete article or incident which, though possibly insignificant of itself, has become invested with value, or is capable of stirring deep emotional and imaginative responses.

"By symbols," Thomas Carlyle wrote, "is man guided and commanded, made happy, made wretched. . . . He everywhere finds himself encompassed with Symbols, recognized as such or not recognized."

TONE. The verbal manner that a speaker or writer adopts; it is the part of meaning which gives the audience an impression of the personality of the communicator and of his attitude toward them and toward himself. A communicator's tone may be serious or facetious, personal or impersonal, condescending or respectful or obsequious, sarcastic or sentimental, ironic or literal, formal or informal, frank or reserved or secretive, assertive or questioning, authoritative or modest, sincere or insincere, enthusiastic or indifferent, etc.

TRANSITIONS. Transitions are words, phrases, sentences, or even paragraphs, which show the reader the connections between the writer's ideas.

Transitions between sentences within a paragraph are established by: (1) using sentence connectives such as *therefore, however, on the other hand, consequently, at the same time;* (2) repeating a key word that has occurred in the preceding sentence; (3) using a clear pronoun reference to a word or idea in the preceding sentence; and (4) putting parallel thoughts in parallel constructions to show the relationships between them.

Transitions between paragraphs are established by: (1) concluding a paragraph with a sentence which leads into the next paragraph; (2) using in the first sentence of a paragraph a transitional word or phrase: *furthermore, as a result, in addition, on the contrary;* (3) repeating a key word used in the preceding paragraph; (4) beginning a paragraph with a sentence which refers clearly to a statement at the end of the preceding paragraph or to its topic idea; and (5) using short transitional paragraphs which summarize the preceding ideas and relate them to the idea which follows.

VALUE JUDGMENT. A value judgment is an opinion. It differs from a verifiable fact in that the latter can be checked and proved to be true or false. That Franklin D. Roosevelt was President of the United States is a verifiable fact; that he was one of the greatest presidents is an opinion or a value judgment. We can assemble evidence to support our value judgments which seems sufficient to us, but others, with evidence that seems sufficient to them, may still support the opposite opinion. See VERIFIABLE FACT.

VARIETY IN SENTENCES. Most skillful writers vary their sentence patterns for two reasons: first, to avoid repetitious, monotonous sentences which might lull their readers to sleep; second, and more important, to suit style to sense, so that the varied pattern of sentences reflects the pattern of their thought. Some of the ways of achieving sentence variety are:

    1. Varying the length of sentences; using occasional short sentences among longer ones, or occasional long sentences if the prevailing style is terse.

    2. Using parallel and balanced constructions, not continuously, but as a change from simpler constructions.

    3. Intermingling loose and periodic sentences. In loose sentences, common in informal writing, the sentence continues after the main thought has been expressed:

> *We know that the young prince died,* although we know little more.

In periodic sentences, more characteristic of formal than of informal style, the meaning is suspended until the end of the sentence:

> *About the subsequent events,* the terrified repledging of loyalty, the whispered conspiracies, the promises exchanged behind locked doors, *we know but little.*

    4. Changing the position of modifiers and parenthetic elements for variety in movement and for better emphasis:

> She is not engaged to Herbert *at present*.
>
> She is not, *at present*, engaged to Herbert.

    5. Changing the subject-verb-object order of some sentences:

> He could never forgive this. [subject-verb-object]
>
> This he could never forgive. [object-subject-verb]

Variety in sentences, it should be emphasized, is not merely a matter of form and style. It is organic expression, in which sound and structure and rhythm all contribute to the full meaning the writer wishes to communicate. The following passage will illustrate. The opening periodic sentence is organically right: the trumpet sound ends the contemplation of the evening scene. Long complicated sentences are used to describe the complexity of darkness and sound and light. Short sentences are used for dramatic action and realization: "Orlando leapt to his feet"; "The Queen had come."

> After an hour or so—the sun was rapidly sinking, the white clouds had turned red, the hills were violet, the woods purple, the valleys black—a trumpet sounded. Orlando leapt to his feet. The shrill sound came from the valley. It came from a dark spot down there; a spot compact and mapped out; a maze; a town, yet girt about with walls; it came from the heart of his own great house in the valley, which, dark before, even as he looked and the single trumpet duplicated and reduplicated itself with other shriller sounds, lost its darkness and became pierced with lights. Some were small hurrying lights, as if servants dashed along corridors to answer summonses; others were high and lustrous lights, as if they burnt in empty banqueting halls made ready to receive guests who had not come; and others dipped and waved and sank and rose, as if held in the hands of troops of serving men, bending, kneeling, rising, receiving, guarding, and escorting with all dignity indoors a great Princess alighting from her chariot. Coaches turned and wheeled in the courtyard. Horses tossed their plumes. The Queen had come.—Virginia Woolf, *Orlando*

VERIFIABLE FACT. Verifiable facts are facts that can be checked and agreed upon and proved to be true by people who wish to verify them. That a particular theme received a failing grade is a verifiable fact; one needs merely to see the theme with the grade on it. That the instructor should have failed the theme is not, strictly speaking, a verifiable fact, but a value judgment, a matter of opinion. Possibly student and teacher will not agree on this matter of opinion. That women on the average live longer than men is a verifiable fact; that they live better is a matter of opinion, a value judgment.

VITALIZING. In descriptive writing, bringing people and scenes to life. Vitalizing a character means describing him in some typical pose or action, rather than completely static or motionless. Vitalizing a scene means carrying the reader into it by providing him with some of the sights, sounds, smells, and feelings which are part of experiencing that scene.

WRITER-READER RELATIONSHIP. The relationship—formal and impersonal; informal and personal; very informal, chatty, and intimate—which a writer establishes with his readers. See TONE.

Index

Abstract words; *see* Concrete and abstract expression, 1137
"Agnosticism and Christianity," by Thomas Huxley, 1003ff.
Aitken, William Maxwell, Lord Beaverbrook, "Present and Future," 784ff.
Allegory, 1135
Alliteration, 1135
Analogy, 737, 1135
Analysis, 1135
Analysis of a concept, 1135
Analysis of a mechanism, 1135
"An American Storyteller: Ernest Hemingway," by the editors of *Time*, 864ff.
"Another Go at F.D.R.," by Hamilton Basso, 769ff.
Anticlimax; *see* Climactic arrangement, 1137
Antithesis, 1136
Apology, by Plato, 892ff.
Arnold, Matthew, quoted, 721
Attitudinal and factual meaning; *see* Inside and outside knowledge, 1143
Attitudinal language, 1136
"Attractions of Stupidity, The," by Howard Mumford Jones, 1120ff.

Balance, 1136
Balanced slanting; *see* Slanting, 1148
Ballou, Robert O., "The Jew and the Christian," 1022ff.
Basso, Hamilton, "Another Go at F.D.R.," 769ff.
"Beau Brummell," by Virginia Woolf, 858ff.
Beaver, Joseph, "'Technique' in Hemingway," 775ff.
Becker, Carl L., "Everyman His Own Historian," 809ff.
  "The Ideal Democracy," 747ff.

"Belief in One God," by John Henry Newman, 1015ff.
Berle, Adolf A., Jr., "Roosevelt's Rendezvous with History," 766ff.
"Bhagavad-Gita and the Perennial Philosophy, The," by Aldous Huxley, 1032ff.
Bible, quoted, 1148
Bowen, Catherine Drinker, "The Business of a Biographer," 846ff.
"Builders, The," by Vannevar Bush, 735ff.
Bush, Vannevar, "The Builders," 735ff.
"Business of a Biographer, The," by Catherine Drinker Bowen, 846ff.

"Calculating Machine," by E. B. White, 1090ff.
Carlyle, Thomas, quoted, 1151
Carson, Rachel L., "The Gray Beginnings," 837ff.
Cause-and-effect arrangement, 1136
Charged words and charged language, 1136
Chronological arrangement, 1137
Churchill, Winston, "Dunkirk," 800ff.
Climactic arrangement, 1137
Colette, "My Mother and the Animals," 1084ff.
Concrete and abstract expression, 1137
Context, 1138

Day, Clarence, "Father Opens My Mail," 1079ff.
Definition, 949, 1138
Devoe, Alan, "The Life and Death of a Worm," 731ff.
Dewey, John, "Does Human Nature Change?" 885ff.

1155

1156 INDEX

Dixon, W. Macneile, "The Human Situation," 1052ff.
"Does Human Nature Change?" by John Dewey, 885ff.
Dominant impression, 1139
Dramatic narration, 1139
"Dreams of the Death of Persons of Whom the Dreamer is Fond," by Sigmund Freud, 787ff.
"Dunkirk," by Winston Churchill, 800ff.

Economy, 1139
Edman, Irwin, quoted, 1146
  "A Reasonable Life in a Mad World," 1065ff.
  "Former Teachers," 1098ff.
Einstein, Albert, "Science and Religion," 997ff.
Emerson, Ralph Waldo, "Self-Reliance," 973ff.
Emphasis, 1140
"Enlargement of Mind," by John Henry Newman, 942ff.
Epictetus, "The Quiet Mind," 928ff.
Epicurus, "Letter to a Friend," 925ff.
Evaluation, 1141
"Everyman His Own Historian," by Carl L. Becker, 809ff.
Exact words, 1139
"Existentialism," by Jean-Paul Sartre, 1040ff.

"Father Opens My Mail," by Clarence Day, 1079ff.
Faulkner, William, "Remarks on Receiving the Nobel Prize," 1050f.
Figurative language, 1142
Flashback, 1142
Formal and informal style, 1142
"Former Teachers," by Irwin Edman, 1098ff.
"Four Kinds of Thinking," by James Harvey Robinson, 875ff.
Freud, Sigmund, "Dreams of the Death of Persons of Whom the Dreamer is Fond," 787ff.

General-to-particular or particular-to-general arrangement, 1143
"Gray Beginnings, The," by Rachel L. Carson, 837ff.
Gunther, John, *Roosevelt in Retrospect*, reviews of, 765ff.

"How Big Is One," by Edward Weeks, 1125ff.
"Human Situation, The," by W. Macneile Dixon, 1052ff.
Huxley, Aldous, "The Bhagavad-Gita and the Perennial Philosophy," 1032ff.

Huxley, Thomas H., "Agnosticism and Christianity," 1003ff.

"Ideal Democracy, The," by Carl L. Becker, 747ff.
"I Get a Colt to Break In," by Lincoln Steffens, 1072ff.
Impersonal style; *see* Personal and impersonal style, 1146
Informative writing, 1143
Inside and outside knowledge, 1143
Intention, 1144
Interest, 1144
Inverted word order, 1140
Irony, 1145

James, William, "Religious Faith," 1008ff.
Jesus, "Sermon on the Mount," 935ff.
"Jew and the Christian, The," by Robert O. Ballou, 1022ff.
Jones, Howard Mumford, "The Attractions of Stupidity," 1120ff.

"Lantern-Bearers, The," by Robert Louis Stevenson, 1111f.
"Let's Wait," by the editors of *Time*, 771f.
"Letter to a Friend," by Epicurus, 925ff.
"Life and Death of a Worm, The," by Alan Devoe, 731ff.
"Lincoln Speaks at Gettysburg," by Carl Sandburg, 823ff.
Logical argument, 1145

Major premise; *see* Syllogism, 1150
Marcus Aurelius, quoted, 934f.
"Measuring the I.Q. Test," by David Wechsler, 760ff.
Mill, John Stuart, "On the Liberty of Thought and Discussion," 950ff.
"Monster, The," by Deems Taylor, 780ff.
Morgan, Clifford T., "Principles of Perception," 725ff.
"My Mother and the Animals," by Colette, 1084ff.
"Myth of the Cave, The," by Plato, 912ff.

Narrative essay, 1145
Newman, John Henry, quoted, 1148
  "Belief in One God," 1015ff.
  "Enlargement of Mind," 942ff.

Objective style, 1145
"On the Liberty of Thought and Discussion," by John Stuart Mill, 950ff.
Organization, 1145
Organization of the Readings by theme, 723f.
Orwell, George, "The Principles of Newspeak," 737ff.

Pace, 1145
Parallelism, 1146
Pater, Walter, quoted, 1141
Periodic sentence, 1152
Personal and impersonal style, 1146
Persuasion, 1146
Plato, *Apology*, 892ff.
   "The Myth of the Cave," 912ff.
   selection from *Symposium*, 919ff.
Platonic love, 923f.
Pragmatism, 891f.
Preface to the Readings, 721ff.
"Present and Future," by William Maxwell Aitken, Lord Beaverbrook, 784ff.
Principle of selection, 1147
"Principles of Newspeak, The," by George Orwell, 737ff.
"Principles of Perception," by Clifford T. Morgan, 725ff.

Question-to-answer arrangement, 1147
"Quiet Mind, The," by Epictetus, 928ff.

"Reasonable Life in a Mad World, A," by Irwin Edman, 1065ff.
"Religious Faith," by William James, 1008ff.
"Remarks on Receiving the Nobel Prize," by William Faulkner, 1050f.
Repetition, 1148
Rhythm, 1148
"Riddles of Franklin Roosevelt, The," by Raymond Swing, 772ff.
Robinson, James Harvey, "Four Kinds of Thinking," 875ff.
Roosevelt in Retrospect, by John Gunther, reviewed, 765ff.
"Roosevelt's Rendezvous with History," by Adolf A. Berle, Jr., 766ff.

Sandburg, Carl, "Lincoln Speaks at Gettysburg," 823ff.
Sartre, Jean-Paul, "Existentialism," 1040ff.
"Science and Religion," by Albert Einstein, 997ff.
Selection; *see* Principle of selection, 1147
"Self-Reliance," by Ralph Waldo Emerson, 973ff.
"Sermon on the Mount," by Jesus, 935ff.
Simple narrative, 1148
Slanting, 1148
"Slow-Motion Picture of High-Speed Death," by Edgar A. Walz and Carl Wall, 729ff.

Socrates; Plato's *Apology*, 892ff.
Socratic method, 918
Speaker-audience relationship; *see* Writer-reader relationship, 1153
Steffens, Lincoln, "I Get a Colt to Break In," 1072ff.
Stevenson, Robert Louis, "The Lantern-Bearers," 1111ff.
Style, 1150
Subordination, 1150
Summary and presentation; *see* Pace, 1145
Swing, Raymond, "The Riddles of Franklin Roosevelt," 772ff.
Syllogism, 1150
Symbolism, 1151
Symposium, selection from, by Plato, 919ff.

Taylor, Deems, "The Monster," 780ff.
"'Technique' in Hemingway," by Joseph Beaver, 775ff.
Thoreau, Henry David, 1064
   selection from *Walden*, 989ff.
Thurber, James, "Which," 1088ff.
Time, editors of, "An American Storyteller: Ernest Hemingway," 864ff.
   "Let's Wait," 771f.
Tone, 1151
Transcendentalism, 987f.
Transitions, 1151

Value judgment, 1152
Variety in sentences, 1152
Verifiable fact, 1153
Vitalizing, 1153

Walden, selection from, by Henry David Thoreau, 989ff.
"Walden, 1939," by E. B. White, 1092ff.
Walz, E. A. and C. Wall, "Slow-Motion Picture of High-Speed Death," 729f.
Wechsler, David, "Measuring the I.Q. Test," 760ff.
Weeks, Edward, "How Big Is One," 1125ff.
"Which," by James Thurber, 1088ff.
White, E. B., "Calculating Machine," 1090ff.
   "Walden, 1939," 1092ff.
Woolf, Virginia, quoted, 1140
   "Beau Brummell," 858ff.
Wordsworth, William, quoted, 1064f.
Writer-reader relationship, 1153